THE CHURCH
IN THE LAST DAYS

THE CHURCH
IN THE LAST DAYS

PASTOR DAVID J. BOWERS

ARPress
ILLUMINATING IDEAS.
EMPOWERING VOICES

ARPress
45 Dan Road Suite 5
Canton MA 02021

Hotline: 1(888) 821-0229
Fax: 1(508) 545-7580

Ordering Information:

Quantity sales. Special discounts are available on quantity purchases by corporations, associations, and others. For details, contact the publisher at the address above.

Printed in the United States of America.

ISBN-13:   Softcover   979-8-89356-408-2
              eBook   979-8-89356-407-5

Library of Congress Control Number: 2024904014

CONTENTS

Appendices

For more information on terms marked with asterisks, see Appendix E: Excerpts from Glossary of Terms.

*Turn you at my reproof: Behold,
I will pour out My Spirit unto you;
I will make known My Words unto you.*[1]

*He that has an ear,
let him hear what the Spirit says
unto the churches.*[2]

---

1   Prov. 1:23
2   Rev. 2:7, 11, 17, 29; 3:6, 13, 22

PREFACE

Dear reader:

The author has written this book to empower and prepare Christian believers to face the last days with a biblical New Testament perspective. If we seek truth independently and fervently, the Holy Spirit will enable us to reclaim the original *sense of Scripture* and history. For this to be effective, proper and contextual comparison to the Standard of New Testament Scripture must be a given. This applies especially in those areas where *traditions and dogma* have biased or distorted the meaning, in however innocuous and unintentional a way it may have been. Faithful and diligent students of the Word always *compare Scripture with Scripture* to realize the goal of doctrinal accuracy. Any true believer can do this with the faithful Paraclete that we have in the person of the Holy Spirit, *the Spirit of Jesus Christ.* Seek to visualize the *Truth as the Holy Spirit reveals it within* and let the meaning filter in and percolate into our minds. Jesus once said, "Let these sayings sink into your ears;" "Be careful how you hear."[3]

Moreover, it is the author's heartfelt desire that through it all, the reader would keep an open mind. In *this rite of passage* that every believer must pass, indoctrinated religious beliefs can be difficult from which to break free and can form a real barrier and hindrance to true biblical *conversion.* Since the *only goal is the Truth itself,* the reader will find no hidden agendas here. Many years ago, I received a piece of very good advice from a pastor's son. He was going through a difficult transition from *believing what others had taught* to a truly biblical perspective. His advice to me was, "Disregard it all; read the Scripture *for yourself,* and *see what comes back.*" Believe me, the Holy Spirit is trustworthy to reveal to anyone the very character of Jesus personally and independently.[4]

---

3   Luke 8:18; 9:44. *Author Note: For more info on terms marked with *Asterisks* see Appendix E: Excerpts from Glossary of Terms

4   John 16:13–15.

Since the Bible is God's Word, the author only writes that this book provokes independent study of it. The Bible teaches that one does not need the teachings of a religious nonprofit organization or a degree from a seminary or Bible school to know the truth of the Word of God! [5]

Jesus also reveals the ways one could tell whether someone is just promoting their own opinion[6]

So when the truth is *the real objective*, you have nothing to worry about!

The purpose of this book is manifold. First, the author teaches that believers must be set free from *their slavery to religious dogma* that betrays Christ and neutralizes spirituality. The second is that *the proper priorities for the church must be reestablished* according to *the original standard. This is the New Covenant of our Lord and Savior Jesus Christ.* Yes, one can historically verify that the author is in fact affirming the original truths as recorded in the New Testament accounts. Thirdly, that we must properly teach believers *the necessity of Biblical conversion!* Unconverted Christians invariably end up conforming themselves to the world.[7] As a Christian who received Christ very early in life, I grew up in the organized church "since I was knee-high to a grasshopper." As a son of a church leader, I have seen more than my fair share of the wicked dishonorable things that Christians can do to each other.

Frankly, "churchianity" grieves me to tears with their humanistic ways. Nevertheless, as a biblical pastor, I still love the church, *warts and all.* So because of this love for God's people, I am determined to do something about it. Long ago, God told Ezekiel that, "You dwell among rebellious people." God told him to "tell them, whether they listen or respond or not."[8]

The harsh truth is that many are just too stubborn to change because of their pride. Nevertheless, as Larry Norman once said, "Here I am— talking about Jesus, just the same."[9]

---

5   John 14:15–17,21–23; 1 John 2:20,27.
6   John 7:15–17; 8:12–36
7   Matt. 18:3.
8   Ezek. 2:3–3:27
9   Matt. 16:6–14; 2 Tim. 2–4

Was not it Jesus who told us about leaving the ninety and nine to go and look for the one lost lamb, and that there is *rejoicing in heaven* when one sinner repents? Yes, I believe that it was worth Jesus coming down and giving his life to save *just one soul!* God loves us so much! However, it was *this very* Jesus who was so unmistakable about his distaste for the way *religious leaders have bound up the Gospel* and have *stood in the way of those seeking salvation!*[10]

Therefore, this provides a more than adequate biblical precedent and basis for us to be doing the same today if we follow the rules God has given us in His Word.

The Holy Spirit is seeking to "conform all believers into the image of His Son, Jesus Christ." *Jesus is only coming back for a pure, spotless, and chaste bride!* However, to achieve even a modicum of revival requires that we make major changes!

Maybe this book is a "stab in the dark," but it *speaks what must be spoken* these last days! God is seeking to break up and through the fallow ground of hardened traditions and those convenient coverings that religious people use to *veil their unbelief!*[11]

If *we really want revival*, the church needs to go back to Second Chronicles chapter 7, verse 14 and to abide by the Christian application of the ancient fourfold admonition: "*If My people*, [who name ourselves after Christ] will *humble themselves* and *pray* and *seek God's face* and *turn from their wicked ways—then* will I hear." Widespread apostasy has blinded far too many to the *truth*. Many Christians have even failed to discern the difference between simple confession and *true biblical repentance!* Very few possess the maturity or spirituality to *differentiate between the soul and the spirit.*

Many leaders have lost their moral compass and the ability to separate the sacred from the profane, watering down even the most basic of moral standards to people-please and get the pews filled. The conditions are intolerable and even getting worse. Yet, it seems that mostly everybody is putting on blinders and vainly thinking *that if the problems are ignored long enough, they will go away.* Nevertheless, they

---

10   Matt. 23; Luke 13,21
11   Isa. 28–30; Jer. 4:1–4; Hosea 10:12; Matt. 15:1–20; John 8:12 ff.

do not, and if anyone dares to point out the source of the problems, they attack the messenger! Many have been "wounded in the house of their 'friends.'" Have you been "redeemed from the vain traditions of your ancestors?" Yes, it is "time that judgment begins with the house of God."[12]

How do we get back to where we should? The first step is to gain *the eternal perspective!* Let us learn to see things as God would see them and learn to *think like God thinks!* We can do this if we begin to receive His higher wisdom.

We do this by repenting, being broken and walking in the light daily. By doing this, God can transform us by the *renewing of the mind* and we can be on our way to revival.

Yet, my friend, this is a *colossal order*. To fulfill it, believers must *establish the proper priorities*. Yet we only need to "look unto Jesus, the author and perfecter of our faith."[13]

Moreover, this same Jesus said, "Seek ye first the Kingdom of God and His righteousness, and all these [other] things will be added unto you," and "He who seeks to save his own life will lose it, but he who loses his life for my sake, will save it to life everlasting."[14]

Finally, the doctrines, assertions, and conclusions contained in this volume are *not just the opinions of a man*.

That is because the author did not make the rules. *Jesus makes the rules!* As such, I merely restate in paraphrased form, what the *Living Word of God personally teaches as the Truth*.

Your friendly neighborhood biblical pastor,
David J. Bowers

---

12 Prov. 28:13; Isa. 1,6; Jer. 2-11; Ezek. 3-18; Zech. 13:6; Matt. 13,16:21-26; Luke 11-14,16,19; John 12:37-50; Rom. 1,2; 2 Cor.11:12-15; 2 Thess. 2; 2 Tim. 3; 1 Pet. 1:18; 4:17,18 *See also the book "Spiritual Guidelines for Restoration,": "Historical Review" section and Chapter 20: "Spiritual Law Eight: The Separation of the soul from the spirit".*

13 Heb. 12:1,2

14 Matt. 6:33; 16:21–26

## PART 1

Laying Down the Proper Foundation

Chapter 1

Gaining the Eternal Perspective

Introduction: The Call to Repentance

From the beginning to the end, God's voice calls out in His Word (written or spoken Scripture), in history and in nature. These three universal witnesses all proclaim the fact that human beings are special creations. As such, the one true living Father God who is in heaven has designed us to worship and serve Him only! St. Paul's comments recorded by Dr. Luke will teach us that God is never so far away from us that we cannot reach Him.[15] His Word says that we need only to cry out in penitent and humble submission, and he will answer. To start that process, God first requires that we admit (confess) our condition before him as needy sinful creatures who need a relationship with God to survive! Second, God expects us to be willing to repent of all those things standing in the way of His love. Christian believers who have done this are incredibly privileged people! Through the wonderful grace of Jesus enabled by his perfect work on Calvary, we can have a personal relationship with Almighty God and experience life to the fullest degree!

Even Christians *continue to need God. Indeed, our awareness of that need should even be more acute. We should acknowledge our abject need of the Savior* to deliver us from this present evil age we live in and from the evil that lurks within our own human nature. Pay close attention to what Isaiah wrote to God's people long ago.[16]

---

15   Acts 17:24–31
16   Read Isaiah 55:6–9 in *The Amplified Bible Version*

I. Notice the contrasts between God's ways and man's ways.

Paul describes this contrast well in Romans 8. *The spiritual mind versus the carnal mind* illustrates these ways. God's Word says that the spiritual mind is *the mind of Christ*, and that it brings life and peace. Conversely, the carnal, self-centered or *humanistic* mind is death to us. This mind-set cuts us off from God because Scripture tells us this attitude is the *enemy* of God. Not only that, it inevitably causes *conflict*. This is so because those living in those ways are in rebellion against God, seeking to *go their own way!* [17] Moreover, since *God is Spirit*, the truth is that believers must progress from the carnal state to the spiritual first to form a *lasting personal relationship with God* and to reach spiritual maturity. It also follows that one cannot ever hope to attain *the eternal perspective* without first undergoing a *radical transformation of the mind!*

One must realize that it takes *godly and spiritual wisdom* to be able to discern the sacred (the spiritual and godly) from the profane (soulish, humanistic, and ungodly). Isaiah's prophecy to Israel echoes King David's correct spiritual attitude about God that the Scripture overall teaches us.[18] Nevertheless, notice that "God does not contend forever." To avoid judgment, we must reach a point of repentance!

Yet God knows everything—and He always perfectly preserves the delicate *balance* between judgment and mercy![19] Scripture tells us that in God's eyes, God always intended mercy to *triumph over judgment*.[20] Dear reader, that highlights the *over-arching precept of Agape love* in technicolor. God's Word has mirrored this kind of love in the New Covenant understanding of the *Christian Gospel!* That is because, *in Christ, mercy does triumph over judgment* in real time and in real lives, and "on earth, [just] as it is in heaven." All you have to do is seek the truth from God's Spirit, who will break it down to the fundamental elements for you.

---

17   Isaiah 53:6
18   Psa. 32, 51; Isaiah 57:15
19   Psa. 107; Matt. 9:13; 12:7
20   2 Cor. 2:14; James 2:13

That is how you can *understand it from a spiritual vantage point.* If you do this, you find that this precept is *a central tenet of New Covenant theology!* Believers must understand that the New Covenant gospel is verily the *fruition of all covenant history* up to this present point in time we call the *age of grace.* In the Old Testament, according to Paul's derivations in Romans and Galatians that we also see in writings of the undisclosed writer of Hebrews, God used various temporary arrangements with man.[21]

The most recognizable of these was the time when God gave Moses *the Law—which developed into biblical Judaism,* which Paul calls *the Schoolmaster* (based on the *Tanakh, not* the *Talmud*). Thus, God shaped a special people who would *provide the Seed.* Paul identifies this seed as the Messiah, Jesus Christ, who would fulfill the original promise made to Abraham in the book of Genesis. This promise was that *the seed* of Abraham was to provide a *blessing to all the nations.* This we know as the New Covenant of Jesus Christ or Christianity (original definition).

God's original plan was always to *redeem humanity* using the sacrifice and perfect work of Jesus Christ, the Seed and Lamb of God. This is also the *eternal paradigm* that contains God's *eternal perspective for* believers today.

God's will is that *His holy presence live in man.* The Holy Spirit does this via the new birth of the human spirit—regeneration.

At the *consummation,* after Jesus Christ comes back, the kingdom is restored to the Father. The outcome will be that the tabernacle of God will be with man in a new set of heavens and earth.[22]

In the interest of maintaining a focus, we will be dealing primarily with those events that directly concern the church during the period called *the last days,* which includes the following:

A. The *great apostasy.* This leads us into

B. The *tribulation of those days* including the period called

C. The *great tribulation,* which also includes

---

21 Romans 1–8; Galatians 2–5, and Hebrews 1, 7–10 *See the book Basic Christian Doctrine and the papers entitled "Fulfilment Prophecy" and "Principles of Fulfillment Theology"*

22 Dan. 9:26; Luke 21:8–33; 1 Cor. 15:20–28; Phil. 1:6; 1 Thess. 4:13–17; Rev. 21

D. The event called *the second coming of Jesus Christ*, which includes

E. The *rapture of the saints* and

F. The *day of the Lord*

Moreover, in preparation for understanding these very significant events, we will attempt to lay down some fundamental biblically-based New Covenant doctrines. These will serve to provide us a more detailed understanding of what our responsibilities are as believers in the last days.

The reader will notice the intentional use of repetition to emphasize specific doctrines that are *crucial elements* during biblical conversion and for survival in the last days.

II. Consider the doctrine of law vs. grace**

Again, Paul gives us many insights in his letters to New Covenant churches of the first century. In Romans, First and Second Corinthians, and Galatians, he develops the precept of faith that first divides into two spiritual streams of *law and grace* that recombine and flow into the New Covenant river. By grace, God gave faith to the patriarchs. Then, God gave the Law to Moses=Old Covenant / Testament= (Biblical) Judaism. God intended this temporary arrangement to bring man to the ultimate realization that he could not relate to God because of *sin*. The law told him that *the universal penalty for that sin was death!* Yet the old covenant used a stopgap measure that enabled man *at least to have a limited relationship to God* via the *Mosaic-Levitical-Sacrifice System* God inaugurated this because of Israel's intransigent rebellion in the wilderness. It was a complex and very messy set of ritual acts that the sinner would have to undergo. Yet this was the way God used so that people could worship a holy and righteous God and avoid destruction.

However, God never intended to continue this system indefinitely. Paul explains to us that the two main purposes of the law were: 1) *to bring the consciousness of sin to the surface*, 2) to make man realize that nobody can be justified with God by compliance with the law! Nobody can keep the whole law, *not even one point of it, no matter how righteous they think they are.* This is *because* God says that even if we *err only in one point*, we are *guilty of all!* [23]** Notice that it was this aspect of the law that Jesus frequently raised when discussing matters with the Pharisees! However, these facts, as important as they are, were still subservient to God's greater plan of *Redemption*. God's Word points to the only solution: once the Seed Sacrifice Lamb that *Jesus Christ Himself provided* was in place, humanity could be freed from the "curse of the law." Then the doorway was finally opened for all sinners to receive that *once-for-all perfect sacrifice of Christ by faith*. This is how we become *righteous before God without the works of the law.*[24]

In the New Covenant, *the blood of Christ does all the work* that the old covenant could never hope to attain to in man's lives: that is, *to cleanse the conscience from guilt; forgive all sins* that would have exacted eternal penalties and place the sinner-convert in a *favored position before God* where he is justified and righteous in his sight. Spiritual *regeneration* *requires that God extend a special type of grace* we call *prevenient grace*.

However, once God has established this restoration of the spiritual functions in a life, God requires that we also maintain a personal relationship *by engaging our reborn human spirit*. Yes, it is *every believer's responsibility* to abide in Christ *by our daily choice!* The New Covenant enables man to commune with God. Moreover, the regenerated sinner can accrue gifts and benefits never available before! Yes, the *perfect sacrificial atonement of Christ* provided a *perfect elegant solution* to the ancient problem of reconciling a sinful humanity to a Holy God while *simultaneously maintaining both His justice and mercy!* The New Covenant does it all in Christ, the *over-arching principle* being none other than *divine grace.*

First, God operates by *prevenient grace*, by which God freely advances faith to every person to provide a way in the door to the Kingdom of Heaven and Salvation. God operates in us by the process of *infusion grace* after the person responds in receiving the sacrifice of Christ. *God's spirit transposes* the very mind and nature of Christ *directly to us*. God's Spirit is the agent of grace in all.

---

23   James 2:10 **See also the book Basic Christian Doctrine, Appendix F
24   Rom. 3:19–26; Gal. 2:16–21; Heb. 7:11–10:39

The beauty of it all is that the very presence of God can live in us *during the same time* he does this special work of internal metamorphosis and transformation within us that we call *conversion* Of course, we must realize that once God has commenced this process, *it requires our cooperation* all the way through. The crucial point is that the regenerated sinner must develop (by transformation only) the spiritual *mind of Christ*, which in turn enables us to think like God thinks. Subsequently, we can *visualize the eternal perspective that he sees.*

Let us also continually realize that this very special and sacred process of *salvation* *is not automatically permanent* after the time we initially decide to receive Christ. We must *repent daily* and *actively cooperate with God continually* to escape the tyranny of the carnal mind and to move on to achieve the things that are His will for you! Moreover, God *does not consider this active cooperation to be work,* but rather it is our *God-ordained responsibility* that *fulfills our part of the New Covenant agreement.*

Whether we realized it or not, we accepted this crucial condition when we first signed on with Jesus, for it is part and parcel of the New Covenant. Finally, we must understand that the heavenly things concerning the Kingdom of God must *gain the place of highest priority. Not only that, we must do this while we are living here on earth* to be ready for Jesus Christ to come![25] **

III. Christian, beware of the Esau mentality!

Can we recognize the utter futility of a self-centered and worldly focus in our own lives? Consider the responses Jesus had in John 6.[26] The outside crowd of supposed believers could not handle the truth and left. Jesus asks Peter, "Will you also leave?" Peter responds, saying, "Where shall we go? You have the Words of eternal life." Yet, why did the crowds leave? Why could they not see what Peter saw? That is the problem I believe the church is facing right now in these last days! Can we see the big picture that God sees and *act according to faith and not*

---

25   Luke 9:23–26; John 1:1–14, 29–34; 3:3–8; 4:23,24; 5:19–30; 6:27 ff.; 8:12 ff.; Rom. 6:1–8:39;12:1 ff.; 1 Cor. 1:17–2:16; Col. 3:1; 2 Tim. 2: 11–13; Heb. 2:1– ; 3:14; 4:9–16; 6:4–12; 10:26–39; 2 Pet. 1:2–11 f. **See the paper entitled "Figure One: Illustration–Comparison"
26   John 6:35–63

fear? Do we have the courage to stand out *from the crowd*—even the *compromising Christian crowd?* Many have already bartered away their eternal future for that "mess of pottage" that we can identify today with: popularity, acceptance, and many transitory temporal things of this world like financial gain, job security, houses and lands, family traditions and national customs, all of which are ephemeral and will not last![27] Nevertheless, the truth hardly ever seems to slow the downward slide to more compromise, does it? Admittedly, the illusion of temporal security is a powerful mirage, is it not? Yet, God's Word tells us that the *only guarantee of absolute security is in Jesus Christ!* To be there and *continue, we must choose to follow and obey Christ.* This age of cynicism and hopelessness has bred a generation obsessed with self-interest, and this mentality has greatly penetrated the church. The question Christians should be asking one another is: Do we really cherish Jesus most of all? If so, then we *should plan to count the cost of serving Him.*

This is not the time to be feathering our nests or to be "building sandcastles by the seaside." This is because God knows that the waves of circumstance that are coming will wipe away all worldly supports! Is the house that represents your life built upon the *Rock* (Jesus)?[28]

The truth is that the only security that we can count on is found within total dependence and faith in God. True saving faith in God includes *following Christ's commands at face value* and letting the chips fall as they may. Yes, unbelievers out in the world may be selfish, but they are not stupid. They are watching everything we do to see what Christians do under pressure! Are they going to *sell out like everybody else?* If you do, that is what Jesus means by being *a foolish virgin!* In the parable they *thought* they were OK, didn't they?

Oh yes, they *had oil,* but their supply was eventually exhausted, yet they *still presumed* they had their "so-called ticket" in their back pocket. Nevertheless, something went very wrong, didn't it? Somewhere along the way, their priorities got mixed up. Foolishly, they *waited too long* to buy more oil, a symbol in God's Word representing the necessary *ongoing spiritual faith-walk of the Christian life.* Why did this happen? Perhaps they just got discouraged or distracted. Possibly, like many

---

27   James 4:13–17
28   Matt. 7:13–29; Luke 6:46–49

Christians today, they got *caught up in the worldly influences* of pride, fear, ambition, and disbelief. In any case, *they chose unwisely,* just what Esau did! Esau became *addicted to his own desires* and ordered his life around *himself.* Since selfishness drove him, he then undervalued (despised) his birth-right. Sadly, like Esau, *many Christians* have *despised their birth-right and the spirit of grace,* trampling the blood of Christ in the dirt by their wicked attitudes! What did Jesus say that a king would do with those subjects who despise him and flout his laws? Scripture infers that Esau *could have* redeemed his birth-right, *had he acted in time,* but he did not. Possibly he just procrastinated too long! Take warning, my friend, it could happen to you!

Jesus teaches plainly that salvation requires that you must faithfully endure true to Jesus *all the way to the end.*[29]

Yes, we have a *kairos* moment—a window of opportunity that we dare not miss! The Latin phrase "carpe diem" tells us to *seize the moment of opportunity while it is here.* Jesus said that "we must work while it is day, for the night is coming when no man can work." The "window of opportunity" is fast passing. *Many will say* the same things said outside Noah's ark, "Let us in," but it will be too late! When Jesus comes back, He must tell *many Christians,* "Depart from Me, I never knew you." So, *do not let it be you!* You have a choice, so choose Jesus now! Get right with God before it is too late! Where is the eternal perspective today that will protect us from the eternal cost of being a *foolish virgin?* [30]

In the midst of all this, we must consider the advantages of living in these times! We are at the *climax of the ages! True believers are incredibly privileged of God!* This is so in spite of all the negative things that have been happening in the world around us. Yes, we still have an *excellent opportunity to show the world what true Christianity is!* Yet the big question looms before us: *Are you willing to pay the cost?* No excuse for ignorance exists. This is the cost that we should expect to pay and the circumstances we know we must endure, about which Jesus has taught every believer.

---

29   Matt. 24:13; Luke 19; Heb. 2:1–3; 3:1–6, 12–19; 6:3–12
30   Ezek. 18:30; 33,34; Matt. 7:13–21; 25:1–13; Luke 21:34–36; John 15:1–7;2 Cor. 11; 1 Tim. 6; 2 Tim. 2; Heb. 3:1–6,12–14; 4:1–16; 6:1–7; 10:26–39; 12:1–18.

Jesus also told His disciples in his time here on earth that many prophets and righteous men have longed to see what you have seen, *but we have seen much more yet than they have!* More than the heroes of Hebrews 11! We stand to inherit such a great blessing *If we but endure just a little while longer!* Yet, why are we in such trouble? Of course, we know that the great apostasy will precede that great day. Precisely because of that, we know that Judge Jesus is almost here! Let us supplicate for His mercy to triumph over judgment!

IV. We must examine ourselves and ask some probing questions:

What kind of Christian do you think is going to be *pleasing in Jesus's sight when He comes?* To Whom will Jesus say, "Well done, good and faithful servants?"[31]*

What are the things that you *now savor, enjoy, and cherish the most in this life you are living here on earth?* [32]

Do you believe that you have "chosen the better part" like Mary of Bethany? [33]

What do *you* believe has *such eternally lasting value* that you are *willing to sacrifice everything* in this world for to preserve that *one thing intact* for heaven? Can you say goodbye to all the advantages that the world places so much value on? The respect of colleagues, power, material gains, jobs, security, retirement benefits, houses, lands, etc.? Of course, you would not be so foolish as to think that you could *have your cake and eat it too,* do you? For Jesus was clear in teaching us that is impossible! Remember that "pearl of great price" Jesus talked about.[34]

Do you emulate those *stand-up heroes* of yesteryear that they have recorded in those glowing accounts in Scripture? Can you match their commitment and zeal and *prove it by the way you live?* What is the eternal perspective worth to you in a materialistic, cynical, and unbelieving age? The Bible records how Job, Abraham, Joseph, Moses, David, and Daniel served God in their time. Have you thought about

---

31   Matt. 24:45,46; *Luke 18:8 *See also Appendix B.*

32   Psa. 119:9–11; Matt. 6:9–13; 16:21–26

33   Luke 10:38–42; 2 Cor. 4; Eph. 3; Col. 3,4

34   Matt. 13:46 See the paper entitled *"Biblical Prosperity"*

the sacrifices that Stephen, James, Peter, Paul, Titus, and Timothy made? What about the price Saint Martin of Tours, John Wyclif, and John Huss paid?

History occludes so many more Christian believers that apostate religion has erased from man's memory "of whom the world is not worthy." These saints paid an *awesome price to serve Jesus in purity.* "Good Christian people" despised them too. Did that make them losers? Does that mean that God was not blessing them?

So, *consider that price* that Jesus said *all Christians must be willing to pay just to be His disciples!* People of this world do not seem averse to working hard for something, spending years learning a profession or trade or paying truckloads of money for the things that they value so much. So why is it that I keep hearing those *what-if questions* from Christians so often? [35]

Could there be many calling themselves Christians who really do not value the things of God's heavenly kingdom after all? Could it be that they really doubt that Jesus will take care of them?

Do you *truly believe* what the Scripture says and follow up and *prove that belief* by our respect, honor, and emulation of Jesus and His way? Was the price paid by those blessed martyrs who *have blazed the trail before us in vain?* You know the answers to those questions, don't you? Yes, the Christian life is based on an either-or proposition: It is *all or nothing at all!* Jesus will *not take second place!*

That is, either you *consider Jesus as Lord of all* in your life, *or you do not consider Him Lord at all!* He said that you chose to serve either *one master or the other.* That means that you are *unable to serve both simultaneously, you must choose between them.* You either choose to follow the world and all those ephemeral advantages with which Satan tempted Jesus in the wilderness, recorded in Matthew 4 and Luke 4. Otherwise, you choose to do what Moses did *and turn your back on all that the world offers and choose to follow Jesus all the way.* God allows *no neutral grounds of compromise in that war!* Both Jesus and John call it "the patience of the saints." Paul calls it "the fight of faith," and many early Christians call it *"the way."* Essentially, the bottom line of this

---

35   Luke 6:20 ff.; 1 Tim. 6:3–10; 2 Tim. 2:1 ff.

crucial doctrine that we cannot dismiss for being 'irrelevant' is what the writer calls *faith-based pacifism, * a *foundational lynchpin of the true complete Christian Gospel!* [36]

Indeed, this indispensable element is one of the "forgotten parts" of the complete Gospel that Scripture tells us would be "spoken against" by many because it flies in the face of all *humanistic ways of "salvation."* [37]

Jesus said that at any given time we could choose to walk on only one of two paths. These paths also correspond to the two masters and represent the only *two possible destinies we have.* Consequently, Jesus says that you inevitably choose to follow *one of two ways:* one is through the *wide gate*—the popular and broad way or through the *line of least resistance* that leads the crowd down the garden path to destruction and perdition. The only other way (the only way to heaven) is that you choose to persevere to the end by going through "the strait gate" and by continuing on "the narrow way that leads to eternal life." Jesus tells us that few will find it. *Fewer still will stay on it.* Ultimately, as a Christian, you must evaluate your choices seriously. As always, our greatest choice remains. What have you done with Jesus the crucified? [38]

V. What do you really believe about Jesus Christ?

Do you really worship God in spirit and in truth? Is your life adorned by your continual pledge of allegiance to Christ alone? As Moses did, do you *follow through in your actions, not fearing the wrath of any earthly king?* Have you even come to the point of enduring the scorn of your friends and family because of your stand for Jesus Christ? [39]

Are you 100 percent *committed to obey Jesus Christ to the best of your ability, so help you, God?* Yes, Jesus Christ is eternal wisdom personified. He is the *bright and morning star.* His Example is the *living eternal perspective* that we have revealed to man. He has personally commanded every Christian to follow him here on earth (just as it is in heaven)! This is so because of His preexistence and preeminence *regarding all things*

---

36   1 Tim. 6:12; Hebrews 11:23–29
37   Matt. 5:43–48; Luke 2:34; 21:19; John 14:21–26; Acts 28:22; Rom. 12:9–21; 1 Tim. 6:3; 2 Tim. 2:10–15; 4:1–8 Heb. 12:1–3; 1 Pet. 2:12; Rev. 12:10,11; 14:12,13
38   Matt. 7:13–21; 24:13
39   Ibid. Footnote 21

in the Christian life whether private or public! Scripture teaches that Jesus Christ is entitled to this because he is first.

First, in being with God from the very beginning. The Scripture defines Jesus Christ *as the same species as God.* Father God, Jesus Christ, and the Holy Spirit together form the Tri-Unity, where all three is One. He is also first because *Jesus Christ created all the heavens* and the earth, and by His power *Jesus Christ holds together all things.* Verily, Jesus Christ is the 'cosmic glue' that holds all 'matter-space-time' together. This entire universe *belongs to Christ and exists for his use and glory:* thrones, dominions, resources, and nature. Every man and institution *of it is subject to the all-encompassing absolute authority of Jesus Christ!*

Jesus Christ is also the *direct head of His body, the church.* Scripture also defines the church as the "elect" or the saints. *All legitimate authorities* of earth exist by the permissive will of Christ alone. Their authority is conditional, indirect, provisional, and subject to Christ because He created them for his use.[40]

Second, let us "look unto Jesus, the author and perfecter of faith." Besides His person, what has Jesus done, and what does Jesus continue doing that we should even more respect, honor, serve, emulate, and obey him? 1) Jesus is our advocate. 2) Jesus is our high priest. 3) Jesus is the only Mediator of the Holy Spirit, our vital link to the Kingdom of Heaven. He gives us the ability to develop a personal relationship with Father God!

Third, the judge of all is coming! God the Father has declared Jesus Christ the righteous to be supreme judge of all, including His body, the church!

One day Jesus Christ Himself will summon every believer to appear before Him personally. Those who make it there must give account of themselves for everything they did or did not do in this life they lived here on earth![41]

Therefore, as we view all these things, consider the following:

---

40   John 1:1–14; 3;27–30; 8:58; 10:30; 1 Cor. 1:17–2:16; Eph. 1:17–23; Phil. 1:19– 21; 2:5–11; Col. 1:12–2:10

41   Matt. 24:1 ff.; 25:1 ff.; Luke 12–19; John 5:19-30; 9:39–41; Acts 10:36–43; 17:24–31; Rom. 2:11–16; 14:10; 2 Cor. 5:8–10; 1 Pet. 4:17,18.

VI. What manner of conversation (lifestyle) should a person who claims to be a Christian be aiming for? Where is the way in which we should walk?[42]

We are directed by the Word of God to *humble ourselves* at the feet of Jesus for our Daily Bread. Believers must also do our part in *obedience*. Continual abiding in the following activities enables the continued supply of grace.[43]*

One, we must *confess our sin*. Part of this is admitting that you may have been holding to *false doctrines*, among which two are very common among modern Christians: defending immorality and the sanctioning of homicide. Two, we must *repent from all sin*. Three, believers must *engage in heartfelt worship* of God in spirit and in truth. Four, we must *exercise our faith in Christ's righteousness*. Five, believers must *submit to the Holy Spirit* who infuses God's grace for the ongoing process of *conversion.*

The following universal spiritual relationship at work here is patent: the only possible way we can have revival is that we must see *the whole unified action of the body of Christ* following Christ. In order for revival to reverse the apostate slide the church is presently in, the church must exercise diligence, honesty, and repentance from the top on down. That is, we must hold leadership to the *same biblical standard* as everyone. Yes, the body of Christ is crying for substantial, honest, forthright, and *humble-minded reform*. The church can no longer afford to be more concerned with image consciousness than with people! Churches must put out a welcome mat for the prophetic proclamation of God's Word. The *true condition* of the body of Christ must get out in the open, and *we must deal with* it instead of playing this dangerous denial game.

We must acknowledge that *constructive and biblical criticism is not being divisive!* In fact, Jesus Himself was the first Christian to do this. We see it frequently in His discourses with the Pharisees! Such a biblical precedent gives us the same basis to hold church leadership accountable today! Remember Jesus sees everything we do. Nobody is

---

42   Isa. 30:15–21; Matt. 6:9–15; 1 John 1:5–10

43   *See Appendix B and the papers "The Amazing Doctrine of God's Grace" and "Conditions of Salvation"*

going to get away with anything with God, so we might as well come clean now.

VII. So what can we do to "prepare the bride for the coming of the Bridegroom, Jesus?"

Believers must become (and stay as) *wise virgins* who are diligent and zealous for his cause, waiting patiently for His coming. Meanwhile, this means doing what Jesus commands us. Therefore, the subject of last days revival is of primary concern to all wise virgins. Wise virgin believers need to "set the example" for younger or weaker believers, so they can have the "reference points" we all require to properly live the true Christian life. Mature believers are also always ready to give answers to anyone who asks about their faith, responding with respect, clarity, and gentleness.[44] Wise virgin saints may at times, however, be required to "get in the face" of those who persistently remain in rebellion against God's Word with strong and timely reprimands. Yet, these blunt messages are only directed at those who show blatant disregard and arrogant disrespect for the Word and way of Jesus Christ. Others may occasionally require more gently but nonetheless forthright exhortations and reminders to stay faithful to Jesus. Yet, you have to ask yourself, *"Who is out there obeying* the Word of God's clarion calling to repentance and vigilance?" Yes, we know that God's Word has told us that the "true *remnant*" is out there, however, you just do not see them often, do you? Who will respond in time to avoid the fate of becoming another Esau? Our answer lies in the sacred wisdom of Scripture.[45]

VIII. How do we deal with the problem of apostasy?

We are living in the last days. We are also in the early stages of the period called "the great apostasy." This is a crucial period and God's Spirit is *testing believers* to the limit. As Jesus told His disciples (Christians) in Matt. 7, *two separate and distinct groups are going to develop* within *the outward professing Church:* first, we have those who

---

44   1 Pet. 3:15
45   Matt. 7:13–21; 24:1 ff.; 25:1 ff.; Heb. 6:1–7; 10:26–39; James 1:1–8, 17, 18, 21– 27; 2:14–26

will fall back into apostasy, following the crowd on "the wide road." Unfortunately, you will not have to look far to see those who are following the Christian crowd— blindly conforming to societal norms, ordinary human responses, and national traditions that will lead them along the garden path to the fate of Judas and Demas. Then, second, we have the believers who are resolutely determined to *follow Jesus no matter what the cost.* That is what it is going to take for Christians to survive. We must pass "through the strait (pressured) gate and the narrow way (the only way) to eternal life, and few find it."

As time goes by, you will be hard pressed to find these, however, *identifying them will be very easy!* They are the ones who have discovered the *sublime value* of the eternal perspective of the Kingdom of Heaven. This heavenly mind-set from the Holy Spirit teaches them that spiritual things *are worth the sacrifice of anything in this world to maintain!* Consequently, they are willing to *pay any price* to ensure their spiritual vitality! They also have accepted some harsh facts about being sojourners and foreigners while in this world. This means that the apostate religious system (the great harlot of Revelation 17, which is guilty of the blood of the saints) will continue for some time.

Unfortunately, the "false cross" and "great prostitute" of churchianity (the cults and "corporation churchianity") will still continue to persecute the genuine saints. They will ignore, dis-fellowship, revile, and hate them because they stand for the *real* Jesus Christ. Have you the fortitude and courage to withstand those conditions and remain *true to Jesus?*

IX. The purpose of this book is to inform and to empower.

This book is for you "if the jury is still out" on what you consider to be *true Christianity,* or if you are one of those who have not fully committed your life to Christ. Yet, you still need to know that *He loves you* more than you could ever know! Are you *really seeking the* truth? Moreover, are you willing to consider new vistas of the truth although you still have your doubts about what the *real standard of Christianity is?* If so, then please read on. Are you one of those privileged ones who know Christ? Then I beseech you to keep an open mind and to be willing to reconsider some things you have been brought up believing, but are *really not sure why you believe those things.* The doctrines and truths herein are also directed toward the ones that the religious establishment has ignored and to the ones who are just following the mainstream crowd for fear of being alone. Yes, the author has written this book for you! Finally, have you *made the greatest commitment of all? Have you accepted your own death up front for your faith in Christ?* If so, then this book should be a great encouragement for you, for this period we are entering is going to be *the church's finest hour!*

Your friend and fellow servant *in Christ,*
Pastor David J. Bowers

## Chapter 2

Vital Issues Affecting Christianity in the Last Days

For Christians, these are sobering times, especially in view of the "big lies" imbedded in high profile events (like the 9/11 attack) and the rapidly unfolding concurrent prophecies regarding the formation of a global dictatorship. If you truly believe the Bible to be the verbally-inspired Word of God, then you cannot ignore the gathering facts that the time is getting very close for the second coming of Jesus Christ. This is no time to be playing games with God! Not only that, Paul clearly warned, "That God would send 'strong delusion' upon all apostates… That they might be damned who *refused to love the truth that God might save them!* [46]" However, I believe that many Christians have lost all hope of the Lord's coming. Consequently, they act like the foolish ones in Jesus's prophetic discourses.[47]

Satan has caught the vast majority up in the things of this world, *"selling out" in droves* for temporal gain, the transient enjoyment of material things, and for pleasures of the moment. Wholesale compromise is the order of the day. *Many churches lower the standard to the ground* to cater to and entertain the masses to get people in the doors, whatever it takes. Pleasing people is a dangerous game to play, my friends. It is like playing Russian Roulette with your eternal destiny. God will not take second place in your heart! Harsh judgment awaits all those who work for Satan (whether they know they do or not!).[48]

---

46   2 Thess. 1:8–2:12; Rev. 13
47   Matt. 24,25; Mark 13; Luke 13,21
48   Isa. 14; Ezek. 28, 32; Matt. 25:41–46; Mark 9:42–48

Where are the ones whom Jeremiah said are "valiant for the *truth?* "[49] Where are the Timothys of today?

Where has the teaching of the complete Gospel of Christ gone? You see many churches full of people, but most are going through the motions, acting like ignorant sheep with no clue of direction. Worse yet, we have precious few biblical shepherds to guide them. What kind of witness do you think the world gets if believers themselves lack commitment to Jesus?

How do you protect against widespread hypocrisy and self-indulgent lifestyles without a *consistent* New Testament standard of morality or ethics being preached? Will Jesus accept *that* kind of bride? I love the church, and in their best interests, I must tell the whole truth. The *vital issues* we must face are:

I. Issue 1

The teaching of the *false gospel of easy-believeism.* It is a tragedy that most mainstream *nominal Christians* have never heard the *complete gospel.* This discrepancy exists because most are led to believe that *mere mental assent about Christ is sufficient for "salvation."* Consequently, many *erroneously believe they can possess a get-out-of-hell free card* to stick in their back pocket and still go on with unchanged! However, that is *far from the original truth of the gospel* that either Jesus or the early apostles taught. This was *certainly not* what the early church consistently taught for the first three centuries after the ascension of Christ either. In the light of Paul's clear condemnation of compromise, let us see what has happened. Throughout the centuries religious hierarchies have sought to evade being *true to the original gospel.*

They have used several foils, all of which employ misinterpretation and false doctrine:[50]

---

49   Jer. 9:3; 1 Tim. 4:1–5; 2 Tim. 3:1–9; 4:1 ff.
50   Matt. 24:21–51; Luke 12:1–12; 21:7–19, 25–28, 34–36; Rom. 8:1 ff.; 1 Cor. 15:20–34; 2 Cor. 4:1– 6; 10:3–6; 11:10–15; Gal. 1:6–12; Eph. 1:7–10; Phil. 1:6; Col. 2:16–23; 2 Thess. 1:3–2:12; 1 Tim. 4:1–6; 2 Tim. 3:1–4:8 *See also Glossary of Terms entry *Determinism* and the papers entitled Christian Guidelines for Spiritual Warfare, Part Three: "Cracking the False Doctrine code" "The Doctrine of the Elect" and "Fallacies of Determinism."*

One is that many conspire to sub-divide or partition off the New Testament, claiming that what Jesus taught in the Gospels was "just for the Jews." Jesus's own ministry soundly refutes this.

Two, we can also spot a common doctrine found among "fundamental evangelicals"—they claim that "we did not form" the church until the day of Pentecost in Acts 2. Nevertheless, who has originally ordained the church and to whom does it *rightfully* belong? Nonetheless, they use that pitiful excuse to *dismiss or disqualify by fiat* nearly all the sayings of Jesus that way! They just write them out and ignore them. Convenient, is it not, especially when you come to some of those *hard sayings,* but does that do them any good regarding God?

Three, another sophisticated one, favored by mainstream organized Christianity overall, is that *they consider* the doctrines of Christianity to be like "a body of laws" that religious authority has "developed and protected" throughout time.

Yes, sixty years did elapse before they wrote down the New Testament. Yet, they willfully ignore the fact that the *true church thrived during that time!*

However, *they* claim that it took centuries to "decide what was canonical" or not. They also claim that it took many wise men and the decrees of "so-called infallible popes" and innumerable councils for *them to "establish"* just what the beliefs of Christianity are. Obviously they are not telling us the truth!

Apparently, as time passed, many of these accreted humanistic traditions of religious leaders and elders followed a similar pattern as the Rabbinical and Talmudic traditions of the Jews before them, evolving into a tainted 'Christian' *Orthodoxy* that diverged significantly from the original Gospel of Christ! Again, they continue to assiduously foster the false notion that 'authority is the truth' and not the correct reverse: *truth is the authority!*

Four, many authorities also have formed this modern gospel on a loose method of *interpretation that uses indiscriminate averaging of texts* from both the Old and New Testaments. In doing so, they ignore the higher wisdom of God's Spirit. They bypass true spiritual exegesis that teaches us that the New Covenant alone is our rule of law. However,

Bible schools and seminaries still routinely teach using humanistic methods like *empiricism.*

Five, as a result, modern-day believers have inherited a confusing and highly syncretized conglomeration of dogma that religious leaders call *the Judeo-Christian tradition*. Most likely, it is *this* compromised modern gospel that they have taught you when you first began to believe in Christ. Worse yet, the authorities treat anyone who questions those traditions with high-minded scorn, saying, "Who do you think you are to question this long list of intelligent and gifted 'preservers' of Christianity throughout the world for two thousand years? How could it be possible *that many could be wrong,* and that *you are right?*" Of course, what Jesus said so clearly just could not break through their hard heads, could it?

Six, then we have various forms of a doctrine called *determinism,* alias "predestination." All types of *determinism* employ *dualism*. They also violate the great command and are essentially equivalent to *fatalism.* The New Covenant upholds the doctrine of "the sovereignty of God and the responsibility of man," teaching that total depravity *does not absolve human beings from the accountability of free will!* Predictably, most religious organizations oppose this because it disproves many of their pet doctrines! Consequently, few through history who rejected traditional religious dogma and policies escape unharmed.

**May the reader take note: The author has covered this volatile subject in detail in two other books, *Jesus' Way,* and *Spiritual Guidelines for Restoration.*

II. Issue 2

What does the original and real Gospel of Jesus Christ teach us? The New Testament Gospel clearly teaches that *Christ is the only owner of salvation.* He is the only one who died to make us free (in all ways) by virtue of *purchase by His precious blood!* Moreover, our salvation is a product that is contingent upon our use and exercise of a special quality called *faith.* God extends faith as *an initial* gift or a privilege granted to every person so that they *can believe.* From then on, however, one must exercise *their own free will.* First, *choose to abide in Jesus by implicit obedience.* Second, cooperate with God every step along the way. Third, *seek His wisdom and power* to give us ultimate success in that *lifelong discipleship and conversion* process we know as the Christian life. *The true gospel* teaches that *no discount tickets to heaven exist.* The gospel teaches that we must count the cost of continuing to pay a *high price* for living the true faith that really is Christianity! In fact, *the whole idea of a ticket* presumes the fallacious assumption of *ownership.*[51] In the sum, we must *abide true to Jesus* to the end of our life or when Jesus comes, whichever comes first, to be assured of *eventual* salvation. Yes, we must be careful to be aware of the tenses and conditions of salvation to properly understand what Scripture *truly* says!

Whenever Scripture speaks concerning salvation, it is always with these conditions in mind. *Notice the ifs and the words before, such as "unto salvation,"* which reveals that an underlying process is requiring our cooperation. Take for example the phrase "to them he gave *power to become* the sons of God." Notice that Scripture does not teach that this transformation is automatic! *Let us carefully examine* the New Testament with an *open mind.* You will find that the New Covenant is very specific about the *conditions we must satisfy* to qualify for the benefits we may have assumed were automatic before! When you are considering Scripture, you must know that you are *dealing with spiritual quantities.* You dare not rely on ordinary human responses (the way of the flesh, the crowd, and the world). If you are foolish enough to choose to follow that way, your perception of God's Word *will be flawed!*[52] Believers must observe the following overall biblical precepts:

1. You must acquire the spiritual mind of Christ. We develop this mind of life and peace only by undergoing the expensive and crucial process of the transformation (*conversion*) of the mind!

2. You must respond in faith biblically *at the heart level,* including obedience to the direct literal teachings of Jesus, for God has commanded you to do this.

3. God expects you to continue to place the entire weight of your life upon what you claim to believe about God, which is the Gospel of

---

51   Rom. 8; Eph. 1,2; Col. 1; Titus 2:11–15. *See the papers: "Conditions for Salvation" and "God's Definition of Salvation"*

52   Matt. 6:24; Luke 10:22; John 1:12; Rom. 1:16,17; 6:1–8:39; 10:9,10; 2 Tim. 2:1 4:8 *See also Appendix A*

Christ. You will receive the doctrine in truth *only if all these conditions are satisfied!* Only biblical Christian faith is sufficient for salvation. Anything less is *worthless unbelief.* [53]

4. Biblical responses always result in *marked changes* in attitude and in lifestyle alterations as measured from the time the person initially commits their life unto the Lord Jesus Christ. Change (repentance) is the *first proof of faith!* This proves that easy-believeism is worthless, simply because it produces *no substantive ongoing change.* The Scriptures also teach us the following truths:

III. Issue 3

Maintaining a daily active faith relationship in the performance of all spiritual disciplines is mandatory for spiritual survival!

The New Testament teaches that each blood-bought believer in Christ is both responsible and accountable for doing the regular daily activities that form the *normal Christian life.* This responsibility commences immediately after we first truly receive Jesus Christ as our personal savior when the Holy Spirit introduces us into the body of Christ. God intends that our *progression into receiving the lordship of Christ* is a rapid process. Without any impediments to our moving into biblical discipleship, these changes should come quickly, *unless something has led us into error.* Believers backslide and become apostatized either by their own self-delusions or by the false or misleading teaching of others. *Since God always plays by the rules,* we must be zealous and repent daily by the following:

1. We must continually seek His presence and be sensitive to His holy Word. *Delight in His will for your life,* continually *worshiping in spirit and in truth.*[54]

2. We must *submit our lives daily* to the work and leading of the Holy Spirit. He is the *divine translator of God's* *infusion grace*. Not

53   Matt. 5:1–20; 24:13; John 7:15–18; 14:12–23; 15:10–12; Rom. 8:1–11; 1 Cor. 1:17–2:16; James 1:4–9; 2:14–26
54   Luke 11:1–13; John 4:23,24 See also Psalms 1,5,8,9,15,17,24,27,34

only that, God's grace is far from being irresistible. God requires our ongoing cooperation to enable the continued supply of grace.[55]

3. We must be faithfully obeying the teachings and commands of Jesus Christ as given in the New Testament accounts.[56]

4. We must be daily confessing and repenting from all known sin. Knowing the consequences, we must always *keep short accounts with God*.[57]

5. Our time in prayer with Jesus in secret must be *top priority business*. True disciples of Jesus Christ consistently cherish and treasure the central relationship they have *in the spirit*, and focus intently on becoming like Christ, building their lives upon the Rock. They absorb their entire lives in *prayer*, and in *cultivating the supreme values of the Kingdom of Heaven*. Overall, Spiritual things are their number one priority! These are the things like Agape love, faith, righteousness, peace, truth, etc.[58]

6. May we deny self and cheerfully *take up our cross daily!* This is the flip side of the priority process. That means that *if* you have truly prized the things of the Kingdom of Heaven, you will do those things that *prove that claim!* Moreover, this means "putting your money where your mouth is!"

If it is true about what you say, that is that you love Jesus, you will find yourself doing those things that *please Him,* will you not? *If* you love God, you will *not grieve His Holy Spirit* by continuing to rebel against him or to tolerate known active sin in your life. Scripture tells us that we are *no longer obligated* to sin like we were before we received Christ. Therefore, it follows that God looks at the *choices we make,* and that *no valid excuse* exists for failing to obey what Jesus has told us to do.[59]

---

55 John 15:1 f.; 16:13–15; Phil. 1:6–21; Rom. 6–8; Gal. 5 2:12.13. *See also Appendix E Entry "Grace"*

56 John 14:12–23; 15:10–12; 1 John 5:3.

57 1 John 1:5–10

58 Matt. 5–7; Luke 6:20–49; Col. 3:1 f.; 1 Thess. 5:16–24; 1 Tim. 6.

59 Luke 9:23–26; Rom. 6; 2 Tim. 2; 1 John 5:3. *See the papers entitled "an Analysis of Faith," "the Gravity of Sin," "How Does Christ's Blood get to us," "the Insidious Nature of Sin," "Living the Complete Gospel," "Obedience to Christ" and "the Way of the Cross"*

7. We must follow Jesus in *truth*. However, this is only possible *if* we have fulfilled all the conditions specified above. *Yes, it is* hard. It was never supposed to be easy! Following Jesus is incredibly tough and for very good reasons! Think about it. Why would Jesus have commanded His followers to do these things so specifically if doing so were not crucial to their survival as believers? Yes, Father God *fully expects Christians to comply with Jesus's literal commands* to the best of their ability, making no excuse! You need the power of God's Holy Spirit working in you to live the Christian life! It is also the only way we can truly fulfill the great commission. However, beware: you dare not take any "credit" for doing anything! *If* you could live the Christian life in the flesh (which is really impossible), then you could boast that you did it on your own. *Nobody steals glory from God* without paying a great price! That is why Satan and his angels are going to hell! Always remember that it is "not by works, lest any man boast."[60]

IV. Issue 4

*The principle of choice and consequence: divine windows of opportunity that we dare not miss!*** [61]Since the salvation process is *not automatic,* at every point in life we must *choose* to follow on, or we risk a relapse by default. During our lives, God has graciously given us numerous *windows of opportunity* at crucial junctures in life that are also used as tests to see if we are in right relationship. Missed opportunities can have dire consequences. What was the moral of the story in the parable of the talents? What happened to that servant, who having received the one talent, went and *buried it?* Remember Jesus's teaching in the parable of the great supper and the parable of the wedding guests. What was the destiny of the privileged ones whom God originally invited but who refused to come? If you look carefully, you will find a common *theme of choice and consequence in all Jesus's *parables*.* The primary issue that surfaces is always that God requires a specific choice, and that specific consequences always follow the chosen path because they are associated with that choice. The pattern is always the same:

---

60   Isa. 41–45; Eph. 2:8,9

61   **See Jesus's Major Parables, and the books entitled Basic Christian Doctrine (Area Twelve)* and Spiritual Guidelines for Restoration (Chapter 20, Law #10)*

CHOICE=MASTER=DESTINY or consequence.[62] Jesus plainly says that *it is the identity of the master you have chosen* at any particular time that *determines your destiny.*

Jesus is saying that if you were to die then or if He were to come back then, you will *inherit the destiny of that master you are truly following at that precise moment!* Procrastination is a very dangerous thing: the harsh truth is that *people are seldom able to change their ways instantaneously!* We have only two sets of destinies/masters: heaven/in Christ *or* hell/in Satan. "No man can serve two masters" (simultaneously).

Either he will love one and hate the other or hold to one and despise the other.** You cannot serve God and Mammon. *Mammon* is a symbol of the world system because the world system runs on money and power and all the associated activities used to get those things. Of course, we know that *the root of all that is selfishness,* which is another way of saying the *flesh.* This *humanism*, the carnal nature of man, is the archenemy of God because of its central theme of pride and independence (from God). That is why everything and everybody associated with the world system will follow Satan and his angels to hell! So if you have to serve somebody, who will you choose to serve?[63]

Beware, if you as a Christian seek to evade this issue, you will find yourself reverting back to the old master (guess who?) by default! *No neutral grounds exist!* You must abide on the path of life to inherit eternal life. Obedience and *perseverance are not works!* Nevertheless, God knows our frame. He is merciful and will forgive, pick you up again, and restore you if you fall. Yet you *must be honest with him and repent.* Keeping close accounts with God is serious![64] Consider Esau again. Esau was the firstborn son of Isaac and by tradition, had the *birth-right* of the family/clan. That meant that he stood to inherit the lion's share of his father's goods and the authority to act for the family. However, he was a man ruled by the desires of the flesh. One day, when he came back from a hunting trip famished, he saw his brother Jacob cooking a pot of lentils. A combination of factors caused him to act rashly as he did.

---

62 Matt. 6:24; 10:32,33; 2 Tim. 2:11,12; Heb. 10:32–39

63 Josh. 24:13; Isa. 14; Ezek. 28, 32; Matt. 6:24; 20:25–28; James 4:1–8; 1 John 2:15–17.

64 Matt. 24:13; John 15:1 ff. (Matt.) 7:13–23... Rom. 6–8; Gal. 1:6–12; 2 Tim. 2:11 15; Heb. 2–4;6:3–12; 10:26–39

First, Scripture says in Hebrews 12 that he was a profane man who was a slave of his lower appetites. Do you remember the rule of wisely choosing your master? He did not. However, since his desire was the immediate gratification of the moment, lust blinded him to the consequences of his action. He also thought little of his birthright at the time. Jacob, ambitious supplanter that he was, seized the opportunity to obtain the birthright by finagling using the uncontrolled desire Esau had for the lentils as the pressure point. This familiar pattern has caught many victims throughout the centuries! The results are astonishingly predictable. Later, we read that he tried to regain the lost birthright, but failed, *having lost the window of opportunity* (by that time)![65-]

We should take heed. Esau made his bed and had to lie in it. The lesson is a serious warning to all. Every compromise or foolish decision based on selfish interest exacts a price. Foolish believers will pay a similar high price for following the crowd or in believing the usual humanistic imperatives of the culture and national traditions of this present age. Even many *good things* in and of themselves can be a serious impediment to our spirituality if they divert our attention from our primary focus of life: serving the Lord Jesus Christ! Which of the two masters do you cherish the most? Remember also the parable of the prodigal son. Consider the decisions made by both the wanderer and the older brother.[66]

Another New Testament example illustrating this *principle of choice and consequence* was when Jesus was leading Peter, James, and John to the Mount of Transfiguration.

Jesus was warning the disciples that he was going to be betrayed to the authorities and executed. Peter interjected and blurted out the usual human response to such things: "This cannot happen to You!" (Assuming that Jesus was to be the new king and lead an armed revolution against the Romans and usher in a new kingdom of Israel right then!) *Wrong answer!* Jesus bluntly rebukes Peter, saying,

"Get thee behind me Satan, for you cherish the things that are of men and not the things that are of God." Do you *understand the reason that* Peter's seemingly innocuous concern for Jesus's welfare was such a

---

65   Heb. 12:16,17
66   Luke 12-16

serious threat to his own spiritual security?[67] Our assurance of salvation is a lot like a birthright. The application to us is *extremely sensitive to what we choose* in this life. So do not be like Esau! *Following self-interest,* vain ambition, or man's myopic visions about what religious people expect you to do in the world is a potential one-way ticket to perdition's halls! Consider Jesus's next saying, "He who seeks to save his life [soul] will lose it, but he who loses his life for My sake will find it." That is the *ultimate decision* that every Christian must make. Is the life you have in Christ more important than all the things in this world that you could ever hope to gain? You are *in serious trouble* if this is not so! For that is exactly what the Gospel of Jesus Christ demands!

I ask again, Christian, *what have* you *done with Jesus, the crucified?* Have you *treasured His ways* and value them like the man who found "the pearl of great price?" Remember that when finding it, He sold all he had to buy the field where it was.[68] Let us take notice of Jesus's statements about the significance of what this "pearl of great price" means—"the Kingdom of Heaven is like… a pearl, and it is like a dragnet that men use to harvest fish, and when they bring up the catch, they sort it out, placing (saving) the good (fish) into baskets and discarding (throwing away) the bad." I believe the angels of God are doing this now. So are you going to *survive the cut?* Are you qualified to be one of the *good?* The last days are upon us, *and we have no time to lose.* What *are the choices you will be making?*

Remember what God said about Jacob and his brother, "I have loved Jacob [in spite of his shortcomings he became Israel, the contender who received the blessing], but Esau I have hated." Why did God "hate" Esau? Was it not because of *his self-centered attitude* that refused to change *even when he had the opportunity?* This attitude of Esau can be found in many Christians today as well, sowing within them the *seeds of calamity!*

We dare not be overconfident in our *own strength,* somehow thinking we are better than others. Will stubborn humanistic pride

---

67   Matt. 16:21–26
68   Matt. 13:44–51 *See also Appendix B" What Type of Christian are You?*

be your downfall? Remember that the higher the position you have in leadership, the worse the problem of pride can become![69]

V. Issue 5

God intends Christian ministries to serve and glorify Him. These are vehicles to do the will of God *"on earth(just) as it is in heaven."* The vital operation of divine *infusion grace* *plays a major part in this*, for the Scripture tells us that a man cannot receive anything from God, unless it *comes from heaven by His Spirit.* All genuine spiritual gifts are the tools and gifts of grace to accomplish God's will in God's way. God intends them to work with God's Holy Spirit such that we develop the greatest gift, *the fruit of the Holy Spirit, which is Agape love.* All the subsequent attributes that Agape love is associated with will follow.[70] Vigorously spiritual life underlies the development of all true Christian ministries. God's Word defines how they work in Scriptures like Romans 12, 1 Corinthians 12, and Ephesians 4. However, proper New Covenant maintenance of all these spiritual things is dependent upon the dispensation (godly stewardship) of Agape love in our lives.

Agape love is the prime characteristic of God. If we abide under those conditions, we will always exhibit the kind of character that is *consistent with the love of God!* Agape is the unmistakable, undeniable attribute that cannot be counterfeited. This love was present *in manifold profusion* in the early church and was the secret of their power! The presence (or absence) of Agape love essentially becomes *the litmus test* of genuine Christianity itself. It is also the primary *evidence of a work of divine grace* in a person. The New Testament defines *true Christian ministry.* Vibrant and effective ministry exists as an organic outflow of a healthy supernatural spiritual life within the believer. Graduating from seminary or Bible school, quoting Scripture, confronting people on the street, or being a good orator or public speaker does not qualify one for ministry. Scripture tells that the early Christians did not need any of those things to be successful! Neither does our following the pet traditions of a particular denomination's distinctive.

---

69   Prov. 8:13; 16:18; Jer. 49:8; Mal. 1:3; Heb. 10:26–39; 12:1–17.
70   John 3:3–30; 1 Cor. 12–14; Gal. 5:22,23; James 1:17,18; 3:13–4:4.

VI. Issue 6

Let us behold the power of true Christian unity! Here we should see the potential power of unified fellowship in Christ or spiritual *synergism or body-life at its finest.* Most assuredly, it is the will of Father God that believers *walk together in unity.* Paul tells us that we should be "endeavoring to keep the unity of the Spirit in the bond of peace."[71] However, we must be ever careful not to let the *tail wag the dog* here! Let us review some fundamental New Covenant precepts: *first,* Scripture teaches us that the *vertical relationship we have with God in the Spirit is the source* and wellspring of ministries and thus gives us the authority to minister. These things are not the property of any organization, corporation hierarchy, or method of man![72] *Second* is that the *horizontal relationships* we have among fellow believers are based on an *outgoing sense.* This means that *they are not the source or uplinks,* but are the *downlinks.* That is, where ministry outflows to others. God's will is that *His spirit controls ministry.* Since God gives man free will, let us acknowledge that in biblical New Covenant theology, the "downlink" of the ministry is *not the control link.* However, human organizations have effectively co-opted this mandate. Like it or not, we must now bring up and deal with a very serious problem in Christian circles.

Many Churches are even teaching that *conformity* is the same as *unity!* They are leading them to believe that "unity" is just following the crowd and doing what everybody else is doing or by *not making waves,* etc. These are dangerous waters where we commonly find authoritarian organizations using these ploys *to coerce a false unity* under the lead and control of man. Some misuse Scripture to manipulate dissidents by *feigning that they have a weak conscience that* your teaching of Jesus's truths has offended! However, believers can find the clear standard in Scripture found in Jesus's high priestly prayer.[73] In this Scripture, Jesus teaches us that it is God's will that we become one with each other in *the same way* as Jesus Christ is one with the Father and the Holy Spirit! Therefore, since *God is love,* that means that *God solely bases genuine Christian unity upon abiding in Agape love.* This means that we only

---

71   Eph. 4:1 ff.; Phil. 2:1–11.
72   Gal. 1:6–12; Eph. 3:5–7; 1 Pet. 4:1–5:5.
73   John 17:11, 20–26

preserve true unity in the church when we are *loving each other in the same way* as Jesus loves the Father and the Holy Spirit!

Three, Jesus Christ also defines genuine Christian unity as existing solely within the confines of obedience to His commands, since Jesus Himself defined love as the equivalent to obedience to His commands!

So the equation regulating all these crucial quantities together is: UNITY=LOVE=OBEDIENCE TO JESUS.[74] Scripture gives us no other valid definition. This means that true Christian unity issues only as a byproduct of our *organic union with Jesus Christ.* This also means having the *Spirit of Jesus Christ!* Accordingly, the conclusion is inescapable: our observance of the literal teachings of Jesus also entirely circumscribes the context and presence of *Agape love* and of Christian unity! Believers must understand that Scripture clearly defines and allows for only *one kind of unity* for being New Covenant Christian. Agape love and biblical unity both are solely dependent upon the unique *life-stream of the Spirit.* This is the source of all good things that flows to us *only from the throne of God in heaven.* Know that all other forms of "unity" are based on *conformity to humanism,* which is *not of God.* The crucial point of truth here is this: God shares His very *special kind of life, love, and experience* only with those individuals and groups of believers who really *submit to Christ.* These are the ones who have renounced humanistic ways and diligently seek to obey the commands of Jesus Christ *from the heart, making no excuses whatever.*

VII. Issue 7

Question: What does all this teach us about *how the true body of Christ is governed?* Answer: We govern the true church that is the body of Christ that is in actuality connected to its head solely upon the *higher and heavenly wisdom contained within the New Covenant.* Jesus Christ personally ordained this covenant for us as our law. *The New Covenant* shows us that it is the *spiritual body of laws* that originate with God's divine wisdom and *grace* by the Holy Spirit that must govern *the body of Christ*.

---

74   John 14:15; 15:10–12; Rom. 8:9; Acts 4:11-13.

Notice that this is the *only* body that God organically connects to Jesus Christ the head in heaven! The fallible traditions and methods of man carry no weight whatsoever with Him. Scripture teaches that only abiding consistently by New Covenant doctrines *in actuality* qualifies us to be part of His body, the church. Consequently, any group that gathers must also simultaneously obey Christ to have a *valid claim to be a church.*[75]

God's Word teaches that any person, group, or organization that fails to pass this test and biblical definition does not work for God or belong to Christ.[76] **

VIII. Issue 8

The issue of assurance. Can a Christian reach the point where we "know that we know that we are going to heaven?"

Yes, I believe that we *can,* however, that presumes *some very specific conditions about our heart-level commitment!* For example, as a Christian believer, have *you made that once-for-all irrevocable commitment of following Jesus Christ and all His commands, no matter what happens* unto the death? *If you truly have,* then you know that God assures your eventual salvation *and that no power in this world can stop you!* However, this condition is true *if and only if* we *have* no *part in us that Satan can get a handle on and cause us to turn away.* Beware and remember what happened to Judas Iscariot! *Only if the Spirit of Jesus Christ is in control of your entire being will you know what assurance is. If so,* then you know what it means to have assurance. Let us never forget the underlying fundamental operation of the New Covenant that applies: salvation *belongs to Jesus Christ alone.* Jesus teaches that we must continually abide *in Him* all the way unto death (or until he comes) to survive spiritually.[77]

---

75   John 3:27; Acts 2:1 ff.; Rom. 12:1 ff.; 1 Cor. 12,13; Eph. 4:1 ff. *See also the paper entitled "Basics of Biblical Church Governance"*

76   Rom. 8:9 ***See also the paper entitled "(What is) The Body of Christ"*

77   Luke 11:33–36; 22:31–53; John 13:1–8

Finally, have you let discipleship crucify the world to you? Have *you* chosen to let God crucify *you* to the world, like Paul wrote in Galatians 6?

If so, then I think you already know what is the whole truth Scripture teaches us about salvation.

## Chapter 3

The Pillars of the Christian Gospel

Introduction: In this chapter we will summarize the Spirit of *the New Covenant Gospel of Jesus Christ*. This New Covenant gospel contains the *dynamite* within so that we can live the way God has intended us to live despite circumstance and the acts of others who oppose us.[78] In doing so, we must know that we must make specific and conscious choices, continuing to follow up on them accordingly, for the fullness of God's plan to be personally effective in us. For example, the operation of spiritual baptism by the Holy Spirit introduces us to the family of God (the body of Christ) when one first receives Christ. Nevertheless, from then on, God requires us to cooperate with him to make the transition from the self-life to the Christ-life. Scripture defines this process as *conversion*. As God is converting us, the Holy Spirit disciplines and guides us into the paths of righteousness and away from the paths of iniquity and sin. God's Holy Word tells us that the Holy Spirit will chastise and discipline *every person that God receives*. If we do not go through this procedure, God will disavow us as "illegitimate!" Yes, if you cut yourself off from Christ, God disqualifies you if you fail to "stay with the program" or follow through to the end. Insistence on going *our way* by dependence upon *works or on human goodness, strength, or soul power* incurs the same result.[79] Always remember that even though God is love, He will not force you to comply. You must individually *choose yourself* to obey God's Word. *These are the main pillars:*

---

78   Acts 1:1–11

79   Ezek. 18:30–32; Matt. 18:3–11; John 15:1–7; Acts 3:19–21; 1 Cor. 1:17–2:16; 9:27; Gal. 2:16–5:26; Heb. 12:1–14

I. The reality, character, love, and justice of our wise Father God will combine to form the first lynchpin of the gospel: our view of God.*[80] Scripture records God's character being expressed in the interactions God has engaged with mankind.

First, God created mankind to be a race of sentient beings who have been given free will to choose their way. This free agency has remained undiminished after the "fall."[81]

Second, God has progressively revealed himself to man in a series of arrangements we call covenants.[82]

Third, God has regularly tested man to see if they respond. The response God seeks is that man would express a heartfelt desire to know, serve, and love God in return.[83]

Fourth, God teaches and disciplines everyone who responds by the instruments of His Holy Word, the Bible, and the Holy Spirit, the inspirer and interpreter of Scripture to the human heart.

God guides them to follow those things that are good for them in the end.[84]

Fifth, God loves man and can give each individual believer the capability to love God in return. He also gives them the ability to love their fellow human beings, no matter where they live or what they have done. This is the highest purpose for man in this world.[85]

Sixth, God's Word also couples this kind of love (Agape) with his strong desire that no human being fall for any deception or follow the lies of the world. However, all those who believe, live, and love the lies of the world and religion will follow Satan and the rebel angels

80   *See the book: Jesus Way, Chapter VII.: Basic Christian Ethics, Part One: 'Our View of God' and the booklet: A Seeker's Guide to Biblical Faith*

81   Genesis 1–2 *See also the papers "Destiny and Free Will" and "The Doctrine of the Elect"*

82   Hebrews 1, 7–11 *See also the papers entitled "Fulfilment Prophecy" an "Principles of Fulfillment Theology"*

83   2 Chr. 16:9; Job 23:10; Jer. 29:11; Matt. 6:33; Rom. 8:28

84   Neh. 9:20; Psa. 1, 19, 25, 27, 32, 86, 119; Rom. 8:28; Heb. 12:1 ff.

85   John 14–17; 1 Cor. 13; 1 John 1–5

to hell.[86] Yes, God must judge all those who continue to rebel against God's authority or *disregard His Holy Word.*[87]

II. The sin problem is very real, and we must deal with it. Every person born from the seed of a man is a sinner. We inherit the trait of sin along with its inherent characteristics: selfishness, rebellion, independence, and disobedience from our human ancestor, Adam, who chose to rebel against God's specific command in the *garden* of Eden. Moreover, each of us has <u>individually</u> offended God by our personal expression of that sin, in whatever way it comes out. Our very lifestyle contains an inward *attitude of rebellion* that disregards God's sovereignty in our life. This fact is true despite whether we recognize it or not.[88]

III. Our Father God's love and mercy are expressed in the giving of the greatest gift of all.

This is the gift of His Son, Jesus Christ, to be the Savior for the world of sinners. He is also the perfect example of *love* to emulate. In the person of our Lord Jesus Christ, we see God's extension of *prevenient grace*. This is expressed in the supreme act of Christ's vicarious sacrificial atonement/ reconciliation on the cross. Yes, our sin caused the shedding of His precious blood.

Yet, the blood sacrifice of Jesus the Lamb of God on the cross of Calvary makes salvation available to all humanity. This is the only pathway to the New Covenant and to the eventual salvation from eternity in hell. However, it only works that way for the ones who obey Jesus Christ.[89]

IV. We must first be born of the spirit by regeneration (of the human spirit) within to become part of Christ. When a person is reborn, the Holy Spirit does the following:

---

86   John 3:16,17; 10:16,17; 13:34,35; 15:13; Rom. 5:5–8; 8:28–39; 2 Pet. 3:9; Rev. 21:7,8

87   Rom. 1:18 ff.; 2 Thess. 2:10–12

88   88 Eccl. 7:20; Psa. 51; Isa. 53:6; Hos. 14:9; Rom. 3:23; 6:23; Col. 1:21; Heb. 2:1- 4:16; 6:3-12; James 2;10 *See also the book: Basic Christian Doctrine, Appendix B: The Nature of Man*

89   89 John 1:10–14, 29–34; Rom. 5:9–18; Phil. 2:1–11; Heb. 2:1-4:16; 6:3-12; 7:11– 10:23; 1 John 2:1,2 *See also the book: Basic Christian Doctrine, Appendix B: The Nature of Man*

1. When we truly receive Christ, the Holy Spirit *restores* the lost functions of *intuition* and *communion* and (initiates) us into the body of Christ and granting us spiritual gifts.[90]

2. The Spirit of Christ, the *baptizer in the Holy Spirit,* also performs a unique *spiritual baptism,* progressively identifying us with Jesus. These baptisms usher believers into the presence of the family of God, the *fellowship of the saints in light.*

3. *The Holy Spirit* is the link that connects every *genuine member of Christ's body,* the church, to the head in heaven, Jesus Christ. The Holy Spirit of Christ *is the only vital link* we have to the throne. According to Scripture, Jesus is our high priest and advocate. The following names also describe this *body of Christ*: the "elect," the saints, and the church (singular, universal).

4. The Holy Spirit also connects all the parts of Christ's body all over the world together. The symbols of *communion* also point to these spiritual realities and remind us of the supreme sacrifice that Jesus made that we might have this kind of life! The Holy Spirit of Christ is *the heart and central source* of this special association Scripture defines as the church.

5. Within this framework of *New Covenant* relationship, Jesus Christ is the sole Mediator of all the affairs of the believer's life, *private and public.* True members of the body of Christ are *his by right of purchase by His blood.* The true church of Jesus Christ is solely composed of those who are *truly united in Christ* organically by the Holy Spirit. Not only that, since His body is so special, we should know that it is most *certainly against God's will* that believers allow the constraints of *any type of human organization* to *interfere with any of its biblical functions.* This is because *God intends the true church to be governed by the New Covenant.*[91-]

---

90 John 3:3–8; Rom. 12; 1 Cor. 12–14; Eph. 4
91 91 Matt. 3:11,12; 6:27–68; 7:14–17; 16:18; 18:18–20; Rom. 6:1–11; Eph. 1–6; Col. 1–4; 1 Tim. 2:5; Heb. 7–11 *See the paper entitled "the Basics of Biblical Church Governance"*

V. As Christians, we receive our justification and righteousness only by faith.

This *faith* is the *initial and provisional* (positional and temporary) gift of God that comes along with the package of *prevenient grace*. Faith is a universal capability and choice given by God to every man. Faith is also the vehicle by which God the Holy Spirit transfers (imputes by *infusion grace*) God's righteousness to all who subsequently continue to exercise that choice throughout life by doing the following: One, we must maintain our profession of the reality of Christ's sacrifice, bodily resurrection, and lordship.[92] Two, we must maintain our confession of the reality of our sin. The extent of our confession extends and relates to the level of the particular person or persons one has sinned against. If we have sinned against God, we confess only to God, but if we have sinned against man we must also confess to man in the appropriate venue. We decide this by the context of the particular sin and whether it is a private or public matter.[93] Three, we must truly *repent* from sin.[94] Four, we must walk daily by faith (trusting in God). God intends this fourfold dynamic of the New Covenant to become the *fundamental operating mechanism in our individual lives,* and it is God's will that we uphold it faithfully. This covenant is the central theme of genuine Christianity. It defines the only kind of Christianity that exists.[95]

Scripture clearly reminds us that Christianity *requires human cooperation* at every turn. This is necessary to enable those marvelous *supernatural provisions* that Father God so graciously has made available. *Are you repenting? Are you being broken? Are you walking in the light?* This New Covenant also teaches that when we are *born of His spirit by regeneration* (of the human spirit) within: the Holy Spirit (of Christ) baptizes (introduces) us into a *special heavenly spiritual organism* that the Scripture speaks of as the *body of Christ. * Spiritual baptism

---

92 Matt. 10:32,33; Luke 12;8–10; John 9:22; 12:42; Rom. 10:9,10; Phil. 2:5–11; 2 Tim. 2:11–13; Heb. 10: 22–39; 1 John 4:1–6.

93 Matt. 18:7–17; Acts 19:18; Rom. 3:23; James 5:13–16; 1 John 1:5–10.

94 Matt. 3:2; 4:17; 21:28–32; Mark 1:15; 6:12; Luke 13:3; 15:4–7; 17:1–4; Acts 2:38,39; 3:19; 17:24–31.

95 Luke 9:23–26; John 8:12–36; 12:35,36; Acts 9:31; Rom. 3:19–5:5; 6:1–11; 8:1 11; 2 Cor. 5:7–10; 10:1–6; Gal. 2:19–21; 5:16–25; Eph. 2:8–10; 4:1 ff.; 5:1 ff.; Phil. 2:12,13; 3:16–21; Col. 1:10; 2:6–10; 1 Thess. 1:1–10; 2:12. *See the papers entitled "the Amazing Doctrine of God's Grace," "Conditions for Salvation" and "God's Definition of Salvation"*

ushers believers into the presence of the family of God, the *fellowship of the saints in light.* The Holy Spirit links every genuine member of the body individually to Jesus Christ, the head in heaven.[96]

He is the only vital link we have to the throne.*[97] He is also the *central source* of this special association we call the church. The symbols of *communion* also point to these spiritual realities. Thus Scripture reminds us of the supreme blood sacrifice that *Jesus alone has* made that we might have God's life and love and have liberty in all ways spiritually and physically! If we allow any other entity to claim credit for these things, it becomes an *idol to us by definition!* Within this framework of New Covenant relationship, Jesus Christ is the sole Mediator, high priest, advocate, and highest *authority* in all the affairs of the believer's life, *private and public.*

All true members of the body of Christ are *the property of* Jesus. Christ has *redeemed us* by the purchase of His blood. Since His body is so special, believers must never allow the constraints of any particular human organization to interfere with or coopt the operation of spiritual life. We should never quench the Spirit of liberty in *body-life.*

The following names also describe this body of Christ: *the "elect," the saints, and the church* (singular, universal). Moreover, the body of believers that Jesus Christ calls *His church* is solely composed of those who are *truly United in Christ* organically by the Holy Spirit.[98] When we enter the family of God, we are also responsible for the following:

VI. His spirit leads us into the lifelong process of conversion, expressed in the warp and woof of Christian discipleship and *sanctification* (holiness).

Salvation is a process, not *a possession.* Eventual salvation will only come to those who have *persevered in the pathway of righteousness "unto the end."* The end refers to the time when the Lord comes back or to our physical death, whichever comes first. Meanwhile, it is the will of

---

96   *See the book Jesus' Way and the three-part series entitled Christian Conversion "the Doctrine of Jesus Christ's Real Presence" and "Regarding Christ's Headship"*

97   *See Jesus' Way, Appendix C: Kingdom of Heaven Diagram*

98   Matt. 3:11,12; 16:18,19; 18:18–20; John 3:3–8; 6:27–68: 14–17; Rom. 6:1–11; 1 Cor. 12:12,13; 2 Cor. 3:17,18; Eph. 1–6; Phil. 1–4; Col. 1–4; 1 Tim. 2:5; Heb. 7–11.

our Father that we are "conformed unto the image of His Son, Jesus Christ." The Holy Spirit can accomplish this, but we must do our part. This part is expressed in receiving our *daily bread* of the spirituality and character of Jesus. The Holy Spirit translates the life of Jesus, our daily bread of life, to us. Every good spiritual thing "comes down from the Father of lights, with whom there is no shadow of turning."[99]

Within the dynamic of this relationship, we find a picture of abiding in *the New Covenant relationship to Jesus in the spirit.* Our continual daily choice to abide in Christ upholds the pillars of the gospel. The main points are as follows:

1. Submission to the Father *in Jesus Christ by the Holy Spirit*[100]

2. *Prayer and worship in spirit and in truth.*[101]

3. *Obedience to Christ's commands from the heart.*[102]

4. Daily *seeking truth* and for *more of God.* The study of the Holy Revealed Word accomplishes this. This is His will and becomes a "word-picture of Jesus."[103]

5. Let us love God continually with *all our heart, soul, mind, and strength,* and *our brothers and sisters in Christ.*[104]

All these above *disciplines are not electives* that only apply for the "so-called super spiritual" or doctrines that we can choose to obey or *not.* They are central Christian doctrines for which God holds us accountable for obeying! Viz., Jesus Christ sets His Word before us like the Ten Commandments were set before the Israelites. If we obey and comply, they are *life and good* to us. Yet, if we rebel, they will become *death and evil* to us, which means judgment! Therefore, let us be diligent even zealous to obey His Word, for it is for our best! As Jeremiah put it, "To give you a future and a hope." The beauty of it all is that we marvelously fulfill God's Word when we seek to be *converted*

---

99   John 3:27; 16:13–15; Rom. 8:26-39; Heb. 2:1–3; 3:1–6,12–14; 6:3–12; James 1:17
100   John 15
101   Matt. 6:9–13; Luke 11:9–13; John 4:23,24; Eph. 6:18
102   Matt. 5–7; 10:16–39; John 8:31–36; 14:15–26
103   John 8:31–36; 14:15–24; 2 Tim. 2:15
104   Matt. 22:37

and follow the image of Christ in daily perseverance. We are *transformed* in our hearts and minds to *think like God thinks* and to *appreciate the way he does things!* Yes, it becomes a joy to live the Christian life! This is what Jesus told the disciples just before the betrayers delivered him up for crucifixion.[105]

All these struggles within progress for a purpose. As we cooperate with God, we reap the benefits of living the true Christian life, and God will work wonders within our regenerated being!

VII. God edifies His dwelling place (our heart).

He builds up within us an enduring personal relationship with God that can withstand all the storms of life and the tests of time.

This He does in the spirit by the process of infusion grace, where God pours divine life, love, and character into our heart! This forms the basis of our testimony!

Deep within, the Holy Spirit becomes a veritable artesian well of the water of life, a fountainhead of spirituality that has no conceivable limit!

This is precisely what made the early Christians so attractive to many of those around them! You *cannot hide this kind of light!* Remember what Jesus said about *letting our light shine!* God's Word says this happens whenever Jesus is in control of our lives.

Our obedience to His commands always brings glory to God![106]

---

105   Jer. 29:11–13; John 15:11; 16:20–24; 17:13
106   Matt. 5:14–16, 38–48; John 4:14; 7:37–39; Acts 4:11–13; Rom. 5:1–5; 12: 1ff. 1 Cor. 1:18–2:16; Gal. 5:22,23; Eph. 4:1–32; 6:18; Phil. 2:5–11; 3:7–15; Jude 20

Chapter 4

The New Covenant

I. Introduction:

Scripture uses the term New Covenant to describe the covenant of Jesus Christ or the Christian covenant. We could also label it "Jesus's Way" or "the Christian Gospel" equally. Within its boundaries lie the terms and conditions by which God expects all spiritually reborn believers to abide. The most general description we have readily available to read for ourselves is found, of course, in the New Testament scripture. The writer merely intended the following brief outlines and descriptions to reflect the overall tenor of the entire New Testament gospel that Jesus Christ taught and lived. Essentially the writer intends it to serve as a "condensed version" of the gospel as a whole. Throughout the first century, all the early disciples/apostles also consistently preached this unique gospel. Although it took about two centuries to "codify the writings" in written form, the essence of its truth has not changed one iota since the gospel's beginning with Jesus Christ.[107]

The reader must also recognize that all "translations" made from the original language may contain errors, but the Holy Spirit can bypass all humanly caused problems. For Christians, the New Covenant functions essentially as *the constitution of the Kingdom of Heaven*. It contains all the spiritual laws and precepts Jesus gave to the disciples to carry out here on earth. Not only that, we can use the entire Scripture that we know as the Holy Bible. However, this only works *if we are careful* to diligently *observe its own internal guidelines*. In this manner,

---

107   107 Mark 1:15; Acts 1:1 ff; Rom. 1:16 ff; 2 Cor. 11:1–4; Gal. 1:6–12 *See also the paper "Looking Through the Lens of Jesus Christ"*

if we *look through* the *lens of Jesus Christ*, God can still use the Old Testament scriptures. This is because the Holy Spirit can transform them spiritually through our eyes.[108]

However, the author would caution the reader that we cannot treat Scripture as a "god," or as a weapon to manipulate others. We will never correctly receive God's message from Scripture if we use empirically based schemes of "intellectual interpretation" that are *humanism*.[109]** Also, God's Word clearly warns us that religious leaders frequently use flawed humanistic schemes in justifying false doctrines and worldliness![110] Scripture *is spiritual!* Consequently, wisdom teaches us that when we are "reborn in the spirit," we must consider the entire body of Scripture *in a new light* and let God's Spirit "elevate it to Jesus's Way."

We can do this by simply *seeking the higher spiritual wisdom the Holy Spirit freely gives* to any humble heart who *loves the truth!* This is what *looking at Scripture through the *lens of Jesus Christ** means for us.

When we grow and gain a sense of spiritual maturity, we can also learn to see the Old Testament in its proper context—that it is a rich historical resource that gives us a *prior covenantal backdrop* that we must see as sharply contrasting to the New Covenant. The New Covenant way that Jesus Christ has brought to us is now *"stage center."* [111] Let us now consider the primary elements of the Christian covenant: the central governing "document" of biblical Christianity and the basis for all doctrine and practice.

II. Our basic elements outline of the New Covenant contains three parts:

A. *Christ's universal *atonement**. Jesus Christ is the New Testament Passover Lamb. The *precious blood of Jesus Christ shed on Calvary* crowns Christ's perfect work and forms the *universal (pan-human) sacrifice/*

---

108   108 Deut. 4:2; Proverbs 8; Isa. 8:9–20; 28–30; Matt. 5:17–20; 2 Tim. 3:16; 2 Pet. 1:19–21; Rev. 22:18,19

109   *See Glossary of Terms: Empiricism, Hermeneutics, Humanism, Nominalism, Platonism.* ***See also the paper "Hermeneutics: Basic Principles of Scripture Interpretation"*

110   Matt. 23; Luke 13; 2 Cor. 11:12–15

111   John 6:27–63; 7:15–18; 8:12–58; 14:21–26; 1 Cor. 10:1–13

payment for all sin for all people for all time. Christ's sacrifice is effective throughout the age of grace right to the point when the wrath of God commences. All taken together, we have the gospel basis for universally offered salvation: Christ's perfect blood sacrifice was "shed once for all" on the cross. God's plan couples this with His bodily resurrection and ascension to heaven where Christ reigns. For those who receive that perfect sacrifice and continue by confession of sin and daily repentance, Jesus acts as our high priest and advocate before the Father. Thus, God provides full *deliverance from the universal death penalty that sin causes.* For those who truly receive Christ, this includes the forgiveness of past sins and mitigation of consequences to all who personally abide in daily spiritual relationship with God. Basing His work on that foundation, the Holy Spirit grants all the gifts concerning salvation and godliness: when one receives Christ, God first acts on the gift of prevenient grace to regenerate their human spirit.[112] Secondly, God's Spirit places that person in a *probational* position of *righteousness* before God, enabling one to personally relate to God. God only grants this righteousness by virtue of Christ's perfect sacrifice that paid for all sin.[113]

Thirdly, as we commune daily with God, obeying the commands of Jesus, the indwelling Holy Spirit transmits the characteristics of Jesus to our spirit.

B. *Repentance*, faith, and *baptism* initiate God's life-transforming power. First, when we are Born Again, the Holy Spirit introduces us into God's family, the body of Christ, by spiritual baptism.[114] Second, we receive the ability to commune directly to God's Throne in our worship and prayer. By doing this, we also receive intuition, the ability to receive revelation directly from God's Throne to our human spirit! Of course, God always intends us to use this gift with our study of the written Word of God, the Scripture. This is the only way that God

---

112   *See Glossary of Terms: Grace, Salvation*

113   Universal Atonement: Matt. 26:26–29; Luke 22:14–23; John 1:1–18, 29–34 3:3– 8,16–18; 5:19– 30; 6:27–63; Acts 2:38,39; 3:19; Rom. 3:19–5:21; 1 Cor. 11:23 ff.; 2 Cor. 5:14–21; Eph. 1:3–3:9; Phil. 2:5–11; Col. 1:12–29; 1 Tim. 2:3–7; Heb. 1:1–9; 2:8–18; 5:6–10; 7:1–10:23; 1 Pet. 1:3; 1 John 2:1–6

114   1 Cor. 12:12,13

ordains to accurately transmit the living Word of God, Jesus Christ, to us.[115] Thirdly, we receive spiritual gifts and endowments.

The Holy Spirit decides which of these we need for the ministry and to share in the body of Christ.[116] Fourthly is the completion of the "discipleship to conversion dynamic" process by which God shapes us into Christ's image. Here, the writer must explain a crucial fact: to maintain our personal relationship to God, we must learn to exercise our reborn human spirit, always taking heed to beware of sins' deceitfulness by practicing daily repentance from subsequent sins. Doing these, we enable God's Spirit work within to bypass the soulish and rebellious element of our intellect and reach our spirit directly for us to properly understand God's Word!

Only truly spiritual worship accomplishes this.[117] God created human beings to live with the spirit in control. This, in turn, enables God to translate spiritual sustenance, life, truth, and knowledge internally. Our intellect receives these things only as a secondary action. This procedure is mandatory because our sinful human nature still gravitates to the carnal mind even after we receive the gift of new birth. The carnal mind is always God's enemy, even in believers!

Moreover, it is only after the conversion process is complete do we attain to a "spiritual mind" position that will accurately understand spiritual things like God sees them! Always remember, nothing spiritual is "automatic!"[118]

C. The ministry of reconciliation is the heart of God's will: By choosing love and reconciliation, Christians *will fulfil the great commission requirements of witness and evangelism. When Christ's followers exhibit Agape love, they energize the engine of reconciliation!* Catching the high vision of Heaven's Kingdom is the universal ministry for which

---

115   Matt. 6:9–13; Luke 11:9–13; John 14–17
116   Rom. 12; 1 Cor. 12–14; Eph. 4
117   John 4:14–24; Eph. 4:23,24; Heb. 3:11–19; 4:11–16; 6:3–12; 10:26–39 *See also the paper entitled "the Lord's Supper, the New Covenant Passover"*
118   *Repentance/Faith/Baptism:* Matt. 3:2; 5:17–20; 6:9–15; Luke 9:23–26; Joh 1:33; 4:14–24; 7:14– 18. 37–39; 14:21–16:15; Acts 1:8; 2:38,39; 3:19; *Rom. 3:19– 5:21; 6:1–11; 8:14–29; 10:1–15; 1 Cor. 10:16–18; 12:1–13; Gal. 2:15–3:28; 4:19–26; *Eph. 1:3–2:22; 3:10–21; 4:1– 16, 21–24; 5:17–33; *Col. 1:22–29; 2:8–19; Heb. 4:9–5:14; 12:1–24; 1 John 1:5–10; 1 Pet. 1:1–2:10; Rev. 3:1 22

all Christians are responsible. This means carrying God's Agape love toward all humanity. The ministry of reconciliation is the full-time occupation of every Christian believer. Believers fulfill God's will when we walk in truth and *love the truth*. This is how the Holy Spirit develops Agape love in us. In the following footnote, the writer has listed those Scriptures that describe two parallel concurrent processes of God's Spirit. Notice the asterisked references refer to the twin processes.[119] First, God displays His love to us while we were still unbelievers. Second, after we receive Christ, God develops Agape love in us that God expects us to show to others who have not yet received Christ.[120] In the gospel, Jesus proclaims that if we really love Him, we will obey His commands.

Paul repeats saying, "Let the same attitudes live in you that live in Christ." He also proclaims that we must conform ourselves to the image of Christ. If these things take place, the *Spirit of Christ* will be in you; you will belong to Jesus and achieve "full stature in the image of Christ," for that is our "one hope of glory."

III. Rightly discerning the *body of Christ* is quintessential.

The New Covenant shows us how we properly "discern the body of Christ."[121] Rightly discerning (properly understanding) Christ's body requires that we use our reborn human spirit and the ability of *spiritual self-awareness that accompanies a mature spiritual relationship to God.* Let us consider the relevance of the outward symbols of "The Lord's Supper," baptism, and biblical marriage. The higher significance of these spiritual symbols points us to one thing: the Holy Spirit creates our oneness and unity through a living union with the body of Christ.*[122]

Conforming to human creedal tradition, church membership or observing outward rituals cannot substitute for spiritual realities in which you must *personally choose to participate*. Only as we submit to

---

119   *The Ministry of Reconciliation:* Matt 5–7; 28:18–20; John 12:23–17:26; Acts 1:1–4:37; 5:12–42; *Rom. 5:6–21; 8:1–39; 1 Cor. 13; *2 Cor. 5:14–21; Eph. 3:1–4:16; 6:10–18; *Phil. 2:5–18; 3:1–4:23; *Col. 1:12–29; 2 Tim. 1:6–14; 2:1–22; *Titus 2:11–15; 3:4–8; James 2:14–26; 1 Pet. 2:21–25; 3:18; 4:1 ff.; 1 John 3–5

120   *See Jesus' Way: Chapter XIV The Circle of Love: Principle of the Kingdom*

121   *See Jesus' Way: Chapter IX The Celebration of the Lord's Supper*

122   **See the paper entitled "(What is) The Body of Christ"*

the lordship of Jesus Christ, our divine husband, can we attain unity in fellowship with our heavenly Father and each other.

When we abide in spiritual union with Father God, God's Spirit personally develops spiritual gifts and Agape love within us. This is what it takes for us to exude that characteristic trademark "glow" that others instinctively know could only come from being close to God. In this relationship, we are truly *part of Christ*. Not only that, no human source can "counterfeit" those attributes! Agape love is a spiritual quantity, like everything else in God's Kingdom! Consequently, *no* "religion" or "religious activity" can produce Agape love. This is because all "religious things" are *soulish in their nature.*[123] Moreover, it is imperative that we understand the true *spiritual meaning* of the body of Christ. Herein we see the vital spiritual link relating *baptism, marriage, and* the *body of Christ* to the covenantal transfer that God has planned every believer to undergo. The primary emphasis of our life must shift first *from law to grace* so that we can participate in the atonement/reconciliation process that is central to God's master plan for the church!

Paul tells us, "Therefore my Brethren, you also have become dead to the law *through the body of Christ* that you may be *married to another,* even to Jesus Christ whom God raised from the dead, that we should bear fruit to God."[124]

Our discerning (the function of) the *literal spiritual body of Christ** *(not* the external assembly of believers we usually associate with this term) is therefore the key to success for the church. The early Christians knew what this meant, for they testified that *Christ's real presence* accompanied their worship when they came together.[125]

Sadly, centuries of apostasy and "mass substitution" of rituals clouds many Christians' understanding of this crucial reality. However, the New Covenant has not changed. This *personal presence of Jesus Christ*

---

123 John 1:1–14; 3:3–8; 13–17; Acts 4:8–13; Eph. 1–5; Rev. 21,22 *See also the 3 part series of papers entitled "Christianity versus Religion"*

124 Rom. 7:4

125 *Matt. 18:20; John 15:1–11; Rom. 6:1–23; 7:7–8:39; *1 Cor. 11:23–32; 12:13; Eph. 2:1–22 *See also Glossary of Terms: *The Body of Christ*, the papers entitled "(What is) The Body of Christ," "the Christian Spirit," "Christian Worship and the True Temple," "The Doctrine of Jesus Christ's Real Presence," "the Evolution of Worship," "the Higher Laws of God," "Regarding Christ's Headship" and "Spirituality and Worship"*

is truly the primary *active agent of fellowship and spiritual power* that made them so dynamic and influential a force in the world. The Holy Spirit energizes that power, *introducing us to the dispensation of grace,* the New Covenant Kingdom of Heaven. Thus, God can deliver us from the bondage and "curse of the law." God's will is that we maintain a "death attitude to sin" within us. If we do this, we will be "more than conquerors," victorious through Jesus Christ.[126] However, this dynamic only works *if* we fulfil *all* the conditions Scripture shows us within the following overall steps.

First, we must truly receive the sacrifice of the blood of Christ so God can forgive us our *past* sins. Second, we must engage our reborn human spirit in worshiping God. Third, we must abide in daily confession and repentance concerning any *subsequent sin.* Fourth, we must practice full and unreserved submission to Jesus Christ as *Lord.* Fifth, we must diligently apply all these in all areas of life. Then, if we fulfill these preconditions, the Holy Spirit guides us into the deeper meaning of the atonement and spiritual life overall. Remember always what Jesus said, "It is the *spirit that gives us life.* The flesh profits nothing. The words that I speak to you *are spirit and they are life."* [127]

God's Word tells us that we can have revival, for nothing is impossible with God. However, we *must obey the one He has sent, Jesus Christ.* Remember Jesus also said that "wherever two or more gather in My name, there I am in their midst." This one statement is the fundamental basis and *order of fellowship* that Scripture teaches. First, we must daily cultivate our *fellowship* with Father God in Spirit. When we do this, then our fellowship with other believers will grow "naturally" out of that venue. However, fellowship still cannot exist unless believers submit to Jesus first and then *submit bilaterally to each other!* Remember our spiritual relationship to God is interconnected to our dealings with others. These relations also form a symbolic "cross:"

The vertical part is our relation to God. The horizontal part is our relation to man. Scripture teaches that Father God intends our personal communion in prayer form a center within us. From this center we cooperate with God's Spirit to start building God's Kingdom

---

126   Rom. 6–8; Gal. 3:1–14; Eph. 2:4–10; 1 Pet. 1:2
127   John 6:63; Rom. 3:19–26; 2 Cor. 13:5; 2 Pet. 1:2–11; 1 John 1:5–2:6

right here on earth in vessels of clay. Building God's Kingdom requires active cooperation between believers working together, starting with *fellowship*. The New Testament defines *Christian* body-life fellowship. Fellowship develops as believers gather to freely share the things of Christ equally with each other. Body-life fellowship can only thrive when leaders encourage this condition. Our Father gives us an awesome *responsibility. Biblical fellowship with God carries us into the reign of God.* It starts as "a grain of mustard seed" within and radiates outward like ripples in a pond, expanding to as many as would receive Christ. To these, God's Spirit extends the "right hand of fellowship" and the *invitation and authority to become* the children of God. Notice the sense of this statement. It does not tell us that becoming a child of God is automatic just because once we received Christ. God's Word plainly tells us that our responsibility is this: we must subsequently *cooperate with God to receive those things!*

God's Word and our New Covenant faith both define cooperation as *obedience to Christ.*

This leads us to discipleship and conversion as we have seen above. All the same rules apply equally to everyone, no exceptions.[128] Jesus Christ must always be the *controlling interest and highest authority in our lives.* When we submit to Christ in obedience, the reign of God's Kingdom comes to our part of the earth! We must always remember that *the Holy Spirit* is the only agency of God acting on earth. He is the one that *connects the true body of Christ on earth to Jesus Christ, the head in heaven.* God defines this *body of Christ on earth for being the universal church.* Scripture teaches us that *the church* is God's vehicle to work out the master plan of reconciliation. God's Word also defines *the church or Christ's body* for being the aggregate sum of believers throughout time and place.

Scripture also calls them *the saints.*[129]*

128   Matt. 10:16–42; Luke 9:23–26; 14:26–33; John 1:12; 12:23–26; 15:1 ff.

129   Matt. 27:52; Acts 9:32; Rom. 1:7; 8:27; 12:13; 15:25–31; 16:2,15; 1 Cor. 1:2;6:1,2; 14:33; 16:15; 2 Cor. 1:1; 8:4; 9:1,12; 13:13; Eph. 1:1,15,18; 2:13-22; Thess. 1:10; 1 Tim. 5:10; Philemon 5,7; Heb. 6:10; Rev. 5:8; 8:3,4; 11:18; 13:7–10; 14:10–12; 16:6; 17:6; 18:24; 19:8
       See also the position paper entitled: "What is the Body of Christ" and the book "Jesus' Way," Appendix C: the Kingdom of Heaven

IV. Recapping the salient elements of the New Covenant and gospel, we have the following essence of the New Covenant.[130] One, God forgives, cleanses, and delivers us from sin and its consequences *by the blood of Christ, ministered by the Holy Spirit.* Two, God's Spirit draws us into union with Christ and makes us *part of Christ.* Three, when we obey Christ, God's Spirit daily renews us and transforms us in the discipleship to conversion dynamic process. Four, God's Spirit grooms us for citizenship in Heaven's Kingdom. There we submit to the lordship of Jesus Christ and enjoy fellowship with the saints in light. Fifth, God's Spirit transmits the ability to live Agape love, and we receive our "great" commission and general orders of reconciliation.[131]

---

130   Matt. 27:51–54; Luke 1:30–35; 2:8–14; 24:13–43; John 18:36–38; 21:15–35

131   John 13:34,35; 14:1–15:26; Rom. 3:19–26; 12:1–3; 1 Cor. 12:12,13; Eph. 1–4; Phil. 2,3; 1 John 1–5

PART 2

True Christian Identity in Christ

Chapter 5

The Kingdom of Heaven is the Highest form of Civilization

Part One:
Let us Consider God's Definitions We Find in Scripture.

I. Background: What is "civilization?"

Throughout history, mankind's problems have continually 'spiraled downward,' beginning with Cain's murder of his brother Abel. This singular act confirmed God's assessment of man's sinful condition resulting from Adam's disobedience of God's express command not to partake of the "tree of knowledge" while still in the Garden. It is also obvious that Jesus's reprimand of the Pharisees, saying that the sin of *Blood guiltiness* originated by the killing of Abel was still an outstanding debt, exposes the fact that God still holds mankind accountable for every murder of their fellow man. Yes, the Blood of Christ paid the cost of all man's sin, however, the transfer of that propitiation and *Atonement* can only be made effective on an individual basis by each individual's personal choice of *Repentance* from sin.[1]

The truth remains that virtually from the beginning, because of sin, hatred and lust for power and pleasure, the bloodshed has become widespread, driving mankind down a spiraling vortex of evil. Yet, Scripture still says that "we are our brother's keepers."

Nonetheless, man has continued to deny their responsibility to God regarding the disposition of their sin, which has complicated their condition. Furthermore, the works of Satan have made major intrusions, making things worse yet.

So, despite the so-called 'modern' improvements, scientific technology and medical breakthroughs, man is ultimately left with a flawed system they vainly call 'civilization' which is riddled with insoluble problems! Millions upon millions have been murdered in wars which have continued despite man's claims to be 'civilized.'

The Romans even used murder as entertainment, leading to virtually the same mind set being portrayed in innumerable movies glorifying violence and killing. Indeed, peace among the many nations of the

---

1   Gen. 4:1-16; Psa. 32, 51; Matt. 23:29-39; John 3:16-30; Acts 17:24-31; Rom. 1:16 32; 3:9 ff.; 8:1 ff.; 1 John 2:1-6

world remains elusive as ever, with conflicts raging under the surface. Study history and you will also find that for millennia, religion has been the underlying cause behind many incarnadine conflicts.[2]

Yes, for all mankind's grandiose promises and efforts to 'improve himself,' he still remains "broken inside" being afflicted with the same recurring insoluble problems. However, Scripture declares that the broken can be 'fixed' in Christ. All one has to do is to do the following:

One, admit they are sinners in great need of a Savior. Two, Repent of sin, viz., change your attitude regarding sin. Three, you must receive Christ's Sacrifice that pays for sin. If one does these, following through each day in Faith as God's Word teaches, God's Word promises to remake us anew by the inner work of Grace by the Holy Spirit. Yet, we must know that only Christ can do this, remaking us within, reconciling us with God and if we follow this "Way of Christ" faithfully, we will bring Peace to our fellow man. This is the unique power of the True Complete Gospel taught by Christ and the New Testament writers.[3]

Moreover, it should be understood that God's Plan only works IF you take the Complete Gospel at face value, including all those "hard sayings" of Jesus that the world scoffs at. In fact, the precise truth is that victory is heavily dependent on those 'hard sayings' for, our lifestyle can only be transformed if they are followed, bringing us to the very Heart of God's Will for mankind: living by Agape Love!

However, the problem with the modern church I have seen is that they deny the very parts of the Gospel that would give them the strength to deal with any problem of life and to show to the world the amazing coping power that we read about in the New Testament and which was observed in the Early Church up until the fourth century. I have consistently observed that the main 'hard saying' that sets True Christianity apart from all the apostates and those who compromise is this: the Doctrine of "Faith based Pacifism" also known as the *Patience of the Saints* in Scripture. Unfortunately, the major changes in the fourth century that took place after the takeover of the church by Emperor Constantine the Great, ruined the vast majority of the 'outward attenable assemblies.'

---

2   Jer. 17:9; 23:10 f.; Matt. 23; Rom. 1:18-32

3   Prov. 16:7; Isa. 26:3,4,12; Matt. 5-7; Luke 6-14; Rom. 3, 5-8; 10:9,10; Eph. 2:83:21

After this, the leaders of the time radically altered the doctrines of the Faith to make them acceptable to the world. Thus, the Roman Catholic Church (RCC) was born. The Protestants, however, changed precious little. Moreover, this worldly church system caused the vast majority of Christians to fall away into a state of spiritual impotence that has continued to this day! The author knows that if Christians would return to the original tenets of the Faith as defined in Scripture, the church would regain its spiritual power and finally fulfill the Great Commission. But, alas, because of their fears and desire to please man, almost all the Christians I have encountered have refused to do this, cutting themselves off from God's Blessings![4]

II. Scripture defines the Truth regarding our receiving God's Agape Love.

Verily, one is unable to continue *In Christ, * abiding in the continuance of His Love and commands and concurrently believe in the taking of human life for any reason![5]

Yes, God's Love is also Christian Love! Verily, our strength is in spiritual prayer for "We wrestle not against flesh and blood but against principalities and spiritual wickedness in high places and the (Satanic) rulers of the darkness of this world."[6]

Essentially, as Scripture defines it, the *Kingdom of Heaven,* with the *New Covenant* operating as its law, is verily the highest possible form of civilization that exists! As viewed from God's viewpoint, the New Covenant ordained by Christ in the first century, revealed the zenith of all relationships encompassing humanity.

Indeed, Scripture teaches that no other way works to solve all humanity's problems without any of the negative aspects found in the world system such as selfishness, violence and killing. Yet, in spite of the clear teaching we find in the New Testament, it appears that the

---

4   2 Chr. 7:14; Isa. 48:18; 56:9-11; 59:1 ff; Matt. 23; Luke 21:19; John 3:36; Rom. 5:1-5;12:9-21; 1 Cor. 13; 2 Cor. 6:4-13; Col. 1:11; 2 Thess. 1:3-8; 1 Tim. 6:3-12; 2 Tim. 3:10-12;Heb. 6:12; 10:26-39; 12:1 -14; James 5:7,8; Rev. 2,3 *See also the author's book entitled Spiritual Guidelines for Restoration, "Historical Review" Section*

5   Matt. 5-7; John 3:16; Rom. 5; 1 Cor. 13; Phil. 1-4; Col. 3:1 ff.; 1 John 2:1-6; 3:1 5:21

6   Rom. 12:9-21; Eph. 6:10-12

vast majority of modern "professing Christians" exhibit virtually <u>no confidence whatsoever</u> in what Jesus clearly taught and commanded. Not only that, my experience with many groups throughout the last half century proves that they are clinging to the harmful humanistic ways of the world like a drowning man to a millstone! This obvious truth begs the question: Why is this so? Jesus knew this truth as well and it shows in His Discourses with the Jewish religious leaders of that time. Indeed, when we read the accounts of the Old Testament Prophets, and compare them with the history of the church, you will find <u>an amazing parallel</u> which will illustrate the common problems afflicting both: <u>Idolatry</u>, the deification of man and worldly humanistic ways which form the underlying cause of their towering <u>arrogance, strong delusion</u> and refusal to either respect or submit to the Lord Jesus Christ. In fact Paul wrote the Corinthians, saying the same thing.

Indeed, this issue of humanism is a fundamental symptom of Idolatry that exposes itself in the glorification of 'human saviors': Politicians, soldiers and professionals. All through Scripture, God consistently condemns Idol worship in any form it takes. In the modern world the major problem is national pride, expressed in the sub areas of patriotism, militarism, politics and blind trust of professionals. Indeed, spiritually, National Pride acts like carbon monoxide does in the human bloodstream, displacing oxygen.[7]

The plain truth is that all those who <u>love the world</u> and are invested in defending what they "think they own," like family members and material possessions will inevitably worship and serve the world's Idols, the most insidious of which is the <u>trust in</u> military force and the use of violence and homicide, all of which contradict the teachings of Christ.

Obviously, these apostates <u>fail to see</u> the crucial teaching we must observe within the <u>Precept of *Redemption.*</u> Scripture clearly teaches that when a person initially repents of sin, the Holy Spirit applies the Blood of Christ to the penitent heart, Regenerates our human spirit and <u>transfers our 'deed of ownership' from the world</u> which is owned by Satan and <u>to the Kingdom of Heaven,</u> whose King is Jesus Christ.

---

7   Psa. 2,110; Prov. 10:29; Isa. 1,2, 28:12-30:21; 52:13-53:12; 56:9-57:21; 59:1 ff.; Jer. 2-10; 11:9; 13:15-27; 17:1-10; 18:12; 23:9,10; 26:1-19; Ezek. 3,18,33,34; Hosea 14:9; Matt. 10:26-39; 23:1 ff.; Luke 2:33-35; 11:33-36; John 8:1-9:41; 1 Cor. 10

You cannot continue living the same way you did before you received Christ! Scripture clearly teaches that a True Christian must learn to live a totally unique, God-centered lifestyle which God's Spirit develops in us as we cooperate in the "Discipleship to Conversion Dynamic Process."

Consider this truth very carefully: One crucial belief that every True Believer inevitably must embrace and hold is this: Jesus Christ is the only person whose blood sets us Free Indeed: Yes, Jesus Christ Alone![8]

Not only that, this basic truth stands in direct opposition to the world's dogma and nationalistic propaganda that exalts soldiers, claiming that those who murder others could "free" us. This problem points directly back to the prevailing attitude of the first century Jews who rejected Christ, their Messiah and wanted Barabbas, an avowed murderer. They did so because they disbelieved the Truth taught by Christ and trusted a murderous partisan Zealot instead, vainly thinking that he could "save" them from the Romans. Does this sound familiar?[9]

Scripture declares that only "the Son (Jesus Christ) can make you Free Indeed."[10] Christian: Beware of religious dogma which most "Christians" have been taught regarding their "doctrines of the state" which exalts politicians, soldiers and professionals. Consequently, millions have been enslaved by "half truths mixed with outright lies."

Start thinking for yourself and independently reread Scripture. Then, if you carefully examine the New Testament anew and compare it to what you have been taught by religious leaders you will find a chasm of difference separating religious dogma from the Truth of the New Covenant *Kingdom of Heaven.* Doing so, you will begin to see the Truth that explains the confusion and division caused by Satan's neutralization that has left modern "Christians" utterly impotent in

---

8 John 8:31-36; 2 Cor. 3:17,18 *See also the paper entitled True Liberty is in Christ Alone, especially sect. II-B, the "List of Solas," those precepts in which Scripture points to the fundamental truth that Jesus Christ is the only Savior in all ways and venues.*

9 1Sam. 2:9; Psa. 1, 2, 32,49,51; 110:1 ff.; 115:1 ff.; 118:8,9; 146:1 ff.; Prov. 29:25; Isa. 2:1 ff.; 53:1 ff.; Jer. 10,17; Matt. 5-7; Luke 22:13-25; John 18:36-19:16; Rom. 12:9-21; Eph. 2:13 ff.; Col. 1:13 *See also the papers Emmanuel (1) and Emmanuel 2*

10 Luke 4:18; John 8:31-36; Rom. 8:21; 2 Cor. 3:17,18; Gal. 5:1 *See the paper entitled True Liberty is in Christ Alone*

the face of the impending cataclysms that will soon come in the last days.

Indeed, in His Prophetic Discourse recorded in the Synoptic Gospels, Jesus predicted that a terrible time will come that will be worse than any other in history and which will never be repeated! The only way you can survive this is to rely entirely on the truths Jesus Christ proclaimed and 'let the chips fall as they may.'

Multitudes of 'nominal Christians' are falling away, 'dropping like flies.' The chilling lyrics of Petra's *the Last Days* reveal much:

Cold chills when the Spirit speaks - that some will depart from the Faith - All ends in a calamity, just when you thought it was safe!

They followed the lies. The fables' men devise – In the Last Days, the Final Haze, there was strong delusion to believe a lie.

In the Last Days, before the blaze, they couldn't see beyond the misty trends To grab the Truth and have a fighting chance - in the Last Days[11]

Always remember that Jesus Christ is your only Hope, but even Jesus cannot help you unless you believe what he has said, taking His Commands and Teaching seriously! Remember this "God made man – men make slaves." So, do not believe their sly propaganda you see and hear from the corporate media, whose operatives are the minions of Satan's New World Order, alias the Antichrist: It is a clever delusion!

No doubt, a striking parallel and a similar situation happened during the Holocaust in WW2. The Jewish prisoners were told by their Nazi captors that they were going to get a shower, but in truth they were being led to the gas chambers to be exterminated! Yet, Christians beware: The Great Tribulation is going to get worse than that before Christ Comes in Great Power to rescue the Church and finally judge and destroy the world system. What you do now in this life is going to determine your fate on judgment day. Are you going to follow the crowd, believing the lies like many doomed Jews did in the Holocaust

---

11   CCLI #1126011

or are you going to Believe what Jesus said and refuse to cooperate with Antichrist <u>no matter what happens?</u>[12]

The absolute Truth remains that, <u>besides Jesus Christ, no other Savior exists.</u> Nobody can "liberate" others for long by killing others for that way always <u>continues sowing the seeds of conflict and the 'vicious cycle of hate'</u> that has afflicted the world ever since Cain killed Abel. You cannot have it both ways: You must choose the Way of Christ over the way of the world every day to avoid sharing the world's fate.[13]

Always remember that the world cannot liberate anyone by more violence and killing since <u>violence and killing are only symptoms of the deeper unresolved issues of fear, greed, lust, jealousy, hopelessness and desperation.</u> That is why they can only make more slaves of the power mongers and principalities that control the world system and order the killings!

Unfortunately, many religious leaders and organizations are also being used as their pawns, falsely claiming to represent Christ, disseminating false doctrines, "looking like a lamb but speaking with the voice of the dragon" and acting like the "Scarlet Woman riding on the Beast."

The ones who believe them vainly think they can be 'free' but, in truth, they are slaves being led into the 'spiritual gas chamber' lined with the lies of the system that subjugates the masses making them dependent on the hierarchy and its enforcers, the military.

Indeed, that is the same 'formula' used by the ancients, Egypt and Rome. The present New World Order of Antichrist uses the same method.

---

12   12 Matt. 24:21,22; Mark 13:19,20; Luke 21:12 ff. *See also the papers entitled The Christian Epiphany and Facts of Scripture: The Church and the Tribulation*

13   *See the papers entitled Are You Sure What you Believe is Truly Christian Doctrine, Authority and Conscience (a 2 Part series), The Beauty and Finesse of the New Covenant, Christianity Versus Religion (a 3 part series), Conditions for Salvation, Divergent Belief Systems, the Dynamics of Christian Discipleship, Every Believer can Independently Know the Truth of Scripture, God's Definition of Salvation, God Provides Everything we Need, How should we then Live (a 2 part series), Looking Through the Lens of Jesus Christ, the New Covenant, Only One Savior, Psychotic Hypocrisy, Retaining our Freedom requires Knowing and Applying the Truth and Serious Problems in Doctrine and practices still exist in many modern churches*

Let us also understand the occult purpose of Monuments and Symbols that Satan and his minions use in dominating the world. The main ones are the <u>Obelisk</u> and the <u>Eagle</u>, both of which were used by Egypt and Rome. We can see them today in Washington, D.C., London, England and in St. Peter's Square in the Vatican. They symbolize male dominance maintained by force of arms. The "truncated Pyramid" on the back of the $1 bill is also a form of the obelisk.

By great contrast is Jesus' Way which is able to liberate <u>all people who submit to the *New Covenant*</u> that Jesus ordained in the first century.[14]

III. The True Christian life requires major changes.

A. The Christian life is serious business. The bottom-line issue remains: Are you willing to keep an open mind to consider options you have never thought about before?

Yes, to make significant progress, the True Christian life requires that you "think outside the box" of ordinary human responses. That is how God works with man.

First, God has to "Break up our fallow ground" to get us out of the former humanistic rules and ruts people usually fall into without even thinking about it. Then, when a person is more open to 'new things,' the Holy Spirit will begin to work anew in anyone's life that satisfies these spiritual and mental conditions.[15]

If you are a True Christian, you must know that *Discipleship* is a crucial process in which every believer must first enter and then continue cooperating with God throughout life. Nobody who is a Christian is exempt from that reality.[16]

As you progress through the Discipleship process, the Holy Spirit will gradually reveal to you the reality and importance of spiritual things pertaining to the Kingdom of Heaven.[17]

---

14   Exodus 20; Jer. 31; Ezek. 36; Matt. 5-7, 26; Luke 6-18, 21; Gal. 2-5; Hebrews 7-10,12; Rev. 13,17,18

15   Jer. 4:4; 10:1 ff.; 17:1 ff.; 31:31-34; Luke 8:18; 11:33-36; John 14-17; James 1,2

16   Matt. 16:21-26; Luke 9:23-26, 51-56; John 12:23-26

17   *See the author's book Jesus' Way, c. 2009, Dorrance Publishing, Pittsburgh, PA.*

B. Fact: You should know that the world always works in the following ways:

1. "The Hegelian Dialectic" of 'Problem, Reaction, Solution.' This is how the Antichrist and the minions of Satan Engineer "Deep Events" like the Kennedy Assassination, 911 and the present "corona virus crisis."

2. The "Freudian Logic" of 'Fight vs. Flight,' teaching people the lie that those are the only choices one has. However, both operate by "the Carnal Mind" which makes them enemies of God.

3. "Absolute Power corrupts absolutely" is a maxim that afflicts everyone who covets control over others. Power is subject to the precept that affects every other temporal thing in life: "the Law of Diminishing Returns." That is why they can never get enough to satisfy. All human lusts work the same parallel way: You 'enjoy' them the most only the first time. Every time you participate in them, you have to put more and more effort in to get the same "enjoyment." Finally nothing will satisfy. This is why God made man to be in close relationship with God to truly enjoy life.[18]

All three of these ways illustrate the futility of life without God. Solomon wrote that "all is vanity and vexation of spirit."[19]

Conversely, the True Gospel of Christ refutes Freud, offering us a Third Choice:

The True Gospel's Third Way shows that you can refuse to act the world's way and Trust Christ to make it through without being enslaved to *Humanism* and all of the negative things it brings: Lust, Jealousy, Conflict, killing, frustration, hatred and despair.

Jesus' Way presents the only viable solution to humanity's insoluble problems! IF you follow Christ as the New Covenant teaches, you can truly be Free Indeed. The reason that this is possible is that the New Covenant shows us the way to deal with our sin and find a way of Reconciliation to God and our fellow man.[20]

---

18   See the paper entitled The Higher Laws of God
19   See the Book of Ecclesiastes
20   Matt. 5-7; 6:9-15; 10:26-39; John 8:9-11, 32-36; Rom. 5-8; 2 Cor. 5:14-21; Phil.1:21; 2:5-4:20

Verily, True Christians are part of Christ and live in the Kingdom of Heaven, going by its rules: "On earth just as it is in Heaven." The truth is this: I am convinced that no one could truly embrace Christ and the Way of *Agape* Love and concurrently believe in taking any human life, period! Not only that, the only way people could believe in killing is to lose faith and to live in fear and unbelief.

C. Christians, know this for sure: One thing that cannot be overemphasized is that you cannot (are unable to) succeed in the True Christian life if you do not accept and apply those major changes the New Covenant Gospel requires in your beliefs and practices. Remaining in "ordinary human responses" simply cannot produce the changes you must incorporate and experience to be prepared for the days which are ahead.[21]

Somehow, we must gain the spiritual strength and acumen to rise above the maelstrom of emotion, hysteria, doubt, fear and hate that are engulfing the world of unbelievers. Yes, Satan and his minions will overthrow and neutralize the best defense that humans in the world of unbelievers can devise. Only the spiritually based, divinely empowered Formula that is defined in the New Covenant of Jesus Christ can be Victorious in all cases and that will work in any person who truly Believes that the Teachings of Jesus Christ apply right here and right now![22]

---

21   Matt. 6:9-15, 22-24; Rom. 12:1 ff.

22   2 Cor. 4:3-6; 6:14-7:1; 10:3-6 *See also the 4 part series of papers entitled Christian Guidelines for Spiritual Warfare*

Part Two:
Kingdom Principles

IV. Let us consider the Precept of *Redemption.*

A. Introduction: Christ Purchased you with His Precious Blood, so to be a True Christian you must Fully Trust Christ in all areas of your life, physical and spiritual, and in all situations, private and public. Indeed, God's Word does not support or condone any type of compartmentalization or compromise. We must trust Christ as our Savior in all ways and venues. That is, ALL True Christians trust God in Christ for everything, giving God ALL the Glory instead of man or human devices! Anything less than that is tantamount to Idolatry.

Think about it: Your choices and focus of trust and obedience prove whom you trust, worship and obey. Yes, if you claim to be a True Christian, you must put Christ First in all things, and you live in the truth only when you can "trust God (Christ) when all men doubt you."[23]

B. Examining Scripture, we need to establish the context of *New Covenant* Redemption and what makes it such a uniquely powerful basis for living that did not exist prior to the Advent of Jesus Christ on earth.

First, we need to look back and examine the Old Testament and to reveal its place in the process in which God is establishing a personal relationship to man. Yes, God had to allow many "undesirable" and inconvenient things to "play out" in this Grand Epic we see in human history. The Old Testament shows us how God started this amazing relationship: In the Garden with our original parents living in an apparently ideal setting. However, God was interested in grooming a race of newly created beings that had a unique aspect: Free Will. We also have the subsequent ability to Repent from our previous error, an option which the angels did not have. In addition, God allowed

---

23   23 Matt. 10:26-39; Luke 11:33-36; 12:8-10; John 5:24-30; 12:37-50; 14:1-17:26; 18:36-19:16; Acts 4:1-20; 5:29-32, 38-42; 17:24-31; Rom. 1:18-32; 6:1-8:39; Eph. 2:5-22; Phil. 2:5-13; Col. 1:12-29; 2:9,10; 3:1-17; 2 Tim. 2:10-12 *See also the paper Only One Savior*

an antagonist to be present to act as a test.[24] Let us summarize a brief history: Man, of course, deliberately disobeyed God's first command that required man to limit his curiosity in the light of their respect for God's Authority in their lives. Of course, God knew this would happen. It was all part of God's plan of Redemption. Ejected from the idyllic Garden, Adam and Eve had to learn to survive and 'make their way.' However, self-reliance created a rift between man and God that worsened with each generation. Finally, God had to take one faithful man, Noah, and his family, destroying the rest with a worldwide flood.

After the flood, God started working with the descendants of Noah's sons. Eventually, one of the sons of Seth responded, the Syrian emigre Abraham, who "Believed God and it was accounted to him as *Righteousness.*"[25]

Thus, began the role of the eventual nation of Israel in the *Redemption* process. Abraham, Isaac and Jacob became the formative "patriarchs" of these people. Jacob's son Joseph came to Egypt to escape a famine and his descendants remained there, becoming a race of slaves to the Egyptians. Then God raised Moses up to be their deliverer. At this point, God miraculously liberated Israel with the first (archetypal) *Passover. * This was when God opened up the Red Sea to give them an escape route, closing it up behind them on the Egyptians. This Passover became the "catalyzing event" that God used to refine the meaning of Redemption. In this unique relationship, God is looked to for being the sole deliverer and grantor of Freedom. In that context, God gave Moses the Ten Commandments on Mt. Sinai.

However, Israel "sinned a great sin" by losing confidence in God and reverting to the worship of a golden calf, one of the idols of Egypt. They compounded that sin by caving into their fears of the giants, thereby poisoning the minds of ten of the twelve spies sent out to spy the Promised Land. Based on these events, God had to impose a temporary set of laws and rules to discipline Israel, This discipline involved the imposition of death penalties for various offenses and

---

24   *See Glossary of Terms' entry *(the archetype of the) Garden**

25   Gen. 15:6; Rom. 4:3

allowing for armed conflict with the Canaanites. This is the *Mosaic-Levitical Sacrifice System.*[26]

This is the system that eventually culminated in the "Stone Temple Worship Religion" of Biblical Judaism. However, God was not finished with the relationship he was establishing with man. Jesus Christ was sent by God the Father to bring in an entirely new way of Worship, the *New Covenant* which was prophesied by Jeremiah and Ezekiel, that superseded this system of bloodshed sacrifice and ended God's approval of all types of human bloodshed. In fact, this New Covenant incorporates and carries forward elements from the archetypal Passover. Indeed, The passion Week of our Savior forms a Second Passover, in which Christ becomes our Strong Deliverer from evil and the only One who can totally propitiate and deal with our sin so that all whom Receive His Sacrifice can become sons and daughters of God in a New Kingdom, *The Kingdom of Heaven.*[27]

C. Let us now consider the following aspects of Redemption *In Christ* very carefully, observing also that it is closely interwoven with the Discipleship to Conversion Dynamic Process, in which God's Spirit is shaping us into the image of Christ:

1. IF you claim to be a Christian, you are simply unable to concurrently believe in any doctrine that contradicts the Teachings or Commands of Jesus Christ![28]

2. Christ died for all because God loves all people equally and so we must also.[29]

3. Christ commanded us to "Worship (and pray unceasingly to) God in spirit and in Truth," which enables the ministry of the Holy Spirit who is the Communicator of Agape Love, God's Grace, the Teacher of

---

26   See Glossary of Terms' entry: The *Mosaic-Levitical-Sacrifice-System*

27   Jer. 31; Ezek. 36; Matt. 26; Luke 22; John 2:19-21; Heb. 7-10 See also the papers entitled Christian Worship and the True Temple: A New Covenant Perspective, Emmanuel (1) God is Dealing with His People, Emmanuel 2, the Higher Laws of God the Three Passovers of Scripture and Passover Sequence Chart

28   Matt. 10:26-39; Luke 12:8-10; 2 Tim. 2:10-12

29   John 3:16; Rom. 5:1-11; 2 Cor. 5:14-21; Heb. 2:9-15; 1 John 2:1-6

all Truth and the Grantor of all *Authority* for spiritual Gifts, roles, ministries and offices within the *Body of Christ.*[30]

4. Christ commanded us to "Love your enemies."[31]

5. Scripture teaches us to "Trust in God and not man."[32]

6. Christ Redeemed you and Liberated you by His Precious shed Blood on Calvary's Cross. As such, you Belong to him, and as your Owner, He alone is responsible for your defense. This is the heart of the precept of *Redemption* which irrevocably teaches that Christ Alone* is our owner by virtue of Christ being our *Kinsman-Redeemer*.[33]

7. Not only that, Jesus Christ and Jesus Christ Alone is the Believer's only True Liberator in all ways. The *Blood of Christ* Alone makes us Free in all ways.[34]

V. Unbelief is at the root of all the problems people have regarding God.

A. Sadly, among "professing Christians," this unbelief stems primarily from a widespread doctrine called *Determinism.* The main problems associated with

Determinism (alias, "predestination") are as follows:

1. Fear and hate, generated and "played upon" primarily by the mass media.

2. Materialism and debt

---

30   30 Matt. 13:12-15; Luke 8:18; 21:14-19; John 3:5-8, 27; 4:14,23,24; 6:27-63; 7:37-39;14:15-26; 15:26; 16:13-15; Acts 1:8; 2:38,39; 3:19; 4:7-13; 5:29-32; Rom. 5:1-5; 8:1 ff; 1 Cor. 2:7-16; 12:1 ff.; 13:1 ff.; 14:1 ff.; 2 Cor. 3:3-5:21; Gal. 1:6-12; 5:14-25; Eph. 1:13; 2:13-3:21; 4:1-16,23,24; 5:17,18; 6:10-18; Heb. 2:3-14; 4:12-16; 8:10-13; 9:11-15; 1 Pet. 1:18-25; 1 John 4,5
      See also the papers entitled the Amazing Doctrine of God's Grace, Christian Worship and the True Temple, the Doctrine of Jesus Christ's Real Presence, Every Believer can Independently Know the Truth of Scripture, the Holy Spirit is God's Revelator, How does Christ's Blood get to us Today, the Progression of our Redemption requires Spiritual Development and Spirituality and Worship

31   Matt. 5:43-48

32   Job 13:15; Psa. 18:2,30; 20:7; 25:1 f.; 27:1 ff.; 31:1 ff; 37:1 ff.; 40:4; 44:1-8; 91:1 ff.; 118:8,9; 146:3; Prov. 2:8; 3:5,6; 29:25; Matt. 21:18-22; Rom. 10:6-17

33   Ruth 4:10; Acts 20:28; Eph. 1:14; Col. 1:12,13

34   Matt. 16:21-26; John 8:31-36; Rom. 6:18; 2 Cor. 3:17,18; Gal. 5:1,13; Heb. 2:9-15; 1 Pet. 2:16
      See also the Hymn Faith of our Fathers, verse two.

3. National pride, expressed in "Patriotism"

4. Organization by the imposition of "Corporation-based Bylaws"

5. Bigotry and racism

6. Paganism, usually found in cultural holidays and nationalistic customs

Of course, unbelief is also carefully camouflaged so people do not recognize it, because it stems primarily from a modern version of an ancient practice defined in Scripture as the sin of Idolatry! Nonetheless, God calls it an abomination. It is also a violation of the First Commandment of the Decalogue, found in the Old Testament book of Exodus. This commandment also categorically refutes the "giving of glory and worship" to Politicians, Soldiers and professionals, which practice is soundly denounced throughout the Bible.

God clearly told the Israelites (God's people of the Old Covenant) that he would not tolerate giving human power the glory and credit that Scripture tells us belongs solely to God! This precept also applies to giving credit to human power 'making us free' when the truth is that the sole source of true freedom and liberty are plainly ascribed to God alone.[35]

B. The fundamental issues concerning True Faith are these:

One, to be a True Christian, you must put the entire weight of your life in God's hands. Two, you must wholly Believe the Truth of the Word of God as taught by Jesus Christ and live according to the *New Covenant* Jesus ordained. Three, you must know that "whatsoever is not of Faith is sin."[36]

Moreover, no 'excuse' exists for any person that claims to be a Christian. We must live *In Christ* according to the New Covenant, for Scripture says that "His Commands are not burdensome."[37]

---

35   *Ex. 6:6,7; *14:13,14; Isa. 42-45; Matt. 6:22-24; John 8:31-36; 2 Cor. 3:17,18; Phil. 2:5-11; Heb. 2:9-15 *See also the O.T. account of the Archetypal Passover in Exodus 3-15 and the paper True Liberty is in Christ Alone, especially Sect. II-B, the "Solas of Christ"

36   Rom. 14:23 See also The Christian Epiphany and True Liberty is in Christ Alone

37   Matt. 10:16-42; Luke 8:18; 12:8-10; 14:26-33; 19:26; Rom. 1:16-32; 2 Cor. 12:9,10; Gal. 1:6-12; 2:19-21; 3:26-28; 6:14; Phil. 1:21-2:13; 3:7-15; Col. 1:23-29; 3:1-17; 1 Tim. 6:3- 12; 2 Tim. 1:7-12; 2:1 ff.; Heb. 2:9-15; 3:14; 4:12-16; 7:11-12:29; 1 John 5:3.

VI. Kingdom Precepts, continued: "The Faith versus Fear Factor," Part 1:

A. What do you truly believe and practice? Always remember, IF you are a True Christian, the "Cup and Baptism of Jesus Christ" concerns all aspects of your life.

Beware: If you claim to be a Christian and think you can still live and believe like the world does and 'get by' you are sadly mistaken! Remember that 'drinking the cup unworthily will drink judgment back in your face for God does not take hypocrisy lightly! Not only that, if you deny the contemporary applicability of the Teachings of Jesus for any reason, you are a hypocrite.[38]

Verily, trusting Christ and living by His Teaching fully is the only way that contains the power for victory in this life and eternal life to come. However, it only works IF you Truly Believe in your heart of hearts and that afterward you openly confess that truth with your mouth.[39]

B. Know God is watching. You cannot "fake" the Christian life and 'get away with it.' Nobody gets away with anything with God! Not only that, you are unable to "mix Christianity with worldly ways" and succeed. Scripture teaches that your Lord Jesus Christ requires your total loyalty and Holiness: He must have Holy Brethren who have made hard choices that cost them much in the things of this world.[40]

Beyond that, Scripture teaches that God demands our unilateral, single-minded Fear, Allegiance, Worship and loyalty. Again, God considers anybody who trusts in any other "source of Salvation" to be guilty of the abominable sin of Idolatry.[41]

Also, a key part of Truly Christian Doctrine is that the Scriptures teach that God commands that we implicitly Trust Him and wait upon

---

38   Matt. 23; Luke 12:49,50; 1 Cor. 10:1-21; 11:23-31; 2 Thess. 1:8 f.; 2:3-12
39   Matt. 5-7; Luke 5:12-14;6:20-42; 8:18; 9:23-26, 51-56; 11:9-13, 33-36; 12:8-10; John 3:18-21, 27; 5:22-30; 6:27-63; 8:12-58; 9:39-41; 12:23-50; 13:34-17:26; 18:36,37; Rom. 6:1- 8:39; 10:9,10 *See also the paper Principles of Fulfillment Theology*
40   Matt. 10:26-39; Heb. 12:1 ff.; James 1:5-8; 2:8 ff.; 1 Pet. 1:3 ff.; 3:13-5:11
41   Exodus 20,32; Psa. 115; Prov. 1:7; 9:10; Isa. 42-46; 57:15; Jer. 10,1-16,23;Acts 4:9-20

him <u>alone</u> for direction, inspiration <u>and for our daily safety from evil of any type, fearing and trusting nothing else!</u>[42]

C. Beware: One of the most insidious types of "intoxicating" and 'strong delusion type' areas of <u>Idolatry</u> is that of <u>National Pride, expressed in patriotism and militarism.</u> All these are central elements of the <u>world's way</u> of trusting in human power to save. Know this: <u>All these ways rely heavily on the use of violence and long term exposure to them results in a 'conditioned' state of mind called "brainwashing" that is very difficult from which to recover.</u>

Even during the Old Covenant we can see that it is recorded plainly that God did not want His People to continue relying on those ways. God was "progressively training" Israel to be "weaned away" from this way of "dealing with evil" that had started with Cain's killing of Abel <u>because it does not correct the underlying</u> cause, sin. The archetypal *Passover* is a great example. The story of "Gideon's Three Hundred" is another perfect example, as was Elijah's "confrontation" of the false prophets of The Baal on Mt. Carmel and Jehoshaphat's experience in heeding the righteous Prophet's voices telling him to trust God for the victory instead of the military. Also, consider God's summary judgment of King David's numbering of Israel's army. Another prime example is Zechariah's proclamation that "It (victory) is not by might, nor by power but by My Spirit, declares the Lord." So, Worship God Alone![43]

Beware also of the doctrine of *Determinism, * alias the beliefs of "Calvinism" (predestination) which serve to deify human government, political figures and military force. The serious implications of this false doctrinal system underscores God's extreme disapproval and condemnation of all types of idolatry because idolatry always gives glory to human "saviors" <u>instead of God!</u> Indeed, one of the most egregious of all is the Satanic-based practice of <u>human sacrifice</u> in sending our youth to fight and kill. God's revulsion of this is recorded repeatedly in the Prophets.[44]

---

42   Ex. 6-15; Psa. 23, 24, 27, 31, 37, 42, 46, 51, 59, 62, 71, 73, 84, 91,94,118; Isa. 40:31

43   Exodus 6, 12-15; Judges 6,7; 2 Sam. 24:1 f.; 1 Kings 18:21; 1 Chr. 17:3-14; 21;1 f.;22:2-9; 2 Chr. 20; Zech. 4:6

44   Psa. 20, 44, 83:18; 94, 118; Prov. 10:9,29; 14:12; 16:7; 21:30; Isa. 1-8, 28-34, 42-47; Jer. 2-19; Ezek. 18:30-32; 23:37-39; Dan. 3:1 ff.; 6:1 ff.; Hosea 10:12,13; 14:9; Matt. 5:43-48; John

A major problem with *Humanism* is that it always <u>drags you down to the world's level of simplistic "Freudian Logic,"</u> simply because it is idolatry and idolatry always does this because it is <u>"double-minded."</u> <u>Only One God exists!</u>[45]

D. One thing we can do, which Glorifies God, is have <u>Faith in His Protection.</u> Verily, God's Word promises that if we are <u>totally true and loyal to Jesus Christ in our heart,</u> that we have nothing to fear or worry about! As long as we are walking in "the Heart of God's Will," we are essentially <u>invincible! Do you believe this?</u>[46]

VII. The "Faith versus Fear Factor,"

Part 2: Your Choice of Master shows that, each day you live, "you choose whom you will serve, fear and trust" because <u>that is the one which controls you!</u>

A. The following precepts should help establish the fundamentals:

1. You must Always put <u>Christ and His Teachings First.</u>[47]

2. You must Acknowledge that Jesus Christ <u>is your Creator, Captain and Lord</u> and that He has Authority over all.[48]

3. <u>Only one God exists and God's Word= Christ</u>: You must also know that <u>His Word always takes precedence over man's</u> or you will become an <u>Idolater</u> and a slave to man's power.[49]

18:36,37; Acts 4:11-15; 5:29-32; 16:16-34

45   Exodus 20; Deut. 4:29-39; 6:4-6; 32:1-39; 1 Sam. 2:6-9; 15:22,23; Psa. 24, 95,96; 111:10; Prov. 1:7; 29:25; Isa. 30:1, 15-22 ; 42:1-9; 44:6-20; 45:5-12, 20-25; Jer. 10; Dan. 2:20- 22; Matt. 6:24; John 1:1-5; Acts 17:22-31; Rom. 1:18-32; 1 Cor. 2:4-16; 2 Cor. 4,5; Gal. 1:6-12; Phil. 2:5-11; Col. 1:12-27; Heb. 10-12; James 1:5-8; 2:10-26; 4:1-8; 1 John 5:19-21

46   Exodus 14:13,14; 1 Sam. 2:6-10; Psa. 23-28, 31-37, 42, 44-46; 49-51, 55-57, 61-63, 71-73, 84, 91, 103, 145; Matt. 8:1-4; 28:20; Mark 1:40-42; 16:15-18; Luke 5:12-15; Rom. 8:26-39; 1 Cor. 10:12,13 *See also The Christian Epiphany, Sect. VI: "An Affidavit," Sect. A-5 for a list of God's "Protection Scriptures"*

47   Matt. 6:24; 10:26-32; 16:21-26; Luke 12:8-10

48   Josh. 5:13-15; Psa. 2,110; Matt. 28:18; John 1:1-18; Acts 4:1 f.; 5:29-32; Eph. 4:1-13;Corl. 1:12-29; 2:6 ff.; Rev. 4,5

49   Ex. 20:1-7; Deut. 4:32-39; 1 Kings 18:21; Psa. 44, 94, 110, 115, 118; Isa. 43:10-12;44:6-10,20; 45:18-23; Jer. 10:1 ff.; 17:1-10; John 1:1-18; 18:36,37; Acts 5:29-32

4. A True Christian is always willing to lay down his or her life for Christ. However, no True Christian would ever justify or approve killing despite circumstance.[50]

5. You must fear God <u>more than</u> you fear man or circumstance.[51]

6. Nothing is 'too hard' or 'impossible' with the Lord.[52]

7. Your worship, trust and fear operate as an "either-or proposition": It is God's infallible Word and authority OR the fallible word and authority of man and his 'media.' So, "Why are you vacillating between two positions?" And, IF God is God, then Why do you not believe our report?[53]

8. You must learn to "let go," forgiving others of their sins o God will not forgive you your sins.[54]

9. Let us consider some General Scriptural references to "the fear of God versus the fear of man."[55]

10. In particular, let us contrast the Scriptures describing the gaping chasm of difference that <u>separates those who truly fear and worship God from those who worship idols because they fear man and circumstance.</u>[56]

B. Not only that, you must know that no neutral ground exists in life. You are serving either <u>one</u> or the other of the two masters that are possible: God in Christ or self, the world and <u>Satan</u>.

Moreover, IF you claim to be a Christian, you must singl mindedly serve Christ <u>Alone</u>, or you will <u>revert to serving the old master by default!</u> You are simply <u>unable to serve both concurrently.</u> Unfortunately,

---

50   Matt. 10; Luke 9:23-26, 51-56; 14:25-33; John 15; Phil. 1:21; 3:7-15

51   Psa. 111:10; Prov. 1:7; 3:5,6; 9:10; 29:25; Matt. 10:16-39; John 18:36,37; Acts 4:12-20; 5:29-32

52   Gen. 18:14; Isa. 53:1; 59:1,2; Jer. 32:17,27; Matt. 19:26

53   1 Kings 18:21; 2 Chr. 7:14; Psa. 1,2; Prov. 1:7; 3:5,6; Isa. 53:1; 59:1,2; Ezek. 3,18,33,34; Matt. 6:24; Luke 16:13; 18:8; Rom. 1:16-25; 2 Cor. 3:17,18; Gal. 1:10; Phil. 2:5-11; James 4:4

54   Matt. 5:3-48; 6:9-15; Luke 6:20 ff.; 17:1-4;

55   Exodus 14:13,14; 15:26; Deut. 7:15; 1 Sam. 2:6-9; 1 Kings 18:21; Job. 28:28; Psa. 23-28, 31-37, 91; Prov. 1:7; 9:10; 29:25; Matt. 10:26-39; Luke 21:12-19

56   1 Sam. 2:1-10; 2 Sam.23:3; 2 Chr. 20:20,21; Neh. 5:9,15; Psa. 19:9; 111:10; Prov.1:7,33; 2:1-16; 8:13; 9:10; 10:27; 14:27; 19:22; 22:4; 23:17; Isa. 11:1 ff.; 33:6; Matt. 10:26-28;Luke 12:5; Rom. 11:16-23; Heb. 12:14-29; Rev. 15:4 *Then, contrast these to the following:* 1 Sam. 15:22,23; Psa. 36:1; Prov. 1:23-32; 29:25; Isa. 53:1-6; Jer. 10:1 ff.; 17:1-10; Rom. 1:18-32; 3:18

religion makes' people think they can and that is why religion is a false belief from Satan that is cast to deceive Christians. However, nobody fools God![57]

C. Now, let us consider the following regarding the recent "corona virus hysteria":

1. Ask yourself: Was Jesus ever afraid of touching lepers?[58]

2. "Death is nothing to fear if you have Faith." Verily, if we Love Jesus, a True Christian's identity is bound up with Jesus Christ, our Risen Lord and "For me to live is Christ and to die is gain."[59]

3. However, for anyone who claims to be a Christian, confessing Christ as their Savior, to "cave into fear" is essentially the same as denying everything for which Jesus lived and died![60]

VIII. Question:

In the light of all the above, why are so many "Christians" still thinking that Jesus's Way is "so hard?" Think about it: You have to know that it is the Gospel He proclaimed and IF you live it, it will make you happy in the end. Think about its basic tenets and how they diverge completely from the ways of the world:

- Love God with all your heart, mind, soul and strength.[61]
- Deny self and taking up the cross.[62]
- Selflessly care for the poor and needy.[63]
- Forgive others of their offenses.[64]

---

57   Matt. 4:1-10; 6:22-24; Luke 4:1-8; 2 Cor. 4:1-6; 11:12-15 *See also the 3 part series of papers entitled Christianity Versus Religion and the 4 part series of papers entitled Christian Guidelines for Spiritual Warfare*

58   Matt. 8:1-4; Mark 1:40-42; Luke 5:12-16

59   Psa. 33:4; Phil. 1:6,21; 1 John 4:18

60   Matt. 10:26-39; Luke 12:8-10; 2 Tim. 2:11-13

61   Matt. 22:36,37

62   Matt. 16:21-26; Luke 9:23-26; John 12:23-26

63   Matt. 5:3 f.; Mark 12:40-44; Luke 6:20 f.; 14:13,21; Gal. 2:10

64   Matt. 6:9-15; 18:21,22

- Holy harmlessness: Loving others, even our enemies and the ones who hate us.[65]

Yes, the "formula" is simple; even a child can understand it. In fact Christ taught that unless you become *like a child* you could not even enter the Kingdom of Heaven that the Gospel describes.[66]

Yet, the True Gospel always points us to the real answers in life that no other way can provide!

The True Christian Gospel poses the stark contrast between the preoccupations the world has with materialism, self-centeredness, power-mongering and uncontrolled lust and the simple pleasures shown by those who love God and have made Jesus Christ the center of their lives.

Indeed, the lifestyle Jesus ordained shows the only way out of the hopelessness, fear and despair engendered by the world system, offering instead the Wellspring of real satisfaction, joy and sense of purpose that always remains just out of reach of those who are consumed by selfishness, hatred, greed and fear.

Yes, it is utterly amazing how effective the Gospel of Christ can be once you finally come to the realization that it is truly logical and practical to live!

Not only that, just think about how miserable those Pharisees, Sadducees and Herodians were! They were so obsessed with legalism that they lost sight of the Truth that was "right before their eyes."

Yes, true civilization is not sophistication, but reconciliation![67]

Finally, let us beware of the flood of "misinformation" that is being pushed upon the masses by the corporation-owned media regarding the "manufactured corona crisis," another "Deep Event" that is cast to "divide and conquer" by isolating people and taking away their rights! This is particularly evident in the way the world is using this "crisis" as a juggernaut to deprive Christians of their Constitutional right to Freely Worship.

---

65   Matt. 5:43-48
66   Matt.18:1-14; 19:13-15 *See also the author's book Jesus' Way Chapter XVI, "The Formula"*
67   2 Cor. 5:14-21

Evidently, the goal of the "elite controllers" is what it always has been: to deceive (brainwash) people into thinking they were "free" when the Truth is that they are the dupes of the New World Order's "Agenda twenty-one," which is designed to incrementally enslave the world, step by step, using these "events" we are told are caused by something or someone else. Of course, that is just another way of defining what has been always known as "the Hegelian Dialectic." Let us remember what Paul and John had said about the Antichrist that rises to power in the "Great Tribulation Period" that has been recorded as prophecy in our New Testament.[68]

If you claim to be a Christian, you must remember: The Way of Christ remains as the "road not taken" by the ones that follow the crowds down the "wide road to perdition," living by "ordinary human responses." Only those who Covenant to follow Jesus Christ with all their heart, soul, mind and strength no matter what happens will survive the 'cut' after the oncoming onslaughts of "lying wonders" in the Great Tribulation. The present "crisis" is only a taste.

Remember what Jesus said about the coming 'mega storm': To make it through intactly you must choose sides and clearly "strike your colors" or you will fall away into apostasy and be lost![69]

---

68   2 Thess. 1,2; 1 Tim. 4:1,2; 2 Tim. 3,4; Rev. 13,17,18
69   Matt. 10:26-39; 24:21,22; Luke 12:8-10; John 16:33; 2 Tim. 2:11-13 \

Chapter 6

The Major Missing Aspects of the Original Christian Gospel

The Major Missing Aspects of the Original Christian Gospel		
#	Description	Page #
I.	Introduction	
II.	Amazingly, the major problem areas of the modern "corporation church system" directly correspond to the Major Missing Aspects of the Original Christian Gospel	
III.	Let us consider now the "Major Missing Aspects of the Original Christian Gospel" . . . in detail	
IV.	"The Truth is the First Duty," Part One	
V.	"The Truth is the First Duty," Part Two	
VI.	Let us review some basic observations about what has happened to most Christians over the years	
VII.	Conclusion	

I. Introduction:

For at least the last forty years, I have researched Scripture, carefully examining it with a mind that is open to the "still small voice" of God's Spirit. I have found that two very good rules in studying Scripture are these:

One is to "Look at every text through the Lens of Jesus Christ." Two is to "Compare Scripture with Scripture." Doing these you will find that no interpretation or doctrine is a Christian belief if it contradicts Christ's Teachings and Commands!

Verily, Paul also told us that he taught the <u>same Gospel as Christ taught</u> and that if anyone taught otherwise that they were cursed by God: Only <u>one true *Gospel* exists</u>! In Revelation, John gave us a clue in Christ's description of the Seven Churches of Asia Minor. In this analysis <u>only two out of seven churches</u> were given a passing grade by God and that account was written <u>in the first century!</u> Much deeper apostasy came about in the fourth century, further degrading the Church's Witness.

Church history reveals to us a series of <u>choices</u> in which crucial leaders took the "path of least resistance" instead of holding to the Truth Christ taught. Not only that, if we continue to follow church history through the "dark ages" to the modern era, the apostasies of the "mainline groups" continues. The only exceptions were the small groups of Believers outside of their system who followed Christ's Teachings that <u>both Catholics and Protestants mercilessly persecuted!</u>

Now you should be able to see the pattern of how through the centuries, the Dragon (Satan) has infiltrated and transmuted what was formerly the early church into a worldly caricature that <u>acts like God's enemy</u> and even <u>teaches the precise opposite</u> of what Christ taught.

Long ago, I dedicated my life to <u>seeking truth and loving the truth</u> with all my heart soul, mind and strength. I rejoiced whenever the Holy Spirit would reveal a new perspective on a doctrine I had previously 'assumed' to be valid, <u>but which in reality was not.</u>

This process has been repeated in several crucial areas in which I had been erroneously "catechized into" in the past or "led to assume were true," along with many others, by religious leaders when I was young.[1] -

Subsequently, after discovering there were "serious errors" in Christian doctrine, I have found that an excellent way to research Scripture and

---

[1]   Daniel 2; Matt. 4:17; 9:35; 24:14; 26:13; 28:18-20; Mark 1:1,14,15 ; 8:34-38; 13:10-13; Rom. 1:16; 15:18-20; 1 Cor. 9:11-17; 2 Cor. 4:1-6; Gal. 1:6-12; 1 Tim. 6:3; Rev. 2,3 *See the book entitled Life-Songs in the Key of Jesus*

to reveal errors is by carefully examining it with a mind that is open to the "still small voice" of God's Spirit. In addition to the two very good rules mentioned above, another tool in studying Scripture that is extremely effective in exposing previously unrecognized false doctrine is this: "Disregard all 'religious catechisms' you may have been taught in the past, reread the Scripture individually and independently and see what comes back." Also, remember this: No interpretation of Scripture or doctrine is a Truly Christian belief if it contradicts Christ's Teachings and Commands!

Think about it: "Can two walk together and not be in agreement?" Can a person claim to be a Christian and not believe what Jesus Taught? I do not think so! Yet, this fact exposes a "deep-seated level of disconnecting" from reality that exists in the hearts of the vast majority of modern "professing Christians." Moreover, it cannot be denied that they are deeply compromised. Consequently, their influence is at the nadir!

God's Word teaches that we must cultivate a humble, submissive 'childlike attitude to receive what we need from God. Consider the sheer volume of Scriptural evidence and warnings predicting what happens when God's people lose their way. The reader will also find the following list of the writer's position papers very helpfully in reestablishing a "beachhead" of truly New Testament Truth that would serve you well in the hard times to come that all True Christians must face.[2]

---

2   Daniel 4,6; Amos 3:3; Matt. 7:13-21; 10:32-40; 16:24-26; 18:20; 24:9-13; Mark 4:11-14; Luke 2:33-35; 4:18,19; 6:20-49; 8:18; 9:23-26, 49-62; 10:16-27; 11:17-36; 12:8-12, 49-53;16:10-17; 18:16,17; 19:26; 21:8-18; John 1:1-18; 3:16-36; 4:14-24; 6:27-63; 8:12-58; 9:39-41;12:23-26,32,46; 13:34-17:26; 18:36,37; 21:15-17; Acts 4:12-20; 5:29-32; 2 Cor. 11:12-15; 1 Tim. 6:3; Rev. 2,3 *See the books entitled Basic Christian Doctrine, Life-Songs in the Key of Jesus and A Seeker's Guide to Biblical Faith See also the papers entitled Authority and Conscience (A 2 part series), Introduction to Christian Conversion (A 3 Part series), Christianity Versus Religion(A 3 Part series), Conditions for Salvation, the Doctrine of the Elect/ Ekklesia, Dynamics of Christian Discipleship, Every Believer can independently know the Truth of Scripture, Fallacies of Determinism, God's Definition of Salvation, Hermeneutics: Basic Principles of Scripture Interpretation (A 2 Part series), the Higher Laws of God, Investigating the Symptoms of Latter day Problems, Jesus' Major Parables, Key Aspects of the Christian Gospel, the Key to Understanding Scripture is Spiritual Exegesis, the Kingdom of Heaven is the Highest Form of Civilization, Looking Through the 'Lens of Jesus Christ,' the New Covenant, Our Preparations for God's Service, Patriarchalism in the Church, Principles of Fulfilment Theology, Psychotic Hypocrisy, the Spiritual Laws of Revival and True Liberty is in Christ Alone*

II. Amazingly, the major problem areas of the modern church system directly correspond to the "Major Missing Aspects" of the Original Christian Gospel of the New Testament. Indeed, the following significant problem areas that I have observed for decades answer to those major areas of false doctrine and practice that are endemic to what I loosely call the "modern church system." Not only that, I positively know that all these areas require major changes just to bring the church back to the New Covenant Standard!

One, many teach that the spiritual gifts somehow "expired" with the passing of the early Apostles of the first century.

Two, they teach that it is "acceptable" for Christians to believe in the intentional (knowledgeable or premeditated) killing of others which secular "authorities," whether they are political or military leaders, have deemed to be "enemies" or "criminals" and that, according to them, "deserves to die."

Three, they lead the masses to believe that religious leaders somehow possess the "sole authority" to understand and interpret Scripture and that they lead you to believe that you can always trust religious leaders to be 'telling the truth.'

Four, leaders mistakenly think they "own the church" and that "worldly nonprofit corporation organization" is an acceptable basis for controlling church affairs.

Five, they have misled male "Anglo" Christians to mistreat their Christian sisters and Christians of other races, unfairly subjugating them and limiting their possibilities for the ministry.

Six, You have most likely been erroneously "led to believe" that "Salvation" is something that you can "own" and that it only applies "internally" or to "the Bye and Bye" of the afterlife.

Seven, if you have been "raised up in organized churches," it is most likely that you do not know the reality of true spiritual worship. Worse yet, you have probably been taught a woefully inadequate "intellectually-based" concept of what "worshiping

God" is like. Indeed, most "professing Christians" are woefully ignorant of the fact that, in the *Kingdom of Heaven,* Jesus has inaugurated an entirely new venue of *New Covenant* worship where the center of activity is the Reborn human spirit, deep inside the body of the worshiper, not in a building made of wood, metal and stone! Yes, this is part of the "New Wineskin" to which Jesus referred.[3]

Indeed, the vast majority of "churchgoing Christians" are misled to believe that a "church" is a building, in which meetings are controlled by "boards and committees" whose actions are regulated by "nonprofit Corporation bylaws" designed the same way as secular businesses, thereby making these organizations part of the world, not God's Kingdom! That is so because their decisions are being surreptitiously molded by "the carnal mind of *Humanism,*" the same way that Satan controls the rest of the world system, of which religion is a part! However, as Scripture defines it, True Christianity is not like that at all! So, if you are willing to accept these truths, you can move onto knowing what the major problem areas are that we are up against.

Moreover, in the remainder of this paper I will conduct a comparison of these areas with the spiritually minded and "properly divided truth" attitude wherein we "walk in the Light" to properly understand the teaching of Scripture. This way one can have the confidence that what we are reiterating is what the Scripture actually says regarding these areas. Indeed, this was the way I discovered that works amazingly well in applying what the Holy Spirit had consequently revealed to me at various crucial times during my search for the truth during the last forty years.

Let us remember what the Scripture tells us about how we receive the Truth by listening to the Holy Spirit Who will spiritually discriminate the messages you hear, discerning the Truth, separating it from the lie. Also know that Scripture says that "Jesus never lied."[4]

---

3   Matt. 5:17-20; 6:9-13; 16:15-20; 18:20; Mark 2:21,22; 16:15-18; Luke 17:20-37; John 2:19-21; 4:23,24; 6:63; 14:6, 15-26; 16:13-15; 17:17; 18:36; Acts 7:48; 17:24-31; 1 Cor. 2:9-16;Rom. 8:1-11; Eph. 2:13-22; 2 Tim. 2:15-26; 2 Pet. 1:16-21 *See also Sect. III-G below and the papers entitled The Spiritual Laws of Revival and Spirituality and Worship*

4   Psa. 49:19; 97:11; 119:105; 130,; 139:12; Prov. 6:23; Isa. 5:20; Jer. 2-11,13,18; 23:9 ff.; 31:31-34; Ezek. 3,8,9,10,14,18, 20-22, 33,34,36; Matt. 4:16; 5:14-16; 6:22-24; Luke 11:33-36; John 1:4-18; 3:16-36; 7:15-18; 8:12-58; 9:5,9,10, 39-41; 12:35,36; 14:6-17:26; Rom. 8:1-18; 13:12; 2 Cor. 4:3-7; 11:12-15; Eph. 5:8,13; 2 Tim. 1:7-14; Heb. 1,2,7-12; 1 Pet. 2:22; 2 Pet. 1:2-11,19-21; 1 John 1:1 ff.; 4:1-6 *See also the 4 part series of papers entitled Christian Guidelines for Spiritual Warfare, Every Believer can Independently know the Truth of Scripture, From Whence do Lies come and God's "Universal Attitude Test"*

Let us also be advised that another serious problem underlying all the others is the apparent human penchant for "assuming" that because someone who is an "authority figure" teaches or tells you something that it is "automatically" true [Sic.]. Worse yet is the sad fact that most Christians know not who they are and are inherently lazy and like others to tell them what to believe without "checking it out for themselves" in the Scripture to make sure that what they believe is actually true or not!⁵

III. Let us consider now the "Major Missing Aspects of the Original Gospel" that were revealed to me in detail:

*A. The first was rediscovering the reality that the Spiritual Gifts, along with the truth regarding miracles and divine healing, are just as viable today as they were in the first century, so long as we clearly understand the Scriptural conditions by which God regulates them.

Let us also be advised that another serious problem underlying Let us examine the overall background: The existence of spiritual Gifts has been catalogued in Scriptural history from the beginning. They were present in Abraham's wisdom and in the miraculous birth of Isaac. They were manifest in the miraculous dream interpretations of both Joseph and Daniel. Right from the start of Israel's history God gave unique abilities to Moses during the first *Passover* as a part of his commission from God as the spiritual leader used in God's Plan for their eventual liberation and formation as a Nation. Later, in the "wilderness experience," God also endued the seventy elders with "Prophetic Gifts." Also, God gave special Gifts of wisdom and power to all the Old Testament Prophets.⁶

Let us focus our inquiry: The most controversy seems to center around the "gift of tongues." From the beginning, God gave man the "ability to formulate and use language" as a means of communication. However, the incident of "the Tower of Babel" showed that if all people

---

5   Ibid. Fn. #3 Acts 17:11 *See also the papers entitled Are You Sure What you Believe and Practice is Truly Christian Doctrine, (the 2 part series) Authority and Conscience, A Biblical Disclosure of Antichrist, (the 3 part series Christianity Versus Religion, The Dangers of Conformity and Do You Know Who You Are*

6   Gen. 12:1-9; 15:1-15; 21:1-7; 22:1-18; 32:22-30; 37:1-11; 40:1-41:57; Ex. 2-15; Numbers 11:1-30; Deut. 1-7; Dan. 2:19-45

spoke the same language that they would transgress their boundary and begin thinking that they could 'reach' God by their own efforts, which is the main fallacy behind all "religion." So God confused their tongues, resulting in the dispersal of man and the proliferation of many dialects.[7]

In the New Testament, God began to solve this problem. When Jesus was concluding His Ministry, He promised the Apostles that they would "receive power, after the Holy Spirit came upon them" and that they would be witnesses to God's marvelous power that was released because of Christ's Perfect Work of Reconciliation on the Cross.[8]

Another crucial fact we need to know is that all spiritual beings, including Regenerated humans, possess varying degrees of an ability we call Telepathy. It is well known that Angels, both holy and fallen, have the ability to "impress thoughts" to human minds.

However, only the Triune Living God can "read" a person's mind!

So, when Jesus Christ came on the scene, teaching the revolutionary precepts of the New Covenant Gospel, the doorway to direct communication and *Fellowship* with God for all True Believers was opened. Indeed, the Gift of Tongues was given as proof that this ability and privilege still exists in the *Body of Christ!*

Of course, we should know these things are true despite the fact that we all have seen many abuses and counterfeits of these. This is because of the Scriptural precept of "free will." However, those anomalies also explain why God wrote the rules regarding Spiritual Gifts. One of these rules is that the Holy Spirit is the One who decided each Believer's own unique "gifts mix" that fits their specific ministry area in the *Body of Christ.* So, you should be able to see that most of the problems with abuse of spiritual gifts arise because those people fail to submit to the Holy Spirit, mistakenly thinking that they can "pick and choose" whatever they want. Of course, that is not how the *Body of Christ* works. Always remember that Jesus Christ is Lord and Scripture tells us that ever since Jesus Ascended to the Throne, the Holy Spirit is the only member of the Divine Tri-Unity (God) acting on behalf of Christ here on earth!

---

7   Gen. 11
8   Acts 1:8; 2:1-39

Nonetheless, Jesus's final words before the Ascension also confirms the fact that the dispensation of these special abilities will continue "unto the end of the Age," that is, unto Christ's Second Coming! You should always know this also: Counterfeits are only there when there is a genuine article. Not only that, you should also know that "throwing the baby out with the bath water" does not do us any good to solve these problems. Also, many have misunderstood what Paul was saying in those two verses in First Corinthians thirteen. However, you must understand the fact that when Christ returns we would no longer require "spoken language" to communicate for we would have received our glorified bodies in which are always "telepathically tuned" to God.[9]

*B. The second missing aspect concerns the New Covenant precept called: *The Patience of the Saints,* a.k.a. "Faith-based Pacifism," which also unequivocally upholds the precepts of Jesus's and the Apostles' Teaching on loving enemies. This type of Love, Agape, is God's Love and is the same type of Love that the Holy Spirit gives every True Christian Believer. This categorically refutes any "so-called Christian" doctrine that would ever rationalize or approve the knowledgeable killing (murder) of any human being despite circumstance.[10]

Also, know this: All belief in killing people (murder) is always associated with evil. Verily, its root is Sin and is the source of hate, savagery and fear, all of which plague the human race worldwide! Not only that, Killing is always linked to Darkness and never Light. It is linked to hatred and never to Love! Moreover, killing is also associated with Idolatry, since the rationale for all types of killing people rests on their innate trust in human power to 'save,' not God. IF they were trusting in God, they would trust God's Power to save, instead of killing! Again, know that hatred for anyone is always associated with darkness and never light. Not only that, True Christians always fight "in the spirit," not by the "flesh."[11]

---

9 Matt. 28:18-20; Mark 16:9-20; John 6:27-63: 14:15-26; 15:26; 16:13-15; Acts 1:8;2:1-39; Rom. 12:1-16; 1 Cor. 1:17-2:16; 12:1-14:40; 2 Cor. 1:20; Eph. 4:1-16

10 Matt. 5:43-48; 26:51-56; Luke 6:20 ff.; 9:49-56; John 18:36,37; 1 John 3:15 f.; 4:7-21

11 Exodus 20:13; Isa. 5:20-30; 8:20-22; 29:13,14; 30:8-22; Jer. 4:22; 11:17; 13:15-17; 17:5-10; Hos. 14:9; Matt. 6:22-24; 8:11,12; Mark 3:1-5; Luke 11:33-36; Rom. 12:9-21; Eph.5:5-11; 6:10-12; Col. 1:13; Heb. 11:13-16; 2 Pet. 2:1 ff.; 1 John 2:9-17; 3:11-15

Know this: killing others can never solve humanity's problems because all humanity's problems are caused by his sin. That is also why the only solution that works is Jesus's nonviolent Way of Faith in God and Reconciliation to our fellow man. That is also why the True Christian must renounce all recourse in trusting human Power to 'solve' because those ways always involve killing!

Not only that, God's Word consistently warns against the concentration of power and its penchant to control others. Of course, this is precisely why the world system is like it is. Indeed, it is that way because it is being controlled by Satan and his minions in the "New World Order." Jesus acknowledged this reality while being tempted in the wilderness.[12]

Unfortunately, most religious leaders, because they have abandoned the True Christian Faith for the falsehoods of worldliness, have become part of the world. That is also why they falsely teach they have a "corner" on interpreting Scripture. Indeed, all this has evolved into a 'cozy' system of compromise in which they teach deluded "so-called Christians" to think they can 'hold on to an illusion of salvation' that is literally riddled with contradictions.

However, Scripture does not agree with any such delusion! Incredibly, these apostates mistakenly think they can "hold onto Christ" while at the same time keeping their worldly friends and still believe in nationalism, militarism and the killing by others. Unfortunately, they vainly think that the blood of those whom they approved to be murdered would not be on their hands! However, they are sadly mistaken: Yes, God still holds them accountable, just like the Pharisees!

---

12   Matt. 4:1-10; 6:9-13; Luke 4:1-8; John 8:12, 31-36; 9:39-41; 18:36; 2 Cor. 3:17,18

Nonetheless, evasion of truth never 'cuts the mustard' with God! To be a True Christian, you must "Walk in Agape Love" every day and totally abandon trust in human devices of 'salvation,' wholly trusting in Christ for all types of salvation, physical or eternal.[13]

The Complete Truth of God's Word warns all who are foolish enough to believe Satan's lies, vainly thinking that they can "save themselves" by using man's schemes, intelligence or murder weapons. All the military power of the world still cannot make you free. Only Jesus Christ can do that! However, even Jesus is unable to save them unless they repent from their Idolatry!

Not only that, Scripture teaches that IF you are a True Christian, a Citizen of the *Kingdom of Heaven,* your venue of warfare is strictly spiritual in nature! Furthermore, any 'culture,' empire, nation or city or portion thereof that is founded on murder is condemned by God and simply unable to endure!

Contrariwise, all True Christians live in the clarity of mind that can only come from a confident Faith in God's Word, coupled with a clear mental state, having a true, clean and pure *Conscience,* guiding their lives by what Christ plainly Taught for being the Truth. So, as far as I am concerned, my motto is: "I would rather die saving lives than to live believing in taking them."[14]

*C. The third area is based on the basic underlying Truth Scripture teaches about how we can understand Scripture independently and individually.

1. Verily, Scripture teaches that we can only understand the Bible properly by examining it with spiritual ways that are endued by God's

---

13   Ex. 6:6,7: 14:13,14; Deut. 1:26-33; 3:21,22; 32:39; Joshua 24:14-24; Ruth. 1:14-18; 1 Sam. 2:9; 1 Kings 18:21; Neh. 9; Psa. 20:6,7; 23:1 ff; 31-37; 46, 51, 61-63, 73, 84, 91, 118, 139; Isa. 42-46; Jer. 31:31-34; Ezek. 20-23, 36; Matt. 6:9-15, 24; 10:16-42; 23:1 ff.; Luke 6:20-49; 9:23-26, 51-56 (KJV); 11:33-36; 12:4-32; 14:15-33; 17:20-37; 19:8-27; John 3:3-8, 16-36; 4:13-26; 5:19-30; 6:27-63; 7:14-19; 8:12-48; 9:5, 9:24-41; 10:9-16, *27-30; 11:25,26; 12:23-32, 37-50; 13:34-17:26; 18:36,37; *Acts 16:25-35; Rom. 5:1-11; 6:1-8:39; 10:1-17; 1 Cor. 10:12-16; 13:1 ff.; 2 Cor. 4:1 ff.; 6:1-7:1; Gal. 1:6-12; 2:16-5:1; Eph. 1:3-2:22; Phil. 1-4; Col. 1:12-3:17; 1 Tim. 6:3-12; 2 Tim. 1:7-15; 2:15-26; Heb. 11:1-6, 12-16; James 1:5-8, 17-27; 4:1-8; 1 Pet. 1:3-25; 1 John 3,4 *See also the papers entitled* The Amazing Doctrine of God's Grace *and* The Christian Epiphany

14   Matt. 5:39-48; John 18:36,37; Rom. 12:1 ff.; 2 Cor. 10:3-6; Eph. 6:10-18; Phil. 1:21; 3:7-20 *See also the 4 part series entitled* Christian Guidelines for Spiritual Warfare

Holy Spirit, the source of spiritual Gifts, including the Revelation of Scriptural Truth, not by intellectualism, *Empiricism* or any other worldly method. Yes, the Holy Spirit can personally reveal the deepest level of Truth and Wisdom to your Reborn human spirit.

If you truly believe Jesus, you should now see that this amazing way makes anything Jesus Taught possible and reasonable to carry out right in today's world! It also refutes the carefully couched religious lie that Jesus's Teaching is "unreasonable in an imperfect world" Not only that, if you live life by using the truths of Jesus Christ, we can break the unbiblical control system upon which apostate religion depends to control the masses, teaching them lies in God's Name![15]

2. Relating to enabling this, it must be recognized that one of the most important transitions that every diligent Christian Disciple needs to do to protect them from undue interference from the "Soulish factors" that are akin to our "flesh" (which God does not undo when we receive Christ) is to specifically ask God to enter their life and perform the "Separation of the soul from the spirit."

If a Christian undergoes this "spiritual surgery" and follows through, faithfully observing all the requirements that are shown in the Complete Gospel, they will gradually reach a point where our Reborn human spirit regains control of our being. When that is accomplished (and, again it must be reiterated that nothing in the realm of spiritual growth is "automatic."), A Disciple can move onto doing the Will of God that is ordained for that particular individual.[16]

*D. The fourth discovery was seeing the shocking truth that the vast majority of modern Churches were not being governed by the ways that are described in the New Testament. The way of Governance that God has ordained for the *Body of Christ* is very specific: The *New Covenant* of Jesus Christ's Gospel is based upon a format of spiritual Governance that regulates church affairs by the dynamics of

---

15   Job. 28:28; Psa. 111:10; Prov. 1:7; 8:13; 9:10; Isa. 11:2,3; 33:6; John 14:15-26;15:26; 16:14-15; 1 Cor. 1:17-2:16 *See also the paper entitled Every Believer can Independently know the Truth of Scripture*

16   Luke 2:34,35; John 6:63; 14:15-26; 15:13-15; Heb. 4:12,13 *See also the paper entitled The Spiritual Laws of Revival Chapter 2, "Spiritual Law Eight is the Separation of soul from the spirit" and the book Jesus' Way*

New Testament *Body-Life* which actively uses the *Bilateral* sharing of all the members in the assembly setting. This way uses all the Gifts inherent in all, thereby creating a dynamic Synergism that transcends the ordinary sum of all the individuals if they were separated. This is the combination that made the Early Church such a powerful force for Peace that "turned the world upside down" (or, should I say: "turned it right-side up!") in the first century! The harsh truth is that, over the years, our leaders have lost the original Christian ideals of the New Testament, because they are governed by the unbiblical "business" methods of that are akin to the world system.

Of course, the most pernicious of these is the device of the nonprofit corporation organization, which is essentially a Satanic Trojan Horse which the enemy of our souls uses to neutralize Christian influence and to fool Christians into serving the state instead of God! Indeed, that is exactly how Satan destroys True Biblical Fellowship: By ensnaring sincere but deceived Christian leaders who think they can use "incorporation" to "protect themselves." Yet, the result is essentially the exact opposite, since it follows the "Hegelian Dialectic" of "Problem, Reaction, Solution" that the New World Order uses to infiltrate, corrupt and then neutralize the true Witness of Jesus Christ, substituting a clever world-serving counterfeit.

This counterfeit works by displacing Biblical governance with corporation "Bylaws" that impose a 'pyramidal' control system that operates by the "carnal mind" which is an enemy of God, constantly working at cross purposes against God's Spirit right in the church! Yes, "Incorporation" is totally inconsistent with the New Covenant.

Of course, this entity "looks like a lamb but it speaks with the dragon's voice" and fits the description of the "Scarlet Woman & Beast System," falsely claiming to be "Christian." As such, it offers "lip-service to God," however, the hearts of those who receive their lies and false doctrines are truly unbelievers failing to respect or fear God, let alone obeying God's Word, Christ! [17]

---

17   Isa. 1-6; 28:9-22; 29:13-30:21; 44:20,21; Jer. 3-33; Ezek. 3-34; Matt. 23:1 ff.; John 15:18-16:4; Rom. 8:1-11; 2 Thess. 2:3-12; Heb. 12:25-28; 2 Pet. 1:16-3:16; Rev. 13 *See also the Papers entitled Basics of Biblical Church Governance, Christian Guidelines for Spiritual Warfare, Part Three: "Cracking the False Doctrine Code," Facilitating Revival, The Fallacies of Determinism, Guidelines for Renewed Leadership and Psychotic Hypocrisy*

*E. This led to the fifth revelation that I received, which is the realization that many religious leaders we all had trusted had in truth at some point in time 'defected (apostatized) from Christ' and had become operatives of the world who have essentially "brainwashed" us to believe "lies in the Name of God." One of the most pernicious of these lies is believing in racism and sexism: That is, they harbor prejudice against "colored" races and also believe our sisters in Christ are somehow "inferior to men." For centuries these sick doctrines have led to the unjust subjugation of many in the assembly venue, excluding them from many ministries in which God had ordained for them to serve the *Body of Christ.* The Catholic Church started this with their false accusation of Mary Magdelene being a "prostitute!" Protestants have also misconstrued Paul's statements regarding the 'silence of women' to mean that they are not allowed to participate in *Body-Life* worship or minister in a Teaching capacity in the public venue. Of course, they also totally ignore Luke's clear recitation of Paul's address at Athens, telling all that God created all races as equals! Paul's statement in Galatians also guarantees the defacto equality of women and "slaves" of all colors to "white" men in God's eyes just as Jesus had obviously treated them as equals before in the Gospels![18]

Tragically, part of it is that they should know that Satan hates women and will use any scheme to hurt them! Not only that, these influences are essentially the same <u>Satanic Principalities that are controlling religious leaders to teach Idolatry: That political leaders are "automatically ordained of God [sic]" so Christians would be docile slaves worshiping the Baal (state)</u>! Even in the first century, both Jesus and Paul warned Christians that "false prophets" would arise, deceiving many.[19]

I can only confess that the Grace of God sovereignly delivered me from the heady delusion of the false doctrines. I believe I escaped by diligent seeking of the Truth, coupled with my <u>Love of the Truth</u>, which had finally enabled God's Spirit to "break the spell" of lies, transporting

---

18   Acts 17:26; Gal. 3:28 *See also the paper entitled Patriarchalism in the Church which identifies the original Greek words Paul used, exposing their lying doctrine that abuses women*

19   Gen. 3:14-16; 1 Sam. 2:9; 1 Kings 18:21; Psa. 94:20-23; 118:8,9; 146:3; Matt. 5:38-48; 6:24; 7:13-15; 10:16 f.; 23:1 ff.; 24:4-13; Luke 2:34,35; John 18:36; Acts 4:12-20; 5:29-32;28:22; 1 Tim. 4:1,2; 2 Tim. 3:1-7; James 3,4; 2 Pet. 2:1 ff.; 1 John 4:1 ff.

me out into the bright sunlight of God's Truth as seen through the face, viz., the Lens, of Jesus Christ.[20]

*F. The sixth discovery is that the True Complete scope of *Salvation* that is taught in Scripture is far more extensive than most "professing Christians" ever have been "led to believe." Indeed, the vast majority of modern Christians have been subtly misled to believe that "Salvation" is an 'Internal' intellectual thing that only comes into play in the afterlife. However, Scripture tells us a much different story: The True Definition of Salvation is effective immediately after we receive Christ in all three areas of our being: Spirit, Soul and Body! [21]

Of course, all the benefits depend upon our continuation in being single-mindedly Faithful to God, knowing all the time that God's Promises are Dependable. Yes, if you want to live in God's Best Will for your life, you must know the Full Complete Gospel Definition of Salvation! [22]

This is because of the serious problem of "prior catechisms" which lead one to incorrectly "assume" that "ordinary human strength and wisdom" is the only 'source' of physical deliverance from evil in this life. However, that belief is part of *Determinism,* a sophisticated system of subtle bald-faced lies that have, over centuries of time, been concocted by Satan, using perfidious religious figures acting as his minions.[23]

You should know God's Word teaches a much different picture! Verily, to succeed in the True Christian life, you must first learn to maintain your Faith by confronting your fears, controlling them by Trusting God and not man. For true Victory, you must also "cast away every doubt" and confidently Trust that God's Word is absolutely reliable in every situation, bar none, and that "God will make a Way" to negotiate the most difficult problem regardless of what anybody else says!

---

20 Cor. 4:1-5:17; 6:14-18; 10:1-7; 11:12-15 *See also the papers A Biblical Disclosure of Antichrist, (the 4 part series) Christian Guidelines for Spiritual Warfare and Christianity versus Religion, Part Two: The Dangers of Religious Catechism*

21 1 Thess. 5:23

22 Psa. 3:8; 4:8; John 3:16,17; 8:31-36; 2 Cor. 1:20; 3:17,18; Heb. 4:16-19; 7:24,25; 10:22-39; James 1:3-5 *See also the papers The Christian Epiphany and True Liberty is in Christ Alone*

23 *See the book Spiritual Guidelines for Restoration, "Historical Review" Section.*

Not only that, you must learn to Speak God's Word to a situation, Believing that God is in Control of everything! All this is "part and parcel" to Christ's *New Covenant* that is like "New Wine that must have a new wineskin" (I.e., transformed minds and attitudes) to contain it.

However, to understand this and to remain in good standing in God's *Kingdom of Heaven,* you must obey Jesus's Teachings and abandon all trust in and worship of humanly manufactured National Idols. These Idols include all worship and trust in national symbols (including documents, dogma, monuments, flags and such), politics and the brute force of military power to 'save' instead of God!

Contrariwise, All True Christians always gladly follow Christ's Commands and Teachings, making no excuse. They know that this is the only way to remain singularly pure in heart and to do God's Will.[24]

All other ways are false and lead back to the "wide road of destruction" that all the "double-minded" and faithless people end up following to their chagrin.[25]

It bears repeating that many modern Christians are living with a very serious problem: They most likely have been "Brainwashed" to believe "half-truths mixed with outright lies" from childhood to the point that their minds are "locked into" worldly attitudes that stand in direct contradiction to Jesus Christ's Teachings and Commands! This problem can be made palpably evident by comparing their beliefs with Christ's Teaching on "living our lives in *Agape* Love," a type of Love which is identical to God's Love which is universal in scope, applying to all people.

Not only that, the obvious requirements that Scripture teaches about Christians' living by *Agape* Love simply cannot be ignored. This is because they have obvious unmistakable characteristics that separate them from all unbelievers, one major example being that a Christian

---

24   Psa. 18:26; 19:8; 24:4; Matt. 5:3-48; 6:9-13; 9:16,17; 10:16-42; Mark 2:21,22; 16:15-18; Lk. 2:34,35; 11:33-36; 17:20-37; John 4:23,24; 15:1-7; 18:36; Acts 7:48; 17:24-31;28:22; Rom. 12:1 ff.; 2 Cor. 6:14-7:1; 11:12-15; Gal. 1:6-12; Phil. 3:3,20,21; 4:6-8; 1 Tim. 3:9; 2 Tim. 2:10-26; Heb. 10:16-12:29; James 1:3-5, 27; 3:17; 1 John 3:1-4:21

25   Matt. 7:13,14; John 10:27

who lives by True Christian Love Never approves the killing of anyone by anyone, anywhere, anytime!

Search the Scriptures, always observing Covenantal Context, and you will find out that this is true. Carefully compare Scripture with Scripture through "New Testament" eyes that "look through the Lens of Jesus Christ" and you will see that Jesus's Way of Peace is the Truth. You will also find that there is a plethora of Scriptures that tell us about God's Supreme Power to Save us from evil in the "here and now." The main thing to observe is this: Do you Believe God's Word? [26]

Then, at the time when I finally found the Truth, that "Pearl of Great Price" that was the true Complete Gospel, I was shocked to see that many Christian friends and colleagues would not receive these truths, even when I presented sound Scriptural evidence as proof.[27]

*G. The seventh area concerns Jesus' Teaching the essential activity of our True Worship of God "in spirit and in truth." I strong believe keeping our worship of God pure and free from all types of contamination. Therefore, I am alarmed at many "So-called Christians" who take 'worshiping God' in a cavalier way.[28]

Let us now take time to elaborate more on God's Primary rules regarding Worship, paying attention that worship involves every aspect of life, private and public. Not only that, our "Service of worship" entails both benefits and responsibilities that must be taken seriously:

First: Our worship of the One Living God must be pure, uncontaminated by "competing objects of worship." Moreover, we must focus solely on one holy object of attention, our God, upon whom we lavish all Glory and exalt with awe and Reverential Fear.

---

26   *Eph. 2:13-22 See also the papers entitled The Christian Epiphany, Conditions for Salvation and God's Definition of Salvation*

27   *See the Papers entitled Basics of Biblical Church Governance and Guidelines for Renewed Leadership*

28   Ex. 20:2-5; 34:14; Deut. 4:35,39; 8:19,20; 11:16; 30:17; 32:39; 33:26,27; 1 Sam. 2:2-10; 17:47; 1 Kings 18:21; 2 Kings 17:35-41; 18:5,6, 19-19:19; 1 Chr. 17:7-22; Psa. 2:1 ff.; 3:8; 4:8; 5:4-12; 11:1 ff.; 23:1 ff.; 27:1 ff.; 29:2; 31:23,24; 32:1 ff.; 33:1-34:22; 37:1 ff.; 40:1-41:2; 42:1-44:8; 45:1-46:11; 49:1 ff.; 50:2,14,15,23; 51:1 ff.; 59:16; 61-63; 66:5-12; 68:4,17-20; 73:16-26; 81:10; 83:18; 84:11; 86:2,11-13; 91:1 ff.; 94:12-23; 103:1 ff; 110:1 ff; 115:1-13; 118, 146; Isa. 6,12,26-30,42-46; Jer. 10; John 4:14-24; Phil. 2:5-11; Col. 2:8-13; 3:1-17; James 1:5 ff. *See the papers: (The 3 part series) Christianity Versus Religion and Spirituality and Worship See also the book Jesus' Way, Chapter X, Sect. III.: "The Glory of Worship"*

Verily, our worship of God also means giving ALL our allegiance and Loyalty, for "the LORD your God" (God in Christ for all Christians) is our true King. Not only that, we must daily maintain a personal relationship with God *In Christ* because that is what God requires for us to enable God's Spirit to nourish our Reborn human spirit and continue giving us *Agape* Love.[29]

Second, remember the "Ask, Seek and Knock" trilogy Jesus told the Disciples in the "Sermon on the Mount." If we observe correctly the Greek Aorist Tense of those verbs, it clearly indicates that God expects us to <u>continue</u> those actions over a significant span of time. Yes, it is Ask <u>and keep on asking</u>, Seek <u>and keep on seeking</u> and Knock <u>and keep on knocking</u>! Indeed, this forms the basis of the "Discipleship to *Conversion* Dynamic Process" that Scripture teaches every Christian must continually engage to grow spiritually.[30]

Third, the quality of our Worship determines the ceiling of our spirituality as well as the limits of how much God can give you, including the extent and depth of the ministries in which God's Spirit has called us to engage throughout our life here. Jesus taught the Disciples that there are levels of understanding that are "given" only to those who are close to the Lord Jesus, whereas, those who live at a distance do not receive those things. Also, the Apostle Paul wrote Timothy that there is a great variety of "Vessels" that God uses in the Kingdom of Heaven: Some are lowly and mundane but others can become "Vessels unto Honor."[31]

Fourth, I have found that there is a close correspondence relating those "Christians" who are "ambivalent" regarding spiritual worship with the ones who are literally consumed with an <u>inordinate interest in worldly pursuits and the associated worldly beliefs and practices of "patriotism."</u> Evidently, they are so "blinded by their love of the things of this world" that they are unable to see that these activities are <u>totally incongruous with the True Christian Faith!</u>

---

29   Ex. 22:20; Lev. 20:7; Num. 23:9; Deut. 4:29-39; 5:6-11; 6:1-16; 10:17; 11:18-23;26:18,19; 2 Kings 17:36; Job. 28:28; Psa. 29:2; 45:11; 95:6,9; Prov. 1:7; 9:9,10, Isa. 42:8;43:10-15; 44:6-8; 45:5-12, 20-23; Dan. 3:10-18; Matt. 4:10; John 4:14-24; Rom. 5:1-5; 12:1-3;Phil. 2:10; 3:3

30   Matt. 7:7; 16:23-26; Luke 9:23-26; John 12:23-26 See also the papers entitled Destiny and Free Will and The Dynamics of Christian Discipleship

31   Matt. 13:1-23; 2 Tim. 2:11-26; Heb. 10:19-12:29; James 1:22-27

Consequently, their lives are empty and lean and they exhibit little interest in actively participating in the dynamic of Biblical "*Body-Life * Fellowship." Worse yet, these are the same ones who, because of their idolatry in worshiping the state are corrupting the church. Not only that, they cause rampant confusion among groups because their "worship" of God is tainted because they do not acknowledge that Christ is our Savior in all venues: Physical Soulical and spiritual. Their defacto denial of Christ in this area proves that they actually serve the world and the Principalities who control it. They are just like the Jews that wanted Barabbas during Jesus's trial before Pilate! Paul cites other instances in his letters to the Colossians and Timothy.[32]

Indeed, nationalism is Idolatry because it supplants our Trust in God for Salvation that the Scriptures teach and that applies in the temporal venue. Also, many "modern Christians" fail to understand that Jesus Christ is our only Savior and King. Remember what happened to Israel when they "wanted to have a king like the other nations," comparing that to what Jesus proclaimed in the First Century. Of course, we know that God gives us "Free Will," but we also know that Samuel sternly warned the Israelites about what kings are prone to do to their "subjects." The underlying Truth is that God wants us to consider Him to be our King and that we consider God's Laws to be always superior to man's despite the situation! [33]

Fifth, from what I have been observing for many years, it is patently obvious that most modern "professing Christians" are totally ignorant of the basic facts defining the terms and conditions by which Christians must live and worship God in the *New Covenant* Kingdom of God as it is presented in the New Testament by our Lord Jesus Christ. One very important fact is that everything must be seen in a spiritual context and our worship is an integral part of this exalted Kingdom! Jesus Christ and the Early Apostles and period writers also agree that God has transformed all venues of conflict and has "upgraded them to

---

32   Matt. 12:30; 27:15-29; Luke 23:1-18; John 15:18-16:4; 18:19-19:15; Acts 5:29-32; 1 Cor. 3:11 ff.; Col. 2:8, 18-20; 1 Tim. 4; 2 Tim. 3:1-9 *See the papers entitled The Christian Epiphany and True Liberty is in Christ Alone*

33   1 Sam. 8-10; Dan. 3,6; Matt. 6:9-13; Lk. 13:30-35; John 18:36,37; Acts 5:29-32

the spiritual level" whereby all True Christians always "wage war in the spirit" and not in the flesh! [34]

Sixth, this brings up a serious problem that many Christians seldom take into account: They claim to "hear, know and understand" things, but the harsh truth remains that few actually do! This failure to comprehend pure Worship of God is underscored particularly in people's palpable misunderstanding of those texts that define the scope of God's *Authority* compared to the limits of God's delegation of power to human instruments. Because of this, the Scriptures illustrate many situations portraying the "deeper understanding of Truth" by which God would have us live.[35]

Seventh, the issue of leadership's apostasy over the years is overwhelming, causing many to "fall by the wayside!" Succumbing to false doctrine in the area of authority has also been a sore issue for centuries, starting with 'caving into their fears' and subsequent abdication of their Faith in God which has severely degraded their quality of worship, which has been supplanted by the worship of human Idols!

The bottom line and the sad fact that still torments many Christians even today is that church leadership has failed to Trust God and consequently have failed to teach us many things that God's Word says are True and trustworthy! Indeed, The true Gospel teaches that when one truly Receives Christ by Faith they will receive God's Love via the Holy Spirit, leading us to know that all human life is Sacred to God! Indeed, God's Agape Love must also be the central aspect of the True Christian's life, giving them the overflowing confidence that God's provisions included in True Complete Salvation will be more than enough for everything we need in this life: Supply, Protection and Health.

---

34   Matt. 5:38-48; 6:9-13; Luke 9:51-56 (KJV); John 18:36,37; Rom. 8:1-11; 12:1 ff.; Eph. 6:10-12
35   1 Sam. 2; Joshua 2; Psa. 1, 2, 94, 110, 118, 146; Prov. 29:25; Jer. 5:1-5. 9, 20-22, 29-31; 6:10-19; 7:13,27; 8:4-11; 9:6-9; 10:1-11, 14-17; 11:10; 13:8-17; 17:5-10, 23; 18:11-16; Ezek. 3:3-11; 20:8-44; 21:24-27; 22:1 ff; 23:37-39; 36:16-32; Dan. 3,6; Luke 13:31,32; John 18:36-19:16*; Acts 5:29-32; Rom. 13:1-7* *Note in the asterisked refs that God's delegation of authority to humans is limited. Two examples are in Rom. 13:1: One, God is the greater power and two, the Greek word Tagma should have been translated Allowed, not 'ordained' The same principle applies to John 19:11 See the 2 part series of papers entitled Authority and Conscience

So, consider the Testimony of Scripture about the <u>serious after effects of leaders who apostatize</u>. Indeed, it can be proven that it is verily the <u>Sacred Responsibility of leadership</u> to have been telling Christians to follow and obey the Teachings of Jesus Christ all along! However, as God told Jeremiah to tell ancient Israel: "My people have forgotten me days without number." [36]

IV. "The Truth is the First Duty," Part One:

Far too many "So-called Christians" are hiding behind a very carefully disguised lie! They are being taught that carnal soldiers are their 'saviors,' vainly thinking that they can 'give you liberty' by murdering other people. Contrariwise, Jesus Christ clearly told the Disciples that "If you continue in My Word you will know the Truth and the Truth will set you Free!" Paul also tells us that wherever the Holy Spirit is there is Liberty.[37]

Know also that Scripture defines the Precept of *Redemption*: This is how we become part of God's Forever Family by Christ's <u>Purchasing us from the "slave market of the world"</u> and joining us to God's *Kingdom of Heaven* by God's *Grace* which is enabled (spiritually) by the *Blood of Christ* shed on Calvary. Moreover, <u>God's Amazing Grace then Flows down from Heaven to all those who obey Christ</u> from the Throne of <u>Jesus Christ our new owner,</u> becoming our Defense, Liberator and provider of everything we need here on earth! [38]

Christian, beware, you must continually evaluate your doctrine and the condition of your own soul very carefully to <u>make sure you are in "Right Relationship" to God</u>. Indeed, I am extremely alarmed at the <u>defacto Idolatry</u> in which many "Professing Christians" are engaging, trusting in false gods, impersonated by The Baals of military power, politicians, national images and their 'symbols' for being their 'saviors'

---

36   Isa. 1-6, 28-30, 42-46; 56:6-59:21; 63:7-65:25; Jer. 2-13; 17:5-10; *18:11-17; 23:9-40; Ezek. 3,7-14, 18, 20-22; 23:37-39*; 33,34,36; Hos. 1-14; Amos 3-9; Mic. 3,4; Mal. 2*; Matt. 5:38-48; 22:36,37; 23:1 ff.; Luke 6-14; John 14:15-26; Rom. 5:1-5; Phil. 4:13-19; 1 John 3-5 *See also the papers entitled Analysis of Church Governance and Questionnaire, the Christian Epiphany, Guidelines for Renewed Leadership and A Questionnaire for Church Leaders*

37   John 8:31-36; 10:27; 2 Cor. 3:17,18

38   Matt. 6:9-13; John 14-17; 18:36,37; Rom. 4:1-5:5; 6:1-8:39; 2 Cor. 1:20; Gal. 2:16-4:20; Eph. 1:7,19-23; 2:13-22; Phil. 3:2,20; Heb. 10:9-11:16

instead of God! It shocks me to the core to Think of the price they will pay if they do not repent. Presently, the price is "deadness inside" and the total lack of Love and spirituality! What are they thinking? Do they actually think that the flag will save them from what is still to come in the Great Tribulation?

Read the Scriptures again carefully. The apostates' palpable prevarication cannot be justified. What is the solution? I fear that it must take a <u>major crisis to shock them back into reality of their condition before God</u>. Unfortunately, most of them are totally oblivious of <u>how harmful Idolatry is to the human soul</u>! Worse yet, they care not for how much <u>it hurts God to know that the people who "claim to worship and serve God" will not even Trust Christ to be their Savior Right here and right now</u>! They should read about what happened to ancient Israel and how Jesus responded to their condition when He was here on earth.[39]

As a Christian, do you know what it means to Love and serve God in true Honesty and Purity of heart? And, as Jesus queried Peter: "Do you Love Me more than these?" Jesus also had told him "When you have repented and turned again, strengthen your brethren."[40]

<u>Only the True Christian has a unique characteristic, a spiritual Identity</u> that is able to resist sin, propaganda and opposition with calm resolve. They possess a "shield" through which the world in all its ugliness and evil cannot penetrate, for its source is a supernatural Peace and a Love (Agape) which reaches out to all.[41]

Jesus once remonstrated the Pharisees, saying: Is it permitted on the Sabbath to do good deeds or is it a day to do evil? Is this a day to save life or to destroy it? Of course, in addition to persuading them to reevaluate their stolid ways, Jesus was iterating a general principle: That killing <u>is always evil</u>, being of darkness and never light.[42]

Another thing is that claiming God's Promises is <u>not 'testing' God</u>! This is in fact <u>agreeing with what God's Word already says</u>! The real question we should ask is this: Do you truly Believe what God's Word says, or not? And, if you doubt <u>any part of God's Promises, what makes</u>

---

39   Isa. 1-6; Jer. 2-18; Ezek. 3-36; Hos. 1-14; Mal. 2; Matt. 23; 1 Cor. 10

40   Matt. 22:36 .37; Luke 22:31,32; John 21:15-17

41   Matt. 18:20; John 13:34,35; 14:6-27; Acts 4:13; Rom. 5:1-5; 1 Cor. 2:9-16; 13;1 ff.;

42   Matt. 5:38-48; Mark 3:4; Luke 9:51-56 (KJV); 11:33-36; Rom. 12:19-21

you think that God will honor any other part? The bottom line is this: You either believe and trust in God or do you believe and trust in man. No middle ground exists! However, a gargantuan problem still exists: Many have been "catechized," viz., "Brainwashed" to believe Lies in God's name for a long time, so you must carefully pick the time to show them the errors of their way and lead them back to the truth. Unfortunately, since they have free will, many will not respond and you cannot 'make them receive the truth' that they are worshiping idols by trusting in national symbols, politicians and military power. This is the "fortress mentality" to which people frequently resort when they do not "think for themselves," blindly assuming what they have been taught was true. So, as it was mentioned above, it is more than likely true that they will require a major crisis to 'hit them' before their minds will again properly respond to truth and regain the perspective they need to establish or reestablish a personal relationship to God.[43]

V. "The Truth is the First Duty," Part Two:

Truth: "Physical Salvation" is an integral part of the *New Covenant* that draws truths from both Testaments, including the First (Archetypal) *Passover* and the *Passover* of Christ's Passion.[44]

Overall, Scripture teaches that the *New Covenant* "builds upon" what God had started in the Old Testament, like the "layers of a Cake." In addition, God "transforms the meaning" of Old Testament passages, elevating them to a higher level. Of course, many changes hinge upon the effect of Christ's Perfect Sacrifice, including God's disavowal of all types of "bloodshed sacrifice," animal or human (war casualties and

---

43 *See the books entitled Basic Christian Doctrine, The Church in the Last Days, Jesus' Way and Spiritual Guidelines for Restoration*

44 Ex. 6:6,7; 14:13,14; Deut. 1:26-33; 3:21,22; 32:39; 1 Sam. 2; 2 Chr. 20:11-24; Neh.9; Psa 20, 23, 24, 27, 31, 37, 42, 46, 51, 55, 56, 61, 63, 73, 84, 91, 94, 118, 146 Et., Al.; Jer. 31; Ezek. 36;Matt. 6:9-13; 10:16-42; 26:26-32, 51-54; Luke 22:15-32; John 1:1-18; 3:3-8, 16,17; 4:14-24;5:19-30; 6:27-63; 7:15-18, 37-39; 8:12-58; 9:39-41; 10:1-38; 11:25,26; 12:23-26,32-50; 13:34-17:26; 18:36-19:15; 20:19-23; 21:4-17; Acts 1:7-11; 2:1-7, 17-28, 32-41; 3:1-4:20; 5:29-32;7:37-60; 13:13-46; 17:24-31; 20:31-35; 26:9-18; Rom. 1:16-32; 3:4-5:11; 6:1-8:39; 12:1 ff.;1 Cor. 1:17-2:16; 2 Cor. 1-5; Gal. 1-6; Eph. 1,2; ... Heb. 7-12 (*and many more*)

death punishments). We can see this more clearly by "Looking at them through the Lens of Jesus Christ."[45]

Indeed, every aspect of Salvation applies in God's *Kingdom of Heaven, * existing on all three levels (venues): Spirit, Soul and Body, "On earth, as it is in Heaven." True Complete Salvation includes True Peace, True Liberty (Freedom) and True Provision and Protection within the terms and conditions God's Word specifies for each individual's case. Verily, these aspects are <u>Precious things, my friends, for they represent crucial Doctrines that must be preserved in their Original clarity and distinction</u>, without ever being dulled or compromised to fit "*Humanistic* expectations!" Yes, the Teachings as well as the Person of Jesus Christ represent "The Way, the Truth and the Life" which must be followed faithfully to be realized by any recipient. This is because, as it is expressed in the title: "They are integral aspects of the Original Christian Gospel" which, in turn, accurately represents the character of God's *Kingdom of Heaven* right here on earth! [46]

Beware of those who have <u>supplanted these ideals with "earthbound definitions" that are directly linked to the world system via "nationalism" and which also always rationalize the murder of other people in violation of Jesus Christ's Commands!</u>

I pity them for "they know not what they do" for the palpably anti-Christian practices of patriotism are the primary causes of many <u>flagrant departures from the Basic Truths of the Original Christian Faith</u>. Thus, they fail to <u>love the Truth!</u>

Moreover, we must be always cognizant of Satan's virulent deceptions and all the ways that he <u>incrementally subverts and corrupts the truth</u> over long periods. That is how he twists and distorts people's understanding of Scripture. One example of this occurred during the "so-called Reformation." It is a "tale of two kings": Henry the VIII and James' I, both of which "subsidized" the printing of Bibles, introducing false interpretations of a key verse of Scripture. Viz., the word "ordained"

45   Jer. 31:31-34; Ezek. 36:16-32; Matt. 5:17-20; John 3:16,17; Heb.2:9-14; 7-12; 1 John 2:1-6
      See also the papers entitled The Christian Epiphany, Fulfilment Prophecy, Looking Through the Lens of Jesus Christ and True Liberty is in Christ Alone See also the Diagram entitled The Nine Ages
46   John 14:6; Gal. 1:6-12

in the first verse of Romans thirteen should have been translated as "Allowed." So, the upshot of this is that they 'figured' religious leaders (who, of course, were appointed by the king also), would then lead naive people to believe that the king's authority was "automatically ordained" by God [Sic.]. That is how that abominable doctrine of "divine right of kings" was hatched! Consequently, in the case of the King James Bible (1611), it has been the source of much confusion among Christians concerning the issue of *Authority.* Contrariwise, if you consider the whole of Scriptural examples, you will get a much different picture which teaches that "submission to duly constituted authority" does not in any way imply trust or worship![47]

Indeed, the Truth of Scripture teaches that All True Christians are Reborn as Citizens of a higher Kingdom called the *Kingdom of Heaven,* and that they guide their entire lives by its Precepts which are clearly specified in the New Testament. Moreover, this means that God's Laws always take precedence over man's laws, traditions and culture despite the circumstance! Not only that, Jesus Christ gave His Life so that you could escape (be saved from) the hegemony of the World which is controlled by Satan. Consider the examples listed in the following footnote.[48]

P.S., To whom it may concern: I want the reader to know that I regard the Complete Truth of the Original Christian Gospel to be a Sacred Trust which I will not compromise one iota, despite the circumstance. Yes, deep down inside, every True Christian Believer knows that he or she might have to give their lives in the course of living the True Christian Gospel. That is a given you cannot change, so it is futile to "try and change the rules to fit the circumstances." If you follow Jesus, people are going to hate you no matter what you do, so you had better get used to it! [49]

---

47   2 Thess. 2:3-12 *See also the 2 part series of papers entitled Authority and Conscience*
48   Joshua 2 (Rahab); Daniel 3,6; Matt. 4:1-10; 5:38-48; 6:9-13; 26:51-56; 28:18; Mark 3:4; Luke 4:1-8; 9:51-56 (KJV); John 18:36-38; Acts 4:11-20; 5:29-32; Phil. 1:27; 3:3,20; Heb. 11:13-16, 24-31
49   Luke 2:34,35; John 15:18-16:4, 33; Acts 28:22; 2 Pet. 2:1-3

VI. Let us review some basic observations about what has happened to most Christians over the years.

Yes, most "professing Christians," because they live just like the world does, are cheating themselves of the Great manifold Blessings they could have IF they would only Believe and practice what Jesus Taught for being the True Christian life! Tragically, because they have been wrongly catechized into many false doctrines containing "half-truths mixed with outright lies," many stubbornly refuse to receive the truth regarding the Original Christian Faith. Consequently, they fail to believe that God's Promises regarding physical Salvation that tell us that God will protect and provide all our needs.[50]

Subsequently, they have "fallen backward," viz. apostatized from Faith, having been taught by apostate leaders that you "have to" depend on worldly sources to "survive." Not so according to God's Word! Indeed, all those 'pseudo beliefs' connected to the false doctrine of *Determinism* that are still being taught in most church organizations have led the vast majority of churchgoers into a dead-end street of unbelief. Essentially, in that sad state of affairs, they have lost any truly Christian distinctive that would separate them from the condemned world system they apparently love more than Jesus! [51]

Their so-called leaders should have been more careful. They too have 'lost their way,' being seduced by the desires and glitter of the world. Think about what had happened before to ancient Israel and then weep. Paul also warns us about this, referring us to the Old Testament chronicles of the Jewish people.[52]

The worst part is that most Christians have become inured and literally addicted to believing in killing "enemies and criminals," to the point that they will hate you and "come out of their corner swinging" whenever you point out their obvious prevarication! Yes, if they had been there that dark day of Jesus's trial before Pilate, they would have yelled out the same: "Give us Barabbas" and, what is worse, to Jesus: "Crucify Him, Crucify Him." Of course, the "Piece de Resistance" that

---

50   Matt. 10:16-42; Phil. 4:6-19
51   2 Thess. 2:3-12; James 1:3-7; 4:1-8; 1 John 2:15-17
52   Jer. 2-9, 18; Ezek. 3,18,33,34; Mic. 3, Mal. 2; Matt. 23; 1 Cor. 10

points to their "patriotism" being the culprit, is "We have no king but Caesar." Think you are different? Try to prove me wrong, but it is futile, for people "in the flesh" are the same now and the Scripture cannot be broken! [53]

Think very seriously about these things, and when you have considered how all these "difficult things" fit into the overall paradigm of the True Complete Gospel. I know that many, because of the ubiquitous presence of questionable catechisms, may think I am an "unrealistic radical" but believe me, God definitely uses those who are "bananas for Jesus!" Yes, I stand for the uncompromised Complete Gospel of the Jesus Christ who lived a perfect life, taught the perfect Truth and died on the cross for "sinners such as I." Indeed, this is the Truth for which I stand and which nobody can legitimately deny!

So, IF the Scripture teaches that Jesus Christ is our <u>Savior in all venues, physical, spiritual and eternal</u>, what makes anyone think that they can "claim that they are saved" if they do not truly <u>believe what Jesus taught</u>? The absolute truth is that if you don't believe that Christ is your <u>physical Savior in the present reality</u>, you really don't have *Faith* to believe that He would be your Savior for eternity! IF you are a True Christian, everything connects to the one <u>singular reality that is the *Kingdom of Heaven</u>, * the True Nation of your Rebirth and the source of the Grace of God by which you are being saved.

I would candidly ask the reader this: Why have you been led to think that agreement with and living by what Jesus taught is so hard to do? However, in some ways they are right. Nothing that is truly worth anything in the universe comes without a high cost! So is the True Christian life. Indeed, Solomon wrote that "the way of the transgressors is hard" (compared with Jesus's Way). The real truth Jesus Taught shows that, when you compare the benefits of the Complete Gospel with the way of the world, no comparison needs to be made! So, you decide which way to go.[54]

---

53   John 15:18-16:4; 18:36-19:15 *See the paper Analysis of the causes and effects of apostasy, Divergent Belief Systems, (the 2 part series) How Should we Then Live and True Liberty is in Christ Alone*

54   Psa. 37:3-5; Prov. 3:4,5; 13:15; 14:12; 16:25; 29:25; Isa. 30:10-21;; 45:5-23; Jer. 2:18-32; 23:10; Hos. 14:9; Mal. 2:1-9; Matt. 6:9-13; John 14:6-17:26; Rom. 6:1-8:39;1 John 5:4

VII. Conclusion and FYI:

I will now tabulate the "major periods of declensions" that have afflicted the church and have been responsible for its ongoing apostasy.

A. In the first century, approximately 72% of churches of Asia Minor apostatized.[55]

B. Emperor Constantine the Great carried out a major "Coup d'etat," dominating the majority of assemblies by during the Synods of Arles and Nicea (AD 314-325).[56]

Reader note: Consult good historical sources for the remainder:

C. The hegemony of the Pope Leo the Great (AD 440-461) was established by implementing Augustine's flawed manifesto, The City of God (426)

D. God's first 'level of judgment' on the apostate church came with the Islamic ascendancy (AD 632-732).

E. The rise of the Catholic Empires dominated most of the civilized world. They were the Holy Roman Empire (800-1648) and the Byzantine Empire, which lasted until Saladin took over Istanbul in 1453.

F. A major 'scourge of *Bloodshed* was brought about by the "Crusades" (1096-1240).

G. The first "Reformation" of John Wyclif and John Huss failed. (1250-1310)

H. The second "Reformation of Protestantism" also failed, ending in the "Peace of Westphalia." (1517-1648).

I. The "British Missionary movement," which started with the Welsh Revival (1740-1850), also ended in failure.

J. The remainder of "Christian" groups continued with the splintering of the remaining sects into "Evangelical" and "Charismatic" camps. (1900 to present).

Your friend and fellow Servant in Christ,
Pastor David J. Bowers

---

55   Rev. 2,3
56   *See the book entitled Spiritual Guideline for Restoration, "Historical Review" Section*

Chapter 7

Do You Know Who You Are?

#	Do you know who you are?	Page #
	Description	
I.	Introduction	
II.	Know this: To be a part of God's Eternal *Kingdom of Heaven* you must obey Jesus Christ's Commands and Teaching.	
III.	Let us now consider the following primary truths which you may not have considered before:	
IV.	God's Definition of *Faith* is one integral Whole that cannot be compromised without losing it.	
V.	True Liberty issues from the Precept of *Redemption*	
VI.	Knowing the difference between "respect" and Trust, Jesus shows us the Truth.	
VII.	Only One True Freedom Exists	
VIII.	Only one Truth Exists	
IX.	Beware of any "false certainty"	
X	Summary	

I. Introduction:

Most modern "professing Christians" have a serious problem: They fail to see the world's ugliness and corruption <u>as God sees it</u>. Yes, multitudes have been taught to live only within artificial and narrowly defined limits. Worse yet, untold numbers of confessing Christians have 'blindly assumed' that everything they had been taught by 'religious leaders' was true without ever 'checking it out' or comparing what they had been taught with the Teachings of Christ. Indeed, because they have relied on others' teaching too much, most have never delved into the Scriptures enough <u>personally</u> to reach the point where they would be confident to know just what they truly believe is the Truth!

Worse yet still, many have been told that the principles that Jesus taught regarding the way we respond to evil are "unrealistic in an imperfect world." Not only that, many regard Paul's teaching on the areas of spiritual Gifts, offices and callings are 'not for today,' not realizing that all the doctrines of the *New Covenant* will continue unchanged <u>until Christ returns!</u> [1]

Always remember: Jesus Christ was very specific in teaching the terms and conditions of our New Covenant:

One, Christ teaches clearly that his followers adhere to the precept of "Holy Harmlessness" which precludes believing in or supporting the killing of any human being by anyone, anywhere or at any time!

Two, Christ makes a wondrous opportunity available to all true Believers via the Holy Spirit of Grace: An impressive array of spiritual gifts that we see defined in the New Testament. Jesus expects us to use our Reborn human spirit to receive as many of these as the Holy Spirit has chosen for each individual to use in the ministry to others, thereby glorifying God in the process. These are the tools God's Spirit uses to guide us along the narrow pathway of *Righteousness.* [2]

Christian: I ask you this question: Do you know who you are and to whom you belong? Also, do you know what you have been destined by Christ to do during the time you are here on earth? Moreover, let us always <u>keep that goal in mind</u>. [3]

Furthermore, if you know the Truth of what Christ taught, you also know that you are <u>unable to remain *In Christ*</u> and to concurrently

---

1   Matt. 5:43-48; 28:18-20; Luke 6:27-40; 9:51-56; Rom. 12:9-21
2   Matt. 7:13-29; Rom. 12; 1 Cor. 12-15; Eph. 4:1-16
3   Eph. 2:5-10; Phil. 3:7-15

support killing in any way, type or form! This is true because Christ died for everyone.[4]

Warning: Many are unaware of the fact that in basic training, when soldiers are drilled to kill other human beings without hesitation, it causes a massive breakdown in the *Conscience* that cannot be restored without Confession that killing is sin, *Repentance* and inner healing! People should know that killing is evil, arising from fear and hatred and is always associated with darkness (the world) and never with light (The *Kingdom of God*)

Because he had killed so many people during his flight from Saul, King David addressed this serious problem in the Psalms when he wrote about the nightmare of *Blood guiltiness,* A dark blot on the soul that is caused whenever people participate in or approve of any type of knowledgeable murder. Notice also that Jesus indicted the Pharisees for being guilty of the same! [5]

Another corollary precept to this is that fact that you cannot defeat evil by using evil because every time you do this you will cause the evil to gain even more strength! It is an undeniable law of responses: Evil begets evil. Sooner or later, it inevitably "boomerangs back at you" and makes the situation worse than before.

This illustrates the obviously futile idolatry of *Humanism,* which relies on human power, vainly thinking that you could solve humanity's problems that way. The Way of Christ is the only way that works, but you must commit your entire life to it or it will not work! Of course, this is also why Jesus said "Resist not (by force) the one who does evil."

The world will always mock Christians for believing this way, but that is because they fail to understand that it is man's sin nature that is the cause of all the evil in the world and that man's sin must be dealt with first before any change can come. This brings up the problems that always afflict every way that the world uses. A classic example is the Freudian "Fight vs. Flight" dichotomy. This is just another rendition of the old illogic: the "us vs. them" argument partisans use to label others, trying to force them to espouse their brand of politics!

---

4   John 3:16; 1 John 2:1-6
5   Psa. 32, 51; Matt. 23:31-39; John 18:36,37

However, what the world refuses to acknowledge is that a viable Third Path exists which is Jesus's Way as it is defined in our New Testament.

Of course, the world's controlling elite does not want you to know that a Third Way exists because they want to use those oxymoronic syllogisms as part of their agenda to dominate and enslave the world. These controllers work for Satan's minions: The "Principalities and powers and rulers of the darkness of this world" about which Paul told the Ephesians.[6]

Christians should know that Jesus commands us to Worship and serve the only One God of *Agape* Love Who also has, via Jesus Christ, ordained a totally unique set of Laws and Precepts for all whom truly Believe what we call the *New Covenant. * According to God's Word, the *New Covenant* supersedes all human laws and policies that conflict or contradict God's supreme Word, Jesus Christ.[7]

Yes, you must learn, know and apply the Truth Christ taught to gain victory over evil and experience true *Salvation* which applies both temporally and eternally. Whereas, All the world system works on an opposing pagan basis, worshiping many false "demigods" that are Satan's minions. It all started with Adam's sin while he was still in the *Garden. * Consequently, a cascade of events resulting from Adam believing Satan's lie led him to relinquish his authority over the earth to Satan. This also caused an internal breakdown in the way human beings make decisions. As God warned, Adam's human spirit suffered the most, with the abilities of *Intuition* and *Communion* that had enabled him to Fellowship with God being deadened. With these abilities gone, this left only the vestigial function of *Conscience.* Also, deliberate continuance in sin "sears the *Conscience*" as well. After this, what we call the "Soul-Body Complex" that Scripture calls the 'flesh' gained control of man's choices, alienating them from God and plunging humanity into a downward vortex of evil, in which unbelieving mankind has remained ever since.

---

6   Eph. 6:12 *See also the paper entitled What is Collectivism*
7   Matt. 6:24; Luke 16:13; John 4:23,24; Acts 4:13-20; 5:29-32

After this, man's worship degenerated into idolatry, beginning with the ancient Sumerians, whose leader, the one they call The Nimrod, who was the one who organized the building of the Tower of Babel.

Their religion evolved into what we know as *Zoroastrianism*, whose main 'deity' was Bel or the Baal, a pseudonym for a Satanic controlling Principality which was taken up by the Canaanites, which brings us to their influence in the middle east, where Biblical history takes place. Let us not forget what God did to the cities of the plain, Sodom and Gomorrah, as well as what God's judgment did in bringing about the destruction of Jericho and the Canaanite dynasty in Joshua's day.

However, one must also realize that God's ways of "summary judgment and destruction" of those who persist in idolatrous behavior that we see executed in the Old Testament was changed when we come to the "Age of Grace," wherein Jesus Christ ordained an entirely new way to deal with sin and evil to save mankind.[8]

Paul also wrote to the Romans, describing the downward spiral of man's sinful ways that brought mankind down to the depths of degradation and to the disgusting practices that arise from idolatry! The application to Christians is obvious: Any True Christian who loves God with all their heart would never consciously consider worshiping an idol. However, that is precisely what multitudes of "so-called Christians" have been led to do when they are told to "pledge allegiance" to any worldly ensign (flag) or claim that soldiers who kill others or had their blood shed by another on some battlefield would ever make us "free!"

Know this: Only Jesus Christ's Precious Blood, Shed on the cross makes us free! You must choose one or the other, but you cannot serve both![9]

As mentioned above, we know that in His Temptation sequence, Jesus acknowledged Satan's hegemony over the world. So, I ask the reader this: Does Satan or the world have control of you? You should know that many "so-called definitions of freedom" exist. Beware of

---

8   Genesis 19; Joshua 1-12 *See also the way God obsoleted "judgment by murder" when He ordained Christ's *New Covenant* See Matt. 5-7; Luke 6:27-40; 9:51-56; John 18:36; Rom. 1:18-32; 1 Tim. 4:1,2; Heb. 7:11-10:23 See also the book Jesus' Way*

9   Matt. 6:24; Luke 16:13-15; John 8:31-36; Romans 1:17-23; 2 Cor. 3:17,18

trying to forcefully change your circumstance! Every way of "so called salvation from evil" but one is based upon worldly ways that involve killing. Jesus's Way is the only way to true freedom of the human soul and *Conscience* that works without doing harm to any other person and that exists no matter what circumstance in which we find ourselves. This is because True Christians, like God does, always observe human Free Will, never advocating the use of force of any type to change them![10]

Paul also unequivocally said: "You cannot partake from the table of God's Kingdom and the table of devils at the same time." You must choose between them. Remember the conflict Elijah had on Mt. Carmel with the prophets of The Baal and what he said about choosing.[11]

This precept forces us to decide "Who we will serve."[12]

By the way, why do modern Christians even dare to think that they can compromise the Holy Christian Faith by worshiping national idol symbols and "get away with it" with God? Indeed, they are not even worthy to use Christ's Holy Name that so many faithful followers throughout the years have persevered and even died for to keep their Faith intactly even in the face of terrible persecution and torture! Always remember: Jesus died for us First because He First Loved us![13]

II. Know this:

To be a part of God's eternal *Kingdom of Heaven* you must obey Jesus Christ's Commands and Teaching.

Not only that, this obedience is defined by the Greek word *Huperkoe* that is used in Scripture meaning "super hearing." It is all part of the Biblical precept of *Faith.* We also should know that God's Word says the following: "To obey is better than sacrifice," "if you love me you will keep my commands" and "whatsoever is not of faith is sin." Indeed, no intermediate area of "independence" exists![14]

---

10   Matt. 4:8-10; 5:43-48; Luke 4:5-8; 9:49-56; John 18:36,37; Acts 4:12-20; 5:29-32
11   Psa. 3:3-8; 4:1-8; 9:9,10; 20:6,7; 27:1 ff.; 32:6-11; 46:1 ff.; 91:1 ff.; 1 Kings 18:21; Isa. 44:6-20; 45:20-23; Nah. 1:7; Matt. 6:24; Luke 16:13; 1 Cor. 10:14-22; 2 Cor. 6:14-18
12   Joshua 24:15; Matt. 5-7; Rom. 8; 1 John 1-5
13   John 3:16; 1 John 4:19
14   1 Sam. 15:22; John 14:15-27; Rom. 15:23

A. Scripture clearly teaches that <u>Only One integral set of Laws governs the *Kingdom of Heaven*: The Law of Christ</u>. Anyone who truly belongs to God's Kingdom gladly submits to Christ's Lordship.

On the other hand, *Sin* comes in many ways and types, all abhorrent to God! Yes, you should know that all sin belongs to "the mind of the flesh" which boldly contrasts with God's Way, "the mind of the spirit." Jesus remarked that this contrast illustrates the <u>incongruity of all humanistic ways</u> for being unworkable for God in his classic Truism: "You are unable to serve two masters." Paul also makes this truth painfully clear in his letter to the Romans.[15] The main types of sin are as follows:

1. Idolatry is the primary root of all the other types since it follows Satan's "big lie" that falsely asserts that we could become "our own god."

Yes, <u>this is the sin lurking behind all the false claims of "worldly salvation"</u> that you have been brought up believing to be "true," among them being <u>the big lie</u> that humanistic power and intelligence "saves you," whether it is by the brute strength of the military, political intrigue or 'academic' or 'scientific' advancements! Not only that, <u>Idolatry is extremely addictive</u> in that the people who become ensnared by its tentacles <u>want it to be true so much that they will attack you</u>, "coming out of their corner fighting" whenever these beliefs are challenged. The primary areas are Patriotism, politics, immorality and materialism.

What is worse is that their "worldly-centered" beliefs that rationalize killing are actually tethered to <u>the abominable practice of human sacrifice!</u>

Think about this and realize that these 'modern humanistic adaptations' are no better than the ancient practices of their 'ancestors' that are typified by the ways of aboriginals, Hittites, Canaanites, Egyptians, Babylonians, etc., that God condemned in the Old Testament.

---

15   Matt. 6:24; Luke 16:13; Rom. 8:1-11

The Scriptures are full of warnings about this sin, but it seems that modern Christians are totally stone blind to their present day practices that are essentially the same in God's eyes![16]

2. Immorality is a large area of sin based on the mistaken relativistic notion that you can be or do whatever you want, regardless of what God's Law specifically teaches about these sins.[17]

3. The general area that Scripture describes for being "the mind of the flesh" is typified by the term *Humanism, * the driving force that has made the "world system" like it is. Of course, what underlies this is the control Satan has over all people who rely upon human power and intelligence to "save." Standing in bold contrast to this, Jesus's Teachings directly challenge all the assumptions of Humanism, showing all Believers that another Way of Living exists that does not rely on any humanly generated "method, strategy or power."[18]

4. Review Summary: Scripture tells us that God gives man "free will," so we must choose the way we live. However, only two ways are possible: Jesus's Way and the world's way: No independent way exists. Not only that, Jesus is painfully clear in saying that "He that is not with me is against me" and that the True Christian Way defined in the New Testament will always "Be spoken against" by the world and by all those who follow the world's ways! In particular, notice also that any rationale for killing other human beings is against Christ's Teachings. Belief in killing is always associated with the darkness of this world and never with light! Not only that, All True Believers know that only Jesus Christ is (the source of) our Peace! [19]

Finally, because God is *Agape* Love, this affects every aspect of the Way we live and extends to the way we fight evil. Yes, we fight, but always according to the "Law of Love" Jesus pioneered in the *New Covenant,* where in Christ, "Love is stronger than death." Viz., "we

---

16   1 Sam. 2:9; 15:23; Psa. 96:5; 106:36; 115:4; Isa. 2:8,18; 45:16; 48:5; 57:5; Jer. 2-10,17,18,23; Ezek. 2:1-3:11; 5:5-6:14; 8:10; 14:3,4,7; 16:36; 18:6-30; 21:24-27; 22:23-28;23:37-39; Hos. 4:17; 10:12,13; 14:9; Zech. 13:2; Mal. 2:1-13; Matt. 23; Luke 2:34,35; Acts 7:41-48; 17:16; 28:22; 1 Cor. 10:14; Gal. 5:1,13; Eph. 2:13-16; 1 Tim. 6:3-12; 2 Tim. 2:19

17   Rom. 1:18-32

18   Matt. 4:1-10; 6:9-13; Luke 4:1-8; 11:33-36; John 14:6; 18:36; Rom. 8:1-11; 2 Cor.4:3-7; Rev. 13

19   Matt. 12:30; Luke 2:34; 11:33-36; John 14:15-27; Acts 28:22; Eph. 2:13,14; Phil.4:6-8

wrestle not against flesh and blood, but (spiritually) against principalities and powers and the (unseen) rulers of the darkness of this world."[20]

B. Yes, God uses a "Pattern" of event-situations to prove the mettle of the Saints. It starts with a "crisis" when God begins to show us a pattern of purification and preparation for divine service.

First, a person chooses to Receive and Follow Jesus Christ.

Second, after the initial "honeymoon period," God frequently will bring a person "to the edge" of a situation, testing them to see if they really Believe what God's Word teaches.

Third, God then evaluates our response to see if we continue to obey His Word (Truth) and His Voice (the Holy Spirit) within us that teaches us to differentiate right from wrong.[21]

Then, to start, let us think about the witness of the Saints in the past, among them being Abraham, Jacob, Moses, Rahab, Joshua, Ruth, Samuel, David and many others.[22]

Always remember that God expects absolute (100%) Allegiance from every Reborn Believer/ Child of His Kingdom. Our Identity begins with our recognition of God's overall Sovereignty. Every true servant of Jesus Christ has a particular Identity that is unmistakably not of this world! Our Love for God and for all humanity begins the Transformation Process. Consider the following comments recorded for us:

"I have lifted up my hands unto the Most High, Possessor of Heaven and earth" … "Fear not, I Am your exceeding Great Reward" and "Abraham Believed God and it was counted unto him as Righteousness."

C. Know this: The True Christian's Identity arises from a personal relationship with Jesus Christ that places us in the *Kingdom of Heaven* where Christ's Teachings are the "Rule of Law" which we know as the *New Covenant* which is primarily the New Testament,

---

20   Song 8:6,7; Matt. 5:38-48; Rom. 12:9-21; 2 Cor. 10:3-7; Eph. 6:10-12
21   Matt. 5-7; Luke 6-12; John 8:31-36; Rom. 8:26-39
22   Gen. 12-14, 22; 28:10-35:35; Exodus 3-15; Joshua 2:1 ff.; 24:14-27; Ruth 1:16-18;1 Sam. 2:1-10; 3:1-14; 1 Chr. 17; Psa. 18,19, 77:19; Isa. 43:16; Heb. 11

but which also contains precepts that are "carried over" from the Old Testament.[23]

A great part of that Identity is the well-known characteristic defined in many Scriptures for being Holiness, described by *(the Doctrine of) Sanctification.*

Indeed, *Sanctification* is so important to God because all the issues that are related to Holiness are inexorably and integrally connected to the associated central Christian doctrines of *Redemption* and *Baptism.*[24]

This will lead us to the underlying Truth that the *Kingdom of God* is <u>above all the world system</u>. This principle also points us to one of the most glaring areas of apostasy that exists in the "modern corporation church system," what is defined in Scriptural symbolism for being the church's sin of having had "Fornication with the kings of the earth" via the blasphemous "doctrines of the state" in which they lead Christians to worship the state as "god," viz., patriotism. All such doctrines arise from the false doctrinal base of *Determinism.* The writer has covered this problem many times in other papers, so he will not belabor it further here, but only to leave a message of warning that this practice is none other than "bald-faced Idolatry!"[25]

Verily, the Truth of God's *Kingdom of Heaven* defines the <u>True Christian Walk</u>, which is indeed "self-evident" to those who truly "<u>Love God with all their heart, soul, mind and strength.</u>" The words of Christ and the early Apostles are "self-teaching," but only <u>IF you love the Truth and God above all else!</u>[26]

---

23 Ex. 20; Deut. 4, 29-32; 1 Sam. 2; the Psalms, Proverbs, and the Prophets, including Jer. 31; Ezek. 36; Dan. 2:44,45; 4:3; 7:18-27; Matt. 5-7; 13:1 ff.; 16:18-26 et. Al.; Luke 1:33; 9:56-62; 11:33-36; John 1,3; 18:36; Acts 4,5, 14:22; 17:24-31; Rom. 4-8; 1 Cor. 4:20; 10:1 ff; Col. 1:13-16 *and so forth* See also the books *Jesus' Way, The Church in the Last Days, Basic Christian Doctrine and Spiritual Guidelines for Restoration and well as the Papers Emmanuel 1,2*

24 Lev. 20:7; Psa. 9:10; 22:3; Isa. 6:13; Ezek. 22:26; 44:23; Hag. 2;11-14; Matt. 7:6; John17:11; Rom. 11:16; 1 Cor. 3:17; 2 Cor. 6:14-7:1; Col. 3:12; 2 Tim. 1:9; 1 Pet. 1:13-25

25 Josh. 2; Psa. 94:20; 96:5; 118:8,9; Isa. 2:8,18,20; 28:5-23; 29:8-30:21; 42-46; Ezek. 6:4,5,13; 14:1-8; 18-23 (esp. 23:37-49); Dan. 2:44,45; 3:1 ff.; 6:1ff.; 7:13-28; Hos.4:17; 14:8,9; Matt. 6:9-13; Luke 13:24-35; Acts 4,5; 1 Cor. 3:16-32; 6:9-11; 10:1-13; 2 Cor. 6:14- 7:1; Phil. 3:20; Rev. 17:1-8; 21:8; 22:15

26 Matt. 6:9-13; 10:16-42; 22:26,37; Luke 2:49; John 18:36; Acts 1-5. 7:48; 17:24-31; Rom. 8; Gal. 1,2; Phil. 1-4; Eph. 1-6; Col. 1-4

"Kingdom Living" includes a wide spectrum of doctrine encompassing the grand vistas of spirituality we can see with the "eyes of our mind and consciousness."

They include *Redemption* and *Righteousness* on one side and *Sin* and *Judgment* on the other, with both revealed by God's Holy Spirit.[27]

Not only that, "Kingdom Living" is always connected to the ongoing Process we should recognize as the "Discipleship to Conversion Dynamic." This embodies God's exalted Way of doing things that is always "higher than our ways." Not only that, God's *New Covenant* requires that every Believer practice Daily *Repentance* which enables us to continue in the *Conversion* process.[28]

D. For True Believers, Our Identity with Christ begins with our Recognition of God's Sovereignty. Part of this is the obvious requirement of our "Fear of God," which is essentially our confession of God's Reality, Power, Knowledge and ability to reward and/or punish.

Moving onward from that beginning point, we can then begin to form a lasting personal Relationship with God where the incipient fear transforms into respect and eventually to Love. Consider again God's comments to Abraham and compare them to Paul's comments in his letters.[29]

God's great promises made to and the tests in which God led Abraham, Jacob, Joseph and others also reveal the ongoing process wherein God shapes and purifies His Saints.[30]

E. As you think about those whom God shaped in the past, also think also about who you are.

Let us examine the events of Scripture that illustrate the elements and stages that make our process of transformation into a Saint of God,

---

27   John 14:6-17:26; Rom. 5-8; 1 Cor. 1:17-2:16
28   Isa. 55:9; Acts 3:19; 1 John 1:5-10 *See also (the 3 part series) Christian Conversion, the Doctrine of Repentance, God's Definition of Salvation and the Role of Conscience*
29   Gen. 12:1-3,8; 13:3; 14:22; 15:1-6, 12-18; 17:19-21; Rom. 4:9.13; Heb. 11
30   Gen. 18:10-18; 22:1 ff.; 28:10-35:36; Jer. 7:23; John 3:16-36; 15:17

a "Vessel unto honor" that is more than adequate for serving the King of kings and Lord of lords.

- God called Abram, saying "Get out of your country."[31]
- God gave Moses the Ten Commandments.[32]
- God essentially told the Israelites that you are Mine by saying: "You must be holy because I, the Lord, am holy. I have set you apart from all other people to be my very own." Note also that the Identity of God's People was first established, being 'Purchased' by the Lamb's Blood shed at the *Passover.* In a like manner, the *Blood of Christ* established the Christian's Identity in the Second *Passover* in the first century.[33]
- Joshua proclaimed "As for me and my house, we will serve the Lord."[34]
- David, the 'sweet psalmist of Israel' and "a man after God's own heart," wrote: "For who is God, except the Lord... and the Lord is my rock, my fortress, my deliverer ... (For) We are the people saved by the Lord."[35]
- In the New Testament, know also that Jesus proclaimed that "Nothing is impossible with God."[36]

Adding it all up, we can easily see that Jesus's Teachings are viable today just as much as they were in the first century. Yes, God's Word tells us the "straight skinny" of undiluted Truth:

First, you must confess your sinfulness and "empty yourself" of all the indoctrinating "worldly claptrap" of humanism that you have no doubt been "catechized" from childhood by the poisons of 'half-truths

---

31   Gen. 12:1 f. Cf. Heb. 11:12-16
32   Ex. 20,34; Deut. 5
33   Lev. 20:26; Num. 8:17; 23:9; Psa. 74:2; Isa. 43:1; John 10:14-18; Acts 20:26-32; Eph. 1:7-14
      See also the paper entitled The Three Passovers of Scripture
34   Joshua 24:13-20
35   Psa. 18, 19,45; 1 Chr. 17:7-14, 20-22; Acts 13:22
36   Matt. 17:20; 19:26 Cf. Luke 1:37; 18:27 and Jer. 32:17,27

mixed with lies' that are endemic to the "blind patriotism" of nationally-based religion that worships the idols of the world system.[37]

Second, we must daily practice the basic commands of Jesus Christ as they were delivered to the Disciples in the New Testament: "Deny self, take up the cross and follow Jesus." Remember always what Jesus said: "Don't you know that I must be about My Father's Business?"[38]

Third, accept the fact that you are not part of the world because of whom you are *In Christ,* the Identity we possess because we Trust in God and not in the ways of man (the world) which rationalize killing and many other types of immorality![39]

III. Let us now consider the following primary truths which you may have not considered before:

A. The basic precept is that only two kingdoms exist:

One is God's *Kingdom of Heaven* which exists both "on earth, (just) as it is in Heaven"[40]

Two, all that remains on earth are all the kingdoms belonging to the world system, which is controlled by Satan. Three: Several corollaries apply to this primary rule:

---

37   Matt. 6:9-13; 16:21-26; Luke 9:23-26; 11:33-36; John 8:12, 23-58; 12:23-26;18:36,37; Acts 5:29-32; Rom. 6:1-8:39; 12:1 ff.; 1 Cor. 1:17-2:16; 10:12-21; 2 Cor. 2:14-7:1;Gal. 1:6-12; 2:19-5:4; Eph. 2:8-22; Phil. 3:20; Col. 1:13-18; 2:8-3:17; Heb. 11:12-16; James 4:1-8; 1 John 2:15-17

38   Luke 2:49; 9:23-26; John 14:6-16:26

39   1 Sam. 2:1-10; 1 Kings 18:21; Job. 19:25-27; Psa. 3:8; 4:8; 9:9,10; 16:1 ff.; 20:6,7; 23:1 ff.; 24:1. Ff.; 27:1 ff.; 31-37, 40-42, 45 (the Kings Daughter), 46, 50,51, 55, 61-63, 73, 84, 91, 94,95, 115,118, 146; Isa. 42-46; Jer. 31:31-34; Ezek. 33-36; Dan. 3,6,7; Zech. 4:6; Matt. 5-7; 10:16-42; John 11:25,26; 13:35-17:26; Acts 5:29-32; 17:24-31; 28:22; Rom. 1:16- 8:39; 1 Cor. 1:17-2:16; 15:20 ff.; Gal. 1:6-12; Eph. 1:7-14; 2:13,14; Phil. 2:5-11; 3:3,20; 1 Tim. 2:5; 6:3-12; 2 Tim. 1:7-14; 2:11-26; Heb. 1-4,10-12 *See also the papers entitled Are You Sure What You Believe is Truly Christian Doctrine, The Beauty and Finesse of the New Covenant, The Christian Epiphany, (the 3 part series) Christianity Versus Religion, Do You Truly Know and Believe the Complete Gospel of Jesus Christ, Fulfilment Prophecy, God's Kingdom is a Whole New World, (the 2 part series) How Should We Then Live, the Key to Understanding Scripture is Spiritual Exegesis, Looking Through the Lens of Jesus Christ, Major Missing Aspects of the Original Christian Gospel, Only One Savior, the Price of Living for Jesus, Principles of Fulfilment Theology, the Reality of God's Kingdom and Eternal Life, Regarding Christ's Headship, Retaining our Freedom requires Knowing and Applying the Truth and the Spiritual Laws of Revival*

40   Matt. 6:9-13 *See also the paper The Spiritual Laws of Revival, Chapter 3, Law #11 and the writer's book Jesus' Way*

1. Only One True Living God exists, the One that created the universe, the earth and the unique race of mankind.[41]

2. No neutral ground exists between the two abovementioned kingdoms. Verily, God judges by the individual case: You are either Part of Christ and a Citizen of the Kingdom of Heaven where Christ is our King, living in the Light in *Righteousness* by *Faith* OR you are part of the world system, living in the darkness of unbelief. Know this also: God does not grant entry into His Kingdom by any form of proxy. That is, you must make a deliberate personal choice to Receive Christ and to become a Disciple who, from that point onward, follows Christ's Teachings to the best of your ability to qualify for being a True Christian. Church 'membership,' associating with other Christians or by merely being a "moral person" does not count with God and always remember: God has no "grandchildren!"[42]

3. Jesus Christ is LORD: God's only divine Legate relating to all human affairs here on earth.[43]

4. Satan is the "demigod" that rules all the kingdoms of this world system of nations and empires. Jesus even acknowledged this because Jesus knew what Adam had done when he disobeyed God in the *Garden.*[44]

Via Christ, all True Christians have been given *Authority* over Satan and his minions.[45]

B. All true Christians are Part of Christ and Citizens of the Kingdom of Heaven where Christ is our King. Whereas, all unbelievers are part of the world system, which remains under God's Judgment.[46]

---

41 See the book Basic Christian Doctrine and Gen. 1,2; Exodus 3,20; Deut. 4:32-42; 32:3,4,39; Josh. 24:14 ff.; 1 Sam. 2:1-10; Psa. 90, 121; Isa. 43-45; John 1:1-5; Acts 17:24-31

42 Matt. 6:24; 10:32-40; 12:30; Mark 3:24-30; Luke 2:34; 11:17-23; 12:49-53; Acts 7:37 ff.; 13:21 ff.; 28:22; Rom. 8:1-11; Gal. 1:6-12; Eph. 6:12; Phil. 3:3,19-21; Heb. 12:1 ff. See the papers Are You Sure What you believe is truly Christian Doctrine; the Beauty and Finesse of the New Covenant, Conditions for Salvation, Divergent Belief Systems, Examining the Original Imperatives of the Christian Gospel, Fallacies of Determinism and Living the Complete Gospel

43 Luke 10:22; Eph. 1:21,22; Phil. 2:5-11; 1 Tim. 2:5; Heb. 4:12-16; 9:9-15

44 Matt. 4:8-10; Luke 4:5-8; Eph. 6:12

45 Luke 10:18-23; 2 Cor. 10:3-6; Eph. 6:10-18

46 Matt. 3:2; 4:17; 6:9-13; 12:30; 13: 10-17; 16:18-26; 19:13-26; Luke 12; John 3:36; 18:36,37; 1 Cor. 10:12-21; 2 Cor. 6:14-7:1; Phil. 3:20,21; Col. 1:13

When Jesus gathered together the Disciples, it was with the understanding that he was forming an entirely New Way of Living that was completely different from all the worlds' ways.

As the Gospels describe, initially, all twelve Disciples followed Christ's Teachings, even the two *Zealots, Simon and Judas Iscariot.

Of course, we know that somewhere along the way, Judases' loyalty was coopted by Zealot dogma to the point that he 'fell away from the Truth and was then influenced to betray Christ.[47]

There is one thing we can know for certain: That Jesus Christ never approved of the Zealot's agenda of terrorism and murder. Indeed, Jesus never approved of killing anyone, anywhere, at any time or in any way or type under any circumstance.[48]

Author's Explanatory: We should know that the New Testament specifically teaches that all types of murder fall under the umbrella of *Humanism,* which is the source of every rationale for killing.

Not only that, ALL humanism, including patriotism, descends from some type of Idolatry, for God considers all trust in human power to deliver from evil, whether it is political maneuvering, military force, state-sanctioned death punishments or the use of deadly force for defense for being classified as Idolatry!

Moreover, you should know that God's view of idolatry and of ALL knowledgeable murder has not changed, even though in the past God had allowed killing as judgment and for some limited specific situations in the Old Testament where God used Israel as a tool of His Judgment. However, God never intended for modern Christians to think that these instances constituted an overall pattern to be extended to the present! C. I ask the reader again the primary question this paper addresses: "Do you know who you are, what Kingdom of which you are a Citizen by Royal Rebirth and to Whom do you Worship, Serve and belong?" Moreover, know this clearly: Since Jesus is the defacto King of all True Christians, all the Scriptures advising "submission to civil authority" must never be construed to imply that we should worship or "pledge allegiance" to any earthly potentate or state symbol!

---

47   *Observing context, you should know that the word "Zealot" is another word for 'partisan' or 'patriot'

48   Matt. 5:43-48; 26:51,52; Luke 9:49-56; 21:8-19; John 18:36; James 3:13-4:8

This great truth leads us now to consider the primary problem area relating to Idolatry afflicting multitudes of modern "professing Christians." The problem is the issue of Nationalism and the worship of national symbols. Know this and think about it: Ask yourself this very relevant question: Did either Jesus, Peter or Paul ever teach that Christians should "offer incense to the Roman Emperor" or to "Pledge Allegiance" to any Roman Ensign (Flag)? I do not think so!

Of course, if you truly know what True Christianity stands for as it is presented in the New Testament, you would intrinsically know that this is because they all knew that to do any of those things would constitute committing Idolatry in God's eyes, and, of course, you should also know that Idolatry is also considered by God as an Abomination! Not only that, the same precept applies to Christians today in America and every other nation! We are part of Christ and not of this world!

Can you hear this message in your heart and receive it, knowing that receiving this extremely important Truth will require you to make major changes regarding your attitudes and doctrines that will cost you dearly? Yes, it will mean that you will lose many "so-called friends" and the 'respect' of 'Fair-weather' colleagues that have not understood the reality of Genuine Christianity![49]

D. A fundamentally universal underlying precept regulating this is that only Genuine Christianity is truly Monotheism, for all True Christians worship and serve only one God Who is the primary source for everything in their lives. However, you should know by now that, all around the true church, the world is polytheistic in nature, even those who supposedly "claim" to worship 'God,' yet the Truth is that they actually worship many 'gods' because of their obvious worship of human power, expressed as "the military's raw might," political intrigue, National pride (Patriotism), economic influence, the "arts," sports and cultural sophistication.[50]

---

49   Matt. 6:24; John 3:36; 8:31-58; 10:27; 12:35-50; 14:27; 15:19; Rom. 12:1-3; 1 Cor. 2:1-16; 10:1 ff.; 2 Cor. 11:12-15; Gal. 6:14; Col. 2:6-3:10; 1 Tim. 2:5; 1 John 4:1-8; 5:4,5,19

50   Ex. 20:1 f.; Josh. 2:1 ff; 24:14-21; 1 Sam. 2:5-9; 1 Knigs 18:21; Isa. 42-46; Jer. 5,7.10,17,18; Ezek. 18:30; 21:24-22:16; 28:1-19; Daniel 2,4,6,7,11; Matt. 24; Luke 16:13; 21;1 ff.; 2 Thess. 2; 2 Pet. 3; Jude 1

Again, think about it: You should know that Satan is no fool. He has had 6,000 years of experience observing what people respond to, want, love, hate, fear, enjoy and take pride in. Yes, Satan plays all the angles with deft alacrity, tuning his appeals to every desire of the flesh with all its quirks and secret desires.

Verily, Satan is a consummate advertising genius, seeking advantage in all situations, using propaganda to the max! So, if you are not <u>100% loyal to Jesus Christ</u>, Satan will find a "chink in the armor" and drive a semi through it!

His favorites are National pride, glorifications of political manipulation, the brute force of the military, sexual desire, ambition, power, greed and the accumulation of wealth and possessions! You need to know that Jesus Christ acknowledged that Satan controls the entire world system. However, as a Christian, it is very probable that you have not taken this truth seriously.

This is because virtually all the organized churches have 'surrendered' to the hegemony of 'worldly prerogatives' and thereby have fallen into apostasy and control by the state that always comes with any organization that operates by "Non-profit Corporation" bylaws. Beware of them.[51]

Unfortunately, the condition of the majority of America's churches has been greatly influenced by their unbiblical trust in human devices, which is evidenced by their obsessive attachment to politics and defacto worship of the state and its symbols. Verily, more than one hundred fifty years before, President Abraham Lincoln had bemoaned the fact that the country's spiritual and moral condition had seriously been compromised, being compared with the <u>obvious ideals of the original settlers</u>. It is interesting to observe the distinct historical parallel that exists between Israel's apostasy and the manifest apostasy of the church![52]

Let us now consider "Lincoln's Warning":

---

51   Prov. 1:19; 15:27; 16:18; 22:7; 29:25; Isa. 8:9-20; 28:9-20; 29:9-16; 44:6-20; Jer. 10,17; Ezek. 21:25-27; 22:1 ff.; Matt. 16:26; 23:1 ff.; Mark 8:36; Luke 9:25; John 18:36; 2 Cor. 4:3-7; 10:3-7; 11:12-15; Eph. 6:1-12; Phil. 3:7-15; 1 Tim. 6:3-12; 2 Tim. 2:7-26; James 4:1-8; 1 John 2:15-17

52   Compare 2 Chr. 7; Neh. 9; Jer. 2-18; Ezek. 3, 7-23,33-36 with Acts 20:25 ff.; Rev. 2,3 *See the papers entitled Emmanuel (1) and Emmanuel 2*

"Intoxicated with unbroken success, we have become too self-sufficient to find the necessity of redeeming and preserving Grace, too proud to pray to the God who made us. We have grown in numbers, wealth and power as no other nation has grown but we have forgotten God, we have forgotten the Gracious Hand that preserved us to peace and multiplied and strengthened us. We have vainly imagined that all these things were produced by some superior virtue and wisdom of our own."

Abraham Lincoln, April 1863

IV. God's Definition of *Faith* is one integral Whole that cannot be compromised without losing it. The *New Covenant,* our set of laws *In Christ, * is also One.

A. The only Way we can be Christian is to follow Jesus, "overcoming evil with good" as Paul wrote the Romans. Yes, our God is real and His Promises are absolutely reliable. However, IF you do not truly Believe this, your 'faith' is worthless![53]

The naked truth is that nobody is able to 'fight or destroy evil' by using evil for it always will "boomerang back" right in your face. Not only that, anytime you use or approve those worldly methods that always rationalize killing to "solve" problems will certainly make you just like the ones you hate! Victory in the battle against evil only comes by doing things' Jesus's Way which demands that you respond to evil with the opposite spirit, with *Agape* Love! The Truth of the Complete Gospel always teaches this fundamental way which is always opposite to any way "of the flesh," which Scripture teaches is by definition, always "at enmity with God."[54]

The undeniable Truth of the Complete Gospel is that Truth is also One integral Whole that cannot be "parted out," nor can we "pick and choose" what parts to believe or not to believe, whatever the reason! The Gospel was written by God and Christ forged out the details in

---

53   Psa. 105; Luke 24:49; John 10:27; Acts 2:33-39; Rom. 4:13-20; 12:9-21; Gal. 3:14- 5:26* Cf. Matt. 5:17-20 *Notice that Gal. 3:19 says when the promised child, Jesus, came, the New Covenant became the rule of law for Christians;* See Eph. 1:13,14; 2:11-22; Heb. 6:13-20; 9:14,15; 10:19-39; 11:1 ff.; 12:26-29 *See also the book Jesus' Way, Chapter V, Sect. II*

54   Matt. 5:38-48; 26:51,52; Mark 3:4; Rom. 8:1-11; 2 Cor. 4:3-7; 10:3-7; 11:12-15; Eph. 6:10-12

His own Blood shed on Calvary, so what right has any mortal man to question what God has ordained for being the Gospel? I will forthright tell you this: Anyone who presumes to "redefine the Gospel" or take any part out, is a traitor to Jesus Christ just as much as Judas Iscariot was! Judas was a Zealot just like Barabbas who thought he could "use Jesus" and get away with it. Well, he was dead wrong, and so is anyone else who presumes they can alter that precious Gospel that Christ paid for with His own sacred Blood on Calvary! And, Yes, this goes for anyone who believes that "approval of killing could ever be a part of the Christian Gospel!" The underlying Truth is that Jesus Christ is our Savior in all ways and venues: Physical, Soulical and Spiritual. Jesus Christ IS our *Righteousness* and *Peace* and He is well able to Save anyone from evil IF you Trust Him! God considers any other belief that condones killing to save to be Idolatry! The Gospel is 100% Light and does not contain any Darkness of which killing is a part.[55]

B. The bottom line is that we must abide by all the Terms and conditions of the *New Covenant,* which includes our commitment to engage evils only with Good and to fight only "on Holy Ground" which means we always live and fight "in the Light" of Jesus's Teachings and never to rationalize any 'method of Darkness,' for to do so would be falling into Idolatry![56]

Indeed, nation-worship, Idolatry, is the "pink elephant in plain sight" that is causing most Christians to apostatize. Verily, because of most church's corporation-based organization, this corruption has successfully infested the vast majority of churches in the modern age. The worst part about this is that, because their leaders seem to "bend over backwards" to popularize Christianity and make it more "palatable" to the world (they should have known that this cannot work!), Bible schools and Seminaries have evolved so much that they have come to assiduously teach their leaders to defend this idolatry.

The basis of this abject corruption of truth is the false teaching that God has "automatically ordained" political authorities. [Sic.] However, that belief can be proven false by a proper exegesis of the very Scriptures

---

55   Isa. 5:20; 8:20; Matt. 6:22-24; Luke 11:33-36; 16:13-15; John 1:4-9; 3:19-21; 8:12, 31-58; Gal. 1:6-12; 5:1-25; Eph. 2:13,14; 5:5-16; 1 Tim. 6:3-12; 2 Tim. 1-4; 1 John 1-5

56   1 Kings 18:21; Luke 11:33-36; John 1:1-18; Eph. 4; 1 Tim. 6:12 1 John 5:21

they use to teach this! The main problem lies in the mistranslation of the Greek word *Tagma*, which should have been translated as "allowed" instead of 'ordained.' It is patent that if Christians knew that crucial bit of information, they would not have fallen for nation worship in the first place. But of course, even Christians are subject to the same temptations that all people have: They inherently have this penchant to find "shortcuts" around the difficult parts of the Gospel and consequently become 'suckers' for every wind of doctrine that seems to satisfy that desire. Among those temptations is the strong desire to "fit in" to the group in which they want acceptance and they are willing to compromise to 'achieve' that goal. Unfortunately, God's Word tells us that you are unable to do this, for it always ends up with people "loving the world" and vainly trying to "serve two masters!"[57]

Another fact they all seem to forget is that because Christ is the Redeemer of every True Christian, He has become our new Owner! Yes, Jesus Christ is our True King, who is superior to all other kings, and that as subjects of our King, "we must obey God rather than man" whenever man's laws conflict with God's.[58]

Not only that, God's Kingdom is universal in scope and Scripture teaches that God's Kingdom must take precedence over all parts of the Believer's life. Moreover, because Christ is new Owner and Savior in all venues, physical, Soulical and spiritual, our "Banner" or Flag is now the demonstrative existence of Heaven's (Gods') signal characteristic, *Agape* Love. No other ensign or symbol of Identity can be allowed to compete with this central aspect of True Christian living!

Anything or anyone that presumes to take the place of our Total Allegiance to Christ in any area of life is an Idol! Indeed, National symbols, like flags and the state's hegemony over people's lives are part of the ancient idol defined in Scripture for being "the Baal." Essentially, God's Law is the *New Covenant,* the overarching source of *Authority* that applies in every venue of life, private and public. Of course, that fact is what makes the True Christian a threat to Satan's hegemony over the world system which he controls. Jesus also acknowledged this when

---

57   Josh. 2; Dan. 3,6; Psa. 20:6,7; 46:1 ff.; 94:20; 95:6; 118:8,9; 146:1 ff.; Prov. 29:25; Song. 2:4; Isa. 42-46; Matt. 6:22-24; Luke 16:13; James 4:1-8; 1 John 2:15-17 *See also the papers entitled Authority and Conscience, the Basis of Liberty and True Liberty is in Christ Alone*

58   Acts 5:29-32

He was tempted by Satan in the wilderness. That truth is also why true Christians are persecuted, regardless of how they try to mollify the situation or pacify the world. The Early Christians understood and accepted that harsh truth very well, knowing that <u>no other way of doing thing works to preserve our integrity *In Christ.</u>* Unfortunately, down through the years, Christians have lost that "crucial edge" of devotion to Jesus Christ which <u>must be preserved intactly as the hallmark of True Faith in Christ, regardless of circumstance.</u>[59]

The reason these "disaffected so-called Christians" do not is because they have lost their <u>True Identity *In Christ,*</u> having exchanged it for a <u>false one that is tethered to the world system!</u> In simple terms, modern Christians have "traded" their eternal heritage for a "mess of pottage" <u>just like Esau!</u> Consequently, they <u>fail to recognize the Primary Truths of the Gospel</u>, the first of which is that <u>Jesus Christ is the Living Word of God</u> that shows you that the Original Teachings of Jesus are <u>still viable today, just as much as they were in the First Century.</u> His *New Covenant* Word is Truth and Light and is the only effective message that can penetrate the "false shield of the world's propaganda" that seeks to neutralize the Power of the Gospel and to enslave you by "buying into" the world's ways of violence and killing. Yes, what Jesus taught is the only True Fulfillment of the Law and Prophets.[60]

Of course, to recover the original truths of the Gospel, you must recognize the 'awful truth' of the "Trojan Horse" that has succeeded in neutralizing the vast majority of "Professing Christians," which is that "pink elephant in plain sight," Nation-Idolatry, which has poisoned the minds of millions.

Indeed, <u>why are they so consumed by fear?</u> The answer is obvious: Their *Faith* in God for being their Savior has been <u>supplanted by trust in man,</u> viz., *<u>Humanism*</u> has become their new 'god.'

---

59   Song 2:4; Dan. 2:44,45; 4:24-27; 7:13-28; Matt. 4:1-10; 6:9-13, 22-24; Luke 4:1-8; 16:13; John 14:6-16:4; 18:36; 1 Cor. 13; Gal. 5:22,23; Eph. 6:10-12; Heb. 10:26-11:6; James 4

60   Gen. 25:23-34; 27:1-40; Psa. 1,2,19,45,46, 110, 118, 146; Prov. 8; Jer. 31; Ezek. 36; Hosea 14:8,9; Zech. 4:6; Matt. 5-7; 26:41-52; Luke 2:34,35; 9:23-26, 49-56; 11:33-36; John 6:27-63; 8:12, 31-36; 18:36; Acts 2:38,39; 3:19; 4:12-20; 5:29-32; 7:48-60; 17:24-31; 20:28; 28:22; Rom. 1:16-32; 1 Cor. 1:17-2:16; 2 Cor. 4:3-7; 6:14-7:1; Gal. 1:6-12; Heb. 4,7-12

That also explains why they do not respond to truth. Consequently, they have become part of the World and, because of that, they love the world.[61]

Contrariwise, the only effective way to neutralize evil is by living in *Agape* Love from a Pure Heart which loves Jesus more than anything else and implicitly follows his teachings! Yes, our only 'sword' is the powerfully wielded "Sword of God's Word," the Truth. Then, finally, remember this: Killing is always associated with evil and darkness, never as light! No, you are never able to 'neutralize evil' by using evil![62]

C. Let us reiterate: There is a very good reason why Jesus taught the Disciples the way He did. That is, to follow Jesus, you must come "as a child," open-minded and willing to learn new things.[63]

1. That reason is further revealed when we understand that, when children are young, they receive and assimilate truth very quickly and easily, whereas, when people grow up to be adults, that spontaneity is largely lost for most. The exceptions are those, like me, who consider themselves to be "professional students" who seek to keep learning throughout life.

However, to remain that way, you must be willing to change your position whenever new information becomes your way that can be verified by reliable sources, the Scripture being the most reliable of all.

Clue: Our ability to learn is regulated by how we receive and give Agape Love, the signature aspect of Father God! The underlying precept remains that whenever we choose to open ourselves up, we enable God's Spirit to minister the Original Truths of the Gospel to our inward Reborn human spirit so that we can now see a new 'vista' of truth that we would have never seen otherwise.

The First part is to think about and compare the reality and possibilities God's Word will show you as time goes by with the

---

61   See 1 Kings 18:21; Psa. 20,46,91, 94:20; 95:6; 118:8; Prov. 29:25; Dan. 2:44,45; 4:24-27; 7:13-28; Matt. 6:9-13; Luke 12:32; 19:12-15; 22:29; John 18:36; Phil. 3:20; Col. 1:13; Heb. 12:28; James 4:1-8; 1 John 2:15 17

62   Mark 3:3,4

63   Matt. 10:14; 16:21-26; 18:2-10; 19:13,14; Mark 10:13-16; Luke 9:23-26; 18:16,17

"humdrum" false reality of the world's propaganda that is saturated with *Humanism.*[64]

The Second part is learning to overcome your fears by accentuating your focus on your Faith in God, which neutralizes the false reality of the world and resets the True Reality of God which will eventually lead to your Home and to the True Doctrines and Practices of Original Christianity as Jesus Taught at the beginning! However, to fail to love the Truth as Scripture requires, has dire consequences![65]

The Third part is to faithfully follow through with receiving and righteously employing the gifts and abilities That God's Spirit grants to every True Believer who obeys Jesus Christ. Having done so, they will fulfill God's Purpose as promised in the Scriptures.[66]

2. Not only that, it seems as though many "Christian people" today are just 'going through the motions' of life, not really understanding what they read in Scripture or what they experience. It is like they were "in a fog" where they act like automatons, only believing what they are told by 'the authorities.' No, they are not thinking for themselves like they should! The truth is that "religions" of any type are vain, useless trappings of man, providing no peace or deliverance from evil or the monotony of their lackluster lives. The undeniable tragic truth underlying it all is that because they have been wrongly catechized by religious leaders who should know better, they have become slaves of the world. Thus they are 'puppets on a string of lies' ever since childhood, thinking they can "serve two masters" concurrently, which Jesus taught was impossible. They practice bald-faced Idolatry because they are essentially taught the false doctrine of worshiping the Baal, which is now being redefined for being the state, their actual "god," not the True God of the Bible they vainly claim to worship! Of course, the source of that "whopper" is Satan, the "god of this world" that has blinded the minds of naive "Christians" to believe a lie, thereby keeping in darkness, preventing them from seeing the "Light of the

64   Matt. 13:10-15, 37-46,52; Rom. 8:1-11
65   John 1:12-18; 8:12, 31-36, 39-47; 14:6; 16:13-15; 18:36,37; Rom. 1:16-32; 2:7-11; 2 Cor. 4:1-7; Gal. 1:6-12; 2:1-6; 3:1-7; 4:1-19; Eph. 4:1-16; 6:10-14; 2 Thess. 2:3-13; 1 Tim. 2:4,5; 6:3-12; 2 Tim. 2:15-26; 3:7-9; 4:1-8; Heb. 10:26-39
66   Luke 24:49; Acts 2:33-39; 3:19; Rom. 4:13-20; 2 Cor. 1:20; Gal. 3:14-29; 4:28; Eph. 1:13; 2:12-14; 3:6-13; Heb.6:12-17; 9:11-15; 10:36-39; 2 Pet. 1:4

Glorious Gospel of Jesus Christ" that could deliver them IF they only would obey the Truth![67]

3. Again, I ask: "Christian, Do you know who you are?" Unfortunately, most "professing Christians" are totally oblivious to what that actually means. Most utterly fail to realize that truth, even though many have had a "spiritual rebirth experience" in the past, but over the years they have drifted away from Christ and have "lost their first love," assuming they even had it to start with! The Truth taught in Scripture is that all true Christian Believers belong to a very special Heavenly-based Kingdom which is governed by a set of Rules that is totally different from the world. God's Rules that are found in the *New Covenant* describes a unique and powerful way of living and dealing with evil and problems that is vastly different from all humanistic "rationales" and schemes that always fail to solve anything. Jesus's Teachings form the Foundation of this Way of Living and all the Early Apostles concur that this Way is the only way that works![68]

The Bible describes this amazing Kingdom, which started in Old Testament times with certain key individuals whom God knew that Trusted God's Promises. Because they Trusted God, God became the center and governor of their lives: Job, Abraham, Isaac and Jacob, whom God renamed Israel, the father of the Twelve Tribes. In all these and many others we read about in Scripture, one aspect stands out in contrast to all other groups of people on earth: They recognized God for being the only Living God and they trusted His Word, guiding their entire lives by it. The writer of Hebrews reiterates the high points.[69]

Jesus said that "Thy Kingdom has come; Thy Will must be done, on earth, (just) as it is in Heaven" and "My Kingdom is not of this world, therefore, My servants do not fight (like the world does)." Neither do you, IF you are a true Christian. Yes, only one Living God exists and

---

67   Matt. 6:9-13, 22-24; Luke 11:33-36; 16:13; John 18:36,37; Acts 5:29-32; Rom. 1:16-32; 2 Cor. 4:3-7; 11:12-15; 2 Thess. 2:3-12

68   Matt. 5-7; Luke 6-12; John 1-21; Rom. 8; James 1:5-8; 4:1-8; 1 John 2:15-17; Rev. 2:1-7; 3:14-22

69   Gen. 15:6; Ex. 3-15; Deut. 4,7,8,11,12; Josh. 2,24; Ruth 1:16-18; 1 Sam. 2:1-10; 1 Chr. 17; 2 Chr. 7; Neh. 9; Various Psalms; Isa. 2,4,6,12, 28-30, 42-46; Jer. 2-18, 31; Ezek. 3,18,33-36; Dan. 2,3,6; Mark 3:4; Luke 6-12; John 5:24-30; 6:27-63; 7:15-18; 8:12,31-58; 10:1-16; 11:25,26; 1 Cor. 1:17-2:16; Gal. 1:6-12; 2:16-4:19; Eph. 1-4; Phil. 1-4; Col. 1-3; 1 Tim. 2:4,5; 6:3-12; 2 Tim. 1:7-2:26; Heb. 1-12

God has designated His sole Son Jesus Christ as Legate and beneficiary to Rule on earth. Only One True God exists and His Legate teaches clearly that you are unable to get Peace or Liberty by killing other people: Only One man can make you Free, Jesus Christ! Jesus is the only Savior from evil in all venues and "Death is nothing to fear IF you have Faith."[70]

V. True Liberty issues from the Precept of *Redemption, * which includes the associated areas of "Spiritual Rebirth" and Resurrection, both which connect to our true Identity for being Citizens of the *Kingdom of Heaven.*

These principles form the basis of our True Nationhood, that is, being aware of "Whom we are" *In Christ,* our only King, Lord and Master! This Fundamental Truth regarding True Christianity flies in the face of the false teachings of *Determinism* which falsely teaches that earthly kings are our overlords, leading Christians into defacto slavery, when God's Supreme Word tells us much differently! Compare Scripture with Scripture carefully. Then, Believe God's Word for being Truth and you will see that you have been lied to by religious leaders you thought you could trust.[71]

A. What other aspects are integral parts of God's Kingdom that we must observe and practice?

1. The issue of Holiness is central to *(the Doctrine of) Sanctification.* The spiritual precept is that our body is God's Temple and that God

---

70 Psa. 2,110; Isa. 42-46, 53; Matt. 5:38-48; 6:9-13; 17:5,6; John 8:12, 31-36; 18:36,37; Phil. 3:20; 1 Tim. 2:5; 2 Tim. 1:7-4:18

71 Matt. 5:38-48; 6:9-13, 22-24; 26:47-54; Mark 3:4; Luke 2:34,35,49; 9:49-56; 11:33- 36; 16:13; John 1:1-18; 3:3-36; 4:14-24; 6:27-63; 7:15-18; 8:31-36; 10:1-16; 14:6- 17:26; 18:36,37; Acts 4:12-20; 5:29-32; 7:48-59; 17:24-31; 20:26-38; 26:12-18; 28:22; Rom. 1:16-32; 12:9-21; Gal. 1:6-12; 2:16-4:19; Eph. 2:13,14; Phil. 3:3,20; Col. 1:13-16; 2 Thess. 2:3- 12; Heb. 11:12-16 *See also the papers entitled (the 2 part series) Authority and Conscience, The Christian Epiphany, (the 3 part series) Christianity Versus Religion, Divergent Belief Systems, Do You Truly Know and Believe the Complete Gospel of Jesus Christ, Every Believer can Independently know the Truth of Scripture, God's Kingdom is a Whole New World, the 'Higher Laws of God' that unify both Scripture and Doctrine, (the 2 part series) How should we then live, the Kingdom of Heaven is the Highest form of Civilization, Looking Through the Lens of Jesus Christ, Major Missing Aspects of the Original Christian Gospel, One Covenant for All, the Price of Living for Jesus, Principles of Fulfilment Theology, Psychotic Hypocrisy, Serious Problems in Doctrine and practice still exist in many modern churches and True Liberty is in Christ Alone*

is very protective about *His Temple.* Indeed, Scripture tells us that "anyone who defiles God's Temple will be destroyed." This shows us the degree to which God is dedicated to this end! According to God's Word, defiling comes from any type of contamination, be it in body, soul or spirit.[72]

2. Let us now catalog the specific areas of sin that greatly diminish our dedication to Jesus Christ in all three sectors of our being, Spirit, Soul and Body:

A) Idolatry is false worship of any type, which is defined in Scripture as the worship of anything except the One, True Living God. This sin stems from man's believing Satan's original lie that someone could be "their own 'god.'"

The primary idol in modern times is the "repackaged form of worshiping the Baal." Namely, it can be proven that many "Professing Christians" are presently committing Idolatry by their defacto worship of a worldly Nation or State along with its attendant symbols, such as flags, politicians and the military, all of which are regarded for being Saviors, instead of Christ! Indeed, Jesus specifically tells us that our Freedom (Liberty) comes directly from God via our *Faith. * This precept derives from the principle of *Passover, * in which God's original people were delivered from slavery in Egypt. Any 'interloper' who presumes to substitute a 'phony god' or worldly "kingdom" in the place of God for being the 'Savior' is universally condemned by God along with their deluded followers![73]

B. Sexual sins such as fornication and adultery also affect all three parts of our being since God also allies this sin with idolatry.[74]

C. Greed and selfish ambition both arise from the same source, with man vainly thinking that he could "be his own independent source." Again, the seeds of Idolatry have borne fruit here also.

---

72   John 2:19-22; Acts 7:48; 17:24-31; 2 Cor. 6:14-7:1

73   1 Sam. 15:22,23; 1 Kings 18:21; Psa. 96:5; 106:7 ff.; 115:1 ff.; Isa. 2:1 ff.; 44:6-20; 45:15-23; 46:1,2; 56:9-57:13; Jer. 7:1 ff.; 10:1-10; 17:5-10; Ezek. 6:4,5,13; 14:3-7; 18:30-32; 21:24-27; 22:1 ff.; 23:37-39; 33:10-30; 36:16-32; 37:20-24; Hos. 4:17; 14:8,9; Mic. 3:1 ff.; Zech. 13:1-9; 1 Cor. 10:14-21; Gal. 5:20; 1 John 5:21

74   Ex. 20:14; Deut. 5:18; Jer. 3:8,9; 7:1-11; 13:27; 23:9-14; Ezek. 16:15 ff.; Matt. 5:27; 15:19; 19:18; Gal. 5:19; 2 Pet. 2:14

D. Materialism and 'power-mongering,' along with obsessive desire for "entertainments" and diversions like spectator sports are the predictable results, however, no amount of material possessions, power over others or entertainments could ever satisfy the "God-shaped void" inside their souls!

B. Review Summary: In view of all these above things it must be acknowledged that God's Laws are there for your protection because Idolatry of any type surreptitiously destroys from within by supplanting our worship of God with Satanically inspired falsehoods!

Yes, "Satan is alive and well on planet earth" and is assiduously working in the modern world, redefining Idolatry. Yes, Satan has revived it, including some very well camouflaged forms and characteristics!

Know this: God's attitude toward idols has not changed However, God's People need to know that the "rules of engagement" have been redefined by Jesus Christ's *New Covenant* which teaches us how to deal with evil without using any humanistic methodology.

Yes, as Christians, we must employ Christ's Way to deal with those who have been ensnared by Idols, using the magnificent power of God's Agape Love as the New Testament shows us.[75]

Yes, Scripture tells us that, in the end, God will deal directly with the evil into which Satan has led the Nations, and they will be destroyed.[76]

C. Another important part of our Identity *In Christ* has to be our Love for the lost. Evangelism is also a very important element of the Complete Gospel which defines God's Love for being Universal in scope with no exceptions!

So, this means that All True Christians share God's Love for all sinners. This also becomes part of their true Position regarding our Love for enemies, individual, group or national!

---

75   Matt. 5:38-48; Rom. 5:1-5
76   Ezek. 20-23, 28-32; Dan. 2:44,45; Luke 24:44-49; Acts 17:24-31; 2 Thess. 2:3-12; 2 Pet. 3:7; Rev. 11:15-19

We mistakenly think that we "have all the time in the world" but God only allows us a brief time to reach the crucial point of *Repentance* to find our way back to the Father's Love, just like the "Prodigal Son."[77]

Are you willing to look past the confusion and darkness of wrong catechisms into the bright light of sincerity and Truth that is in Jesus's Teachings? Time is running out and I hope you will choose life soon enough! So, if you become aware of these evident truths, let us know this: "Blessed are those whose hearts are set on Pilgrimage." Of course, Scripture teaches that the True Pilgrimage of Christians is an underlying message that tells us that we are "coming out of many foreign lands into the Kingdom of Heaven" where we govern our lives by heavenly standards "On earth as it is in Heaven." Do you share this ideal? "Let us also be grateful for receiving a Kingdom that cannot be shaken." Do you believe this?[78]

Yes, "The Law of the Spirit of Life in Christ Jesus has set you free from the law of sin and death." Jesus alone has the Power to Save and Liberate from evil and God's Spirit shows us the "Deep things of God."[79]

Consider Ezra the Priest's speech to the survivors of Israel's Babylonian captivity recorded by Nehemiah. It is in this speech that Ezra encourages the people trust God and the "the joy of the Lord is your strength."[80]

Comparing history, we can see an amazing parallel between the history of Israel and its long period of apostasy and if we observe the history of the church, we can observe that, by enlarge, it has taken a similar track. Human nature, of course, lies behind the similarity because people always seek "the line of least resistance." The Scripture is quite clear: Enjoying the benefits of God's Promises requires adherence to God's Rules, to which every believer must exercise constant vigilance to prevent falling back into the trap of using humanistic ways. So, you can deduce the result that has taken place: Over the course of many years, just like Israel had done in the past that Paul had warned about,

---

77   Matt. 5-7; Luke 6-12, 15
78   Psa. 84:4; Dan. 2:44,45; 7:15-27; Matt. 6:9-13; Heb. 12:28; Rev. 11:15 f.
79   Eccl. 3:11; John 8:31-36; 11:25,26; Acts 4:12; Rom. 8:1,2; 1 Cor. 2:9-16; 2 Cor. 3:17,18
80   Neh. 8:10

the church has sunk deeper and deeper into the abyss of apostasy. The church's apostasy has eventually resulted in its defacto <u>Captivity to the world</u>, in stages, beginning with John's depiction of the "Seven Churches of Asia Minor" in which only two of seven churches were given a "passing grade."

A much more serious declension occurred in the fourth century consequent to the Synod of Nicea in 324-325 AD.[81]

As you carefully compare the Scriptures describing Israel's apostate history with that of the church, you can find many common aspects that link the two histories together. Of course, that reveals the reason why we have the Old Testament in our Bibles. Paul's admonitions in the letters to Romans and Corinthians confirm this.[82]

Yes, you may not want to believe it, but nonetheless the modern church is languishing "in Captivity" to worldly idolatry and unbelief. <u>If you realize this truth and admit this condition</u>, then you can begin the *Repentance* process and reclaim the original Truths of the Gospel that were taught by Jesus Christ and the Early Apostles. However, if you continue to believe the false doctrines of apostate organizations, especially the "Calvinistic" dictates of *Determinism* and blindly cling to "religious catechisms" you will lose that opportunity and thereby remain outside of God's Righteousness. That, of course, is how apostasy, especially the heady Idolatry that stems from nation worship, gains control, overriding the sensitive truths of original Christianity! Now, then consider the many Scriptures warning Israel and the content of Nehemiah's penitent Prayer calling for Israel's Repentance and compare it to God's admonition to Solomon in Second Chronicles and Jesus's diatribes against the Pharisees.[83]

The harsh truth remains that false doctrine is an insidious thing, especially breeding a 'false sense of security' that comes from "automatically" believing what others have taught us. In many ways it acts like the 'spirit of suicide'. The attitudes into which many 'professing

---

81   See Matt. 24; Luke 21; 1 Cor. 10 *See also the book Spiritual Guidelines for Restoration, "Historical Review" Section and the papers entitled Emmanuel (1), Emmanuel 2*
82   Rom. 15:4; 1 Cor. 10
83   Ex. 32:9; 33:3; Deut. 9:13; 10:16; 2 Chr. 7:14; 30:8; Neh. 9; Matt. 23; John 9:39-41; Acts 7:48-60 Also, Ibid. Fn. #81 *and the paper entitled the Fallacies of Determinism*

Christians' have slipped have literally caused a mental psychosis to persist among most mainstream Christians.

Indeed, most of them have gotten that way because they have essentially "assumed" what religious leaders have taught without question. Bad choice!

However, that is a very dangerous thing to do! Living the True Christian life requires our maintaining a daily personal relationship to God in which you must independently think about what you are believing and doing. If you fail to do this, blindly assuming what other have taught you, you will reach a point where you think you are O.K.. Yet, you will eventually become "locked into," that is "brainwashed," into a particular mind set from which you are unable to see any other point of view! Unfortunately, "religious catechisms" inculcate a dependent mind set which has a negative side-effect which views all others who espouse different beliefs for being "enemies," alias, the "fortress mentality." Consequently, people who think like that and have been ensnared by false doctrine always find it very difficult to change. The issue of Identity comes into play here: People naturally want to 'belong to something' and when they think they 'belong' they become "one-sided" in their attitudes. "Religion" exploits this trap with alacrity, however, True Christianity categorically excludes this aspect because of Jesus's specific teachings about living by *Agape* Love which requires us to have compassion and concern about others, regardless of whom they are![84]

VI. Knowing the difference between "respect" and "Trust," Jesus shows us the Truth of the Complete Gospel which is the only way to resolve our conflicts. This truth highlights the pan-biblical teaching that humans are created to Trust in God and not man.

---

84   Matt. 5-7; Luke 6-12 *See also the papers entitled A Writer's Commentary, An Analysis of the Causes and Effects of Apostasy, Are You Sure what you Believe and Practice is Truly Christian Doctrine, Authority and Conscience (a 2 part series), Christianity Versus Religion (a 3 part series), Conditions for Salvation, the Dangers of Conformity, Divergent Belief Systems, Every believer can independently know the truth of Scripture, the Fallacies of Determinism, God's Definition of Salvation, God's Universal Attitude Test, Only One Savior, Regarding Christ's Headship, A Synopsis of Modern Idolatry among 'professing Christians' and What is Collectivism*

Paul writes the Ephesians, telling them about the most basic precept of the Christian life, that "He (Christ) is our peace, who, with his own body, has broken down the hostile dividing partition separating people."

Indeed, Christ's work on the cross works on the same two 'axes' that illustrate our relationships: The Vertical, between people and God, and the Horizontal, between people at all levels, individual, group and national.

Not only that, All this is true because of Christ's work "God has transferred us from darkness into His Kingdom of Light."

The underlying truth is that Jesus's Way is the only existing pathway of Light, Liberty and Peace which stands in bold contrast to the entire world that is darkened by man's sin and evil. No other way to Life, Liberty, Peace and Salvation exists.[85]

Again notice that no Scripture exists telling us to "trust in man." Indeed, the exact opposite is taught quite clearly! So, why are Christians being taught to trust in the state and to glorify politicians, soldiers and professionals for 'salvation' and 'freedom' when Scripture teaches otherwise?[86]

A. Verily, True Peace and Freedom can only be experienced by observing all the rules, terms and conditions of the *New Covenant* of Jesus Christ.

The main elements are as follows:

- Confession and *Repentance* of *Sin,* including the necessary parts of admission of error and reversal of attitude that God requires for these initial requirements.

These must be in place and continue to be throughout our mortal lives.[87]

---

85 Psa. 49; 119:105,130; Isa. 8:20; 9:1,2,6,7; Luke 1:76-79; 11:33-36; John 1:4,5,7-9; 3:19-21 (Isa. 5:20); 8:12, 31-36; 9:5, 39-41; 12:30-36,46; 18:36,37; Rom. 13:12; 2 Cor. 3:17,18; 4:4-6; Eph. 2:13,14; 5:8; Phil. 3:20; Col. 1:12-16; 2 Tim. 1:7-14; Heb. 11:12-16; 1 Pet. 2:9; 2 Pet. 1:19; 1 John 1:5-10; 2 :9-11,15-17; 3:11-17; 4:7-21

86 Ex. 6:6,7; 14:13,14; Psa. 94:20; 118:8,9; 146:3; Prov. 3:5,6; Isa. 36,37; Jer. 7:4 f.; 10:1 ff.; 17:5-10; Matt. 5:1-12, 38-48; 6:9-15; Luke 1:75-79; John 8:31-36; 2 Cor. 3:17,18; Col. 1:13

87 Eccl. 7:20; Prov. 28:13; Ezek. 18:30; Mark 1:15; Acts 2:38,39; 3:19; 17:24-31; 26:15- 18; Rom. 6:1-7:25

- True *Faith* (Trust) in Christ <u>alone</u> for <u>all venues of deliverance</u> and *Salvation* as they are defined in Scripture:

These are the Physical, spiritual, temporal and eternal.[88]

Our initial experience is God's Spirit's *Regeneration* of the functions of our human spirit: *Communion*and *Intuition.* Following this, we must maintain an <u>ongoing Personal Relationship with God. This includes Worship in spirit and in Truth, "conversational prayer,"</u> ongoing *Repentance* <u>from subsequent sin and "Loving God with all our heart, soul, mind and spirit."</u>[89]

- We must always maintain the healthy attitude that is defined in Scripture as "the Fear of God." As such we must come to know and understand the <u>Reality of God's Power, Love and capability of Judgment for all unrepentant sin.</u>

Also, we must revere Jesus Christ for being our <u>True King who reigns over </u>the entire *Kingdom of Heaven* which includes <u>all aspects regarding the lives of True Christian Believers, commanding our absolutely Total Allegiance in all venues of life: Private and Public.</u>[90]

- A corollary to this is that we do, in a human way, "respect" the positions of authority that Jesus Christ originally created <u>for His use.</u>

Under this rule, to live in a civilized way, we respect and submit to all "duly constituted authority" that upholds the good and restrains evil, which is like the respect we accorded to our parents when we were growing up. God's Word teaches that respect and honor comes in <u>Two different levels:</u> One, the overarching level of <u>God's superior Authority is mentioned in Scripture as "the higher power"</u> and Two, the secondary level of human authority that is <u>Provisionally Delegated by God,</u> being dependent upon their obedience to Christ. However, we

---

88   *See the papers entitled The Christian Epiphany, Conditions for Salvation, The Conditions of God's Protection for Believers, God's Definition of Salvation and True Liberty is in Christ Alone*

89   Matt. 5-7; 22:36,37; John 4:14-24 *See also the papers entitled The Dynamics of Christian Discipleship, The Higher Laws of God, The Spiritual Laws of Revival and Spirituality and Worship: A Study of Worship*

90   Job 28:28; Psa. 2:1 ff.; 110:1 ff.; 111:10; Prov. 1:7: 9:9,10; Eccl. 12:13,14; Isa. 33:6; 42:1-46:13; Jer. 7:4 ff.; 10:1-0; 17:5-10; Mal. 2-4; Matt. 10:16-42; Luke 2:34,35; John 18:36,37; Acts 28:22; Rom. 1:18-32; 8:1 ff.; 1 Cor. 3:11-17; 11:23-32; 2 Cor. 11:12-15; Gal. 1:6-12; Phil. 3:3,20,21; Heb. 10-12

must know that whenever man's power infringes on God's or conflicts with the Teachings of God's Living Word, Jesus Christ, this provisional authority is null and void since all positions of legitimate authority were originally created to Serve Jesus Christ. Consequently, this also means that no governmental agency or power of man possesses "automatic" authority over Christians!

Contrariwise, God holds all rebel or satanic authorities which arise to refuse, resist or thwart Jesus Christ's Lordship responsible and will judge them![91]

However, for the True Christian, any respect we may have for human power that is allowed by God must never be allowed to interfere with our God-ordained responsibility to Honor God much more than (above and beyond) that which we have for any earthly ruler! Yes, know this: In every instance where human authorities conflict with God's greater overarching *Authority, * "we must obey God rather than man." This is the very important part of Christian Doctrine we call "The Law of Godly Civil Disobedience."[92]

Mark God's Word: If anyone has taught you differently from this, they are cursed for doing this because they have essentially betrayed Christ and delivered you to the enemy of our souls and the enslaving power of Idolatry which serves the state as a god instead of God. Yes, "patriotism" is tantamount to Idolatry for it interposes corrupted authority above God in the eyes of people! Remember that God's Word says that "God's People are not reckoned to be a part of the Nations" but we are a Holy People separated unto God to serve Him alone![93]

Long ago, Elijah the Prophet faced this awful situation in his confrontation with the "Prophets of Baal" on Mount Carmel. Since you have free will, you must also make the choice: "Why do you vacillate between two opinions?: If the Baal (the territorial principality that controls all the Nations of the world)" is the god, then serve him. But, IF God is your God, then you must be Holy and serve Him only.

---

91   Matt. 4:1-10; Luke 4:1-8; Acts 5:29-32; Eph. 6:10-12; Col. 1:15,16; Rev. 13:1 ff. *See the 2 part series of papers entitled Authority and Conscience*

92   Josh. 2; Dan. 3,6; Acts 4:12-20; 5:29-32; Eph. 1:15-23; 6:10-18; Heb. 11:24-31

93   Lev. 19:2; 20:7,26; Numbers 23:9,10; Deut. 7:6; 14:2,21; Josh. 24:14-19; 1 Sam. 2:5- 10; 1 Kings 18:21; Psa. 2:6; Isa. 6, 43-46; Matt. 4:1-10; 16:21-26; Mark 8:34-38; Luke 9:23-26, 49-56; John 8:12-58; 9:39-10:18, 27,28; 12:23-36; 14:15-27; 15:1-16:4; 17:3 ff.; 18:36,37

Jesus essentially reiterated this challenge in the Sermon on the Mount. He reiterated that holy uniqueness of God's People and their separation from the world to Pilate also.[94]

- We must always fear God rather than man or circumstance. This follows the precept that must "discern the difference between 'respect' and Trust" regarding our ongoing protection and salvation by God.[95]

Scripture never teaches us to trust in man! So, religious leaders teaching "nationalist propaganda" exalting the state do so because they are part of the world.

Remember God's warnings. The world will hate you no matter how hard you try to placate it! God will judge those "false prophets" that have infiltrated the church for what they have done in deceiving people!

Remember also that it is recorded in two Gospels that Jesus did not contest Satan's claim that he controlled all the kingdoms of the world. Not only that, John tells us not to love the world! Not only that, if American "So-called Christians" cannot see that obvious truth, they are deceived and are holding to false doctrines that are tantamount to Idolatry in God's eyes![96]

- Think: Where is any contextual Scripture which would legitimate trusting in the power of the state and military for 'salvation' and 'freedom?'

No, you will not find it because that would constitute idolatry, repackaged by Satan's minions by the deliberate misconstruction and misinterpretation of Scripture to "make it signify" something totally different from God's intention in the original. Yes, Scripture is painfully clear in teaching that only one God exists and that God is well able to save His people in every context conceivable: Temporal and physical or spiritual and eternal! However, like everything else in the *Kingdom of Heaven,* you must believe that this is true to receive that benefit! God

---

94   1 Kings 18:21; Matt. 6:24; Luke 16:13; John 18:36,37; Rom. 12:1-3; Gal. 6:14-16

95   Psa. 3:8; 4:8; 9:9,10; 37:1 ff.; 44:1 ff.; 46:1 ff.; 91:1 ff.; 94:20; 111:10; 115:1 ff.; 118:8,9; 146:1 ff.; Prov. 3:5,6; 14:12, 26; 16:25; 29:25; Matt. 19:16-42; 16:23-26

96   Matt. 4:1-10; Mark 8:36; Luke 4:1-8; John 15:18-16:4; 17:5-16; 18:36,37; Rom. 12:1-3; 1 Cor. 1:17-2:16; 3:18,19; 2 Cor. 4:3-6; Gal. 1:4,6-12; 4:3,4-16; 6:14; Eph. 6:11,12; Col. 2:6- 23; 2 Thess. 2:3-12; Heb. 10:26-12:29; James 4:4; 2 Pet. 2,3; 1 John 2-5

considers all types of "Double-mindedness" for being unbelief and no unbeliever can receive anything from God other than conviction of their sin. Among others, the imagery of the *Passover*plainly conveys this truth.

Case in point: Many unbelievers slavishly quote the first few verses of Romans thirteen, thinking that this legitimates their worship of the state. Wrong answer! Essentially, the truth is that King James the first deliberately fostered the mistranslation of the Greek word *Tagma* in verse one to be the English word "ordain," whereas the truth is that *Tagma* means only "to tolerate, allow or to permit" which is under the overarching "Doctrine of the Sovereignty of God and the Free Will of man." Of course, their fallacious doctrine is part of a widely-held system of belief called "Predestination," A.k.a., *Determinism,* which is an offshoot of "Platonism" and "Aristotelian logic" that teach that "God" is 'way out there in the distance' and does not get involved in human affairs.

Yet, that is a bald-faced falsehood that is founded on paganism![97]

Obviously the statement "no authority exists other than that is 'ordained' by God" cannot be true unless you correctly change the words 'to ordain' to 'tolerate,' permit' or 'allow' because Jesus Himself told us that Satan exercises authority over the entire "world system." Paul also wrote clearly about "Satanic authorities" using the same Greek word, *Exousia*, in Ephesians six.

• The Scriptures plainly teach that God alone is the source and grantor of all types of true salvation and true freedom.

Certainly, Scripture never teaches us to commit idolatry like the world does because all those beliefs issue from a common root: The "Deification of man." This means that all the world system operates under the satanic delusion that man could be 'his own god.' This exposes their ludicrous assertion regarding what they mistakenly call 'freedom': That "X" number of soldiers killing "Y" number of "enemies" would 'make others free!'[Sic.] Consequently, they are literally "stone blind" to Satan's deception. Indeed, basing 'salvation' on brute force being inflicted on others only produces a very sophisticated type of Slavery

---

97   *See the two part series of papers entitled Authority and Conscience," the 3 part series Christianity Versus Religion and The Fallacies of Determinism*

that must be reinforced and "redefined" by a continual blitz (a 'snow job') of patriotic propaganda! Folks, "wake up and smell the coffee" for that is the source of the "so-called American dream."[98]

B. It is very important to observe the Precept of Christ's Lordship.

Yes, Jesus Christ is <u>Always First</u> and <u>Above All</u>. Consequently, whenever man's laws, policies or traditions conflict with God's Word, True Believers must "Obey God rather than man." Yes, it is very important that we observe this rule because True Christians "are not of (attached to) this world" for, like Abraham, <u>"We look for a (new) country whose Builder and Maker is God."</u> This primary truth is based on our knowledge that <u>every earthly state</u> is controlled by Satan's minions (the "New World Order")[99]

Moreover, you should intrinsically know that Jesus would <u>never have advocated patriotism</u>, for in that day, partisan patriotism was precisely the agenda of the Zealots, of whom Barabbas was the leader! Notice also that it was at the instigation of the <u>Jewish religious leaders</u> that the crowd was manipulated by <u>nationalistic propaganda</u> to reject Jesus and to call for the avowed <u>murderer Barabbas</u>, vainly believing that he would "save them!" Of course, that would also mean that the main body of Jews had <u>abandoned their *Faith* in God and had turned to worshiping idols, just like the world!</u> Tragically, most modern Christians also place themselves in the same position by the world-serving beliefs in which they have been instilled by their religious leaders. Essentially, like ancient Israel, they have also abandoned any trust in God that they may have had by deliberately placing their trust in man's power, the

---

98   Psa. 3:8; 4:8; 9:9,10; 83:11; 94:20; 118:8,9; Prov. 29:25; Isa. 43-46; Matt. 4:1-10; 10:16-42; 12:30; Luke 4:1-8; 11:33-36; John 8:31-36; 18:36,37; 2 Cor. 3:17,18; Gal. 4:4-9,16; 1 John 5:18-21 *See also the papers entitled A Biblical Disclosure of Antichrist, the Basis of Liberty, the 4 part series Christian Guidelines for Spiritual Warfare, the Dangers of Conformity, Destiny and Free Will, Divergent Belief Systems, Do you Truly Believe that God is Real, Examining the Original Imperatives of the Christian Gospel, From Whence do Lies come, God's Universal Attitude Test, the 2 part series How Should We Then Live, Living the Complete Gospel, Looking Through the Lens of Jesus Christ, One Covenant for All, Principles of Fulfillment Theology, Retaining our Freedom requires Knowing and Applying the Truth, True Liberty is in Christ Alone and What is Collectivism*

99   Num. 23:9; Josh. 2:1-7,14-18; Daniel 3,6; Matt. 4:1-10; 6:9-13; Luke 4:1-8; John 18:36,37; Acts 4:12-20; 5:29-32; 2 Cor. 4:3-7; 10:3-7; Phil. 3:3,20,21; Col. 1:13-16; Heb. 11:13-16,24-31; James 1:5-8; 4:1-9; 1 John 2:15-17

"splintered rod of 'Egypt' and the "Stumbling block of their iniquity" before their faces, loving the world and 'finding fault' with God![100]

C. Think about it: In every "deep event" there are many factors that lead up to it: Some are apparent, but others are hidden. The worst part is that worldly "authorities" are acting as agents of Satan (Antichrist) under the veil of secrecy, have undermined the stability and structure of 'civilization' to gain power, control, amassing huge profits for the elite. Their agenda is to "plant fear" in the minds of the masses, producing doubt, distrust and "failed Expectations." Of course, all this is prophesied in Scripture to happen during the period called "The Great Tribulation." (GTP) These events parallel what happened to Israel in the wilderness when the twelve spies returned with horror stories about the giants. The masses reacted emotionally, fearing the loss of their children. I have been seeing this same attitude among most modern Christians! Solomon wrote that "the fear of man is a snare." Satan does this by planting "false ideas and images in your mind." Know this: Because God plays by the rules and you are responsible for your thoughts and actions, If you do not Discern these for what they are you will be enslaved by sin, the world and Satan! Contrariwise, God is totally reliable, but this only works for you IF you Believe what God's Word says! Remember that fear of loss is the path to Darkness. "God is Light and there is no darkness in Him."[101]

You should also know that this is why Christ's Gospel tells us to mentally "let go" of everything you fear to lose and Trust God implicitly thereafter! Of course, that is because succumbing to fear cuts you off from God and points you toward destruction.

The only way to reverse this situation is this: You must first Repent of that sin of unbelief and reaffirm your *Faith* in God![102]

---

100   Jer. 2:1-13; 10:1-10; 17:5-10; Ezek. 7:1-12,19; 14:3-7; 18:30; 20:13 ff.; 21:24-27; 23:37-39; Hos.10:12,13; Mal. 2; Matt. 10:32,33; 11:28-30; 23:1 ff.; Mark 3:3,4; Luke 11:33-36; 12:8-10; Rom. 8:1-11; 2 Thess. 2:3-12; Rev. 2:1-7, 12-3:6; 3:14-22 *See the papers Destiny and Free Will, Fallacies of Determinism and the 2 part series How Should We then Live?*

101   Numbers 13,14; Prov. 10:29; 19:23; 28:18; 29:25; 30:5; Hosea 14:9; Matt. 6:22-24; 10:16-39; Luke 11:33-36; John 1:1-18; 8:12; 12:35,36, 46; Rom. 13:12; 1 Cor. 4:5; 2 Cor. 4:3-6; Col. 1:12,13; Heb. 10-12; 1 John 1

102   Matt. 16:21-26; Luke 9:23-26; John 12:23-26; Acts 3:19

D. Let us clarify the fundamental difference between God's Kingdom of Light and the entire world system. Ask yourself the question: Do you know why Jesus did not approve of Barabbas and the Zealots (Viz., patriotism)? It should be obvious, but religious leaders have literally ruined the gospel by their "mixing in worldly propaganda" in their misplaced desire to be "accepted by the world." You never will, so get used to it. Consequently, the problem with many "professing Christians" is that they have not thought through what the Truth means in terms of their daily life. Therefore, they fail to see the truth about human nature as God sees it!

God's Word, the *New Covenant,* says that all humans are sinners. And no "good people" exist in God's eyes. Moreover, as true Christians, we are unable to make substantive distinctions, labeling people for being "good" or "bad." According to God's Word, a person can only make moral assessments discerning right from wrong. However, because people's obsession is to "make things right by force," the outcome always ends up with hatred which, in turn leads to some type of Judgment that rationalizes killing! This brings us to the most offensive part of *Humanism *: Their approval of killing other people they "label as criminals and enemies."

Know this: In God's eyes no "good murderers" exist! No matter what the rationale in man's opinion, in the *New Covenant* of Christ, all murder is evil and comes from Darkness and never from Light, regardless of whether it is in war, capital punishment or abortion. Verily, all intentional murder arises from hate or fear and the *New Covenant* universally condemns all who knowingly kill. God considers hate for being equivalent to murder and "No murderer can enter Heaven."

Not only that, God's overall attitude about this has not changed since Cain killed Abel. God even forbad David to build the Temple because "he had waged great wars and shed much blood." Beware of the sin of *Blood guiltiness.*[103]

---

103   Gen. 4; Psa. 32, 51; Matt. 5:38-48; 6:22-24; Luke 6:35-49; 9:51-56; 11:33-36; John 5:19-47;
        7:24; 8:31-58; 9:39-41; 14:6-17:26; 18:36,37; Rom. 8:1 ff; Gal. 1:6-12; 2:16-21; 3:11- 4:20;
        5:1, 14-26; 6:14-16; Phil. 3:3,7-21; 1 Tim. 6:3-16; 2 Tim. 1:7-14; Heb. 10:26-39; 1 John 3:7-15
        See also the paper entitled The Nature of Man and the book Basic Christian Doctrine

VII. Only one True Freedom exists.

That is the Truth of Christ's Gospel: The only <u>authentic source of true Liberty and Freedom is *In Christ* Alone!</u>

All others are fakes: Cheap imitations of Satan that dominate the world of nations and which are in reality nothing but <u>sophisticated types of Slavery based upon human devices and control grids which inevitably condone and practice violence and murder.</u> Indeed, anyone who believes that way stands under God's Judgment. Not only that, God's Word teaches and also the writer of the hymn *Stand Up, Stand Up for Jesus,* George Duffield agrees: That "the arm of flesh will fail you; you dare not trust your own." Also, know this:

All the main precepts governing *Salvation* connect to the great Doctrines of Scripture that define its parameters: *Passover,* *Redemption* (Viz., Christ's Purchase and Ownership of all True Believers) and *Atonement.*

You must know also that because we Fear and Love God more than man or circumstance, the Word of God specifically teaches that the True Christian's venue of conflict is <u>in the spirit and not the flesh!</u>[104]

Christians need to learn to appreciate <u>just how marvelous, incomparable and wonderful God's *Agape* Love truly is!</u> Not only that, we must also recognize that God's Love can be transferred to us via the Holy Spirit, so that we have no excuse not to obey and follow what Christ Taught for being <u>the Truth!</u>[105]—

<u>God's Love is so incredibly unique and special</u> because <u>no other type of love can compare with it. Verily, experiencing God's *Agape* Love is the pinnacle of the Christian Life</u> and anyone who has received it cannot live without it. This is true because all the other Genuine Characteristics of the Authentic Christian Life issue from this Godly Love that cannot be counterfeited! Not only that, it is *Agape* Love that is the source of the Christian's "Edge" and supreme advantage that

---

104   Ex. 6:6,7; 14:13,14; Deut. 3:22; 4:10; 5:29; 6:2-13,24; 10:12,20; 1 Sam. 2:1-10; 25:29; Psa. 1-5 ,9,17,20,23,31,34,37,44,46,51, 73,84, 111, 115, 118; Prov. 1:7; 2:5; 3:7; 9:10; 10:27; 14:26,27; 15:33; 16:6; 19:23; 29:25; Isa. 33:6; Matt. 5:38-48; 11:25-30; John 3:36; 8:31-58; 18:36,37; Acts 2:38,39; 3:19; Rom. 8:1-11; 12:1 ff.; 2 Cor. 3:17,18; 4:3-7; 10:14-18; 11:12-15; Gal. 5:1; Eph. 6:10-12

105   John 15:1-17; 21:15-17; Rom. 5:1-5; Gal. 5:22,23; 1 John 4:7 ff.

empowers us to literally "Overcome evil with Good!" The flesh profits nothing.[106]

So, always keep in mind the contrast between "flesh and spirit." Indeed, One of the most important actions we need to take early in our Christian experience is to ask God to "sever the motions of our soul from the spirit."

This gives the Believer a powerful internal ability to resist the lies and propaganda of the world and religion. Paul's letter to the Galatians gives us much information on this crucial point of doctrine and experience as did Jesus in His Discourses with the Pharisees.[107]

Unfortunately, most "professing Christians" fail to understand the Truth regarding True Freedom. They are so catechized (brainwashed) into Nation worship by apostate religious leaders that they do not see the ugly reality in which they live and to see "America" for what it truly is: A cleverly disguised sophisticated slave state. Its people, including most "So-called Christians," have been slyly deceived and conditioned to believe that they are "free." However, they have been led into an "invisible cage" by the media's Propaganda machine' through which they are duped to believe lies like telling the masses that the military keeps them 'free.' The deception works like this: One is in the political and military venue where the elite controllers of the "New World Order" teach naive listless people to exalt "heroes" whom they are led to worship as "saviors." Yet, in the end they will be unable to even save themselves! Two, economically, the masses are being stripped of their earnings and substance by the "Federal Reserve System" which is controlled by offshore Global Banking Cartels. Put in place in 1913, this despicable "Trojan Horse" enables banks to expand or contract the money supply at will, thereby creating the vicious cycle of "booms and busts," including the infamous Great Depression! Furthermore, coupled with their pushing of the "Credit purchase system," they have created a nightmare of mass debt which they will use to institute the "Mark of the Beast" as their final 'deathblow' to any liberty that remains.

---

106   John 6:27-63; Rom. 12:9-21; 2 Cor. 10:3-7

107   Luke 2:34,35; John 7:1-24; Rom. 8:1-11; Gal. 1:6-12; 2:19-5:13; Heb. 4:12,13 *See the paper entitled The Spiritual Laws of Revival, Ch. 2, Law #8: "The separation of the soul from the spirit"*

Remember Solomon's warning about "debt slavery." Thirdly, add to all that the "rachet effect" whereby inflation is used to greatly increase income taxes which essentially destroy the middle class. In addition, ballooning sales tax rates grind the poor even further into the dust! Worse yet, people are not being told that a countrywide surveillance net has been put in place with cameras everywhere, virtually eliminating any remaining privacy. The "Coup de Grace" is the Department of Commerce being the issuer of "Birth Certificates." Of course, they do not tell you that all those documents are being used as a database to determine the "lifetime income potential" of every 'citizen-slave' of the system![108]

VIII. Only One Truth Exists: "There is One Lord, One Faith and One Baptism."

Moreover, regardless of how many gather to believe otherwise, Jesus proclaimed "God's Word is Truth and I AM the Way, the Truth and the Life; no one comes to the Father, except by Me and IF you continue in My Word, you will know the Truth and if the Son sets you Free, you are Free Indeed." Yes, God's Living Word plainly teaches us that the Truth will set you Free (that is, if you obey and practice that Truth). Furthermore, nothing or nobody else can grant that benefit! Yes, in the *New Covenant* only One overarching seamless Truth applies that is the Genuine Complete Christian Gospel, the one Gospel that exists.[109]

All other corrupted or 'truncated' versions are condemned by God! Remember this: Although Scripture does teach us to "respect" earthly authority we must acknowledge that God's "Higher Power" trumps all other order, law, policy or tradition of man in every case where these two would conflict. Moreover, mark God's Word right well: The complete Gospel of Christ does not include any attitude or course of action that constitutes 'trusting in man to save!'[110]

---

108   Prov. 22:7 See also the papers entitled True Liberty is in Christ Alone and What is Collectivism?
109   John 8:31-36; 14:6; Gal. 1:6-12; Eph. 4:4
110   Matt. 4:1-10; Luke 4:1-8; 13:32; John 8:12-47; Acts 4:12-20; 5:29-32; Rom. *13:1 (*always know that God is the "Higher Power"); Eph. 6:10-12; 2 Cor. 3:1-4:7; 6:14-18; 10:3-7; 11:12-15; Gal. 1:6-12; Col. 1:15,16

Nor does it approve giving glory to "human saviors": "Politicians, soldiers professionals or religious leaders," regardless of their "positions or functions." Indeed, God originally ordained all the structures of civilization to serve Jesus Christ. However, if they do not, God considers them to be rebels like Satan and cancels their legitimate authority. In any situation, the True Christians' Trust in God's ability to save always takes precedence over that of any agency of man! The watchword in all this is David's bold statement: "I will not fear what man could do to me."[111]

The upshot of all this is that trusting in man is a dangerous and deadly snare of Satan that always leads to Idolatry and the original "Big Lie" of the deification of man: Believing he could be his "own god." The basic precept to which we must always adhere is that only One True Living God exists and that one must Fear God much more than man![112]

Moreover, IF you are a true Christian, you should know by now that IF you truly Trust God you also know that you cannot trust in man without being guilty of Idolatry! Know also that a good maxim is this: Respect is not the same as trust![113]

However unfortunate it may be, we must acknowledge that modern Christians have been very cleverly "Catechized" by corrupt apostate leaders to believe "Half-truths mixed with lies," the worst part of which is their exaltation of the raw power of the military for being their "savior" instead of God! The New Covenant teaches no such *Humanistic* gobbled gook. Jesus even called King Herod a fox, a wily predator which cannot be trusted. Also, Peter exclaimed that "we ought to obey God rather than man." You cannot have it both ways: If the Baal (the symbol of a Nationalistic Principality) is your god, then go and serve him, but if your true object of worship is the Living God,

111 Psa. 3:8; 4:8; 9:9,10; 20:6,7; 27:1-3; 31:1 ff.; 32:7; 34:1 ff.; 37:1 ff.; 40:4; 41:1,2; 43:1-44: 46:1 ff.; 51:1 ff.; 56:4,11,13; 61:1-3; 84:1 ff; 91:1 ff.; 94:20; 115:9-11; 118:8,9; 146:1 ff. ; Prov. 3:5,6; Dan. 3,6; Jer. 5:1-9; 17:5-10; 18:6-12; Matt. 5:38-48; 6:9-15; 23:1 ff.; John 18:36,37; Acts 5:29-32; Rom. 12:9-21; 2 Cor. 6:14-18; 10:3-7; Eph. 6:10-12; 1 John 3:10-15

112 Ex. 6:6,7; 14:13,14; Deut. 4:32-40; 32:3,4,38,39; 1 Sam. 2:1-10; 25:29; 1 Kings 18:21; 2 Chron. 7:14; Job 28:28; Prov. 1:7; 9:10; 29:25; Isa. 33:6; 36-38

113 Psa. 44:1-8 (notice also that, in the *New Covenant* God has translated the venue of war to spiritual warfare); 94:20; 118:8,9; 146:1 ff.; Prov. 29:25; Isa. 42-46; Jer. 7:4-14; 10:1- 10; 17:5-10; Zech. 4:6

then you must worship and serve Him Only! You are unable to do both concurrently! So, have you "Seen the Light" yet?[114]

Remember this Only Jesus Christ is your True Savior in all venues, physical and spiritual! Scripture declares that (eventually) Christ will return to earth in Great Power and "Every knee will bow and every tongue will confess that Jesus Christ is Lord" even though many of those will be the damned who had refused to obey His Commands beforehand. "There is One God and One Mediator between God and man, the man Christ Jesus." "Whoever listens to His Word, listens to the One who Sent Him." "God's Word is a quick and powerful 'two-edged sword,' cutting all the way down to the separation of soul and spirit, and is a Discerner of the thought and intents of the heart." "He (Jesus) IS our Peace, and has broken down the wall of hostility." Do you believe this?[115]

One more thing we all must consider is that our fundamental attitude toward others and their obvious sins must be in accordance with Jesus Christ's Teachings: That is, we must live in *Agape* Love to satisfy God's requirements. Remember the ancient Chinese proverb about dragons: Inevitably, we become like the ones we hate If we veer off into worldly schemes of the 'flesh' that justify hatred and killing, thereby cutting ourselves off from God and Salvation![116]

IX. Beware of any "false certainty" that is based on your past "catechisms" by religious leaders who have "conditioned you" to believe contradictions in doctrine and "half truths mixed with lies in the name of God."

Know this: You can only legitimately say "I will not be moved" IF you Believe the Complete Gospel of Jesus Christ. That is, the Truth that includes all the ramifications of *Agape* Love.

This signifies that you truly have been endued with God's *Agape* Love by the Holy Spirit and have been "spiritually circumcised" by the disciplinary hand of God so that you respond biblically to all

---

114   1 Kings 18:21; Zech. 4:6; Matt. 5:38-48; Luke 9:51-56; 11:33-36; 13:32; Acts 5:29- 32; 1 John 1:5-2:17

115   Matt. 21:22; Luke 1:34-37, 78,79; John 5:24; 8:47; Rom. 8:1 ff.; Phil. 2:5-11; 1 Tim. 2:5; Heb. 4:12,13

116   Matt. 5-7; Luke 6-12; Rom. 5:1-5; 8:1-18; Gal. 5:13-26; Eph. 2:1ff.

the commands and teaching of Jesus Christ without reservation or complaint. Indeed, it also means that you are willing to die for what you believe, but at the same time, you are unwilling to use or approve violence and killing by anyone to "defend."

Of course, that also means that you know you have been *Redeemed* by the Blood of Christ and know you are not your own. Moreover, All true Christians know that you must Trust God in all situations, regardless of what happens, proclaiming as Paul did: "For me to live is Christ and to die is Gain."[117]

God's Word is Truth; man's is not. But do you believe this? Know this: ALL the benefits of receiving from God Hinge on this one truth: You must "Single-mindedly Trust God," erstwhile shrinking back from any resort to using force on anyone or approving the use of force by anyone else! We serve God and not people.[118]

If we want to be used of God to reclaim those who have become inured to lies, we must play by the rules, just as God does. They have Free Will so you cannot 'make them' believe.

First, you must Trust in God's work and Pray for them.

Second, set the example by your testimony in "unlearning" the false way of manipulation by religion and political entities allied with Satan's "New World Order."

Third, stop "assuming" the negative but rather reassert the positive by believing that "Nothing is impossible with God."[119]

*Consider the Scriptures listed in the following footnote.[120]

X. Summary:

Always remember that our worship of God always entails the existential part of serving our Lord Jesus Christ wholly and loyally with

117   1 Sam. 2:1-10; 2 Sam. 22:33; Jer. 4:22; 5:1-5; 6:16,17; 18:12; Matt. 5:38-48; 10:16- 42; 26:51,52; Luke 6:20 ff.; 9:51-56; 11:33-36; John 18:36,37; Rom. 5:1-5; 8:1 ff.; 1 Cor. 1:17-2:16; 2 Cor. 3:17,18; Phil. 1:21; 3:3,20,21; 1 Pet. 1:3-25; 2:21-25; 1 John 1-5
118   Eph. 6:7; James 1:5-8
119   Matt. 17:20; 19:26; Mark 10:27; Luke 18:27; *Heb. 6:4; 1 Pet. 3:15
120   Ex. 15:11; 1 Sam. 2:9; Psa. 5:14,15,23; 9:9,10; 23:1 ff.; 76:11; Isa. 35:4; Matt. 6:22-24; Luke 16:13-15; Eph. 2:13,14

a pure heart as a "living Sacrifice." Thereby, we may "know the good, acceptable and perfect will of God" for our individual lives.[121]

If we do these things from the heart, Loving God as we are commanded, we will experience the Presence of God personally![122]

This is the reality of the Normal Christian Life of personal intimate Fellowship with God as it is defined in Scripture and what history records for being the normal that Christians practiced up until the fourth century when massive apostasy quenched the witness of the Pre-Nicean Church. Regardless of what errors our predecessors may have made in the past, the *New Covenant* still stands Faithful and True: Yes, in spite of our imperfections, God still offers us a quality of life that far transcends all our human possibilities.[123]

Finally, a gentle warning reminder is in order: For all those who hanker after "worldly pleasures," wealth and power, a universal law always governs all those things: "The Law of Diminishing Returns."[124]

Yes, many persist in thinking they can "pick the best from both worlds," but that is a lie of Satan. The more you try to gain enjoyment or "get high" from some activity, the less you will receive, until no enjoyment is left.

This precept is mirrored in what Mick Jagger said: "I can't get no satisfaction." Read Solomon's writings and you will get some good advice. However, for those who stay true to Loving God and following Jesus Christ's Teachings, you will nonetheless be required to "endure all the way through to the end to be Saved." God's Promise, of course, stands true: He will give you all the Grace you need to make it through intactly![125]

Yours truly from Heaven's Kingdom Ground, I remain,
Pastor David J. Bowers

---

121   Rom. 12:1-3
122   Matt. 5:8; 22:36,37; Rev. 22:1
123   Phil. 3:7-15; Heb. 7:11-10:23; Rev. 3:20 *See also the book Spiritual Guidelines for Restoration, "Historical Review" Section*
124   *See the paper The Higher Laws of God*
125   Matt. 24:13

## Chapter 8

Following in the Footsteps of Jesus

The author writes this chapter to correct some false impressions of belief concerning the person, teachings, and work of the Lord Jesus Christ. Biblical *Christology* defines two distinct natures in Christ: human and divine, combining to form one person—God the Son. So when we cite the teachings, commands, and the example of Jesus Christ to apply to contemporary lives and situations, we do so because Christ is God! I believe that Jesus intentionally did what he did and taught the way he taught for a good reason. That is, that if Jesus's followers were to be able to follow him, it would be on his terms, and nobody could claim that they could live the Christian life in their own strength! Jesus already knew that the precepts he taught were going to cause fireworks of conflict and division. That is why Jesus told the disciples that believers must be converted and be "wise as serpents and harmless as doves." Christians require this to exercise perseverance and to hold fast to the moral courage needed to succeed as a Christian in an alien world. We must acknowledge that *the New Covenant* regulates believers' lives in the following areas: first is knowing that we are responsible for following His commands recorded in Scripture.[132] Thus, being a disciple leads us to relational obedience, in which is the will of Jesus for every believer to abide. Second is that His teachings and example are truly practical and relevant for every Christian. Third, the *Christian* lifestyle is significantly and observably *different* from the traditions of the surrounding world culture and social norms. Christianity is a positive faith. Still, we must avoid many things to preserve the quality and integrity of the Christian lifestyle. They originally called Christianity *the Way* because it closely

---

132   *See the paper entitled Obedience to Christ*

followed *Jesus's Way.* They called the early believers *Christians* because their lifestyles so closely followed Jesus's commands and teaching that they acted like *little Christs.*

I. The main elements of Christian responsibility are these: One, believers must acknowledge the *absolute primacy, authority, and lordship of the Lord Jesus Christ* in their lives. Jesus is our *commanding officer.*[133] This becomes especially apparent in the way believers consider or regard their obligation or accountability in the next area. Two, the New Covenant Christian must consider *obedience to the specific commands and teachings of Jesus Christ to be priority one general standing orders.* Every believer is responsible for carrying out His orders until death or when Christ comes. In Scripture, the term's *hearken and observe* also directly imply obedience.

When Jesus comes, He is going to place us according to our response to His commands. All the parables illustrate this law of accountability in one way or another.[134]

Three, *Christians must follow Christ's example both implicitly and explicitly.* This applies to all areas: words, deeds, our innermost thoughts, attitudes, and intents. *Man is judged by God at the heart level* of the spirit. This brings us to the central theme within the New Covenant Gospel of Christ: when we live as a true disciple of Christ, His *spiritual life within* leads us to the "altar" of absolute surrender.

This is when we dedicate our entire being—spirit, soul, and body to the will of God the Father in Christ.[135]

Four, believers must daily live *in relational union with and in submission to the yoke of Jesus Christ and His New Covenant.* The picture that Jesus gave His disciples was that of the yoke, by which they would link an untrained animal to an experienced one, such that the novice could learn. This is the crux of discipleship. Jesus says to "learn of me," and that "His yoke is easy and his burden is light."

---

133 Eph. 1:9–23; Col. 1:12–29
134 Mat. 5:3–7:29; 25:1 ff.; 28:18–20; Luke 6:46–49; 10:16–28; John 5:19–30; 13:34,35; 14:6–24; 15:10–17; Rom. 14:10; 1 Cor. 4:4,5; 2 Cor. 5:10 *See also the paper: "Jesus' Major Parables"*
135 Matt. 4:17–20; 8:19–22; 9:9; 16:21–26; Mark 1:14–17; 2:14 f.; 8:31–38; Luke 5:27 f.; 9:23–26, 51–62; 18:22

Verily, this means that you have nothing to worry about or to fear when you completely submit your life to Jesus! He will never let you down! Scripture tells us that God has promised us that the Holy Spirit will faithfully *express all that we need to live like Jesus.*[136] In other words, God's Word says *that you can do what Jesus says,* in spite of what others may have told you in the past about the *so-called* "hard sayings" and "impracticality" of Jesus's teachings! The central issue that forms the crux of it all is, *are you willing?* However, you must understand that these things only come one way! No one can receive anything from God unless he receives *it spiritually by faith from heaven,* just like you were *born from above* (heaven).

God's ways of heaven are higher than all the humanistic ways of the earth. God's ways are so different that many teachers, religious people, and many scholars even have dismissed them as irrelevant or fanciful in their nearsighted world of blinded and carnal-minded vision! *Nevertheless, none of these things alters the truth one iota, does it?* Despite what any teacher (or a preacher) who may have taught you in the past that "Christ's teachings were impractical," does that make a single letter of Scripture or command of Christ invalid?

Does it change what Christ taught, *that you know to be true,* just because some "earthly authority" tells you that they did not believe it? Of course not! Neither does what anyone says to you, *no matter who they are,* make void, invalidate, nor make even one of Christ's commands impractical either![137] Moreover, if one truly considers and shoulders the biblical responsibility of being a Christian like he or she should, we would never raise what-if questions. They should not even enter our minds, should they? Not only that, Paul even tells us to disregard humanistic interpretations. We can only reach the essence of true doctrine when you *follow the truths of original biblical Christianity.* Always remember, nothing is impossible with God—so Jesus fully expects Christians to do what He says we can do without murmur, complaint, or making excuses. This includes practicing the central Christian doctrine of *faith-based pacifism.**[138]

---

136   John 16:13–15; John 14:15-26
137   Matt. 11:25–30; Luke 11:1–13; John 3:3 ff.; 15:1–7; 17:7–15; Acts 4:10–20; 5:29–32; Rom. 8:1 ff.; Gal. 5:1–10; Phil. 2:5–11; 3:8–16; Col. 1:12–29; 2 Tim. 2–4
138   Matt. 5–7; Luke 6,12; 21:19; Rom. 12:9–21; 1 Tim. 4:7; 2 Tim. 2:1 ff.; Rev. 12;10,11; 14:12,13

II. Costly discipleship leads us to biblical conversion.

First, we must define discipleship so that it includes the full recognition of New Covenant responsibilities including *taking up our cross, dying to self, and living for Jesus.* These tenets are at the very foundation level of Christianity. Throughout the New Testament, Jesus exhorts us, and the Apostles confirm that God requires us to take a *death attitude to sin.* This must be so that we can continue to receive righteousness and Agape love and that the Holy Spirit might form the life of Christ in us. Yes, these are *central issues at the heart of conversion.*

We must traverse them so that we might be *transformed into the image of Jesus Christ!* [139]

The second function of discipleship relates to our fellowship and placing within the body of Christ, the church. We should realize that when God's Spirit liberates us from the tyranny of sin, we should seek to be *transformed by the renewing of our minds.* Biblical prayer and worship in spirit aid greatly in this inward metamorphosis. When we begin *thinking like Jesus,* then we begin to *follow in the footsteps of Jesus!* At this point, the Spirit of God enables us to truly share in the spiritual continuum of the body-life of Christ. Fellowship and body-life arise from the *common ground of our identity with and in Christ.* Under these conditions, we *can minister the life of Christ to others. We do this by* sharing *His life* in fellowship with other believers.[140]

Thirdly, discipleship *includes our enduring trials and afflictions for the sake of Christ and His* gospel. Yes, the true Christian life is *tough!* God intentionally designed it that way to prove our faith! Jesus said to His disciples that if they were diligent in following him, "All men would hate you because of me." He also said that God would save the one that endures to the end.[141]

Fourth, we cannot separate *the precepts regulating the governance of the church* (the true body of Christ) from those same commands and example that issue from the person of Jesus Christ. Moreover, this very

---

139   Matt. 10:16–42; 16:21–28; Luke 9:23–26; 14:26–33; John 12:23–26; 2 Cor. 4:1–18; Gal. 2:16–21; 6:12–14

140   Matt. 6:9-13; John 4:23,24; Rom. 6:1–8:15; 12:1 ff.; 1 Cor. 12–14; 2 Cor. 3:17–4:18; Eph. 1–6

141   Matt. 10:16–39; 24:13; Mark 2:21,22; Luke 14:26–33; John 12:23–26; 13:3-38; 15:18–16:4; Phil. 2:5–3:21; Col. 1:10–29; 2 Tim. 2:1 ff. 1 Pet. 4:1 ff.

New Covenant (testament) tells us that *the church belongs to Christ.* This is the New Covenant that Jesus Christ inaugurated during his earthly life here. It is *sealed with His own precious blood* and ratified by Father God and tells us we are to govern the body of Christ *by His rules!* [142]

III. Agape love is the litmus test.

The actions and attitudes of believers prove the *presence (or absence) of Agape love.* This test shows which master is *in control of their life.* The actions of the worshiper reflect the characteristics of the true object of worship. Only the Spirit of Christ can give us the Agape love of God! "He who has not the Spirit of Christ is none of his." *God is also a title, not just a name.* Just *name.* Just like the Pharisee in Luke 18, many believe in a *fictitious god (idol),* trusting only in human power and intelligence to save. Consequently, they only take seriously or believe what they can conceive with the human senses. This is *pure nominalism,* and is the carnal mind at work. In reality, their god is Satan, *god of this world,* the author of *humanism,* the world's religion! Their object of worship drives them to hold doctrines that are patently contrary to the true Gospel of Jesus Christ. This is why most professing Christians in organized Christianity hold many doctrines that contradict each other. This disconcerting truth remains: most Christians *cannot reconcile* their present "state of conscience and belief" with the *whole truth of the Gospel of Jesus!* Yes, the ultimate conclusions that Agape love forces us to acknowledge will inevitably contradict many beliefs and practices that mainstream organized churches routinely hold. The major areas of concern are as follows: one is the seemingly widespread "acceptance of sexual immorality." The second is the unabashed abandonment to worldliness and materialism exhibited by many. The third is the obvious betrayal of Jesus's clear commands regarding the way Christians believe they should respond to evil.

The only way to get back to a consistent doctrine is for professing Christians to renounce humanistic *empiricism* and its twin, *nominalism,* and return to the *original standards* of *the New Covenant.* To have

---

142   Matt. 16:18; 18:18–20; 20:20–28 *See also the paper: "What is the Body of Christ" See also the paper 'Basics of Biblical Church Governance'*

true revival, we must guide our lives by *comparing our lives and beliefs to the standard of the New Testament scripture.*[143]**

IV. Summary and Conclusions

One, the preceding spiritual laws should be patently obvious in the eyes of any serious and unbiased reader of Scripture that approaches it with an open mind and observes its own guidelines. Since Scripture says clearly so, the modern church is responsible for governing itself by the *same set of rules as did the first century early church.* This is so even if all the written documents we have today had not yet been in circulation. Two is that God does not approve any influence of *humanism.* Humanism inevitably co-opts, negates, and dilutes the authority and truth of Jesus Christ or His New Covenant as God presents it to us in the New Testament accounts. This is true no matter what tradition of man it arises from, who it is, or from what organization it may be. Three, Christian believers are personally responsible for obeying the true and *complete Gospel of Jesus Christ.*

---

143   Matt 5:38–48; Luke 9:51–56; John 15:1 ff.; Rom. 8:1 ff.; 12:19–21; 1 Cor. 13; 2 Cor. 4:4–6; 1 John 2–4; Rev 12: 19-21. *See also Appendix E entry: *the patience of the saints*, viz., *faith-based pacifism**

## Chapter 9

The Role of Conscience

Determining the quality of spirituality, doctrine, and practice in the body of Christ is extremely important. To do so, believers need to know and use the basic relationships establishing and governing the parameters of the human conscience. In particular, we need to know its relationship to God, to spiritual matters, to the world and society, and to the other components within man's being and make-up. First, we examine those things regarding:

I. The Conscience and Salvation

Question: In relation to the conscience and the gospel, *when* does the evident ignorance of the individual affect the eternal outcome in God's eyes? One big problem we face is that many believers have blindly *assumed* that everything their particular church taught them was true. Second, many have *assumed* that certain rituals and ceremonies conducted by a priest or minister really *does something for them* such that they *need not act on their own.* Third, the dogmas of apostate religion have led millions to erroneously *assume that they can really be Christians and simultaneously hold on to humanistic doctrines.* Religious authorities have concocted these false doctrines from worldly traditions awash in *syncretism*, paganism, and the cult of nation worship. *They even taught many of us that these false doctrines were originally part of Christianity!* Nevertheless, the truth is that they are decidedly toxic to spirit, neutralizing spirituality, and diametrically opposed to the spirit of love and of true New Testament Christianity! As a result, in the modern church we have a wide range of conditions from the good, the ignorant, and innocuous all the way to the extreme of the arrogant, reprobate, and agnostic. Paul wrote about former believers who had *"made shipwreck,"* *having relapsed and fallen back into a reprobate, unsaved* condition, "Having their consciences seared as with a hot iron."

Yes, many veer off the path of faith into false doctrine that is contrary to the New Covenant.[144] Then, we have those many thousands of apparently true and sincere believers who nonetheless continue to believe in questionable and unbiblical doctrines. Where do these stand with God? This last condition applies with many mainstream Christians who have grown up in traditional denominations and have followed the lead of the majority. Where can we find *the testimony of a good conscience in Christianity* these last days?

This brings us to some big questions:

1. Where is *that thin blue line* that separates true New Testament Christians from all the others?

2. How do we *identify* those who form the true body of Christ, His church?

3. Can *we tell the difference between the ones that really are being saved* (the saints and the elect), whom the Holy Spirit has connected to the head, Christ, from the ones who are not?

4. Can we *specify a verifiable standard* by which we can detect that boundary with by using Scripture and with prudent observation of lives and fruit?

5. Which New Testament doctrines then must we observe in determining and using *that holy standard?* [145]

6. Can the testimony of the conscience help us know *who is who?*

Jesus tells us that "by their fruits [works] ye will know them."[146] What a professed believer *does* becomes a very specific indicator or *litmus test* that others can legitimately use to detect or verify the *identity of their*

---

144 Matt. 7:13–21; Rom. 1:18 ff.; 2 Cor. 11:1 ff.; 1 Tim. 1:18-20; 4:2; Jude 3–19. *See Glossary of Terms' entry *casuistry**

145 John 7:24

146 Matt. 3:8; 7:13–21; 12:33–37; 25:14 ff.; Luke 3:8; John 7:7; 8:34–47; 10:25–30, 36–38; 9:4; 14:9–12; 15:24; Gal. 5:19–23; Eph. 5:1–21.

source of life. Observe the fundamental habits and patterns of speaking along with the professed beliefs and acts that form the person's lifestyle. Over a judicious time, one can use this *as a reliable means to identify just who or what is their real "God," and primary object of trust.* We can observe and accurately resolve the following guidelines:

1. Organized churches are composed of *mixed multitudes,* containing both believers and unbelievers. So we cannot use baptism, church attendance, or membership as determining factors for people being Christian believers.

2. We *can* make certain kinds of *judgments.* These are moral decisions involving right and wrong where we *do not* prescribe *specific* punishments or categorically condemn individuals or churches. *This is valid since* we solely base our judgment upon the larger truth of the counsel of God as expressed in Holy Scripture.

3. Holding onto the traditional beliefs of others *cannot save us.* Assuming you can trust in the *human organizations* of even the best of churches is extremely hazardous to spiritual life.

4. We cannot judge another individual's own conscience, per se. However, we *can* make honest value assessments. By observing, we *can evaluate* the presence, absence, or the quality of fruit in individuals, in groups, or in churches, *without compromising the law of love.*

II. What is the relationship between knowledge and the conscience?

It is God's will that we receive and use the crucial New Covenant precepts governing our trust in Christ. These must enter our conscience as knowledge, and we must practice them in our daily lives. It is God's will that we have a *clear and good conscience.* This is necessary to assure that the testimony of Scripture may enter unhindered into our mind. By that, the Holy Spirit can translate spiritual life inwardly to build up the conscience.

We require the testimony of *conscience* very often. Christians must make daily choices regarding the issues of life. These involve morality, determining truth and to the shades of meaning showing us how Scripture applies in our lives. This we can do both for ourselves (provided we are honest) and for others also as we observe their works over a span of time.[147] In addition, in all these matters, we must always observe that the conscience is a spiritual organ. Consequently, it is not to be confused with soulish organs such as the emotions, intellect, or the subconscious mind.

III. Let us explore the issues of idolatry and ignorance.

Deception is a large part of Satan's agenda. Idolatry and ignorance are two main areas of human life that Satan exploits with deceptive alacrity to subvert the conscience! The enemy hides *false doctrine* within and behind both. First, let us know that idolatry arises from humanism. Humanism contains the occult mantras of idols and Antichrist. We can see the deceptive idolatry of humanism in many things: *materialism, nationalism, fear, ambition, greed, pride, and in the lust of the flesh.* Giving glory to man and his ungodly devices are common to all these.

However, it is detestable in the sight of God.[148] Deception, which can *subvert faith from within,* is a multiple pincer attack strategy. The enemy orchestrates it well with propaganda, false doctrine, advertising, projected or imagined fears of all kinds, appeals to pride of ownership, disinformation, confusion, and misinterpretation. Believing in lies *desensitizes the conscience and masks the operation of demons.* These disable the godly mechanisms that limit deception, opening the capability for us to commit sin and believe more lies without *even being aware of it!* Secondly, what should we *know about ignorance?* The mind of the person shares *all three parts of the human* make-up and the *conscience shares all that the mind knows.* An old truism states that "wherever you go, there you are!"

You cannot escape your own self-consciousness! Can a true Christian not know that something or someone has deceived them and *still be saved?* Can you handle the truth? Principle: ignorance of God's law is not an excuse. Willful ignorance is worse yet. For far too many, however, ignorance is a deep trap and a dangerously thin veneer for unbelief (faithlessness). For any person to qualify *for being ignorant at*

---

147   2 Cor. 4:1
148   Luke 12:15; 16:15; 1 Tim. 4:1,2; 2 Tim. 3:1–9.

all, they must have an actual primal absence of knowledge. Believers cause or complicate this by one or more of the following: They did not exercise diligence after the initial experiences of salvation. They *assumed* or expected others to do something for them. They may have suffered a traumatic incident or accident that causes amnesia or that otherwise *masks or suppresses* the memory. However, if the person resorts to a deliberate and willful act to *hide the truth* from their own mind and heart, they *have no valid claim of ignorance.*

The *main possibility* of exemption the New Covenant allows is for those people who *have never passed that indeterminate boundary* of *the age of accountability* when sin is *first* imputed. This only applies to infants or to those having a genuine debilitating congenital condition such as mental illness or retardation. God's Word teaches that all normal and self-aware humans *are wholly accountable* for *the complete truth of the New Testament gospel in their own conscience.* Yes, God expects you to follow through to the best of our ability in *seeking the whole truth.* Jesus was quite clear that this also means counting the cost of following Jesus, our very lives![149] Still, one must know that even legitimate ignorance *may not* shield one from eternal judgment! That is up to God alone. Ignorance is extremely dangerous! I believe that God saves some of those believers who are legitimately ignorant. Still, God will hold church leaders responsible for many lost souls.

That is because many *failed to teach the whole truth* of the Gospel of Jesus Christ. Remember the warnings that God gave the prophet Ezekiel.[150] Nevertheless, countless Christians have failed to understand the richness of the gospel or to arrive at the *unavoidable implications of Agape love.* Let alone do they understand the radical changes in life that result from adhering to the complete message of New Covenant Christianity that the early (Ante-Nicean) church was practicing before the gross compromises. This reveals an abysmal shortfall due to cultural adaptation and complicated by long-term teaching of false and misleading doctrines especially in the area of God's word that teaches us how we should respond to *authority.*. The cost to the church has been extreme.

---

149   Matt. 10:16–42; 16:21–26; Luke 9:23–26; 14:26–33; Rom. 1:18–2:16.
150   Ezek. 3,11, 18, 33, 34

That toll is being exacted on all believers. These losses are expensive in personal lives and at the congregational level. What you do not know *can hurt you!* We must also realize that *by definition,* sin cuts off *the natural man* from God because of its source, the innate way of thinking of the carnal mind. Scripture condemns the carnal and soulish humanistic nature, even in believers. Even receiving Jesus as our personal Savior does not automatically change our human nature! These changes require our subsequent cooperation with divine *grace*. This explains why so many who claim to be believers cannot truly understand these things, especially the *hard sayings of Jesus!* This explains the many unbiblical doctrines that arise. They arise because the carnal mind twists the meaning of Scripture inside them *because they have no root within (the spirit),* as Jesus puts it in the parable of the sower. One major missing element anyone needs before they can see the truth God's way is the transformation of the mind.[151] So to accomplish this, we must first acknowledge that the *conscience* is an organ of the human *spirit,* not the soul! Consequently, it must also have an outlet compatible to spiritual things to properly preserve its integrity. Remember that the carnal mind only sees spiritual things as garbage—it just *does not compute.* What is worse, if our conscience is left to itself unchanged, the carnal mind will corrupt, contaminate, and poison the conscience because of the interconnection to the *volition!* Yes, *renewal of the mind* is a necessary part of *conversion.* In this process, the Holy Spirit gives us wholeness, and all parts of our being are being sanctified—holy and dedicated unto Him, spirit, soul, and body. *Salvation means health.* Jesus knew and taught these precepts consistently, for they are integral to His New Covenant, the basis of true Christianity![152]

---

151   Matt. 13; 15:6 14; 16:21–26; Rom. 8:1–11; 12:1–3; 1 Cor. 2:9–16; 1 John 1:1-10; 3:5–9.

152   John 5:6; Acts 9:34; Rom. 8:1 ff.; 12:1–3; Eph. 4:23,24; 1 Thess. 5:23. *See also the papers entitled "the Higher Laws of God" and "The Spiritual Laws of Revival" and the book* The Spiritual Man *by Watchman Nee, Christian Fellowship Publishers, Inc., NY, 1977*

IV. Let us investigate the relation between the *conscience*, the baptism of Jesus Christ, and worship.

Christian baptism means that one accepts their own death ahead of time. Baptism is spiritual. Baptism is also used as a test by God to see if you really trust him to do what he promises to do in our lives. Similar to the elements of communion, Christian *believer's baptism is a symbol of our identity of being part of Christ*. The Holy Spirit immerses us into the body of Christ and into the spiritual framework of the New Covenant Kingdom of Heaven. It is within *the context of this consciousness that* God intends the organ of conscience to function in! We can only properly appreciate and experience the fullness of these and many other New Testament truths with the spiritual senses that a believer can (by free will) receive directly from God.

The Holy Spirit has accomplished this via another organ of the spirit called *intuition*. This is how the new birth (regeneration) gives us the ability to pursue and apprehend spiritual things. We must first receive all spiritual things in our human spirit by intuition. As a reborn Christian, your spirit also contains the organ of *communion*. The function of communion enables you to worship God in the way Jesus commands: "God is Spirit, and we must worship (God) in spirit and in truth." Worship contains all the important things for which the Christian life stands! (Spiritual) Baptism leads us to worship *in spirit and in truth*. God intends spiritual worship to be our full-time occupation and service to God.[153] See Figure 1 below.

---

153   John 4:23,24; Rom. 6:1 ff. 12:1–3

V. The human make-up is divided into three major sections:

Spirit, soul, and *body.* It is God's will that all three parts of our being glorify Him and take part in spiritual worship. To help in visualizing this, let us view an illustration of the human make-up: Figure 1:

AN ILLUSTRATION OF THE HUMAN MAKE-UP:

FIGURE 1.

There are three major sectors of the human make-up as we were created by God Cf. Genesis 1:26,27; 2:7-9

OUTSIDE SECTOR=BODY

MIDDLE SECTOR=SOUL

CENTRAL SECTOR= SPIRIT

4-12-00
Rev. 1: 2-21-07

A. Outside Sector=Body

B. Middle Sector=Soul

C. Central Sector=Spirit

A. *The human body is the external and corporeal part of our being.* See Figure 1 above. This includes all the physical structures and systems of the human body inside and out. Using these structures, man can move about and relate to his environment by the sense organs that are *hardwired* to the central nervous system and to the brain. Within and intertwined like a program within this external structure, we have:

B. *The human soul.* The act of God breathing originally created this unique part upon the formerly lifeless flesh of Adam. In doing so, the *interaction of God's gift of spirit being breathed upon the body produced the unique human soul—* thus, man became a living soul.[154]

The three organs of the human soul are *volition, intellect,* and *emotion,* all of which center on the *mind,* which in turn occupies the same space as the physical brain. These three organs, when developed, define the *personality* of the person. We observe the following attributes*:

---

154   Genesis 1:26,27; 2:7.

- Volition *proves the existence and visible exercise of the power of choice or will that* God granted to all humankind at creation. Moreover, God has preserved this function intact as a central part of his program of redemption and salvation. Original sin has not defeated it—neither by *the fall of man,* nor by *total depravity. Man still has both the advantages and the responsibilities of free will, and is wholly accountable to God for all decisions he makes!*

- Intellect (or the mind) proves *the existence and capability of man to exercise sentient reasoning power.* Within the human mind are *two distinct compartments: the conscious mind and the subconscious mind.* Neither one of these can directly relate externally to spiritual things, however, many people still mistakenly identify the latter with the human spirit. Author note: God's Word disallows using any function of the subconscious mind to relate to God. God judges as sin all soul-power methods, including those which make uses of the subconscious mind to attempt to relate to or worship what they think is a god! God has forbidden these methods commonly used by deceived Christians and the Cults, such as hypnosis for good reason—they open one up to serious demonic influence, deception, and harm!

- *Emotion.* The existence of human feelings proves emotion. These are affection, sentiment, love, hate, fear, jealousy, etc. Nevertheless, again the truth remains: we must always acknowledge that the organs of the *soul cannot relate directly to God, for they are* not spirit.

Since the higher functions of the human spirit are dead in unregenerate man, the Bible teaches that overt choice is necessary for the unbeliever to receive the sacrifice of Christ! That exception involves both *the created and intact power of choice* (volition) and the human *conscience.* God intends that these two parts of our being *point to a single* decision that remains as the single most important choice that any person can make during this lifetime here on earth. That decision is, "What will you do with Jesus Christ, the crucified?" That is the same Jesus Christ who is the *only pathway to the new birth of the spirit* and of any possibility of *eventual salvation.*

C. The human spirit. The human spirit *is the most important part of man.* However, in an unregenerate man, it is dead (except the conscience) because of sin. Only *an act of God called regeneration can restore the original created functions of the human spirit.* This is only possible when an individual confesses sin, repents of sin, and receives by free will *the perfect once-for-all sacrifice of Christ.* When a person truly receives Jesus Christ, the Holy Spirit enters their spirit and *regenerates* our original spiritual abilities.

These are the functions of *intuition* and *communion* that Adam's sin destroyed. In the process, God's Spirit forgives the receiver of all pre-existing (past) sin, and *baptizes them into the body of Christ.* This event is what most Christians have called *salvation.* However, more accurately, they should call it *initial salvation*, since it is *provisional and probational* in nature at the beginning. Note also that salvation is different from conversion. Eventual salvation requires our being *converted first.* Conversion requires our subsequent cooperation with God's Holy Spirit in effecting the changes God has commanded, such that we can live the *New Covenant Christian life.* Principle: *God is a triune being.* Since God Created man *in His own image* (the divine nature), it follows that *man is also a triune being.* Let us also realize that the mind includes (affects) *all three parts of our being:* spirit, soul, body.[155] In review, the fully functional *regenerated human spirit* in man is composed of three parts: One, *intuition* is the function by which man *can personally receive relational guidance* directly from God on a spiritual level by the Holy Spirit. This function operates the best when used with biblical faith and the diligent study of God's holy written Word, the Bible. Two, *communion* enables man to *worship* and have *personal fellowship with God,* enjoying God's company on the personal relationship level of *righteousness.* This includes our personal access to Father God's throne in biblical prayer.

Three, the *conscience,* least damaged by the fall, gives the person an immediate response whether something is *good or evil,* or whether it is right or wrong. It is clear only when righteous and uncontaminated knowledge build it up. Background: In the *garden*, Adam fell by disobedience, failing to heed his conscience, choosing to disobey

---

155   Ibid footnotes 9–11 and Matt. 22:37; Luke 10:27; 1 Cor. 6:15–20; 1 Thess. 5:23; 2 Pet 1:3,4

the express command of God. He lost the first two spiritual abilities relating to God listed above for all of us. *The same thing can happen to believers* if we are not careful. Therefore, Christians should take heed: spiritual matters are *serious business!* [156]

VI. Conclusion

Ever since God's pronouncement of, "In the day that you eat of it [the tree of the knowledge of good and evil], *You will surely die,"* Adam's sin plunged humanity into the recurring nightmare of *original sin, with each generation receiving it from the human father.* Subsequently, sin has cut off unregenerate man from God, since active sin has permanently darkened the two primary spiritual organs of intuition and communion (communication and worship) because of *sin.* This is the *kind of death* that God spoke of in Genesis 2. *Remaining in that condition,* sin will hopelessly condemn man to an eternal hell. Peter tells us this is not God's will, of course. Therefore, God intends the conscience to point us elsewhere. As we have seen above, the human conscience is the only surviving organ of the human spirit that God has left intentionally intact in man. As a vestige of his former estate, the uncontaminated good conscience is still reliable to convict one internally of sin. That is so, only if one has not tampered with it by continual *willful sin* or by *feigned ignorance.* Both these disastrous actions by man *will numb or sear the conscience* such that it can no longer function as God intended. [157]

As a result, we have psychotic-type individuals that can be very dangerous to everyone around them because they have no sensitivity or remorse regarding their sin or its effect on others! The *only antidote* to these and all other actions, and the eternal consequences and destiny of the unregenerate, sinful or the apostate, is *one thing:* repent and believe (obey) the complete gospel! [158]

---

156 John 15:1–6; Rom. 1:16–2:15; 1 Cor. 9:24–27; Heb. 2:1–3; 3:6–4:16; 6:1–15; 9:11–15; 10:26–39; James 1:1 ff.; 2 Pet. 3:9. *See also the papers entitled "Conditions for Salvation, Destiny and Free Will," "The Fallacies of Determinism," "God's Definition of Salvation," and "The Spiritual Laws of Revival"*

157 John 9:39–41; 1 Tim. 4:1,2; Titus 1:15,16 Cf. Ezek. 3,18, 33

158 Acts 2:38,39; 3:19

The Christian Epiphany

#	The Christian Epiphany	
	Description	Page #
I.	Introduction	
II.	What is preventing most "professing Christians" from seeing these truths?	
III.	Those who know the "Way of Christ" do not "fall for" any of the ways of the world, the flesh and Satan.	
IV.	Christ has ordained for us a Whole New Way of fighting evil: In the spirit.	
V.	What is the New Covenant teaching?	
VI.	The following is "An Affidavit/ Statement for all True Christians"	

I. Introduction:

The "Christian epiphany" happens at that point in time when a confessing Christian believer first begins to realize the full extent of meaning contained in Christ's *Atonement,* personal presence and significance of teaching and doctrine. Yes, "epiphany" is when these fundamental precepts of originally Biblical Christianity finally penetrate our being and we start taking spiritual things seriously.

Of course, that realization, when took seriously, will surely confront many deeply entrenched misunderstandings and outright falsehoods into which many of us have been led into and "catechized" for being "Christian" [sic.] when in fact they are "religious dogmas" that are decidedly anti-Christian since many of them directly contradict Christ's clear teachings on crucial points of doctrine.[1]

However, the Truth remains that everything Jesus Christ taught is true and doable just as much today as it was in the first century. IF you truly "Love God (Christ) with all your heart, soul, mind and strength" as the Great Command states, you will indeed know intuitively that "His Commands are not burdensome" as John wrote.

Moreover, IF you truly Believe God's Word and for being the Truth and know who is your God, you will not flinch at obeying His Commands nor would you give them a second thought! Yes, Christ's Commands are indeed viable right here and right now![2]

God's Word, the Truth, tells us that God provides everything we need: Provision, inspiration and defense. Verily, the Truth of God's Word is available, evident, simple and direct.[3]

However unfortunate it may be, man's machinations contained in religion have muddied up the water of the Gospel, making it appear to be 'complicated' so that corrupt, apostate leaders may control the masses.

Indeed, even today, just like the Jews during Jesus's first Advent, most religious leaders and the congregations that follow them (instead of Jesus Christ) are stubbornly clinging to "traditions of the past" and to "the Doctrines of the State" that entangle them in Idolatry and effectively 'handcuff them to the world.'

---

1   Matt. 13; 2 Cor. 5:14-21 *See also the author's book Jesus' Way, Chapter XI, "The New Covenant," Section Three: "Consider The Deeper Meaning of Atonement"*

2   Matt. 11:25-30; 28:28; Mark 10:15; Luke 10:21-24; John 14:6; John 1:1-5, 10-18; 4:23,24; 5:22-27; 6:27-63; 8:31-36; 10:25-28; 11:25,26; 12:23-26; 14:6, 15-26; 15:26; 16:13-15; 17:14-24; 18:36; 2 Pet. 2:22; 1 John 5:3

3   Psa. 23,46,91; Matt. 6:33 *(and many others!)*

However, that tragic fact alone proves it to be obvious that <u>they love the world more than Jesus!</u>[4]

<u>Know this:</u> <u>the one or thing you believe, fear and trust to be your</u> <u>"savior from evil" is your actual 'God.</u>' However, beware: IF, in truth, if the doctrines you have been taught to believe have led you to <u>trust any other object</u> of Allegiance, worship and trust <u>other than God in Christ, the only source which is defined by Scripture regarding any venue of Salvation, you are in fact committing Idolatry!</u>[5]

Based upon the above facts, it is the certain position of this author that the following changes must be made in the vast majority of "professing Christians" to restore the church to a biblically based relationship to Christ:

1. They must be willing to set aside all previous "indoctrination of religious dogma" and reread the Scriptures independently.

2. They must return to the simple basic application of Scripture, beginning with the New Testament, receiving the Truth readily as a child as Jesus told the early Christians.

3. As the Holy Spirit convinces them of their shortcomings, let them be open-minded to receive the changes necessary to bring them to compliance with the Pathway of Jesus Christ.[6]

One fundamental fact regarding all this is that "the promises of God are all Yea and Amen" to all who really see and appreciate them.[7]

---

4   Isa. 1, 5,6; 28:9-20; 29:13-16; 30:9-22; 42:18-25; 44:6-20 48:17,18; 56:9-57:13; 59:1-18; 65:1-15; Jer. 5:5; 6:16; 8:8,9; 18:12; Ezek. 3,18,33,34; Hosea 1-14; Matt. 4:1-10; 13:1-30;16:23-26; 23:1 ff.; Luke 4:1-8; John 8:23; 14:27; 15:18-16:4,33; 18:36; Rom. 1:18 ff.; 1 Cor.1:17-2:16; 10:1-23; 2 Cor. 4:1-5:21; Gal. 4:1-5:4; 6:7-16; Phil. 2:5-16; Col. 2:6-12,18-23;Heb. 11; James 1:27; 3:13-4:8; 1 John 2:15-17 *See also Glossary of Terms' entry *(the Doctrine of) Sanctification* and the book Jesus' Way, Chapter XIX: "Knowing the Difference between the Church and the World"*

5   Ex. 20:1-7; 1 Sam. 2:1-10; 1 Kings 18:21; Psa. 2:1 ff.; 3:8; 4:8; 20:6,7; 94:20; 115:1 ff.;118:8,9; Prov. 29:25; Isa. 2:8-20; 8:9-20; 28:9-20; 29:9-30:21; 44:6-46:13; Jer. 10:1-11; 17:1- 10; Ezek. 23:37-39; 33:1-36:38; Hos. 14:9; Matt. 27:15-26; John 18:36,37; 19:11-15; Acts 5:29- 32; Rom. 1:16-32; 1 Cor. 10:1-22; 2 Cor. 10:3-7; Gal. 5:1; 6:14-16; Eph. 2:13,14; 6:10-12; Col. 1:12-3:15; 2 Thess. 2:3-12; 1 Tim. 6:3-12; 2 Tim. 1:7-15; 2:11 ff.; Heb. 10-12; James 4:1-8; 1 John 1-5

6   Psa. 16:11; 23:1-6; 27:1-4, 11-14; 32:6,7; 33:4; 34:4 ff.; 36:9; 37:3-5, 18-31

7   2 Cor. 1:20

However, it remains that we must know that faith only works IF you implicitly believe God's Word at face value and put the entire weight of your life (100%) upon that belief!

II. What is preventing most "professing Christians" from seeing these truths? Unfortunately, the biggest problem I see is that most Christians are unable to recognize the Truth for various reasons, the following of which are the most significant:

A. They have been conditioned (brainwashed) to believe half-truths mixed with lies for most of their lives by the apostate religious establishment that is "in bed" with the state. Consequently, they are literally unable to properly respond to Scripture and thus fail to love the Truth as they are commanded by God to do.[8]

Indeed, whether they are aware of it or not, the vast majority of "professing Christians" have been taught by the "catechisms of religion" to speciously avoid the more 'difficult parts' of the Gospel that require a person to use their conscience or to exercise virtually any level of moral courage. Obviously, they are doing this because they have never received the True Gospel or at some point in time have "caved in" to their fears and have reverted back to unbelief.

Of course, that also explains why they have fallen away from those fundamental Truths of Jesus Christ that conflict with the world's humanistic way of thinking, the "carnal mind." That is also why they approve of the killing of others by the state. However, those in that category are totally unaware of the unavoidable consequences of falling away and of the deadening of their consciences from long term disbelief that will inevitably take hold if they fail to repent! They also fail to realize that their approval of others killing human beings, regardless of how they may be defined by the world, they are nonetheless considered by God to be guilty of murder![9]

B. Indeed, precious few of those who claim to be Christians have ever been taught the "straight skinny" of the complete Truth of Jesus Christ

---

8   John 6:45; 8:31-58; 9:17-41; 14:6-26; 18:36,37; Rom. 1:18-32; 2 Thess. 2:3-12

9   Matt. 5:43-48; 10:26-39; 23:1 ff.; Luke 8:18; 11:33-36; 12:49-59; 14:25-33; 16:13-15; 19:26; John 8:21-47; Rom. 8:1-11; 2 Thess. 2:3-12; 1 Tim. 4:2; James 2:10; 1 John 3:15

regarding the cost of the True Christian life, that which the spiritual mind teaches. John Huss spelled it out in his book *De Ekklesia,* especially about the precept of "Relative authority" which correctly teaches that a Believer must choose to "obey God rather than man" whenever man's law conflicts with True Christian Doctrine!

Yes, Scripture teaches that in 'normal life' we can count on God's protection over True Believers in Christ. However, Christ also taught that sometimes God allows us to suffer at the hands of unbelievers (even some of which claim to be Christians) and some have had to pay the ultimate cost, their lives for the True Gospel! Yes, Jesus taught that we must be willing to die for our faith if it is necessary.

Not only that, the Gospel allows no room for compromise, for if you take one step down that way of accommodation, you will be walking in a life of miserable apostasy, whether or not you know that you have betrayed Christ.[10]

However, make no mistake, because God is Love, the New Covenant never gives us any rationale for believing in killing, despite circumstance.[11]

In the outside humanistic world, they cannot conceive of such a high standard, but they do not have a marvelous God like we have! Yet, the fact that God has given Christians such a great legacy of spiritual wisdom, a sound mind and access to God's awesome power of Salvation that every True Believer can have by Faith, those "seemingly impossible" levels of morality, spirituality and amazing coping power are well within the scope of reality in which every True Christian can live. However, none of this will work unless you are truly Believing what God's Word says and put the whole weight of your life upon the promises of God's Word!

If you truly believe what God's Word says you will also know what I am saying is true. That is also why I do not sanction any type of homicide because it does not solve the underlying problems of mankind

---

10   Rom. 8; Phil. 1:21
11   Matt. 5:43-48; John 13:34,35; 1 John 3,4

that sin causes. Only a personal relationship with God via Jesus Christ can solve these issues.[12]

C. All those who approve humanistic ways for 'solutions' are that way because they have never truly experienced *Regeneration* or understood the full ramifications inherent in the Doctrine of *Atonement.* Another reason could be that they had never sufficiently developed their spiritual relationship with God to the point that they could recognize the fundamental spiritual laws, truths and precepts that should be obvious to anyone who truly "Worships God in spirit and in truth."[13]

D. Knowingly or unknowingly they tolerate palpable conundrums, embracing contradictions that cannot remain if they are to be saved. Quite possibly, the worst of these "pseudo doctrines" is part of a tainted *Orthodoxy* religious apostates call the *Judeo-Christian Tradition, * the JCT. However, the JCT. contains obvious errors in it, one of which is the belief that they can rationalize the killing of other human beings. Of course, that is contained in another common doctrine they ascribe to: *Determinism.*[14]

What can we do to escape the 'gravitational pull' of our lower carnal nature of humanism? Knowing God's Will is the Key to our attitudes and actions. Always remember that the one which you give glory and honor is in fact your God.[15]

E. Like the world, most "professing Christians" are 'stuck' in the habitual 'ruts' of 'ordinary human responses' and in the same type of thought and attitude patterns as the world. Scripture indicates that this problem is a serious impediment to repentance for it produces a condition called the "hardened heart." That is why God tells us that something or situation must come about to change the status quo

---

12   Matt. 17:20; 19:26; Mark 10:27; Luke 1:37; 18:27; 12:8-12: 21:8-19; John 14:12; Rom. 7:1-4; 8:1 ff.; 12:9-20; 2 Cor. 1:20; 5:6-21; 10:3-6; 12:9,10; Gal. 1:6-12; 2:19-21; 6:14; Eph. 2:13-16; 6:12-18; Phil. 1:21; 2:5-13; 3:7-14; Col. 1:12-29; 2:9,10; 2 Tim. 1:7-12; 2:3-13; Heb. 2:14,15; 4:6-16; 9:11-15, 27; 10:16-39; 12:1 ff.; James 1:5-8, 16-25; 3:13-18; 5:13-18; 1 Pet. 1:3-19; 4:12-19; 2 Pet. 1:1 ff.; 1 John 1:5-2:17; 4:4; 4:7-5:15 See also Footnote #1
13   2 Chr. 15:15; Psa. 119:10; Prov. 10:9,29; Hosea 14:9; John 4:23,24
14   Gal. 1:6-12 *See also the paper entitled The Fallacies of Determinism*
15   Mark 11:22,23; Rom. 8:26,27; 1 John 5:14,15

of our life. This is why God uses agricultural terminology in telling us to "Break up your fallow ground and sow not among thorns." Unfortunately, it usually takes a "crisis experience" to get our attention and to make us open to the changes that must be made so we may conform to God's Way of doing things!

Unfortunately, people resist change because it upsets their familiar patterns of life, however, that is what it takes to become a True Disciple of Jesus Christ. You cannot keep going the same way: You must Repent and then Receive the True Gospel in its entirety to begin living as a True Christian![16]

F. Many claim to be "Christians," but apparently lack any significant interest in Holiness. Many Scriptures attest to the importance of Holiness or the *Doctrine of Sanctification.* Indeed, Holiness is a very important element that is absolutely necessary in the development of Righteousness, Peace and Victory in a Believer's life.[17]

Why are so many "so-called Christian" people totally oblivious to the clearly defined conditions laid out in Scripture that we must satisfy?

Not only that, it should be obvious that a Believer must possess the necessary self-awareness of spiritual things to be able to progress in the "Discipleship to Conversion Dynamic Process" that every True Christian must remain in to be saved in the end! Remaining in the Discipleship process (abiding and trusting *In Christ*) is the only way we can develop sufficient resistance to sin and reach the level of spiritual Formation that is commensurate with adult spirituality.

Only in this state of being are we able to attain the humility, poise and stability we need to endure the struggles of life that will surely come our way if we persevere in the Christian Walk anywhere beyond the "baby stage."[18]

---

16   Jer. 4:4; Hosea 10:12; Matt. 13; Mark 4; Luke 8

17   1 Chr. 16:29; Psa. 29:2; 30:4; 89:34,35; 96:9; 97:11,12; 110:3; Isa. 35:3-10; 63:9-19; Jer. 2,23,31; Mal. 2; Luke 1:67-79; Rom. 1:4; 6:19-22; 2 Cor. 7:1; Eph. 4:24; 1 Thess. 3:12,13; Heb. 2:10-14; 10:26-39; 12:1 ff.; 1 Pet. 13-19

18   Psa. 1, 19, 23, 27, 34, 37, 40, 42, 45, 46, 50, 51, 56, 61-63, 73, 84, 91, 97, 103, 112, 115, 118, 119, 121, 139, 146; Isa. 32:17,18; 40:28-31; Matt. 11:25-30; John 13:34-17:26; Hebrews 4

G. Beware of those who claim to be "Christians," but who are (knowingly or not) the agents of Satan that, like the proverbial "Trojan Horse," infiltrate the Body of Christ and corrupt its simplicity. "By their fruits you will know them." According to Scripture, every part of the Body of Christ, the True New Testament church, is a part of Christ and is Loyal to Christ and follows the Commands of Christ, never making excuses. True Christians know that they are part of the *Kingdom of Heaven,* pledging total allegiance to Jesus Christ as their highest authority and Worship God in Christ in spirit and in truth. They do not compromise their faith no matter what happens.

Not only that, True Christians are not arrogant or judgmental in their attitudes toward others, but exude the *Agape* Love of God and represent Christ as humble and respectful ambassadors of Truth.[19]

H. Review Summary: As we live in the Discipleship to Conversion Dynamic Process, the elements and value of suffering and affliction for the Gospel cannot be overestimated. Neither can the issue of our own willingness to forgive others of their transgressions. Only in Christ can we be always victorious over sin, fear, persecution, lust and prejudice.[20]

Finally, do not be surprised: All those who are invested in this world's goods and ways, Christian or not, will virulently oppose the True Christian Faith.

III. Those who know the "Way of Christ" do not "fall for" the ways of the world, the flesh and Satan. Yes. All those whom Truly Love the Ways of Christ will not be "fooled" by any of the ways of the world, the flesh or the devil. Beware: Remember Job had feared loss, so this belief worked like a 'self-fulfilling prophecy.' However, he eventually recovered from that lapse of faith and was restored threefold. When

---

19 Isa. 8:9-20; 28:12-30:21; Matt. 7:13-23; 28:18; John 18:36,37; 1 Cor. 12:12,13; Phil. 3:20,21; 2 Tim. 2:3-12; 1 Pet. 3:15; 1 John 2:15-17

20 Psa. 119:65-72; John 15:18-27; Acts 5:29-42; Rom. 8:17 ff.; 1 Cor. 10:12,13; 2 Cor. 1:1-11; 4:1-5:21; 7:9,10; Gal. 6:14; 2 Tim. 1:7-14; 2:3-12; 3:12; Heb. 10:26-39; 11:25; 12:1-29; 1 Pet. 4:1-19; 5:6-11; James 5:10,11 *See also Glossary of Terms' entry *Affliction* and the paper entitled The Indispensability of Affliction*

you fully trust God and are confident of His Loving care, all your fears evaporate like smoke![21]

Beware of the world's ways, for they all come from *Humanism.* However, IF you truly "Delight in the Law of the Lord," "Love God with all your heart, soul, mind and strength" and seek God's Ways in Christ, you will find His Will and Way. If this is true, then you will also know and believe that God will perfect His Will in you so long as you actively cooperate with the Holy Spirit.[22]

Always remember that Jesus will never let you down and the best is yet to come! Let us then "go on to perfection" and press onto the high calling and the prize we have been waiting for us in Christ![23]

Scripture tells us that man has no excuse not to believe in the reality of God and His Kingdom. Yet, man deliberately dishonors God by refusing to acknowledge the obvious: Even many "So-called Christians" can be counted to be in this category because they are giving honor and glory to politicians, soldiers and professionals that belongs exclusively to God! Worse yet, this problem points to the source of it all: Idolatry. The song "He Laid Aside His Majesty" essentially confirms Scripture which tells us that "only one man's Blood makes us Free," Jesus Christ Alone.[24]

Moreover, Jesus Christ is the Word of God and the Truth. Viz., ALL that Jesus taught is the absolute Truth and is reliable and doable just as much today as it was in the first century. Jesus Christ is God to us: His Word and Authority are superior to any man or agency of man. How we give honor and to whom we ascribe glory are serious things that indicate the identity of whom or what we worship! IF in fact that object of worship and trust is not the one True God of the universe defined in the Bible, it is an IDOL.[25]

---

21   1 Kings 18:21; 2 Chr. 20:19,20; Psa. 23, 24, 27, 31-42; Matt. 11:25-30; Heb. 4:9-16
22   Psa. 1,2; 37:3-5; 23,24; John 14-17; Phil. 1:6,21; Heb. 13:15; 1 John 2:15-17
23   Isa. 26:3,4; 40:28-31; Phil. 3:7-14
24   Psa. 2,110; Isa. 44-46; Jer. 10,17; John 2:19-21; 3:16,17; 11:25-52; 12:23 f; Rom. 1:18-32; 1 John 2:1-6 *See also the paper entitled True Liberty is in Christ Alone, especially Sect. II-B, which contains the list of "SOLA's," those benefits which come from Christ Alone*
25   1 Kings 18:21; Psa. 94:1 ff.; 110:1 ff.; 118:8,9; Isa. 43-46; Jer. 10,17; Ezek. 18:30-32; Matt. 28:18; John 14:6; 8:31-36; Acts 17:24-31; Rom. 1

IV. Christ has ordained for us a <u>Whole New Way of fighting evil</u>: In the spirit. Let us establish some "absolute givens" concerning the Genuine Christian Faith. One is this: The whole world was not worthy of Jesus Christ or of one drop of His Blood shed on Calvary! However, "eternal Salvation" in the future was not the entire purpose of Christ's sojourn here on earth. Of course, that particular issue lies behind religion's hold on the masses of "professing Christians," deceiving them to believe that God's Salvation is limited to the "bye and bye." Yes, under this guise, false doctrine has been hiding in plain sight for seventeen centuries. Yet, all is not lost.

We still can correct our attitude and see the "bigger picture."

Moreover, God loved us so much that He saw past our despicable, sinful and earthbound ways, showing us the exalted "Way of Heaven" that redirects our focus to see what Jesus gave us in our well-known Disciple's Prayer: "Thy Will be done <u>on earth (just) as it is in Heaven.</u>"[26]

However, we are still left with a big problem: Many religious leaders have lost their spiritual perspective regarding their relationship to Christ the True Head of the Church worldwide. Not only that, their position concerning the issue of the supreme *Authority* of Christ on earth is questionable at best since they invariably appear to exalt <u>human authority over God's Authority as defined in Scripture.</u>[27]

Is there any way to get religious leaders to see and understand the True nature of the Complete Gospel and to redirect their teaching accordingly? I know that this would usually be considered an impossible task. Yet, despite this, we must pray that this happens soon for this is an especially important change that must take place to bring about true <u>Revival.</u>[28]

Consider the following questions:

One: Do you <u>truly Believe that God is real and, because of this you implicitly Trust Christ</u> completely, following His Commands in every facet of life without reservation to the best of your ability?[29]

---

26   Matt. 6:9-15; John 3:3-8,16,17; 6:27-63; 2 Cor. 4:3-6; 10:2-6; Eph. 6:10-18

27   Matt. 28:18; Luke 10:21-24; John 18:36,37; Phil. 3:20,21

28   *See the papers entited (the 2 part series) Authority and Conscience, (the 3 part series) Christianity Versus Religion and Regarding Christ's Headship*

29   John 1:1-14; 14:1; Heb. 11:1-6

Two, Do you actually trust God's Word to be truthful and effective, so long as we apply it contextually to every situation we face right here and right now in this life on earth?[30]

Three, are you willing to set aside your prior "religious catechisms" long enough for you to open up your mind's eye to the greater truths that Jesus taught?

Explanation: Many are taught that these truths of Christ are "idealistic" or "impractical in the real world," but God's Word says you can believe this way and guide your life by His Precepts despite what others may say, no matter who they are! Compare the proactive teachings of Christ and Paul with those of the Old Testament King David and you can see that, via the *New Covenant,* God has sublimated (changed) the venue of warfare from the physical to the spiritual. When you "see" this truth, you can also see through the lies of religion. This sight reveals that they are in a league with worldly powers and their ways that diametrically oppose what Jesus Christ taught. Study history: It can be proven that the vast majority of Christianity was coopted in the fourth century by Constantine and replaced by a religion that masquerades as "Christian" and has since continued for seventeen centuries to betray Christ. Yes, humanistic religion is the source of all the contradictions, confusion and impotence that has plagued organized churches. Satan's neutralization techniques are amazingly effective, acting very much like 'brainwashing' and that is why they are so deeply entrenched in the psyche of modern Christians. The deception is so pervasive that they "come out of their corner swinging" when are confronted with the entire set of basic truths that comprise the True complete Gospel of Christ![31]

However, the lies of religion can be overthrown by the supernatural operation of "fighting by Love Power in the spirit" ordained by Jesus Christ and subsequently preached by Paul. Also, consider the following references which reveal the amazing "power of Agape Love": [32]

---

30   John 14:6; Heb. 6:15-20; 1 Pet. 2:22

31   Luke 11:33-36; Acts 2:38,39; 3:19; Rom. 1:18-32; Gal. 1:6-12; Eph. 6:12; 2 Thess. 1,2; Heb. 7:11-10:23; 2 Pet. 1:2-21; Rev. 13,17 *See also the 4 part series of papers entitled Christian Guidelines for Spiritual Warfare and the book Spiritual Guidelines for Restoration, "Historical Review section"*

32   Matt. 5:43-48; 6:9-15, 22-24; 10:22-39; Luke 9:51-56; 12:8-10; John 8:12-58; 18:36,37; Rom. 12:9-21; 1 Cor. 13; 2:Cor. 10:3-6; 11:12-15; Eph. 6:10-18; 2 Thess. 2:3-12; 2 Tim. 2:11-13

Also, consider the awesome power of the Word of God candidly spoken so that the listeners were "cut to the heart" with conviction by the Holy Spirit.[33]

Yet, we must always keep in mind that, to be a true Disciple of Christ, one must totally be committed to following Christ, despite the cost. This is the only way we can fully understand the teachings of Christ that alone can Transform our entire outlook on life and way of thinking.[34]

When one truly receives the full import of the above, when, like an odometer, the digits of the mind all turn to the next whole number, one can truly have an "epiphany experience." The "epiphany" comes when the Holy Spirit opens the 'inner window' of your mind and the fog of confusion from humanism lifts. Then "at last you can see the Light" of the Glorious Gospel of Christ with all its exalted majestic truth. It is at this point that we are enabled to see the full extent of the *Atonement* of Christ. Indeed, this inner opening occurs when Christ's Teaching finally "sinks in" and makes sense to us![35]

When a person truly "sees the Light of Christ" and begins to understand its full meaning, their perception of everything in the world radically changes! This awakening also triggers a major alteration of attitude, causing the person to enter a time of inner evaluation and struggle in which the spiritual life within seeks to regain control over the sinful desires of Humanism.[36]

Moreover, when the Christian Believer reaches this point when the spiritual begins to take control, those "so-called hard sayings" that we were taught were "impractical" by religious leaders will come into a sharp focus. But of course, God's Word says they are practical because those particular teachings of Christ that directly contradicts the world's way of thinking are the same ones that are necessary to redirect our attention from self and worldly things and unto Jesus Christ and others. The upshot of this is that when we take the whole of Christ's

33   Luke 2:33-35; 21:8-24; Acts 2, 7; Heb. 4:12,13
34   Rom. 12:1-3; Eph. 4:23,24
35   Matt. 6:22; Luke 8:16-18; 11:33-36; John 1:1-18; 3:21; 6:27-63; Acts 26:12-18; Rom. 13:12; 2 Cor. 4:3-6; 5:14-21;10:3-6; Eph. 5:1-20; Col. 1:12,13; 2 Tim. 1:7-15; 2 Pet. 1:12-21
36   Heb. 10:32; 11:24-28; 12:1-14

Teaching seriously, we realize that there is <u>no other way or means to obtain peace on earth!</u> [37]

Indeed, Jesus warned and the Scriptures also say that the full truth of what Jesus taught, the Way of Agape Love and Light, would be "evil spoken of" by both the world and apostates because it flies in the face of all the humanistic ways the world uses to rationalize their violence, killing and slavery. The fundamental difference that separates True Christian Believers from the world is the fact that they, in stark contrast to the Platonic and Aristotelean beliefs, <u>believe God is directly involved with the affairs of mankind right here and now</u>[38]

V. What is the New Covenant teaching?

A. Jesus is teaching us a whole new level of confronting evil <u>at its source.</u> Know this: It is the <u>only way that works to solve man's problems.</u> Not only that, if you are a True Christian Believer, you know that no matter what the enemy throws at us, the Holy Spirit will teach you how to neutralize it!

However, you must <u>pay attention to details</u>, comparing Scripture with Scripture, searching for corresponding precepts in the Word of God. Then, pray for *Wisdom* and God's Revealed answer from the Holy Spirit that forms a weapon that <u>no enemy can defeat.</u> Notice the sermon/ speeches of Paul and Stephen.[39]

Not only that, IF you truly Believe God's Word is Truth with all your heart, soul, mind and strength, you will eventually overcome and win the battle, enduring faithfully to the end. However, you must also remember that our battle is in the spirit. Also, we must always remember that God works simultaneously on both axes of life, like a "symbolic cross": Vertically, between Believers and God and horizontally between Believers and our fellow man.[40]

---

37   Matt. 4:16; 5-7; 10:16-39; Luke 1:67-2:14; 9:23-26; John 8:31-47; 9:39-41; 12:23-26;14:15-16:33

38   Luke 2:34,35; 6:22 ff.; John 3:19-21, 27-36; 15:18-25; 18:36,37; Acts 28:22; Rom. 1:18-2:16; 2 Cor. 4:2-6; 10:3-6; 11:10-15; 13:5-8; Gal. 1:6-12; 3:1; 4:16; Eph. 4:15-5:20; 6:14; 2 Thess. 2:3-12; 1 Tim. 2:5-7; 6:3-12; 2 Tim. 2:15-26; 3:1-8; 4:1-4; Heb. 10:26-39;; 2 Pet. 2:1-3

39   Isa. 50:7; 54:17; 59:19; Acts 2:14-41; 7:1-60; 17:24-31; 2 Cor. 10:3-6

40   Matt. 5:43-48; Rom. 12:9-21; Eph. 6:10-18

B. Let us observe God's Spiritual guidelines for Spiritual Warfare, that is, how we deal with spiritual enemies. Satan is our primary enemy and he has myriads of minions working for him, However, we must remember that God's forces are far superior to any working of Satan and are effective in all circumstances.

The most significant arena of our spiritual battle exists in the mind. Mental attacks represent the most pervasive and widespread threat to our spirituality since they always act in concord with some sin area in our life. That is also why the issue of Holiness is so important.[41]

Consider the main subareas of sin and iniquity:

1. Idolatry is the defacto worship of human power, expressed mainly in people's "pledging Allegiance" to the State and its symbols and agencies, an apostate condition into which multitudes of "So-called Christians" have been led by religious leaders, along with its attendant trust in politicians, soldiers and professionals to 'save' instead of Trusting God like they should.[42]

2. Succumbing to Fear and intimidation.[43]

3. Unbelief, the failure to seriously take God's Word or the Teachings of Christ at face value.[44]

4. Hatred of any person, group or nation.[45]

5. The 'unforgiving spirit.[46]

6. Adultery and sexual sins of all types.[47]

7. Unbridled ambition and greed, based on the world's falsehood that this "brings happiness".[48]

---

41   John 10:25-30; 17:10-26; Acts 26:12-18; 2 Tim. 2:19-26; Heb. 2:9-15; 10:9-39; 12:1-17; 1 Pet. 1:3-2:10; 1 John 3:3 *See also the 4 part series of papers Christian Guidelines for Spiritual Warfare and Glossary of Terms' entry *(the Doctrine of) Sanctification*

42   1 Sam. 2:6-9; Zech. 4:6; 1 Cor. 10:1-21

43   2 Tim. 1:7 f.; 1 Pet. 5:8

44   John 5:24; Rom. 10:17; Heb. 11:6

45   Rom. 12:19-21

46   Matt. 6:14,15

47   1 Cor. 6:9-11, 16-20; Gal. 5:19-21

48   Phil. 3:17-21

8. Loving and seeking the "advantages" of the world in which they vainly think they can indulge without serious consequences.[49]

9. Dependence on Drugs, regardless of whether they are by prescription or obtained "in the street."[50]

C. Another major area of Satan's work can be found in the illicit use of "Soul Power," a.k.a., "the latent power of the soul." This is something that Satan makes great use of among naive Christians. It follows the same idolatrous track as those who believe in violence which is the dependence on man's power to save. The only antidote to this is to <u>Ask God to sever the motions of your soul from the spirit.</u> Interestingly, this "spiritual surgery" parallels the Old Testament ritual of circumcision and also the act of (spiritual) *Baptism,* in that it serves to disentangle the motions of our fleshly nature that still likes to sin from our Reborn human spiritual life.

The plain truth is that unless this choice is made early in our spiritual adventure with God, our flesh will retain control over our being preventing our growing into the "fullness of the stature of Christ." Unfortunately, few Believers have ever been told about this crucial change we must ask God to perform within us.[51]

VI. The following is An Affidavit/ Statement for all True Christians to consider.

Think about this:

IF you let anyone or any situation take away your God-given Liberty to Worship God to worship freely without <u>any restrictions at any time,</u> you will eventually let the Antichrist take away <u>everything else</u> and make you his slave!

---

49   James 4:1-8; 1 John 2:15-17

50   Gal. 5:21 *(translated as 'witchcraft' in KJV)*

51   Luke 2:34,35; Heb. 4:12,13 *See the paper The Spiritual Laws of Revival, Law #8:"the separation of soul from spirit"*

Ask yourself: Who or what do you worship, fear, trust and serve? Know that Scripture says that, to live as a true Believer, you must fear God and not man or circumstance, for the fear of man is a snare.[52]

A. Consider the application of the following Scriptural truths to contemporary situations very seriously:

1. God's Word tells us that we must trust (have faith) in God and "Worship (God) without any hindrance or interposed influence, barrier or veil on our face" (placed between us and God).[53]

2. Jesus Christ commands every Christian to "Worship (God) in spirit and in Truth" continually. This includes the underlying precept that our worship of God is single mindedly focused only on the one True God. This also means that we fear, trust, serve and pray to the one and only True God.[54]

3. Know also that Scripture plainly tells us that God's Law is supreme in the lives of True Christians and that "We must obey God rather than man" whenever their laws conflict.[55]

4. It is "Not my will (or words) but God's Word," for "Thy Word is Truth" and "Jesus Christ IS the Word of God" and the "Word that is written on our hearts" by the Holy Spirit, the Spirit of Christ.

Beware of those who tout humanistic interpretations of God's Word, for they speak from the "carnal mind," which God defines in Scripture for being an enemy of God. Only that which pertains to the Spiritual Mind will result in life and peace with God and our fellow man.[56]

5. God's Word teaches us that God's Protection is over and around all those who loyally Serve Him with the whole heart. Also, remember God's Deliverance of His People on the First Passover. However, the underlying condition remains that one must personally believe God's

---

52   Psa. 94:20; 115:11; 118:1-9; Prov. 29:25; Jer. 10,17; Matt. 6:22-24, 33; 10:26 39
53   2 Cor. 3:17,18
54   Exodus 20:3; 1 Kings 18:21; Psa. 19, 119; Isa. 44:6-20; Jer. 10:1-15; 17:5-15; Matt. 4:10; 6:1-13, John 4:23,24; Acts 17:22-31; Rom. 1:16-2:16; James 1:5-8
55   Psa. 94:20; 118:8,9; Dan. 3,6; Matt. 22:21; Acts 4:12-20; 5:29-32 *See also the 2 part series of papers entitled Authority and Conscience and Authority & Conscience Part Two: God has established a "Framework of Order"*
56   John 7:16-39; 8:12-58;9:39-10:18; 13:35-17:26; Rom. 8:1-11; 1 Cor. 1:17-2:16; Heb. 8:6-12; Rev. 19:10-13

Word for it to be effective! Asterisked refs refer to God's protection from diseases and poisons and the healing of those afflicted with them.[57]

B. Christians, watch and beware of the "strong delusion" that is coming upon all who fail to love the Truth of Christ's True and only Gospel of Peace.

1. Much compromise comes from the false doctrine of *Determinism,* which falsely teaches that God "ordains" political figures, thus leading their naive followers into gross error with doctrines that combine the church with the state. The "doctrines of the state" result from this unholy alliance which exalts nationalism and state symbols and rationalizes mass murder by the military.[58]

2. To survive as a True Christian in the tribulation, you must know how to discern the Truth and to see the vast chasm between the truth and the "big lies" being foisted upon the masses by the corporate media of Antichrist (the secular part of the False Prophet). They also cleverly use Religion (not true Christianity) as the religious part of the False Prophet. Together, Satan uses them to deceive and enslave the foolish and naive who believe anything they see on TV.[59]

The only source you can fully trust for being The Truth is God's Holy Written Word, the Bible, interpreted by the Holy Spirit as mentioned above.[60]

3. Scripture plainly tells us that in the Last Days will come a time of testing that will be more difficult than any other period before and that it will never be repeated. Scripture tells us that God's Judgment

---

57   Exodus 6:6,7; 14:13,14; *15:26; *Deut. 1:28,30; 3:22; 4:32-39; 7:15; 1 Sam. 2:6-10;*2 Chr. 7:14; 20:20; Psa. 5:11,12; 16:1 ff.; 18:2,6,16,17, 30,31, 46-49; 23:1 ff.; 25:1-12; 27:1 ff.; 31:1-15, 23,24; 32:6-8; 33:4, 18,19; 34:4 ff.; 37:3-5, 18,19, 23-25; 40:1-4; 41:1,2; 42:8; 44:1-8; 46:1 ff.; 50:14,15,23; 54:1 ff.; 59:16; 61:1 ff.; 62:1-8; 73:16,17, 24-28; 80:7; 84:11; *91:1 ff.;97:10,11; *103:1-5; *115:1 ff.; 116:6; *118:1-9; 121:1,2; 145:19,20; Prov. 2:8; 10:29; 12:28;19:23; 29:25; 30:5; Isa. 28:12-16; 29:9-30:21; 33:2-6; 42-46; 50:4-754:17; 59:19;*Matt. 8:1-4; 4:23,24; 9:20-30,35; 10:1; 14:35; *Mark 1:40-42; *16:15-18; *Luke 5:12-15; 6:17; 9:1; John 5:4; *Acts 28:1-6

58   Matt. 5:43-48; John 18:36; 1 John 3,4; Rev. 13,17

59   Matt. 24; Luke 21; 2 Thess. 2:3-12; 1 Tim. 3; 2 Tim. 2

60   Psa. 119:89; John 1:1; 14:21-26; 15:26; 16:11-15; 17:17

is coming soon and that it will fall on all who have failed to love the whole truth, that is, ALL the Truth that Jesus taught.[61]

4. Beware of drugs. The minions of Antichrist are avidly using drugs to "dumb down" the masses, making them docile slaves. "Universal" Vaccines will be used more and more in this agenda, for they will contain the 'poisons' that will accomplish that goal. Another use for vaccines will likely be to slyly administer the miniaturized chips that will serve as "the Mark of the Beast," as defined in the Bible as the way Antichrist will use to control and dominate the world. Interestingly, the use of manmade drugs is listed among grievous sins listed by Paul in the Greek text of his letter to the Galatians.[62]

5. God's promise to Christian Believers remains that God will not allow us to be tested beyond that power God gives by Faith in His Presence which will inspire, guide and safely protect all those who loyally serve Christ with the whole heart, never resorting to compromise of any type.[63]

C. Always remember this: Neither the government, politicians, soldiers nor professionals can truly save you. Scripture teaches that only God's Power can save us from circumstance or from the evil that comes from our sin or the sins of others. God's Word teaches that whenever one places their trust in worldly sources based on human power instead of God, they are committing the sin of Idolatry. If you claim to be a Christian and do this, you will surely "fall away" from faith into unbelief and become like the rest because of the "strong delusion" that accompanies the sin of idolatry! Unfortunately, however, most professing Christians are not being taught about this fact! The undiluted truth teaches us that ALL who fall away into unbelief become subject to God's wrath and, therefore, God's Word expressly tells us that we must subsequently Repent of any sins we may commit after our initial *Regeneration* experience. God's Spirit is always there to convict you of any sin you commit, but it is your responsibility to do the repenting![64]

---

61 Jer. 30:7; Ezek. 5:9; Dan. 12:1; Matt. 24:21,22; Mark 13:19,20; Rom. 1:18-32;2 Thess. 2:3-12
62 *This reference is found in Gal. 5:20 with 'witchcraft' being the English translation of the Greek word Pharmakeia, which is also the root of the English word "Pharmaceutical"*
63 Psa. 15; Luke 21:8-19; 1 Cor. 10:1-21 Ibid. Footnote #6 above
64 Ezek. 18:30; Acts 3:19; 2 Cor. 7:9,10; 2 Thess. 2:3-12; 1 Tim. 4; 6:3-12; 2 Tim. 2,3

Moreover, to pass the tests of the age that are coming, you must be able to recognize the difference between the Truth and the lie. Specifically, you need to see that this present "corona crisis" is a man-made "deep event" that has been set up and managed by the Antichrist as a tool to control, dominate and enslave the masses according to the agendas of the New World Order. Again, reliable sources have indicated that the "corona vaccine" will most likely be used to deliver the implants that the Bible defines for being "the Mark."

D. Question: What is the Divine Standard that All True Christians are being held to by God?

Answer: The Gospel of Jesus Christ describes the *New Covenant,* which is defined throughout Scripture for being God's intended Standard by which all humans can be Saved in all ways, temporal and spiritual. It also contains the set of Godly Moral Standards by which righteous people live. God's Word, the Bible, defines the Body of Christ for being the set of persons that responds to the Living Head, Jesus Christ, Who Reigns alongside Father God on the Throne in Heaven. For all intents and purposes, our Living Head, Jesus Christ, is also our King pertaining to all matters here "on earth, just as it is in Heaven" in both private and public situations.

This means that Christ's Commands and Teachings must take precedence over and above all earthly authorities, despite whom they are. Yes, this means that Christians will suffer affliction, which means tribulation. However, God's promise is that Christ has overcome the world and that we will benefit from that promise.[65]

The New Covenant was put into effect the moment Christ proclaimed from the cross: "It is finished." At that precise time, God's angels rent the veil in the holy of holies and opened the great doors of the temple, signaling that the Father had received Christ's Blood as payment for the sins of the world.[66]

---

65   Matt. 6:9-13; 28:18; Luke 11:1-4; John 16:33
66   Matt. 27:50-53; 1 John 2:1-6

Moreover, God's receiving of Christ's Sacrifice also means that as of the moment of Christ's crucifixion, all types of "Bloodshed sacrifices, punishments and payment for sin" are no longer approved by God. The New Covenant is a covenant of Agape Love wherein God shows His Love to all humankind.

Not only that, we should know that, in God's sight, everyone is equally guilty of sin and that means everybody is guilty of breaking all the law, including murder, even if we have not killed anyone individually. That is also why No True Christian could ever approve of the killing of anyone by anyone, regardless of the reason.[67]

---

67   *Matt. 5:43-48; Luke 6:20 ff.; James 2:10 See also the papers entitled as follows: The 3 part series Christianity Versus Religion, Divergent Belief Systems, the 2 part series How Should we then Live and The New Covenant*

Chapter 11

Examine Yourselves

Let us now go on to the precepts regulating the *crucial use* of the human conscience in continually examining and comparing our lives with the Christian standard of the New Covenant.

I. Consider the primary guiding principles regulating biblical Christianity.

One, the *New Covenant* of Christ is the rule of law for Christian believers. Believers are answerable to this standard. It is the Word of God for Christians, giving us the *divine ruler* by which we can always readily apply *to all situations, private and public.* Let us also realize that the terms *New Testament and New Covenant* are not completely interchangeable. The difference lies in the fact that *the New Covenant* contains doctrines that God has *carried over* from the Old Testament, such as stewardship "worship in song" and the doctrine of creation. To accurately determine *Christian doctrine,* however, one must realize that a substantial and collateral New Testament scriptural witness must also accompany to compare and verify all texts taken from the Old Testament. Thus, in our minds, God's Spirit can transform these texts, upgrading them to the New Covenant level.

Two, now we explore the relationship between the human mind and the Word of God. God commands us to study His Word and to let His Word penetrate our entire being so that the Holy Spirit will have a handle on our lives. However, His Word is no toy. God condemns its use as a pretext for spiritual pride to justify worldly and materialistic lifestyles, or as a club to browbeat other people! God's Word reveals our inward desires. Often in Scripture, we encounter the terms, *incline your heart… and seek…* They tell us that God looks for a submissive, teachable, and inquisitive mind and heart (inner being or human spirit), which seeks the awesome profound wisdom recorded in Jesus's masterful truism: "Blessed are those who hunger and thirst for righteousness, for God will fill them to satisfaction."[159] Do you have this kind of heart, my friend?

This is the most crucial of attitudes that we must cultivate to see and appreciate the incredible depth, value, and diversity that the Scripture holds for the diligent and honest *seeker of truth.* However, we must be constantly on guard because of the potential distortion and misdirection of crucial information caused by the carnal (humanistic) mind, which only sees what human nature wants to see. It is the express will of God that we become *lovers of truth!* Jesus said, "I am the way, *the truth,* and the life, no man comes unto the Father except by Me."[160]

Three, every believer is personally responsible to the *truth before God and their own conscience* for all their thoughts, motives, attitudes, and actions! Paul wrote a chilling truism in his second letter to the Thessalonians: Any failure to act upon *the love of the truth* can condemn us! Moreover, God is going to judge us by Jesus Christ based upon *what we truly do,* not just by what we say! "God is *no respecter of persons."*[161]

**Therefore, it behooves us to carefully observe the response of our conscience and to act accordingly. Yet, to do this, we must also maintain a *clear and good conscience.* We do this by daily obedience to the current level of truth the Holy Spirit has granted us to our mind as it receives information from the Word of God. Yet beware of self-deception! God's Word tells us that *ordinary ignorance* is no excuse! However, God does mitigate this to a degree by also telling us that "His goodness [toward us] leads us to repentance."[162]

God's mercy, however, is not a pretext for delaying our repentance or thinking we have gotten away with sin. However, I am afraid that many Christians think that by hiding behind the authority of others they have evaded those thorny issues of conscience. In essence, these

---

159   Matt. 5:6
160   John 14:6
161   Matt. 7:21; Rom. 2:11–16; 2 Thess. 2:10–12 See also the books" Basic Christian Doctrine, The Doctrine of the Elect/ Ekklesia and Conditions for Salvation
162   Rom. 1:18–2:16

authorities are leading them to believe that they can avoid the hard sayings of Jesus this way! Yet that is a lie! Nevertheless, they couch this lie of the misuse of authority by assuming or teaching that a church gives individuals a cover that takes care of those things for them! They mistakenly believe that the collective consensus of the majority and those in authority in a church organization can substitute for the individuals' responsibility to heed their own conscience before God personally!

This is an incredibly dangerous doctrine exploited by authoritarian organizations! Claiming exemption is very easy for them! They just say, "I was just following orders," or that "everybody says it is OK," or that "my church leaders say [that doctrine] is 'biblical,'" et. al. when deep down in their own conscience they know (or used to know) *that it is not OK with God!* Deception will fill the halls of perdition with those who thought they could get by and that God would still save them, depending on man's fallible standards. Situation ethics (relativism) has very powerful motivation! The powerful sway of false religion exploits the weaknesses of man. They know that people crave acceptance. People want to fit in. Evidently, they like others to tell them what to do and believe. They adapt to the crowd. People "assume" that satisfies all the conditions required by God, and that they are safe (saved).

Yet are they? What you do not know can hurt you! Like the "proverbial frog in the pan," *false doctrine is cooking many* to death because they did not heed their conscience or *love the truth more than the acceptance of man!* Peer pressure greatly distorts our perceptions of right and wrong!

John wrote, "Many leading men believed in Him [Jesus], but because of the Pharisees (influential religious leaders), they did not publicly acknowledge Him for fear that they would expel them from the synagogue (church), for they loved the praise of men more than the praise of God!"[163]

Has anything changed? Jesus was adamantly clear about telling those who (*say* they) believe in Him that they must also *publicly* receive, support, and acknowledge Him. He said that if they did that, He would also support them before God the Father. However, if they

---

163   John 12:42,43

denied Jesus Christ in public, then Jesus would also deny them before the Father![164]

Fourth, we must have the spirit of Christ to be a genuine Christian. *First,* this means *that we belong to Christ* by virtue of purchase by His precious blood. Second, we have been transformed within by the process of biblical *conversion*! Remember the beautiful illustration of *the caterpillar and the butterfly?* Everyone knows that the caterpillar must die before the butterfly can live and fly. The carnal self-seeking (caterpillar) nature with which we were born must die before we can live the Christian life. You cannot make a butterfly by tacking wings on a caterpillar!

The butterfly of the spiritual life in Jesus cannot live unless this required process is completed.[165]

**These two natures cannot peacefully coexist! Deep down inside, we must decide to follow Jesus come what may unto the death! This ties together both baptism and discipleship. However, do not be dismayed. God knows our heart.

Even in our imperfection, if we conscientiously choose to act and respond like Christ would in any given situation, making no excuses, we are blameless before God. That is the standard of biblical Christianity! However, we *prove that Jesus is not* our true master guiding us if we resort to *making any kind of excuse.* This also applies if we attempt to change the rules to fit the circumstances! Jesus said that we could only serve one master at a time, and that crucial decision is wholly up to us!

Every believer is going to *be judged* at the judgment seat of Christ on that same basis! Jesus plainly taught that "God would only save the ones that endure to the end."[166]

Yes, we are responsible for doing what Jesus said to the best of our ability until we die, or to the time he comes back, whichever is first. No "easy ways out" exist, and it is not over until it is over!

---

164   Matt. 7:13–21; 10:32,33; 2 Tim. 2:11–13; Heb. 3:12–15; 6:4–6; 10:26–39
165   Rom. 8:9 **See also *Christian Conversion, Part One: Introduction to Christian Conversion and Figure One: Illustration-Comparison*
166   Matt. 6:24; 24:13; Luke 10:22

Fifth, behold the contrasts! Jesus said to Peter, "He who seeks to save his [earthly] life [soul] will lose it, *but* he who *loses* his [earthly] life [soul] *will find it.*"[167]

The truth is that we *do not lose our fleshly nature so easily!* The caterpillar still lives *until we choose to do something about it!* Jesus said to Nicodemus, "Flesh gives birth to flesh, and Spirit gives birth to Spirit… You must be born again." The Bible teaches that the old nature *must die for Christ to live within!* Scripture bluntly tells us that we must choose to be *single-minded* to receive anything from God. The things we say and do prove who is the master that we serve![168]

However, *if we do nothing* about this and remain unconverted (still a caterpillar and in the flesh), we risk eternal judgment! Jesus says unequivocally that any unconfessed or unrepentant active sin remaining (at death) will result in eternal damnation![169] Here, Jesus tells us that it is the selfish nature of the flesh that is responsible for this. This nature is expressed in the appetites of sexual desire and pleasure and in the "other types of lust" we see in the desires for acceptance, money, possessions, and power. However, we can choose the master that is in control of us at any given time! The Bible teaches that the identity of the master/nature determines the destiny of a person.[170]

The truth is that not only must we be first born of the Spirit of God in provisional, positional, or initial salvation, but that we must also *persevere on.* All the way unto the *end!* The Holy Spirit must lead us in our daily lives to do this. Conversion is not automatic. "For as many [only the ones] the Spirit of God [truly] leads are the sons [children] of God."

Merely holding on to a *mere confession of words,* while still going our own way or following man does us absolutely *no good to justify us* before God![171] Yet, the chilling truth remains that Scripture says that only a *few will be saved!* Scripture tells us, "For the preaching of the cross is

---

167   Matt. 16:21–25

168   Matt. 6:24; James 1:5–8, 17–27; 2:14–26; 3:1–18

169   Matt. 5:20–25; Mark 9:35–50; John 9:39–41. *See also the papers entitled 'Christian Conversion (a 3-part series),' and 'Figure One: Illustration-Comparison of Caterpillar/ Butterfly to Conversion'*

170   Matt. 5:20–25; 7:13–29; Mark 9:35–50; John 14:6; 15:1–7

171   John 1:1–14; 3:3–8; Rom. 2:1–16; 8:1–16

foolishness [absurdity] unto the perishing, but unto us who are [being] saved, it is the power of God."… "We are the sweet fragrance [smell] of God among those whom God is saving… And among those who are perishing… To the latter the stench of death, to the former the aroma of life."[172]

II. How do we conduct a balanced value assessment?

Although we must acknowledge that one cannot judge another's conscience per se, conducting simple observations over a judicious period may obtain a well-balanced value assessment of a life. Wisdom recommends that we first do this for our own life, for then we will have realized at that point how far short of the goal we are! From that vantage point, God's Spirit will give us the opportunity to "remove any beams in our own eye, so we can see clearly to remove the speck in the other's!" This kind of observation evaluates a person's:

1. *avowed beliefs:* what a person says they believe in tells you much;

2. obvious and apparent *attitudes* exhibited toward God;

3. attitudes we express toward others, especially offender types;

4. their actions: what a person does—lifestyle, business practices, language, etc.

We must repeat that it is not the purpose of this examination to *judge* in the sense of condemnation (prescribing specific punishment). The Greek word for that is *Krima* or *Krites*. The word for judge that we seek to guide our consideration here is *Krisis*. Greek lexicons define Krisis as making a *value assessment or a moral determination.* We apply this in what is right or wrong in a given situation, or an analysis of *fruit or behavior in a person's life.* Jesus used the same word when telling his listeners to exercise *righteous judgment.* Therefore, our purpose is to sharpen the focus of true New Covenant doctrine and practice.[173]** In doing this, we can accurately evaluate things (judge) by comparison

---

172   Matt. 7:13–21; Luke 13:23–30; 1 Cor. 1:18–2:16; 2 Cor. 2:11–16
173   Compare Matt. 7:1 with John 7:24; **See also Glossary of Terms entry: Judgment*

to Scripture, and finally relate all this to the process of salvation. *The salient points* are as follows:

One, we must engage in *ongoing confession* of sin and of *repentance from sin on a daily basis.*[174]

Two, we must be diligent in our *ongoing faith* by *daily walking in the light,* comparing our lives to the standard of Holy Scripture.[175]

Three, *ongoing conversion* cannot continue unless we allow God's Spirit to reshape us. The Holy Spirit accomplishes this process first in the mind. Only then we can move from the carnal to the spiritual. This opens the way for the necessary changes we must make in our lifestyle and central belief structure. If we continue diligently in this discipleship, then we are progressively conforming to the image of Jesus.

Four, *ongoing obedience* is essential: following in Jesus's steps by abiding in His Word (commands, teaching) as expressed in the New Testament.[176]

Five, *ongoing seeking:* let us seek more of God. We do this by *our obedience of the great command in loving God* and our brothers and sisters.[177]

Six, *ongoing ministry:* continually seeking to serve Jesus, using the gifts that He has so graciously given by His spirit.[178]

Seven, *ongoing love:* this is the resultant fruit of abiding in Jesus and the quintessential "litmus test" of mature Christianity.[179]

Let us be totally honest in our heart and ask: Can someone legitimately *claim they are a Christian* and not even believe, or even refuse to obey what Jesus taught as the truth, saying it is not for us today? Scripture's unequivocal answer is *no.* We must seek to obey Christ every day all the way!

---

174   Luke 9:23–26; 1 John 1:5–10
175   John 8:12; 9:39–41; 1 John 1:7
176   John 14:15; 15:10–12
177   Matt. 22:37–39
178   Luke 9:51–56; Rom. 12:3–21; 1 Cor. 12,13; Eph. 4:1–16
179   John 15:1–5; Gal. 5:22,23

III. The issue of the lordship of Jesus Christ is important!

How does God view this crucial precept of our faith? We know that the Scripture teaches that our attitude toward and belief in Jesus Christ are important.

The big question we have before us asks: Is it possible for God to save a person who claims *Jesus Christ as Savior, but not as Lord?* However, this very statement of human independence and rebellion is just another restatement of "no, Lord," which is itself a *contradiction* (oxymoron)! So, why do Jesus, Peter, Paul, and James *all* speak concerning a believer's responsibility to obey the Gospel of Jesus Christ if it were of no consequence?[180]

We find a different approach that leads to the same conclusion in Paul's first letter to the Corinthians. This is when he relates the communion elements to the Christian walk. In this familiar passage, the Spirit of Christ admonishes believers to *examine themselves before partaking the communion elements.* Why do you think Paul considered this so important? We can find the answer in Hebrews.[181] Although the communion elements are only symbols, they nonetheless point us to serious underlying spiritual realities. Both *the body of Christ and *the blood of Christ* form very *crucial links in our spiritual lifeline* to righteousness, holiness, and to eventual salvation *without which we cannot live!* Without these things, we will never experience holiness, and as Scripture succinctly reminds us, "Without holiness, no one will ever see the Lord."[182]

Think about it: *If you really consider yourself a true believer, then acknowledge the following realities about Jesus. Yet first,* in your heart, prayerfully ask the Lord, "Search me, O God, and see if there is any wicked way in me, and lead me in the way everlasting."[183] Consider the following:

---

180   Matt. 8:11,12; 13:24–52; 22:1–14; 23:1 ff,; 14:36–51; 25:1 ff.; Luke 13:28; 2 Cor. 13:5; 2 Thess. 2:10–12; James 2:14–26; 2 Pet 1:3–10

181   1 Cor. 11:27–32; Heb. 2:1–3; 3:1–6,12–14; 6:1–9; 10:26–39

182   Heb. 12:10–14

183   Psa. 139:23,24

1. It is *Only* by virtue of Jesus's blood that we are *forgiven of any sin, period!* So we invite disaster and judgment if we *trample the blood of Christ* by rebellion, believing false doctrine, or by willful unrepentant sin![184]

2. It is only the personal and real presence of the body of Christ Jesus that gives us our identity by spiritual baptism. This is so since Jesus is the real baptizer in the Holy Spirit and is our source and ultimate authority! His Holy Spirit (the Spirit of Christ) introduces us to the family of God, the body of Christ on earth. The Holy Spirit also personally *translates Jesus's life to us.*[185] Let us also never forget that:

- Jesus Christ is also *our high priest and our advocate* (defense attorney), defending us against all the accusations of the enemy.[186] And, moreover,

- Jesus Christ mediates the Holy Spirit, the only vital link believers have to the throne of God the Father in heaven![187]

- Since Jesus Christ is in heaven and the only link between us and Christ is the Holy Spirit, it behooves us to be very careful to *"grieve not the Holy Spirit,* by whom you were *sealed for the day of redemption."* This is another *crucial link in the chain of salvation.* Yes, we know that God calls *us to or unto salvation* and that the Holy Spirit *seals us for the day of redemption.* Yet, it remains true that we still can "break that link" by disobedience or abandonment.[188]

- *We must also know* that the judgment (righteousness) of God finally conditions our eventual salvation upon our actual response to the gospel, for it is *not our possession* as of yet. Nor is it independent of what we do in this life. Salvation is only *in Christ.* However, His promise is trustworthy. He says that "if we

---

184   Matt. 10:32,33; Heb. 10:26–39. *See the papers entitled "the Doctrine of Jesus Christ's Real Presence" and "Regarding Christ's Headship"*

185   *Matt. 3:11,12; 6:9–13; John 1:29–34; 16:13–15; 1 Cor. 12:12,13; Eph. 1:19–23; 2:18–22*

186   1 Tim. 2:5; 1 John 2:1,2

187   John 16:7–15

188   Matt. 10:32,33; Eph. 4:30; Heb. 10:26–31, 38,39

endure to the end" (just like Jesus said), we would be assured that *salvation will be our destiny!* [189]

- In the light of these clear statements, what should our attitude be toward Jesus and His commands? I know for some it will take time, but since we have life, we have hope. Remember, it is not where we are at the beginning of this race we call life, *but where we are at the end! Always keep the final goal in mind, for that is what will count for eternity!* See the parable of the workers in the vineyard and the parable of the prodigal son.[190]

IV. Summary

Let us now return to the title scripture: *"Examine Yourselves,* whether you are walking in faith. Test yourselves. Do you not realize that Jesus Christ is in you, unless (in the case that) you are reprobates?" What does this truly mean? Yes, it *means that it is possible* that *many* in the (outward) church who "profess to be Christians" are *not so in actuality!* The same subject surfaces frequently in Scripture. Yes, Scripture clearly teaches that *Christ* will *reject* all those who deny Christ or betray Christ by persistent disobedience! How do you interpret that as meaning? Consider a similar statement of Jesus in Matthew 10. What about the whole subject of "faith without works is dead"? Paul even confides that many Satanic operatives exist that *appear to be ministers of righteousness!* John told us that many Antichrists abound as well! That tells me that we *must know who is who in the zoo!* [191]

189   Matt. 24:13; 25:1–13; Luke 19:11–27; Acts 4:12; Rom. 10:10; Phil. 2:12,13; 1 Thess. 5:8; 2 Thess. 2:13; 1 Pet. 1:5–10

190   Matt. 20; Luke 15

191   Matt. 7:15; 10:32,33; 24:24; 2 Cor. 11:13–15,26; 13:5; Gal. 2:4; 2 Tim. 2:11–13; James 2:14–26. *See reference to Aesop in Bartlett's Familiar Quotations, Little, Brown and Co., Boston, NY, London, 17th Ed., 2002, Page 60#2*

## Chapter 12

Fundamental Issues Regarding the True Christian Faith

	Fundamental Issues Regarding the True Christian Faith	
#	Description	Page #
I.	Introduction	
II.	There is no such thing as absolute freedom or "independence"	
III.	To be a Christian, you must Believe and practice what Jesus Taught and Commanded to the best of your ability, making no excuse.	
IV.	You are not free unless you are Liberated by Jesus	
V.	The Fundamental Issues are as follows.	
VI.	What makes so many "So-called Christians" think that God will "blithely accept" a corrupted, worldly church who has the blood of millions on its hands?	
VII.	Conclusion	

I. Introduction:

Eight hundred years ago Saint Francis is quoted to have cried while walking in the forest near Assissi, Italy: "The Lord is not Loved, The Lord is not Loved ... "over and over again! Many tears have flowed, both before and since then and his voice echoes in my mind today and every day I weep because I see the apostate, fallen condition of the vast majority of Christians in modern times. Indeed, I believe that this condition exists primarily because Christians have "lost their first Love," the Love that God's Spirit gives every new Reborn Believer in Christ when they actually receive Him for being their Personal Savior. I know these truths because I know what the New Testament tells me about the Early Church and that the Early Christians stood for what Christ taught despite the cost.

How long will it be before they "wake up" from the nightmarish dream of unbelief into which they have been led astray by centuries of compromise by their leaders? Yes, they are trusting the wrong object of worship! Yes, in truth, most "Christians" actually trust human strength and worldly intellect for being their "saviors," not God or Christ! Yes, most Christians trust and worship the State for being God, not in God as they falsely claim. The proof is in their avowed Doctrines which have put them into an altered state of mind, in which the enemy of our souls has deluded their thinking into believing that "patriotism" will save them from anything, but it is a trick and lie of Satan![1]

Let us beware of what is known as "Confirmation Bias," the mental condition people fall into when they think they have "figured it out" or "know the truth," however, they have obviously overlooked significant facts and truths that would greatly alter their viewpoint IF they would only see them. Long term mental Conditioning, otherwise known as brainwashing, also lies as the unseen source of this serious problem!

Indeed, most modern Christians have been led into bald-faced Idolatry!

This problem illustrates the ever-present Truth that we must always keep our minds open to new information and be ready to receive new facts that we never considered before! The upshot of all this is that every Blood-bought Christian must continually reevaluate their beliefs regularly to make sure that their loyalty to Christ is not being suborned by "alien influences." Indeed, Satan makes great use of religion's penchant to deceive naive Christians who have been taught to "assume" that whatever the "authorities" teach is the "truth." That is not so: You must continually compare them to the Standard of God's Word!

---

1   2 Cor. 4:3-7 *See also the book entitled Spiritual Guidelines for Restoration, "Historical Review" Section.*

Learn to ask questions and to always question authority to make sure they are doing and teaching *Righteousness* and Truth. Otherwise, you do not know where you stand. Delve into Scripture regularly and God's Spirit will always teach you the Truth. You cannot trust man, only God. However, this always puts you in a difficult position whenever you are "out there in the world" because the world is being controlled by Satan and his operatives in the New World Order that will always seek to censure the Truth of the Gospel. If they cannot do this, they work to subvert the truth by substitution with clever "half truths mixed with lies."

Study history and you will find out that Religion is the result of this legerdemain. Consequently, True Christians are always "under fire" and are hated by everyone who serves the world system, many of whom claim to be Christians, regardless of their claims. Always go back to the Teachings of Jesus Christ and compare their beliefs with that and you will see "who is who in the zoo."[2]

Yes, the Truth of Christ's Word that stands inviolately, no matter what man may say despite their position or authority in the eyes of man.[3]

Indeed, the only way the church or anyone in it can recover from the condition into which it has fallen, is to confess their sins, *Repent,* again and affirm this by again receiving the Truths Christ taught without equivocation!

Answer the following questions: Why did the ancient Hebrews want to worship the golden calf? Hadn't they just been delivered from slavery in Egypt by God's miraculous Hand at the Red Sea? Could it be that they wanted to be slaves? Oh, yes, it's so easy: You do not have to think for yourself, take responsibility for yourself and your family, for all you have to do is do what you are told! Is that what you want? I sincerely hope NOT. But that is precisely what the Christians have done, most of them for the last seventeen centuries! Oh, yes, they love modern Egypt-America and their leaders tell them that "God" has ordained their leaders who teach them that it is O.K. to approve

2   Matt. 4:1-10; 7:15-29; 10:16-42; Mark 1:14-17; 3:1-6; Luke 1:78; 6:20 ff.; John 3:16-36; 6:27-63; 8:12, 31-58; 10:1-16; 12:32-50; 14:6-17:26
3   Psa. 119:89; Rom. 1:16-32; 3:4

mass murder in wars, capital punishment and to abort their unwanted unborn children! THINK about what you believe! Turn away from the lying tongues of the modern "Pharisees, Sadducees and Herodians" who have made "Christianity" a literal mockery. Even the world is laughing at them, knowing that their beliefs are a sham, riddled with contradictions! They should know that they are still slaves, believing the glitzy propaganda of the elite controllers.

Their leaders are blind, helpless tools of Satan who essentially repeat back the same drivel as the world, fulfilling their destiny as underlings who use religion to control the masses. Yet, God knows who they are and what they have done. Like the Pharisees of Jesus's time, they are the most culpable because they have abandoned the Original Standards of Faith and replaced it with a "mess of pottage" so they would be 'accepted' by the world! Remember, that is how Esau lost his inheritance. However, anyone with an ounce of *Conscience* knows that True Christianity cannot ever be reduced to being a "religion" for religion is part of the world! God's condemnation is upon anyone who fails to love the Truth or perverts the Truth.[4]

Finally, the analysis of the grim situations that Christians face in these last days demands that we hold our leaders accountable to the Truth of the Original Gospel as it is presented in the *New Covenant.* Do not trust anyone who does not submit to that One unimpeachable Standard.

Always remember that only two kingdoms exist: One, God's *Kingdom of Heaven* which exists both in Heaven and on earth and Two, ALL the kingdoms of this earth as Scripture teaches.[5]

Furthermore, You cannot "pick and choose" by "parting out" those elements which you like and ignoring the rest. The Gospel and True Christianity is governed by One unbreakable Set of rules. If you do not want to abide by that standard, then you are unable to qualify for being a True Christian. You must choose one kingdom or the other: If you are not part of Christ, then you are part of the World. No intermediate state of being exists. The truth is that all God's true people Fear the

---

4   Gen. 25:21-34; Mal. 2; Matt. 23; Luke 13:34,35; 2 Thess. 2:3-12
5   *See the paper entitled The Spiritual Laws of Revival, Law #11*

Lord and Trust God. Consequently, they are Holy unto God and separate from the world.[6]

Yes, the issue of separation from the world and all its humanistic ways is a crucial issue! You must maintain your absolute Loyalty and Allegiance to Jesus Christ in all areas of life, private and public, by the continual practice of being separate from their ways every day. If you fail to do this, you will eventually adapt, succumb and be "assimilated" into the world system like all the rest, neutralizing and forfeiting every aspect of Righteousness you may have had before God.

Do not kid yourself: No part of the "Discipleship to *Conversion* Dynamic Process" is ever easy! Temptations to find some "easier path" will assail you daily. However, the "path of life" is very narrow indeed. Not only that, no "independent path of convenience" exists because of the primary precept we all must acknowledge: Only two masters exist and you are the slave of one or the other.[7]

One other caution is called for: One of the most insidious of those "temptations" is that which is taught by "mainstream religion": The false 'deterministic doctrines' that teach that worldly governments are somehow "ordained by God" and that you are "duty-bound" to obey them. This false doctrine is based on a deliberate mistranslation of the Greek word *Tagma,* found in Paul's letter to the Romans.

So, beware of those who "manipulate" Scripture to make it "look like" God "ordains" worldly leaders. Look to the original Greek word in Romans thirteen, *Tagma,* which means "to allow or permit" or to be ordered. This means that God has originally ordained a set or order in which people can live in a civilized manner.

We should note in particular that this order was originally set in place by Christ when He created the worlds. In the *New Covenant, * God put these Scriptures there to emphasize Christ's Authority in forming the pillars of civilization and orderly structure of government, telling

---

6   Ex. 19:5; Lev. 20:24-26; Num. 23:9; Deut. 14:2; 26:18; 1 Kings 18:21; Ezra 10:11; Neh. 9; Psa. 115:11; Matt. 4:1-10; Luke 4:1-8; Matt. 6:9-13; 12:30; John 18:36; Rom. 8:1-39; 2 Cor. 6:14-7:1; Eph. 5; Phil. 3:20; 1 Tim. 6:3-12; 2 Tim. 2; Titus 2:14; Heb. 11:12-16; James 4:1-8; 1 Pet. 1, 2* *(Note that 2:13,14 is conditioned by all the other Scriptures regulating our deportment in the world, however, it does not imply that we exalt worldly rulers and authority above God! God's Law is always above man's law whenever they conflict!)*

7   Matt. 6:22-24; 7:13-29 *See the paper The Dynamics of Christian Discipleship*

us that they were there to serve Him! It should be obvious that God does not authorize their power if officials act against that purpose! They also serve to minimize the situations that would lead to martyrdom.[8]

So, why cannot modern Christians see the simple plain Truth that the New Covenant Gospel stands plain for all to see? All you have to do is confess your sins and unbelief and receive the Gospel's complete Truth that Christ's teachings fulfill prophecies and supersede all previous "interim" doctrines of the Old Testament, especially those which temporarily allowed the killing of others. Furthermore, since God is *Agape* Love, IF we believe *In Christ*, we should also be able to see the higher logic of God's Kingdom which illustrates Christ's exalted way of making *Peace* that totally eliminates any resort to violence or killing![9]

II. There is no such thing as absolute freedom or "independence." All people are servants (slaves) of one of the two masters that exist.[10]

The only existing masters are the following:

One, God *In Christ* by the Holy Spirit, The Triune Living God Who has all legitimate *Authority* and Reigns over the *Kingdom of Heaven* as it is defined in Scripture, which exists in both Heaven and on earth wherever Jesus's Commands are being obeyed. In spiritual terms, this is the only Kingdom of Light.[11]

Two, the entire aggregate world system of nations and empires, all of which are controlled by Satan, a fact that Jesus did not contest while He was being tested in the wilderness. In his first letter, John also told

---

8   Neh. 9:6: Rom. 13:1-7; Col. 1:13-16; Titus 1:15,16; 1 Pet. 2:13,14 *See the 2 part series of papers entitled Authority and Conscience*

9   Matt. 5:17-20 *See also the book Jesus' Way and the papers entitled Christian Conversion (a 3 part series), The Christian Epiphany, the Christian Spirit, Christianity versus Religion (a 3 part series), Destiny and Free Will, Do You Know Who You Are, Fallacies of Determinism, Fulfilment Prophecy, the Kingdom of Heaven is the Highest form of Civilization, Major Missing Aspects if the Original Christian Gospel, One Covenant for All and Seeing Through the Eyes of Jesus*

10   Matt. 6:22-24; Luke 16:13-15

11   Matt. 3:2; 4:17; 5:3-20; 6:9-13, 33; 7:21; 10:7; 11:11,12; 13:11-52; 16:18,19;18:3,4,20; 19:13,14,23-26; 20:1-16; 21:28-46; 22:1-22* (Notice the second half of vs. 21); 25:1-34; 26:17-29; Mark 1:14,15; 10:14-25; 12:28-34; 14:24-27; Luke 1:30-33; 6:20: ff.; 8:10; 12:8-12, 22-53; 13:18-30; 17:20,21; 18:16-27; 19:11-27; 22:15-32; John 3:3-8; 18:36; Acts 14:22;28:22,23; 1 Cor. 4:20; 15:20-28, 50; 2 Thess. 1:4 ff.; 2 Tim. 4:1 ff.; Heb. 1:8; 12:28; 2 Pet. 1:2-11; Rev. 1:9; 12;10

us that the whole world lies in wickedness, which is the equivalent of darkness in spiritual parlance. Indeed, the entire world system is under the hegemony of the figure we know as Antichrist![12]

In any case, no intermediate 'territory' of independence exists and all false claims of 'having freedom' that is outside of God's definition in Scripture are delusions and lies fomented by Satan to make people think they are 'free' but, in reality, they are slaves of the world system! IF you are a true Christian, you know that one main attribute of our *Faith* is that it is one integral Whole and that this unity of Faith cannot be "portioned out" or subdivided without destroying the whole in the process! The True Gospel cannot tolerate mixture with the world's ways of any type or at any level, for any such compromise neutralizes the "edge" of God's incredible Coping Power we read about in the Acts that is only present when the Gospel is kept totally intact in its Original form![13]

Reread the New Testament carefully and you will see that the True Christian Faith was a "juggernaut" of powers that, even in the words of their enemies, "turned the world upside down." However, in the intervening centuries, Satan has infiltrated and corrupted the organized assemblies to a great degree, causing untold harm to the *Body of Christ, * eventually in the fourth century, creating a cascade of apostasy that has not been corrected since! Consequently, because of religion, most of the "mainline congregations" have become "part of the world." Only a few "spurts of life and revival" have ever been seen since, such as Saint Francis' witness in thirteenth century Italy and the Wesleyan Revival of the eighteenth century in England. Unfortunately, apostasy persists primarily because most modern church leaders still refuse to accept the Truths that Jesus Taught and stubbornly cling to unbelief and the humanistic ways of the world system which advocate

---

12   Deut. 28: 15 ff.; 2 Kings 19:19; 2 Chr. 20:6; 36:23*; Ezra 1:2* *(note that in specific situations in the Old Testament, God did intervene, using temporal kingdoms for a temporary protector of His people, however, this must not be construed to be a 'general rule' extending to the present.); Psa. 2, 46,110; Isa. 10:5-25* (note also that at any time, because He is sovereign, God can also use 'heathen nations' to discipline His people when they go astray, reserving their judgment for a later time!)* Isa. 37:16-20; Jer. 10:1 ff.; 25:12 ff.; Ezek. 29:1 ff.; Dan. 2:44,45; 7:15 ff.; Zeph. 3:8; Matt. 4:1-10; Luke 4:1-8; Rom. 1:18-32; 2 Thess. 1:8; 2:3-12; 1 John 5:19; Rev. 13-18

13   Rom. 1:20

mass murder in wars and worldly governance formats that ensure that no change can get through.

Essentially, their intransigency is based on a total abandonment of Faith in God for being their Savior, which has been replaced by their fawning sycophancy to world powers which in truth has become their true object of worship instead of God! That is also the reason that patriotism has become organized religion's "new god" that rules their lives because their fear of man and circumstance has supplanted any trust in God that remained. Essentially, modern Christians have been led into abject Idolatry and its abominable approval of human sacrifice, following the lying mantra of Satan: "Sacrifice your children and for you it will be well." Know this, all those who unrepentantly continue to serve the world's master, Satan by approving killing will regret it for eternity, including those who falsely "claim to be Christians!"

This abysmal dichotomy reveals the underlying cause: A collective *Reprobate mind* that has evolved to supplant the True attitudes and beliefs of Genuine Christianity with a "tainted *Orthodoxy*" that is riddled with lies and contradictions. Unfortunately, religious leaders, in their misguided desires to "make Christianity more popular," have allowed this to take place! All you have to do is compare the "deterministic doctrines" you find in most modern churches to the True Doctrines of the "Saved Mind" that exist in all who truly Trust Jesus Christ and not man.[14]

Again, Scripture clearly teaches that to be Saved, we must adhere to the right master every day!

This is the only way to know that Christ is our Savior in all venues: Physical, Soulical and spiritual. Know this for sure: You must choose to be the servant of one master or the other, never both: You cannot claim to be a Saved Christian and cling to the evil ways of the world system.

Clearly, God does not ordain killing, for that would be approving Antichrist, the mind-set of the world system! Beware also of the unavoidable precept of *Bloodguiltiness* that clings to all who kill

---

14   Matt. 23; Rom. 1:16-32; 2 Cor. 13:5-7; 2 Thess. 2:3-12; 2 Tim. 1:7-15; 3:8; Titus 1:15,16; 1 John 3,4; *(note that the reference to Cain and Abel in Ch. 3 that proves that all mankind are our brothers and sisters); Rev. 18 See the paper Fallacies of Determinism See also Glossary of Terms' entry *The Reprobate Mind*

or who justify or approve of killing! Know this also: The *Blood of Christ* is the <u>final payment of bloodshed for sin for all time confirmed</u> <u>w</u>hen He said on the cross: "It is finished," the New Covenant was ratified.[15]

Now, let us again recognize the underlying Truth of biblical servant-hood: We all are slaves to one of two masters. The daily issue is which one we are serving?[16]

Pursuant to our subject of choosing the right master, we need to ask the following question: Why can't those who claim to be Christians Believe the Promises of God's Word? Indeed, I am incredulous that it appears to be that most 'mainline Christians' <u>want to be a slave of the</u> <u>world rather than Christ!</u> Let us review Old Testament history. First, think about the promises God had given in the Passover. Then think about what the ancient Hebrew people did after they were first liberated from four hundred and thirty years of enslavement in Egypt. Read in the Books of Exodus and Numbers about Israel's reversion to the ways of Egypt in their worship of the Golden Calf and their unpersuadable fears about losing their children to the giants after the "evil report" of ten of the twelve spies sent out to reconnoiter the promised land.[17]

Believe it or not, <u>moderns act just the same as they did!</u> The underlying truth is that the vast majority of People, <u>including most</u> <u>"Christians,"</u> <u>do not like to make the effort to think for themselves.</u> Yes, most people <u>want to be told what to do</u> and consequently are very predisposed to and easily become the victims of <u>mental conditioning,</u> otherwise known as <u>Brainwashing!</u> We do not like to admit this, but nonetheless it is true. Virtually all of us have been unconsciously subject to this phenomenon ever since we were children. Moreover, because we were raised in a structured society, we have been "brought up" with a set of "assumptions" that we have been told by "authority figures" were not to be questioned. Thus, most have become slaves.

---

15   Psa. 51; Matt. 4:1-10; 6:24; 23:1 ff.; Luke 4:1-8; 9:23-26, 51-56 (KJV); 16:13-15;John 19:30; Heb. 2:9-15; 7:22-25; 8:6-13; 9:11-28; 10:12-39; 1 Pet. 2:21-25 *See also the paper entitled A Biblical Disclosure of Antichrist*

16   Matt. 6:24; Rom. 6:1-23; 1 Cor. 7:21,22

17   Exodus 6:6,7; 14:13,14 32:1 ff.; Numbers 13,14 and Deut. 1:30; 3:22

However, to become free, every Christian must question these worldly beliefs to be able to recover from the delusions of *Humanism* that society uses to control the masses! Whether we like it or not, the following is True: Among these are the following "tenets of the world" that are "drummed into our minds" just like the "Pledges of Allegiance to the Flag." Yes, you were catechized to unconsciously "assume" that what you were taught was true and that you are "safe" and "free" if you follow the crowd, but in reality you are far from being "free" or "safe!"[18]

The first belief is "Patriotism," the belief that "our country" is the god they taught you to serve and that everything else is arranged around that belief. The familiar phrase they repeat - "God and country," is wrong: It should read "Our Country is God." Concomitant with this is the second tenet, which tells us that we must do whatever it takes to protect that "god," including the mass murder of those which propaganda teaches us are the "enemies of the state" that threaten that entity they essentially worship for being "god."

Returning to our history lesson about the ancient Hebrews, we learn in Scripture that, because of their intransigent rebellion in the wilderness, they prompted God to change the "rules of engagement." Previous to their rebellion, at the *Passover, * God had promised to "fight for them" in battle against all who stood in the way of their inheriting the "Promised Land."[19]

Indeed, the "Precept of *Passover*" is the Original Covenant Pattern and Fundamental underlying premise of God's Plan of Salvation that applies for God's People in all three venues: Physical, Soulical and spiritual. After Israel's rebellion in the wilderness, God digressed into a disciplinary mode, altering the way Israel would have to deal with opposition, temporarily allowing them to engage enemies and to kill. However, this was only a temporary "stopgap" measure used to teach them the ugliness of combat as a form of discipline. The experiences they went through because they "wanted a king to rule over them like

---

18   See the paper entitled What is Collectivism
19   Ex. 6:6,7; 14:13,14; Deut. 1:30; 3:22 See also the Chart entitled "Behold the stark contrast between True Liberty and Slavery (Table One in the paper True Liberty is in Christ Alone) and Passover Sequence Chart which correlates the Precepts of the Passover and the paper The Three Passovers of Scripture

the nations" are mere microcosms of this disciplinary cycle. Samuel had warned them what would happen and they suffered from their stubbornness for centuries because of it![20]

A major problem concomitant to "religion" is that "authorities" have caused and are actively exploiting a "manufactured Wall of Fear" they use with alacrity to intimidate the masses. By deliberately withholding information, they can 'create' mass hysteria, prompting a hyper-reactive mind-set. Antichrist also takes full advantage of the well-known "Hegelian Dialectic," Problem, Reaction, Solution, in which they use people's "herd reaction aspect" that sweeps over people's minds after a "deep event." You would think that Christians are supposed to be resistant to this and they would be IF they actually Trusted in God and not man, but, sad to say, most of them do not! So, would you like to know why they are not Trusting God?

Unfortunately, I already know the answer: Religion has inured them so well to slavery in trusting in man's apostate devices to "save" (the government and military) that they have abandoned their Faith (If they even had faith to start with)! Indeed, in a way the Bible does teach a precept that is very similar to "Achem's Razor." It goes like this: "When all other contingencies fail, whatever remains, whatever improbable, must be the Truth."

The catch is that most Christians have not even tried to understand what Christ Taught for being the Truth and the Only viable Way out of the "vicious maelstrom of sin, slavery and death" that the world has been enmeshed in ever since Adam's sins "opened Pandora's Box" and unleashed Satan's hegemony and control over the course of human events, starting with Cain's murder of Abel. Yet, most "Christians" blindly accept the world's false concept of "liberty" which is just a sophisticated type of slavery to man!

Clue: Remember Jesus's acknowledgment of Satan's control during His wilderness testing period recorded in the Gospels of Matthew and Luke. Later, Jesus said the Pharisees were culpable for all the murders of the Righteous from Abel onward! Do you also remember what John

---

20   Contrast 1 Sam. 2 with 1 Sam. 8-10; 1 Kings 18; Psa. 94, 118; Prov. 29:25; Isa.1,2,6,8, 27-30; Jer. 10,17; Ezek, 36; Mic. 3,4; *See also the application to Christians found in John* 6-8; 18:36; Rom. 8; 1 Cor. 10; Heb. 11:12-16; James 4 and 1 John 2

wrote in his first Epistle about what happens when you become ensnared by your fears and fail to Love your (human) Brother? Remember that "the fear of man is a snare."

Yes, it is a tragedy that most "So-called Christians" are <u>so stuck in unbelief that they fail to Believe the simple Word of God when it comes to Salvation</u>, which <u>the Bible defines in all three venues: Physical, Soulical and spiritual.</u>

Still, most Christians have not even thought out what they believe to see if all their beliefs <u>are consistent with each other.</u> Nor, do they even understand that their "approval of killing others," ostensibly to 'save,' is a <u>lie of Satan</u> which <u>drags them down into the evil vortex of Fear, Idolatry and the nightmarish practice of human sacrifice</u> by sending their children to fight in wars.

Let us duly remember that God had specifically told Ezekiel to upbraid the Israelites for doing this![21]

Also, many Christians seem to be "isolated" by individualism which works against living the True Christian life! The <u>Original Gospel of Jesus Christ and the Early Apostles was in a "group context"</u> in each area, where each member worked together as a team for Christ. Though some leaders were alone at times, most were <u>part of a greater Fellowship that is defined in Scripture as a local *Body of Christ* or Church</u>, a supportive venue in which <u>True Freedom</u> can develop.

As such, the synergism of the entire body of Believers produced <u>much more than the individuals could produce separately.</u> Also, the <u>underlying source of power is always</u> *Agape* Love, ministered by the Holy Spirit to each member who has been given <u>unique spiritual Gifts that are to be used for the benefit of the entire Body of Christ,</u> working specifically within the "Yoke" and Will of Jesus Christ, the Head of all True Christians![22]

---

21   Prov. 29:25; Isa. 8:12-20; 26:3-12; 28:9-30:22; 32:1-18; 40-46, 48:17,18; Jer. 31:10-34; Lam. 3:22-24; Ezek. 23:37-39; 36:16:ff.; Hosea 14:9; Matt. 4:1-10; 23:1 ff.; Luke 4:1-8; 8:22-25; 2 Tim. 1:7-15; 2:1 ff.; 1 John 3,4 *See also the papers entitled Conditions for Salvation and God's Definition of Salvation*

22   Matt. 5-7, 10; 11:28-30; 18:20; 22:36,37; Luke 6, 12; John 8:31-36; 13:34-17:26; Acts 2:42-47; Rom. 6:16-22; 12:1 ff.; 1 Cor. 7:20-24; 12-14; Gal. 5:1, 22,23; Eph. 4

III. To be A Christian, you must Believe and practice what Jesus Taught and Commanded to the best of your ability, making no excuse.

To truly experience the genuine Christian life requires that a person Really Believes that what Jesus Christ taught is actually liveable in the present day world. Indeed, there are only two possible positions of belief and practice and these positions are associated with the two masters about which Jesus taught us:[23]

The First is that you fully Believe and Trust God's Word (Jesus) to be True and that His Salvation in every venue is viable right here and right now.

The second is following the crowd by remaining in defacto unbelief, Idolatry and fear by believing the propaganda of the world and religion's corrupted message that "internalizes" Salvation and essentially calls Jesus Christ a liar!

Now let us consider the following facts that are clearly taught in Scripture:

Another very important fact for every True Christian to remember is that God's *Agape* Love applies to everyone equally, no matter who they are, where they live or what they have done.

Moreover, IF we observe the Sovereignty of God we should know that God intends that His Love to be infused into every Believer by the Holy Spirit! Verily, God's Sovereign *Agape* Love in us requires that we love all others as God does!

Yes, this means that IF you are a True Christian, you are simply unable to rationalize the killing of any person, by anyone, anywhere or at any time! Yes, God's Love, given to us by the Holy Spirit, is meant to be extended freely and unequivocally to every person on the planet![24]

Again, IF God Loves everybody the same, it follows that everyone who is a Christian must do the same. The upshot of all this brings us back to the Fundamental Issue of our Identity *In Christ.* Yes, we must be constantly aware of the underlying reality that True Christians are not part of this world system: Contrariwise, the Bible teaches that Christians are both Citizens and Ambassadors of God's indestructible

---

23   Matt. 6:22-24; Luke 16:13-15
24   John 3:16; 12:32; Rom. 5:1-5; 12:9-21; 13:8-12; 2 Pet. 3:9; 1 John 2:1-6

Heavenly Kingdom that is separate from all nations of this world. Not only that, Christ is our only True King who has also ordained the set of governing rules in God's Kingdom which is called *the New Covenant.*[25]

All the time we are on earth, God's Word commands us to give our utmost and complete (100%) Allegiance to Jesus Christ in every venue, private or public, no matter where you live. Never forget that Jesus Christ is your King, whose commands and teachings supersede all conflicting traditions, laws or policies of man.[26]

Yes, Christ has shown us the only "True and Living Way" that leads to everlasting Life in Heaven and the only way in which we can remain a True Christian.[27]

All other 'ways,' especially those that rationalize the killing of other humans, lead their deluded followers down to the Pit of Hell! Not only that, all worldly ways are classified by God for being one type or another of Idolatry because they always rely on human strength, strategy or intelligence rather than Trust in God as the Scriptures teach. Indeed, all the rationales supporting killing in war, abortion and death punishments constitute the abominable practice of human sacrifice!

No "middle ground of independence" exists! Not only that, whenever a person starts to trust in man, they immediately become addicted to the world and its humanistic ways which puts you on a collision course to destruction for all those ways are against Christ, which means they are of Antichrist!

Again, only two paths of living are possible, with no middle ground between: The Truth remains inviolately: You either live 100% for Jesus Christ or fall away into the world's ways! Another way of saying that would be that you must continue to live in *Agape* Love, following Jesus's Commands, OR you will succumb to fear, unbelief and hatred and follow the world's ways to the pit!

---

25   Lev.20:26; Num. 23:9; Isa. 42:1-4; 43:1-18; Jer. 31:31-34; Ezek. 36:16 ff.; Dan. 2:44,45; 7:9-14; Matt. 6:9-13; 28:18; Luke 9:51-62 (KJV); 12:31,32; 17:20,21; 18:9-31; 22:24-32; John 18:36; Acts 14:22; 28:22,23; Rom. 14:17; 2 Cor. 5:14-21; 2 Tim. 4; Heb. 1:8;10:1-12:29; 2 Pet. 1:2-11; Rev. 1:9; 12:10 *See also the paper Do You Know Who You Are*

26   Matt. 28:18; John 18:36; Acts 4:10-20; 5:29-32 *See also the 2 parts series of papers entitled Authority and Conscience*

27   Matt. 5-7; Luke 6,12; John 14:6-17:26

Know this: All the world system lies in the darkness of wickedness and idolatry, for Only those who live 100% for Christ will live in the Light of *Righteousness.*[28]

For truly Dedicated Christians, I believe we are entering a period of great testing, *Affliction* and Tribulation. Indeed it is going to be used of God to "hash out the dead wood" and to Purify the Hearts of those who refuse to compromise, knowing that they can Trust God's ultimate protection over them, no matter what happens!

Moreover, in the process, because of the work done in them by *Affliction* and suffering, the true Servants of God will be much better prepared for service in God's Kingdom.

The final result will be that the remaining Christians will accurately represent Christ and be a powerful influence so that the church will finally be ready to fulfill the Great Commission![29]

Let us ever remember Jesus's Teachings to the Disciples about the conflicts we must endure to remain a faithful Believer. Above all is the one signal Command: "Love (others) as I have Loved you." All the other virtues and characteristics that define True Christianity Lie within the scope of *Agape* Love!

Not only that, all the aspects of *Agape* Love encompass a Sacred Trust in which All True Christians abide![30]

Indeed, whenever we are Living in God's Love, we see no man as an enemy, only Satan and his demonic horde. Know also the entire world is being controlled by Satan, so you cannot trust human rulers to keep their word or to even act with a view to the good of the people. Be "wise as serpents, but harmless as Doves."[31]

---

28 Matt. 12:30; Luke 2:34,35; Acts 28:22; Rom.1:18-20; 6:3-23; 8:1-11; 2 Cor. 4; Gal. 1:6-12; Eph. 6:10-12; 2 Tim. 2:19-26; James 4:1-8; 1 John 2:15-17; 5:19-21 *See also the paper entitled A Biblical Disclosure of Antichrist*

29 Matt. 28:18-20; Luke 22:31,32; Acts 3:19 *See the papers The Christian Epiphany, Facts of Scripture: The Church and the Tribulation and the book The Church and the Last Days*

30 *Matt. 5-7; Luke 6:20 ff.; 11:33-36; 12:1 ff.;* John 1:1-18; 4:14-24; 5:19-30; 6:27-63; 7:15-18; 8:12, 31-58: 12:23-26; 13:34-17:26; Acts 2-7,17; Rom. 5:1-5; 6:1-8:39; 14:8; 1 Cor. 1,2,10,12-15; 2 Cor. 1-7; Gal. 1:6-12; 2:16-4:19; 5:1 f; Eph. 1-6; Phil. 1-4; Col. 1-3

31 Matt. 5:38-49; 10:16-42; 16:21-26; Mark 3:1-5; Luke 9:23-26, 51-62; 11:33-36; Acts 4:9-20; 5:29-32; Rom. 6:1-22; 12:9-21; 2 Cor. 6:14-7:1; 10:3-7; Eph. 6:10-18; Col. 1:12-29; 2:9-24; 1 Tim. 2:5; 6:3-12; 2 Tim. 1:7-15; 2:1-4:8; Heb. 4:1-19; 6:3-12; 10:19-39; James 4:1-8;1 John 1-5

Never forget: All True Christians belong to God's Heavenly Kingdom, whose only King is The Lord Jesus Christ.[32]

Let us ever continue to observe that "Tribulation is a given" that we cannot avoid IF we are serving Christ, giving 100% of our Allegiance to Him.[33]

Finally, know that following Christ is The Way that "Guides our feet into the Way of Peace." Indeed, "He IS our Peace, Who has broken down the hostile dividing wall of fear separating people."[34]

This issue of "Making Peace" is central to Jesus's Way. Study history and you will see that God has been teaching this way from the beginning. One example stands out in my mind. The reason why Moses was driven into the wilderness for forty years was to "Break up his fallow ground" by taming his murderous temper.

Remember that when he first found that he was a Hebrew, he tried to liberate them by himself by killing an Egyptian overseer. Obviously, that did not work! Let us all take notice of that important precept! The truth is that God's "teaching and discipline" had to work first to *Convert* him, teaching him to depend solely on God! Christians should learn to understand this.

Also the testimonies of Daniel and his three friends align perfectly with the very unique way God teaches His servants to deal with 'hard times,' opposition and persecution. Jesus Christ's specific teachings in this are crystal clear. One cannot ignore the obvious implications of living by *Agape* Love.

Paul learned his lesson after his encounter with the Living Christ on the Damascus road and, following that *Conversion* experience, became one of the most zealous exponents of Jesus's Teachings. His experiences, recorded by Dr. Luke in Acts, unequivocally show that his responses to multiple incidents where he was attacked and even stoned, being left for dead, were totally consistent with Jesus's Teachings on how we deal with evil and hatred from others. The writings of James,

32   Matt. 6:9-15; John 18:36; Phil. 3:20; Heb. 11:12-16; 12:1 ff.; James 4; 1 John 2
33   John 15:18-16:4,33; Acts 14:22; 26:13-18; 28:22; Rom. 5:3;; 12:12; 2 Cor. 1:4; 1 Thess. 1:4; Heb. 11:12-16; James 1:3-5, 21-27; 3:1-4:17; 5:11-20
34   Matt. 5:7; Luke 1:78,79; 2:14; John 14:26,27; 20:19-26; Rom. 8:6; 10:15; 14:17-19; Eph. 2:12-22; Phil. 4:7-9; Col. 1:20-24; 1 Thess. 5:23

Peter and John also concur. Of course, we should also acknowledge that the scope of Jesus's Teachings applies to every venue of life and at all levels of human experience and interaction: Personal, group, national and international.

The ultimate upshot of all this is that only one Perfect Way to bring "Peace on earth and good will toward man" exists: Following Jesus's Way according to the New Covenant! However, God's warnings throughout Scripture predict major judgment against those who trust in idols and refuse to obey God's Word.[35]

IV. You are not Free unless you are Liberated by Jesus

From the time I was five years old I knew I was a Christian. I publicly acknowledged my Faith on Father's Day, 1953 at the First Baptist Church in Foxboro, Massachusetts. I also knew that the legacy of every True Christian Believer is following Christ's Commands and teachings by Loving all other humans. Yes, I knew God's Spirit had told me this Truth. However, as I grew older, I found out that my family members and religious leaders I trusted were telling me a very different story, one based upon worldly values that rationalized selfishness and the use of murder to "defend" the institutions of the state that they told me was "necessary." Of course, I knew that Christ's Teaching must stand uncompromised or the very essence of our Faith in Christ would be a sham! I also came to know that "religion" and the religious Catechisms to which they hold which justified mass murder in war was a direct contradiction of the truth that Christ taught. However, it took many years to finally "crystalize" my Beliefs and "break free" in this area because of the inherent confusion in my *Conscience* that those false teachings had caused! Yet, the bottom line is that I recovered the Truth that God's Word is Truth regardless of what man may say or teach otherwise. The truth is that it took the shock of an "obnoxious brother-in-law" who zealously pounded me with "unpopular" facts, telling me about his horrible experiences in Vietnam. He concluded that

---

35   Ex. 2:1-15; Psa. 4:8; 34:14; 119:165; Prov. 16:7; Isa. 9:6,7; 32:17,18; 48:16-19; Jer. 4:4; 12:14-17; Hosea 10:12; Matt. 5:38-48; 7:12-29; 2:51,52; Luke 2:14; 6:20 ff.; 12:1 ff.; John 4:14-38; 5:19-30; 6:27-64; 7:15-18; Acts 12-28; Rom. 12:1 ff.; 1 Cor. 15:30-33; 2 Cor. 4,6,11; Eph. 2:13,14; 2 Thess. 2:3-12; James 1,4; 1 Pet. 3:8-22; 1 John 1-5

killing was always evil and that the church's advocation of "Christians" participation in combat by "killing communists for Christ" was also evil in the extreme![36]

So, now, after more than fifty years of studying Scripture I know that this is true and that we have all been 'brainwashed' by religious leaders who, in effect, have been used as the tools of the state to "keep people in line" with the national propaganda line. Then, when I began rereading the Old Testament Prophets, I found another "treasure-trove" of information. Indeed, Scripture teaches us about man's fickleness and how they "want to just hear smooth things" that titillate the senses and "do not rock the boat" of the prevailing National doctrines. However, the Word of God is "Sharper than a two-edged sword," "cutting across the grain" of all humanistic conveniences and religious dogma! So, IF you claim to be a "Christian," think very hard and know this: "The Truth is not subject to a popularity contest," but rather it compels us to Believe and do what Christ Taught, despite the cost![37]

Christians ought to know that Christ Alone is our Savior in all venues! Again, reread the Scriptures again carefully. Doing so you will see that many Christians have been conditioned to accept lies in God's Name, thereby leading them into "a velvet cage of slavery to man's idolatrous way," falsely believing that soldiers who murder others could make people "free." Not so! Contrariwise, Jesus Christ gave us the "Keys" to the exalted *Kingdom of Heaven* which Jesus teaches can exist "On earth as it is in Heaven," in present tense Reality. However, this only happens IF you Believe what Jesus taught is the Truth instead of the "twisted, forked tongue of religious authorities" who teach you to worship the state as 'god' instead of the True Living God! Unfortunately most people believe the lies of organized religion which have been leading naive millions into abject Idolatry for seventeen centuries! The only way out of that dark place of unbelief and idol worship is to reset

---

36   Psa. 119:89; Prov. 27:6; Matt. 5:43-48; Mark 3:1-6; Luke 9:51-62: John 7:15-18; 8:31-36; 17:17
37   Isa. 1:18-2:22; 8:9-20; 30:9-22; Jer. 2:23 ff.; 3:16-4:4,22; 5:1-5,9,22-31; 6:13-7:29; 8:1-12; 10:1-11; 11:9-17; 13:8-17; 17:5-10; 23:9-14; Ezek. 18:23-32; 20:3-44; 21:24-22:31; 23:37-39; 33:30-33; John 3:16; 1 Cor. 10:1 ff.; 2 Cor. 5:14-21; Heb. 4;12,13; 8:6-12:29

the confidence of professing Christians back to the Revealed Word of God as Jesus taught it! [38]

Moreover, in many places in Scripture, Christians are taught plainly that Jesus is our King in present tense Reality and that God's Kingdom is our True Country by spiritual Rebirth. Consequently, Jesus is also our Highest *Authority* regarding all affairs and venues of our lives while we are here on earth. This includes all areas of Doctrine and Practice. In the *New Covenant,* God's Law is always superior to any worldly law, tradition or policy of man or of human government or 'religion.'[39]

Yes, the only way we can be victorious is by following Jesus's Teachings day by day. Moreover, can you not see what Jesus's Life, death and Resurrection have done? Do you Really Believe what He Taught? Do you truly Believe that Jesus Alone is our Peace? How many more deaths is it going to take before those who claim to be Christians start living like Christians should - right here and right now? Yes, Jesus Christ Alone is our source of Freedom, not soldiers, guns and bombs or the strategies of politicians and pundits! Only Christ's Blood, shed on Calvary Once for all, has purchased our entire being by the precept of *Redemption,* the only way which makes us Truly Free. However, cost of that freedom is high: We must be willing to die for what we believe, but never willing to believe in killing![40]

V. The Fundamental Issues are as follows:

A. You must Believe that the One True Living God is a Personal Eternal Being existing from Eternity past to Eternity future. God has three main attributes: Omnipotence, Omniscience and Omnipresence. Moreover, Scripture plainly teaches that only One Living God exists: All other "play-actors," no matter what they may "claim to be," are

---

38   *Read Jesus's main Discourses found in the Gospels:* Matt. 5-7,10,13,16,18,20; Mark 3,4; Luke 6-14, 19,21; John 3-17; Acts 1-17; Rom. 1-8; 1 Cor. 1-3,1-15; 2 Cor. 1-7,10,11; Gal. 1-5; Eph. 1-6; Phil. 1-4; Col. 1-3; 2 Tim. 1-4; Heb. 1-4, 6-12 *See also the book entitled Spiritual Guidelines for Restoration, "Historical Review" Section*

39   Matt. 6:9-13; John 14:6-17:26; 18:36; Acts 4:9-20; 5:29-32; Rom. 8,12; 2 Cor. 3:17,18; 11:12-15; Eph. 2:13,14; 6:10-12; Phil. 3:3, 20; Col. 1:12-29; 2 Tim. 2,3; Heb. 11:12-15; James 4:1-8; 1 John 2:15-17; 5:19-21

40   Matt. 16:21-26; John 8:31-36; 14:26,26; 2 Cor. 3:17,18; Eph. 2:13,14; Phil. 1:21

phonies, especially Lucifer, the angel we now call Satan, who attempted to take God's place and was ejected from Heaven with one-third of the other angels.[41]

B. Jesus Christ's Perfect Set of Works, which consist of the following major areas: One, The Whole of Jesus's Teachings and Commands that are recorded in our New Testament.

Two, Jesus's Vicarious Passion Week, the Second *Passover,* concluding with His Precious Blood being shed on the Cross, which, when enabled by Repentance, is more than sufficient for the entire sin-load of the world, which Fulfilled the many Prophecies that were foretold, including Isaiah fifty-three.

Three, Jesus's Bodily Resurrection from the dead after spending precisely seventy-two hours in the lower parts of the earth "taking captivity captive and ordaining Gifts for man." All taken together, these three comprise the essence of the *New Covenant*, which serves as the binding set of rules by which we must abide and the descriptor of True Salvation, including all Christian relationships and benefits.[42]

C. This part is the responsibility of All True Christian Believers in their Obedience to Christ in everyday life by exercising *Faith* in Christ's perfect Works mentioned above. This area contains all the elements of the *Discipleship to Conversion* Dynamic Process in which every Reborn Believer must continue throughout life to inherit the benefits to which we should all be looking forward to receiving in Heaven. This includes the following elements: Daily Confession and Repentance from sin, Worship in Spirit and in Truth, Personal Holiness and separation from the world's ways, God's Granting of Gifts and the Authority to Minister in the *Body of Christ* ordained by the Holy Spirit and the complete set of Ethics and Morality that is befitting an Ambassador of Christ in this dark world of sin.[43]

---

41   Ex. 3:11-14; Deut. 4:39; Psa. 2,110; Isa. 14, 42-46; Ezek. 28 *See also the book entitled Basic Christian Doctrine, Section I: "The Nature of God"*

42   *See the Chart entitled Passover Sequence Chart and the Papers entitled The New Covenant and The Three Passovers of Scripture*

43   *Start with the papers entitled Alive Forevermore, the Gift of God in Christ Jesus, the Amazing Doctrine of God's Grace, the Baptism of Jesus Christ, the Beauty and Finesse of the New Covenant, (the 3 parts series) Christian Conversion and Conditions for Salvation*

D. All Spiritual Gifts and Callings are valid throughout the Age of Grace. These are ordained of God's Spirit and apply to all True Believers who obey Christ's Teachings as defined in the New Testament. As for the writer, I am a "Called Pastor Emeritus," ordained by God's Spirit in the "Five-Fold Ministry" that is defined in the New Testament. Know this for sure: The Gospel that I Preach is the only Gospel that exists and it cannot be "parted out," "compartmentalized" or compromised in any way without calling down a curse from Heaven upon all who attempt to limit it or 'redefine it' in any way, shape or fashion![44]

Moreover, not only that, I have been receiving Wisdom directly from God's Spirit, right from the beginning. When I began seriously studying God's Word, I began receiving much more in the area of Believers' maintaining of a clearly defined Christian Identity while we are here among others in the world. Yes, we must be "out and about" others who are "of the world" to minister to them. However, we must be ever careful not to let their worldly ways corrupt us! That is the essence of the "separation issue" and the Doctrine of *Sanctification.* Indeed, possibly the worst problem that has developed among most "professing Christians" is in that area of "defacto nation worship," patriotism, in which many Christians have become defiled with abject Idolatry, trusting in the "bloodstained" humanistic powers of the state, expressed in the worship of national symbols, politics and militarism, for being their saviors instead of God as the Scriptures clearly teach us otherwise! I will not belabor this subject further, for it has been well covered in other papers.

After over a half-century of intense Bible study and Christian service in leading home Bible studies and in being a Pastor in a local church, the Lord Jesus has qualified me for many wonderful things pertaining to the *Kingdom of Heaven* here on earth! Still, I grieve very much in spirit for those 'Professing Christians' who are languishing in apostasy, being deeply enmeshed in the world and its ways. Nonetheless, I am still hopeful for a "change in the wind" to come soon, especially as the Great Tribulation grinds on, becoming worse every day. They say

---

44   Matt. 5-7; 16:18,19; Matt. 18:19,20; John 8:31-58; Acts 17:24-31; Rom. 12:1 ff;1 Cor. 12,2,12-14; 2 Cor. 3-5; Gal. 1:6-12; Eph. 4:1-16; 1 Tim. 6:3-12; 2 Tim. 2:11-26; Heb. 1-4, 6-12

whenever the pain of iniquity begins to exceed its 'pleasure' that change will start.[45]

Another thing I know is that Christ's overarching *Authority* is absolute, extending to all things pertaining to the Christian life.[46]

Know this: The Fundamental issue of all truly Christian living is the Fact that God's *Agape* Love in us must extend to all aspects of life and Discipleship, in both private and public venues! "God is *Agape* Love" and God's Love is extended equally to everyone on this planet! Moreover, God never legitimates any response to sinful acts that would be inconsistent with Christ's Teachings! Yes, God makes no distinctions. Not only that, "God is no respecter of persons": Not by race, not by color, not by culture or traditions and not by nationality. Moreover, think about it: IF you claim to be a Christian God's Word tells you to "Love all your 'fellow humans, friend or foe,' just like God does, despite any difference or circumstance, which means that you are not able to remain *In Christ* and advocate killing anybody by anyone, anywhere or at anytime! Moreover, if one approves killing, God's Word tells us that the guilt of that sin extends to everyone who believes that way, in spite of the fact that they were not the ones who did the killing. God's Law works the same as the "Law of conspiracy in crime": All members who agreed with the act are equally guilty in the eyes of the Law. In Scripture, the "Law of *Blood guiltiness*" applies to every person who agrees with killing. Of course, if modern religious leaders remain unrepentant, continuing to support these damnable doctrines of *Determinism* that advocate killing like the Pharisees of the first century, they will have to take the brunt of God's Judgment for what they have done![47]

E. Again, IF you are a true Christian, you Belong to Jesus Christ by virtue of your *Redemption* by His Blood Shed at Calvary when you *Repented* of sin and received Jesus's Sacrifice and He became your

---

45   Luke 22:31,32; 1 Cor. 10; 2 Cor. 7:10; 2 Tim. 2:19-26
46   Matt. 6:9-13; 28:18; John 18:36
47   Psa. 51; Ezek. 23:37-39; Matt. 23:29-39; John 3:16; 8:39-58; 1 John 3,4 *(Note in particular, the reference to Cain killing his brother extends to the present to include all humans on earth for being our "brothers and sisters!")* See the papers entitled A Writer's Commentary and The Main Missing Aspects of the Original Christian Gospel

Personal Savior. At that time also you received a Reborn human spirit to Worship God in the process. That human spirit functions in two ways: Being a receiver of messages from God and a transmitter of your Prayers and Worship to God. The Genuine Christian life cannot be lived without that spiritual Reality that is Reborn within by God's Spirit. Any attempt to live "like a Christian" by will power alone or any scheme of "religion" is futile at best and will call down judgment from God because any way of living that is not defined by the terms of the New Covenant described in Scripture is classified for being the sin of iniquity! That is also why Jesus condemned the Pharisees. IF you are a true Christian, you do not belong to any part of the world! You belong to Jesus and His Kingdom of Heaven where you always do things "on earth (just) as it is in Heaven." Know also what Jesus proclaimed to Pilate at his trial: "My Kingdom is not of this world: My servants do not fight (like the world does)." That Truth underscores the Christian Way and it is the Way that I Believe that governs the life God gives me with Jesus's Commands occupying the Highest level of Authority and practice.[48]

F. We must also know and apply the following things regarding *Authority*: One, God does not "ordain" humanistic things, including the way the world governs the nations! The true meaning of the Greek word *Tagma* describes "an allowed order to exist," even when it is clearly alien to the Ways in which God works. This tenet falls under the overall classification of a law called "The Sovereignty of God and the Free Will of Man," which is the way the New Covenant works. Beware of the false doctrine of *Determinism.*[49]

The truth remains that, originally, God *In Jesus Christ* created the universe and all the pillars of true civilization to serve Jesus Christ, the true King. Ever since, God has been in the process of creating and perfecting a Special People that would serve and Glorify God and achieve true Peace and satisfaction in living. First it was ancient Israel, which, in the process of time in spite of their failures, via Mary,

---

48   Matt. 6:9-13; Luke 12:1-33; 13:18-35; John 18:36; 2 Cor. 3,4,6; 10:3-7; 11:12-15; Gal. 2:16-4:19; Eph. 6:10-18; Phil. 3:3:20; Heb. 11:12-16 *See also the paper entitled The Kingdom of Heaven is the Highest Form of Civilization*

49   *See the paper entitled The Fallacies of *Determinism**

produced the physical person, Jesus, whose Father was God. Jesus, the Son, as the only sinless person, lived a perfectly sinless life and was then offered to God as the perfect *Atonement* for the sins of mankind. Jesus then ordained the Church for being the vehicle which would take the Perfect Peacemaking Message we call the Gospel, to the ends of the earth. Then, the Holy Spirit gave as many as there were who Received the Gospel "power from on High" to live life in *Righteousness,* proving that the Message God gave to man was effective. This is also the Message that was preached by the Early Apostles. It is also the same Message that I preach.[50]

However, God also knew that even the church would apostatize after the third century, allowing events to "dovetail" into a period Scripture calls "The Great Tribulation" so that the Great Commission would finally be fulfilled.[51]

VI. What makes so many "So-called Christians" think that God will "blithely accept" a corrupted, worldly church who has the blood of millions on its hands?

Not on your life! No, anyone who knows the True Original Christian Gospel knows that the long-held false doctrines of the apostate church system that approves mass murder in wars and of prisoners must be purged before Christ returns or there will be Hell to pay! I sincerely hope that most Christians will "wake up" and Repent before it really is too late, that is, before Christ returns in Power and great Glory. At that time, all who remain in sin or apostasy must face God's Judgment.[52]

However, before that can happen, the church's leadership must first Repent of its long-held addiction to the "dictates" of *Determinism* that are the lying basis of many false doctrines, including the ones that approve of mass murder! Just compare their doctrines with the Original Gospel Preached by Christ in the first century and you will be literally forced to the conclusion that, long ago, church leadership,

---

50   Psa. 1-4, 8,9,15,16,18, 23-27, 31-37, 40-46, 55-57, 61-63, 73, 83,84, 89,91, 94-100, 103-107, 110, 121, 136, 146, Prov. 16:7; Matt. 5-7; 16:18,19; 18:19,20; John 3-17; 18:36,37;Acts 1-11; 17:24-31; Rom. 1:16,17; 5:1-8:39; 12:1 ff;; 1 Cor. 1-3, 10,12-15; 2 Cor. 1-7; Gal.1:6-12; 2:16-4:19; Eph. 1-4; Col. 1-3

51   *See the papers entitled Facts of Scripture: The Church and the Tribulation and Fulfilment Prophecy*

52   Matt. 25; Rom. 14:23; 2 Thess. 1:8; 2:3-12; Rev. 11:1-15

has apostatized by falling back into the world's ways and, therefore has been lying to Christians for centuries.[53]

Indeed, if one knows this painful truth and realizes just how long that great apostasy has prevailed, it does not take a rocket scientist to figure out that it is going to take a cataclysmic crisis to "Break up this fallow ground" of fear, unbelief and worldliness. Of course, if you have and keep an open mind and follow that up by studying Scripture carefully, you can deduce that this is God's primary purpose for the Great Tribulation Period.[54]

Yes, God is allowing the evil empire of Antichrist to rise up and devastate the world system. Yet, far too many "So-called Christians" Love the world and have been consequently lulled to unconsciousness by its drone of propaganda to the point that they no longer can legitimately be called Christians. By their doctrines, they are identifying themselves with the World and not Christ. Verily, their avowed approval of mass murder in wars, capital punishments and abortions have alienated them from the God of Love they falsely claim to worship! Indeed, their "deterministic doctrines" insult Christ and call Him a liar!

Not only that, the collective *Blood guiltiness* they have been accumulating surpasses the imagination. Remember again Christ's diatribe against the religious rulers of His day on earth that "called them on the carpet" for their gross hypocrisy and iniquity. Their treacherous manipulation of the crowd at Jesus's trial before Pilate is the *Piece de Resistance!* Notice in particular that the religious leaders were behind getting Barabbas released and that later proclaimed to Pilate that "We have no king but Caesar!"[55]

The underlying truth about all this is that you cannot trust people to be honest. They are devious, seeking advantage by doing anything they can do. That is also why modern "Christians" have sunk so low as to believe in bald-faced contradictions because they are loath to be willing

53   See the papers entitled Basics of Biblical Church Governance, Destiny and Free Will, Guidelines for Renewed Leadership, Questionnaire for Church Leaders and the Book entitled Spiritual Guidelines for Restoration, "Historical Review" Section
54   Jer. 4:4; Hosea 10:12; Matt. 24; Luke 21; John 15:18-16:4,33; Rom. 14:23; 2 Thess. 2:2-12; Rev. 2,3 See also the papers entitled A Biblical Disclosure of Antichrist and Facts of Scripture: The Church and the Tribulation and the book entitled The Church in the Last Days
55   Matt. 23; 27:1-26; Mark 15:11-15; Luke 13:18-35; 23:13-25; John 18:36-19:15

to pay the price for being a Real Christian that God's Word clearly tells us we must do every day! Yes, the fawning, sycophantic leaders teach precisely the same as the Pharisees, Sadducees and Herodians did in the first century. The only way to rectify this mess is to <u>Go back to the Original Definitions and refuse to compromise these Truths, no matter what happens!</u> That is also why I believe in *Faith-based Pacifism,* for it totally concurs with Christ's Teaching and that of the Early Apostles and period writers like Tertullian of Carthage. The True Gospel that is defined in our New Testament is verily the <u>only flawless way to neutralize evil at its source.</u> The same truth is here today: True Christians know that <u>the source of evil is with Satan and his fallen angels.</u> Moreover, that is why "We (True Christians) wrestle not with flesh and blood, but against principalities and powers and the rulers of the darkness of this world."

Always remember that <u>nothing spiritual is "automatic"</u>: You must make the right choices every day you live to remain in Right standing with God. All those who follow the world are also guilty of committing Idolatry by 'pledging allegiance' to the false gods of the worldly state religion. Sadly, they will suffer God's judgment unless they Repent in time! On the other hand, ALL True Christians belong to the Heavenly Kingdom described by Jesus Christ in His Teachings. You are <u>unable to go both ways at once: You must choose one or the other.</u>[56]

VII. Conclusion.

All True Christians belong to the *Kingdom of Heaven,* in which the <u>only Reigning King is Jesus Christ.</u> If you Read your Bible very carefully, individually by yourself, not being influenced by anyone else around you, you will begin to see that no Scripture exists that contradicts that ultimate truth. Simply put, the Word of God does not teach like the "poison pen" of modern religion wants you to think! All the Scriptures they twist around to teach fawning obeisance to worldly rulers are being <u>misinterpreted</u>. No Scripture tells you to <u>worship</u>

---

56   Matt. 5:43-48; 6:9-13, 22-14; Luke 16:13-15; Acts 5:29-32; Rom. 12:1-21; Gal. 1:6- 12; Eph. 6:10-12; Col. 1:13-16; Phil. 3:20; Heb. 10:18-39; 11:12-16 *See also the papers entitled The Christian Epiphany, Divergent Belief Systems, Do You Know Who You Are, Every Believer can independently know the Truth of Scripture, The Kingdom of Heaven is the Highest Form of Civilization, Looking Through the Lens of Jesus Christ and True Liberty is in Christ Alone*

the state like religious rulers teach, but rather, God's Word merely advises that we submit to duly constituted civil authority because that is becoming to civilized manners. Remember that Scripture teaches that all the "pillars of true civilization" were put in place By Christ to serve Christ. Therefore, we can tell by comparing what they do with this original imperative to see if they are fulfilling their purpose that God intends in making a peaceful background. However, if what they do is against what Christ teaches, then we know that God no longer authorizes their power! That is the basis of the Doctrine of Godly Civil Disobedience, which must come into play in those situations so that God's People can remain independent of evil influences and thereby keep themselves Holy before God! For example, remember what Rahab did by sheltering the spies in Jericho. Remember that Elijah the Prophet told the Israelites to refuse serving the Baals (national idols) even though both the king and queen commanded it. Remember also what Daniel and his three friends had to do during the Babylonian captivity. Peter taught the same rule to the Early Church.[57]

Yes, sometimes you must suffer for your Faith in Christ. It is all "part of the deal" you agreed to when you first received Christ. IF you Truly Live for Jesus Christ, You are simply unable to avoid controversy and persecution! It is a given.

The bottom line is that whenever man's rules or laws conflict with our clear mandates to live for Christ, then "You must obey God rather than man." For the rest, we must put all things in life into God's Hands. God will "take care of" all those who pervert the Gospel to gain human advantage. Yes, God will judge all the workers of iniquity and false teachers who lead the naive astray, stealing away the liberty of many in the process. I grieve for the multitudes who still languish in the spiritual dungeons of darkness because they are taught by religious leaders to commit Idolatry by worshiping the state (the Baal) and its symbols. They also impugn Christ and trample His Precious Blood in the dirt by teaching Christians that soldiers who murder others on the battlefield, shedding copious blood, would "make people Free."

Indeed, this is possibly the most ludicrous of all heresies that have consumed the church because of false doctrines. How dare they despise

---

57   Joshua 2; 1 Kings 18; Daniel 3,6; Acts 5:29-32; Heb. 10:26-31; 1 John 5:19-21

Christ's Sacrifice so flippantly? Contrariwise, the Scripture clearly tells us that <u>Only Christ's Blood makes a person Free and gives people True Peace!</u>[58]

Not only that, Scripture teaches that "the mind of the flesh (Humanism) is antagonistic to God." This means that all man's corrupt ways of vainly trying to make peace by the use of deadly force <u>are futile in the extreme!</u>[59]

Finally, the bottom line remains: Do you know who you are and that you <u>do not belong to this world</u>? IF you are a True Christian, You already know that you belong to a Heavenly Kingdom in which You Trust Jesus Christ for being Your Savior <u>in all venues, Physical, Soulical and spiritual</u>! So, look to Jesus Christ in all things, knowing that <u>He is your True King</u> and deliverer from all evil, not "Caesar!"[60]

Do you also know that Jesus Christ IS our *Passover* Lamb and that <u>the *Passover* pattern is the universal archetype of all types of Salvation</u>? Indeed, this Pattern of "Jehovah-Jireh," viz., the Lord will provide everything we need, can be seen from the start with God's 'grooming' of the Patriarchs' *Faith* and also in the *Kingdom of Heaven* Imagery we can see, mirrored in Prophecy.[61]

<u>No peace exists anywhere without following Christ's Teachings of Love</u>! Also, at any level, <u>Peace and True Freedom are inexorably linked</u>: One does not exist without the other. <u>Christ's Bloodshed Sacrifice covers all venues of Salvation: Physical, Soulical and spiritual</u>. You cannot "limit it" to forgiveness of sin. The *New Covenant* does not <u>ever</u> tolerate or approve <u>trust in more bloodshed of any human to "save."</u>

---

58 Matt. 27:1-6; Luke 22:15-20; John 8:31-36; 14:26,27; 2 Cor. 3:17,18; Eph. 2:13,14; Col. 1:20-24; Heb. 9:11-15; 10:26-31; 1 Pet. 1:19-21,
59 John 6:27-63; Rom. 8:1-18
60 Matt. 6:9-13; 22:21; John 18:36; Phil. 3:20; Heb. 11:12-16
61 Gen. 12, 15, 22, 28, 32 35, 37-45; Ex. 3-15; Num. 6:22-27; Deut. 28-34; Josh. 1:5-9;24:1 ff.; 1 Sam. 2:1-10; 2 Sam. 22:1 ff.; 1 Chr. 16:1-17:27; 2 Chr 7:12-22; Neh. 1:4 ff.; 9:1 ff.; Psa. 1-9, 15-20, 23-37, 42-48, 51-57, 61-63, 68, 73, 84, 89-91, 94-98, 100-107, 110-119, 121, 130, 135-139, 145-147; Isa. 2,6,; 7:14; 9:6,7; 11:1-12:6; 25-32; 33:6; 35:1-38:22; 40-66; Jer. 31; Ezek. 36; Dan. 2:44,45; 7:9-28; Joel 2; Mic. 3-7; Matt. 5-7,10; 12:18-45; Luke 6,12; John 1:1-18; 4:14-24; 6:27-63; 7:15-18; 8:31-58; 10:1-16; 13:35-17:26; 18:36,37; Acts 17:24-31; Rom. 5-8; 1 Cor. 1,2,12-14; 2 Cor. 1-7; Gal. 2-5; Eph. 1-4; Phil. 1-4; Col. 1-3; 1 Tim. 2:5; 6:3- 12; 2 Tim. 1-4; Heb. 1-4, 9-12; 2 Pet. 1:2-11, 19-2:9, 20; 3:1 ff.; 1 John 1-5 See also Passover Sequence Chart and the papers entitled Fulfilment Prophecy and The Three Passovers of Scripture

Chapter 13
The Great Commission

Before we go into the specific events relating to *the church in the last days,* we need to address this most crucial subject. To be truly biblical, *the great commission* of Jesus Christ refers to its complete message. To do this justice, we should include the full text of all the directives and messages that Jesus Christ gave to His disciples/apostles and followers throughout His ministry. However, in the interest of brevity, we can limit our examination to the crucial period after His resurrection through to His ascension to the right-hand of the throne. The average modern Christian, however, may be quite oblivious to the full scope and significance of this historic compound declaration. Many believers think it is only the concern of *mega-church* corporation organizations with global satellite television networks at their disposal. However, we must be honest and willing to face the truth that these methods of high-tech evangelism that they touted for being so effective only a few short years ago, are failing us miserably. In fact, we are falling behind percentage-wise, not even keeping up with the population increase! What is wrong with this picture? I fear that the major part of the problem is disobedience. The great commission of the New Testament is clear: Jesus has commanded us to go, and He did not mean by proxy. Whatever or wherever your mission field is, He *expects you personally* to be in that field working to the best of your ability! That was also the message of all the parables as well. Not only that, every blood-bought Christian believer has a God-given responsibility to do his or her part. That part is to acknowledge *our responsibility to obey all* the commands of Jesus Christ, the One sent by God. We must do this *first* if we are going to be "teaching them to observe all that I have commanded you."

Christians need to ask themselves, "Just how do we perceive the great commission to be?" Better yet, we should ask, "How did Jesus, the apostles, and the early church originally define evangelism?" Follow the New Testament accounts carefully, and it may surprise you that the early Christians did not concern themselves with *organization* like modern Christians are.

Why? Because when you *really do obey* the one God has sent and follow Him like you should, your cup is full, just like He promised. When your cup is full and overflowing, the spiritual artesian well within you is active and the water of life naturally flows out. This vital spiritual precept of the New Covenant is astonishingly predictable. That means yes, we can find a one-to-one correspondence between our obedience in following Christ's commands and truly spiritual success and fruit-bearing.

However, such statistics like numbers of members or converts and dollars in an offering plate *cannot count as fruit.* Jesus tells us much about *the significance of light and fruit* in places like the Sermon on the Mount, the parable of the sower and the seed, and with His discourses with the Pharisees. Jesus's "Upper Room/Gethsemane Discourse" contains many recognizable references.[192] Fruit-bearing requires spiritual quality.. Spiritual quality both requires and produces *Agape love.* The gift of God's love in us gives us the ability to form lasting relationships. We also require it to maintain relationships, because we must choose to *continue our commitment and obedience* to receive more love. The following *progressive equation emerges:* RELATIONSHIOP + COMMITMENT + OBEDIENCE = FRUIT. That is, if we continually maintain right relationship, commitment, and obedience to Christ, in the end, we will produce fruit.

Notice the prerequisites and the progression, just like with faith, hope, and love. "By these men will know that you are my disciples if you have love one for another." "If you love Me, you will keep My commands."[193] It is a truism that the light, warmth, and bright fire of true Christianity burning in our lives will attract others to Jesus. That is why Jesus said that you did not "hide your lamp under a bushel."

---

192   Matt. 5:13–16; 13:1 ff.; John 7:37–39; 8:12. ff.; 13–17 *(Upper Room/Gethsemane Dis.)*
193   John 13:34,35; 15:1–12; Acts 4:11-13; 1 Cor. 13.

Can we not see the truth? When the true gospel is being lived out and followed *as Jesus gave it,* we need nothing else to "add to it" to make it work!

Yes, the *original gospel of Jesus is all you need!* What does Jesus say about fancy high-minded, humanistic methods, corporation organization political agendas, computerized demographic techniques, and high-technology ways the church has imported from the world system anyway? Where do you think they lead? *God says,* "What is highly prized among men is detestable in the sight of God." So what business does the church have in using those methods? Consider also Jesus's saying to the laborers. What did Jesus say about using the usual human comparisons?[194]

I. What is the text of the great commission?

The first thing we must realize is that "the great commission" is much more than just the one scripture in Matthew 28 we usually hear quoted. In fact, we find at least *five direct Scripture references,* from which we can piece together the main body of the message. **See below.[195]

Before we consider some main elements contained in this very important directive, let us address the issue of *the stewardship of the gospel.* The Greek lexicon defines biblical stewardship as *the keeping of the house,* based upon the Greek word *Oiknomos.* This means *that believers must observe and keep all the rules* that Jesus Christ has left us in Scripture to govern His house. God has placed the New Covenant *standard that every Christian believer is responsible for obeying* to govern His body, the church.

1. Let us pay particular attention to the requirement that we must *obey all of Jesus's commands according to the best of our ability, making no excuse.* This command should be an obvious given and is confirmed as a necessary part of the Christian life by Jesus's specific instructions contained in the "Upper Room/Gethsemane Discourse." We should

---

194   Matt. 10:16–42; 16:21–28; Luke 10:1 ff.; 16:15.
195   **Matt. 28:9–20; Mark 16:9–20; Luke 24:25–53; John 20:16–21:19; Acts 1:1-11

also understand that true believers never try to change the rules to fit any circumstance whatever.[196]

2. The new commandment to love one another, even as I have loved you. Found also in the "Upper Room/Gethsemane Discourse," Jesus commands His followers to love (Agape) one another the same way as Jesus loves the Father and the Holy Spirit and vice versa.[197] All these commands and directives contain the ever-present fact that:

3. We must receive the universal calling: that we seek to be conforming to the likeness of Jesus. This illustrates the central New Testament doctrine of *biblical conversion.* That is, it is the Father's will *that each individual believer* is "conformed to the image of His Son, Jesus Christ." Yes, this mandate is for *every Christian, not just for the "super spiritual!"* [198]

II. Preview types of Christ sending out workers.

First, the "fishers of men mandate" Jesus gave to Peter when Jesus first encountered him, "I will make you fishers of men if you follow Me." Notice both the *command* and the requisites for fulfilling obedience to it.[199]

Second, the "feeding of sheep" discourses and narrative sequences give us a vivid picture of Jesus's concern for the needy and His compassion for the multitudes.

He sees them as they are—as sheep who have no shepherd. This is a large part of the heart of Jesus Christ. They saw it in "The Feeding of the Five Thousand" and Jesus's charge to John that is part of the great commission itself.[200]

Third, the pictures of the seeking shepherd continue this image, reinforcing the same trend in highlighting Jesus's care in all concerns of human life. See the Lost and Found parables.[201]

---

196   John 13–17
197   John 15:10–12
198   Rom. 8:29
199   Matt. 4:19; Mark 1:17; Luke 5:1–11.
200   Matt. 14:1 f.; John 6:1 ff.; 21:15–17; Acts 20:28; 1 Pet. 5:1–5.
201   Matt. 18:12; Luke 15:1 ff.; John 10:1 ff. *See also the paper: Jesus' Major Parables*

** Then Jesus gave the disciples a taste of His evangelism style in the sending out of the laborers. Let us take heed.[202]

III. It is all about a very special kind of building in which we are involved, called the body of Christ.

The great commission is *part of Christ*. Spiritual attributes and qualities are at its core, and *God uses spiritual means to fulfill it.* Consequently, edification is also a central issue. The Holy Spirit uses many callings in the up-building of Christ's body. Among these are *the five-fold ministry* and the diverse spiritual gifts and callings ordained of the Holy Spirit. We can find these in Romans 12, 1 Corinthians 12 to 14, and Ephesians 4. The word *missionary* is not in that list as such, but can be considered *A universal calling* to all believers.[203] Scripture teaches us that to have and continue in a *true calling of God,* one must satisfy the following conditions:

1. We must have *a solid foundation* of spirituality that is *built upon the Rock.*[204]

2. We must have *continual edification* (maintenance) based on spiritual precepts.[205]

3. *Utilization* of outreach or ministry must be based on *spiritual* means and power.[206]

IV. What forms the basis for renewal?

Fulfillment of the great commission happens if and only if we have *all the following in place:* renewed commitment, renewed obedience, renewed spirituality, renewed worship, renewed minds, renewed leadership.[207]

---

202 Matt. 9:39–10:42; 20:1 f.; Luke 10:1 f.
203 Luke 6:46–49; Rom. 8:29; 1 Cor. 3:11–15; Eph. 2:13–3:21.
204 Matt. 16:18; Luke 6:46–49; 1 Cor. 3:11–15.
205 Acts 9:31; 1 Cor. 3:11–15; 8:1; 14:1–5; 2 Cor. 12:19; Eph. 4:1–16; Jude 20.
206 Zech. 4:6; Matt. 20:25–28; 25:34–40; John 15:5; Acts 1:8; 1 Cor. 15:10; 1 Pet.1.
207 *See the booklet: Guidelines for Renewed Leadership*

The final requirement is absolutely necessary. We must have renewed New Covenant-based methodology based on *the Gospel of Jesus*. Jesus, our Bridegroom, is constantly evaluating our motives and those in the church to see *if we really mean business about following Him!*

V. The passing of the final exam requires tests of faith in tribulation.

Absolute loyalty to the cause of Christ is the primary "secret to being successful," both for individual Christians and for successful evangelism by the church collective. Only those whom God has *spiritually* prepared for ministry over years of seasoning will possess *consistent* integrity, godly character, and endurance unto the end. These are the ones who have made conscious and irrevocable choices that have cost them and will continue to cost them dearly in the things of this world! In doing so, they have been abiding by God's timetable, not their own (or from some human logic or format). The true servants of God do not rush ahead of him, nor do they lag behind. However, those who lack sensitivity to the Holy Spirit, who is the communicator of Jesus to believers, will risk serious losses. The same rules work for the congregational level as they do for the individual. Churches need to be prepared as well.

Let us learn the hard lesson given by the parable of the ten virgins.[208] This and other parables of Jesus highlight the absolute necessity of *choosing wisely* and maintaining a healthy and virile spirituality by our obedience of Jesus's commands. The five wise virgins *did*. The five foolish virgins *did not*. Notice that the *only difference* between these two groups was that one group prepared and persevered, while the other did not! Jesus invited them both. Both considered themselves "friends of Jesus." *Both had oil once*. Yet something went wrong with one group, didn't it? The night is coming on and the Bridegroom tarries. Will you be prepared and ready when Jesus comes? Your loyalty to Jesus is very important to Him. Is loyalty to Jesus *as important to you?* Yes, we must count costs as given, whether we like it or not.[209]

---

208   Matt. 25:1–13 See the paper "Jesus' Major Parables"
209   Matt. 10:16–42; Luke 14:26–33; 18:8; John 15:18–16:33; Acts 14:22; 2 Tim. 2:1 ff.

Both Jesus and the apostolic writers warn of trials, opposition, and persecution in the world. As a Christian living in the world, you will have tribulation. *The great tribulation* is only an extension of this precept. We must be ready always, all the way to the end. Yes, the great tribulation relates to the church, contrary to the contemporary escapist mentality of many modern churches. The church's eventual success and deliverance depend upon our diligence *in both knowing and practicing the truth! Scripture connects the great tribulation and the great commission both to the church and to the last days!* Yes, history has proven that the church is the strongest when she is under the gun of persecution and opposition.

Conversely, acceptance weakens her. Now, let us consider the historically proven facts about persecution: First, persecution spreads the church. Second, persecution empowers the church, making it stronger. Third, persecution proves that *true Christianity works* in the world where everyone can see it!

The gospel is *"the power of God unto salvation."* [210] Yes, the great tribulation will accomplish much for God, and the church will finally fulfill one great command of Jesus that has remained unfulfilled in all two thousand years of Christian history: *the great commission.* I hope you will want to be a part of what Jesus is doing now.

*See also chapter 9, section V: Explanatory:
"The Three Microcosms"

The Main Elements of the Great Commission, Part 1: God's Part		
1	The authority of Christ.	Matt. 28:18.
2	The promise of the Spirit/power to believers.	Acts 1:8.
3	I am with you always.	Matt.28:20.
4	Jesus's reproof of unbelief.	Mark 16:14; Luke 24:25, 26: John 21:18

---

210   Rom. 1:16,17

5	Promise of signs to follow believers.	Mark 16:17-20
6	Jesus's opening up of the Scriptures to the disciples (now done by the Holy Spirit)	Luke 24:27-32, 44-46
7	The "blessing at the breaking of bread."	Luke 24:30; John 21:13
8	"Peace be unto you"	Luke 24:36; John 20:19
9	Infallible proofs and demonstrations of the reality of His resurrection (life)	Matt.28;9, 10; Luke 24:38-43; John20:16; 21:7,14
10	The miraculous catch of fish	John 21:6-8
11	The benediction/blessing	Luke 24:30, 50, 51
12	The promise of His second coming/return	Acts 1:11

The Main Elements of the Great Commission, Part 2: Our Part

1	"Go," and "So send I you"	Matt. 28:19; Mark 16:15; John 20:20
2	"Receive the Holy Spirit" and power	John 20:22; Acts 1:8
3	"Make disciples"	Matt. 28:19
4	"Teach all nations"	Matt. 28:20
5	"Baptizing them…"	Matt. 28:19; Mark 16:16
6	"Obey everything I have commanded you"	Matt. 28:20
7	"Follow Me"	John 21:19
8	"Preach the gospel… repentance"	Mark 16:15; Luke 24:47
9	"You shall be witnesses"	Acts 1:8
10	"Cast the net"	John 21:6
11	"Come and dine"	John 21:9–13
12	"Feed My lambs/sheep"	John 21:15–17

## PART 3

The Church in the End Times

Chapter 14
Biblical Precept of Mystery

Fundamental Issues Regarding the True Christian Faith		
#	Description	Page #
I.	Introduction	
II.	The "Mystery of Godliness"	
III.	Consider the following list of Scriptures that sequentially tie together the prophecies relating to the unification of God's People, Jew and Gentile, into One Body *In Christ*	
IV.	The "Mystery of Iniquity/ Apostasy" acts like a "Trojan Horse"	
V.	Let us investigate the following illustrations, observing how context helps us understand the meaning of Scripture	
VI.	Appendices	
	Appendix 1: Diagram One: Correlating Last Days Events	
	Appendix 2: "Chronological Chart of 'writing periods' in Daniel"	

I. Introduction:

In Scripture, the "Precept of Mystery" is a multifaceted Principle composed of the following aspect areas or overall classifications of mysteries:

A. Scripture defines the "Mystery of God" or "Mystery of Godliness," which also can be found in Scripture in other terminology, viz., the "mysteries of the Kingdom of God," the "mystery of Christ," the "mystery of the Gospel," the "fellowship of the mystery" and the "mystery of Faith."[1]

Within the "Mystery of Christ" we have God's Master Plan regarding "The whole Family in Heaven and earth (which is named after the Father of our Lord Jesus Christ)." Jesus referred to this Family for being likened to a "Flock of sheep" which includes members from widely divergent sources but all *In Christ.* John the Baptist, Jesus and Paul all tell us about a Mystery that concerns "Christ and His Church," and that this mystery can be explained in the roles of the Bridegroom and the Bride in the "Jewish Wedding Paradigm."[2]

The main classification of "Mysteries" concerning Christian Doctrine and practice is the "Mystery of Godliness," which also includes all that pertains to God's overall "Master Plan of the Ages": Christ's universal invitation of Salvation and the potential reconciliation of all mankind into one *Kingdom of Heaven* that Christ will eventually deliver intactly to Father God.

Moreover, Scripture tells us that this is accomplished by the Unification of One Body of Believers *In Christ,* (the True Church), that is faithful and loyal to Jesus Christ, taken from all nations, tribes and tongues.[3]

This mystery is also referred to by Jesus for being "the mysteries of the Kingdom of God."[4]

Paul also tells us that the Mysteries of God form a stewardship and that True Believers intuitively understand and speak about the things that God's Spirit reveals to us as would a child whose mind is open to Truth. Jesus had spoken about this earlier to Nicodemus and the Disciples.[5]

---

1   Matt. 13:11; Mark 4:11; Luke 8:10; Eph. 1:9; 3:3-9; 6:19; Col. 1:26,27; 2:2,3; 4:3; Tim. 3:9,16
2   Matt. 25:1-13; John 3:29,30; 10:13-16; Eph. 3:3-21; 5:22-30 *See also the Paper entitled Jesus' Major Parables*
3   John 1:1-14; 3:3-8, 16,17, 27; 10:1-18, 27-30; 1 Cor. 15:20-28; Eph. 1:9,10; 2:11-22;3:1-19 *See also the Papers entitled Fulfilment Prophecy and One Covenant for All*
4   Matt. 13:11; Mark 4:11; Luke 8:10
5   Matt. 18:3,4; 19:13,14; John 3:9-16,27; 1 Cor. 2:9-16; 4:1; Gal. 1:12; Eph. 1:3-14; 3:3-12; 6:19

Not only that, Scripture unequivocally tells us that "God is no respecter of persons" and that although Christ first preached the Gospel to the Jews, it had been God's Plan all along to use the Jews to produce the *Seed,* Christ, so that God's original promise to Abraham: "In your Seed all Nations will be Blessed," would be fulfilled. This Blessing is the universal offer of Salvation through Christ to all mankind.[6]

Paul also tells us the details concerning a 'major detour' that affects this Plan: This involves the "Cutting off of the Jews" because of protracted unbelief and rejection of the Messiah to continue "Until the Times of the Gentiles are fulfilled."[7]

B. Scripture defines the negative type of mystery for being the "Mystery of Iniquity," which also aligns with works and agendas of our adversary, Satan. Satan lies behind many stratagems that make use of the human penchant to find "shortcuts" around the more difficult areas of the Complete Christian Gospel. According to God's Word, this aspect of human nature is called iniquity, which is crookedness, deviousness and stubborn independence, all of which constitute sin in God's eyes!

Other terms for this phenomenon are as follows: The "abomination of desolation," the "Transgression of desolation," the "Stumbling block of their iniquity" and the "Blasphemy of the Holy Spirit." Not only that, all the above are "life dominating type" sins that disrupt any relationship with God.[8]

C. Another aspect of a mystery is that it is not the same as a "secret." A mystery is a spiritual fact, precept or relationship that, although it is not obvious on the surface, it can be understood even by a child by simple Revelation from the Holy Spirit, via the human spirits' organ of *Intuition.* The dreams that were interpreted by Joseph, Daniel and Joseph, Jesus' stepfather, are in this category.[9]

---

6   Gen. 12,18,22; Acts 10:34-38 See also the Paper entitled *The Fulfillment of God's Promise* (to Abraham)

7   Luke 21:20-24; Acts 13:26-49; Romans 9-11; 16:25-27; Eph. 1:10; 2:11-22; 3:1-13;Col. 1:12-29; 2:2-4

8   Jer. 2:7; 6:15; 7:10; 8:12; Ezek. 6:11; 7:19; 8:6; 14:3-11; Dan. 9:27; 11:31; 12:11; Matt. 12:30,31; 24:15; Mark 3:28-30; 2 Thess. 2:7; Rev. 2:9; 17:5,7

9   Gen. 37,40; Dan. 2; Matt. 2; Gal. 1:12

D. A mystery is also very similar to a Parable, in that it is a presentation of a spiritual truth in such a way that it "screens the hearers," separating those who truly seek to love and serve God from all the users and unbelievers.[10]

II. What are the major characteristics regarding the "Mystery of Godliness," which highlights God's elegant process of Unification, including the "Cutting off of the Jews," grafting in of the gentiles and the re-grafting of the Jews after the "Times of the Gentiles are fulfilled?" See also Section IV[11]

A. Let us consider a few "Question and answer couplets" in Scripture, paying particular attention to the words "End, Final, Finish, after and Consummation." 1. Two significant Old Testament examples can be found in Daniel twelve:

Q.: Daniel asks: "How long will it be to the end of these wonders?"

A.: "The man (angel) in white linen which was upon the waters of the River swore by Him who lives eternally said: It will be for 'A Time, Times and dividing of Time,' when he (God) will have accomplished to scatter the power of the *holy people, all these things will be finished." (Both Jews and Christians are 'Holy people.')[12]

Q.: "O my Lord, what will be the end of these things?"

A.: "The words are closed up and sealed until the time of the end (after which time) the daily (sacrifice) will have been taken away* and the abomination of desolation is set up, will be 1290 days."*This event was "prefigured" when God Tore down the Veil in the Holy of Holies at the precise moment Jesus dismissed His Spirit and died on the Cross, installing the *New Covenant.* The First fulfillment of the "Abomination that causes Desolation" took place forty years later when the Zealots and Sicarii occupied the Temple. The second will be during the Great Tribulation. Explanatory: Let us observe two things

---

10 See the papers entitled Biblical Symbolism (Parts One and Two) and Jesus' Major Parables

11 *Dan. 9:26,27; 12:7; Matt. 24; Luke 21:24; Acts 13:17-49; Rom. 11:25; Rev. 10:7 *Observe that the "holy people's scattering" and the 70th Week both take place in two stages, following the "Law of Double fulfillments": One for the Jews and the second for Christians.

12 Dan. 12:6,7. Cf. Dan. 9:24-27 Again, note the last part of Dan. 9, Vss. 26 and 27 both point to " the scattering of the holy people's power" in two installments. Ibid. Fn. #11

about "Prophetic Time Text" (PTT): One, depicted events appear 'foreshortened' when viewed from the past looking forward. Two, these prophecies are cast in "spiritual vision" context which makes great use of "spiritual symbolism." Moreover, in Daniel twelve, after verse four the context indicates that we are looking at the modern age in the time just before the "Great Stone" strikes the base of the statue icon of chapter two.[13]

2. In the New Testament we have three major examples: In Jesus' "Prophetic Discourse," the Disciples ask the following questions:

Q.: "When will these things take place? And what will be the 'Sign of Your Coming' and of the end of the world?" Again notice the questions indicate that they are addressing two separate events.

A.: Jesus answers them by a multifaceted warning about what was to come, both in the near future (for them) and in the "Last Days," saying: "Many will come in my name... and will deceive many... You will be hated by all Nations... The end is not yet... he that endures to the end will be saved... the **Gospel will be preached to all Nations and then will the end come." "When you see the abomination of desolation that was spoken by the Prophet Daniel... stand in the holy place... flee to the mountains."[14]

Q.: In Acts they ask "Lord, will you at this time restore again the kingdom to Israel?" A.: "(Jesus said) It is not for you to know the times or the seasons which the Father has put in his own power but you will receive power, after that the Holy Spirit has come upon you and you will be my witnesses... unto the uttermost parts of the earth." Did you notice how Jesus "changed the channels" by redirecting their attention on spiritual things? Of course, the Disciples' misunderstanding about

---

13 Compare Dan. 12:8-13 with *Prophetic Chronology Two*, Sects. III and IV, *Contextually Comparing Elements ..., Sects. III, IV-B, C, F, VI-B, VII and Sequence of Events See also Fulfilment Prophecy, FIGURE ONE: "The Nine Ages" and Messiah Figures FIGURE ONE: "Seeing the Double Peaks of Teleos Vision"*

14 Daniel 9,12; Matt. 24; Luke 21 *Together, these statements describe two stages: First, the events of the first century Jewish war of AD 67-70 (the 1st half of the 70th Week) with the 'Abomination of Desolation' (AOD) referring to the time when the Jewish Zealots desecrated the Temple by their indiscriminate bloodshed of innocent civilians. See Josephus' Wars of the Jews and the chart entitled Sequence of Events. The Second Fulfilment (2nd TOHY and 2nd Half of the 70th Week) takes place in the Great Tribulation Period, at the end of the "Age of Grace." See also Sect. III, Patterns in Prophetic Scripture II-A, IV-B-2, Cross Reference Guide IV-C, Fn#27,28 and Prophetic Chronology Two, Section IV "Correlating Prophetic Texts and Acrostics"*

Jesus' mission reflected the predominant Jewish thought of the day. By that time, the Jewish concept of Messiah had been clearly corrupted by their reliance on political chicanery and military might, both of which are tantamount to idolatry in God's eyes!

That is also why the Jewish religious leaders totally failed to recognize the "dual fulfillment" precept of "Messiah figures" that first show Jesus as the "Suffering Servant" and "Lamb of God," the "One Father God has Sent" (MFLa). They should have noticed that when Jesus entered Jerusalem on the "foal of a donkey" (not a horse), it was not to "take over" by force and overthrow the Roman occupation but to die for their sins, fulfilling the prophecies of both Isaiah and Zechariah![15]

In Revelation six, at the opening of the Fifth Seal in Heaven, the voice of the martyrs calls out:

Q.: "How long will it be, O Lord, holy and true, until you judge and avenge our blood on them that dwell on the earth?"

A.: "White robes were given unto them and it was said unto them that they should rest yet a 'little season' until after their fellow servants and brethren are killed as they were, will be fulfilled." Notice that this exchange occurs just before Christ's Return to earth.[16]

Review Summary: Notice that all these questions indicate the existence of a fundamental prophetic law: "The Law of Multiple Fulfilments." Consequently, similar to Jesus' Prophetic Discourse, the events depicted apply in sequence to the two halves of Daniel's 70th Week. Also, the cessation of sacrifice/ worship via the "abomination of desolation" takes place at two levels, each representing the two prophetic periods which form the two halves of the 70th Week.

The first half was for the Jews in AD 70. The second half applies to both Christians and Jews when worship of the true Living God is forced underground during the Great Tribulation Period. This can already be detected in the global influence of the New World Order's "Agenda twenty-one" which intends to "replace all religion" with a

---

15   Acts 1:6-8 Cf. Isa. 52:13-53:12; Zech. 9:9,10; Matt. 16:15-23; 20:20-28; 23:1 ff.; Luke 24:25 ff.; John 10:24-38; 11:49-52 *See also the Papers entitled Conditions for Salvation Appendix C: "Sent Me Scripture List," Covenant Principles, Fulfilment Prophecy, Illustrating the Law of Multiple Fulfillments and Messiah Figures*

16   Rev. 6:9-11

universalist secular system which persecutes all beliefs that teach one way for Salvation by one God.

B.**Regarding the "Mystery" of God's Grand Plan of Unification, let us examine the connection that links God's final Reconciliation of the Jews and the point described by the moniker "Until the Times of the Gentiles are Fulfilled" (TGF). In John's amazing vision of prophetic imagery found in the *Apocalypse*, we find a crucial "Time Tag Scripture" identifying a time when "God's Mystery will be Finished" (GMF), i.e., Fulfilled.[17] **

Indeed, this is a signal prophetic "benchmark" that sums up and fulfills the major tributary streams that form "God's Prophetic Time Line" (GPT). If you look closely, dutifully comparing Scripture with Scripture, you will find the common underlying pattern of Scripture that unifies all prophecies, culminating at the end of the Great Tribulation Period (GTP).

The all-inclusive prophetic declaration and the "finishing touch" that we find in the following chapter happens after Christ's final Global Victory over all the forces of Antichrist as the second Messiah Figure, the "Lion of God" (MFLi).[18]

Consider and compare these with the references describing God's archetypal promise to Abraham, the Psalmist's predictions of Christ's hegemony and the prophets' remonstrances regarding the "Day of the Lord."*[19]

---

17   Rev. 10:7 **The text of paragraph B can also be found in the Paper entitled Patterns in Prophetic Scripture, Section IV-C, D. See also Appendix 1: Diagram One: "Correlating Last Days Events."

18   2 Thess. 1,2; Rev. 5:5; 11:15 See also the Papers entitled The Biblical Role of Israel, Facts Concerning the 70th Week of Daniel and The Messiah Figures

19   Genesis 12:1-3; 15:1-6; 17:1 ff.; 22:15-18; Psa. 2, 45, 110, 118:22; *Isa. 2,4, 8:9 20;9:6,7; 11-14, 24-35, 43-48, **61:1-3; Jer. 3-25, 31-36; Ezek. 7-25, 33,34, 36; Dan. 2:34,35,44,45; Joel 1-3; Amos 1-9; Mic. 2-5,7; Zeph. 1-3; Zech. 11-14; Mal. 3,4 *Note that many Old Testament Prophecies have multiple fulfillments that reiterate for as many subsequent generations and times, applying to both Jews and Gentiles, as are necessary to fulfill God's Grand Plan of Unification in Christ! **The reader should also note that, during his first appearing on earth as Messiah Lamb of God (MFLa), Christ stopped mid-sentence in the second verse. See Luke 4:18,19 Whereas, in Christ's Second Appearing as Messiah Lion of God (MFLi), the Judgment part is fulfilled. See 2 Thess. 1,2 See also the Papers entitled The Biblical Role of Israel, Fulfillment of God's Promise (to Abraham), Fulfilment Prophecy, Emmanuel 1 &2, Illustrating the "Law of Multiple Fulfillments" and The Messiah Figures

Compare also to Jesus' Prophetic Discourse, the Letters of Paul and Peter and in other places in John's *Apocalypse*.[20]

III. Consider the following list of Scriptures that tie together the prophecies relating to "God's Prophetic Time Line" (GPT), viz., the unification of God's People, Jew and Gentile, into One Body *In Christ* and the fruition of the *Kingdom of Heaven.*

*Let the reader also observe that the structure of Daniel's Prophecy parallels that of Jesus' Prophetic Discourse in that Two distinct levels of fulfillment exist, both relating to the 70ᵗʰ Week: The first half was fulfilled in AD 70 and the second, relating to the "Great Tribulation Period," is yet to come. See Fn. #11, 14, 19, 20.

- "Sit at my Right Hand, henceforth expecting your enemies to be made a footstool for your feet... (Jesus Christ), the Stone that the builders rejected, has become the Head of the Corner (*Cornerstone)..."

The Isaiah passage is a detailed remonstrance confirming that Jesus Christ is the 'Cornerstone' which relates to God's Grand Plan of Unification/ Salvation.[21]

- Prophecies declare that the "Desolation of the Jews" will continue "unto the End" Viz., in the *KJV* it is translated as the Consummation.[22]*

- (At the end time) "They will mourn for him... as for an only son."[23]

- "Behold that your house is left desolate."[24]

---

20   *Luke 21:20-24; Rom. 4:9-13, 20-5:5; 11:11-36; Gal. 3:6-29; Eph. 1:9,10; 2:11-22;3:1-11; 2 Thess. 1,2; 2 Pet. 1-3; Rev. 11:3-21 *See the Paper entitled Facts Concerning the 70th Week of Daniel (Especially Section I, Paragraphs B, C and Figure One which delineate the partitioning within Jesus' Prophetic Discourse that fits the "splitting" of the 70th Week into two separate fulfillment sequences. See also the Paper entitled Correlating Last Days Scriptures*

21   Psa. 110:1 ff. 118:22; *Isa. 28:16 (Chapters 26-30); Dan. 2:34,35,44,45; Matt. 21:42; Luke 20:40-44; 21:22-28

22   Dan. 9:26,27; 12:7 ff.* *See also the papers entitled The Biblical Role of Israel, Correlating Last Days Scriptures, The Doctrine of Last Things and Facts relating to the Fulfillment of God's Promise (to Abraham)*

23   *Zech. 12:9,10*

24   Matt. 23:29-39

- "This *Gospel* will be preached all over the world... and then will the end come," viz., after the 'evangelical age of Grace' has expired.[25]

- "Immediately after the tribulation of those days... the sign of the Son of Man will appear in the sky"[26]

- "They will be led away 'as captives' into all nations... and Jerusalem will be trodden down... Until the Times of the Gentiles are Fulfilled."[27]

- "I have other sheep which do not belong to this fold: Them also I must bring and they will hear my voice and there will be one fold or flock and One Shepherd," viz., Christ, the *Messiah*[28]

- "It is not for you to know the times or the seasons, which the Father has put in his own power..."[29]

- "(God) has appointed a Day, in which he will judge the world in righteousness by that man (Jesus Christ) whom he has ordained, whereof he has given assurance unto all men in that he has raised him from the dead."[30]

- "For, Brethren, I would not want you to be ignorant of this Mystery... that blindness has happened to Israel... Until the Fulness of the Gentiles has come in."[31]

- "But now Christ has risen from the dead and become the First fruits of them that slept...afterward, they that are Christ's (will be raised) at his Coming... Then the end comes, when he (Christ) will have put down all rule, authority and power, for he must reign 'till he has put all enemies under his feet."[32]

- "For you are all the Children of God in Christ Jesus:... There is neither Jew nor Greek... for you are all one in Christ Jesus."[33]

---

25   Matt. 24:14,15
26   Matt. 24:29-31
27   Luke 21:24
28   John 10:16
29   Acts 1:6-8
30   Acts 17:31
31   Rom. 11:11-36 Cf. 9:6-10:13 *See also the Paper Destiny and Free Will*
32   1 Cor. 15:20-28; Rev. 11:15 Cf. Psa. 110:1 ff.; 118:22; Isa. 28:16
33   Gal. 3:1 ff.

- "Blessed be the Father of our Lord Jesus Christ... wherein he has abounded toward us... Having made known unto us the Mystery of his Will... that in the Dispensation of the Fullness of Times he might gather together in One All things In Christ ..."[34]

- "We are the 'circumcision' which worships' God in the spirit and rejoice in Christ Jesus and have no confidence in the flesh."[35]

- "(Christ) is the image of the invisible God... All things were created by him and for him. He is before all things... And he is the Head of the Body, the Church... For it pleased the Father that in him all fullness should dwell and, having made peace by the blood of his cross... to reconcile all things unto himself... to fulfill the Word of God, even the Mystery which... is now made manifest..."[36]

- "For the Grace of God has appeared to all men..."[37]

- "Being made Perfect he became the Author of Eternal Salvation unto all those that obey him... For (Christ is) this Melchizadek, King of Peace... Unto whom even the patriarch Abraham gave the tenth... Who is made not after the law of a carnal commandment, but after the Power of an endless Life. For (God) testifies (of Christ) You are a Priest forever... By so much was Jesus made a surety of a better Testament... He mediates a better Covenant..." "Behold the days come, saith the Lord, when I will make a *New Covenant*... for this cause (Christ) is the Mediator of the New Testament..."[38]

- "Unto you, therefore, which believe he is precious, but unto them which are disobedient, the 'Stone' which the builders (the Jews) rejected, the same has made the Head of the corner and a

---

34   Eph. 1:3-10; 2:11-22; 3:1-11
35   Phil. 3:3 f.; Cf. Gal. 6:14-16
36   Col. 1:15-29
37   Titus 2:11-15
38   Heb. 5:1-9; 7:1-10:23 Cf. Jer. 31:31-34; Ezek. 36:22-27 *See also the Papers entitled The Fulfillment of God's Promise (to Abraham), Fulfilment Prophecy, The New Covenant and One Covenant for All*

Stone of stumbling and Rock of offence to them which stumble at the Word, being disobedient... "[39]

- "In the days of the 7th Angel, when he will begin to sound, the Mystery of God should be Finished..." Viz., God's Mystery is Fulfilled, (GMF)[40]

- "And the 7th Angel sounded... saying 'the kingdoms of this world have become the Kingdoms of our Lord and of his Christ and he will reign forever and ever'..."[41]

IV. Like many other stratagems of Satan, the "Mystery of Iniquity/ Apostasy" acts like a "Trojan Horse" or a "virus" that is surreptitiously implanted into a target person or group. In the spiritual application we are examining, Satan accomplishes this by a process known as "incremental infiltration."

Regarding God's People (Israel or the Church), this shows just how dangerous false doctrine is. Not only does it corrupt a person or group's Faith in God, but it displaces biblical faith with trust in man, with net result being the "great falling away," which enables Satan to gain control over them!

That also explains why those who are being deceived seldom realize what is happening, even to the point of defending the false doctrines Satan has implanted! The same process is used in a worldly sense by spy operatives or sly propagandists who use "subliminal messages" to "mentally condition" target subjects to corrupt, control or "brainwash them."[42]

Concerning God's People, whether they are Israel or the Church, the primary sense of iniquity, as defined in Scripture, almost always points to sinful acts that come from within the gate. Viz., the "Mystery of Iniquity" is linked to the following destructive sins that are germane

---

39   1 Pet. 2:5-10 Cf. Psa. 118:22; Isa. 28:16; Matt. 21:42; Acts 4:11
40   Rev. 10:7 Cf. Zech. 12:10; Matt. 5:17-20; Rom. 11:25; 16:25-27; Gal. 3:23-29 Ibid. *Footnote #17 See also the Paper entitled Prophetic Chronology Two Sect. IV: "Correlating Prophetic Texts and Acrostics"*
41   Rev. 11:15 Cf. John 10:16; 1 Cor. 15:20-28
42   Jer. 5-13,17,18, 20, 23; Matt. 24:4,5,11,24; Luke 21:8; Rom. 1:18-32; 2 Cor. 4:26; 11:12-15; 2 Tim. 3; Heb. 3:7-4:11

to God's People who have habitually rebelled against God, fallen away from faith in God and have become "easy marks" for Satan's deception! They are the "Stumbling Block of their iniquity," the "Abomination of desolation" and the "Transgression of desolation."[43]

Indeed, the historian Flavius Josephus chronicles the egregious acts of the extremist Zealots, especially the most radical group led by John of Geshala, which included the assassins called Sicarii, eventually forced the Romans to do what they did.

Originally, Josephus was also an ardent Jewish partisan. However, he experienced a miraculous conversion, receiving Christ. He tells us that, while defending Jotopata, he was given a direct Revelation from God that literally changed his mind about everything. Subsequently, he was able to objectively observe and document the incredibly stubborn intransigence and ferocity of the Jewish "Patriots" (Zealots).

In the vision after which Josephus was converted, God revealed to him the meaning of Daniel's prophecy that was reiterated by Christ: That the Jews were going to lose and that Vespasian and his son, General Titus, were going to be God's instruments of judgment against apostate Israel that the prophets had predicted. Not only that, the pattern of judgment follows the overall outline of the Passover.

Unfortunately, this time the Jews were on the wrong side and their barbarous acts of genocide against their own people called down God's judgment following the manner in which they acted.[44]

God's Spirit also revealed the truth to the writer regarding these things while studying *The Works of Flavius Josephus*. In this amazing chronicle of Jewish History I found a host of details that "filled in the picture" of what was truly happening in the Jewish war. The crux of this is the shocking truth: The true underlying cause of the Jews' desolation and the destruction of Jerusalem and the Temple was their own fault!

As mentioned above, the war and final siege was triggered by a nightmarish sequence of rapidly escalating acts of fanaticism and genocide perpetrated by three competing groups of intolerant Zealots.

---

43   Compare Matt. 24 and Luke 21 with 2 Thess. 1,2 *See also Facts of Scripture*
44   Daniel 9:24-27; Matt. 23:33-24:15; 2 Thess. 2:3-12; Rev. 13,17 *See also the Papers entitled Emmanuel 2: God is Dealing with Israel/ the Jews and The Three Passovers of Scripture*

They already had murdered two high priests and threatened to kill anyone else who wanted to get out of the city. It cascaded into a bloody internal civil war inside Jerusalem that precipitated the desecration of the Temple, the "abomination that makes desolate." During the siege, many even resorted to cannibalism!

Not only that, you can see an amazing pattern when you put together the "second fulfillment" of the messages of the older prophets that apply again along with the prophecies of Daniel, Zechariah, Jesus and Paul, the pattern of God's progressively developing Master Plan begins to take shape. Notice also that God uses both positive and negative elements in a perfect balance that, in the end, will produce God's Will for His Unified People *In Christ.*[45]

Note also that God "uses" "Antichrist figures" in His Overall Plan, along with false prophets and corrupt religious figures to test people and to prove their loyalty or disloyalty! Notice Jesus' "concluding statement" to the Jews essentially sets the stage for God's sentence that judgment regarding all the sins committed against Abel to Zecharias would fall on that generation. This "Cuts off of the Jews… until the times of the Gentiles are fulfilled," as Paul also commented later.[46]

V. Let us investigate the following illustration/ aspects, observing how "context" helps us understand the meaning of Scripture. Our example is Daniel twelve.

A. Aspect one, "Historical context": Daniel's prophecy of the "end times" can show us how history will 'play out.' A possible secondary meaning is the "taking away of the daily (sacrifice ritual)" being caused by a law that makes the worship of God illegal. See two shining examples from Joshua (Re: Rahab) and the earlier writings of Daniel that also vividly illustrate God's "Higher Law" of civil disobedience:[47]

---

45   Isa. 8, 28-30, 40-66; Jer. 2-36; Ezek. 3-24, 33,34; Dan. 2,7,9,11,12; Matt. 23; Rom. 9-11; Gal. 2-5 See Footnotes #7, #21 *See also Sequence of Events, which includes references to Wars of the Jews, which is part of The Works of Flavius Josephus Translated By William Whiston, AP&A, Grand Rapids, 1971*

46   Ezek. 13,14; Zech. 11; Matt. 23:33 f.; Luke 21:20-24; Acts 13:26-52; Rom. 9:32,33; 11:25

47   Josh. 2; Dan. 3,6; Acts 4,5 *See the Paper entitled The Higher Laws of God This pattern can also be seen in Luke's account of the early Church's acts of bravery during the early persecutions of Christians by both Romans and apostate Jews.*

1. A great example of "biblical civil disobedience" was when Nebuchadnezzar commanded everyone to bow down to the statue he constructed. When Daniel's three friends refused they were thrown into the fiery furnace made seven times hotter. However, God miraculously delivered them all unscathed, with the added bonus: Having the king see Jesus with them in the fire beforehand.

2. "Daniel in the lion's den" happened because of others' envy and hatred of Daniel because he was a gifted person who loved and worshiped God. His enemies manipulated king Darius to enact a law that forbad all worship for thirty days unless he approved it. Of course, Daniel's enemies also knew that according to the customs of the Medes and Persians, no law could be changed afterward. Daniel prayed to God nonetheless, landing him in "the lion's den," from which God delivered him unharmed but where his accusers were thrown instead and were eaten alive![48]

3. A third example can be found in the book of Esther, also chronicled by Josephus, when king Artaxerxes, unable to change the law against the Jews instigated by Haman, passed another decree allowing the Jews to defend themselves.[49]

See Appendix 2: "Chronological Chart of 'writing periods' in Daniel"

B. Aspect two, "Mystery of God" context:

Daniel twelve is introduced in a "future or 'end of days' context" known as "Prophetic Time Text" (PTT). This same context can be found in the last eleven chapters of Ezekiel.

As we begin to understand this context, we also know that this prophecy must "mesh together" with all other prophecies concerning the "Last Days," in particular our Lord's Prophetic Address, the fulfillment of which clearly applies in two different periods.

Thus, the writer believes this chapter (Daniel twelve) definitely refers to a latter-day persecution of Jews and Christians.

---

48   *Daniel 3,6 See also the Paper entitled Authority and Conscience*

49   Esther 1-10 *See also the book entitled The Works of Flavius Josephus, which includes Antiquities of the Jews* by Flavius Josephus, Bk. XI, Ch. VI, P. 12, AP&A, Grand Rapids, 1971

Revelation ten to twelve also broaches the subject of persecution, which is a regular occurrence in the Great Tribulation Period. Paul's derivations in Romans and Galatians also reveal the same pattern, which culminates in the "Jewish extension period (JEP)" shown in the "Last Days Time Line Chart, Part Two."

Another signal aspect related to the fulfillment of the "Mystery of Godliness" is the "Precept of First Fruits" that Paul mentions in his Epistle to the Corinthians.[50]

C. Aspect three: The "Multiple Fulfilment" context of Prophecies. As mentioned above, when you compare Scripture to Scripture, it is apparent that, in Daniel twelve, we are again dealing with prophecies that have "multiple Fulfilments," of which the most common is the Dual Fulfillment.

You can see this if you examine Jesus' Prophetic Discourse recorded in the Synoptic Gospels and compare it with the prophecies of Daniel and Revelation.

Not only that, if you combine the overall precept of "Multiple Fulfilments" with the "Prophetic Pattern of Parallelism" that exists, linking the way both groups of "God's People," Israel and the Church, have acted, you should be able to ascertain and recognize God's Grand Plan of Unification.[51]

Another very interesting common factor to note in the prophecies of Daniel and Revelation is the "Three and One-half Year (TOHY) period," expressed at least eight times in various forms.

Comparing Scriptures we can link this period with the "dual fulfillment precept" which is illustrated by comparing the prophecies defining the 70th Week of Daniel and the New Testament accounts quoting Jesus and the Apostles' teachings regarding the persecution of true Believers who hold to the doctrine of the "Patience of the

---

50   Daniel 12:1 ff.; 1 Cor. 15:20-28; Rev. 10-12 *See The Church in the Last Days' Chapter entitled: "End Time Analysis: The Tribulation Period, Part One " and The Biblical Role of Israel*

51   See the Papers entitled *The Biblical Role of Israel, Contextually Comparing the Elements of Prophetic Scripture, Emmanuel 1: God is Dealing with His People, Emmanuel 2: God is Dealing with Israel/ the Jews, The Fulfillment of God's Promise (to Abraham), Illustrating the "Law of Multiple Fulfillments" and Understanding Prophecy (a two part series)*

Saints" otherwise known as *Faith-based Pacifism* and God's ultimate Judgment of all unrepentant unbelievers and apostates.[52]

Indeed, all the pertinent Scriptures will be satisfied if we observe that the 70th Week is fulfilled in two parts:

The first half applying to the Three and One-half Year Jewish War of the first century and the second half applying to the Great Tribulation Period yet to come, during which Christ will Return to earth in great power and glory.[53]

Your Fellow servant in Christ,
Pastor David J. Bowers

**See Appendix 1: Diagram One: Correlating Last Days Events and Appendix 2: "Chronological Chart of 'writing periods' in Daniel"

---

52   Dan. 7:19-28; 9:24-27; 12:7 ff. Matt. 24; Luke 21; Rom. 9:25,26; 2 Thess. 1,2

53   Ibid Footnote #'s 12,21,45,49 See the papers entitled *Correlating Last Days Scriptures, The Biblical Role of Israel, Facts Concerning the 70th Week of Daniel and Prophetic Chronology Two: General Facts regarding the timing of "End Times Events"*

VI. Appendices:

Appendix 1: Diagram One:
CORRELATING LAST DAYS EVENTS

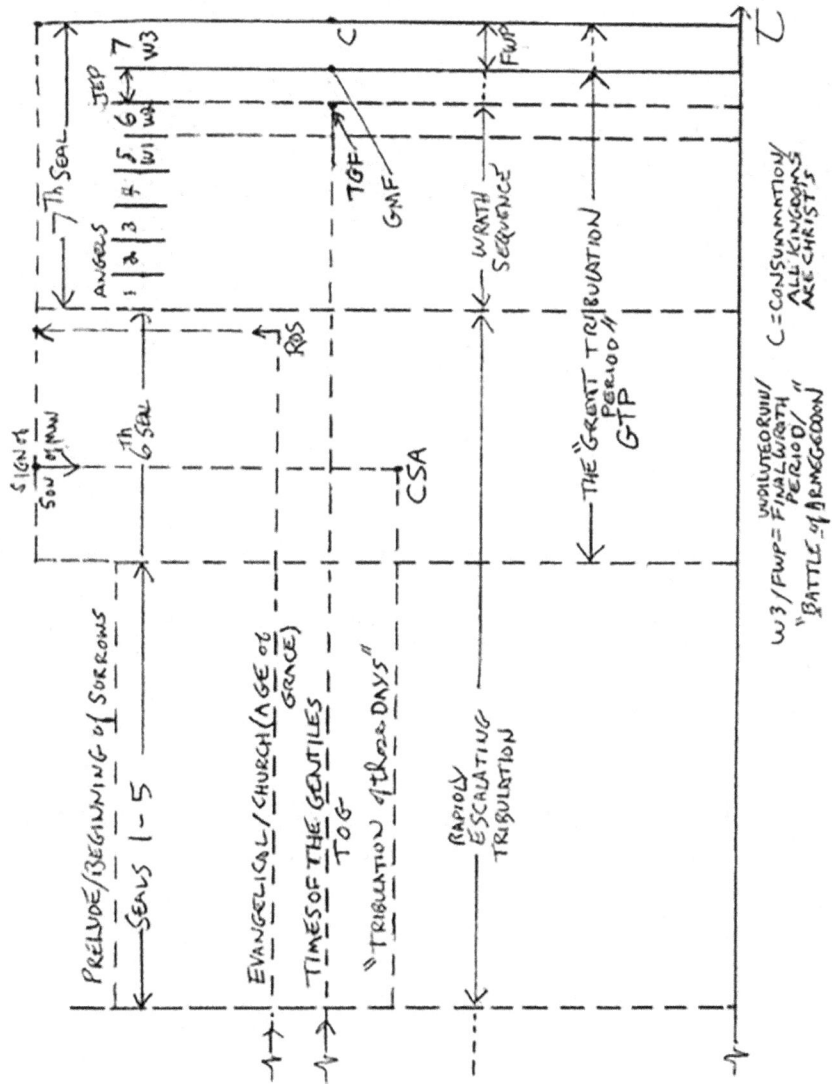

Appendix 2: Chronological Chart of 'writing periods' in Daniel:

Chronological Chart of 'writing periods' in Daniel Portion of Scripture: Date written:	
Daniel 1	606 BC.
Daniel 2	603 BC
Daniel 3 and 4:1-3	580 BC
Daniel 4:4-27	571 BC
Daniel 4:28-33	569 BC
Daniel 4:34-37	562 BC
Daniel 7	550 BC
Daniel 8	548 BC
Daniel 9	539 BC
Daniel 6, 10-12	537 BC

END TİMES ANALYSİS, PART 1

## Chapter 15

The Tribulation Period

The word *eschatology* means the doctrine or study of last things. It is based on the Greek word *eschatos,* meaning the last. The Greek word *eschatos* establishes an *order.* This order can refer to either one of two things: *(the last of) a particular sequence or to the relative significance of something or someone* (e.g., "The last will be first, and the first will be last.")[211] Faithful and careful study of the Word of God also requires that we understand *shades of meaning* so that we do not become confused by assumptions or by cultural or idiomatic differences. In eschatology, we can establish guidelines to pinpoint and use what one might call *time tags.* These are timing references that link the *relative chronological order* within particular events or between one event and another. We can detect these by *the faithful* use of *comparing Scripture to Scripture.* We will use this precept in the analysis that follows. It is well known that various groups bias Scripture to advance their particular doctrines and positions regarding this controversial topic. Consequently, many unknown and unspecified assumptions have arisen as a result. Therefore, *taking an unbiased approach is mandatory* for the reader, letting the Scripture *speak for itself and never to force a meaning or context beyond what it says.* Let us seek to find the real sense of Scripture: First we must consider its context of spirituality. Second, we must look within its historical and cultural background of the first century, and third, within the context of the text itself to the previous verses and the succeeding verses, etc. Thus we can find the answers that God has for us contained within His Holy Word. We must seek to resolve the many misconceptions, confusion, and complexities surrounding end-times terminology.

---

211   Matt. 19:30

Observing the following general guidelines would also be helpful:

1. Let the scriptures speak for themselves.
2. Be willing to set aside any prior dogma regarding these events.
3. Let us always keep an open mind.
4. Let us seek the truth from the Holy Spirit.
5. Let us compare Scripture with Scripture.
6. Let us resolve to base our understanding upon the original context.
7. Seek the etymology of the words from the original language, learning to differentiate the various shades of meaning. For example, the word *tribulation* comes from the Greek word *thilipsis,* meaning pressure.

It is also rendered as *trouble or affliction.*[212] One should see that the word *tribulation* does not mean the same as *divine wrath.* They translate the Greek word *orge* as wrath (i.e., the wrath of God), which requires a direct action of God's judgment.[213] Compare John 16:33 with 1 Thess. 5:9.

Let us now consider the relevant terminology of the period called *the tribulation.*

I. Let us consider the great falling away or apostasy[214]

In 2 Thess. 2:3, they translate the Greek word *apostasia* as *falling away,* but it also means *to fall backward, forsake or to backslide.* The context is always definitely negative. Both Jesus and Paul warned believers that this condition would prevail increasingly among God's people as the times approach the hour of Christ's return. This period of apostasy is now in *"progress."* In fact, one could argue that *great apostasy* has been with us ever since AD 325! Regardless, it will deepen and

---

212   Matt. 13:21; 24:21,29; John 16:33; Acts 14:22; Rom. 5:3; 8:35; 12:12; 2 Cor. 1:3.
213   *Compare John 16:33 with 1 Thess. 5:9 and use any Greek lexicon to look up the words for yourself*
214   Matt. 24:9,10; 2 Thess. 2:1–7. *See the paper entitled "an Analysis of the Causes and Effects of Apostasy"*

worsen significantly in the first phases of the tribulation known as *the beginning of sorrows*. Apostasy has a way of sneaking up on you!

Denial, situation ethics, and insensitivity play a large part, as does rampant worldliness and self-centeredness among modern Christians. Adaptation to a self-centered culture has plagued the last days with a people-pleasing clergy. Resulting from this, modern congregations appear to crave the stroking of egos and abhor *hearing the truth*. By doing so, *the true message of the Gospel of Jesus gets lost in the shuffle* and the church moves away even more from the doctrines that make for being a wise virgin. Not only that, the recent spates of highly speculative movies and novels featuring sensationalistic Hollywood-style depictions of the end-times have not helped the truth in the least either!

In fact, the self-centered, materialistic, and escapist mind-set of modern mainstream Christianity is deeply worsening. You can see evidence of this in the often hostile and hyper-defensive reaction you get when you question many Christians regarding certain doctrines they hold. Many hold to these without even knowing why they believe that way. Far more, never check out or question their validity in Scripture. One of these doctrines is the popular *pre-tribulation rapture theory*. This belief has gained immense popularity although it has no true foundation in Scripture at all. In fact, it is extremely dangerous because its underlying escapist attitude severely undermines our receiving the harder givens of the gospel.

These entail Christ's clear Word regarding the necessary preparation that Christ's followers must undergo to persevere and endure until the end! However, this and other misleading doctrines do *serve to fulfill prophecies* in that they accelerate the apostasy of the latter days and pave the way for revealing Antichrist. This leads us to examine the following.

II. What is the relation between the restraint and the revealing of Antichrist?

Several pseudonyms or aliases apply to the great Antichrist: *the beast, the false prophet, the man of sin, lawless one, the abomination of desolation, and the number 666.* Scripture shows that *Antichrist* has been operative all along in various forms. The "spirit of Antichrist" acts under many aliases and disguises, all taking orders from our enemy, Satan. John refers to the existence of *many Antichrists*. In some places, Scripture calls Antichrist a merely impersonal influence. We can see this in *the mystery of lawlessness (iniquity)*. Elsewhere, Scripture identifies Antichrist as *one* having a personality.

Either case can apply. Scripture says that *Antichrist* will occupy a significant role in the tribulation period. Paul also tells us that Antichrist has been *restrained* and *that something will remove this restraint* sometime before the great tribulation period, precipitating the events that conclude this age. Can we find out what the restraint on Antichrist is? Although Scripture does not specifically say so, we *can accurately postulate a logical scenario of what it is that will fit the rest of Scripture*. In 2 Thessalonians, Paul gives us a disturbing truth many Christians willfully ignore, that *the apostasy of the church* plays a major role!

In fact, the church's apostasy is the *primary direct* cause of the removal of restraint on Antichrist.[215] This is because the great apostasy is antecedent to and occurs simultaneously with the revealing of Antichrist, by that linking the two. Paul would not have specifically mentioned this sequential link if that were not true! The Scriptures tell us in many ways that God is *not* taking the church out of the way before the great tribulation. When taken together, the diligent student of the Word should clearly see the pattern. The Scriptures *literally prove that* the church will enter and endure at least a significant portion of the great tribulation. The church requires this to ready herself for Christ's appearing and to fulfill the great commission. Moreover, one cannot justifiably claim that the Scripture says the Holy Spirit is the restraint. Still, because God allows man free will, the Holy Spirit's lack of interference does affect the result in an indirect way!

Thus, it all adds up:

God's will for the end-times precludes the church being taken out *any time before* the great tribulation. *Scripture does not support the pre-tribulation view* invented by J. N. Darby (ca.1830) and later popularized by Dr. C. I. Schofield. However, one cannot explain the latter's enigmatic change of doctrinal position between 1909 and 1916.

---

215   2 Thess. 2:3

It goes to show how desire for convenience can deceive even the most brilliant people. The upshot is that this "pre-tribulation" view fails the test of New Covenant truth. This illustrates the danger of combining old covenant ways with new. What did Jesus say about the *wineskins?* The truth remains: *no easy ways out exist!* We must be prepared always, eagerly awaiting Christ's coming, just like Jesus commanded His disciples in the gospels![216]

III. Let us consider the tribulation period itself.

This very important period encompasses many diverse and high-profile events. We see them symbolized in John's imagery of the *seven seals:* the aftermath of long-term apostasy, the rise of Antichrist, worldwide catastrophes, astronomical signs, the sign and appearance (*Parousia*) of Jesus Christ, the rapture of the saints, the judgment seat of Christ, and the wrath of the Lamb (Jesus Christ) upon Antichrist and the worldwide system of *Babylon* (the global network of mega-corporations and banks that Antichrist controls). Then, *after the rapture,* God deals in a special way with Israel and delivers them in "the battle of Armageddon" (the seventh angel of the seventh seal). Finally, Jesus Christ descends and assumes power over the earth.[217] Note that the *sixth seal context* of Revelation 6:17 demands that the people on earth are seeing wrath for being *imminent but not striking or affecting them yet.* This is so since Scripture tells us that divine wrath or judgment *does not commence until the seventh seal.* The tribulation period naturally divides itself into *three general segments,* the second two of them *overlapping in time.*

1. *The beginning of sorrows or birth pangs* (seals 1–5). This period concludes the long-term period of apostasy. Clever propaganda will abound in the preaching of false prophets. Because of widespread deception, many believers will succumb to false doctrines, and betrayals of fellow believers will be rampant. In this period *global Babylon* will become a totalitarian empire *using the propaganda ministry of the false*

---

216   Matt. 24:14–28; Mark 2:21,22; Luke 21:34–36; 2 Thess. 2:1–12; 1 John 2:15–23; Rev. 13:1–14:13. *See the book "The Pre-Wrath Rapture of the Church" by Marvin Rosenthal, Thomas Nelson, Nashville, 1990*

217   Matt. 24;21–30; 25:1 ff.; Luke 21:8–27; 2 Cor. 5:8–10; Rev. 6:1–11:19.

prophet=Antichrist.[218] (See Appendix C: "Last Days Timeline Charts," *Part 1, **Part 2.)

2.** *The great tribulation* (seals 6 and 7) is the one-time three and one-half year period Scripture identifies as 42 months, 1260 days, and "a time and times and dividing of time." To avoid confusion, one must be aware that this period includes several main events that *appear to be overlapping in time.* By the time the great tribulation commences, global Babylon (alias the new world order=Antichrist) will encompass all nations and control all economic, social, and political activity. Christians will be forced underground, and the vast majority of the world's populations will take a unique form of implanted *global ID called the "mark."* Besides Christians, I believe many brave freedom-loving unbelievers will also refuse the mark, risking unemployment, persecution, or starvation. The one bright hope for this time will be the promise Jesus made to His disciples: "But for the sake of the elect, God will shorten those days." Therefore, Christ will appear in the sky *before* the end of the great tribulation. All earth dwellers will see Christ. He will send His angels with a loud trumpet and "gather 'His elect' from the four winds," *just like Jesus has promised.*[219]

3.** *The great Day of the Lord begins during the sixth seal and continues through the seventh seal.* It contains the following main components: *the appearing* (Parousia) of Jesus Christ in the air, the deliverance of the saints (the first resurrection and the rapture), the judgment seat of Christ, the wrath of the Lamb (Jesus Christ), the special dealings with Israel, the marriage supper of the Lamb, the great supper of God, and the binding of Satan. *The Day of the Lord* marks the time when Jesus comes back *in power and great glory.* When He first appears, He will take charge, displaying awesome power, magnificence, and splendor *never before seen by man!* He will miraculously deliver His body, the church. Then, *at the commencement of the seventh seal,* Jesus Christ will take vengeance upon antichrist and its world system of government, along with all those who refuse to obey His gospel. This judgment includes all unbelievers and false confessors. He will also deal with the Jews in a special way God has not told us. After that, His bride, the

---

218   Matt. 24:4–13; 2 Thess. 2:3.
219   Matt. 24:4–31; 1 Cor. 15:20–23; 1 Thess. 4:13–17; Rev. 1:7; 3:10; 6:1–7:17.

church, will be presented to Jesus at the marriage supper of the Lamb. After this is the great supper of God, where the final execution of all the world's forces will take place in the "battle of Armageddon" (the third woe).**[220] Some Bible scholars attempt to equate the tribulation period with the OT prophetic period known as the "seventieth week of Daniel." However, Scripture clearly proves that these two cannot be identical. Consider the following:

First, by comparing Scripture we can determine that the seventieth week is a "split prophetic period," the *first half* of which has already been fulfilled by the Roman-Jewish war of AD 67–70. Compare the Scriptures and you will notice that this significant one half week long prophetic period of "3 and ½ years, 42 months or 1260 days" is mentioned many times by both Daniel and John. The remaining *second half* will take place during the great tribulation.[221] *Second,* Christ will personally shorten the sixth seal portion of the great tribulation by an indeterminate time *for the sake of the church* (saints). *Thirdly,* the periods of the beginning of sorrows and the Day of the Lord carry *no specific spans of time* listed in Scripture. *Fourth,* God has a special plan for the Jews taking place *after* the church is raptured and *after* the judgment of antichrist. Daniel prophesies *two special extension periods* (beyond the 1260 days) for God's dealing with Israel (the Jews). In thirty more days, desolation will be complete (1290 days), and deliverance comes after seventy-five days (the 1335 days).[222]

IV. End-game summary

Scripture tells us that *the great tribulation period* (GTP) is a one-time event (that is 3 and ½ years long, *not* seven years) characterized by extreme anguish that *God will never allow to repeat.*[223] Jesus told

---

220   **See Appendix C and Chapter 12, Section V*

221   *Daniel 7:25; 9:24–27 (notice the prophetic 'week' is interrupted); 12:7; Matt. 24:14–31; Rev. 11:2,3,9-11**Notice that John also uses the word 'days' in a similar prophetic context applying to the same period. See also the papers entitled "Contextually Comparing the Elements of Prophetic Scripture," "Correlating Last Days Scriptures, the Biblical Role of Israel," "the Doctrine of Last Things," "Facts Concerning the 70th Week of Daniel" and "Precepts Regarding the Interpretation of End Time Prophecies" Rev. 12:14;13:5*

222   Ibid. Footnote #8; Daniel 12:10–12; Luke 21:24; Rom. 11:25,26; Rev. 10:7. See also Appendix C

223   Matt. 24:21,22; Mark 13:19.

the disciples that it would be a frightful time compressed into two main parts. The latter one contains two overlapping events. The first is *the beginning of sorrows* and the second is *the great tribulation,* during which *the Day of the Lord begins.* John foresaw the tribulation period as a succession of seals announced by seven angels armed with seven trumpets and bowls of divine judgment, with the seventh seal itself consisting of seven angels. Notice that two sections of Revelation, chapters 6 through 11 and chapters 12 through 19, cover the *same tribulation period* in *different ways with different symbols.* Scenes and time frames switch rapidly, so we must be aware of *where each event takes place* and their relative timing.[224]

1. "The beginning of sorrows" starts with a preparatory scene in heaven. Then on earth we have the first four seals—a period of progressively worsening global scale events. The four horsemen of the apocalypse depict the seals: 1) white, meaning imperialism or worldwide dictatorship,[225] 2) the red horse symbolizes the wars that are happening all over the world,[226] 3) the black horse symbolizes worldwide famines,[227] 4) John sees a pale or ashen figure, the symbol of death (very possibly caused by global pandemics).[228] This period completes *the great apostasy.* Apostasy will dramatically reduce Christianity in influence. Their influence will plummet from the level that John foresaw when he received the vision of *the seven churches of Asia Minor* that we read in Revelation 2 and 3. The remaining *remnant* of true believers will fall from 28.5 percent (two out of seven) to approximately 0.5 percent. This small remnant corresponds to the number of the righteous in the time of Elijah.[229] * Notice also that is how "God removes" the restraint on Antichrist. Consequently, the love of many will turn cold because of widespread iniquity; pressures and persecutions will invade every aspect of life. Hatred of true believers, loss of love and sensibility,

224   See Chapter 12, Section V
225   Rev. 6:1–3
226   Rev. 6:4
227   Rev. 6:5–7
228   Rev. 6:8 Cf. Matt. 24:6–8; Mark 13:8; Luke 21:9–11; 1 Thess. 5:9.
229   *See Sections VII and VIII See also Glossary of Terms' entry: the *Remnant**

disillusionment, and betrayals will follow in its wake. However, these conditions will only last a short time, as we will soon see.²³⁰

2. *The fifth seal* takes place in *two places:* 1) *In heaven,* when the souls of many martyrs will appear, asking the Lord,(paraphrased) "How long will it be until You execute vengeance upon Antichrist?" The Lord's reply is that they must wait "a little longer (that is)—until those other believers (including the two 144,000s) whom they will also martyr before I come." 2) *On earth,* this time will be that time when (the great) Antichrist will expand to control a global dictatorship that is hostile to both Christians, Muslims and Jews spurring hate crimes against them.

3. The great tribulation commences with *the sixth seal.* Jesus promised that God would shorten this time "for the sake of the elect," (the true church or the saints). God has counseled them to patiently endure *to our end* of the great tribulation when the rapture takes place. However, before the rapture takes place, the church has much work to do *during* the great tribulation. It is during this time that the great revival will take place and the church will fulfill the great commission! Then, according to Scripture comparison, at *the close of the sixth seal,* Jesus Christ will appear in the clouds and all the saints will be rescued. The first group is resurrected from the graves, then the angels will bodily translate the remaining saints that are living on earth up to the sky to join the rest. Both groups will receive transformed resurrection bodies in transit.²³¹

V. Explanatory

The three microcosms. *In Revelation, we have three special word pictures that the author is calling "the three microcosms":* 1) the two witnesses of Revelation 11, 2) *the woman clothed with the sun and her child* of Revelation 12, and 3) *we have the two 144,000s* of Revelation 7 and 14. All three of these parallel narrative pictorials deal with the issue of the *persecution* of both Jews (Israel) and true Christians by the world system. First, we could interpret the two witnesses for being symbols of Jewish and Christian *martyrs.* God miraculously protects them *for a time.* However, *God allows the world to outwardly "kill them"* (symbolic

---

230 Matt. 24:9–12; Mark 13:9, 11–13; Luke 21:8, 12–18; 2 Thess. 2:1–8; Rev. 2:1-3:22.
231 Matt. 24:29–31; 1 Cor. 15:20–23; 1 Thess. 4:13–17; Rev. 7:7–17

for destroying their influence). *Then, God raises them up to heaven.* Second, the woman clothed with the sun is Israel, and her child is Jesus, symbol of Christianity. The devil uses the world to persecute, but God shelters her during the tribulation. Third, God allows the sacrifice of the two 144,000s. One gives the witness to apostate Israel. The other is a witness to the world. To stay alive, the Christians remaining on earth must exercise *the patience of the saints,* which is the New Covenant term for *faith-based pacifism.*

The majority do not suffer martyrdom. God will *translate them alive,* and they will *appear en masse in heaven at the rapture.*[232]

VI. Let us expand upon the relevance of the second 144,000.[233]

In verses 1 to 5, the scene opens with another heavenly vision similar to the one in Revelation 4 and 5. *In the spirit,* God personally invites John *to "come up here"* into God's intimate presence to receive a very special set of messages. One must take care to note that these kinds of *visions are different from physical assumptions.* Within this vision, we have a *spiritual picture of Mount Zion.* Mount Zion is the *prophetic symbol* of the eternal and heavenly throne of Almighty God! Similarly, *the Lamb* is the symbol of Jesus Christ.[234] Interestingly, John sees 144,000 *special saints* who are already beside Jesus at the throne! These saints have some *very significant* attributes that should alert believers to what is pleasing to God: 1) They have the *"counter-mark" of the Lamb* on their foreheads. Like baptism, this is the *mark of identification with Christ* and is the opposite of *the mark of the beast*, *the mark of the world.* 2) *They are to sing a new song* before the throne and the twenty-four elders and living creatures. Yes, praise and worship of Jesus Christ are definitely high priorities with these saints! 3) They have been ransomed from the world system. They are *separated unto God* and holy, redeemed by the blood of the Lamb. 4) They are spiritually pure and holy *"as virgins,"* signifying that this affirms and reinforces *their separation from the world system,* and of their *holiness and loyalty unto the Lamb.* Note here that *biblical marriage* on earth does not defile one. Defilement

---

232 Matt. 10:24–28; 17:23,24; Luke 12:1–12; Rev. 7:13–17; 13:10; 14:10–12.
233 Rev. 14:1–15
234 Psa. 2:6; 48:1,2; 87:1 f; Rev. 5:6–7:17; 12:10,11; 13:8.

only comes by *sin*. Scripture teaches us that the physical relationship of those who are committed for life in the covenant of godly marriage is undefiled![235] 5) They are those who have *followed Jesus to the best of their ability* and have become "*the first fruits* unto God and unto the Lamb (Jesus Christ)." This says that only those who have been *loyal* to Jesus in this life will be close to Jesus in heaven and that we can expect *many more to come!*

VII. Let us investigate the definition of the first fruits.

The first fruits is a symbolic and spiritual relationship that originates from the ancient Hebrew feast of weeks. It refers to *an advance harvest* that is the tangible evidence of fruit *gathered before the main season*. In New Testament history, "the feast of weeks" *is associated with the holiday Pentecost*. If you recall, that was that great event when the promised Holy Spirit first energized the New Covenant church that Luke records in Acts chapter 2. We can observe the following primary aspects about spiritual *first fruits:*

1. the bodily resurrection of Jesus Christ is the first fruits of them that slept, meaning that *glorified saints also will share the same kind of body as Christ!* [236]

2. The giving of the Holy Spirit as the first fruit or guarantee of God's presence confirms the existence of the regenerated human spirit within an individual. This also proves that God's presence is not just some generic influence. It also means *that redemption itself is an individual and personal event.*[237]

3. In doctrine, first fruits can be *representative symbols* identifying the source of life, and they show us how spiritual things operate in the Kingdom of Heaven. Using the characteristics of the first fruits as a gauge, we can identify the source that sustains spiritual life, *infusion grace*. In this way, the doctrine of first fruits is an integral part of *the*

---

235   Mark 10:1–12; James 1:27; Heb. 13:4; 1 John 2:15–17.
236   1 Cor. 15:20–23; 1 John 3:1–3.
237   Rom. 8:23–27; James 1:17,18.

deeper spiritual meaning of Christ's body, that we can also see in Jesus's discourses.[238]

The New Testament teaches that to stay alive spiritually, we must continually receive sustenance (spiritual life) from Jesus, the source of first fruits, *imputed* by the Holy Spirit. This brings us to a spiritual precept that links first fruits, the rapture, and the *remnant*: the doctrine of the elect.[239]

VIII. Yes, the doctrine of the elect intertwines two precepts.

The first fruits and the *remnant* Scripture tells they are "gathered" sequentially in the "great ingathering of saints" and the rapture.

In this doctrine, the *identity, attributes, and characteristics germane to Jesus,* the *source of our spiritual life,* find expression in all those who "love His appearing!" However, *we do not escape our responsibilities* just because we call ourselves the body of Christ, the saints, or by the term *elect.* God plays no favorites. *God still holds us accountable for* all *the things we do.* Above all, first fruits are first. They are the *souls suddenly appearing in heaven* with Jesus at the time of His second coming that John saw in his vision, the *Apocalypse.* Notice that all these (the "dead in Christ") have passed through the gate of bodily death.[240]

The *remnant* refers to two meanings: They are those *who remain true to Jesus to the end.* Also they are those true believers *who remain alive at the coming of the Lord.*[241]

In Revelation 2 and 3, John tells us that the vast majority of Christians will fall away from Christ and that only a small *remnant* will remain true to Jesus. The reference to *the Jezebel* is significant. Remember that God had told Elijah that he had saved *seven thousand* who had not succumbed to worshiping Baals, symbol of national or imperial *idols.*

---

238 John 4:23–38; 6:27 ff.; 14:21–26; 15:1–6; 16:12–17:26
239 *See also the entry *Ekklesia* in Appendix E: Excerpts from Glossary of Terms*
240 Matt. 24:29–31; 2 Cor. 5:8; 1 Thess. 4:13–17; 2 Tim. 4:8; 2 Pet. 3:9–18; Rev. 7:9–17
241 Matt. 20:16; 22:14; 24:13; Mark 13:20; John 15:14–23; Rom. 8:23–39; 11:1–5; 1 Cor. 15:20–23; Heb. 2:1–4; 3:6; 6:3–12; James 5:7

Yes, I know that "seven thousand" figure *looks like* it is a lot, but look closely. Compare the relative percentage of these with the entire population of Israel then living. Doing the math we find that the remnant would only be 0.4 percent! In Romans 9 through 11, *Paul also links first fruits to the original lump or* whole *of God's people.* This means that *all* who are *in Christ,* Jews and Gentiles, are *one body,* whose members belong to God and are holy in his sight.[242]

---

242   John 15:1–7; Rom. 11:16–32; Rev. 2:18–23 Cf. 1 Kings 17–19 *See also Glossary of Terms entry *Remnant/Gather/Harvest* See also Dan. 9:20–27 and the paper entitled "Facts Concerning the 70th Week of Daniel"*

END TİMES ANALYSİS, PART 2

Chapter 16

The Tribulation Period – The Characteristics of Antichrist

We can generate a profile of Antichrist by combining the multifaceted characteristics we can glean from both history and the Scriptures. Several different *milieus of Antichrist exist:* (in) a person, philosophy, agency, organization, culture, religion, media, entertainment, advertising, technology, attitude, etc. *The spirit of Antichrist* can be personal or impersonal. It can even be a machine that possesses artificial intelligence, like a specialized computer, but the common thread in all these things is always the same. By definition, Antichrist *always acts against Christ.* Not only that, the spirit of Antichrist reinvents and repackages itself in every age. John says *many Antichrists abound.* Just like the serpent in the *garden* of Eden, Antichrist can *appear beautiful,* and it can present itself as logical and reasonable and in a plethora of other ways. Eventually, because of its inherent *nature,* the *pit viper* (serpent=dragon=Satan) *always attacks.* Then, from the bite, Satan *releases his poisonous venom, devouring and desensitizing* the victim. Frontal attack is only one strategy; Antichrist often stalks prey with the stealth of a cat. It also *"strikes" under a disguise, foil, or shield.* This shield includes the use of psychological warfare and *subterfuge,* like when they deliberately conduct a "false flag operation," an attack used to terrorize people and seize power and blame-shift the onus onto others! Remember Satan's strategy is *world domination!* One constant remains: it *always opposes the true Jesus Christ.*

This includes all acts against freedom, liberty and the attributes, teachings, commands of the historical Jesus. Yes, Antichrist at times can *even appear to defend Christianity as a "religion,"* however, even this is a false ruse. Satan betrays everyone who serves him! One of the most effective of his corruptive schemes is to fool Christians into *associating worldly ways with Christianity.* Of course, this is but another scheme *to neutralize its spiritual power base.* Satan uses unequal yokes assiduously to pervert Christianity from *within.* This is the basis of all *syncretism—that of mixing* foreign influences, using them like "Trojan horses."*[243] Like a broken record, Antichrist repeatedly uses the same methods: treachery, cunning, deceit, slander, pretense, flattery, infiltration, disinformation, and always appeals to pride, fears, and the lusts of the flesh. Savvy believers who are *"wise as serpents, but harmless as doves,"* know that if Satan's hidden agendas fail, Antichrist does not hesitate to use the *"big guns" of persecution and intimidation just as well!*

The most insidious part of this scheme is that he is simultaneously using many people who *claim to believe in Jesus* to attack his true followers! John gives us two vivid pictures of the "false flag Trojan horse" of Antichrist: 1) "A beast *that looks like a lamb,* but *speaks with the voice of the dragon"* (Satan) and 2) *a "scarlet woman riding upon a beast."* John implies that these pictures all point to a symbolic (spiritual) common source *vehicle* of worldly evil that Satan orchestrates—a *global entity called "Babylon,"* which uses an *alliance of big business, religion, and the state.* That is, Antichrist employs an impressive arsenal of weapons, all connected to Satan's sophisticated array of tools, including *public institutions, cultural icons, corporate business, religion, and corrupt government* to dominate the world and attack the servants of Jesus Christ. Today we know this as the "new world order." We also know that Satan used the religious leaders of Judaism with the Roman Empire to kill Jesus! Consider the Roman Catholic Church, which for centuries had conspired with empires and nations using political alliances and stratagems to *persecute Christians in the name of Christ!* Lest we point fingers so hastily, Protestants and other Christian groups have followed the same pattern as the Catholics! Antisemitism is also a priority target, since Jesus's earthly heritage was Jewish! We begin with some main areas Antichrist uses, always knowing that the word Antichrist does not necessarily mean one person. It can be also present in a cultural or societal bias or a system of business. It can exist in a government agency, the military, or in the media. Even now, it prevails in most

---

243   1 John 2:15–24; 2 John 4–11 *Note that a "False Flag Operation" is a pre-planned event in which others are "set up" for the blame. See also What is Syncretism*

public institutions like the media, entertainment, television networks, professions, scientific fields, and in medicine. Scripture predicts it will soon be a *global* governmental system.[244]

I. Antichrist and the state (the new world order)

In the *agendas of master politicians, propaganda, coverups, and occult spin doctors,* Satan weaves the spirit of Antichrist to subvert duly constituted government. In doing this, Satan loves to exploit ambitious politicians, especially since they are usually pretenders who espouse grandiose claims that they have no intention of fulfilling. *Politicians appear* as something that they are not. Politicians like to associate with influential groups. They appeal to *Christians* because their surveys tell them that they are a large bloc of votes to exploit. However, all these pretenses, masquerades, and clever masks are always cast with a view to grasp or maintain *power.*

Jesus used this label to apply to the *religious leaders* of Judaism: Pharisees, Sadducees, and Herodians when He walked this earth. Yes, the Antichrist spirit is very clever. We can see it in corrupt politicians who frequently appeal to pride and nationalism in patriotic speeches, alternating between *flattery* and *domineering belligerence.* Their propaganda machine tells people what to believe by saying that this is what they want to hear. We can count upon the masses to swallow the big lie. That is what got Hitler into power. They define everything in *vague* generalities, making people *assume* this is what they want. That is how they cement together in one political bloc many divergent groups who mistakenly think their leaders are going their way! *This is how the false prophet gains power.* Yes, the mouthpieces of Antichrist have "both hands full of reason," encompassing the consummate pragmatist better than any other. They create and bankroll both sides of wars and political controversies. Their agenda is clear: "create the problem" and then present their "solution" by compromising or stealing something belonging to someone else (usually either a resource or a freedom)!* Many poor victims always lose, do they not? It should not surprise

---

244   Dan. 2:34,35,44,45; Luke 13:31–35; 21:8–19; Eph. 6:12; Rev. 12,13,17 *See also the author's book Spiritual Guidelines for Restoration, "Historical Review Section" and the references regarding John Wyclif and John Huss in the book The Reformation by Will Durant, Simon & Schuster, NY, 1957 Pages 30–37, 163–168*

us, because *they think* that "the end justifies the means!" See how they run: Politicians always parrot back the *three big lies:* "war is the way to peace," that "slavery brings freedom," and that "oppression gives security." Christians, remember Constantine I and weep! Yet I fear that most are so well-indoctrinated that they know not what has been lost. The *specialty of the house* is Lord Acton's quip that "absolute power corrupts absolutely" by that enabling Antichrist *cleverly and craftily to manipulate government,* using it as a weapon *against its own people.*

This is so because of their obsession to control everything. Soon, the *mark* will accomplish this. The "Patriot" Act of 2001 is just a prelude. At first, like with credit cards, they pressure people to take it to "enable" trade and business. Then they claim that it will eliminate identity theft, child stealing, drug smuggling, and counterfeiting. Of course, the "new world order" spirit of Antichrist does not stop there. This regime is so hyper-security conscious, power-mad, and paranoid to the extreme that it exploits technology, computers, paid spies, and informants to monitor people's movements and acts. Soon Joe McCarthy will look like a Sunday school teacher! (John D. Rockefeller was!) Like the Soviet KGB and Mao's Red Guard, the authorities will sedulously profile and keep detailed dossiers on *everyone who takes the mark* of the universal global-positioning ID Let US beware: Teddy Roosevelt wisely said that "No man is justified of doing evil on the ground of expediency."[245]

II. Then, we have the perfidious doctrine of war, religion, and politics.

To achieve its goal, Antichrist uses a masterful and sophisticated mixture of religion and politics, playing them like a violin! The history of the Roman Catholic Church and the devious ways of the Papacy readily tells us what John's vision of "the scarlet woman upon the beast" is all about, doesn't it? Many cannot see that this vision also illustrates the same modus operandi of Babylon, mother of Harlots, being advocated today by Protestants and even by many evangelical and charismatic organizations. By enlarge, although they look like a

---

245   Rev. 13 *Viz., the "the Hegelian Dialectic." *See also Appendix A and the paper entitled "A Biblical Disclosure of Antichrist Ibid. Bartlett, Pages 554, #12 and 615, #2"*

lamb, these religious nonprofit corporations of men are being used as tools of the state.

Notice in particular *religion and the state operate using the same patterns.* With few exceptions, they all speak the same language, "the counsel of the ungodly," which echoes the "voice of the dragon." *Their common beliefs,* mainly stemming from "corporation organization," prove this: their *avowed resort to using violence and of killing their enemies,* falsely claiming that "God" ordains it! This crass substitution of worldly humanism stands in blatant defiance of the commands of Jesus Christ! *If* they were the true body of Christ, they would obey Christ.

Since they do not, this proves that *their "god" is not the father of Jesus. Who is their god?* Daniel tells us that *Antichrist serves "Mauzzim"* (or Molech), *the god of forces.* Paul identifies this monstrous imposter as "the god of this world," who is Satan. This *spirit of Satan, as Antichrist,* the false prophet, is also the *lying spirit* behind *the false gospels* taught by many mainstream churches that tell Christians that they should hate and kill enemies. They approve Christian participation in combat and support the execution of prisoners. Then they have the audacity to turn around and say that they serve God! Yet, they *still* fail to see or to take seriously the fact that these very beliefs betray the Spirit of Jesus Christ! This abandonment of genuine Christianity will eventually call down judgment from on high! Why do these false beliefs continue to exist? They exist precisely because *man intentionally* organizes and governs modern churches using the ways of man.[246]

In stark contrast to this, Jesus said to Pilate, "My Kingdom *is not of this world—if* it were, then my servants would fight."[247] By co-opting genuine authority, Antichrist adroitly manipulates *its prey! One of the biggest lies* that Satan leads Christians to assume is that *God directly appoints authority.*

Satan frequently uses religious leaders to teach Christians that if someone is in power, that "automatically means that God put them

---

246 Matt. 5:38–48; 22:15–22; Luke 13:31–35; John 16:1–3,33; Gal. 1:6–12; 2 Thess. 1,2 *See also the book Spiritual Guidelines for Restoration Appendix A: "A Critique of Soul Power" See also the 3 part series of papers entitled "Christianity versus Religion"*

247 Dan. 11:35,36; Matt. 7:13–21; John 18:36,37; 2 Cor. 4:4–6. *See the papers entitled "Basics of Biblical Church Governance" and "Guidelines for Renewed Leadership"*

there." Sorry, wrong answer! First, we should know by now that *God is a title, not a name!* Second, the English word "ordained" found in the King James's version of Romans 13 is an *incorrect translation* slavishly referred to by many misguided leaders. The original Greek word is *tagma,* which means an *allowed* arrangement, *not a direct appointment.*

Yes, God's Word teaches that man has free will in governing himself. Moreover, by this permission, God also *allows rebel authority to be alive and well on planet earth* and that Antichrist is the *lying spirit taking advantage of it!* Christians should know that Jesus Christ is the only authorized legate of the true Father God for us. We must obey God over man when human law conflicts with God's law.[248]

Jesus's statements to religious authorities frequently reveal this truth. Both John and Paul also point the finger at Satanic (rebel) authority. The ultimate truth is that the New Testament does not teach the *false doctrine* of *divine right of kings.* Who then is responsible for teaching this big lie? Antichrist uses a remarkably effective and lethal combination: *Religion + Politics + Propaganda=Power + Death.*

Tribal chiefs, kings, and potentates have used this equation for millennia as a powerful tool to control the masses, keeping monopolies on power, and economic activity worldwide. Satan deftly *combines the secular with religion* using the occult and secrecy to infiltrate all the bastions of government, business, and organized religion to the highest levels.

III. Babylon gathers a cartel of multinational banks and big businesses.

Babylon (the global plutocracy or new world order) gains worldwide power by the widespread use of *fiat money.* This is what the banks *"create" out of thin air* by computer entries! Fiat money is the prime cause of the manufactured "boom and bust cycle" that business tycoons exploit. Multinational (global) corporations are the perfect vehicles to do this, for their ubiquitous presence worldwide even today guarantees that Satan will bring all nations and economies under subjection.

---

248   Matt. 7:13–29; 10:16–42; John 6:27–29; 7:15–27; 8:31–59; 10:1–30; 12:31–50; Acts 4:8–20; 5:17–32; 2 Cor. 4:4–6; 10:3–6; 11:2 ff.; Eph. 6:10–12; 1 John 2:1–20; 4:1–6; Rev. 12:1–13:7
See also the book Jesus' Way, Appendix B

Global central banks complete the economic picture by fostering long-term loans to developing countries to get them to amass huge debts. These colossal debts pressure them into playing ball with the system of global capitalism. Notice also that *capitalism* is very different from "free enterprise!" Carefully review the description found in Revelation 18.

"Babylon" is a colossal *secular religion* of money, politics, and power that Antichrist shrewdly uses to exploit and enslave people for gain! It uses political, military, and legal muscle to ensure the maximum flow of profits to the global oligarchy. Rigid control of all the *means of production and distribution of both durable goods and food supplies* assure *dictatorship!* If you look carefully beyond the thin veneer of respectability, we can readily see the spirit of Antichrist in the attitudes of *greed and selfish ambition.* We can see it in the works of Adam Smith in his book *The Wealth of Nations.* We are led to believe that *The Prince* by Macchiavelli teaches us that "the end justifies the means." Yet, this quote originally comes to us from St. Jerome (c342- 420) Letter 48. Caveat Emptor let the buyer beware! The big lie gets many converts by appealing to pride of ownership, greed, and self-interest. Thus, they buy into the world system and all its evil ways used to defend and protect all those privileges they covet. God's Word tells us that the carnal nature of man is consistently evil.

When man becomes an owner, he will use any means and go to great lengths to protect that investment. These things include unethical business practices, underhanded legal procedures and technicalities, and even murder! Think you are different? Wait and see. Always remember: man is not "god"; religion is not "god"; the state is not "god"; Antichrist is not "god." *Only God is God!* At the great white throne judgment, all the big tycoons of Babylon will end up saying the same thing as Pharaoh in Cecil B. DeMille's *The Ten Commandments,* "His God is *God!*"

IV. Let us categorize other "types of Antichrist."

1) God can use Antichrist *as a tool of judgment.* God uses Satan to discipline disloyal, deceitful, apostate, and rebellious people who have persisted in disobedience. God reserves the right to use this possibility to apply to any of God's people anytime. Yes, God allows this to happen

to the Jews or to the church.[249] 2) History and Scripture also depict Antichrist (the works of Satan) in prophecies as a warlord, a dictator, or a tyrant who amasses power by using many devious schemes. These include *flattery,* trickery, craftiness, brute force, and cunning deceit. Among these were Antiochus Epiphanes, Herod the Great, Nero, Constantine I, Mohammed, Ghengis Khan, Napoleon, Stalin, Hitler, and Chairman Mao.[250] 3) As the spirit of Satan either in person or in sinful and evil acts of men, Antichrist is an adversary, accuser, betrayer, tempter, or faultfinder. The spirit of Antichrist fosters division "sowing discord among brethren." Antichrist is a *blasphemer of God,* that is he vigorously opposes and vilifies the person and character of the true God.

Because he hates God so much, Antichrist uses any means possible to desecrate God's creation.[251] 4) In the pervasive philosophy of *dualism* (the depiction of "good vs. evil") that saturates the media and movie industry with adventure, intrigue, and "action heroes" in cleverly crafted situation dramas glorifying human ways. Their glorification of soldiers and politicians for being saviors is pure humanism and *idolatry! Like Satan's puppets,* the politicians take up their soliloquy in their Machiavellian rationalizations of war. Again, they first create the situation and then craft the "solution."

V. The ultimate goal of Antichrist has always been world domination.

It has been Satan's agenda ever since he was cast out of heaven. When, as Lucifer, the bearer of light, sinned by attempting to usurp the place of God. Satan craves *the worship of man!* Satan expects to take over the world by the same methods he has always used.[252] However, we must realize that this nightmarish endgame concoction of Satan's emissaries is *not an entirely monolithic system.* Big holes still exist. Daniel's prophecy tells us the key in his interpretation of King Nebuchadnezzar's dream of the great statue. Daniel explains that the statue represents successive

---

249   Psa. 101:7; Jer. 5:27; 8:5; 9:6; Dan. 8:12–14; 9:1 ff.; Mark 14:1; Luke 21:24; Col. 2:8
250   Gen. 3:1; Dan. 8:23–26; Eph. 6:10–12; 1 John 3:8; Rev. 13:1 ff.
251   Job 1:6; 2:1; Dan. 8:11; 11:36; Matt. 4:10; 16:23.
252   *See Appendix D for more details*

empires that will rule the world until the time Christ returns, starting with Babylon, the "head of gold." Each empire would be *inferior* to the previous. Moreover, Daniel tells us that the feet of the statue are composed of iron and clay. Iron and clay are insoluble. They cannot coalesce or mix in a unified way. This tells us that *no cohesion exists* in the end-time empire of Antichrist.[253] If you follow the sequence, you will notice that the statue "splits" during the Roman (iron) period into two branches (legs). Yes, these could very well represent the western and eastern blocs of civilization. Coming back to the feet, we know that each foot has a "big toe." Consider the following postulated scenario as a logical application. I am not being dogmatic about this possibility, but it fits. Each "big toe" could represent the "lead nation" or empire in the particular bloc (foot). 1) We would have the west bloc (American Union) with the U.S. as the predominant power. 2) We have the east bloc (Eurasian Union) with England or another European or Asian nation as the dominant power of it.

Yes, Antichrist will control the world through these instruments as an "axis of power" fulfilling end-time biblical prophecies that will prevail until Christ comes in great power, delivering the saints and judging the world.

Yes, Jesus Christ is the Stone not made with human hands! He will strike the base (feet) of the statue and pulverize it to powder (destroys the humanistic hegemony of Antichrist, including all "falsely confessing" religious organizations) and grows to a great mountain that engulfs the world. Thus, Christ assumes power over planet earth.[254]

Scripture Profile of Antichrist, Part 1: New Testament	
1. Pretender, hypocrite, child of hell	Matt. 23:1 ff.
2. False prophet, messiah	Matt. 24:4–15
3. Deceiver	Luke 21:8 f.

---

253 Compare Daniel 2:19–45 with Rev. 13:8 ff.
254 Psa. 2,110, 118:22; Isa. 28:16; Dan. 2:19–45; Matt. 21:42; Luke 20:9–18; Rom. 9:33; Eph. 2:13–22; 2 Thess. 1,2; 1 Pet. 2;1–10; 4:12–19

4.	Loveless, people-pleaser, murderer	John 5:39–44; 7:18; 8:40 ff.
5.	Greedy, opportunist, betrayer=Judas Iscariot	Matt. 26:45-50; Luke 22:47–53; John 12:6; 13:18–30; 18:2–6
6.	Violent, murderer, revolutionary patriot=Barabbas	Matt. 27:15-26; Luke 23:18,19;John18:39,40
7.	Reprobate mind, misrepresents truth as lie	Rom. 1:18–32
8.	Distracts, diverts attention from truth	2 Cor. 4:3,4
9.	Stronghold of Argumentation	2 Cor. 10:3–6
10.	Masquerades as Christian, corrupts, boasts	2 Cor. 11:2– 4,11–15
11.	Exalts self above law, awesome lie, false wonder	2 Thess. 2:1–12
12.	Argumentative, greedy, materialist	1 Tim. 6:3–12
13.	Willful sin, man of sin	Heb. 10:26–31
14.	Merciless, faithless, warmonger	James 2:12- 26; 4:1-8

Scripture Profile of Antichrist, Part 1: New Testament

15.	Lover of the world, denier/betrayer of Christ	1 John 2:13– 23
16.	Man-hater, murderer	1 John 3:1–18
17.	Inhuman, opportunist	1 John 4:3–7
18.	A wolf Masquerading as a lamb	Rev. 13:1 ff.

Scripture Profile of Antichrist, Part 2: Old Testament References

1.	Serpent, deceiver, liar = Satan	Genesis 3
2.	Betrayer, murderer, coverup = Cain	Genesis 4
3.	Abuser of fellow man = Sodomite	Genesis 18,19
4.	Despises birthright = Esau	Genesis 25:21 ff.

5.	Jealous; hater, betrayer of brother = Simeon	Genesis 37 f
6.	Enslaves God's people = Pharaoh	Exodus 1–12
7.	Greedy opportunist = Balaam	Numbers 22–24
8.	Mixture with pagans, syncretism	Numbers 25; Joshua 23
9.	Sows discord, civil war, blood feuds	Judges 19–21
10.	Slanderer, false accuser, friendly fire = Saul	1 Sam. 15–31
11.	Corrupter, idolater = Jeroboam	1 Kings 11,12
12.	Seducer, entices to evil = Ahab and Jezebel	1 Kings 16– 19; 2 Kings 21
13.	Rebellion against God = Lucifer, Prince	Isa. 14; Ezek. 28
14.	Proud revolutionary patriot = Ishmael, son of Nethaniah, and Johanan, son of Kareah	Jer. 40–44
15.	Warlord, dictator=Gog, Magog	Ezek. 38,39

Scripture Profile of Antichrist, Part 2: Old Testament References

16.	Flattery, intrigues, deception	Daniel 7–11
17.	Mockers, revilers, mob mentality	Ezra 4:1–16; 5:5–17
18.	Racial hater, ethnic cleansing = Haman	Esther 3–10
19.	Mixed marriages, syncretism	Ezra 9,10
20.	Heckler, conspirator, hinderer = Sanballat	Neh. 2:19,20; 4:1–23
21.	Greedy, heartless opportunists	Neh. 5:1–13
22.	Predatory stealth, craftiness = Geshem	Neh. 6:1 f.

END TİMES ANALYSİS, PART 3

## Chapter 17

Facts Concerning the 70ᵗʰ week of Daniel

Facts concerning the 70th Week of Daniel		
#	**Description**	**Page #**
I.	Introduction	
II.	Let us now examine the Scriptural evidence	
III.	The following elements explain "prophetic texts" concerning Daniel's 70ᵗʰ Week	
	Fig. One: Partition of 70ᵗʰ Week	
IV.	Review Summary	
V.	Consider the following specific points tying togetherthe events of the Great Tribulation Period and the 2ⁿᵈ Half of the 70ᵗʰ Week of Daniel	
VI.	Appendix One: The following chart is a legend for acronyms in text and Fig. One	

Let us examine the Facts concerning the 70ᵗʰ Week of Daniel, seeing how they fit into God's overall Plan to Unify all God's People.

Introduction:

To reach an accurate exegesis that reflects the masterful order of God's Great Plan of the Ages, it is very important that we carefully compare Scripture with Scripture, letting God's Spirit reveal the underlying Truth we must have to properly comprehend the Heart of

God's Will. This is only way that works to reveal the Complete Truth. Another fact we cannot ignore is that "the Testimony of Jesus is the Spirit of Prophecy." This means that no interpretation of Scripture can be true if it contradicts Christ's Word.[1]

In sorting out these things, let us first see how all the Prophetic Messages fit together into one whole, God's Prophetic Time Line, integrating all the elements that comprise "the Mystery of Godliness" and God's Plan to unify all Believers. These elements also perfectly mesh with a prophetic pattern we call the "Passover Paradigm," which reaches its final fulfillment in the events of the "Great Tribulation Period."[2]

The following primary elements or levels of God's Master Plan can be seen and they align with the "Major Rivers of Prophetic Thought" that join together into one whole that describes the correct eschatological picture:

A. The first is the amazing Prophecy of Daniel which includes predictions involving virtually all the major developments of world history from the seventh century BC to the present time and beyond! The great pictorial image of the "Great Statue and the Stone from Heaven" and the Parallel imagery of the "Four Beasts" provides the underlying structure. The Prophetic Message of the "Seventy Weeks" is superimposed over that and includes "God's Six Point Disciplinary Process" that completes the pacification of the Jews, integrating (re-grafting) them back into the Body of God's People *In Christ* and completing God's Judgment regarding all unrepentant unbelievers.[3]

---

1   Luke 24:25-49; Rev. 19:10,13 See the Papers entitled *Covenant Principles, Fulfilment prophecy, Hermeneutics: Basic Principles of Scripture Interpretation, Hermeneutics, Part Two: Major Tools in Revealing Scripture, The Higher Laws of God, The Holy Spirit is God's Revelator, Illustrating the "Law of Multiple Fulfilments," Jesus' Major Parables, The Key ... is Spiritual Exegesis, Looking Through the 'Lens of Jesus Christ,' One Covenant for All, Principles of Fulfillment Theology, Prophetic Chronology and Prophetic Chronology Two*

2   Mal. 3:16-18; John 10:1-16; Rom. 11:11-32; 1 Cor. 15:20-28 *See the Papers entitled The Biblical Precept of Mystery, The Biblical Role of Israel, Correlating Last Days Scriptures, The Doctrine of Last Things, Fulfilment Prophecy and The Three Passovers of Scripture*

3   Psa. 110; Daniel 2,7,9,12 *See also the Papers A Biblical Disclosure of Antichrist, Correlating Last Days Scriptures, "Correlating Major Events to Prophecy Chart," Emmanuel 2 and The Messiah Figures*

B. The second is Jesus' Prophetic Discourse*, which is included in all three "Synoptic Gospels." Of course, we should also know that, since Jesus Christ is God, all true interpretations of Scripture and doctrinal conclusions must align with Jesus' Word, for Jesus is the Word of God. Moreover, when we observe this standard, all things begin to make sense. Also, these conclusions include the chronology of events during the Great Tribulation Period (GTP) and the "Day of the Lord" (DTL), which includes the "Ingathering of the Saints," otherwise known as the "Rapture."[4]*

C. We can identify a third stream in Scriptures' River: The "Messiah Figures." Two main spiritual pictorials stand out that are sequential in nature: The "Lamb of God" (MFLa) and the "Lion of God" (MFLi). Also, keep in mind the fact that God's Prophetic Time Line (GPT) does not go in reverse.

The first expresses the perfection of God's Plan for the Atonement of sin, the lynchpin of the *New Covenant* whereby Jesus' Sacrifice on the Cross provides the Way for mankind to reestablish a personal relationship with God. This figure was prophesied by Isaiah in the vivid vision of the "Suffering Servant."

The second figure expresses Christ's awesome power in executing Judgment and Justice in the last days via the pictorials of the "Stone from Heaven," the Lamb who is transformed into a Lion who opens the seven Seals and destroys Antichrist, Babylon and the Great Harlot.[5]

---

4   *Matt. 24*; Mark 13*; Luke 21*; Rev. 19:10,13 *With careful examination it is apparent that Jesus' Prophetic Discourse contains two levels of predictions, some applying to the Roman Jewish war of 67-70 AD, which was a direct judgment of Israel for rejecting Jesus as the "Lamb of God Messiah," (MFLa), forming the first half of the 70th Wk, and others which "look forward" to the Great Tribulation Period yet to come, associated with Jesus as the "Lion of God Messiah" (MFLi) in the second half of the 70th Wk. See Section III, Footnote #17 and the Papers entitled Correlating Last Days Scriptures, Sections II, IV and VIII, The Doctrine of Last Things, Section V and Facts of Scripture: The Church and the Tribulation*

5   *Isa. 53; Matt. 24:1,2, 32-35; John 1:29-34 (MFLa) and Dan. 2:34,35,44,45; Mal. 3:1-18; Matt. 24:14-31, 36-51; 2 Thess. 1,2; Rev. 5:5; 14:1-19:21 (MFLi) See also the Papers entitled The Biblical Precept of Mystery, Illustrating the "Law of Multiple Fulfillments" and The Messiah Figures*

D. The Prophetic Book of Revelation (*Apocalypse*) contains the most detail concerning the Great Tribulation Period. Revelation also contains similar spiritual pictorials that we find in the Book of Zechariah and is a source by which we can sort out many apparent anomalies so long as we diligently compare these messages and details with the above classifications.[6]

II. Let us now examine the Scriptural evidence for the 70ᵗʰ Week of Daniel being split into two halves, each being Three and one-half years in length.

First, we must acknowledge that, to understand Prophetic Scriptures, one must realize that Prophecies are part of God's way for presenting His Will to mankind. More specifically, Prophecies are germane to God's overall "Plan of Unification" that eventually brings all God's People into One Body in Christ.

Moreover, the writer believes that all the Scriptures are satisfied if you place the first half for being the first century Jewish War, culminating with the destruction of Jerusalem in AD 70.

The upshot of this means that the second half must be fulfilled at another time, of which many Prophecies indicate, that will apply during a "Last Days event" called the Great Tribulation Period (GTP).

1. Consider the profuse number of references about a specific Three and one-half year period, expressed in varying forms, all concerning "tribulation periods" and "Antichrist figures."[7]

2. The only mention of a "one week" period is truncated "in the midst of the week." This took almost a year, starting with open conflict in May of AD 66 between the minions of Procurator Cestius Gallus and the radical Zealots, which included the *Sicarii* or 'dagger men.' Cestius' siege of Jerusalem in September 'interrupted the daily sacrifice' setting the stage for the First Half of the 70ᵗʰ Week.[8]

---

6   *See sections II, III and IV below for details*
7   Dan. 7:25; 9:26; 12:7,11; Rev. 11:2,3; 12:14; 13:5
8   Dan. 9:26 *See the historical chronicles contained in The Works of Flavius Josephus, which includes the following section: Wars of the Jews, Bk. II, Ch. XVII-XXII*

3. The Roman-Jewish War escalated rapidly after the Roman army of General Titus entered the area in February 67 AD, continuing for three and one-half years (67-70 AD), the First half of the 70th Week, culminating in the destruction of Jerusalem and the *Third Temple on August 7, AD 70, after which "(the Roman Prince) caused the daily Sacrifice (stone temple worship) to permanently cease."[9]

4. In the Prophetic Discourse, Jesus accurately prophesied the total destruction of the Temple by the Romans, confirming Daniel and also precisely predicting that this event would be concluded at a time "this generation will not pass until these things are fulfilled."[10]

5. Scripture tells us that the progress of the "Six Point Disciplinary" for the Jews would go "on hatius" "Until the Times of the Gentiles are fulfilled."

Knowing that the Jews had rejected Christ for being the Messiah, the contexts of Jesus' Prophetic Discourse and Paul's Address at Antioch both specifically tell us that God was going to shift his emphasis to the Gentiles during the "Age of Grace," which eventually led to an interruption or break in the 70th Week after 70 AD.[11]

6. The only reference period concerning the "hegemony of the Antichrist figure" is three and one-half years (not seven years), which also coincides with the testimony period of the "Two Witnesses" in the 'parenthetical period' during the Second Woe of the Seventh Seal.[12]

7. This position (of the second half of the 70th Week) is bolstered further by Daniel's prediction in chapter twelve of an "extension period" that takes place after the 1260 Days for the express purpose of God's dealing with the Jews.

---

9   Ibid. Fn. #5 *Note also that a footnote in Josephus' Antiquities of the Jews, Book XV, Chapter XI (Pg. 334) specifically states that the temple the Romans destroyed was the Third Temple! See the Set of Charts entitled Sequence of Events (leading to the destruction of Jerusalem in 70 AD). See also Section VI below

10   Dan. 9:26; Matt. 24:1,2,34

11   Dan. 9:24; Matt. 23:37-39; Luke 21:24; Acts 13:38-52; Rom. 11:25

12   Ibid. Fn. #7

III. The following elements explain "Prophetic Texts" concerning Daniel's 70ᵗʰ Week:

A. First, let us review the major factors that affect our understanding of prophetic Scripture.[13]

1. Spirituality: We must acknowledge that Scripture is a spiritual quantity that requires spiritual means to interpret.[14]

2. We must observe all the pertinent rules regarding scriptural contexts relating to the subject matter.[15]

3. Knowing the relative timing of the "writing/ speaking periods" of Scripture will help us greatly.*[16]

4. We must recognize any "Time-Tag" Scriptures that are present.[17]

5. The student needs to recognize the salient "prophetic monikers" within a text that links it to other similar prophecies.[18]

6. It is important that we associate the relevant "Messiah Figure" of which the text refers to discern the particular application of the prophecy.[19]

7. We must observe the chronological relation that each element of the prophecy has to the "Age of Grace."[20]

---

13 See also the Papers entitled The Biblical Precept of Mystery, The Biblical Role of Israel, Contextually Comparing the Elements of Prophetic Scripture, Correlating the Prophecies concerning 'TOHY Periods,' The Fulfillment of God's Promise (to Abraham), Emmanuel 1, Emmanuel 2, Fulfilment Prophecy, Hermeneutics (1), Hermeneutics, Part Two, The Key to Understanding Scripture is Spiritual Exegesis, The Messiah Figures, Patterns in Prophetic Scripture, Prophetic Chronology One and Prophetic Chronology Two

14 See the Papers entitled Hermeneutics, Hermeneutics Part Two and The Key to Understanding Scripture is Spiritual Exegesis

15 Ibid. Footnote #14

16 *For example, see The Biblical Precept of Mystery, Appendix 2: "Chronological Chart of 'Writing Periods' in Daniel

17 See Appendix E: "Time Tag Scriptures"

18 See the Papers entitled Contextually Comparing the Elements of Prophetic Scripture, Section VII, Correlating the Prophecies concerning 'TOHY Periods,' Patterns in Prophetic Scripture and Prophetic Chronology Two

19 See the Paper entitled The Messiah Figures

20 See the Papers entitled Facts of Scripture: The Church and the Tribulation and Prophetic Chronology One

B. Regarding "Prophetic Texts," whenever we examine prophecies we must observe that these texts contain "multiple fulfillment segments" and "snapshot-type" references with both "near and far" time contexts. Know this also: "God's Prophetic Time Line" does not go in reverse, since the context of all prophecies is God's Master Plan for the Unification of all God's People in one Body in Christ!

Another fact that is very important for us to understand is that when you compare Scripture with Scripture, you find that the "biblical restoration of Israel" is also part of God's Unification in Christ. To maintain a proper exegesis of Scripture, you must know that it is not a 'political restoration' made by military force, nor will it take place until the end (Consummation), which is at a time during the "Great Tribulation Period" and after the "Times of the Gentiles are fulfilled," which means after the evangelical "Age of Grace" has run its course. Moreover, beware of the many false doctrines germane to the "deterministic-based" system of belief known as the "Judeo-Christian Tradition."[22]

Moreover, when comparing the TOHY** or "tribulation period" references applying to the 70th Week from different books, observe that they were written in different times and, depending on context, may apply in separate periods of fulfillment.

The texts in Daniel chapters seven and nine (550-537 BC) apply to "tribulation periods," the first segment/ "tribulation period" of which would take place 'before that generation would have passed' and was fulfilled in AD 70. Jesus later predicted this in the Prophetic Discourse recorded in the Gospels (AD 29) with other parts of the discourse applying to the second segment. Notice that the "Six-point Disciplinary Process" of Daniel nine concerns both periods.[23]

---

22   Dan. 9:26,27; Matt. 24:14; Luke 21:20-24; Acts 1:6-8; Rom. 11:7-33; Eph. 2:11-22; Rev. 11:1-3 *See also The Biblical Role of Israel and The Biblical Precept of Mystery and the Glossary of Terms' entry "The Judeo-Christian Tradition" found in the last Appendix*

23   Matt. 24:1,2, 32-35; Luke 21:5,6, 20-24 *(1st half), with Luke 21:24 as pivotal verse and Vss. 8-19, 25-28, 33-36 pertaining to the 2nd half. See also the papers entitled Correlating the Prophecies concerning 'TOHY Periods,' Correlating Major Events to Prophecy Chart and Correlating the "Horns of the Fourth Beast" of Daniel seven...*

However, the references in Daniel twelve and Paul's letter to the Romans, Circa AD 50, concern the Jews' future restoration. They line up with the Revelation texts *(Circa AD 90) which were written after the Roman Jewish war of AD 67-70, all pertaining to a future second segment/ "tribulation period" that Daniel says would take place much later, after the "Times of the Gentiles are Fulfilled." (TGF)

Taken together, all these Scriptures point to a double (split) fulfillment sequence of the 70th Week. Moreover, carefully comparing Daniel, the accounts of Jesus' indictment of the Pharisees and Prophetic Discourse, Paul's Letter to the Romans and John's *Apocalypse* yields a very significant pattern regarding the 70th Week that cannot be ignored.

Verily the events of the 70th Week contain the final corrections God brings to bear in fulfilling the "six point disciplinary process" we find in Daniel chapter nine. The writer believes that when you correlate all the statements concerning "TOHY (three and one-half year) periods" that it sets the stage for a previously unrecognized pattern that can explain what God's Spirit is telling us:

Indeed, the result you get when you compare all the Scriptures concerning these "event types" is that God's overall message is teaching us that the Seventieth Week is split into two halves.

Not only that, each half is Three and one-half years (TOHY) long, separated by the crucial "hatius period" separating the two halves of the prophecy. Indeed, Scripture designates the unique "hatius period" by two main monikers: One is that of the Jews' "Desolations unto the End" (DUE) and two is "the Times of the Gentiles" (TOG), which ends at the specific point in time defined in Scripture as (when) "the times of the Gentiles are Fulfilled" (TGF).[24]

C. Another very significant "Time-Tag" Scripture that links the first half of the 70th Week to the beginning of the abovementioned "hatius period" of "desolations" is Jesus' statement "*this generation will not pass until these things are fulfilled" (TGNPU). To understand how

---

24   Dan. 7:25; 9:24-27 *In Matt. 24 and Luke 21 it appears that* Matt. 24:1,2, 32-35 (Luke 21:5,6,20-24) apply to the first century tribulation/ war and that Matt. 24:3-31, 36-51 (Luke 21:7-19, 25-28, 34-36) *apply to the last days' Great Tribulation Period along with Dan.* 12:4-13; Rom. 11:25,26; Rev. 11:1-3,11; 12:6,14; 13:5 Ibid. Footnote #22

this all fits together we must also see that Jesus' Prophetic Discourse recorded in the Synoptics has two levels, installments or sets of prophecies imbedded and interwoven within it, each lining up with one of the two Messiah Figures, Lamb (MFLa) and Lion (MFLi):[25]

The first level applies to the first century Roman Jewish war of AD 67-70, which is directly related to God's Judgment of the rebellious Jews of that century.

This judgment stems from two things: One, their rejection of Christ the "Lamb of God" as their Messiah and two, their rejecting the *New Covenant* for being God's New Way of worship.

In the "Age of Grace," this is the "new way" in which Jesus' Teachings ordain the human body as the central venue and focus point of our worship of God, the "New Temple" wherein God's People worship "in spirit and in truth."[26]

Jesus' proclamation to the Jewish religious leaders also sets the terms for their judgment by saying that (paraphrased) "the judgment from all the righteous blood that was shed upon the earth ... from Abel to Zecharias will fall upon your generation. Verily I say unto you: All these things will come upon *this generation." A 'double meaning' imbedded within this says that Christ took all the sins of the world upon himself as "the lamb slain from the foundation of the world," mentioned in Isaiah's Prophecy and by John the Baptist and the Apostle John.[27]

The second and final installment (half) of the 70th Week aligns with the coming Great Tribulation Period (GTP), mentioned in Jesus' Prophetic Discourse, during which Christ will return in Great Power and Glory.

Moreover, in the interpretation God gave Daniel concerning king Nebuchadnezzar's dream of the Great Statue, the "Great Stone from Heaven" that strikes the Statue's base is the prophetic moniker for Christ's Second Coming. This is the Day of the Lord (DTL), wherein Christ will Gather up all the Saints, execute judgment on Antichrists'

---

25   Ibid. Footnote #4, #23 and #24 See also Fig. One: "Partition of 70th Week"
26   John 2:19-21; 4:23,24 See also the Paper entitled *Christian Worship and the True Temple*
27   Dan. 9:2, 24-27; Matt. 23:29-24:31; Luke 21:20-24 See also Isa. 52:13-53:12; John 1:29-34; Rev. 5:6-13

New World Order and <u>confront the remaining Jews</u>, after which they will repent and be restored and "re-grafted" into the Body of Believers in Christ according to Zechariah's Prophecy and Paul's declaration in Romans eleven.[28]

D. Moreover, it must also be emphasized that God's Grand Plan of Unification (UNIF) of all Believers in Christ has <u>two major aspects</u>: Judgment and Unification. These two intertwine into one whole that is also described by Daniel's "six point disciplinary process" (SPD), delineated in chapter nine.[29]

It is also interesting to note that Zechariah's Prophecy has many of the same patterns within it, so we must be ever so careful to observe the "cut away" portions that refer back or forward to different times and/ or events.[30]

D. The 70th Week and the *Passover* Paradigm.

It cannot be ignored that the multifaceted pattern of the 70th Week contains many of the same elements as the *Passover,* beginning with the Archetypal *Passover* we find in the Book of Exodus that launched the Hebrew Nation: Judgment and *Redemption.*

Let us now pause, taking a long hard look to clarify this <u>major aspect of Biblical Prophecy.</u> This part of Biblical Prophecy has many believers confused and unable to see the Truth mainly because the teachings of *Determinism* have presented a "false view of prophecies" that has been inculcated by centuries of "religious Idolatry," causing a flawed view of the doctrine of Salvation to exist in the minds of multitudes.

Addressing the subject of "properly understanding Scripture" is a daunting task but it can be done IF we first "set aside all prior religious catechisms" and then <u>open your mind and Listen to God's voice in your innermost being!</u> This is how we begin understanding Scripture

---

28   Dan. 2:34,35,44,45; Zech. 12:9,10; Matt. 24; Rom. 11:7-33 *See also the Papers entitled Correlating Last Days' Scriptures, The Doctrine of Last Things and the book The Church in the Last Days*

29   Compare Daniel 9:24-27; Matt. 24: Luke 21; John 10:7-16; 2 Thess. 2; Rev. 13,17

30   Zech. 9:9,10; 11:12-14; 12:9,10; 13:6,7

and Prophecy as well, letting the Holy Spirit teach us the Truths of Scripture anew![31]

If you progress down that road for some time, God's Spirit will show you the multidimensional characteristics of Jesus Christ's Gospel and *New Covenant.*[32]   Then, relating this all to the subject of "Passover," we can begin to piece together what God's Spirit would have us know.

The first thing is to realize that the Archetypal Passover is indeed the "Catalyzing Event" that sets the tone for God's Salvation in the Physical venue, commencing a personal relationship in which God's People solely depend on God to save and liberate, not by human power! Not only that, God classifies any dependence on human power to save for being Idolatry! So, beware of those who seek to "limit God" by teaching that "salvation" only applies internally or to the "bye and bye" of some future time! God's Word specifically teaches that Only One Living God exists and that God is our Savior in all venues of life: Physical, Soulical and spiritual! [33] Subsequent to this event, Scripture also describes two other Passovers that we can recognize for having the same overall elements as the first.

They are as follows: The Second *Passover* is the Passover of Christ's Passion, wherein Christ, as the *Lamb of God* Messiah Figure, paid the price for all sin by shedding His Precious Blood on the cross! This one event launched the *New Covenant* foretold by Jeremiah and Ezekiel and is found in three of the four "Synoptic" Gospels. Again, however, we must note that Scripture plainly teaches that for any absolution of sin to occur, a person must personally Confess and *Repent* from sin and engage in ongoing human cooperation in the Discipleship to *Conversion* Dynamic Process that leads eventually to Salvation.[34]

31   See the book Jesus' Way: God's Guaranteed Blueprint
32   See the papers entitled Looking Through the Lens of Jesus Christ, The New Covenant and Principles of Fulfilment Theology as well as the book Basic Christian Doctrine
33   Exodus 6-15; Deut. 1:30; 3:22; 4:39; 32:39; 1 Sam. 2:9: 1 Kings 18:21; Psa. 3:8; 4:8; 20, 23,27, Isa. 42-46; Hosea 10:12,13; Acts 16:31 and may others See also the papers entitled The Christian Epiphany (espec. Sect. VI-A-5, Fn. #57), Conditions for Salvation, God's Definition of Salvation and True Liberty is in Christ Alone
34   Jer. 31:31-34; Ezek. 36:16-33; Matt. 26:26-29; Luke 22:15-32; Rom. 5:1-11; Eph. 1:7;2:13,14; Heb. 2:9-15; 6:17-20; 7:19-10:39; 11:12-31

The Third *Passover* is the "End Times Passover" when Christ Returns, gathering His Bride, the Church and executing Judgment upon Antichrists' World System.

Moreover, the 70th Week is a "Passover Type" Event.[35]

In the first Half, because of their rejection of the Messiah, the Jews played the negative/ Judgment part, suffering for their error becoming like a "branch cut off from Christ the Root." In the Second Half, they will play the Restoration/ Redemption part, being "Re-Grafted in" at the end of the age, fulfilling God's Plan of Unification.[36]

Not only that, by itself, the Second Half of the 70th Week "fits the Pattern of the third Passover" in the following elements:

1. First, God allows evil things to reach a "crescendo" or "climax."

2. Second, God provides (Jehovah-Jireh) a "Way of escape" for the Righteous to endure and survive.

3. God's Judgment intensifies, falling upon the Rebellious, reaching the point of "undiluted wrath" (in the Third Woe or the 7th Angel of the 7th Seal) which brings about the "Apotheosis," the final *Reconciliation* of all Believers and the establishment of Righteous Rule by Christ all over the earth.[37]

Of course, this is none other than the Fulfillment of "God's Prophetic Time Line" (GPT) which is essentially also known as "God's Mystery Fulfilled" (GMF).

---

35   *See the paper entitled The Three Passovers of Scripture*
36   Rom. 11:17-24
37   2 Pet. 3; Jude 8-16; Rev. 11:15 ff.; 16:17-18:24

PARTITION OF 70TH WEEK

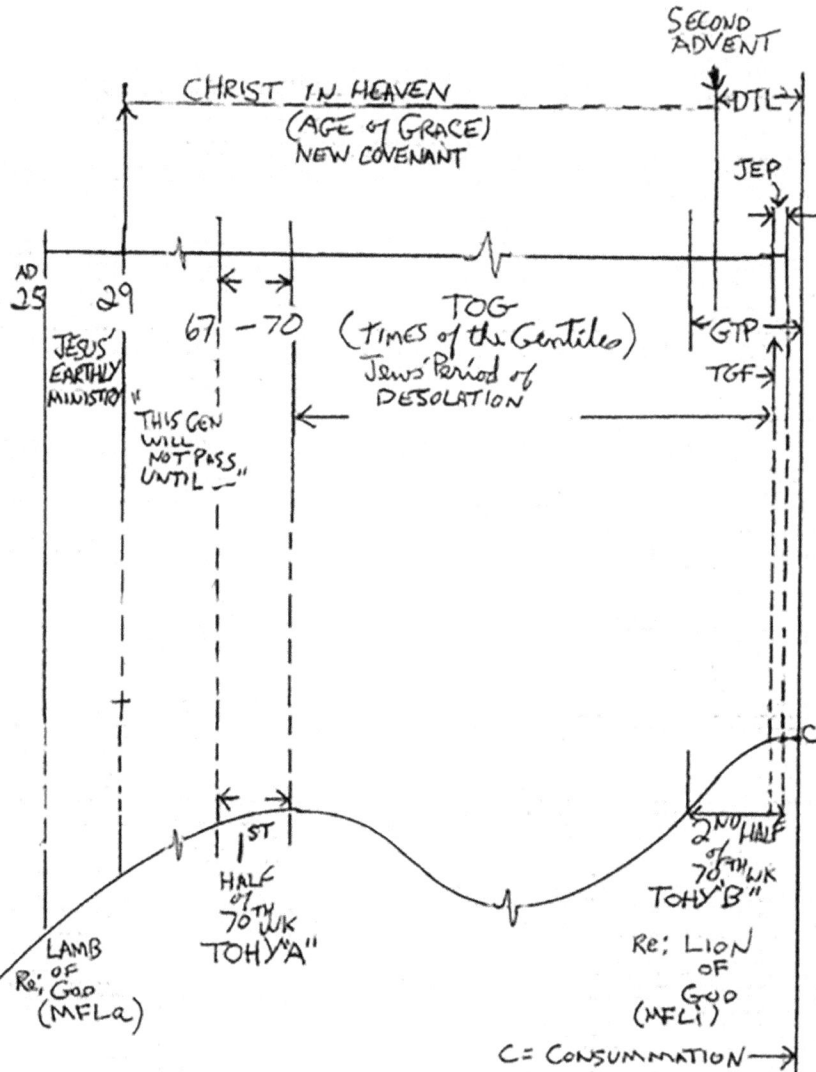

FIG. ONE

Review Summary:

Let us now elaborate on what God is telling us. Daniel twelve, verses' six and seven form a "question and answer couplet." The question asks "how long will it be until the end of these wonders?" The answer is the oft mentioned "Three and one-half year" period the writer refers to as the "TOHY." Observe that verses' seven and eleven both show a "looking forward" viewpoint. In particular, notice that verse seven tells us that this TOHY (Three and one-half Year) period connects to a time which is after the "power of the holy people had been scattered." If you also consider the word 'from' in verse eleven to be 'after,' then the same relative chronology is satisfied.[38]

Clearly, the "Law of Multiple Fulfilments" plays a part since all the "Three and One- half Year" periods apply to prophecies of "tribulation-type" events. This signifies that a "Double Fulfillment" most likely applies to verses seven and eleven, the first portion (half) concerning the cessation of sacrifice and the desolations of the first century Jewish War and the second portion (half) being placed in the "post-Sacrifice (New Covenant) Era" in which Scripture tells us that the Jews will experience "Ongoing Desolations Unto the End" (DUE) which, of course, indicates that God places these events into another point in time after AD 70.[39]

Moreover, this "future tense statement" is another reason why the writer believes the 70th Week is split and that the second half happens during the Great Tribulation Period to come. After this, God will have pacified the remaining repentant Jews, fulfilling the prior prophecies of Zechariah, Daniel, Jesus and Paul.[40]

Not only that, in Revelation ten and eleven, John specifically mentions an interruption (parenthetical period) of the second Woe,

---

38   *See the Papers entitled Correlating Last Days' Scriptures, Correlating the Prophecies concerning 'TOHY Periods,' The Doctrine of Last Things, Patterns in Prophetic Scripture and Prophetic Chronology Two*

39   *To understand this, let the reader observe the corrected syntax in the latter part of Daniel 9:26 and which is reiterated in verse 27, both which tell us that God is extending the Jew's Desolation unto the end (Consummation). Jesus' statement in Matt. 23:37-39 also confirms this. See also Section VI*

40   Zech. 12:10; Dan. 12:7 f.; Matt. 23:37-39; Luke 21:20-24; Rom. 11:25,26 *See also the Papers entitled The Biblical Precept of Mystery, Sect. III, The Higher Laws of God, Sect. III, Illustrating the "Law of Multiple Fulfillments"and Prophetic Chronology Two, Sect. II*

during the Great Tribulation, which directly relates to Daniel's prior mention of the Jews' "extension Period" (JEP), first to 1290 days and finally to 1335 days.

Also the "advanced future time context" of Daniel twelve clearly places the final "three and one-half year period" (TOHY)* in "modern times" at the "end of days," the final segment of "God's Prophetic Time Line" which sums up all the prophetic Streams into one. This also refers back to the "Great Image Prophecy" recorded in Daniel chapter two which predicts the arrival of Christ, the "Stone from Heaven." Of course, this is during the final "Great Tribulation Period" (GTP), which is the time of the Second Half of the 70th Week of Daniel.

Of course, this takes place after the "Falling away First" when "the lawless one" (Antichrist) sets up "the abomination that makes desolate" (AOD). Then, "after the Tribulation of those days" (TOTD) reaches its peak, Christ appears in the sky and Gathers the Saints.

Finally, after the Rapture (ROS) when the "times of the Gentiles are fulfilled" (TGF), Christ and his army vanquish Antichrist and pacifies the Jews.*[41]

V. Consider the following specific points tying together the events of the Great Tribulation Period and the Second Half of the 70th Week of Daniel to the common denominator linking both: The Three and one-half Year (TOHY) periods.[42]

Let us review some very important facts:

A. In the Prophecy of the Seventy Weeks, found in Daniel nine, we have statements (written in 539 BC) that indicate four different "event periods" that are separated in time, which start to be fulfilled in 458 BC. Note that Nehemiah's Temple, the Second Temple, had already been completed in 517 BC.[43]

B. The first two periods cover the events happening during the first 69 Weeks. The first is connected to the "Restoration" period referring to

---

41   Compare Dan. 9:24-27 with Matt. 24:34; Luke 21:24; Rev. 10:2,3; 12:14; 13:5

42   Compare Dan. 9:24-27 with Matt. 24:34; Luke 21:24; Rev. 10:2,3; 12:14; 13:5

43   *See the Papers entitled Prophetic Chronology and The Three Passovers of Scripture*

events relevant to the reconstruction of the <u>city of Jerusalem</u> after the decree of Artaxerxes the First, king of Persia.[44]

The second refers to the period that included Herod's dismantling of the Second Temple and rebuilding of the *<u>Third Temple</u>. Soon after, the Prince who is the "Messiah," Jesus Christ, comes on the scene. Thus, the 7x7 + 62x7= 483 year period brings us to AD 25, just before the ministry of Jesus Christ commences. He is crucified <u>after</u> the end of the 69 Weeks.[45]

C. After a delay of a generation, specifically prophesied by Jesus Christ, the 70th Week starts with the Jewish War with Rome, but 'clocks out' "in the midst of the week" when the Roman army destroys Jerusalem, <u>causing the Sacrifice to permanently cease</u> in AD 70. Again, this perfectly meshes with Jesus's Teaching that the *New Covenant* was <u>totally replacing the "stone temple worship system"</u> with <u>Spiritual Worship,</u> wherein the <u>Regenerated human spirit</u> becomes the central focal point from which we worship and *Commune* with the Living God and to which God's Spirit gives us *Intuition* and spiritual Gifts. Collectively, in this way God's Spirit unifies all believers into <u>One Body, the New Testament Church!</u>[46]

D. After this, another delay then ensues, which continues to this day. Viz., according to Scripture, the <u>Jews' desolations will continue until the end (DUE)</u>. That is, "for (because of) the overspreading (ongoing increase) of abominations, he (God) will make it desolate <u>until the *consummation</u>." Essentially, this means that the Second Half of the 70th Week will not resume until the commencement of the Great tribulation Period.

---

44   Dan. 9:25 Cf. Nehemiah 2-13 *See also the Papers entitled Correlating Last Days Scriptures, which includes "Correlating Major Events to Prophecy Chart" and Prophetic Chronology*

45   Dan. 9:26a *See also The Works of Flavius Josephus: Antiquities of the Jews, Transl. By William Whiston, AP&A, Grand Rapids, 1971 Book XV, Ch. XI. P. 1 Note that the Editor's comment there confirms that the Temple the Romans destroyed in AD 70 was the Third Temple.*

46   Dan. 9:26b, 27; 12:7; Matt. 23:37-24:2; 24:34; John 2:19-21; 4:14-24; 14:15-27; 16:13-15; Acts 1:8; 2:1 ff.; Rom. 8:11-17,26,27; 1 Cor. 12-14; Eph. 4:1-16 *See also the Papers entitled Illustrating the "Law of Multiple Fulfillments" and Messiah Figures*

Then, near the end of the Great Tribulation, at the conclusion of the 6th Seal, Christ Himself will come, Catch up (Rapture) the Church in midair and then directly intervene with powerful demonstrations, proving to the remaining Jews that he is the Messiah! Then they will repent and "mourn for him as with an only son," saying "Blessed is he that comes in the Name of the Lord."[47]

E. The original Hebrew word for "consummation" (also rendered as"end" in some translations) is Kalah, Strong's #3617, meaning finish, completion or end, the alternative word being consummation.*[48]

This is an unmistakable reference to the vision of the "Great Statue" in chapter two that Daniel interpreted for king Nebuchadnezzar. At the end of this vision, a huge "Stone from Heaven" comes and strikes the base of the statue, destroying it and then expanding to encompass the entire earth. This, of course, is none other than a prediction of the "Second Coming of Christ," the Messiah, which begins the period we call "The Day of the Lord" (DTL). Know this also: The "Day of the Lord" is a two-sided *Passover* type event, bringing forth both the Salvation of the Saints and the Judgment of the wicked. According to Scripture, this unique event is scheduled to happen during the 6th and 7th Seals of the Great Tribulation Period (GTP).[49]

F. Another significant fact is that in Daniel nine verse twenty-six some versions show an improper syntax which confuses the reader. It should read as follows: "Until the *end there will be war (and) to the *end desolations are determined," that is, until the consummation, viz., the end.[50]

---

47   Zech. 12:9,10; Matt. 23:37-39; Rom. 11:11-32

48   *See The Interlinear Bible by Jay Green, Vol. Three, AP&A, Evansville, IN., 1978*

49   Compare Dan. 2:31-45 and Joel 2,3 with Matt. 21:28-46; Luke 21:20-24; 2 Thess. 1,2 and other *references to the "Day of the Lord." See also Chapter 19: "The Event Sequence of the Second Coming of Jesus Christ" and the Papers Emmanuel 2: God is Dealing with Israel/ the Jews and Facts of Scripture: The Church and the Tribulation, Appendix 1*

50   Dan. 9:26*; 1 Cor. 15:20-28; Rev. 11:15 Cf. Dan. 7:9-28 *The word used for 'end' here is Qets, meaning (to the) extremity, end, infinite or after. Note also that the New American Standard translation of the Bible has the correct syntax for this verse.*

G. Another interesting term we find in verse twenty-seven is the word *Kanaph*, meaning the 'furthest extremity.' The translations vary here, but the idea being conveyed is unmistakable: That <u>God is still very displeased</u> with the ongoing unbelief, rebellion and abominations perpetrated by the Jewish 'patriots' (Zealots). Let the reader note: If you read the chronicles of Flavius Josephus, describing the fanatical and murderous actions of the Zealots during the Jewish War of the first century, I believe you will understand just how bad it was even in the first century! Not only that, the message delivered to Daniel tells us that the Jews' rebellion against God will not stop, but will continue, <u>spreading to the extreme</u>, thereby calling down Judgment upon them again "until the Times of the Gentiles are Fulfilled."

So, for the second time this also fulfills the prophecies of Jeremiah and Ezekiel and other prophets, all of which had already expressed God's extreme displeasure regarding Israel's apostasy in voluminous detail, starting even before Solomon's Temple was destroyed in 586 BC! That is why God's Word, via the Prophets, Jesus and Paul, tells us that <u>the Jews' desolation will continue to the end</u>, not ceasing until Christ Himself returns and deals with them personally! Jesus said that "Your house is left to you as desolate and you will not see me again until you say 'Blessed is he that comes in the Name of the Lord.'"[51]

Not only that, the apostasies of most "mainline Christians" essentially follows the same track as the Jews <u>because of human nature.</u> Yes, all people who base their decisions in life on <u>humanly generated assumptions and doctrines will go the same way</u>. Tragically, they have become unbelievers, even though they may still cling to "vestigial religious beliefs" that were catechized into them as children. However, in the main, they are <u>reprobates, having abdicated any scrap of true Faith</u> they may have had because they love the world, believe like the world and have followed the world and its ways. Of course, the major area by which you can tell this is the case and that reveals <u>what master they are truly serving</u> is their <u>adamant holding to idolatry in nation worship and militarism,</u> both of which depend upon the use of

51   Dan. 9:27 Cf. Jer. 3-31; Ezek. 3-34; Zech. 12:9,10; Matt. 23:37-39; Rom. 11 *See Strongs Exhaustive Concordance of the Bible, Hebrew and Chaldee Dictionary section, #3671 and The Works of Flavius Josephus See also the set of Charts entitled Sequence of Events (leading to the destruction of Jerusalem)*

violence and killing they think is the main source of "salvation" from evil instead of God! [52]

VI. Appendix One: The following chart is a legend for acronyms in text and Fi. One:

Acronym:	Description:	Application/ Reference
AOD	Abomination of (that makes) Desolation	[53]
DTL	The Day of the Lord(sign of the Son of man)*	[54]
DUE	"Desolations Unto theEnd"	[55]
GPT	*"God's Prophetic TimeLine"	*See *Prophetic Chronolgy Two,* Sect. IV
GTP	The Great TribulationPeriod (the Second TOHY period)	[56]
JEP/JR	Jews' Extension Period/Repentance	[57]
MFLa	Messiah Figure/ Lamb	[58]
MFLi	Messiah Figure/ Lion	[59]
SPD	Jews' "Six Point Disciplinary" Process	[60]
TGF	"the Times of the Gentiles are Fulfilled"	[61]

---

52 1 Sam. 2:1-9; 15:22,23; Matt. 5:43-48; 6:24; 23:1 ff.; 26:51,52; Mark 3:4; Luke 9:51-56 (KJV):16:13-15; Rom. 1:16-32; Gal. 1:6-12; 1 John 1-5 See the papers entitled *A Synopsis of Modern Idolatry among 'professing Christians', Are You Sure What You Believe is Truly Christian Doctrine, (the 3 pt. series) Christianity Vs. Religion, Emmanuel (1) and Emmanuel 2*

53 Dan. 11:31-35; Zech. 11:12-14; Matt. 24:14,15; Luke 20:17,18,; 21:24

54 Dan. 2; Mal. 3,4; Msatt. 24: Luke 21; Acts 17:31; Rom. 2:16; 2 Thess. 1,2; 2 Pet.3 *A.K.A. Christ's Second Coming*

55 Dan. 9; Matt. 23:36-39

56 Matt. 24:3-31, 36-51 *(see also next Fn.)*

57 Dan. 12; Zech. 12

58 Isa. 53; Dan. 9; Zech. 9:9,10; 11:12-14

59 Psa. 2, 110, 118:22; Dan.2:34,35,44,45; Matt. 21:42: Luke 20:17,18

60 Dan. 9:2, 24-27

61 Luke 21:24; Rom. 11:25,26

TGNPU	"this generation will not pass until . . ."	[62]
the TOG	"Times of the Gentiles"	[63]
TOTD	"the Tribulation of Those Days"*	[64]
TOHY	the "Three and One-Half Years" (a.k.a. a time, times and dividing of time and 1260 days)	[65]
UNIF	"God's Plan for the Unification of All God's People in Christ"	[66]

---

[62]   Matt. 23:29-39; 24:34 *See also references in the following papers: The Biblical Precept of Mystery Pg. 9, Contextually Comparing the Elements of Prophetic Scripture Sect. IV, Pgs 11-18, Correlating Last Days Scriptures, Pg. 12, The Doctrine of Last Things Pgs 5,6,22, Fulfilment Prophecy Pg. 18, Illustrating the "Law of Multiple Fulfilments" Sect. III, Pg. 9, Prophetic Chronology One, Pg. 8, Fn. #26 and The Three Passovers of Scripture, Pgs 3,14

[63]   John 10:7-16; Rev.11:1-3

[64]   Matt. 24:29-31 *Note that Jesus's statement "the tribulation of those days" refers to that portion of the Great Tribulation Period (GTP) prior to the "Day of te Lord" DTL, viz. Christ's Second Coming. Clue: An easy way to sort this out is to always remember that, during the GTP 'tribulation is man-caused, whereas 'wrath' is God-caused. This is also how we can accurately place the timing of the "Rapture of the Saints" (ROS). See also the book The Church and the Last Days and the papers entitled Correlating Last Days Scriptures and The Doctrine of Last Things

[65]   Dan. 7:25; 11:31-35; 12:6 ff.; Rev. 11:1-3; 12:6,14; 13:5

[66]   Dan. 7:22; John 10:7-16; Eph. 2:11-22

## Chapter 18

The Three "Passovers" of Scripture

God's Paradigm for Salvation and Judgment:

See how in each case, by their own actions, the "vessels fitted unto wrath" confirm God's Way of Salvation and their own sentence of Judgment.

#	Description	Page #
THE THREE PASSOVERS OF SCRIPTURE, God's Paradigm for Salvation and Judgment		
I.	Introduction: The Pictorial Paradigm	
II.	Notice the paralleling conditions	
III.	God's enemy . . . sets the specific means of their own judgment.	
IV.	The Passover is the primary pattern by which God saves the righteous and destroys the enemies.	
V.	Let us examine "the two sides (bipolarity) of Passover."	
VI.	We must also take notice of some "Unique aspects of Passover Chronology"	
VII.	Summary and conclusion	
VIII.	P.S.: Let us "Tell it like it is"	
IX.	Scripture unequivocally reveals that <u>God knows</u> who are the perpetrators of evil	

Introduction:

The pictorial paradigm of the Passover is a wonderful representation of God's Ways of Salvation and Judgment. In studying Scriptural history, you will find three distinct main examples of 'Passover'. May the reader also take note of how the pattern they show to us is mirrored in many other subsequent events, extending even to our modern age.

The First is the Archetypal Hebrew Passover (Passover #1) that reached its fruition in circa 1462 B.C. This was the 'catalyzing event' of emancipation when God used Moses to lead the Hebrew slaves to freedom out of Egypt. At that time God used the evil plan of Pharaoh to exterminate the Hebrews' firstborn sons as the very method of Judgment against Egypt. Upon freeing the Hebrews, God then brought them into the desert where Moses, who had been prepared previously by God in a forty-year sojourn to refine his character to be their human leader and to issue God's special set of Laws we now call the Ten Commandments.[1]

The Second is the Passover of Jesus' Passion Week (Passover #2), climaxing in circa 30 A.D., which was the culmination of Jesus Christ's earthly Ministry when Jesus assumed the role of the "Passover Lamb" Slain from the foundation of the earth.

In the events leading up to Jesus' Crucifixion, we can see the same pattern of God's using the evil plan of the Chief Priests, Pharisees and other Jewish religious leaders to destroy Jesus' influence, because they saw Jesus as a distinct threat to their power base in Jerusalem. Notice that their 'presumption of power' is similar to the way many modern religious leaders' gain their influence: Not from God, but from political finagling! Not only that, the Jews' religious leaders' power was gained illicitly in two ways: Both being against God's law. One was by their continued violation of the Mosaic Laws of Priesthood that was started by the Maccabees which became the "Hasmonean Dynasty." The second was by their cooperation with the Roman occupation system under Herod the Great and his son, Herod Antipas.

---

1   Exodus 3-15; Lev. 23

However, according to the pattern, God used their ambition and hatred against Jesus, the True Messiah, to usher in a inaugurate the *New Covenant* foretold by Jeremiah. Forty years later, *precisely* according to Jesus' Prophecy that "This generation will not pass until these things take place," God's 'axe' fell on the religious leaders' entire corrupt system with Titus' destruction of the Temple and the city of Jerusalem in 70 A.D.[2]

The Third (Passover #3) is the one that many call the "Last Days Passover" because it climaxes in the End Times. However, this Passover begins development even in the first century. Major prophetic 'undercurrent themes' then emerge during the fourth century. Then, according to Scripture, this final Passover reaches its zenith during the Great Tribulation period when Jesus Christ will return in Power and Great Glory. This is the "Great Ingathering" when the True Church will be "Caught Away" and when God's Angelic Army, Jehovah Sabaoth, will summarily execute final Judgment upon the last form of the shape-shifting "Beast," Antichrist's "New World Order!"

According to "God's Higher Law" of "Partial and Multiple Fulfilments," each Passover contains the same basic Two-edged Paradigm of Salvation and Judgment: Salvation to those who have "Endured Faithfully to the End" as Jesus Commanded the Disciples and Judgment (Destruction and damnation) to all the rest who have rejected God's magnanimous offer of Salvation.[3]

This "Last Days Passover" is mentioned in many ways in Scripture. Some of the common terms that identify it are "The Day of the Lord," "Day of Judgment" and the "Great Day." God's "Higher Law" of 'Sowing and Reaping,' which includes the corollary "Law of Choice and Consequence," also mirrors The Passover Theme. In addition, both David and Solomon wrote pithy sayings about the 'just deserts of the wicked' that fall into this same category that some now refer to

---

2   Matt. 23:36; 24:29-34 *See also Passover Sequence Chart*
3   *See the Papers Biblical Symbolism, Section III, Facts of Scripture' Section XII and Appendix 1, Fulfilment prophecy, Sections IV, V and VII, Emmanuel: God is Dealing with His People, Section III: "Exile and Gathering Part Two: The Passover and the End Times," Covenant principles, Section III-C-2, The Higher Laws of God and the book The Church and the Last Days, Chapter 12: "Event Sequence" (of the Second Coming of Jesus Christ), which includes the section entitled "Explanatory of the Term 'The Day of the Lord.'"*

as "Karma." These sayings all apply to the brazen arrogance, idolatry and pride of those who would conspire to dominate, enslave and kill others, revealing also Lucifer/ Satan's 'calling cards:' Pride, exploitation, oppression, hatred and murder. However, we know that God allows these things for a greater purpose, also knowing that the actions of the wicked (secular or 'religious') always "boomerang back" upon them sooner or later![4]

II. Notice the Paralleling conditions in all these signal events: In all three "Pass- overs" we can find common elements that unify the underlying Doctrinal Teaching about God's Conditions for both Salvation and Condemnation that we find interweaved within all Scripture. That is, throughout history, two distinct groups are apparent, as mentioned above: The saved and the damned. No intermediate ground between them exists! This is evidence of the "Higher Law" that states that "Only Two Kingdoms / Masters Exist": One is God's Kingdom *In Christ * where people serve Christ. The only other is all the world system that lies in Satan's hands and in every sinful heart that, by default, serves Satan by serving self.

The "Passover Pattern" includes the following main elements that take place over extended periods of time:

A. God seeks for someone who "Finds Grace" in God's eyes by doing what is righteous when others around them are drawn away into selfish and vain pursuits. God works with that person (E.g., Abraham) to develop a community of faithful persons that seeks God's Way.

B. Yes, God's People are human beings with the same foibles as all the rest. However, the primary difference is that a unique person, a critical mass or 'core group' at one time has responded to God's call on their lives and had worked with God's Plan, receiving manifold Blessings, a Future and Hope.

---

4   Psa. 2, 5, 9, 10, 14, 37; 46, 53-59, 68, 73, 97, 109, 110, 137; Prov. 16:18; Eccl. 10:8; Isa. 24-26; Ezek. 22; Joel 2; Amos 6,8,9; Mic. 3; Nahum 1; Matt. 24; Luke 21;John 10:10; Gal. 6:8; 2 Thess. 1:3-10; 2 Pet. 3:7-18; Jude 3 ff. *See also Section IV-B below, and Footnote #18*

C. God's People have apostatized and fallen away from their relationship to God by trusting human devices (Idolatry), thus losing their God-given power and influence. Thus, they have lapsed into a state of servitude in the world, requiring an act of Divine Power to free them. Not only that, the enemy (Satan) incites "Evil thoughts" and plans to destroy God's People to arise in those who would enslave them.

D. God's Power intervenes in a miraculous way to deliver His People and brings them once again 'under the Yoke' of Covenantal Relationship.

E. God's Power neutralizes or destroys the worldly power enslaving, exploiting and conspiring to kill God's People. This God does in an unmistakable demonstration of God's Superior might and command of History.[6]

III. It is notable in all three Passover cases listed above that God's enemy actually set the specific means of their own Judgment expressed in their own statements andactions!

Let us review: In the first it was Pharaoh's plan to exterminate the firstborn sons of all the Hebrews. In Jesus' time on earth, the Jewish religious leaders (Priests, Pharisees, Sadducees and Lawyers) hated Jesus so much that they used Caiaphas' 'Prophecy' of 'one man to die for the Nation' to 'set Jesus up for crucifixion' thereby also sealing their fate as well as that of Jerusalem in AD 70.[7]

In the Last Days it is Antichrists' psychotic agenda of extermination of large populations such as the U.N.'s "Agenda 21." This Luciferian plan is being carried out by an entity they call "The New World Order," from the Latin Phrase "Novus Ordo Seclorum" found on the back of the U.S. $1 Bill under the picture of the truncated Pyramid, another occult symbol. These symbols can all be traced to occult organizations that go back many centuries, even as far as "The Tower of Babel," the

---

6 *Notice the sequence in points C to E are repeated several times in the book of Judges in the Old Testament. Remember also that Paul wrote the Corinthians that the things that were chronicled in the Old Testament were put there for our admonition so that we can learn from their (the Hebrew Nation that became ancient Israel) experiences. 1 Cor. 10; Cf. Ezek. 38:10*

7 *Exodus 12; John 11:49-53 Cf. Matt. 23,24; Psa 118:22; Isa. 28:16; Jer. 2-10; Ezek. 24:21-27*

founding of the Empire of Babylon, which John refers to many times in the *Apocalypse*. All occult entities have come into being because of Lucifer (Satan or the Devil) and his insane hatred of God and of God's bringing man to earth, a territory he claims. He even tempted Christ using this claim.[8]

Of course, the main goal of Satan (alias, Antichrist) is world domination. He also recruits many operatives from the ranks of government officials, corporation executives, scientists, educators, the medical establishment, bankers and religious leaders. Many belong to satanic cult organizations like "Skull & Bones" and the higher orders of Freemasonry. They all work for Antichrist, which is nothing more than a mask or facade Satan uses to hide his activity, hence the term 'occult.' In essence, all occult figures and operatives worship Satan, thus sealing their destiny. In one of their documents planning 9/11 as a Coup D'etat to enslave America they state that they needed a "Catalyzing event" like a *new* "Pearl Harbor." However, God sees it as a "New Passover."

IV. The Passover is the primary Pattern by which God saves the righteous and destroys the enemies. Note again that <u>God uses the evil thoughts and plans of the enemy</u> against them to eventually destroy those who hate God and God's People. It is also a very recognizable characteristic which we can identify in Scripture. This pattern occurs in several places in addition to the main three:

A. Consider the evidence, first in the Old Testament:

- Isaiah's proclamations regarding the fate of Babylon, Tyre and other nations who, in their lust to control, violate the laws of nature God put in place to maintain order.[9]

- God's categoric condemnation revealed to Jeremiah that "The false gods that have not made the heavens and the earth will perish from the earth."[10]

---

8   *Matt. 4:1-1-; Luke 4:1-13; 10:18; Rev. 12-20 Cf. Isa. 14; Ezek. 28, 38 Note also that in Scripture, "Babylon," "Gog and Magog" and "Tyre" are spiritual symbols referring to occult sources or principalities that incite rebellion against God. See also Glossary of Terms' entry *(the archetype of the) Garden* See also the Paper A Biblical Disclosure of Antichrist*

9   Isa. 14-30

10   Jer. 10

- Examine Ezekiel's succinct chronicling of the intertwined fates of Israel ("Israel" is also a general prophetic moniker for God's People) and the "king of Babylon," which also carries other prophetic pseudonyms such as "Gog and *Magog," "king of Tyre" and the "Dragon" (Pharaoh, the king of Egypt).[11]

- Think about Habakkuk's vision that highlights the <u>vivid contrast</u> between those whose pride causes them to oppress others and those whose Faith acts a protective barrier curbing their lust.[12]

- God's Judgment "turned the tables" on the evil Haman, enemy of the Jewish people in Persia who conspired to commit genocide.[13]

- Daniel's Prophetic Interpretation concerning the destruction of the Great Statue of Nebuchadnezzar.[14]

B. In the New Testament era we have:

- Jesus' Christ's Statements about the destruction of those who reject God's True Messiah, Jesus Christ.[15]

- Consider Paul's description of Jesus' Second Coming "With flaming fire, taking vengeance on those who do not obey the Gospel of Christ."[16]

- John's Vision of *Apocalypse* contains much more detail. In *Apocalypse* we can see 'two sides' of the Passover Paradigm: Destruction and Salvation, mirrored in vivid symbolism:

These are the "Second Beast" and the "Scarlet woman riding on the beast" on one side and the <u>Son of God riding on the White Steed</u> coming to the rescue, executing judgment on the other side. See how God "sets them up like ducks in a shooting gallery" and knocks them

---

11   Ezek. 17, 21, 28, 29, 38* Cf. Rev. 13 *Magog is also the secret moniker for a well-known ex-President that belongs to the Satanic Cult of "Skull& Bones"
12   Hab. 2
13   Esther 1-10
14   Daniel 2
15   Matt. 21:42-46; 24:1,2; 26:52; 27:19-25; Luke 19:41-48; 20:17,18; 21:5,6
16   2 Thess. 1,2

down, Glorifying His Salvation of the Faithful who recognize the Truth and Repent.[17]

Compare all the accounts and you will see the remarkable truth concerning the eventual fate of those who conspire to dominate the world! Think about what will happen to all those who work for Satan to 'destroy the earth.' Yes, God's Word teaches that all the so-called elite 'destroyers of the world' will be destroyed themselves in a similar manner that they inflicted it on others!

Some already have "done themselves in" or have been 'judged' in this world, like Hitler and many of the Nazis after World War II because of the Holocaust. This generally follows God's "law of Karma" (Sowing and Reaping) we see throughout Scripture.[18]

However, God sees everything Yes, God sees all the figures down through history which never repented, having exploited and exterminated populations, created depressions, planned world wars and engineered 9/11 and other "False Flag events." Many think they have "gotten away with it," however, they will all fall under God's Wrath at the Judgment. God revealed a preview to Ezekiel that all these 'warlord type' figures will all be lying in Hell with their swords beside them.[19]

V. Let us examine the "two sides (bipolarity) of Passover" (the 'Down side' and the 'Up side') and the amazing correlation between 911 and Prophecy:

This illustrates God's Sovereignty and command of history: Yes God allows evil events to happen, but this is all part of a greater "overall Master Plan" in which the Passover Paradigm is a central theme. We can see it in the "Kenosis Trail" where Christ was first humiliated (by living in human form and being crucified) and then Glorified to Blaze the Trail of New Covenant Salvation in those who receive His Sacrifice and Follow His Way as Disciples.[20]

---

17   Rev. 11:15-19; 19:1 f. Cf. Jer. 10:11; Joel 2

18   Deut. 32:1 ff.; Psa. 1:1 ff.; 7:11-16; 94:13; Prov. 26:27; Isa. 61:1 f.; Mark 9:42-50; Luke 21:20-22; Rom. 12:19-21; Gal. 6:7,8; Rev. 12-21

19   Ezek. 21:1 ff.; 32:17-32 Cf. Isa. 14; Ezek. 28; Rev. 19:11-21; 20:7-15; 21:8

20   *See Glossary of Terms' entry *Kenosis**

Based upon their <u>choices</u>, God saves the ones who cooperate and judges all the others, who, as Paul declares, are "Vessels fitted unto Wrath." Paul also tells us that God has interwoven a second level of 'duality' in dealing with His People, within the paradigm of Salvation itself, linking the "Great Apostasy" with the down side and those who "Endure unto the end" with the up side. Again, <u>you decide</u> which 'side' you are on <u>by your choices</u>! This reinforces the "Universal Law of Choice and Consequence." Notice the "bipolar" nature of these spiritual truths! Enfolded in this is the fact that the "Great Apostasy" of the church (i.e., the neutralization of its influence) is the primary antecedent cause of the rise of Antichrist.[21]

The <u>biblical chronology</u> of the "Tribulation Period" events show us clearly that the 'Sixth Seal' is when Christ will return. "<u>After</u> the Tribulation of those days," Christ will appear in the sky in full view of the entire world and "Gather in" the Saints from the four winds. This is the biblical timing of the "Rapture." Then, at the breaking of the 'Seventh seal,' Christ will begin the execution of Judgment upon the Antichrist system of the New World Order.[22]

Let us now note some very interesting facts about all 'deep' or "Catalyzing Events" that parallel the nature of Passover. As we have seen, comparing to Scripture, we can see that both are bidirectional in nature, having a 'Down side' and an 'up side.' True Believers can take comfort in the fact that, even though God permits such terrible things to happen, the Company of the Faithful knows the deeper underlying truth that everyone who worships the True Living God acknowledges: "All things work out for good to those who Love God..."

Moreover, <u>IF</u> we are living by Faith and not sight, God can use negative events in our lives as an opportunity for God's Spirit to <u>Transform our thinking.</u> Wise Solomon wrote that he wanted God to "Turn my heart, O Lord, like Rivers of water."[23] However, to take

---

21   *Romans 1:18 ff.; 5:8 ff.; 9:17-23; 2 Thess. 1:4-2:12 See also the Papers entitled A Biblical Disclosure of Antichrist and Destiny and Free Will, the book Spiritual Guidelines for Restoration, Chapter 20, Spiritual Law #10 and the book The Church in the Last Days, Chapter 12, "The Event Sequence"*

22   Matt. 24:29-31; 2 Thess. 1:7.f

23   Prov. 21:1

advantage of this, you must first embrace change and seek to be Conformed unto the image of Christ.

Consider the amazing correlation between 911 and Prophecy: The 9/11 attack which destroyed the Twin Towers in N.Y.C. is a "Catalyzing Event" that also closely parallels specific details in Scripture:

Consider the following significant references to Antichrist's latter-day takeover that fit perfectly with the modus operandi of The New World Order: One, Daniel's Prophecy of the Great Statue and the "Fourth Beast." Two, Christ's chilling warning of future Judgment quoted above that was given as a part of Jesus' pointed castigation of the Jewish religious leaders. A Third can be found in Paul's description of the "Lawless one" or "man of sin." The Fourth is the reference to "Fervent Heat" in Peter's Second Epistle and the Fifth can be found in John's *Apocalypse*. In particular, in the last reference, notice how the Scripture perfectly describes Antichrist's crafty weapons that constitute a Coup D'etat: Deception, "lying wonders" and the imposition of "the Mark of the Beast." The latter one is the Global Economic Controls, starting with "currency control," which gives the Antichrist system the 'Carte Blanche' whereby they can regulate all transactions of buying and selling (the credit system managed by super computers).[24]

Now, compare the abovementioned Prophetic Scriptures to 911, taking notice of two key characteristic elements of the Twin Towers' destruction: One is in their Pulverization and the second is the amazing residue of molten steel they found at the bottom of the rubble. This amazing degree of complete destruction was brought about by one of the New World Order's carefully occluded high-tech 'weapons of mass destruction:' Computer-timed "Controlled Demolition Technology" techniques, coupled with the use of a substance known as military grade "Nano-Thermate." Nano-Thermate is an amazingly effective incendiary agent which, when used with explosives, creates such a "fervent heat" (up to 5100 degrees' F.!) that it vaporizes solid steel and pulverizes the rest into a fine 'talcum powder' like dust! It also leaves 'telltale' residues of aluminum oxide and 'pockets of liquid steel' that

---

24   1) Dan. 2:31-45; 7:7 ff.; 2) Matt. 21:42-26; 3) 2 Thess. 2:3-12; 4) 2 Pet. 3:9-13; 5) Rev. 13:11-18 Cf. Psa. 118:22; Isa. 28:14-22; Luke 20:17,18

they found <u>still</u> <u>molten</u> under the rubble of the Twin Towers six weeks later!

Moreover, <u>Controlled Demolition technology</u> was the main cause of the pulverization and molten residue. It is also the <u>only reason why</u> the Towers fell straight down *precisely into their foundations/ footprint* with the <u>speed of gravity in free fall</u>!

Of course, you can also easily see why they 'had to destroy' Bldg. Seven the same way to destroy the evidence, since it had housed the 'control center of operations' during the event. Essentially, <u>all</u> the planes were remotely controlled <u>military drones</u>, the "stories" about the 'airliners,' 'hijackers' and the 'passengers' were fabrications full of inconsistencies and the fire was a diversion. Despite all this, any engineer worth their salt knows that the laws of physics concerning these structures do not allow for any steel building built like they were to be brought down by fire alone. In the third reference in Paul's second letter to the Thessalonians cited above, he names Antichrist as the "man of sin" or "lawless one."

Both these monikers relate to the brazen anarchistic arrogance of those who consider themselves to be "above the law." This also fits the fifth reference which depicts the acts of the "lawless bankers' cartel" which puts in place the <u>economic dictatorship</u> of Antichrist that regulates all transactions, thereby enslaving the world. Yet, on the other side of the coin, because of their intransigent unrepentant arrogance and blatant disregard for human life, they have also 'sealed their fate' and will be held to answer before Almighty God just like their instigator, Lucifer/ Satan, at the end of the "Tribulation Period." The fourth reference fits another example of the World's evil rulers setting God's future Judgment upon themselves, where the "Elements will melt with fervent heat."[25]

The future destruction of their empire that God describes in Prophecy is so complete that the only thing that remains is "like the chaff of the summer threshing floors." Jesus said "Upon whomsoever it (the Stone) falls, it will grind him to powder." Not only that, Scripture tells us that <u>God's future Judgment</u> of all the "vessels fitted unto wrath," including those who perpetrated   this heinous crime against the

---

25   *See the book The Church in the Last Days*

American people, was <u>already</u> in God's perfect foreknowledge from the beginning! As we have already seen in prophecies, God's Spirit has told us in advance about the <u>specific details of the destruction of God's enemies</u> when Jesus Christ, the "Stone not made with hands," will annihilate Antichrist and its N.W.O. empire![26]

Review Summary: In particular, let us note again that the way the Twin Towers were destroyed on 9/11 point directly to the End-Time Prophecies in Daniel concerning the details of the Great Statue's destruction, Jesus Christ's pointed statements about "Being <u>ground up to powder</u>" (i.e., <u>pulverization</u>) and Peter's prophecy about "Elements melting with fervent heat." These Scriptures all apply to God's sure Judgment and destruction of the World System and all perpetrators of 'evil plans' to destroy and dominate the world. Both these prophecies refer to what will transpire during a very special Event we call the Second Coming of Christ.[27] In his second letter to the Thessalonians, Paul points to another aspect which also accompanies Antichrist's takeover: The widespread disseminations of "<u>strong</u> <u>delusion to believe a lie</u>," which amounts to <u>mass deception.</u> They accomplish this by using the corporate media, which is owned by agents of Antichrist. Therefore, it acts in deliberate complicity with the elite controllers. That is how they dupe, demoralize and brainwash the masses into believing a Big Lie. Of course, one of the most outrageously ludicrous Big Lies is telling the American people that some religious fanatic living in a cave has caused these things![28]

However, <u>God knows who the real perpetrators are,</u> and Believe Scripture, they will not escape God's Wrath! They have not fooled at least half of the people in New York City either! Remember what the Scripture says about those who think they can sin with impunity and not face God's judgment or outwit God and 'get away' with sin: "Your sin will find you out." There will be no place left for them to hide when Christ comes.[29]

---

26   *In particular, compare Dan. 2:35, noticing the description of the destruction, with Matt. 21:44 See also Romans 9:17-23, keeping in mind that God's perfect foreknowledge is not the same as the "Calvinistic' misinterpretation of "predestination." See the Paper Destiny and Free Will*

27   Dan. 2:34,35, 44,45; Matt. 21:42-46; Luke 20:17,18

28   *2 Thess. 2:7-12 Cf. Rom. 1:18-32 *Note that God is not the source of evil or deception, but allows these things to happen to fulfill prophecies.*

29   Rev. 8-11, 14-21

Those who have Faith know that God will make things right eventually. Remember what Jesus and Paul said: "He that endures to the end will be Saved" and "Leave place unto wrath, for it is written 'Vengeance is Mine, says the Lord.'"[30]

VI. We must also take notice of some "Unique aspects of Passover Chronology": In God's Grand Master Plan depicted in Scripture, some very unusual "timing aspects" cannot be ignored if we, as God's People, are to understand what is going on and not get disillusioned or succumb to "failed expectations." As such, the "Relative Timing" of elements within the Passover Paradigm is very significant.

A. To understand this better, let us now look at the Passover Paradigm as a "Play" that contains Three Acts.

Act One is the "perpetration of evil" phase which also may contain elements of God's own peoples' apostasy that God is planning to expunge by discipline.

Act Two is the "Salvation of God's People" Phase, which we also need to clearly understand is taking place on a variety of different levels, among them the Spiritual, Attitudinal and finally, the Physical.

Act Three is the phase where God makes all things right: The "Judgment and punishment of evildoers," which is always the final in the series.

In particular, we must always keep in mind that, after the first act and before the last act, God progressively refines, purifies and perfects a Godly *Remnant* from among "God's people" in manifold ways. They are those who have responded to God's Call through various trials, afflictions and persecutions, emerging from them mature and stronger and "sufficient for the Master's use."[31]

That is why the "Passover Paradigm" is so important, for it also serves as an excellent test of faithfulness and commitment to perseverance, no matter what happens, over the long haul of life and even extending to

---

30   Matt. 24:13; Rom. 12:19-21
31   Psa. 78; Isa. 6, 30, 63; Jer. 31 *See the Paper Emmanuel: God is Dealing with His People*

many generations of the faithful.[32] Always know that God's Timing is not like ours! God does not 'settle accounts' every Friday. Note Jesus' statement to the workers sent into the Vineyard. It all hinges on the fact that <u>God is the owner</u> and not us![33]

Not only that, because of God's Great Mercy, He gives people more than enough time to make the right decisions and Repent. However, we must also realize that God has set a "deadline" in place that, beyond that point, we may not be able to "Find a place of repentance," like Esau.[34]

Another aspect is that those who are righteous must often suffer because of the unrepentant sin of others over extended periods. This is a given, about which many Christians are not properly taught. That is also why God cautions us to develop that aspect of Agape Love that is called *The Patience of the Saints,* that indispensable characteristic that the writer calls "Faith-based Pacifism." God's Promise still remains, however, that "All things work together for those who Love God..." Not only that, those whose Faith is secure know that God <u>will eventually make all things right.</u>[35]

B. Let us examine the specifics of timing within the three main Passovers.

1. In the First Archetypal Passover, Act One lasts more than four centuries when the Hebrew people were in Egypt, most of that time being as slaves.

Act Two, the "Salvation Phase," takes only a very short time, possibly only weeks, after which the Hebrew people emerge emancipated from Egypt and enter the wilderness. However, their true complete "Salvation" was not even close to being complete at that time. Only the temporal physical deliverance from bondage was evident then and many trials, afflictions and tests awaited them. That is what the "Wilderness Experience" is all about, and it applies to Christians as well!

---

32   See Hebrews 11
33   Matt. 20; 2 Pet. 3:9
34   Heb. 12:14-17
35   Luke 21:15-19; Rom.5:1-5; 8:23-28; Heb. 10:26-39; Rev. 12:10,11; 13:10

In Act Three, at the Red Sea crossing, God summarily judges and dispatches Pharaoh (the Dragon) and his army. Of course, this also prefigures the end time destruction of Antichrist.[36]

2. In the Second Passover, the Passover of Christ's Passion, "the Jews" had been in a state of apostasy for more than nine centuries, with the development of the *New Covenant* being 'in the wings' for six centuries.

Their 'perpetration of evil' had been exposed by the Prophets, many of whom were murdered by their religious leaders. During the Passion Week, Jesus pointedly castigated the Jewish religious leaders and pronounced God's sentence of impending judgment of evil acts that dated "From Abel to Zecharias," all being levied upon that generation.

The final act of Act One was their crucifying Jesus. Of course, this simultaneously was the fulfillment of Isaiah's Prophecy concerning the "Suffering Servant Messiah figure."[37]

Act Two, the Salvation Phase, is the institution of the New Covenant's Terms which commenced with Jesus' inaugural Sermon at Nazareth and was sealed the moment Jesus said "It is Finished" and dismissed His Spirit on the Cross. This Phase that continues today is God's open invitation period that we call the "Age of Grace."[38] Act Three (the judgment phase) of this Passover took place in AD 70 with Titus' destruction of Jerusalem and the Temple according to Jesus precise statement. The "Salvation Phase" of this Passover also extends into the Third Passover period.[39]

3. Concerning the Third Passover period, we can see the following prophetic elements that span all ages:

In Act One Prophecies identify the 'perpetrator' for being the "fourth Beast" by Daniel and the "Second Beast" and the "Scarlet Woman riding on the beast" by John. It is the 'reinvented Roman Empire,' elements of which also have gone by other pseudonyms, 'shape-shifting' itself over

---

36 Exodus 3-15; Ezek. 29:3 f. *See also* Glossary of Terms' entry *Affliction*

37 Isa. 52:13-53:12; Matt. 23:35; Luke 11:51 See also the Paper entitled *The Messiah Figures and the set of Charts entitled Catalogue of Events which includes the Passover Sequence Chart, which covers the details of Jesus' passion Week*

38 Jer. 31:31-34; Matt. 26:26-29; Luke 22:15-20; John 19:30; Heb. 1,7-10

39 Isa. 53; Jer. 31; Matt. 23,24

time: These are the Roman Catholic Church (RCC), the Holy Roman Empire (H.R.E. or 'western' Roman Empire), the Byzantine Empire (the 'eastern Roman Empire), the Protestant Church system (nation-oriented part of the 'Scarlet Woman'), the New World Order and the Antichrist system.

It came on the scene in AD 325 with Emperor Constantine's takeover of the Early Church's affairs at the Synod of Nicea. It was crystallized into an Empire, based upon a flawed manifesto, Augustine's *the City of God* (426), by the Pope Leo the Great (440-461).[40]

The Second Act, the Salvation of God, is a multifaceted epic that takes place on different levels, as mentioned above. On one hand, throughout the intervening centuries, you have God's nurturing of the True Church, the *Body of Christ.* On the other hand (remember the 'bipolar' nature of Passover), in contrast, we have God's developing judgment sequence upon the "Scarlet Woman."

Still, the suffering of God's servants and the True Church will continue into the future, with *The Patience of the Saints* being the watchword.

In the future, the last Act three is commenced at the "Seventh Seal" during the "Great Tribulation Period" (G.T.P.) as a part of Christ's Second Coming![41]

VII. Summary and Conclusion: The Three Passovers of Scripture all prefigure God's Way of both Salvation and Condemnation (Judgment).

God's Word is clear: Every person has been given free will and an opportunity to make a choice in receiving God's Salvation. However, only those who truly receive Christ, the only True Messiah, and follow Christ faithfully to the end, will receive a Heavenly inheritance in the *Kingdom of Heaven* and be delivered from the ultimate dark destiny and punishment that was only created for the Devil and his angels.[42]

---

40   See the Paper entitled *A Biblical Disclosure of Antichrist*, the book *Spiritual Guidelines for Restoration*, "Historical Review" section and Appendix C: "Historical Timeline Chart

41   See the book *The Church in the Last Days* and the Paper *Facts of Scripture: The Church and the Tribulation*

42   Matt. 24:13; John 10:27; Acts 20:17 ff.; Rom. 8; Col. 1:13,14; 2 Tim. 1-4; Heb. 10:26-39; 1 Pet. 1:1 ff.; 2 Pet. 1:2-11

Notice in particular the remonstration Jesus issued to the Disciples against the use of force while being arrested in the Garden of Gethsemane. What Jesus says is that all those who advocate or use deadly force against others will regret it![43]

The exalted Wisdom of the New Covenant inaugurated by Jesus Christ sees everything as through the *Lens of Jesus Christ. * Once we begin seeing through the Eyes of Jesus, we can also see that All those who disobey Christ and the True Gospel (including those who use or advocate deadly force intending to kill other human beings) and remain unrepentant, are part of the world. As such, they will be judged with Satan, notably those who have conspired with the archenemy of souls to destroy God's Earth and God's People.[44]

VIII. P.S.: Let us "Tell it like it is!" With regard to recent events, especially of the last century, it is simultaneously interesting and tragic to note the 'Twilight-Zone' type responses you frequently get when you finally find the truth and confront people with the truth about "deep events," such as Pearl Harbor, the Kennedy assassination and 911. It parallels the responses you get from 'religious people' who have been indoctrinated in false doctrines all their lives. Yet it makes you think: "I cannot believe that people could be that stupid" to believe the outlandish lies they continue to 'spin' regarding these events! The explanation is found in a common factor that applies to both: Brainwashing, a procedure that totalitarian societies frequently use to maintain control of their 'subjects' and keep them as docile slaves of the state. The worst part is that Americans have been led astray to believe that we live in a "free country" and that things like brainwashing, torture, mind control using psychotropic drugs, 'gulag-style prisons' and regimented conformity only exist in places like North Korea and Red China. Guess again.[45]

The unvarnished truth is that the American people have been subjected to long-term brainwashing concocted by the mass media that has been intentionally calculated to produce a "Conditioned

---

43   Matt. 26:52 Cf. Matt. 5:43-48; Luke 9:51-56
44   2 Thess. 1:3-12; Heb. 10:26-39; Rev. 21:6-8
45   *See the Paper Christianity Versus Religion*

Response," a state of mind that avoids the harsh truth about an event, preferring to believe disingenuous fables. It is the same method that corporation advertisers use to sell products and that the entertainment industry does, using movies as propaganda.[46]

Another large part of this brainwashing scheme is the "induced hysteria" that is applied by reports of the event they inflame to 'herd people' into a preconceived response that benefits the elite controllers. Above all, war is a huge moneymaker that Banks and multinational corporations use to profiteer from both sides! Rothschild pioneered this evil pattern during the war of 1812 and the Rockefeller family used it to make fabulous profits by selling oil to both sides in both world wars.

The psychosis regarding deep events also exists because of incredulity: I.e., in their 'Alice in Wonderland' false reality, they apparently 'just cannot conceive' that the Government is capable of such crimes: Wake up folks, they have, they are and they continue to be! Watch the documentaries containing the original archival footage and hear the testimony of the witnesses that spoke during and immediately after these events transpired and the evidence is plain and clear! The Government is lying!

Consider also the ubiquitous lies surrounding the currently manufactured "Corona Virus Event."

What is also clear is that we are seeing John's Prophecy about the Antichrist recorded in the *Apocalypse* coming true right before our eyes. Clue: The "Antichrist" is not just a man, it is a system! One particular aspect of this Antichrist system of which we must take special note, is that it is not a "political dictatorship" but an "Economic Dictatorship" using currency control by a syndicate/coven of Thirteen Global Central Banks. The cult-based elite cabal which controls them also controls the economic systems of the entire world. Verily, this is what John saw as the "Second Beast" and the entity we call Antichrist.[47]

Their upper echelon leaders are "hard-core" Satan worshipers and megalomaniacal psychotics who have proven that they will kill

---

46   See the 1929 book Propaganda by Edward Bernays
47   Rev. 13:9-18

Presidents in broad daylight and commit mass murder without blinking an eye to keep their power![48]

Mayer Rothschild once boasted that "If the banks control the currency, I care not what laws they enact." This "Federal Reserve" system was enacted in December 21, 1913, disguised as a "banking reform law" signed into law by President Woodrow Wilson. So, with the device of currency control, in conjunction with variable <u>Fractional Reserve Banking tactics,</u> the Central Bank can control <u>all other aspects</u> of the economy and bypass any "political interference."[49][798]

Note also that "the FED" is <u>not a 'federal government agency'</u> at all, but a <u>private bank</u> that is not subject to direct control by *any* government agency. This places unknown people that are not elected or appointed by the American people, many of them in <u>foreign countries,</u> in the driver's seat to control <u>American policy decisions</u> like the prime interest rate! Not only that, their decisions are essentially "above the law" of either congress or the Presidency! Now think about what could be the "lawless one."[50]

Then we have the unconstitutional income tax that reaches into the pockets of millions to pay the <u>interest payments</u> on the Federal Reserve Notes most people mistakenly think for being 'money.'

The banksters also promote the "credit system" at all levels (national, corporate and individual) that lures the unsuspecting into the deep black hole of <u>debt.</u> The fostering of massive debt is another unseen <u>control mechanism,</u> making slaves of those who are ensnared by it. Solomon warned against being indebted.[51]

Yet, for a century now these controls have been integrated into the 'ordinary business landscape' by using "fiat currency" via government decrees they have dictated in advance. Thus, the American people do not even know what is causing all these things because the elite controllers own the media and the politicians are paid off to tell them lies. So,

---

48   *See the Papers A Biblical Disclosure of Antichrist, A Profile of Antichrist and What is Collectivism?*

49   *The "Fractional Reserve" device is the practice of only requiring banks to keep a 'fraction' of the depositor's 'cash' on hand, while concurrently tallying 'on paper' or in computer files, the full amount of value they do not actually possess, but with which they nonetheless grant loans.*

50   2 Thess. 2:3-12; Rev. 13:9-18

51   Prov. 22:7

since 1913, these shadowy figures have deliberately manipulated the economy at will, extending credit (expanding the money supply) or denying credit (shrinking the money supply).

Of course that is how they create "booms and busts," including the "Panic" of 1907 that was deliberately caused so that they could get the Federal Reserve Act passed! They also instigated the Stock market crash of 1929 and the "Great Depression." Allied with the 'fractional reserve tactic' is the "Midas Touch," the little known Bankers' device that produces money out of thin air simply by granting loans or by making money 'disappear' by denying loans.

Worse yet, the election process has been corrupted by the semi-secret elitist "kingmaker" organizations, like the Council on Foreign Relations (CFR) and the "Bilderberger Group," both of which the elite controllers use to "select" the candidates for major political offices, especially those who run for U. S. President. Then we have the 'toadies' that also aid in this rape of the world to round out the picture: The Wall street investment houses and Multinational Corporations which include the mainstream media that they own and control.[52]

Beyond this, knowing the existence of "Agenda 21," It should be no surprise that the psychotic operatives of the "New World Order" have, since the mid twentieth century, been surreptitiously using Government agencies and government-sponsored entities against us that are supposed to be used to protect us!

These include the U.S. military, the CIA, the pseudoscientific propagandists, NASA, the EPA and the FDA, various and sundry corporations and the telecommunications industry that is used by the NSA. The only logical conclusion that explains their obvious secrecy, lying statements and intransigence is that an "unknown Agenda" exists that they are protecting that is harmful to the American people.

If it were not, they would be telling us the truth. However, it appears that they are actively working with major pharmaceutical corporations to systematically 'drug down' and poison the American people! In fact, this poisoning has also been going on in at least 14 other countries as well.

---

52 *For more reading on this subject see the book The Creature from Jekyll Island by G. Edward Griffin*

They do this in many ways:[53]

1. By using Fluoride compounds similar to "Prozac" in the water supplies of more than 60% of the major cities.

2. The widespread marketing of 'Antidepressants' that cause suicidal and homicidal urges.

3. Countrywide Aerial Chemical spraying of biological agents and other chemical compounds (Chemtrails) into the atmosphere, including Barium, which cause asthma, bronchitis, memory loss and other 'flu-like' symptoms.

4. They are trying to force people to take <u>vaccinations containing poisonous agents</u> like mercury, aluminum and arsenic that have been linked with 'engineered outbreaks' of polio, autism, influenza, measles and now, the "Corona Virus."

5. They are marketing food products laced with chemical additives and animal hormones as well as <u>Genetically modified </u>(GMO) 'foods' that they use as a weapon to alter our DNA.

Be that as it may to know these things, <u>IF</u> you are a true Christian, you should know that <u>our real battle is in the spiritual realm</u>. We may or may not be able to stop all these things from affecting us. Yes, we should inform others to these dangers and do everything we can within the legal process to protect ourselves from this onslaught of filth, poison, lies and evil. However, "We wrestle not with flesh and blood but with (Satanic) Principalities and Powers, the rulers that control the darkness (evil) that saturates the World System."

Moreover, we must take the High Road and not depend upon human methods or to resist these evils in our own strength. Yes, it is a difficult path to negotiate, but know that Jesus also warned us to be "Wise as serpents, but harmless as doves." Always remember that God's Word and the <u>Truth</u> are our primary weapons, knowing also that "The pen is mightier than the sword." Notice also that they, like the Devil they work for, cannot stand exposure to scrutiny for the light always

---

53   *See the papers A Biblical Disclosure of Antichrist and What is Collectivism?*

overcomes darkness. Also remember that God's Word tells us that our Faith in God and the Power of Love will eventually overcome evil.[54]

IX. Scripture unequivocally reveals that <u>God knows</u> who are the perpetrators of evil, who they work for (Lucifer or Satan) and exactly what they are doing.

They may think they can hide in their "ivory towers" and do these things with impunity, disregarding the welfare of the American people. They know they are breaking the law, even though they have <u>sworn oaths to obey</u> the Constitution, the "Supreme Law of the Land," yet they flagrantly ignore it.

However, they <u>will not escape God's Wrath</u>: Most assuredly, they will be <u>held</u> <u>accountable for their actions</u> at the "Great White Throne" Judgment!

The "Passover-like" vengeance that God has ready, waiting for them, will be 'tailor- made' to fit their presumptive arrogance, egregious malice and wanton disregard for human life![55]

Yes, <u>right now</u> Antichrist is 'alive and well' using the secular arm of the "False Prophet" (the corporate media) to animate the 'living image' that speaks fluently with "the voice of the Dragon." Its "lying Wonders" are orchestrated by shadowy Luciferian operatives like the 'man behind the curtain' in *the Wizard of Oz.*

Their deft use of propaganda over decades of time, has developed the deep level of brainwashing, manipulation and demoralization that we now see in the American public. Consequently, those who believe the media's lies are acting like captivated 'huddled masses' that live in a man-made fog of contrived preposterous <u>lies</u>.[56] Lest we forget, <u>the 'religious arm' of the "False Prophet"</u> also does their nefarious part for Antichrist by religious leaders' sycophantic bolstering of a falsely based blind patriotism that reveals its alliance with the state. Indeed, many religious leaders, like Paul tells us, are Satanic operatives that worship false gods in secret imagery like the Priests that Ezekiel wrote about.

---

54   Matt. 5:43-48; 10:16; 26:52; Luke 22:53; John 1:1-5; 16:33; Rom. 12:19-21; 2 Cor. 10:3-6; Eph. 6:12
55   Isa. 14:12-15; 24:17-23; 66:4,22-24; Jer. 10:11; Rom. 1:18-32; 3:10-18; Rev. 11:15-18
56   Rev. 13:12-18

Their "corporation church system" is also a 'dead ringer' for the "Scarlet Woman" that John depicts in the *Apocalypse* for being "in cahoots" with the 'Beast' with which she fornicates.[57]

If you truly are a Christian, you know you cannot be a part of this. God's Word is unmistakable: You must make the harsh decisions that have to be made if you expect God to 'save you.' This means maintaining a distinct separation from the world system (which includes "religion") in all aspects of your life, private and public, despite cost.

Above all, the bedrock of our Faith is rooted in God's Power, God's Command of history and the assurance and knowledge that "All things will (eventually) work out for good IF you Love God." Indeed, God's Word declares that you are unable to follow Christ and the world concurrently, for "Without holiness, you will never see the Lord."[58]

Reread the New Testament with an open mind, listening to the Holy Spirit's "still small voice" of Truth and trust God's Living Word, Jesus Christ, not the platitudes of apostates who are allied with Antichrist.[59]

Your friend and fellow servant in Christ, I remain,
Pastor David J. Bowers

---

57   Ezek. 8; 2 Cor. 11:12-15; Rev. 17:1 ff. *See also the Paper Authority and Conscience, also found in the writer's book Jesus' Way, Appendix B*

58   Rom. 8; Heb. 12:14

59   Rev. 19:10,13 *See also the Papers What is Liberty? and What is Collectivism?*

Chapter 19

The Church's Finest Hour

I. Introduction: Antichrist and the Church

At this juncture, the need for following the *sense of Scripture* should be patent. This applies especially so when it comes to dealing with end-time Scripture exegesis. A crucial question arises if we examine the facts we have. What could possibly be in common between Antichrist and the church which claims to worship and serve Jesus Christ? Simply comparing the conditions, doctrines, and practices of modern Christianity to the known divine standard of the New Testament reveal the naked truth. In the previous chapter, we learned the definition of Antichrist. You can find it present in *all attitudes, beliefs, doctrines, or acts that serve to neutralize or dull the keen edge of the true New Covenant gospel message of Jesus Christ.* I believe that definition is inclusive enough to cast a net over most of the hidden snares and big lies which Antichrist has imbedded in many common traditions of men.

The pervasive influence of Antichrist is closer than you could ever dare to think! Many Christians do not even know that some of their own beliefs contain these lies! *This is how* Antichrist has *squeezed many Christians into the mold of this world. Thus, the world system* virtually strangles the spiritual life out of them in the process, allowing the enemy to frustrate the grace of God and obstruct the truth of the gospel in many ways. Yes, Antichrist is feeding countless believers lies, propaganda, and half-truths under a *clever* guise. This artifice makes *people assume they can trust *Orthodox* [sic] religion!* Yet, you should know by now that religion is part of the world system! So you can easily see that the lying spirit of Antichrist (the false prophet) is also leading them to believe *many false assumptions and doctrines.* Thus, they ignore their responsibilities to follow and obey Jesus Christ, the leader they claim to worship and serve! Remember what Jesus said to the author of Antichrist: "[Satan] You *will* worship *the Lord, your God,* and *Him alone you will serve.*"[255] Later Jesus told the disciples that *you are unable to serve two masters (simultaneously).* Christian, beware. You must choose the one you will serve wisely. The spirit of Antichrist, like the serpent in the garden, *is very subtle* and crafty. He will make you think that you can have the best of both worlds, but that is a big lie! Using religion, Antichrist subverts the truth to such a degree that religious leaders may have taught you *that the true gospel is a lie!* [256] Lies are the native language of Antichrist, just like its source and namesake, Satan.

Jesus told the disciples that Satan is the father of lies and murder. He is a monster, a dragon, or a ravaging wolf that hides within the warp and woof of everyday things, feeding and exploiting our fleshly nature and devouring our spiritual life! This monster *hides in plain sight* in many respectable places of life: in doctrines, attitudes, laws, governments, business practices, philosophies, cultural traditions and icons, media propaganda, provocative and flashy entertainment and advertising clichés, in educational institutions at all levels, in *scientific methods* and *techniques of reasoning like empiricism,* in technological marvels, and even in *organized religion.* Operating from this globally-based juggernaut (the "new world order"), Antichrist puts pressure on believers from every conceivable direction! It is no wonder that many Christians have compromised their faith and beliefs. The constant barrage, like Scripture tells us, "wears down the saints." God has permitted this to be the final test of loyalty for true believers and which will fulfill many prophecies.

What we must realize is that the fact remains that *Antichrist has the world in his pocket.* What he or it *does not possess* is the true church that is the body of Jesus Christ! Can you guess where Antichrist is concentrating its effort to overtake? What strategy has our enemy used to achieve this end? History gives us the answer: the spirit of Antichrist has already co-opted the vast majority of outward organized

---

255   Matt. 4:1–10; Luke 4:1–13.
256   John 8:37–59; 10:10; Rom. 1:18–2:16

Christendom seventeen centuries ago! It was a masterful piece of strategy of the Roman emperor, Constantine I. "Beware of Greeks bearing gifts" and in AD 313, the *Trojan horse* arrived! How did the enemy succeed? It was so easy! Emperor Constantine *pretended to approve the church and make it a part of the society of the Roman empire.* The result is the *Roman Catholic Church!* At first, the gullible early Christians were so exhausted enduring ten major periods of persecution that they *bought the big lie hook, line, and sinker!* This sad fact of history goes far to explain how Antichrist has *infiltrated, subverted, and mutated* the outward church from within, even using it as a weapon to persecute true believers. This was how Antichrist has *demonized the truth and driven the true complete Gospel of Christ* underground. Using this new weapon, Antichrist continues to stigmatize and vilify the servants of Christ to this day, even using many misguided Christians as his dupes! All this has happened because believers fail to recognize the signature of Antichrist *in the outward organized church!* Yet we must know this: Antichrist *has not overtaken* the true body of Christ![257] So it does not take a rocket scientist or a nuclear physicist to figure out that there is not going to be *any* "grandiose public announcement" of a takeover by Antichrist. *He (it) is already in power!*

Yet Christians are so asleep in the light that they fail to even see it! Think about it. If you are a believer, you must not let the evil Antichrist spirit deceive you.

Consider that the Son of God had to leave His heavenly home and die an ignominious death for us. *Consider* the *millions* of believers whom the Antichrist world system has martyred for their courageous stand for Jesus Christ down through the centuries. If these things are true, then *why* should we have the audacity to expect God to deliver rich American Christians from the great tribulation? Whom do they think they are? That scenario just does not fit the overall scriptural pattern and what Jesus so clearly proclaimed!

Contrariwise, the presence of Christians in the tribulation *highlights the unique power of genuine Christianity.* Thus, we can see the way believers face the persecution and manifold trials that life confronts us with perseverance, boldness, and courage. One cannot ignore the

257   Matt. 16:18; Rom. 1:18–2:16; 8:31–39; 12:1–3; 2 Cor. 10:1–9; Eph. 6:10–18; 2 Pet. 2.

tenacious determination of Christians who follow their Lord Jesus without regard to the cost involved. Think about it: *Why would God take His best representatives out of the world just when they are the most needed and will shine the brightest?* Then think about who would stand to gain the most if God prematurely removed the Christians before multitudes could be saved? Do you think that God's work would ever benefit the devil?

So in Revelation 12 and 14, to whom does John refer to and during what time do the scenes in the following footnote take place?[258] Question: "How do we then live" the Christian life in these last days? Answer: *Just like the early Christians who were true to Jesus!* Just read it for yourself. No power on earth could stop them. According to worldly observers' comments they "turned the world upside down" for Christ! So can we believers today if we but obey the One sent! It was this Jesus that said, "I am, the One [that is] sent by God the Father," and that we must listen to and *obey Him.*[259]

I ask the reader: Has God changed the terms of the New Covenant since the first century? *I do not think so!* What was the secret or key to success of the early church? The New Testament has all the answers, *and these all point to one person, the Lord Jesus Christ!*

Wherever you go in the New Testament, *Jesus Christ is the main focus!* Jesus also said, "If you love Me, you will keep My commandments." John wrote later that "His commandments are not burdensome." That means that Christ's commands are verily practical, *and you can do them* in present tense reality of life here on earth!

The will of Father God is that we, as New Covenant believers, *are conformed to the image of His Son, Jesus Christ!* What is the single most important of the attributes of *His image? Is it not Agape love?* John tells us that *Agape love is the primary attribute of God the Father!* God the Father seeks all humankind to participate in *this kind of love,* and to share in the Kingdom of Heaven right here "on earth, [just] as it is in heaven." Consequently, one can easily understand that *Agape love* is

---

258 Rev. 12:10,11; 14:12,13
259 Luke 4:18; John 3:16,17; 5:24,37–47; 6:27–29; 7:29; 8:16–18; 26–29; 13:16; Gal. 4:4. *See also the papers entitled "Are You Sure What You Believe is Truly Christian Doctrine," "Bonehead Christianity," "Divergent Belief Systems," the 2 part series "How Should We Then Live" and "Key Aspects of the Christian Gospel"*

a primary target of Antichrist. Satan knows that if he can neutralize Christians in this area, he can destroy the keen edge of their witness! Notice the harsh evaluation that Jesus gives about the pre-tribulation condition of the church in Revelation 2 and 3. God's Word has given only two out of seven (28 percent) a passing grade! Far fewer will pass the test before apostasy gives way to revival! This should behoove us to make sure that *nothing* is between our soul and the Savior. Can you be absolutely sure that the evil spirit of Antichrist has not *poisoned your mind* or blinded you to the truth? A vital spiritual truth Christians must learn to use is that we only become aware of our *true* condition before God as we abide in the New Covenant Gospel of Christ. Therefore, let us be ever motivated to be a *transparent witness of the vital truths of the complete Gospel of Jesus Christ!* Beware of losing your first love like the ones in Laodicea that John wrote about. Let us be faithful to commit ourselves to being like Jesus always—while we fellowship within the church and when we must be "outside in the world!"

By definition, the body of Christ is *part of Christ!* It cannot be part of the world system! God's Word declares, "Come out from among them, and be ye separate, says the Lord, and touch not the unclean thing and I will Receive you (unto Myself)." "Have no fellowship with the unfruitful works of darkness. [You should] expose them… Redeeming the time, for the days are evil." "Cast out the bondwoman"—the Great Harlot of Babylon, symbol of apostate religion that "consorts with the state."[260] We must be ever vigilant to preserve *all* the key aspects of the Christian gospel.** That is the way we consistently *showcase the love of God* in us toward those who are the objects of God's love, everyone. We do this by continuing to observe the following things:

1. We must maintain *a personal commitment to Jesus Christ* as the Lord of our lives, and to place His cause as our life-long priority one focus.[261]

2. We must reaffirm daily our love and devotion to Jesus and His holy cause by *pledging our absolute allegiance to him* alone.**

---

260   2 Cor. 6:14–18; Gal. 4:30; Eph. 5:8; James 3:1–4:8; 1 John 2:15–17; Rev. 17.
261   Matt. 10:16–42; 2 Tim. 2:1–12. ** *See the paper "Key Aspects of the Christian Gospel"*

True Christians acknowledge that Christ's authority is the overriding consideration above all others in the lives of kingdom believers. We fulfill this by obeying His commands and by implicitly following His teachings and example. Moreover, we do all these things solely as a matter of faith, despite the cost to our person or to anything in our lives![262]

3. We must make a daily personal covenant to repent, to be broken, and to walk in His light. Let us always embrace the cross of Christ that mortifies all trust in humanistic ways and that leads us to renounce all of their methods and so-called solutions to combat evil.[263] Following this *central gospel truth* inevitably leads the believer to embrace *faith-based pacifism*. The world system will devour all those who seek to avoid this issue!

4. Let us abide in Christ's ways of *Agape love*. It must be the *central theme of our* lives. Let us live in spiritual union with our Lord Jesus Christ constantly. His Spirit teaches every believer to love every other human being with Christian love=God's love (Agape). This is the Same kind of love (Agape) that God the Father has shown to us in the person of Jesus Christ![264]

5. Let us seek *fellowship of like-minded believers* wherever we go. Let us always be diligently and authoritatively "apt to teach" others with respect and reverence. Meanwhile, we must teach others *the heavenly precepts of the New Covenant*, Amen.[265]

II. What is the proof of saints?

One thing that the end-times are doing is to sift and separate those who are claiming to be Christians into two very distinct groups, purifying the faithful few in the process. Jesus clearly and consistently emphasized that ultimate salvation requires his followers to "endure to the end." The context of the end means the time of our bodily death or His second coming, whichever comes first. Meanwhile we must be

---

262   John 14:6:16:15; Eph. 1:19–23.
263   Matt. 5:38–48; 16:21–26; Luke 9:23; John 12:23 ff.; Col. 3:1 f.; 1 John 1 ff.
264   John 17:1 ff.; Rom. 12:9–21; 13:8 ff.; Col. 3:12,13; Titus 2:11–15; 1 John 2:1– 4:21.
265   Matt. 18:18–20; 28:18–20; 2 Tim. 2:15–26; 1 Pet. 3:15.

prepared to deal with the reality of the daily conflicts that life brings our way here on earth. This is where the rubber meets the road in the Christian life. In addition, the great tribulation will be the ultimate final examination for every believer on earth. However, one must not become too concerned or worried! In fact, I wonder where the "pre-hysteria" about the so-called "omnipotence" of Antichrist comes from? Think about it: the promises of God's Word are still "yea and amen" anytime. God is still on the throne. Jesus Christ is still our faithful advocate and protector. The Holy Spirit will continue as the faithful communicator of Christ.

He will be at your side right up to the precise moment that the angels have translated us into the presence of Jesus Christ to see him in person in the sky! Let us always know that no matter what happens *the great Antichrist is not God. God is God!* We should know that *no power of evil,* be it human, angelic, or otherwise, can separate us from the love of God in Christ Jesus. However, this is true only *if* we abide 100 percent faithful to Christ, *trusting His Word.*

Now you should see *why* obedience to the commands of Jesus Christ, the One sent, is not an elective! Yes, the proof of the saints is in great tribulation. In fact, the greater the pressure that they apply, the more *the true saints and followers of Jesus Christ* will shine! John tells us that in the end, the Christians *will emerge victorious, overcoming Antichrist:* "By the blood of the Lamb, the word of their testimony and [because] they loved not their own lives unto the death."[266] Will you persevere all the way unto your destiny as a true believer in Jesus Christ? Are you willing to endure those things that Jesus has told us we must be willing to endure to be in His blessed presence for eternity? Do you *really believe* in your heart of hearts that everything that Jesus said while he walked this earth is *the absolute truth today?* Christians are responsible and accountable to abide in His Word, obeying implicitly and explicitly the whole gospel and New Covenant that bears His name. Do you also recognize that receiving His righteousness is a daily *choice* and that it is *not automatic? What does the Scripture say regarding the polarization of believers?* According to the gospel accounts of Jesus

266   Rom. 8:28–39; Rev. 12:10,11

and the apostolic writers, even Christians are *very much divided by the Gospel of Jesus Christ!*

In fact, Jesus frankly told the disciples that His message was going to divide families (spiritual and biological) and that "all men would hate you because of me." *Yes, Jesus is divisive!* His very presence in one produces vigorous division, opposition, and contention *especially* among groups *composed of mixtures.* Unfortunately, virtually all corporation churches are like this. There we find true believers mixed with *nominal Christians* and unbelievers who still operate according to the *carnal mind* and humanistic formats of governance. Scripture tells us that *humanism* (the world's religion) is constantly at war with the Spirit, since it (the flesh) always operates according to the carnal mind, which is an avowed enemy of God! Consequently, when you first receive Jesus Christ as your personal Savior, your identification with Christ thrusts you into a *battlefield!* Your new nature, born of God, produces a vigorous reaction from your innate human nature.

That is precisely why Jesus told the disciples that they *must be converted.* However, conversion requires all believers to enter the discipleship process and *die to self.*

This means that we must cease ordering our lives around those human ways that drive the unconverted world around us.[267] The church must recognize this, since God's Word tells us that all unregenerated and unconverted human beings follow the world. This is so because the flesh always acts according to the "law of sin and death." One must therefore come to the unavoidable conclusion that believers cannot use the same humanistic methods that the world uses to govern the church without incurring catastrophic consequences! The *true* church is a living spiritual organism vitally connected to God. God's will *demands that we govern* the body of believers the Scriptures define as the church, *by spiritual guidelines and laws!* God's Word calls this set of laws *the New Covenant*, and it operates by "the law of the spirit of life in Christ Jesus." *The Word of God also teaches* us the doctrine of *holiness or *sanctification*.* God considers any contamination of the church that arises *from adulteration, that is* sins of mixture with worldly ways, such as syncretism, humanism, and nationalism, *to be unfaithfulness*

---

267   *See the paper: "Christian Conversion, Part One: Introduction to Christian Conversion"*

(spiritual adultery) by Christians! This is *such a serious issue because* the special association and kind of life, love, and spirit we know as the body of Christ, *cannot survive the competition* of such alien things! John's vivid picture of the scarlet woman riding the beast shows the disastrous consequences of allowing worldly ways to contaminate the church! This goes back to the maxim of Jesus: "You cannot serve two masters (simultaneously)"[268]

The world is a Trojan horse. It is a harsh and domineering taskmaster. However, *true believers are part of Christ.* Our only head is Christ in the Kingdom of Heaven. The church cannot function with two heads! The Holy Spirit of Jesus will not tolerate such things. "If any man has not the spirit of Christ, he is none of his." You are either part of Christ or you are part of the world system! This is the ultimate and immutable dividing point and the *crux of discipleship and of biblical conversion!* You cannot serve two masters. We simply are *unable* to hold on to *two irreconcilable sets of beliefs simultaneously!* One or the other must die for the other to live. That is one big reason that we have so much confusion and division within the modern church system today.[269]

Two distinct groups concurrently develop:

1. *The wheat,* which represents *the revolutionized and faithful few* who will persevere unto the end no matter what the cost. These are the ultimate God-pleasers who follow Jesus, remaining true to His way, being zealous and ardently loyal to his cause, never compromising truth unto the death. These are the *spiritually-minded* who are obedient unto the Spirit of Christ and to the gospel of His grace. They will be a special cadre of *holy=saints,* separate from the world system. They shrink from every form of iniquity, yet simultaneously remain *Fervent in Agape love!* These believers will form the *nucleus for the greatest revival in history!* They will be the front-runners of the *great feast of ingathering* that great *harvest of souls* that God will glean just before Christ's appearing in the sky. In contrast, Jesus tells us that:

268   Matt. 5:27–48; 6:24; 12:39; 1 Cor. 6:9–20; Rev. 17:5 *See "What is the Body of Christ"*
269   Matt. 6:22–24; 7:13–23; 13:24–30,36–43; 16:21–26; Luke 6:22; 9:51–62; 13:5–9; 22–35; 14:26– 33; 16:13; John 7:7,15–18; 12:23–26; 15:18–25; 17:1 ff.; Rom. 8:1 ff.; 1 Cor. 1:17–2:16; 2 Cor. 3:17–4:18 *See the papers "Basics of Biblical Church Governance," "Guidelines for Renewed Leadership" and "Two Divergent Belief Systems"*

2. *The tares* (chaff) are *the many who fall away into apostasy,* who *have culturally adapted* to their ruin by following the crowd. The old illustration of the "frog in the water" applies incredibly well. Yes, apostasy is sin. Sin is an insidious enemy. Sin first binds, and then it blinds the sinning one. Eventually it deadens them inside in the conscience such that they no longer feel the need to change or repent! Many organizations claiming to be Christian have "transformed" iniquity into *orthodoxy, * teaching it as tradition! Here we find the people-pleasers and the carnally-minded who depend upon *humanistic solutions and methods.* They *pay lip-service to Jesus in public,* but in reality they act like *unbelievers* who ignore Christ, painting Jesus's cause and commands as "irrelevant in a modern age." Essentially, they call Jesus a liar and a fraud. Failing to count the cost, they compromise truth and pacify iniquity, ultimately failing God's test to *remain in Christ and abide in His love.* Consequently, they readily pervert the doctrines of Christianity to fit the circumstance, diverging away from Christ into "the spirit of error," which leads to the spirit of antichrist, whose mark they will inevitably take. Still, God is allowing them to flourish to *test Christians' loyalty to Christ!* [270]

In the final analysis, I believe that the sense of Scripture suggests that the Great Tribulation will give Believers the greatest opportunity for Evangelism in history The grinding tyranny of antichrist will cause many unbelievers to seek deliverance. Although God permits antichrist to "Overcome Saints" at first, this will only be in an outward and temporary way. Yes, the world will despise, discredit and ignore organized Churches even more.

Nevertheless, the underground Church will thrive and grow tremendously and become a spiritual powerhouse! Very quickly, the Saints will go on to victory!

In Revelation, John shows us a dramatic groundswell of response to the *true* Gospel *during the Great Tribulation!* [271] Several reasons explain this:

---

270 Matt. 13:24–30, 37–43; 2 Thess. 2:1–4; 1 John 4:1–6. *See the papers entitled "Analysis of the Causes and Effects of Apostasy,' 'an Analysis of Faith' and 'Investigating the Symptoms of latter-day Problems afflicting the Church'*

271 Rev. 7:9–17

1. Many formerly apostatized believers will repent, be converted and restored to full spirituality, becoming spiritual dynamos, fervent in love and zealous for the truth of Jesus.

2. The Critical Mass of spiritually virile believers will rise all over the earth, bringing in countless millions to Christ.

3. The Church will truly fulfill the Great Commission for the very first time in history. The world's seeking lost will have seen the tenacity and faithfulness of the Christians under fire, and during this time, many will break ranks from the antichrist, renounce the mark and follow Christ.

We must note that Scripture shows that *the Empire of antichrist will not martyr most of Believers* during The Great Tribulation. Moreover, Scripture never specifies that a person could not repent and renounce the *Mark* before the judgment sequence starts in the Seventh Seal. How else do you explain the one hundred million plus converts coming out of the Great Tribulation?

III. We can readily identify the true saints by the ones who love His Appearing.[272]

1. They are the Patient and Loving Saints Enduring "Until the Coming of the Lord." They are the persevering ones who count the cost of *dying daily* to sin, self, Satan and the world. They persist unto their death if need be.[273]

2. These are the ones who are Faithful to the Cause, tenaciously loyal to Christ, keeping the Way of Christ, walking in Love. True Believers love their enemies and *Never Compromise the Standards that Jesus Christ gave us in the Gospels* for any system of man.[274]

3. They are the faithful few who *remain distinct and separate* from the world system. The True followers of Jesus Christ know that they are Citizens of the Kingdom of Heaven, and that their Constitution is the

---

272   2 Tim. 4:1–8
273   James 5:7,8; Rev. 12: 10,11
274   Matt. 5:38–48; 1 John 2:1-11

New Covenant Gospel of our Lord and Savior Jesus Christ. Their *flag represents their allegiance to the Kingdom of Heaven, and the only Banner over them is Agape Love!* [275]

4. *True Believers* wisely maintain Absolute Confidence in God's overall Sovereign Control over their lives. As such, they entrust their lives unto Jesus irrevocably, renouncing dependence on any other gods. Nor do they rely on any arm or power of the flesh to save from evil either internal or external.[276]

5. The Enduring ones live and teach the Complete Gospel of Jesus Christ consistently! This is the only foolproof way to empower Believers to face, endure and overcome in the harsh reality of the last days, and to emerge victorious in time at the end *when Jesus Christ comes* in Power! Yes, Scripture teaches that *The Church,* also defined as *The Saints and the Elect,* will remain on earth *right up to The second coming event.* Then all Believers on earth will be Caught Up and away at the Rapture. If you follow this scenario to its logical conclusion, *all the Scripture fits together* and dovetails in without confusion or forcing the context.[277]

IV. Let us review the general conditions applying to all believers.

1. *Jesus Christ is lord in all matters, whether they are private or public.* This rule applies to all situations in the lives of true believers. No exceptions. See the New Testament en toto.

2. God's Word commands believers to be *responsible and accountable to abide in Jesus;* to obey Christ's commands and to follow his example and remain *personally loyal to Jesus* keeping our vows "while we live."[278]

3. Scripture allows for *only one second coming of Jesus Christ.* Scripture *does not support* a secret (or separate) rapture that is "artificially detached" from or before the great tribulation or His second coming.

---

275 Song 2:4; John 13–17; Phil. 3:7–21; 1 John 2:12 f.;4:7-21; James 4:1 ff.
276 Matt. 28:20; Acts 17:24–31; Rom. 8; 1 Cor. 10:12,13; 2 Cor. 5:8; 2 Tim. 1:7–12; 1 John 2:1–6; 4:1–6; 5:1–12.
277 Matt. 10; 24:1 ff.; 28:18–20; Gal. 1:6–12; 2 Tim. 4:1–8.
278 John 15:1 ff.

Scripture clearly teaches that "we [will]… remain unto the coming of the Lord."[279]

4. God's Word guarantees *no automatic immunity from persecution* or even *great tribulation.* Why do you think Jesus was so clear about his followers *enduring faithful unto the end?* In fact, the very strength of original Christianity lies in the *incredible coping power of God* that is present in God's *true* worshipers. True faith knows that *no matter what happens, He will care for us!*[280]

5. Only those who pass *all* these tests will share in the first resurrection and rapture portion of the second coming that transpires at the end of the sixth seal when the true Christians living on earth then will all be *caught up in the air* to meet Jesus.

Yes, "in the twinkling of an eye" we will be with our Lord Jesus and rejoin our loved ones who have gone before![281] Up there, Jesus Christ invites us to *two major special events that are unseen by the world below:*(1) The glorious *judgment seat of Christ* where Jesus will evaluate us, and we will receive our *final grades and heavenly assignments.*[282] (2) *The marriage supper of the Lamb,* when Christ, our Bridegroom, will begin to consummate the spiritual bond of love that He has been cultivating with His people and creation since the beginning of time.[283]

V. Summary

Let us consider the end-times within the context of the entire Christian experience.

First, God is *always sovereign.* He has promised us that he will preserve us and keep us intact and save us if we choose to trust *in Christ* fully!

---

279   Matt. 24:27–31; Luke 21:8 ff.; 1 Cor. 15:23; 1 Thess. 4:13–17; James 5:7–9; Rev. 1:7.

280   John 16:33; Rom. 8:35–39; 1 John 4:1–6; Rev. 12:11; 13:10; 14:12.

281   1 Cor. 15:50–58; 1 Thess. 4:13–17; 5:1–11.

282   Matt. 5:1–12; Rom. 14:10; 1 Cor. 3:9–16; 4:4,5; 2 Cor. 5:10.

283   Luke 14:16–24; Rev. 19:6–13.

Second, think about it, would Jesus Christ have ever commanded what He commanded or said the things He did the way He did *if He did not seriously intend for His followers to obey Him?*

Third, if you want to be on that train, you buy the ticket. *Everyone pays the full price!* Jesus said that no bargain basement specials and no discount tickets to heaven exist!

We must satisfy the following conditions:

1. Always be ready for Jesus Christ to come.

2. We must endure faithfully unto the end.

3. Prepare for and deal with crises of all kinds.

4. Know that we will experience victory only by persevering in faith no matter what happens!

5. We see final deliverance *only when Jesus returns!*

## Chapter 20

The Event Sequence of the Second Coming of Jesus Christ

Scripture mentions the second coming of our Lord Jesus Christ in various places and names including the appearing (Parousia in Greek), the Day of the Lord, the coming of the Lord, the blessed hope, the Day of Jesus Christ, and the wrath of the Lamb. Scripture refers to this event repeatedly throughout the New Testament: by our Lord Himself, by the apostolic writers, and even by angels. We must see the second coming as *one event sequence* taken as a whole to preserve the original sense of Scripture. This way we can easily resolve the *truth* and eliminate the confusion. Let us observe the following: The second coming of Jesus Christ is *the beginning point of a series of events called "the Day of the Lord."* The day of the Lord pertains to the *earthly reign of Christ.* The second coming event is composed of several main components: the appearing or Parousia, the gathering of the elect, **the judgment seat of Christ (postulated time placement), the vengeance (wrath or judgment) of the Lamb, the special dealings with Israel, the marriage supper of the Lamb, and the reign of Jesus Christ on earth. This is decidedly a *two-sided event:* To true believers who are part of Jesus Christ, it will be the long-awaited vindication of their faith and patience. Yet to anyone who is part of the world system, it will be their worst nightmare come true. By comparing Scripture with Scripture, the discerning Bible student can identify the major *sub-events* contained within. Note that the Scriptures support *only one* second coming of Jesus Christ—a *contiguous event sequence that is one* *cloth.* No part of it, such as the rapture, can be biblically placed out of that event sequence context, simply because *it is part of it!* [284]

**The numbers in parentheses (through 13) are keyed to the Last Days Timeline Chart in Appendix C, Part 2. The main sub-events are as follows:

I. The Parousia: (1–3) This includes:

A. (1) The initial precursory signs and celestial happenings. [285]

B. (2) *The sign of the Son of Man* in the sky. His great glory and splendor are visibly displayed worldwide, so all can see. This is what *the appearing* of Jesus Christ means. Finally, every person on earth will see the reality of the Lord Jesus Christ *with their own eyes!*

Yet, only the ones who have served Christ by faith will have the privilege of enjoying it. This corresponds to the time of the sixth seal after tribulation, but before the wrath portion of the great tribulation. [286]

C. (3) When they see Him, *the response of the peoples* (nations) of the world system is to run and hide. They can run, but they have no place to hide. [287]

II. The gathering of the *elect* to Jesus is the event where all true believers are rescued (4–7) and is the event that every true Christian believer should be eagerly anticipating! This is the true blessed hope, when we reunite with our loved ones who have passed away in Jesus. The great ingathering is a time of celebration when true believers receive the fulfillment of one of the greatest promises God has given His followers! Our great deliverance commences with:

A. (4) *The great trumpet call of the archangel.* Every Christian should be eagerly anticipating and patiently living and waiting for this. Yes, He is *coming for those who love His appearing!* [288]

---

284 Matt. 24:27 f.; Mark 13:24–37; Luke 21:27,28; Acts 1:11; 1 Cor. 1:7; 15:23–25; Phil. 1:6; Col. 3:3; 1 Thess. 1:3; 2:19; 3:13; 4:13–17; 5:2,3,23; 2 Thess. 1:6–10; 2:1; 3:5; 1 Tim. 6:12–14; 2 Tim. 1:10; James 5:7,8; 2 Pet. 3:4–13; Rev. 1:7.

285 Matt. 24:29

286 Matt. 24:27–31; Luke 21:27; Rev. 1:7; 6:12–17.

287 Matt. 24:30; Rev. 6:15–17.

288 Matt. 24:30; 1 Cor. 15:50–54; 1 Thess. 4:15; 2 Tim. 4:8.

B. (5) The *first resurrection* is the raising up *of the dead in Christ.* They are all the saved (saints) who have passed away in Jesus before this event takes place. God will instantaneously clothe them with immortal bodies and personally gather them up to Jesus in the sky![289]

C. (6) The *catching away* or *rapture* of all the saints living bodily then. The holy angels will translate believers into the presence of Jesus Christ in the sky! Scripture context demands that this event take place sometime *after* the onset of the great tribulation period. This is since it is *an integral part* of the second coming event. No doubt, this event includes the multitudes of believers that will receive Christ *during* the great tribulation, but *before the seventh seal when the judgment sequence commences.*[290]

D. (7) The *judgment seat of Christ**. This is when Jesus Christ will debrief and evaluate all believers, granting them their rewards, assignments, and placing in the Kingdom of Heaven.

*See chapter 13 for details.[291]

III. The seventh seal includes the *wrath of the Lamb, the three woes,* the third of which is the battle of the Armageddon *(the great supper of God),* and concludes with *the touchdown of Christ on Mount Olivet.*

Explanation: The seventh seal is *at the very end* of the great tribulation when Jesus Christ vents His wrath and rains divine *retribution down upon Antichrist* and the entire unrepentant world system he controls, including all who disobey *the Gospel of Jesus Christ* and then deals with the Jews.

The *seventh seal* includes the following:

A. (8) *The trumpet and bowl judgments* of the seventh seal's angels, one through six, the last two are *the first two woes.* Scripture tells us that this period includes the first part of the execution of the rain of ruin and judgment pronounced upon *the great harlot* (apostate religion) *and all of Babylon* (the new world order). God's judgment condemns all

289 1 Cor. 15:23; 1 Thess. 4:15,16.
290 Matt. 24:27–31; Luke 21:27,28; 1 Thess. 4:17; Rev. 7:9–17. *See the papers entitled "Correlating Last Days Scriptures," "The Doctrine of Last Things" and "Facts of Scripture: the Church and the Tribulation"*
291 Matt. 5:21,22; Rom. 14:10; 1 Cor. 4:1–5; 2 Cor. 5:8–10.

godless humanism in the world, wherever it may be found: religions, governments, economies, arts, education, atheistic science and medical and pharmaceutical establishment, philosophies of professionalism, syncretism, and paganism. His judgment applies to everything that represents, undergirds, enables, or supports any part of the evil empire of Antichrist in any way![292]

B. (9) *The special dealings with Israel.* God will *interrupt the progress of the seventh seal* and deal directly with the Jews in a special way. To do this, God will use a *special extension period* to the great tribulation, to which comparing Scripture leads us. It has something to do with *the seven thunders* that John the Revelator heard from God and wrote about in Revelation chapter 10.

During this period, the Jews, liberated from the delusion of Antichrist, will finally recognize Jesus Christ as their Messiah, and "God will save all Israel" *then.*[293]

C. (10) *The marriage supper of the Lamb* takes place in the air and is unseen by those on earth. Believers are all waiting for this one main event. Remember the parable of the ten virgins? If you are a true believer, then the experience of *this event alone* will make all the sufferings, troubles, and trials of this life unworthy with which to compare! All the sorrows of more than twenty centuries *will pale into insignificance in the Bridegroom's brightness!* Seeing His blessed face will be worth it all! Behold His cheery smile, when Jesus says, "Well done, good faithful friends!"*[294]

D. (11) *The great supper of God.* This event occurs during angel seven or the third woe of the seventh seal. Most likely, this is that famous "battle of Armageddon" John writes about.[295] It is at Armageddon when Jesus Christ and the Angelic Army will carry out the actual physical destruction of Antichrist and the slaughter of his armies worldwide, personally! Then God annihilates all the infrastructures of the world system as described above.[296]

---

292   2 Thess. 1:6–10; 2 Pet. 3:3–12; Rev. 8:1–9:21; 14:14–18:24.

293   Dan. 9:24–27; 12:10–12; Luke 21:24; Rom. 11:25,26; Rev. 10–12. *See also* The Doctrine of the Elect/Ekklesia

294   *(Postulated timing)* Matt. 25:1–13; John 14:1–3; Rev. 19:1–10.

295   Rev. 16:16

296   Psa. 2,110; Eph. 1:17–23; 2 Thess. 1:6–10; Rev. 17:1–18:24; 19:11–21.

E. (12) *Touchdown.* Jesus's return to earth is the time when Jesus *descends* in a cloud of angels and saints to take over all rule, and reign on earth, fulfilling the promises made by our Lord Jesus before He left. This is when the saints reign beside Christ in power and glory, fulfilling all the promises of the Bible, such as the prophetic pictures of the Old Testament and the parables of Jesus. Then, Jesus will separate, judge,** and rule all the nations on earth.[297]**Note that *judgment, including* the judgment seat of Christ, is a multi-phase *process.*

F. (13) *The binding of Satan.* After Christ overthrows the Antichrist and his empire destroyed, the Lord will send down an angel to bind Satan and to cast him into the abyss.[298]

G. 14 Jesus Christ reigns on earth "with a rod of iron," including the judgment of the nations.[299]

**See also V below: "Explanatory" and chapter 13, "The Judgment Seat of Christ."

IV. Chart of Events within the Second Coming of Jesus Christ
Numbers in parentheses are also keyed to text and Appendix C, Part 2

	A: The Parousia	
1)	The Celestial Signs	Matt. 24:29
2)	Matt. 24:29	Matt. 24:30; Luke 21:27
3)	The Response of the Peoples	Matt. 24:30; Rev. 1:7
	B: The Great Ingathering	
4)	The Great Trumpet Call of the Archangel	Matt. 24:31; 1 Thess. 4:14, 16
5)	The First Resurrection	Matt. 24:31; 1 Cor.15:51–55; 1 Thess 4:15,16

---

297   Zech. 14:1–4; Matt. 12:1 ff.; 25:14 ff.; 28:20; Luke 19:11–27; Acts 1:11; Phil. 2:10,11; Rev. 11:15; 19:11–21; 20:1–6.

298   Rev. 20:1–6

299   Matt. 19:28; 25:14 ff.; Acts 17:31; Rom. 2:1–16; Rev. 2:26–29; 11:1–4; 12:5; 19:13

6)	The Catching Away or Rapture	Matt. 24:31; 1 Cor. 15:23; 1 Thess. 4:17
7)	**The Judgment Seat of Christ	Rom. 14:10; 2Cor. 5:10
C. The Seventh Seal		
8)	The Trumpet/Bowl Judgments of the Seventh Seal, Angels 1–6.	2 Thess. 1:6–10; Rev. 8:1– 9:21; 14:14 – 18:24.
9)	The Special Dealings with Israel.	Rev. 10:1–4
10)	The Marriage Supper of the Lamb.	Rev. 19:1–10.
11)	Angel 7: This is the Third Woe and includes Armegeddon, The Great Supper of God.	Rev.16:16,17; 19:11–21.
12)	Touchdown: Jesus Returns to Earth	Acts 1:11; Zech. 14:4.
13)	**The Binding of Satan	Rev. 20:1–6
14)	**The Judgment of the Nations/ Tribes	Matt. 19:28; 25:14 ff.; Acts 17:31; Rom. 2:11– 16

2-10-04

V. Explanatory of the term "the Day of the Lord." In Scripture, the term "the Day of the Lord" has several different contexts and meanings.

A. In the Old Testament, the phrase "the Day of the LORD" is a term for the judgment of God. The Prophet Joel wrote that the Day of the LORD is darkness and not light. This is so because of its purely *negative context in the Old Testament* under (original, biblical) Judaism. To properly understand Old Testament prophetic contexts, one must realize that the word "Lord" (usually all capitals in KJV) Only refers to Father God. Evidently, many Believers may be confused about pronouns referring to God. The Hebrew Lexicon lists the word LORD (or Lord sometimes) as Jahweh or Jehovah. In contrast, New Testament references use a generic word, *Kurios,* meaning *lord or boss.* The word

Lord refers to deity when capitalized and is primarily used with the name Jesus Christ.

B. God the Father has an Angelic Army called *Jahweh Sabaoth in Hebrew* (The LORD Sabaoth). In the *Old Testament context, God employed this army to execute judgment on three different categories of people:* 1) *the heathen nations* such as Babylon, Assyria, Edom, and Egypt, etc.,[300] 2) the earthly kingdoms of Israel or Judah (God's wayward people in the Old Testament), 3) combinations of both.[301]

C. Zechariah 14 is a rare specific OT prophetic reference to the New Testament Jesus Christ (the Messiah) as also being the executor of divine judgment. It refers to Christ's coming at the end of the tribulation to deal with and pacify apostate Israel during the seventh seal (9).[302]

D. Why was God the Father so violent in His execution of judgment in the Old Testament? Three main reasons explain this: 1) because Israel was *under the law of the old covenant* (biblical Judaism), otherwise known as Mosaic Law. 2) Israel had abandoned their covenant. God in prophetic Scripture describes them as *stiff-necked and rebellious!* [303] 3) because Christ had not yet been sacrificed as the Lamb of God to pay for sin.[304] 4) because God's people did not have a permanent *mediator yet between them and Father God,* except the angels that were primarily used as communicators of law and judgment.[305]

E. Now, let us consider the Day of the Lord in the *New Testament context.* When we come to the *New Testament* references of the Day of the Lord, *we encounter a very different context for those saints who have served Jesus Christ faithfully.* Therefore, for the New Testament believer, the Day of the Lord is not judgment, but *deliverance!* The Day of the Lord is *only judgment to the world—those serving Antichrist!* This is the judgment that Jesus Christ will mete out after he appears at the

300   Isa. 13:6–14:27; 34:8–17; Jer. 46:1 ff.; Ezek. 30:3 f.
301   Isa. 1:1 ff.; Joel 1:1–2:32; Amos 5:6; Mal, 3,4; Isa. 2:12–22; Joel 3:1 f.; Obad. 1:15
302   Zech 14:1–9 Cf. Zech. 9:9; 1 Cor. 15:20–28; Rev. 10:7–11:15
303   Heb. 9:9,10
304   Heb. 9:9–15
305   Heb. 8:6–9

end of the tribulation period. Thus, *the Day of the Lord* begins with the sixth seal and continues through the period called *the seventh seal,* which contains *the seven trumpet and bowl judgments.* Now, compare Revelation chapters 6 to 11 with Revelation chapters 14 to 20.

In these two narratives, we can see that God gives us *double coverage,* with the second using a sequence of seven angels with seven bowls. Thus, we have two accounts of the *same scene* or period. In the latter set, we have two scenes. First, a heavenly scene reads like a preview of coming attractions or like a parade of military forces going off to fight an enemy. Secondly, we have an *earthly scene* where God transmits to John a message to admonish and encourage the saints to exercise patience until Christ arrives![306] When God gives the order to strike, the seven bowls are emptied upon the earth below. John's accurately symbolic description of the Antichrist empire of political and religious alliance allows us to see vividly the elements of a *satanic trinity: the dragon, the beast, and the false prophet.* This evil trinity is the heart of the Antichrist system, Babylon, and animates the entire worldwide empire it controls. First, in Revelation 13, John describes this empire *as an animal with ten horns that correspond to ten kings.* They slay this beast, but miraculously *it reinvents itself in a new form* that John describes as arising from the ruins of the first. However, this *second beast* has a new adaptation—it *cleverly disguises itself to look like a Lamb.* Of course, this cover of deception and lies is none other than the "religious arm" of the sophisticated propaganda ministry of *the false prophet.* It is also clear from comparison of Scripture to Scripture that "the false prophet" is the *mouthpiece of Antichrist* who uses many branches, including the *media, politics, and religion* to dupe the masses.

To this lying "mouthpiece of Antichrist" John ascribes the lying wonders and Satan's big lie: "Sacrifice your children, and for you it will be well."[307]

---

306   Rev. 14:12,13

307   2 Thess. 1:1–12; Rev. 16:12,13 See also Chapter 10, Sect. II and the paper entitled 'a Biblical Disclosure of Antichrist'

The false prophet also introduces the *mark.* In detail, John also describes this second beast as the symbol *"Babylon."*[308]

At the end of the great tribulation, after Jesus sends the angels to deliver the saints, He will execute His wrath upon Antichrists' global empire of Babylon. In Scripture, various names describe this event: the third woe of the seventh seal, the seventh angel, (the battle of) Armageddon, and the great supper of God. This is the end when Jesus Christ and the Angelic Army, Yahweh Sabaoth, will destroy all the armies of Antichrist at Armegeddon.

The term *Babylon refers also to the entire global empire complex of Antichrist* (the new world order) that Christ comes to destroy.[309]

---

308   Rev. 17:1; 18:24
309   Rev. 11:14–19;16:16,17 *Armageddon is the Hebrew: 'Ar Megiddo=Mt. Megiddo*

Chapter 21

The Judgement Seat of Christ

The judgment seat of Christ is going to be one of the most significant events of history! Those who are true believers in Jesus Christ who *love His appearing* will be very privileged, since the Scripture tells us *that they will stand* at this judgment. In this glorious judgment, Christian believers of every nation, tribe, and tongue will be *judged personally* by Jesus Christ without partiality using the *same standard* we already know in Scripture! Not only that, Jesus now employs the identical *New Covenant standard* by which Jesus gave the apostles 2000 years ago to measure us! This standard *applies to all situations no matter what* the circumstances may be! Moreover, this New Covenant standard demands that we *love all others with the same kind of love* that God the Father, Jesus Christ, and the Holy Spirit share with one another![310]

By comparing Scripture with Scripture, we can closely estimate the timing of this event to be during the *series of events* Scripture calls the second coming of Christ or *the Day of the Lord.* Scripture tells us that the judgment of God is *a multi-phased process.* The first part is a "pre-screening" judgment of the body of Christ that is taking place in the present.[311] Secondly, we have the judgment seat of Christ (which pertains to *true Christian believers only)* that takes place *in heaven* immediately *after the great ingathering of the saints* in the air to meet him.[312] Thirdly, Christ will *also* judge the nations and tribes after he assumes power on earth.[313]

---

310   John 15:1–12; Rom. 2:1–16.

311   Matt. 13; 22:1–14; 25:1–13; 2 Cor. 11:2; 1 Pet. 4:17.

312   Rom. 14:10; 2 Cor. 5:8–10.

313   Matt. 19:28; 25:14 ff.; Acts 17:31; Rom. 2:11–16.

More important to us now, however, are the following:

I. The precepts regarding the judgment seat of Christ are as follows:
1) God the Father has committed *all judgment* into the hands of His Son, Jesus Christ.[314] 2) We know that all true Christians must appear before Jesus one day.[315] 3) We will be judged and evaluated personally by Jesus Christ according to His rules of determination. Jesus bases this upon our deeds done in the body during the time that God has allotted us here on earth in this life.

The outcome of His judgment will determine our final placements and rewards. Will you be close to Jesus in His Kingdom?[316]

II. Yes, the choices we make *now* can make for very *major differences in our eternal destiny and rewards!*[317] Both Jesus and the early apostles teach us that these differences center on the Christian believer's responsibility to obey the commands of Jesus. This means that we must consistently strive to carry out the kind of character, love, and morality that Jesus Himself showed. We must remember that Jesus said that we would do this as well if we choose to follow him—showing that same Agape love to the world of sinners and to each other. Always remember that *nothing is impossible with God!* Never forget that John tells us that "His commands are not burdensome!" This means that we can follow them today!318 Furthermore:

III. Our obedience to Jesus Christ fulfills the spirit of the great commission. Jesus personally admonished Christians to teach by example those same commands He gave the first apostles. The New Covenant states clearly that God expects believers to comply with Jesus's commands in whatever time we live, and this applies no matter what country our temporary home might be. We can fulfill the great commission if we order our lives by and continue upon the basis of being Kingdom citizens first! Do you seek that country that is above? Is your citizenship in heaven first and before all earthly concerns? Even

---

314   Luke 10:22; John 5:22,23.
315   Rom. 14:10; 2 Cor. 5:8–10.
316   Matt. 5:10–12; 6:4,6,18; 10:42; 16:27; 25:1 ff.; Luke 6:23,35; 1 Cor. 3:1–4.
317   Matt. 6:24; Heb. 12:1 ff.
318   1 John 5:3

today, Jesus is judging based on how the ones who call Him Lord claim to believe and how well they follow that belief in reality![319]

IV. Let us now consider the pertinent scriptures relating to the judgment seat of Christ:

1. *Who will make it* to this special event?[320]

2. That God the Father has granted Jesus sole authority to judge His own, and that He will be completely impartial.[321]

3. That this summons *applies to all genuine believers.*[322]

4. That we will not know the complete picture until then.[323]

5. That *we must rightly discern* the New Covenant and body of Christ.[324]

6. The basis by which Jesus will be judging us ahead of time.[325]

7. The type of **foundation** upon which we really base our lives determines our rewards.[326]

Yes, we must pay particular attention that the New Testament considerably *deepens accountability to the thought and motive level regarding our choices,* thoughts, attitudes, and actions! This is part and parcel to the entire body of teaching that Jesus Christ taught!

V. Let us now examine the importance of stewardship regarding our obedience to Christ's commands!

The Holy Spirit intertwines the precepts regarding **stewardship** throughout Jesus's ministry. This doctrine is found in the whole of Scripture. In particular, Jesus's **parables** are striking in their

---

319 Matt. 28:18–20; Luke 22:15–22; John 14:12–24; 15:10–17; Phil. 3:19–21; Col. 3:1–7; Heb. 11.

320 Matt. 25:1 ff.; Acts 17:30,31; Rom. 2:1–16.

321 Matt. 5:21,22; Luke 10:21,22; 21:36; John 5:22; 8:15,16; Acts 10:34–43; Eph. 6:9.

322 2 Cor. 5:1–21

323 1 Cor. 4:1–5

324 1 Cor. 11:23–32

325 Gal. 5:13–25; 2 Tim. 2:1–14; 1 Pet. 4:17.

326 Luke 6:46–49; 1 Cor. 3:9–17.

illustrations.**[327] Jesus places significant emphasis *on his followers to obey Him* and to follow His teachings and example. This accountability directly relates to the destiny of man. Every human being born of sinful man will answer to God, either at the judgment seat of Christ or at the great white throne judgment. The latter functions only as the *sentence hearing* for all those who *failed to meet the conditions of salvation that Jesus gave us in the New Covenant!*

1. The parable of the ten virgins and the parable of the sheep and goats, recorded in Matthew 25, give us a keen insight into what Jesus expects disciples to be like and to do.

There, Jesus delineates specific consequences that are the direct results of our *actions,* which in turn are the result of our *fundamental attitudes* and beliefs concerning the person and work of our Lord Jesus Christ.

2. The parable of the unjust steward is a stark warning to those who *try to walk the picket fence.*[328]

This parable teaches that we cannot please people and be comfortable in the world and serve Jesus Christ simultaneously! Jesus declared, *"You cannot serve two masters"* (simultaneously). The plain facts of the New Covenant echo the first of the ten commandments, telling us that the *Lord* Jesus Christ *will not take second place to anything* in the life of a believer.

3. The parable of the sower, found in Matthew 13, gives us a comprehensive overlook of the different types of responses humans have to the Gospel of Jesus Christ, which is the Word of God. In this marvelous parable, Jesus tells his listeners that the results of their lives are dependent upon *the condition of their hearts!* [330]** He cites four primary conditions:

Case one: The hardened heart, where the "seed of the Word" cannot penetrate. These hearts are the *trampled paths of lives* where people follow the crowds where their "authorities" teach them to believe and follow the traditions of men.[331]**

---

327 *See "Jesus's Major Parables"*

328 Luke 16

330 **See Appendix B: What Type of Christian are you?*

331 Matt. 15:7–14 **See also the position paper: Authority and Conscience*

Case two: The shallow heart, where the "seed of the Word" penetrates at first, but after it sprouts up, finds no basis or support to continue growing.

Lack of commitment, lukewarmness, and equivocation and compromises of beliefs are the common responses you find here. Whenever persecution or opposition arises because of the Word, they are *down the road and gone!*

Case three: The crowded heart is where *competition crowds the seedlings of spiritual life out.* If you, as a believer, do not *prioritize* the things in your life, always placing the highest value on spiritual things, then worldly things will *quickly co-opt your will!* The world will surely choke out the tender and vulnerable beliefs that Jesus brings by the gentle Holy Spirit if you fail to do this. You must be ready, willing, and diligent to *weed out your heart!* One thing you quickly learn is that *the Agape love of God cannot survive competition.* Always remember that God will never force you to receive deeper spiritual truths. To receive these, you must act individually, choosing to seek first God's Kingdom.

Case four: The good heart is the life that has *counted the cost* of the Christian life and has decided to *follow Jesus no matter what.* Within this category are the varying *degrees of success* in spiritual things "some thirty (times what they sowed), some sixty (times what they sowed), and for some, a hundred (times what they sowed)." The results that people see in a life we also can measure as *fruit or works.* Scripture also defines them as *characteristics of the Holy Spirit* that grow in our lives as we submit our lives unto the Lord Jesus Christ.

The main attribute is Agape love.[332] All the rest are formed out of this central kernel of God's kingdom within our lives! God also shows fruit in Scripture as reward or recompense. It is considered the value of the harvest that God will reap at the end of the age. The parable of the sower also gives believers some very stern warnings in the subsequent second parable section concerning "the wheat and the tares." Jesus also mentioned the importance of the "harvest."[333] Not only that, believers need to constantly evaluate their own motives.

---

332   John 13–17; 1 Cor. 13; Gal. 5:22,23.
333   Matt. 13:24–43; John 4:34–38

Ask yourself: *Why am I really serving Jesus?* Is it just because you receive these spiritual gifts now? Is it because you will *reap a reward in heaven?* Are you motivated to serve Jesus *solely because you love Him?* [334]

VI. The way Christians regard the stewardship of the body of Christ has great significance.

The quality of relationships within the body of Christ accurately reflects *the level and quality of spirituality within it.* God's Spirit vividly reflects these in the commands our Lord Jesus taught the disciples in the Upper Room/Gethsemane discourse, chronicled by John in his gospel, chapters 13 to 17. *Agape love* plays a major role in maintaining righteous relations between believers.[335] John also deals with this crucial subject as well in his later letters. The epistles of Paul also address the many serious ongoing problems with factions, personality cults, and moral issues. All the New Testament underscores a vital New Covenant truth:

It appears that Paul was merely reinforcing the spiritual precept that there was a direct spiritual connection between stewardship and interpersonal relationships within the body of Christ. This appears prominently in the pastoral narrative that Paul wrote to Timothy in his last letter. Moreover, we must acknowledge that:

VII. Christians will be judged by the Lord Jesus Christ concerning the following areas:

1. *The infiltration of false doctrines,* especially those related to *humanism.* Smooth talkers hawking high-minded and "logical" methods, schemes, and ideas easily take in people. *They exalt humanistic solutions* that foment troubles, cause legalism, exalt self-righteousness, stifle love and liberty in worship, and cause a host of relational problems in the church. However, these problems are part of a larger issue: the deification of man—*idolatry.* People do not like others to tell them that, but the problems remain and keep worsening.

---

334   Luke 14:7–24
335   John 13:34,35; 1 Cor. 11:28–32

Although they cleverly mask themselves, spiritually minded believers can see and identify the idols by various names: high-minded professionalism, materialism, humanism, paganism, intellectualism, nationalism, syncretism, and so forth.[336]

2. *The serious ongoing factional problems* (encountered early in Christian history) are still afflicting the church. We must deal with them. Paul knew what the consequences of these fleshly attitudes were and warned that leaders must be careful in how they deal with these problems.[337]

3. We cannot overemphasize the *central issue of our faithfulness and personal loyalty to Jesus Christ.* Maintaining *the integrity* of the true and complete Christian Gospel is indispensable! This issue *relates to the fundamental identity we have in Christ* as true believers, baptized into His body, and being *part of Christ.* Loyalty to Christ means that we place Him above all other concerns of this life and of the world around us.[338]

4. *Our willingness* to endure suffering and *persecutions for His sake* are a measure of our loyalty. These are central to the gospel and should be the crowning glory of a Christian's baptism.[339]

5. The way we believe concerning our response to evil or to what others do to harm us is the acid test of biblical Christianity. It is a tragedy that church leadership has taught most believers that worldly responses to evil are acceptable. The New Covenant teaches us about a progression fatal to spiritual life associated with all casuistic doctrines that condone hatred, violence, or homicide! This pattern is a familiar part of Satan's web of lies and deceit.

---

336   Acts 20:17–38; 1 Cor. 1:17–2:16; 2 Cor. 3:1–4:7; Gal. 1:6–2:21; Col. 2:1 ff. *See the papers entitled "Facilitating Revival," "Investigating the Symptoms of Latter-day Problems," and "Patriarchalism in the Church"*

337   1 Cor. 3:1 ff.; 2 Tim. 2:19–26. *See the papers entitled "Basics of Biblical Church Governance" and the 3 part series "Christianity Versus Religion"*

338   Matt. 24–38; 16:21–26; Luke 9:23–26; 14:26–33; Acts 20:19–38; Gal. 1:6–12; 2 Tim. 2:1–15. *See the papers entitled "Failed Expectations" and "God's Universal Attitude Test"*

339   Matt. 5:10–12; 10:24–38; Luke 12:49–53 14:26–33; Eph. 6:10–18; 2 Tim. 2:1–15. *See the papers entitled "the Baptism of Jesus Christ"*

The predictable progression goes like this: *Pride or lust* (including all the desires to make things right by force) + *Fear* + *Anger* + *Hatred*= *Violence* + *Death.* Eventually, if we follow that way, one is "overcome of evil" and "gives place to the devil." The rules work the same for everyone. Jesus clearly teaches that we can only survive the storms that life brings our way when we build our lives *"upon this Rock."* To be truly living *on the Rock,* this means that we follow Jesus's teachings that inevitably lead us to **faith-based pacifism.**

When persecution intensifies, we can effectively protect our hearts securely against perdition only when this central doctrine is the paradigm and basis of our response to evil! [340]

VIII. Summary

The Lord Jesus Christ will judge Christians on our faithfulness and diligence in following the commands of Jesus—*both within the church and in the outside world.* We should note that the *usual, traditional, and organizational methods* commonly used to deal with the church's problems have failed primarily because of disobedience. This is largely because far too many Christians refuse to submit to Jesus Christ *as their true head!* The truth is that, to gain any measure of true success or revival, the body of Christ *must repent* and return unto the archetypal (biblical) doctrines of *the New Covenant.* This truth is readily found in the *New Testament Gospel teachings of Jesus! God has given us the solution! Yet, are Christians willing to use it?*

---

340   Gen. 4:7; Matt. 5:22–25,38–48; 26:51,52; Luke 6:46–49; 9:51–56; Rom. 12:9– 21; Eph. 4:26–31; Col. 3:8; James 1:14,15; 1 John 3:1–15; 4:7–21 *See Glossary of Terms entry *Faith-Based Pacifism* See also the author's book "Jesus' Way," Dorrance Publishing Co., Pittsburgh, 2009*

Epilogue

In concluding our analysis on the church in the last days, let us seek the divine light of prophetic Scripture in directing our belief and faith. One must be careful to observe that spiritual visions of prophecy can have multiple meanings. One must also understand that in many accounts, the phrase "[I was] In the Spirit" does not necessarily refer to a physical translation or assumption of the body itself.[341] What is ultimately important, *however, is that* we gain a truly spiritual understanding of Scripture! Let us observe the following:

I. Scripture teaches us that God continues the proclamation of the eternal gospel during the great tribulation. This is the same gospel that God always ordained for redemption. This is that the blood of the Lamb, Jesus Christ, would be the sacrifice intended to *redeem* human beings from the power of sin, death, and the grave.[342]

II. In Revelation 14, John reminds us that the saints (the church) are definitely going to be here during *at least for a significant part of the great tribulation.* God admonishes them to continue exercising *fundamental gospel truths.* Among these is the patience of the saints, which is the spiritual term for the *original Christian position of *faith-based pacifism*.* This is the total commitment to non-violence in response to evil, based on Jesus plain teachings and the New Covenant.[343] The writer would

---

341   2 Cor. 12:1–4
342   2 Pet. 3:9; Rev. 14:6,7
343   Isa. 53:9; Matt. 5:1–7:29; 10:16; Luke 9:51–56; Phil. 2:12–16; Heb. 7:26; Rev. 12:10,11; 14:12,13.

gently remind the reader to please continue to observe the crucial difference between tribulation *(thilipsis)* and wrath *(orge).*

III. Then we have the second coming event, when Christ becomes visible to earth-dwellers. Jesus Christ first appears in a cloud of angels and saints. Jesus then gathers the saints to Him in the clouds that is the first resurrection and rapture.[344] Following this, we have the judgment sequences of wrath.[345]

IV. Believers must prepare for the judgment seat of Christ. The Bridegroom requires widespread repentance of the church, both *as individuals and as a whole.* Believers must *get their house in order* and make ready for the Bridegroom! Judgment must begin at the house of God.[346]

Moreover, Christians need to *forgive each other,* come together, and work together to encourage prayer for the mending of the torn garment and for the healing of the body of Christ! Jesus is watching right now, looking down, and probing our hearts to see whether the people who call him "Lord, Lord" will do what he says to do. Verily, we must *do whatever it takes* to implore God's great mercy and love for us, for we have sinned greatly![347] Consider the penitence God would have us cultivate in the responses God's Word has recorded for us in the past.[348]

V. The most difficult area within the scope of repentance that we must now consider is that God commands Christian people to "turn from their wicked ways."

Wicked means *anything that is harmful or hurtful!* Christians have hurt each other terribly, and the ones who have done these things must acknowledge these things as wicked and make amends according to what Jesus has taught us in Matthew 18.

---

344   Matt. 24:27–31; 1 Cor. 15:23; 1 Thess. 4:13–17; James 5:7; Rev. 7:9-17
345   2 Thess. 1:6–10; 2:1–12; 2 Pet. 3:10 f.; Rev. 14:14 ff.
346   Matt. 25:1–13; 1 Pet. 4:17.
347   2 Chr. 7:14; Dan. 9:4-19; Matt. 6:1–15,33; Luke 11:1–13; 1 Cor. 11:23–34
348   2 Chr. 7:14; Psalms 32, 51; Neh. 9; Dan. 9 *See the paper entitled "the Doctrine of Repentance"*

Leaders must take the lead, encourage exchange, and *actively foster and encourage biblical repentance.* In doing so, Christians must be willing to *deal biblically* with things like the following:

1. *Christian Arrogance.* The high-minded, aloof, and proud *holier-than-thou* attitudes commonly exhibited by Christians that falsely represent Jesus Christ must change! Jesus commands Christians to "become like little children," and to exude *His fragrance.*[349]

2. *Sectarianism.* The unbiblical *walls* churches build up to protect are insulating them from other believers they themselves need. *These walls must come down!* We cannot continue to tolerate unbiblical organizational forms and legal technicalities used to drive Godly ministers away.[350]

3. *The Fortress Mentality,* where they consider religious dogma, church traditions, and denominational distinctive for being more sacred than Scripture or even God Himself! *How do you think God feels* about the bitter hostility directed by both church organizations and leaders alike toward anyone who challenges their comfortable worldly system? What does God feel about *the unmerited forced exits and* unbiblical *disfellowshipings?* Many churches even rigidly enforce *a false facade of unity.*

Many treat the genuine messengers of God like enemies just because they are honest enough to tell them the truth![351] These things should not be so!

4. *The apparent total acceptance of any kind of immorality* within the church if leaders believe it is "legalized by the state." This travesty exists in part because "church growth mad" modern Christianity has admitted a whole generation of "practical infidels," marginal Christians, and "habitual church hoppers" who commit sin with impunity and dilute the holy standard.

---

349   Matt. 18:1 ff.; Luke 9:44–48; 2 Cor. 2:14–17.

350   Matt. 18:1 ff.; Luke 9:44–48; 2 Cor. 2:14–17.

351   Matt. 15:1 f.; Mark 9:38–40; 1 Cor. 3:1 f.; Gal. 4:16. *See the paper entitled "Christian Guidelines for Spiritual Warfare, Part 4: Knowing Your Enemy" and the 3 part series entitled "Christianity Versus Religion"*

Yet, leaders *appear to intentionally look the other way* when a decision requires the slightest exercise of *moral courage!* We cannot avoid these problems. We must face them squarely and *deal with them biblically!* A common scenario involves adultery. These "so-called Christians" expect others to ignore their gross arrogance and lawlessness. Not only that, they think they can avoid repentance and "wipe their slate clean," escaping accountability They simply get a secular court document of divorce or marriage and switch churches!

It grieves me to the core to have to say this, but it does put ministers on the spot. Yet, the error is compounded when church leaders continue to approve these ungodly evasive maneuvers. Like Pilate, many leaders try to "wash their hands of it," all for several different reasons *all related to pride:* 1) their fear of man is palpable, 2) they are *people pleasers at heart,* 3) they are afraid of *losing members (numbers and dollars),* 4) *their fear of losing their position and influence,* and 5) because *religious authorities taught them to consider man's law above God's law!* Do you really believe that the leaders who persist enabling this gross miscarriage of righteousness will escape the judgment of God? I do not think so.[352]

5. *Their "definition of success" is far afield from God's!* They think "success" is temporal popularity, material wealth, numbers in the pews, and dollars in the plate. What can I say about *wishy-washy morality, bend-over-backward people-pleasing and blatantly worldly entertainment methods?*[353] How wrong they are!

6. Then, we have the *flagrant use of simplistic legalism* as a dodge to evade the tougher issues Christians face in life. This is the coward's way out! Churches place a higher value and premium on man's law than God's. Evidently, they despise the deeper truths of the Word of God, ignoring the New Covenant! They should be ashamed! Yet, *Jesus is watching* every day, every moment, everywhere. Jesus is carefully evaluating the church's responses to the New Covenant.

---

352   Matt. 5:17–32; Mark 10:1–12. *See the 2 part series of papers entitled "Authority and Conscience"*
353   Matt. 23; Luke 16:1–15.

7. Yes, *Jesus sees* all *the unbiblical responses to the messengers* that he has sent to them to bring the message of *prophecy, repentance, and biblical reconciliation* that Jesus would have them to hear. Yet, do they even care to glorify Jesus and *be ready for His coming?*

Christian, *what is your focus on?* Beware. The subtle latch of pride and the fear of public shame prevents far too many from repenting.

Will they find the place of repentance in time? [354]

---

354   Luke 11:29–14:35; 1 Cor. 4:8–21; Heb. 10:26–39; 12:1 ff. *See also the papers entitled "Two Divergent belief Systems" and "Facilitating Revival"*

APPENDİCES

Profile of Antichrist

The following outline is an addendum to the information in chapters 9 and 10. *The global empire of Antichrist/Babylon is a totalitarian system* characterized by the following:

I. Imperialism. Babylon (the new world order) controls a worldwide dictatorship and global empire with unrestricted power. It is a system within which and from which the ruling party and its leader rule.

A. *The lawless one:* Viz., the leaders of "Babylon" disregard duly constituted authority, including the Constitution, considering themselves "above the law."

B. They are obsessed with control and security everywhere.

C. Babylon commands global control over all government, laws and courts.

D. The system commands a global outreach of Military operations.

E. They manipulate and control information by a sophisticated propaganda machine headed by the false prophet.

F. They regulate public transportation carriers.

II. It controls a worldwide (global) economic monopoly including:

A. It will become a closely controlled cash-less economic system that uses an *imbedded financial transfer chip* regulating all legal transactions *by a master computer.*

B. It is a worldwide network of multinational banks and corporations owned and controlled by an occult group of major stockholders whom the ruling party (global oligarchy) then controls. An even more secretive cabal of ultra-rich figures owns and sets the policies for all.

C. They ensure their ever-tightening control and the maximization of profits by using the ubiquitous presence and power of the military being unconstitutionally used as police, to enforce illegal laws that deny citizens their freedoms that are guaranteed by the "Bill of Rights."

D. Worldwide propaganda reinforces media control, which they also repackage as advertising to sell products using human appetites and perceived needs as lures.

III. Worldwide secularized professionalism. This system monopolizes, permeates, and rigidly controls all outward professions, including all corporate business organizations whether they are *for profit or nonprofit,* governmental agencies, organized religion and licensing of ministers, entertainment, transportation, education, medical, psychiatric, and scientific Fields. They gear technologies to serve the world system and ruling "oligarchy." Widespread use or promotion of the following characterizes the entire professional, legal, and justice system which Antichrist selectively biases.

A. Pseudoscientific *atheism* permeates all fields.

B. They forbid prayer and religious activity in schools.

C. They falsely teach the "theory of evolution" *as a fact.*

D. Prescription and use of psychotic drugs, such as antidepressants, are used for mind control.

E. The use and teaching of *occult and psychic meditation techniques for counseling and "therapy"* permeate both government and business venues.

F. The system maintains and funds a network of specialized clinics that they dedicate to the practices of infanticide and abortion, protecting it vigorously with laws and military (police).

IV. "Police State" style totalitarian tactics ensure complete control and guarantee maximum profits for the oligarchy.

A. The system starts by employing legal technicalities to deny and deprive people of civil rights including those guaranteed constitutional rights in America we now call the "Bill of Rights." We can see this already *in the "Patriot" Act of 2001.* They then defeat constitutionally legal protections that true law would adjudicate or uphold. This "lawless system" selectively bypasses due process of law by the selective withholding of relevant evidence to obtain either convictions or exonerations. We can see this today as legalized jury tampering, and by unlawful detentions that suspend the fundamental right of Habeas Corpus.

B. Martial Law. Expanded powers of the police that violate "Posse Comitatus," the Constitutional protection against using the military as the police. These include unannounced searches and seizures, warrantless wiretapping, and the keeping of detailed dossiers on everyone. They tell the duped masses that this is necessary to *"fight terrorism,"* which is exactly what *the government is doing! Remember how Hitler did this to seize power in Germany after the Reichstag fire.*

C. The "new" world order (global fascism) uses spy agencies with private armies as terror and death squads. They use them to carry out "false flag operations" even within the most prosperous "countries" to ensure docile compliance of the slave population and maximum profit to the multinational corporations. This leads to

D. Total Military control and administration of technological development, the space program, global business, and of all resource exploration and management. Babylon (the new world order) also sedulously controls all government-sponsored technologies that they have geared to favor the politico-military-industrial complex.

E. The new world order *(the beast) uses computers as the universal linchpin* of all corporate business operations. First, they will use the Internet to link them to mandatory government controls over all transactions. Then these will be all keyed to the "implanted chips" that will become the mark *of the beast.*

F. The authorities of *global Babylon* will supervise the issuance of a universal global ID chip. Comparing this to Scripture, this would fit what John envisions as a "mark" that they will "implant" in either the right hand or forehead.[356] These chips will contain a GPS (global positioning system) and a complete "dossier" of the subjects' (slaves') whereabouts and background. They will issue electronic program code numbers to every *global citizen*. This controls all financial *transfers*. This effectively eliminates paper currency and identification papers. These implant devices will enable the global government of Antichrist to track and monitor the enslaved masses by using a master computer (the beast). They will initially introduce it as a *"foolproof method"* to eliminate the problems with "terrorists" (their false definition), counterfeiters, drug dealers, bank robbers, identity thieves, and child abductors.

V. Worldwide media ministry headed by the false prophet who deviously slants propaganda to glorify and deify men for being the saviors!

Globally controlled consortiums have already "bought out all major media publishers." We can see this agenda today in the glorification of human prowess, especially in the movie industry, politics, and the military. The system gives nearly all the glory to the exploits of man. The media also exalts soldiers they depict as "freedom fighters and heroes." Using this mechanism, the voice and agenda of Satan is broadcasted worldwide through the medium of entertainment. Yes, the false prophet *adeptly uses entertainment as propaganda* in cleverly crafted "situation dramas" showcasing and *exalting humanistic "solutions"* according to the "Hegelian Dialectic."

Like a giant commercial advertising message, the image of the beast will come alive for everyone to see, portraying his agendas worldwide on giant LCD screens (just like in Times Square).[357]

---

356   Rev. 13
357   *See Chapter 10 and the paper "A Biblical Disclosure of Antichrist."*

VI. "The beast" will inaugurate a worldwide conglomerate secular religion based on humanism that is integral to Babylon.

The UN already has the blueprint of this "religion" ready to carry out! It *has the number of men*. It is a system wholly based on the Satanic formula of: Humanism=Man is god=WWW=666. Its foundation is pure humanism, mixed with occult methodology and syncretism.

A. It persecutes all Christians, Muslims, and Jews, especially because they claim to have the sole path to a single God outside man.

B. Global Babylon, overall, follows the historic structure of ancient cults and modern cults like *freemasonry*. Of course, we already know that Lucifer (Satan) has long held world domination as his goal and agenda. Among many others, we can see Antichrists' symbol in *the all-seeing eye* and pyramid capstone on the back of US $1 bill.

C. It serves the global state's agendas of maintaining absolute power.

D. It follows the ancient pagan pattern of religion and state being combined.

E. Babylon echoes the original lies in the garden foisted by Satan, the former Lucifer: "You will be as gods, knowing good and evil."

VII. What do you think qualifies for being Antichrist and the head of "the new world order" even today? Ask yourself the following questions:

Q1: Who or what has the most economic clout worldwide?

Q2: Who or what has the strongest and largest military might worldwide?

Q3. Who or what has made an "alliance treaty or agreement" to "protect" Israel? [358]

Q4. Who or what "pretends to be Christian" (looks like a Lamb) yet betraying the very central person of Christianity (speaks with the voice of the dragon) by their avowed imperial policies? [359]

---

358   *Note that Scripture does not say that "Antichrist will make a covenant with Israel."*
359   Rev. 13

VIII. Conclusion

Because of the *intense delusions* that are very much a part of Antichrist, the church must be aware of any false assumptions. God's people must endure much difficulty and extreme pressures in the future. Traditional forms and organized churches will effectively disappear from view. So it is imperative that our focus is on Jesus Christ alone to survive that portion of the great tribulation that God is allowing the body of Christ to pass through as a final test! Take heart, all God's promises are still truly effective then and now. God's Word promises us *that no test that we must endure is beyond the power His grace will provide at the time of our need!* [360]

---

[360] 1 Cor. 10:12,13

What Type of Christian Are You?

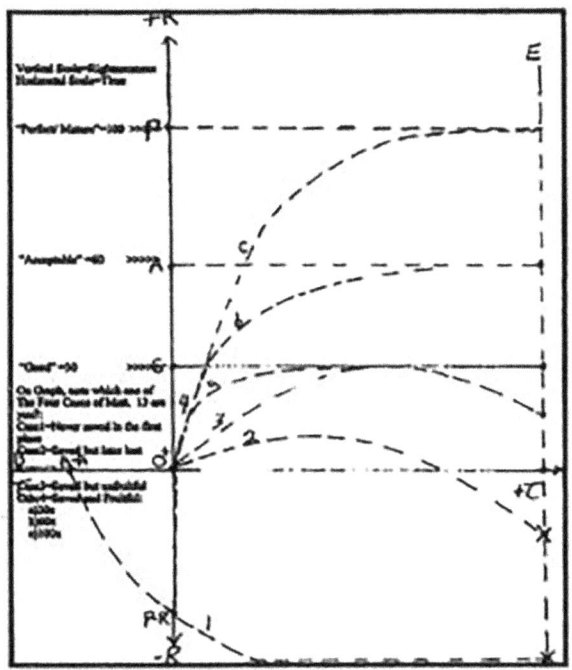

For Legend, see the list on following Page:

Legend for Appendix B:

1. +R, – R is scale axis of righteousness. To inherit salvation, one must remain on the positive side and finish at least at 0+ on this scale. Zero or anywhere below zero is unacceptable to God.

2. P= "perfect" or mature. This means that we exhibit the fullness of the stature of Jesus Christ. Matt. 13; Rom. 12:1,2; Eph. 4:13.

3. On curves, a positive slope shows *repentance* or restoration is in progress.

4. Conversely, negative slope on a curve shows either apostasy or rebellion is in progress.

5. B= our time or birth

6. A-A is our "age of accountability," when we first have "knowledge of the law," and know what right and wrong are, and sin is first *imputed.* Rom. 5:12– 14

7. E= the "End," either of life, or when Jesus comes, whichever is first. Matt. 10:22, 24:13.

8. P-R is the point at which one first receives Christ as Savior, when the gift of *faith* imputes provisional/ positional righteousness to us by *prevenient grace.* Rom. 3:19–26; 4:4 ff.

9. The four cases of Matt. 13:1 ff. and Rom. 12:1,2. In review, we can see:

Case one: Never saved (born from above) in the first place. Matt. 13:4,19

Case two: Saved at first, but later lost by *cutting ourselves off from the Vine,* apostasy, blasphemy, or becoming a reprobate, castaway, or shipwreck. Matt. 13:5,20,21; Luke 12:8–10; John 15:7; Rom. 1:28; 1 Cor. 9:27; 2 Cor. 13:5,6; 1 Tim. 1:19

Case three: Saved but becomes unfruitful due to competition. Matt. 13:7,22.

Case four: Condition a, b, and c saved and fruitful. Matt. 13: 8,23.

See also Matt. 5:20; 18:3; Heb. 6:1–7; 10:26–39.

Rev. 8A:7-30-09

Correlating Last Days' Scriptures

A spiritual discipline that is necessary for attaining the fullness of Truth in God's Word.

IX.	Conclusion	
X.	Appendices:	
	Figure One: "The Seventy Weeks"	
	"Correlating Major Events to Prophecy Chart"	
	"Postulating Overlaps/ Offsets" in Last Days Diagram	
	Legend for "Postulating Overlaps/ Offsets"	

I. Introductory explanations: In general, properly correlating Scripture involves <u>comparing</u> Scripture to Scripture in such a way that we observe its primacy and preserve its integrity. Following this guideline is absolutely necessary for any Bible student to understand the teaching of God's Word. Moreover, coming to know the Truth that Scripture teaches is a foundational part of Salvation's Process which includes Worship, Prayer and all the other elements of Discipleship. "Thy (God's) Word is Truth" and learning the Truth as accurately as possible is indispensable for we must know how to discern "The Spirit of Truth from the spirit of error." God will honor all those who love seek and practice the Truth, but judges all those who avoid, corrupt, manipulate or contradict Truth.[1]

Two <u>levels</u> of Truth are apparent: First, the personal or existential Truth and second, the Written Truth (God's Holy Written Word, the Bible) which reflects the first.

Also, two main <u>areas</u> of Truth exist, paralleling the two levels:

The first is the *Logos*, which is the foundational set of precepts (the source) from which God's Word proceeds. Not only that, Scripture tells us that the <u>Person of Jesus Christ IS the Word of God.</u>[2]

The second is the *Rema*, which is the communication, teaching or transfer of that Truth to others. We cannot ignore the utter seriousness of attaining, maintaining and practicing the Truth of what we know as the *New Covenant* Christian *Gospel,* which is the Word of God

---

1   1 John 4:1-6
2   John 1:1 f.; 17:17; 1 John 1:1; 5:7; Rev. 19:10,13

for our times, as seen thru the *Lens of Jesus Christ.*[3] This broaches the subject of context, of which we will have much to say about as we delve into this crucial subject. Let us list the aspects/ types of Scripture and the types of context we find therein:

- Spirituality is the underlying bedrock context which interweaves all Scripture at differing levels.

This explains how God "reinvents" the meaning of Scripture for each Age, thereby keeping its meaning relevant for each generation. Always remember these facts: God is Spirit, Scripture is spiritual and that we must Worship God in Spirit to access and attain the Truth that only the Holy Spirit can give. The fact that Scripture study is a part of Spiritual Worship clearly tells us that all "intellectual methods" are insufficient and, if used by themselves, will fall short of the goal.[4]

- To understand "Prophetic" Scripture we must also be aware of the "General rules of context" that apply to the study of any written work.

Viz., you must consider these conditions: Know who is speaking, to whom are they speaking, the subject matter and the applicable tenses: Past, present, future or *Aorist*, which is present continuing into the future.

- Whenever you study, you must observe the type of Scripture. These are Prophecy, Discourse, Narrative story, Parable, poetic or a lyrical passage or historical chronicle, et al.[5]

- The student must be especially careful and always diligent to submit to God and seek the underlying truths God has imbedded in these "multilevel" texts, "letting the Scripture speak for itself."

Author note: You cannot overestimate the value and necessity of submission to the Holy Spirit. Regarding Prophetic and eschatology texts especially, far too many have been 'led astray' by intellectual schemes and other humanistic factors that cause people to artificially "twist Scripture," ignoring the underlying spiritual prerequisites and

---

3 Jer. 31:31-34; Matt. 24:14; Acts 17:24-31; Heb. 1:1 f.
4 Psa. 73; John 4:23,24; 8:31-36; 1 Cor. 1:17-2:16 See the Paper Fulfilment Prophecy
5 For more details on these guidelines see the paper: *Hermeneutics: Basic Principles of Scripture Interpretation*

conditions and thereby "jump to falsely based conclusions." One of the most insidious problems that cause this is man's innate penchant for 'people-pleasing' and desire to find "shortcuts" around seemingly difficult subjects.

The amazing truth about all this is that God's Spirit stands by ready, willing and able to impart Spiritual *Wisdom* to <u>anybody who truly submits to God</u> and perseveres onward to the fullness of Truth. God is no respecter of persons. In fact, Jesus' Teaching about coming to God <u>like a little child who is always willing to learn</u> shows us the "secret" and key to comprehending all Scripture![6]

However, in many cases the problem is that we have blindly trusted the earthbound traditions of many religious leaders who have another agenda that conflicts with God's Will. As Jesus succinctly told the Disciples, they are the stumbling block standing in the way of the deeper truths the Holy Spirit teaches about how God is working to <u>unify all Believers</u> into One Body *In Christ.*[7] This fact makes it all the more important that you <u>individually seek the Truth independently</u> and not "assume" that what you have been taught in the past by church leaders was true![8] Let us investigate some of the most significant Prophetic texts in God's Word that profoundly affect doctrine in this area.

II. Concerning the major "Event Types," Correlating and comparing the Scriptures that impinge upon doctrine leads us to the "<u>common statements</u>" within that <u>link them</u> <u>together</u>. Let us consider the major terms regarding our understanding of eschatology and the Last Days. They are the "Falling away First" (FAF), the "Antichrist figure" (ACF), "the Great Tribulation Period" (GTP), "The Day of the Lord" (DTL), the "Rapture of the Saints" (ROS), the "Three and ½ Year periods"** (TOHY), the "Seventy Weeks of Daniel" (SWD), "Until the Times of the Gentiles are Fulfilled" (TGF) and the "Jews Extension Period" (JEP).[9]**

---

6   Matt. 18:3,4; 19:13,14
7   Matt. 15:1-14; 23:1 ff.; Luke 11-13 See also Footnotes 15,28,34
8   *See A Seeker's Guide to Biblical Faith*
9   ***Note that the TOHY periods are a.k.a. "1260 Days," "42 Months," "a Time, Times and a Dividing (a half) of time," "in the midst of the week" and sometimes "3 ½ Days": Dan. 7:25; 9:27; 12:7; Rev. 11:2,11; 12:6,14; 13:5 See also the book The Church in the Last Days and the following: A Biblical Disclosure of Antichrist, Facts of Scripture: The Church and the*

Then, by carefully comparing Scripture with Scripture, maintaining submission to the Holy Spirit and diligently listening to the 'still small voice' in your Reborn spirit you will find the Truth, for God's Spirit will gladly give it to you.

Amazingly, when you listen to God, the comprehending of spiritual things is not as "complicated" as you might think! Know that God's Holy Spirit always teaches precisely the same as Jesus Christ would teach, if he were here as a man speaking to you.[10] As you compare the Scriptures' references to the above terms, you will find that some appear 'offset,' staggered' or 'overlapped' in time. Just taking this one important fact into consideration goes a long way in clearing up the "Last Days Picture" and toward unifying doctrine so that it satisfies all the Scripture.[11]*

To understand what God's Word says about the Last Days, we must do the following: First, take Jesus Christ's statements and chronology in the main "Prophetic Discourse" and the "Emmaus road Discourse."[12]

Second, compare this to Jesus' Parables that concern the "Jewish Wedding Theme," like the Parable of the Ten Virgins.[13]

Third, compare to Jesus' other Parables that tell us about a Householder, business man or dignitary who entrusts his tenants to manage his affairs while he goes on a long trip and then when he returns requires to give account on what they did.[14]

Fourth, compare to Jesus' Parables and teachings that use the "Sheep-tending" venue, like the "Lost Sheep," the "Sheep fold Illustration" in John that reaffirms God's Plan of unification and the "Parable of the Sheep and Goats."[15]

Tribulation, The Doctrine of Last Things, The Three Passovers, Last Days Time Line Diagrams and Historical Time Line Chart See also Section IV and the Appendices

10   John 14:6-9, 15-26; 15:26; 16:7-15

11   *See the diagram "Postulating Overlaps" in Appendices. See also The Church in the Last Days, Chapter 12: "Event Sequence" paragraph V: Explanatory on "The Day of the Lord."*

12   Matt. 24; Mark 13; Luke 21,24

13   Matt. 25:1-13

14   *See the Paper Jesus; Major Parables*

15   Matt. 18:10-14; 25:14 ff.; John 10:1-16

Fifth, having done this, then compare to Jesus' other pertinent statements on similar subjects such as "In this world you will have Tribulation, but be of good cheer: I have overcome the world."[16]

Sixth, then compare the above to Paul's statements in his letters.[17]

Seventh, compare to James's letter.[18]

Eighth, compare to Peter's Second epistle.[19]

Ninth, compare to John's statements in his First epistle and in the *Apocalypse* about Antichrist [20]

Tenth, when we compare all the above, Daniel's Prophecy also links these with the chronological placing and partitioning of the 70th Week and the Jews' extension period at the end of the Great Tribulation Period.[21]

Having completed these comparisons, you should clearly see how God's Word is centered in spirituality and is one cloth. Then, when you let the Holy Spirit interpret the meaning, you will eventually see the Truth that unifies all Doctrine so that it satisfies and fits all Scripture without "twisting it around." Of course, the constant underlying maxim is, that to be valid, every interpretation of prophecies must agree with Jesus Christ. Another crucial element is that when a prophetic text is introduced by a "spiritual vision" venue, the reader needs to observe that context since the descriptions given there are meant to be understood primarily in a spiritual sense.[22] The Bible student must always keep an open mind that is ever ready to receive new information. Think of Scripture inquiry for being similar to the "Scientific Method," with one major difference: Recognizing that spiritual things are real. Thus we are always ready to modify our beliefs whenever we sense the Holy Spirit giving us new information and avoid the pitfalls of narrow mindedness and dogmatism.

16   John 16:33
17   Rom. 11:25,26; 1 Cor. 15:20-28; 1 Thess. 4:13-18; 2 Thess. 1:7-2:12; 2 Tim. 3:1-7
18   James 5:7,8
19   2 Pet. 2:2-3:10
20   1 John 2:15-27; Rev. 6:12-7:17; 11:1 f.; 12:1-11; 13:5
21   Dan. 2:19-45; 7:25; 9:24-27; 12:7,11,12; Matt. 24; Luke 21
22   *E. G., Ezek. 40-48 is a "pictorial vision – prophecy" written during the captivity that "looks forward" to the New Covenant. In that way it is similar to Ch. 37, Zechariah and Revelation. FYI.: See also the Paper Biblical Symbolism, Section D, #24-26 (Pgs 26-32)*

III. Overall, the "Passover Paradigm" traces a four-phase pattern that can be seen throughout Scripture. It also contains the elements of a spiritual Pattern of Advent/ Manifestation, Humiliation and Exaltation we call the *Kenosis.*

The last three (underlined in the left column) also form "God's Passover Pattern" of Salvation for the Righteous and Judgment for the wicked:

The "Passover Paradigm"		
Historical:	**Spiritual:**	**Common Figures:**
(+) Ordination and initial Investment by God, E.g., the Exodus of Israel and the Passion week of Christ.	"Grafting in"/ Advent Establishment of a Covenant/ Atonement of sin (See Passover Sequence Chart)	Noah, Abraham, Moses and Christ, "The Vine"
–Perpetration of evil: Apostasy/ Captivity/ Divestment [23]*	"Cutting off"/ Humiliation/ "Valley of Dry Bones"	"Messiah is cut off"
Sanctification: Separation and God's promise is given for future deliverance after discipline.	Projects the "New Covenant" vision of "Taking Captivity Captive and giving gifts to man"[24]	"Emmanul": God is dealing with us
(+) Rectification: The Restoration, preservation and unification of all Believers and God's Judgment of the wicked.	"Re Grafting in"/ Revival and restoration of life, empowering, Exaltation and Resurrection [25]	"The Ancient of Days" (Jesus Christ) overcomes evil and reigns overall.

---

23   Ezek. 36:16-23; 37:1-1-3; Dan. 9:24-27 *See also the Paper entitled: The Three Passovers of Scripture, Paragraph VI: "Unique Aspects of Passover Chronology"

24   Psa. 68:18; Isa. 7:14; 9:6; Jer. 31:31-34; Ezek. 37: 4 ff.; Matt. 26:26-28; Luke 22:20-22

25   Dan. 2:44.45; Matt. 10:24-42; Acts 17:24-31; Rom. 11:25,26; 1 Cor. 15:20-58; Phil. 2:5-11

IV. _We can also clarify doctrine by correlating and classifying Scriptures according to their application in tabular form._ The main factors are the person or group to which this Scripture applies, the approximate date which it was written and the particular hegemony, event or events to which it is linked: The "Apostasy" or "falling away first" (FAF), "The Antichrist Figure" (ACF), The "Day of the Lord" (DTL), the "Three and ½ Year" (TOHY) periods that are connected to a period of "Great Tribulation" (GTP), the "Seventy Weeks of Daniel" (SWD), the "Rapture of the Saints"(ROS), "Until the Times of the Gentiles are Fulfilled" (TGF) or the Extension Period for the remaining Jews at the end of the Great Tribulation (JEP).

Correlating Scriptures:		
Date of the source:	**It applies to:**	**Related Events:**
536 B.C. (Daniel)[26]	Jews primarily	ACF, SWD, DTL, TOHY
536 B.C. (Daniel)[27]	Jews only	JEP, DTL, SWD
520-516 B.C. (Zechariah)[28]	Jews, Christians and finally the Jews remaining after the GTP	JEP, DTL, SWD
AD 29. (Jesus Christ)[29]	The Saints or Elect: Jews and Christians	ACF, DTL, GTP, SWD, TGF
AD 53. (Paul).[30]	The Saints or Elect: Christians and Jews	FAF, ACF, DTL, GTP, ROS
AD. 90. (John).[31]	The Saints or Elect.	DTL, TOHY and GTP

---

26   Daniel 7:25; 9:24-27; 12:7

27   Daniel 12:11,12

28   Zech. 3-6*; 9:9-17; 12:10 _Note: This Scripture* first applies physically to Nehemiah's/ Zerubbabel's rebuilding of the Jewish Temple (#2) and second, spiritually, to the cessation of "ritual Temple worship" and God's restoration of spiritual worship by the New Covenant way of Faith in Jesus Christ, The BRANCH. John 4:23,24 See also the Papers entitled Biblical Symbolism, Christian Worship and the True Temple and Spirituality and Worship_

29   Matt. 24; Luke 21

30   1 Thess. 4:13-18; 2 Thess. 1:7-2:12

31   Rev. 7:9-17; 11:1-4; 12:7; 13:5 Cf. Zech. 4

V. God's Spirit <u>links together</u> the elements of "Last Days Theology" into the larger venue of the "<u>Mystery of Godliness</u>" which unifies all Scripture and Doctrine into one Whole. Before we continue, we must learn to see that only a spiritually based understanding of Scripture yields the <u>Full Truth</u>. In the archetypal Parable of the Sower, Jesus tells the Disciples that "It has been given unto you to know the mysteries of the Kingdom of Heaven." This brings us again to the crux of the issue of understanding Scripture: Revelation by the Holy Spirit, the source of Scripture's inspiration and its only reliable interpreter.

Moreover, obedience to Christ and submission to the Holy Spirit are the Key factors in unraveling the <u>Great Mystery of Godliness.</u> This ties directly with <u>God's Prophetic Timeline</u> (GPT), which will be Finished (Fulfilled) during the Seventh Seal of the Great Tribulation Period (GTP).

Of course, when we look with <u>spiritual eyes</u> within <u>"God's Prophetic Timeline"</u> (GPT), we also can see the Grand process whereby God is <u>unifying all things In Jesus</u> <u>Christ</u>, the original Creator of the Universe and the race of Mankind. Yet, we must clearly understand that <u>this Timeline never goes in reverse.</u> In particular, this precept warns anyone who attempts to "go back to Old Covenant ways" that they are incorrectly interpreting Scripture. Indeed, the popular belief that a "new temple" would be built falls under that classification.[32]

Again, the centerpiece for God's Prophetic Timeline process is the <u>Unification of all Believers</u>, whether they are Jews or Gentiles, into <u>one Body in Christ</u> that will Worship in spirit, fellowship, serve and Glorify God. Essentially, in various terminology, this body is what Jesus Christ defines for being the Saints, the Ekklesia, the church or the *Kingdom of Heaven.* It is also the theme of God's *Tapestry* the writer refers to in the book *Jesus' Way.*[33]

Paul expands on this theme and Foundational Truth in his letters. As we diligently seek the Truth with our whole heart, the Holy Spirit

---

32   See the Papers entitled *The Biblical Role of Israel, Sect. IV-D, The Doctrine of Last Things, Sect. VII, (Pg. 20, Footnote #33), Facts Concerning the 70th Week of Daniel, Sect. III* and *The Higher Laws of God, Pg. 7, Footnote #16*

33   Matt. 13:10; Mark 4:11; Luke 8:10; 1 Cor. 1:17-2:16; 1 Tim. 3:16; Rev. 10:7 See the Papers entitled *The Biblical Precept of Mystery and The Key to Understanding Scripture*, Section II

reveals the purpose of this Tapestry to our inward Reborn human spirit. Then, as it percolates into our being, we begin to 'see it' in our conscious mind and it begins to inspire us onward to unbounded zeal for the Faith and the *Patience of the Saints.* Indeed, this is God's Will for all who Love God.

As we continue to Abide in this process, God's Spirit gives the sublime byproduct that graces our lives when we live life in obedience to Christ, *Agape Love.* God also honors us with the manifold mantle of *Wisdom.* Divine Wisdom also includes the instant recognition of spiritual truths and the perseverance and courage we must have to live life according to Christ's Commands despite cost. Walking in <u>Wisdom and Agape Love</u> gives us the supernatural ability to endure faithfully to the end despite circumstance as Jesus Commands all True Disciples.[34]

The "Mystery of Godliness" also includes the theme of *Kenosis* mentioned above whereby God carries us through the stages of <u>progressive Sanctification</u>: Manifestation, Humiliation and Exaltation.

This pattern can be seen in God's dealings with the Jews: "God Plants," "God Cuts off" and "God Re-grafts in." Then, at the end of the Age, "<u>G</u>od's <u>M</u>ystery will be <u>F</u>inished" (GMF) and <u>All True Believers will be unified into one Whole in Christ</u>. This is the essence of the "Mystery" that God's Spirit revealed to Paul and the writer of Hebrews and it permeates their works.[35]

VI. Let us now correlate all the above elements in the Gospels epistles and Prophecy and we can see how God integrates the "Last Days' Scriptures" into the Great Eternal *Tapestry* of His Word which also aligns with <u>God's Prophetic Timeline</u> (GPT).

A. In particular, notice the timing reference John records in Revelation chapter ten: "When the Seventh Angel is *about to sound his Trumpet*

---

34   Job. 32:8; Prov. 1:7,23; 8:1 ff.; 9:10; Matt. 10:22; 24:13; Luke 21; Rom. 5:1-5; 8:1 ff.; 1 Cor. 4:1-5; 13:1 ff. ; Eph. 1:8,17; Col. 1:12-27; Heb. 1-4, 6, 9-12; James 1; 3:13-18; 2 Pet. 1:19-21; Rev. 12:10,11; 14:12

35   John 10:1-16; Rom. 11:25,26; 1 Cor. 15:20-28, 51-58; Eph. 3:1-11; Col. 1:12-29; 2: 1-3; Heb. 1:1 f.; 10:12-39; 12:22-29; Rev. 10:7 *See the Paper entitled The Biblical Precept of Mystery, Sect. II-B and IV*

(i.e., before God's wrath has finished), the Mystery of God will be accomplished."[36]

Compare this to the "Six Point Disciplinary" (SPD) of Daniel chapter nine: "Seventy sevens are decreed for your people... to finish the transgression, to put an end to sin, to atone for wickedness, to bring in everlasting righteousness, to seal up the vision and prophecy and to anoint the most Holy." Although this passage applies first to Jews, when you 'put it together,' both these Scriptures point us to God's overall Plan that leads to the Unification of all the Saints (Jews and Gentiles) into One Body in Christ's *Kingdom of Heaven.*

Notice in Daniel seven that God shows us the purpose of the Fourth (iron) beast which symbolizes the Roman Empire and its first Emperors from Caesar to Vespasian. This illustration is one of several, all being linked to the Vision of the Great Statue in Daniel two which is essentially God's incredibly masterful overview of earth's latter-day history all the way to Christ's Second Coming! [37]

B. Using these illustrations, Scripture teaches us that during the Multiple Fulfilments* that all refer to "periods of Great Tribulation," God will continue using the "Antichrist figure" (ACF), of which the Emperor Nero and Hitler are prime examples, to progressively test, sort out and purify the Saints on earth prior to Christ's (the Ancient of Days) return.

First, one central common reference links them all, the "Three and ½ Year" periods, the TOHY's, which are expressed in varying terminology.[38]

Second, Daniel nine, Jesus' Prophetic Discourse and John's *Apocalypse* all show us "multiple imagery" that points to the same type of Event with the linking common denominator of the "Three and ½

---

36   Rev. 10:7 *See also the Papers entitled The Biblical Precept of Mystery, The Biblical Role of the Jews Sect. IV-D, The Doctrine of Last Things, Sect. VII, Facts Concerning the 70th Week of Daniel, Pg. 3, One Covenant for All, Sect. V-D, Patterns in Prophetic Scripture, Sect. IV-C & D, Prophetic Chronology Two, Sect. IV*

37   Daniel 2:31-45; 9:24-27

38   Daniel 7:7-28; 2 Thess. 2:3-12 *See also the Papers entitled: A Biblical Disclosure of Antichrist, The Higher Laws of God, A Historical Sketch of Antichrist Figures, and *Illustrating the 'Law of Multiple Fulfillments' Ibid. Footnotes #9 and #30*

Year" periods, expressed in various ways, all telling us that the Saints will be present on earth during the Great Tribulation.

C. Among many others, the following references confirm this truth: All through "God's Prophetic Time Line" we can see a pattern of juxtaposing positives and negatives.

1. Among the positive symbols are the "Two Anointed ones," the "two olive trees" (also called "the Two Witnesses" in Revelation) which stand on either side of the "Oil-Delivering Manoreh" with the two tubes connected to it. Overall, this forms a combined symbol describing the *New Covenant* Mediatorship of Christ, the Holy Spirit's function of purifying, sealing and empowering the Saints and in Unifying all Believers into One Body in Christ.[39]

2. The negative is symbolized by the "Antichrist figure's" waging of "war against the Saints," the "Gentiles' Treading underfoot," the "Dragon chasing the Woman clothed with the Son" and the "Beast with seven heads and ten horns" that is also miraculously 'reincarnated' and issues the "Mark." The "Scarlet Woman & Beast" system is another figure that describes the Saints' enemy that persecutes both Jews and Christians.[40]

D. Not only that, IF you properly interpret them, the teachings of both Christ and Paul say the same thing. They also gave unequivocal warnings about extremely difficult conditions that will develop in the world (during the Great Tribulation) that all Christians must acknowledge for being the reality they must face sooner or later! So, beware of those who teach false doctrines of escapism. Consider well and take the Scriptures about this issue very seriously:

1. First is Jesus' prediction that "in the world you will have Tribulation." Think about it: If God did not prevent the unbelieving Jews and Romans from persecuting Christians in the first century, what makes you think that God will "magically deliver" modern Christians in the twenty-first century? Yes, in some cases' God does supernaturally

---

39   Zech. 3,4; 14:4-9; Rev. 10:7; 11:1-18 Cf. Jer. 31; Ezek. 36; John 10; 1 Cor. 15; Eph. 1-4; 1 Tim. 2:5 See also the Paper *Biblical Symbolism*, Sect. IV-C, P. 19-21, D, P. 24 and O, P. 3,4,10,11

40   Rev. 12:1-14; 13:1 ff.; 17:1 ff.

deliver Believers from persecution. However, read history: Many True Christians suffered greatly and were not delivered. This harsh Truth may be hard to take but it is nonetheless true.

2. Second, Paul's statement to the Thessalonians that Christians are "Not appointed unto wrath" certainly does not exclude the reality that we will have to experience "great tribulation," since John also specifically shows us a vivid preview of this very thing.

Carefully examine the sequence in Revelation seven: At a point just before the opening of the Seventh Seal, the sequence mentions the "Rapture" as the vast multitude of Christians "which came out of the Great Tribulation."[41]

E. The Great Tribulation, including the reign of Antichrist, takes place before Christ's Second Coming and the Rapture. Simply compare and correlate the following Scriptures again.[42] Consider the following:

1. If you see what the whole of Scripture is teaching, you cannot dissociate the Rapture from Christ's Second Coming since it is part of it!

2. The "Great Falling away first" mentioned by Paul in Second Thessalonians can only refer to the apostasy of the outward organized assemblies who no longer qualify for being Churches in God's eyes. Viz., the church's apostasy is the primary cause and enabler of the rise of Antichrist.[43]

3. According to Scripture, the Great Tribulation Period is Three and One-half Years long, not seven years. Not only that, according to Daniel, the termination of the 'daily sacrifice' is the dividing point that separates the first and second halves of the 70th Week.[44]

---

41   Dan. 9:24-27; Zech. 2; Matt. 24:15-22; Luke 21:20-28; *1 Thess. 5:9; Heb. 11; Rev. *7:9-17; 11:1-13 See the book *The Church in the Last Days and the Paper entitled Facts of Scripture: The Church and the Tribulation See also Fox's Book of Martyrs*

42   Matt. 24:29-31; Luke 21:20-24; John 16:33; 1 Cor. 15:20-23; 1 Thess, 4:13-17;5:9; 2 Thess. 1:5-2:12; Rev. 7:14-17 *Notice also that all these Scriptures tell us that the Rapture comes after the Tribulation, taking place during Christ's Second Coming.*

43   Matt. 24:21-31, 36,37,42-46; Mark 13:24-27; Luke 21:34-36; 2 Thess. 2:1-7; 2 Pet. 2:1-3; Rev. 2,3 *Notice that these warnings relate to a runaway apostasy in the church, rendering it impotent, neutralizing its influence against evil, thus unleashing antichrist. For more details concerning this see the papers entitled A Biblical Disclosure of Antichrist and Facts of Scripture: The Church and the Tribulation*

44   Compare Daniel 9:24-26 to Matt. 24 and Luke 21

4. God's purpose of the *New Covenant* is the <u>Unification of all Believers into one Body in Christ</u> (the Mystery of God to which Paul refers) and it will be fulfilled <u>during the sequence of events that will take place at Christ's Second Coming.</u>[45]

5. Christ's Second Coming is a Two-sided event: "The Day of the Lord" (DTL) is <u>Good News</u> for everyone who truly Loves and serves God.

However, it is very bad news for everyone who does not serve the True God, regardless of whom they are![46]

VII. Correlating the 70th Week to the "Three and ½ Year" periods, the "Great Tribulation Period" and when the "Times of the Gentiles are fulfilled" yields some very interesting facts.

Introduction: Reese's *Chronological Bible* annotates the events of the Bible in chronological order, which greatly helps to sort out these types of issues. Reese places the Prophecy of Daniel, chapters 5,6,9-12 for being written in 539-536 BC. This includes the crucial rebuilding reference that starts the clock of the "Seventy Weeks" prophecy. Yet, this prophecy has some 'irregularities' that cause many to be confused and led astray if you do not strictly adhere to a proper exegesis. In the book of Ezra you can find the chronicle of the Decree of King Artaxerxes the first, which Reese places at 458 BC. This then leaves a "gap" of 81 years from the time of the prophecy until the event took place that "started the clock." Reese also shows that the 483-year period, summed up by the "Seven weeks and sixty-two weeks" brings us to the launching of the Ministry period of Jesus Christ (Messiah/ Prince), in C. 25 A.D.[47]

Three and ½ years after this, in C. 29 AD, "Messiah will be cut off," which is <u>after</u> the 483-year period expired. <u>After</u> Christ was crucified (cut off), <u>another delay</u> ensues until the next major event, which I believe fits the pattern of the "Three and ½ Year" periods we find in other prophecies. This is the Jewish War of 67-70 AD, culminating with Roman Emperor Vespasian's son General Titus destroying

---

45   John 17; Acts 17:24-31; Rom. 11; 1 Cor. 15:20-23; Phil. 1:6; 1 Thess. 4:13-5:12

46   Isaiah 2; Joel 2; Micah 3,4; Matt. 24; Luke 21; 2 Thess. 1,2; Rev. 6,7

47   Ezra 7:6-28; 8:32-36 *See The Chronological Bible by Edward Reese, c. 1977 Regal Publishers, Nashville, Pages 1161 and 1210 -1214*

Jerusalem and the 3rd and last "Stone Temple" in August of AD 70, fulfilling the predictions of Jeremiah, Ezekiel, Daniel and Jesus Christ's Prophetic Discourse.[48]

A. The writer believes that the only way you can fit this together and satisfy all the Scriptures is to "split" the 70th Week in half: The First Half pertains to the Jewish Revolt Period which ended with General Titus' destruction of the Temple, "In the midst of the week (after the first Three and ½ years)... he* will cause the sacrifice... to cease." Jesus Christ's prediction aligns perfectly with this apportionment. Viz., Scripture does not support God's ever approving a resumption of "Old Covenant-based Sacrifice" after this point.

This is because the *New Covenant* was placed in force at the precise moment when Christ died and God Tore down the veil in the Temple, permanently ending the Old Covenant dispensation and inaugurating the Age of Grace, wherein God Commands us to Worship in Spirit and in Truth.

This command of Christ is the foundation of the New Covenant. It also describes the personal relationship between God and faithful people that is enabled by the contact point of the Reborn human spirit of every individual who lives *In Christ.*[49]

B. The Second Half of the 70th Week will be fulfilled at the end of the Age of Grace during "the Great Tribulation Period," which includes the last of the "Three and ½ Year periods" references that are common to three passages in Daniel and at least four in Revelation, during which Jesus Christ the Messiah, the "Stone uncut by human hands that comes from Heaven," will return. After this, Christ will confront the remainder of unbelieving Jews and they will finally repent![50] Let us review:

---

48   Jer. 3:12-19; Ezek. 20:33-24:27; Matt. 24:1 ff.; John 2:19-21; Acts 7:48;17:24-31
49   Jer. 7:1-12; 31:31-34; Dan. 9:26,27; Matt. 27:50-54; John 2:19-21; 4:23,24 *For more info see the Paper entitled The Doctrine of Last Things *The Roman Prince, Titus*
50   Dan. 2:44,45; 7:25; 9:24-27; 12:7,11,12; Zech. 12:10; Matt. 24; Luke 21; Rom. 11:25,26; Rev. 11:1-4,11; 12:14; 13:5 Ibid. *Footnote #9*

1. Comparing history and Daniel nine, at least three gaps can be discerned: The delay from the Prophecy concerning rebuilding Jerusalem to its fulfillment (81 years), the break between the time "Messiah (Christ) was cut off" and the great Jewish revolt (29-66 AD) and the third break between AD 70 when the last (3rd) Temple was destroyed and the Beginning of the Great Tribulation Period.

2. The writer postulates that since the only periods mentioned in Scripture regarding the prophecies of the 70th Week are Three and ½ years long, it leads one to conclude that two "Three and ½ Year periods" exist, separated in time: One in the first century connected with Jesus' Prophecy of "This Generation will not pass until these things are fulfilled." This was Titus' destruction of Jerusalem in AD 70, "in the midst of the week (when the prince) will cause the sacrifice... to cease." The second is in the Great Tribulation Period. This fits the other Scriptures as well.

3. The other Prophecy that aligns with this in the same chapter is that Jerusalem's "Desolations will continue to the end," which points us again to Two distinct Fulfilments of "Tribulation Periods": The Jewish Revolt period that Jesus predicted that "This generation will not pass" experienced and the one immediately before Christ's Second Coming that ends with the fulfillment of "Until the Times of the Gentiles are Fulfilled."[51]**

4. Moreover, no Scripture can be found that would tell us that God would go back to approving "Ritual Temple Sacrifice" ever again. Also, remember that God's Prophetic Timeline (GPT) does not go in reverse. This is because Jesus' Teachings all point to the human body for being the New Temple where Spiritual Worship takes place.[52]

5. In the end Daniel prophesied that God will also execute Judgment upon the Desolator, i.e., the reincarnated "beast" or the "Antichrist."[53]

---

51   Dan. 9:26,27; Matt. 24:2,3, 15 ff.; Luke 21:20-24 **See Figure One: "The Seventy Weeks" and "Correlating Major Events Chart" at the end of this Paper and the companion Paper: Sequence of Events (leading to the destruction of Jerusalem and the Great Temple in 70 AD).

53   Dan. 9:27; 2 Thess. 1:6-10; Rev. 11:15-18

C. Notice that when you compare <u>all pertinent Scriptures</u> that <u>all prophecies</u> fit when you split the 70th Week into two halves that are separated in time.

First, compare the following references in Daniel.[54]

Second, consider Jesus' statements during His Prophetic Discourse in which the narrative clearly indicates that Jesus is referring to <u>two different events that are separated in time.</u>[55][66]

Third, observe the following crucial terms: The "Times of the Gentiles" (TOG), which shows us the 'separation time between the two of the TOHY (Three and One- half Year) periods that form Daniel's 70th Week. Jesus tells us that His Second Coming will happen just after the "Times of the Gentiles are Fulfilled" (TGF). At that time God's Great Mystery will be fulfilled and all the elements of God's <u>unidirectional</u> Prophetic Timeline (GPT) will have come together.[56]

Fourth, another Scripture also shows this same timeline: "Christ the First Fruits… and then <u>when he Returns</u>, (He will Gather) those who have served Him." Of course, that is another reference to the Rapture which clearly takes place <u>after the Tribulation Period</u> and before the Wrath sequence, just as Jesus had told the Disciples.[57]

Fifth, notice the clear sequence: Tribulation escalates, the Antichrist takes power after the Church's apostasy and then finally, Christ Comes back and rescues the loyal Believers and destroys Antichrist, reestablishing order on earth. Always remember James' admonition: "Be patient <u>until the Coming of the Lord</u>."[58]

---

54 Dan. 2:31-45; 7:24,25; 9:24-27*; 12:7 *Verse 27 shows the "split point" occurring "in the midst of the week"

55 Carefully read Matt. 24 and Luke 21 and you will see

56 See the Papers entitled Correlating the Prophecies concerning TOHY Periods, The Doctrine of Last Things, Emmanuel 1 and Emmanuel 2, Facts Concerning the 70th Week of Daniel and Fulfilment Prophecy

57 1 Cor. 15:20,23 Cf. Matt. 24:29-31

58 Matt. 24;29-31; Luke 21:5-28; Rom. 11:11-26; 1 Cor. 15:20-23; Phil. 1:6; 1 Thess. 4:13-17; 5:9; James 5:8

VIII. In correlating the apostasy and the Rapture to the "Three and ½ Year" periods and the "Day of the Lord," we confirm the following truths:

Among others, three major references in God's Word plainly tell us that God allows the Saints to experience Tribulation. Despite this, however, God's promise stands that in the outcome all those who Trust in Christ will emerge victoriously. This is the

Patience of the Saints, a.k.a. "Faith-based Pacifism," that Jesus clearly taught for being a necessary part of Christian Discipleship that prepares us to faithfully "endure to the end." This means that we must be prepared to endure unto the time of our physical death or when Christ returns, whichever is first.   God's Word Promises to give us the Grace to endure and that IF we persevere on that path, abiding in Christ and loving the Truth despite circumstance, we will inherit eternal Salvation.[59]

Now compare this with Jesus' unequivocal statement pertaining to the chronology of the Tribulation Period and the "Day of the Lord" that follows, given in the Prophetic Discourse recorded by Matthew and Luke. Doing this will prove to you that the sequence of events has been set in place by God. The upshot is that all interpretations and doctrines must align with Christ's Teachings or they are false doctrines! Paul also told us that only One Gospel exists and that 'his Gospel' is the same as Christ's. Not only that, the Holy Spirit always teaches precisely the same as Christ.[60]

Moreover, Christ ordains that His Church (the only real one) is" Built upon the Rock." This is of course, the One we see throughout Scripture and Prophecy: Jesus Christ and His Teachings, which form the Firm Foundation and "Cornerstone" of life and Living Head to which God fully expects every Believer to place their entire Trust and Allegiance. Yes, as Jesus said: "In this world you will have tribulation, but be of good cheer, I have overcome the world."[61]

---

59   Daniel 7:21,22; John 15:18-16:3; 16:33; Rom. 8:26-39; 1 Cor. 10:12,13; 2 Cor. 1:1-22; 2 Thess. 1:4-2:12; James 5:7,8; 2 Pet. 3:8-18

60   Matt. 24:29-31; Luke 21:20-28; John 14:26; 15:26; 16:13-15; Gal. 1:6-12; 1 Tim. 6:3-5

61   Psa. 110; 118:22; Isa. 28:16; Matt. 21:41-46; 1 Cor. 10:12,13

These rules apply all the way to the end of the Age until Christ Appears. This is the "Day of the Lord" which Scripture (Jesus) teaches will commence "Immediately after the Tribulation of those days" which is during the last "Three and ½ Year" (TOHY) period of the Great Tribulation. Near the end of the 7th Seal (the 'hatius period of the 6th Angel/ Second Woe') "the Times of the Gentiles are fulfilled" and Christ deals with the Jews. Finally, the 7th Angel executes undiluted wrath.[62]

IX. Review summary and conclusion: One detail we must keep in mind is that Prophetic Scripture contains Multiple Fulfilments. For example, once you know this characteristic of prophecies, when you compare one set of references to the others, this general rule will point you to a possible set of Fulfilments of which the double fulfilment is the simplest form. The one regarding the "Three and ½ Year" (TOHY) periods mentioned earlier linking the 70th Week of Daniel to Revelation is one of the most important.**[63]

However, as the Age of Grace progresses, Scripture warns us that the majority of the outward church will continue to apostatize. Moreover, it is the church's apostasy that Paul had warned the Thessalonians about that aligns with the "Mystery of lawlessness" (Greek *Anomia*, meaning iniquity) which then enables the rise of the "Antichrist figure" (ACF), the "man* of sin" that will usher in the Great Tribulation period and the "Day of the Lord" (Christ's Second Coming). Put all these together and correlate them without any bias or 'preconceived interpretation model' and the Truth concerning God's Plan to unify all Believers will become apparent![64]*

---

62 Matt. 24:29-31; Luke 20:9-19; 21:24; Rom. 11:25,26; Rev. 10:7; 11:15-19; 15:1 16:21; 19:1 ff. *See also the Papers entitled Jesus' Major Parables, Correlating Prophecies concerning "TOHY" Periods and Facts Concerning the 70th Week of Daniel*

63 **Dan. 9:24-27; Rev. 10:7; 11:1-4; 12:14; 13:5 See also the Papers entitled *Biblical Symbolism, The Doctrine of Last Things, The Higher Laws of God, Illustrating the "Law of Multiple Fulfillments" and The Key to Understanding Scripture is Spiritual Exegesis*

64 Matt. 24:29-31; John 10:1-16; Gal. 2:16-5:25; *2 Thess. 1:3-2:12; 2 Tim. 3:1-7; 2 Pet. 2:3-3:13; 1 John 2:15-4:6; Rev. 2,3; 6:9-7:17; 11:1 ff.; 13:1-18:24 Ibid. Footnotes 15,28,34 *Note also that the moniker 'man of sin' is a general characteristic germane to the negative consequences of humanism that afflict people worldwide: It does not necessarily indicate that 'antichrist' is an individual person, but rather a "global system of government" which fits perfectly with John's descriptions in Apocalypse. See also the Papers entitled Facts of Scripture: The Church and the Tribulation and Prophetic Chronology Two*

As an exercise, consider the asterisked passages in the following footnote that first point us more specifically to the first fulfillment in the Great Jewish Revolt of 66-70 AD when General Titus "caused the sacrifice to cease" after a Three and ½ Year siege. Then observe that the verses after each of these tend to be more general in scope and apply to both Fulfilments. Of course, for Christians, they mainly apply to the secondary fulfillment at the end of the age that climaxes during the Great Tribulation Period.[65]

Sincerely, Your friend and fellow servant of Christ,
Pastor David J. Bowers

---

65   Matt. 24:4-6*, 7-14, 24:15-28*; 29-51

**See also the following Appendices

Figure One: The "Seventy Weeks"

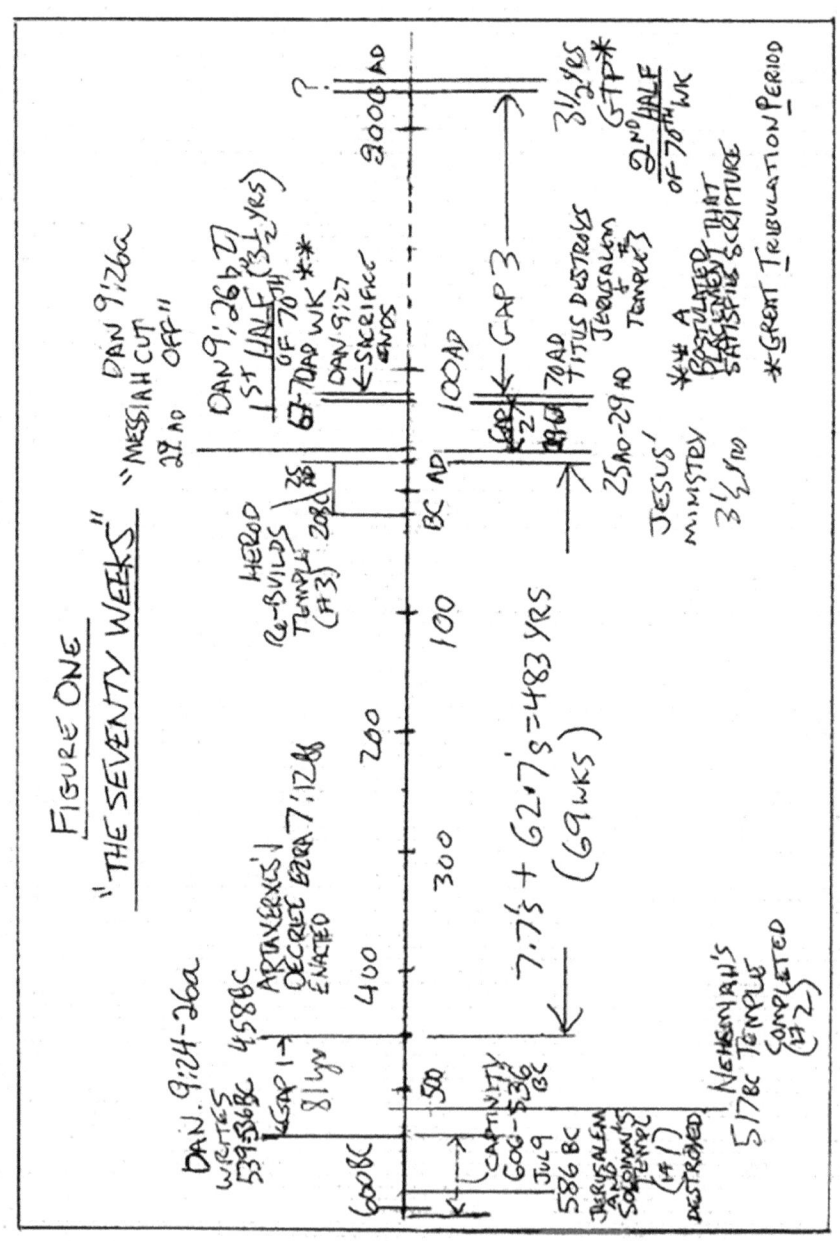

Correlating Major Events to Prophecy Chart:		
Relation to Date:	**Event:**	**Prophecy, history, "Statue":**
612 B.C.	Babylon/ Nebuchadnezzar rises to power	Tool of Judgment and Discipline/ "Head of Gold"[1]
604-603 B.C.	Daniel is brought to Babylon and writes chapters one and two.	Daniel reveals the meaning of the "Great Statue."[2]
586 B.C.	Jerusalem and Solomon's Temple destroyed	God's radical restructuring of worship begins making way for the New Covenant.[3]
580-573 B.C.	Daniel writes chapter three. Ezekiel writes his messages to the captives, including a "Vision/ Prophecy" that aligns with the New Covenant.	God exhorts those who are enduring trials to keep up their hope for the future.[4]
570-562 B.C.	Daniel writes chapter four. Nebuchadnezzar goes mad.	True sanity only comes after our submission to God.[5]
		""
550-548 B.C.	Daniel writes chapters seven and eight	Daniels' vision of the "Four Beasts" (parallel to the four metals of the Great Statue) and of the "Ram and the he-goat," the latter of which is Alexander the Great.[6]

1   Dan. 2:38
2   Dan. 2:36-45
3   Jer. 31:31-34; John 4:23,24
4   Dan. 3; 4:1-3; Ezek. 33-48
5   Daniel 4:4-37
6   Cf. Daniel 2

539-536 B.C.	Medo-Persia overthrows Babylon.	God reveals future history and the "Seventy Weeks" timetable/ "Thorax of Silver"[7]
516B.C.	Nehemiah/ Zerubbabel complete Second Temple	The First fulfillment of Restoration is accomplished.[8]
Gap one (81 years)		
458B.C.	King Artaxerxes the first enacts the Decree.	"Starts the clock" for the first 69 weeks.[9]
337 B.C.	Alexander the Great gains hegemony[10]	The "Belly and thighs of Bronze"
		""
337 B.C. to 146 B.C.	Period of the Greeks and Seleucids	See the Chart showing "Postulated Sequence of Events" in Daniel eleven.[11]
146 B.C. to 63 B.C.	Rome rises to power	The "Legs of Iron"
20B.C. to 4B.C.	Herod rebuilds the Third Temple.	Note the editors' comment in Josephus confirming that this was the third temple.[12]
4B.C.	Jesus born in Bethlehemc. March[13]	See the Prophecies of Isaiah, Daniel and Micah and the historical chronicles of Josephus.[13]

7   Dan. 5,6,9-12

8   Jer. 32,33

9   Ezra 7:6,7, 11-28 *The Chronological Bible by Edward Reese, Regal Publishers, Nashville, 1977, P. 1210,1211*

10 Daniel 8

11 *See The Story of Civilization, by Will Durant, Vol II, "The Life of Greece," chapters XXII to XXX*

12 *See Flavius Josephus' Antiquities of the Jews Bk. XV, Ch. XI. P. 1*

13 *See The Works of Flavius Josephus, Flavius Josephus, Translated by William Whiston, AP&A, Grand Rapids, 1971, Antiquities, Book XVII., Ch. VI., P. 4. See also Isa. 7:14; 9:6; Dan. 2:44,45; Mic. 5:2*

AD 6 to 25	Various repairs and maintenance to the temple are made after the riots in AD6.	Comment made by Pharisees to Jesus recorded by John.[14]
		" "
AD 25 (483 years from the decree)	Jesus' Ministry begins	"Messiah the Prince"[15]
AD 29	Jesus, the Lamb of God, is Crucified.	"Messiah cut off" after 69 weeks expired, fulfilling prophecies.[16]
Gap two (AD 29-66)		
AD 67-70	The Great Jewish Revolt	First Half of 70th Week [17]
Gap three (AD 70 to?)		
AD 476	"Fall of Roman Empire"	This starts the period of the "Feet of Iron and Clay."[18]
?	The Great Tribulation Period	Second Half of 70th Week[19]
?	Christ's Second Coming.	Jesus Christ is "The Stone from Heaven"[20]

---

14   John 2:20
15   Dan. 9:25
16   Isa. 53; Dan. 9:26
17   Dan. 9:27 a See also the Chart entitled Sequence of Events (Regarding the Jewish War of the First Century)
18   Dan. 2:41-43
19   Dan. 9:27 b; Rev. 13:5; 17:1 ff.
20   Dan. 2:44,45; Matt. 24:29-31; Acts 17:24-31; 2 Thess. 1,2; Rev. 11:15

"POSTULATING OVERLAPS/ OFFSETS" IN LAST DAYS

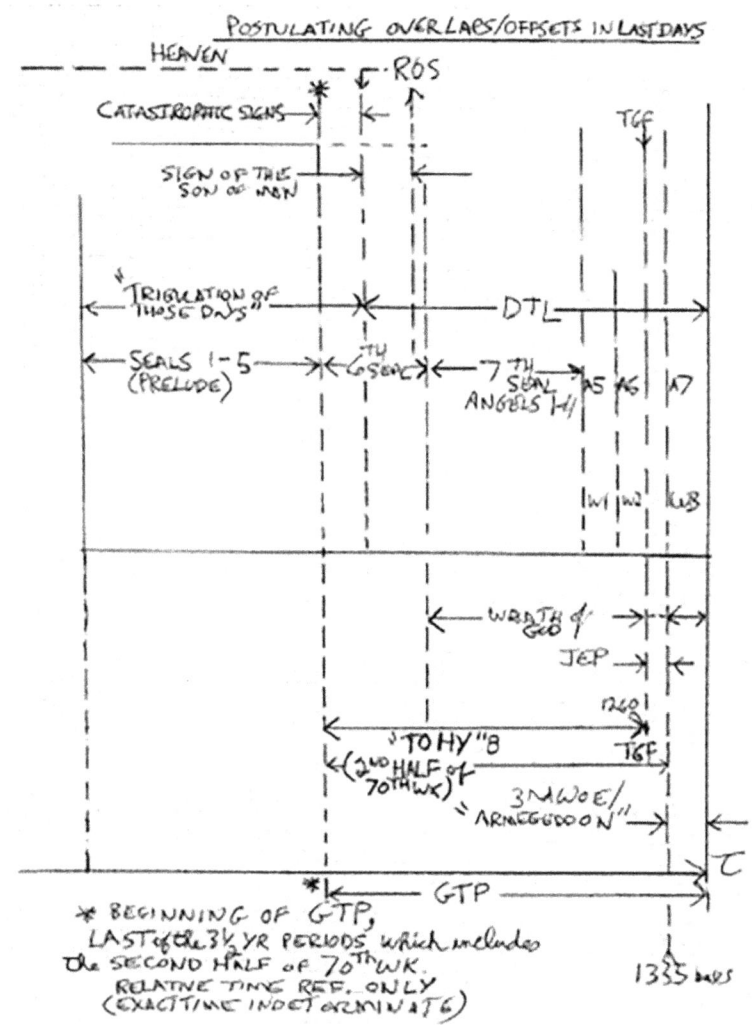

LEGEND FOR ACROSTICS IN "POSTULATING OVERLAPS"

A5= Fifth Angel of the Seventh Seal (W1)

A6= Sixth Angel of the Seventh Seal (W2)

A7= Seventh Angel of the Seventh Seal (W3)

DTL= "The Day of the Lord"

GTP= "The Great Tribulation Period"

JEP= "Jews' Extension Period"

ROS= "Rapture of the Saints"

TGF= "Times of the Gentiles are Fulfilled"

TOHY= "Three and ½ Year Period"

W1= "The First Woe"

W2= "The Second Woe"

W3= "The Third Woe"

Correlating the Prophecies Concerning "TOHY" Periods

Correlating the prophecies concerning "TOHY" periods		
#	Description	Page #
I.	Prefatory Note	
II.	The following is a chart correlating the prophecies concerning "TOHY" periods.	
III.	Analysis and summary	
IV.	Scripture teaches that every Christian must be prepared to "Endure until the end."	
V.	Appendices: Appendix one: See also the following Diagrams	
	Appendix two: What does Prophecy tell us about the identity of the "Two Witnesses"...?	

I. Writers' Prefatory Note: The following chart depicts the sequence of events of the two halves of Daniel's 70ᵗʰ Week, which can be roughly associated with the various Scriptural descriptions of the common spiritual symbol that links them together: Viz., The Three and one-half

Year (TOHY) periods that are mentioned in Scriptures that are defined in varying terminology.[1]

As mentioned in several of the writer's Position Papers, when one compares the 'future context' of Daniel Twelve, portions of Christ's Prophetic Discourse and the narrative sections of John's *Apocalypse* (Revelation), the deeper meaning strongly implies a Double Fulfilment taking place in two separated periods.[2]

Moreover, since "holy people" can refer to both Jews and Christians, the fulfillment applies in two periods: In the first place to Jews in the 1st Century (first half of 70th Wk.) and in the second place regarding Believing Jews and Christians during the Great Tribulation. Most likely the Second Half of the 70th Week starts with the 6th Seal and ends with the 'hatius period' of the Second Woe (6th Angel of 7th Seal). It is a very eventful period that includes Christ's Second Appearing and the Rapture of the Church. This period also lines up with the final verses of Daniel twelve concerning an 'extension period' describing Christ's final dealings with the remainder of the unbelieving Jews which finishes God's plan of unification. It also fits with all the other Scriptures in "God's Prophetic Timeline" that concludes when all God's People are unified in one Body in Christ and "God's Mystery is Finished."[3]

Due to the fact that the Prophecies in both Daniel and Revelation are cast in a spiritual venue with "flashback" and "flash-forward" scenes, the student must understand that these prophecies cannot be simplistically arranged according to a single chronological sequence. Overall, the "end times chronological sequence" of the "Tribulation Period" can be identified in the following sets of Scriptures:

---

1   *That is the following, in order of their appearance in Scripture: "A Time and Times and the Dividing of Time" (Dan. 7:25), "in the midst of the Week" (Dan. 9:27), "a Time, Times and a Half" (Dan. 12:7; Rev. 12:14), "a Thousand two hundred and threescore days" (Rev. 11:3; 12:6),* "Forty-Two Months" (Rev. 11:2; 13:5) and "Three Days and a half" (Rev. 11:11) See also the Paper Prophetic Chronology Two, Sect. IV: "Chart One: Correlating Prophetic Texts and Acrostics" *Note: Jewish Ext. Period (JEP) adds 75 Days Cf. Dan. 12:11,12*

2   *See the following Papers: The Biblical Role of Israel, Contextually Comparing the Elements of Prophetic Scripture, Correlating Last Days Scriptures, The Doctrine of Last Things, Emmanuel 1, Emmanuel 2; Facts Concerning the 70th Week of Daniel and Facts of Scripture: The Church and the Tribulation*

3   *Rev. 10:7 This Scripture is part of a "parenthetical vision" including Revelation chapters ten to twelve. See line #4 in chart and the Paper entitled The Biblical Precept of Mystery*

*The First is seen in two strikingly parallel overviews of future events that when you compare them, describe a "double fulfillment" of prophecies imbedded within them. One is recorded by Daniel: The first concerns the "fourth beast" that is different from its predecessors (the Roman Empire) having Ten Horns (Emperors) the last of which is a 'horn' that will arise "after three horns are plucked up" (Vespasian and his son, Titus who became Emperor afterwards). Nero first sent General Vespasian to the region (Alexandria) to 'pacify' the region in February AD 67 at the beginning of the three and ½ year Jewish-Roman War. Vespasian also called Titus, whose army was the one who destroyed Jerusalem and the third Temple in AD 70.[4]

A second version of this is reiterated by John in *Apocalypse* for being the "first beast having Seven Heads and Ten Horns" that describe the entity antichrist that plays a major role in the Great Tribulation Period (GTP).[5]

John's narrative received from Christ also describes the Great Tribulation Period as a progressive series of "Seven Seals" that reveal the events of that tumultuous period yet to come.[6]

*The Second is a "deeper level," a "parenthetical overview summary" that concentrates on the consummation of "God's Prophetic Timeline," the centerpiece of which is God's Unification of the Saints into one Body in Christ. The last piece of this puzzle/ Tapestry takes place in the "extension" or period of 'hatius' during the 2nd Woe when Christ will confront the Jews and finish the reunification (re-grafting) of the remaining Jews. Soon after that time, Christ's Victory will be complete.[7]

*The Third, found in chapters thirteen to eighteen, reveals much more pictorial detail about Antichrist's system (The 'shape-shifting beast' and the Scarlet Woman & Beast System) that Christ destroys

4   Dan. 2:40-45; 7:7,8, 19-26 See the book entitled Wars of the Jews, by Flavius Josephus, translated by William Whiston, AP&A, Grand Rapids, 1971, Book III, Chapter I See also the writer's Historical Chart entitled Sequence of Events
5   Rev. 13 Ibid. Footnote #8
6   Rev. 6-9
7   Rev. 10-12 Cf. Dan. 9:26b,27; 12:11,12; Zech. 12:9,10: Matt. 23:37-39; Rom. 11:25 See also line #6 in the chart (Section II below)

soon after He Comes. This narrative also covers the events of the 7ᵗʰ Seal recast with different symbolism, using "Bowls" instead of "Angels".[8]

II. The following is a chart correlating the prophecies concerning "TOHY" periods.

Let us examine the Scriptures and correlate the prophecies concerning "TOHY" periods:		
#	Application/ Fulfillment Period:	Prophecy Description:
1.	These events are Fulfilled in the First Century (First Half of the 70ᵗʰ Week)	A terrible time of tribulation happens during a "Time, Times and Dividing of Time": General Titus, son of Vespasian "shatters the power of the holy people" and causes the sacrifice to be terminated.[9]
2.		"The (daily) Sacrifice ends, being terminated...In the midst of the week"[10]
3.	These events are fulfilled twice: First in AD 70 and Second in the last days before the end of the 7ᵗʰ Seal.	During this time "both Christians and Jews are being persecuted for 1260 Days" after which "The power of the holy people is shattered."[11]*
4.		In this "flashback" parenthetical "The 'outer court' is given to the gentiles."** This aligns with the Jews' Desolation "Until the Times of the Gentiles are Fulfilled." [12]

---

8   Rev. 13-18 Cf. Dan. 2:44,45; Matt. 21:33-44; 24:29-51; Luke 19-21; 2 Thess. 1,2; 2 Pet. 3:9-14
       See also line #3 in the chart and the Paper A Biblical Disclosure of Antichrist

9   Dan. 7:19-25

10   Dan. 9:24-26

11   *Dan. 12:1-10 Cf. Rev. 7:9-17; 12:6, 14; 13:5

12   **Rev. 10:1-11:13 Cf. Matt. 23:37-39; Luke 21:24; Rom. 11:25 *See also next page line #5*

Let us examine the Scriptures and correlate the prophecies concerning "TOHY" periods:		
#	**Application/ Fulfillment Period:**	**Event/ Prophecy Description:**
5.	These events are <u>Fulfilled during</u> the 6th and 7th Seals of the Great Tribulation Period.	"The Two Witnesses Prophesy/Preach for 1260 Days."[13]
6.		"The Two Witnesses" are 'overcome and killed,*' and after three and ½ Days they are raised by God's Spirit and "Gathered into Heaven."*[14]
7.		Christ's Heavenly army wages war against antichrist / Babylon. The <u>unbelieving Jews remain under God's Judgment</u> until "the Times of the Gentiles are Fulfilled" (TGF), after which Christ also confronts the remainder who then will finally recognize him as the Messiah and repent.[15]*
8.	This is fulfilled after God's final wrath in the 7th angel (3rd Woe) ofthe 7th Seal.	The Sequence ends with Christ's Final Victory. [16]

III. Analysis and summary: It cannot be overemphasized that the Student of Scripture must acknowledge that Scripture is a spiritual quantity that is multifaceted. In a very special way Prophecy stands out as the most complex part of this divine Tapestry. However, the Holy Spirit can readily "cut though the fog of complexity, confusion

---

13   Rev. 11:3 Cf. 12:14; 13:5 See also Zech. 4:1-5, 11-14

14   Rev. 11:7-14 Cf. 7:9-17: 12:1 ff. *Apparently, all these Scriptures describe antichrists' persecution, "wearing down of the Saints" and the subsequent major event we call the "Rapture," in different terms and symbolism See also the book The Church in the Last Days, Chapters 9-12 and Facts of Scripture: The Church and the Tribulation

15   Dan. 9:26,27; 12:11,12; Zech. 12:9,10; Matt. 23:39; Luke 21:24; Rom. 9:6-8; 11:11-33; Gal. 3:1 ff.; 4:19-26; 6:15,16; Rev. 14-18 *Ibid. Footnote #7 (Pg. 4)

16   Rev. 11:15; 17:14 See also Appendix two

and uncertainty" to reveal God's deepest Truths to the childlike, open-minded Disciple.[17]

FYI, With diligent study of Scripture, the reader will find that specific texts from many books in the Bible point to the same basic underlying spiritual truth that points to "God's Prophetic Time Line" (GPT) that is unidirectional in nature. That is, it always moves forward to the final goal of the Unification of God's People in Christ, Jew and Gentile, who will all "Worship God in spirit and in Truth" according to the *New Covenant.*[18]

Indeed, pursuant to our main topic, Daniel twelve is one of those unique "futuristic" texts. In it we find a "crossover text" that affects both Jews and Christians, with the common denominator of both being the "TOHY" period reference that links them together.

Not only that, when you carefully compare the Scriptures that define the "70th Week," you will find that two distinct Fulfillments 'fall out.' Daniel's mention of a break "in the midst of the week" demands that the 70th Week comes in two installments separated in time.[19]

The First, regarding Jews, took place in the first century (AD 67-70).

The Second, yet to come, applies to both Jews and Christians during the Great Tribulation Period (GTP).

All these prophecies also refer to an archetypal prophecy given to the Patriarch Abraham in which God declares "In your *Seed* all the nations are blessed."

Of course, the word "Seed" is a prophetic Symbol of Jesus Christ, the Messiah, who is progressively revealed in Two Figures: The Lamb of God (Mfla) and the Lion of God (MfLi). God's Promise/ Prophecy to Abraham is also a foundational anchor and 'signpost' along "God's Prophetic Timeline" (GPT) that links all prophecies together with God's Master Plan of the Unification of all God's People into One Body in Christ.

---

17   Prov. 8; 1 Cor, 2:9-16

18   *Among these are the "Messianic Psalms," the prophecies of Isaiah, Jeremiah, Ezekiel, Daniel and Zechariah, Jesus' Prophetic Discourse in the Synoptics, Paul's letter to the Romans and second letter to the Thessalonians and John's Apocalypse (Revelation)*

19   Dan. 9:27; 12:1-13; Zech. 12:9,10; Matt. 23:37-24:51; Luke 21:20-24; Rom. 11:25

At that time, which Scripture indicates is very close to the end of the Great Tribulation Period, God will have "re-grafted" all the Believing Jews and thereby united all Believers. Thus, as Scripture declares, "God's Mystery is Finished," that is, Fulfilled. (GMF)[20]

The writer has also noticed an overall distinct Scriptural pattern in the "TOHY" periods describing "Tribulation Type Times," during which God's People are put to the Test. Finally, in each case, after the situation reaches a climax, God sovereignly intervenes, neutralizing the threat and "saving the Day."[21]

Interestingly, this pattern also closely parallels the "Passover Paradigm" of which the writer refers in other Position Papers and books. It also meshes with the writer's assertion that Scripture indicates that the last "week of years," the "70th Wee Prophecy," is split into two halves. Moreover, both halves work according to the general pattern of Passover. They are also separated in time, with each Three and one-half Year period applying to one of two fulfillment installments.

First, consider the parallel between the week-long sequence of events in the "Original Jewish Passover and Feast of Unleavened Bread" and the events of Christ's Passion Week. Notice that we can see that Christ's Passion Week is also "split" into two segments of Three and one-half days: The first starting from the "Triumphal Entry" to Christ's Death on the Cross and the second from Christ's Death to the Resurrection. Understanding prophecies this way then gives us a distinct "Prophetic Timing Marker" (Time Tag Scripture) by which we can discern the "Signs of the Times" and as Jesus taught the Disciples, enabling us to prepare for hard times and successfully endure all the way through to the end!

Second, consider also the "reprise" of the "TOHY" that played out during the three and one-half year Jewish-Roman War of AD 67-70, the 1st Half of the 70th Week.

---

20   Gen. 12:3; 22:18; Dan. 2:44,45; Acts 3:25; Gal. 3:8 See also the Papers *The Fulfillment of God's Promise to Abraham, The Biblical Precept of Mystery, The Biblical Role of Israel, Fulfilment Prophecy* (see the Diagram: "The Nine Ages") and *The Messiah Figures*

21   *Compare the contexts of the aforementioned "TOHY" references: Dan. 7:25; 9:27; 12:7; Rev. 11:2,3,11; 12:6,14; 13:5, associating them with the appropriate historical "Tribulation Type" period in which the reference or references applies, also considering the "multiple fulfillment" precept that underlies many prophecies.*

Then finally, third, study the prophecies that describe the events of the Great Tribulation, the 2ⁿᵈ Half of the 70ᵗʰ Week, and compare them all together.[22]

IV. Scripture teaches that every Christian must be prepared to "Endure unto the end": Our physical death or when Christ returns, whichever is first. Prophecies clearly reveal that the placing and conditions of the last "TOHY" period, the Great Tribulation Period, plainly show us that <u>Christians will be here on earth up to the end</u> of the 6ᵗʰ Seal. Consequently, they must <u>prepare themselves</u> to face the very difficult times that will come upon the earth during the time of Great Tribulation.

Notice also that the contexts of prophecies regarding the Great Tribulation show us that in that period <u>tribulation is man caused</u> but <u>wrath is God-caused.</u> Not only that, it can be shown that Christ's Prophetic Discourse has <u>two levels</u> imbedded in it. Moreover, since Christ did not come back in AD70, this means that Jesus' statement "Immediately <u>after</u> the tribulation of those days" in the Prophetic Discourse must then refer to the 2ⁿᵈ Half of the 70ᵗʰ Week, which is fulfilled during the Great Tribulation Period!

Putting all these facts together should also help the Bible student to clear any confusion they have regarding Christ's Prophetic Discourse. These inescapable truths are also underscored by Jesus' subsequent declaration that "He that endures to the end will be saved."[23]

It is patent that any True Believer who has learned to receive *Intuition* from God in their Reborn human spirit via the Holy Spirit should by now be able to see past the artificially maintained fog of confusion generated by the False Prophets of antichrist which include worldly religious leaders who serve the state instead of Christ.

Those in the know can see Satan's agenda and the way the world system is being "globalized." Essentially the New World Order has

22   Dan. 2:44,45; Matt. 24,25; Luke 21; Rom. 9-11; 2 Thess. 1,2; Rev. 6-11, 12, 13 *See Catalogue of Events, Correlating Last Days Scriptures Sect's II-IV, Destiny and Free Will, Emmanuel 1,2; Event Sequence, Fulfilment Prophecy and The Three Passovers of Scripture*
23   Matt. 24:29-31 *See also the book The Church in the Last Days Chapters 8-12 and the Paper Facts of Scripture: The Church and the Tribulation*

established a universal currency system (the credit system) and that control of transactions by computers has already been put in place.

Unfortunately, because of their selfishness and greed, God has allowed the system's "strong delusion to believe the lie" to dupe, deceive and brainwash multitudes of Christians who are being assiduously taught a false sense of security with "prosperity doctrines" and a corrupted "Pretribulation Rapture theory," both of which fly in the face of many Scriptures that refute their position. Not only that, notice Paul's statements in his letters unequivocally tell us that the Gospel he preached was <u>identical to Christ's.</u> Moreover, that means that any doctrine that contradicts Christ's Teaching is a <u>false doctrine!</u>[24]

Consider the following "Basic Christian Responsibilities" that God is holding us responsible for observing:

One is obedience to Christ's Commands and Teaching. The second is Total Relinquishment of everything we have. The third is Worship in spirit and in truth. The fourth is Ongoing Repentance from subsequent sin. The fifth is our willingness to share our faith with others whenever God opens the door.

FYI: The reader is encouraged to study the "New Covenant Series" Resources listed in the following footnote.[25]

Your fellow servant in Christ,
Pastor David J. Bowers

---

24   Gal. 1:6-13; 1 Tim. 6:3

25   *See the books Jesus' Way: God's Guaranteed Blueprint, The Church and the Last Days and the reference entitled Basic Christian Doctrine. See also the Papers entitled A Biblical Disclosure of Antichrist, Are You Sure What You Believe and Practice is Truly Christian Doctrine, Authority and Conscience, Authority and Conscience 2, Basic Observations regarding God's Rules, The Beauty and Finesse of the New Covenant, The Biblical Precept of Mystery, Biblical Prosperity: God's Definition Vs the World, Bonehead Christianity; The Three part Series on "Christian Conversion": Introduction to Christian Conversion, Christian Conversion Part Two: Factors in the Conversion Process and Christian Conversion Part Three: The Necessity of Conversion; Christian Conversion and the True Temple, Christianity Versus Religion (A Three Part Series), Cracking the False Doctrine Code, Destiny and Free Will, Divergent Belief Systems, The Doctrine of Repentance, Facts of Scripture: The Church and the Tribulation, Fallacies of Determinism, God's Definition of Salvation, God's Universal Attitude Test, The Higher Laws of God, The Holy Spirit is God's Revelator, How Should we then Live (A Two part Series), Jesus' Major Parables, Key Aspects of the Christian Gospel, The Key to Understanding (Scripture) is Spiritual Exegesis, Looking Through the Lens of Jesus Christ, The Major Elements of Biblical Salvation, The Messiah Figures, The New Covenant, One Covenant for All, The Primacy of the Christian Gospel, Principles of Fulfillment Theology, Regarding the Headship of Jesus Christ, The Role of Conscience, The Spiritual Laws of Revival, Spirituality and Worship and The Way of the Cross*

V. Appendices:

A. Appendix one: FYI: See also the following Diagrams that are found in other Papers:

1. "Partition of the 70th Week" [26]
2. "Last Days Time Line, Part Two" [27]

B. Appendix two: What does Prophecy tell us about the identity of the "Two Witnesses," the "two 144 thousands" and the "true Israel of God?"

1. The writer believes that the "Two Witnesses" are Prophetic Symbols referring to the two parts of God's witness of the Gospel in the Great Tribulation Period: One is sent to the remainder of Jews and the second concerns the Gentiles who will respond to the "Everlasting Gospel" up to the end of the 2nd Woe. Notice also the distinct parallel in Zechariah regarding the "Two Olive Trees/ Anointed Ones" (Witnesses) who testify of the Mission of Christ (Messiah the Branch) to build a New (spiritual) Temple.

Notice that many prophecies use multiple symbols to describe things. E.g., in Revelation ten and eleven, the sense of Scripture points to a "parenthetical flashback period" in which some events prior to the Seventh Seal are reiterated to emphasize their importance. The undiluted Wrath of God does not commence until the commencement of the 3rd Woe. The chronological sequence resumes in chapter eleven, verse fourteen.[28]

2. Prophetically, God's allowing the witnesses to be "neutralized" by antichrist is also symbolic of the "great Falling Away First" (FAF) predicted by Paul. Their "resurrection" after "Three and one-half Days" strongly points to this description being yet another prophetic symbol of the great Ingathering of Saints otherwise known as the "Rapture."

---

26 *See the Paper Facts Concerning the 70th Week of Daniel*

27 *The Diagram entitled "Last Days Timeline Chart Part Two" is in the book The Church in the Last Days, Appendix C. It can also be found in the Papers entitled Facts of Scripture: The Church and the Tribulation, Appendix 3 and The Doctrine of Last Things, CC. 2*

28 Rom. 11:25-33; Rev. 7:1-8 *(the 144k of Jewish Witnesses)*; 14:1-7 *(the 144k of Gentile Witnesses)*; 7:9-17 (the Rapture); 11:1-11 Cf. Zech. 4:1-7, 11-14

Yes, the underlying truth still remains that even after the Rapture, some Christians will be present during the Great Tribulation Period up to and including the 2nd Woe. After the "Jewish Extension Period," They will join with the repenting Jews to whom Christ confronts and proves His Messiahship. Then, all Believers will be Unified into One Body in Christ, the true Israel of God.[29]

3. Putting all Scriptures together clearly shows us that Daniel's prophecy of an added 75 days to the TOHY period associated with the 2nd Half of the 70th Week (for Jews) precisely fits with all the other Scriptures that align with "God's Master Plan of Unification": Zechariah's Prophecy, Christ's Prophetic Discourse, John's Gospel and Paul's Letters to the Romans and Galatians.[30]

---

29   2 Thess. 2:3 f.; Gal. 6:15,16; Phil. 3:3; Rev. 10:7; 11: 1 ff.

30   Dan. 9:26,27; 12:11,12; Matt. 23:37-39; Luke 21:24; John 10:7-16; Rom. 11:25; Gal. 3,4,6 *See The Church in the Last Days, Facts of Scripture and Facts concerning the 70th Week of Daniel*

Appendix E

Last Days Timeline Charts

Part One

THE BEGINNING OF SORROWS

Horizontal Scale~time
Vertical Scale~ %Spiritual Efficiency, Re: the Church
Relative timing and Relationships between Events determined by Comparing Scripture

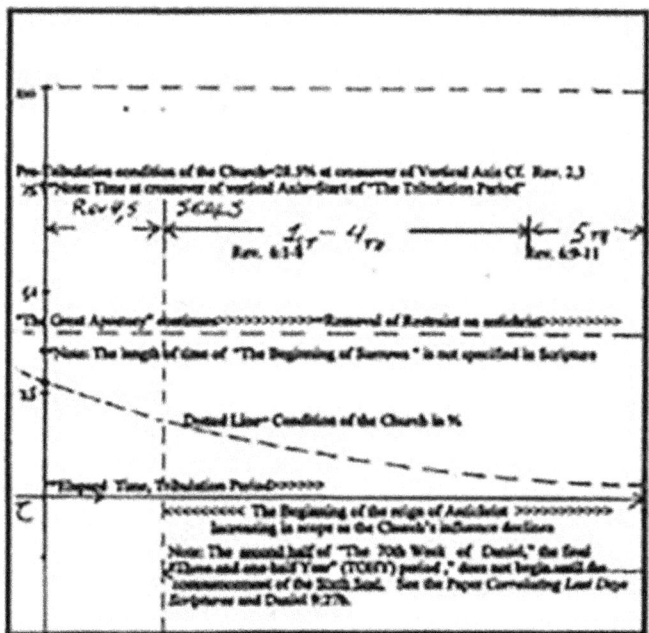

11-9-03/ Rev. 1: 1-17-04/ Rev. 2: 8-1-10
Rev. 3:2-8-15
For continuation see Last Days Time Line, Part Two: The Great Tribulation Period

Part Two

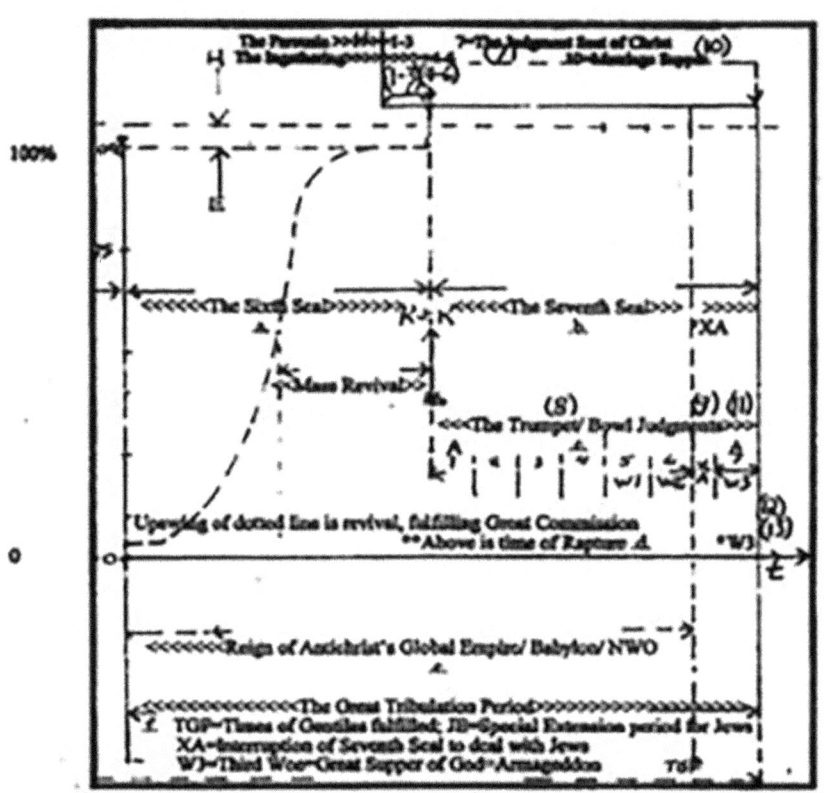

Legend for "Last Days Timeline Chart, Part 2

a. = Rev. 6:12--7:17

b. = Rev. 8,9,13–18

c. = Rev. 8:1–9:21; Cf. 2 Thess. 1:6–10

d. = Rev. 7:9–17; *11:9–12; Cf. 1 Thess. 4:13–17; Matt. 24:29–31

e. = Rev. 13:1–14:13

f. = The Great Tribulation Period (GTP)

TGF: Luke 21:24; Rev. 11:1,2

XA: Rev. 10:7–11:15

W3: Rev. 16:12–21; 19:17–21

*Note 1: The experience of the "two witnesses" is spiritually symbolic of the "wearing down of the saints" (God's people: Jewish and Gentile believers) during the tribulation period.

Note 2: The period known as "the day of the Lord" commences with the "Parousia" during the sixth seal and continues to the conclusion of the great tribulation period (GTP).[361]

Note 3: The GTP overall refers to the acts of the great Antichrist (the *second* beast of Rev. 13) and God's sequential responses of delivering the saints and pouring divine wrath and destruction on Antichrist that will occur during the three and one-half year period (TOHY) that is also referred to in several different places in Scripture as "a time and times and a dividing of time" and "*twelve* hundred and *sixty* days." See the following references.[362]

Note 4: Daniel tells us that God has granted a unique extension period for dealing with the Jews. This will occur near the end of the seventh seal during the "hatius period" of the sixth angel (the second woe).[363]

8-1-10

Rev. 1:11-19-13

Rev. 2: 8-5-14

Rev. 2A: 8-28-16

---

361 *See the book entitled The Church in the Last days, Chapter 12, Paragraph V: "Explanation of the Term "The Day of the Lord."*

362 Matt. 24:9–31; Luke 21:8–24; Rev. 11:3,9; 13:11–18

363 Dan. 12:4–13; Rom. 11:25–27; Rev. 10:7

Appendix F

Time Tag Scriptures

For many years, I avoided the subject of the last days. This was because of the confusion with each church having its own pet dogma. I considered it insoluble and at the least controversial. In 1983, I read Revelation through in one sitting, and some missing pieces began to fall into place. Recently I began a concerted detailed study of the gospels and found a treasure-trove of information from the words of Jesus. Putting it together from the more familiar references in 1 Corinthians and the letters to Thessalonica, a discernable pattern emerged to find out the relative timing of some crucial events. Consider and study the following scriptural references and the events they portray:

1. The description of the beginning of sorrows.[364]

2. The description of the great tribulation.[365]

3. The description of the conditions at "the second coming event" occurring *after (the onset of) the great tribulation.*[366]

4. Luke also describes the angel's promises of Jesus Christ returning (to earth) in the same way in Acts.[367]

5. The context of Scripture demands that we include the judgment seat of Christ in the second coming event sequence.[368]—

6. Scripture describes what we know as the "catching away" or the "gathering of the elect" (also known as the church or the saints), which

---

364 Matt. 24:4–8; Mark 13:5–8; Luke 21:8–19
365 Matt. 24: 9–22; Mark 13:9–20; Luke 21:20–24
366 Matt. 24:27–31; 25:1–13; Mark 13:24–27; Luke 21:25–33
367 Zech. 14:4; Acts 1:7–11
368 Matt. 25:14–30; Rom. 14:20; 2 Cor. 5:10

divides into two sub-events: the first resurrection and what believers call the rapture. Even a casual examination of Scripture shows that this must occur as part of the second coming event and takes place after Jesus appears in the clouds in the sky.[369]——

7. The New Testament describes the conditions under which the church remains on earth. Notice the marked distinction between the words *tribulation* and *wrath*. *Tribulation* happens because of man's actions that God tells us are sins. However, *wrath* means a specific and active end-time execution of divine judgment upon man.[370]

8. In detail, Scripture describes the "divine judgment sequence" that is first pronounced and then executed upon Antichrist and Babylon.

This sequence is separated into two events: the wrath of the Lamb that is the trumpet and bowl judgments of the seventh seal, angels 1 to 6, and the final detached section of the seventh angel (the third woe), which is the great supper of God, during which we find the final pronouncement of Christ's assumption of power on the earth.[371]

Many believers consider only this part of the sequence to be the day of the Lord. However, one needs to realize that, *in the New Testament, God defines the day of the Lord differently.*

In the New Testament, the day of the Lord refers to Jesus Christ's reign on earth or to the earthly kingdom of God, which commences with (and therefore includes) the second coming event.

**See chapter 12, V.: Explanatory of *the day of the Lord.*

9. In the suspension period between the two judgment sequences of the seventh seal, we find what we can call *the special dealings with Israel.* God's Word has not told us much in the way of specifics about this period. One fact we know is that it is a special extension period at the end of the great tribulation that completes the seventieth week of Daniel. Notice that it takes place after the first judgment sequence and before the second. See number 8 above.[372]

---

369   Matt. 24:29–31; 1 Cor. 15:51–55; 1 Thess. 4:13–17; Rev. 7:9–17
370   John 16:33; Rom. 1:18–32; 2:5–16; 1 Thess. 5:9
371   2 Thess. 1:6–10; Rev. 8:1–9, 21; 11:15–19; 14:14–18:24
372   Daniel 12:4–13; Rev. 10:1–11:14

Excerpts from Glossary of Terms:

The Age of Accountability:

This refers to the age a person reaches when they first recognize the difference between right and wrong, and have made a knowledgeable choice. This is also the time when God would first impute sin (count as applying) to the individual, thus removing their name from the Lamb's Book of life. God's Word tells us this sinful condition remains until that person chooses of their own free will to repent of sin and receive the shed blood sacrifice of Christ. If a person fails to biblically repent during their lifetime allotted here on earth, God must unavoidably condemn them (judge that one). The chronological age corresponding to this awesome responsibility varies with each individual. In the ancient world they assumed that this was about twelve years of age. However, in the corrupted techno-culture of modern times, exposure of young children to powerful stimuli has considerably shortened this time. See Impute, Sin and The Lamb's Book of Life.

Atonement:

Atonement describes the terms, conditions, events, relationships and spiritual processes that God has used to deal with sin and thus produce the desired effect of Reconciliation. This process has changes significantly with time: The determinant being the context of Covenantal Dispensation that changes the terms. We can see the way God arranges things in Old Covenant times in the meaning of the Hebrew word *Kaphar,* meaning to *cover up.* This meant that under the Old Covenant (Dispensation of Law), all the worshipers' sacrifices combined still could not directly deal with *the price of Sin*. God permitted all the Bloodshed sacrifices of animals and human death punishments to serve only as IOU's in an extensive *temporary arrangement*. The writer is calling this 'stopgap' arrangement the 'Mosaic- Levitical-Sacrifice-System.' God had always intended to replace this system and told us in many ways in Scripture. We can see examples of this in the prophets Jeremiah and Ezekiel, in the Epistles of Paul and by the unknown writer of Hebrews.[373]

When Jesus Christ came on the scene with the first Coming, He established and inaugurated an *entirely new* way. Scripture calls this way *The New Covenant* that now deals effectually with the sin problem *at its source*. God ratified this New Covenant while Jesus still hung on the cross. Precisely when Jesus dismissed His Spirit, God personally tore down the veil that occluded the Holy of Holies inside the Jewish Temple. That single act of God ended Judaism as a God-ordained religion. Father God's ratification of Christ's Sacrifice also simultaneously ordained its replacement, New Covenant Biblical Christianity. In God's new Way of dealing with sin, the meaning of Atonement greatly expanded to completely pay the price that God's justice demanded for all the sin of humanity.

The perfect Sacrifice of Christ also blazed the trail that granted humanity the possibility of reconciliation to both God and their fellow man. The Greek word *Katallage* describes this way as the only valid way to *Biblical Salvation and Reconciliation*. One may also find other perspectives on Atonement by looking under the following terms: Bloodshed, The Mosaic-Levitical Sacrifice System, The New Covenant, Reconciliation and Sacrifice.

Authority:

I. Overall precepts: Expressed in the Greek word Exousia, authority represents right or privilege granted or permitted to exercise that power or ability that originates with God. Believers must realize that the basic underlying assumption is incumbent that God retains the ownership of all genuine authority. In the New Covenant, Father God has delegated

---

373   Jer. 31:31-34; Ezek. 36:26,27; Gal. 2-5; Heb. 7-11 *See also the book Jesus' Way: God's Guaranteed Blueprint*

all authority to Jesus Christ who sits at the right hand of the Father. From thence, it flows via the Holy Spirit to the grantee who fulfills the conditions specified in the New Covenant.[374]

A. *Unconditionally Absolute, Inherent or Original authority* only inherently exists in the Persons of the Godhead: Father God, Jesus Christ and the Holy Spirit. Only God can exercise this type of authority that is unconditional, determinative, imperative or mandatory.

B. *Conditionally Delegated Authority* is the common type that God delegates to man. This is the primary type present on earth where God delegates it to specific human beings. Conditionally delegated authority applies only to individuals who fulfill the specific conditions that we find in the Word of God. God always retains the ownership of all *genuine* authority. God's Word gives us the terms that apply. We must remember that even duly constituted organizations carry no more weight than the authority delegated to those *specific individuals* God has granted authority to within them. Conditional authority is *limited in scope for good reasons:* Because of Adam's fall, human nature is not trustworthy. Not only that, God only grants conditional authority with the proviso that the one granted authority acts as the legate of God. This is also indicated according to the terms of our agreement, the New Covenant. If any such person violates that proviso, the 'line of authority' is broken and the authority ceases to be valid.

C. *Conditionally Permitted,* tolerated or allowed authority remains as the main type one finds *outside the Church in the world.* This is so since God always allows man a free agency and permits or tolerates man's governments to 'use' authority. Yes, God even allows Satan and tyrants to exercise 'rebel authority.' Ephesians chapter six tells about the commonplace reality of *Satanic or rebel authority on earth.*

II. **Corollary guidelines:** God's Word also specifies exclusions that directly affect or limit that authority. One such scripturally mandated privilege that exists to preserve the integrity of our conscience is legitimate Civil Disobedience. Christians *should cherish* Biblical Civil

---

374   Matt. 28:18; John 1:12; Eph. 1:19-23; Col. 1:11-29; 2:9,10

Disobedience and the legitimate right of passive nonviolent resistance and dissent. Examining the chronicles of Scripture and history reveals that these costly archetypal precedents follow the heroic and *Prophetic* tradition of *confronting leaders and speaking truth to power.* God has gone to great lengths to preserve these intact to assure the integrity of conscience among God's People. This tradition applies in all those cases when man's *fallible* laws or 'justice' conflicts with the absolutely infallible authority of God's higher law.[375]

The Scriptures highlight heroes like Moses, Rahab the Harlot, Ruth, Nathan, Elijah, Elisha, Jeremiah, Daniel and his three Hebrew friends and the brave Early Christians. All these Saints were forced to *disobey man to Obey God.*

Many others also paid an awesome price just so we could read their story in the Bible. Consequently, the whole of Scripture teaches that no government can assume they can exercise 'automatic' authority over their constituency. For example, the American government exercises authority only because *the American People have consented to and have enacted laws to support the existence of said authority.* All these terms and conditions are evidence of the general spiritual law of Scripture that teaches us about *the Sovereignty of God and the responsibility of man.* This is the way that God preserves the individual's conscience before God. However, on the other side of the coin we can see a tragic pattern of history. This pattern tells us that many 'Have failed to learn the lessons of history and their actions continue to condemn them to repeat it.'

Moreover, throughout the centuries, countless church leaders have been guilty of equivocating away our legacy to keep their influence in the world. *Consequently, they have done despicable 'Violence to the law of God'* in doing so! *They have created mountains of confusing and flawed dogma that contorts and twists Scripture around.* Many religious leaders have made it appear that the Bible teaches that Christians are always duty bound to obey man's law, when Scripture paints to us a far different picture! We must come to know *for ourselves* the true meaning of scriptures such as Romans Thirteen.

---

375   Daniel 4; Acts 4,5

If we do homework in this, God's Spirit will reveal to us that man has *willfully mistranslated this Scripture*. The original Greek word *Tagma* means that God has chosen to *Permit, allow or tolerate man to govern himself*, whether the form of governance be democracy or dictatorship. However, when God directly ordains or appoints someone or something, Scripture uses a much different word. In Greek, Jesus used the word *Poema* when our Lord ordained the Twelve. Yes, we know that at specific times in the distant past, God did appoint *certain Kings*. However, this *did not* establish a general pattern. Scripture tells us that God only 'appointed' the following: King David of Israel, the Babylonian King Nebuchadnezzar and Cyrus, King of the Medes and Persians. Not only that, with each case God had a specific contemporary purpose in mind. *Overall, however, God has chosen to allow man to choose his own form of government.* However, man must also live with the consequences of choices. Consider what Samuel said about what God felt concerning the Israeli's determination to 'get a King' and become like the Nations around them.[376]

The New Covenant teaches us a vital precept regarding how much authority that man can command. Scripture teaches that *God regulates* the *relative degree of submission* that a human authority can command any subject.

The New Covenant also specifically regulates the terms and *the extent of our obedience to any human authority.*

The fact remains that *the authority of Jesus Christ is superior to any human authority in the life of a Believer.*

Scriptures teaches the essential truth that God *never commands* Believers that they are 'duty-bound' to absolute or 'blind obedience' to man precisely because human authority is subject to infiltration by our enemy, Satan! Consequently, we can prove "Divine Right of Kings" for being a false doctrine. Those leaders who teach that doctrine prove that they love the world more than Jesus! I suspect another possibility is that they are fawning cowards who fear standing up for Jesus Christ in the face of opposition. Not only that, one cannot 'hide behind' the authority of others or an organization to 'sanctify' an act that would be sin for an individual.

---

376   1 Sam. 10; Psa. 94:20-23

Yes, God holds everyone accountable to the same standard! Moreover, this also means that even though one may be 'acting under the orders of others,' it nonetheless does not give them a shred of an excuse to disobey God's law any more than others would. For example, God holds the soldier responsible for acting according to their conscience individually before God despite 'man's orders' to the contrary notwithstanding! Not only that, God holds them just as accountable for everything they do on the battlefield as much as under any other condition. Viz., acting 'under the orders' of fallible humans of any position does not absolve anyone from their accountability before God. Let us remember the remonstrance John the Baptist gave the Roman soldiers and Jesus' plain statements about loving enemies.

If Christian leaders had been teaching these truths consistently, then they would have armed Believers (like me) with the truth when they most needed it. That way many more could have been spared the nightmarish consequences of being involved with war and combat, since human law allows us to register as conscientious objectors. Even if this were not the case, a True Christian would be willing to endure any punishment of man to keep Christ's Commands!

Not only that, I strongly suspect that many would have made *very different* choices if had they known that killing another human being (the sin of knowledgeable murder) incurs such an awesome price to their soul!

That is not to mention the potentially eternal judgment God prescribes for unrepentant murder, regardless of the circumstances! Yes, this means that under the *New Covenant* of Christ, God still defines any type of hatred of enemies and intentional or knowledgeable killing as the sin of *murder*. All the rules of God apply equally to everyone in every situation. That is why God is holding Christian leaders accountable for teaching the whole truth to new converts from the beginning! [377]

---

377   Matt. 5:43–48; 26:52: Luke 3:14, 15; 9:51–56; Acts 5:29-32; 1 John 3:11-15; 4:7-21; Rev. 13:9,10; 14:12,13 *See also the Papers entitled Authority and Conscience and Authority & Conscience, Part Two: God has established a Framework of Order*

III. Other related words and precepts:

A. Authority is to establish: God either ordains (appoints) or allows the establishment of a 'Covenant,' a 'House' or a 'Steward/Householder' who acts as a tenant, managing God's Estate (Vineyard).[378]

B. It is to ordain (Appoint), Call, Grant or Send: For example, Jesus ordained and Sent the Seventy. He also sent the workers (Prophets) to serve and, eventually, His Son (Jesus Christ) to the Vineyard in the Parables of the Householders and of the Citizens and Talents.[379]

In the other places, Jesus says 'He has Sent Him (Jesus)… On Him (Jesus) Whom He has Sent… (Jesus), the One whom the Father has Sent is True… Et. Al.[380]

C. It means to Set or Place: E.g., Jesus' quote of Isaiah the prophet: 'To set at liberty those who are oppressed…'

D. A Throne: Two senses: One relates to God's absolute authority proceeding from Heaven via Christ and the Holy Spirit.

See Jesus' Way Appendix C: "The Kingdom of Heaven Diagram."[381]

The other relates to man's delegated authority.

E. Another word refers to a specific event, 'The Great White Throne (Judgment),' where all unbelievers will receive the ultimate sentence: eternal damnation in the lake of fire.[382]

See the New Covenant, Basic Christian Doctrine, EKKLESIA and the Kingdom of Heaven.

Baptism:

I. Basic precepts: Baptism has multiple meanings. Although most Believers consider 'Baptism' only to be an outward 'ceremony' done by a priest or minister, however the Biblical understanding is far deeper

---

378 Gen. 6:18; 9:9–17; 17:7, 19,21; 1 Chron. 17; Daniel 2:44,45; Matt. 13,21; Mark 12; Luke 20

379 Matt.21; Luke 19

380 John 5:38; 6:29; 7:28,29; 8:26,29,42

381 1 Kings 22:19; 2 Chron. 18:18; Psa. 11:4; 45:6 (Heb. 1:8): 47:9; 89:14,29,36,44; 97:2; 103:19; Isa. 6:1; 22:23; 66:1 (Acts 7:49); Jer. 17:12; Ezek. 1:26; 10:1; Matt. 5:34; 19:28; 23:22; 25:31; Acts 2:30; Heb. 4:16: 8:1; 12:2: Rev. 4:1–10: 5:1–13; 7:17; 8:3; 14:3–5; 19:4,5

382 Rev. 20:11

and significant. Baptisms occurred in the Early Church at the point when a Believer chose to publicly declare their allegiance to Christ. However, the primary meaning of Baptism as defined in Scripture goes beyond any outward action.

A. *Spiritual Baptism* points us to that internal unseen process that progressively identifies a person with Jesus Christ. Spiritual Baptism begins when God's Spirit introduces us into God's kingdom and then continues to serve in the Believer's odyssey of *Conversion*. This adventure begins at *Initial Salvation* when the person first confesses that they are sinners in need of God and choose to receive the sacrifice of Christ. If we carefully study Scripture and follow the way God's Spirit teaches, we always find that the process of *Spiritual Baptism parallels the process of Conversion. The Holy Spirit first Regenerates the functions of the human spirit within us.* Second, He *introduces us to the Fellowship of the True Body of Christ.* Third, He comes alongside and helps the Believer in their journey of self-discovery, self-confrontation and continual repentance that God requires of us to lead us to Conversion.

B. Consequently, we can only rightly call the common form of outward 'Baptism' that describes one of a set of outward liturgies commonly used in organized Churches *Believers Water Baptism.* Christians should know that this Baptism is *only secondary in importance.* We must learn to distinguish it from inward spiritual Baptism that is entirely independent of it.[383]

Let us always remember that *outward forms of Baptism cannot save us!* This means that simple comparison with Scripture can prove all humanistic doctrines containing Baptismal Regeneration for being *false doctrines.* This includes infant baptism because an infant could not be an active participant making a rational and informed decision. We can only regard Infant Baptism as a form of *dedication only,* and is a service primarily concerning *the responsibility of parents* to raise up the child "In the nurture and admonition of the Lord." Again, Scripture plainly teaches that *the most important type of Baptism is only Spiritual in nature.* Man cannot control spiritual things other than to decide whether we obey the ones God has outlined for us in Scripture.

---

383   1 Cor. 12:12, 13; Eph. 4

I. Other symbolic meanings: To Wash, which even when it is externally done in water, still speaks of an inward 'change of heart' that John the Baptist referred to as the 'Baptism of Repentance.' It is also related to anointing with oil, since both are actions that God's Holy Spirit does in our inner being. In fact, starting with John's Baptism, Christian Baptism arose from the ancient Jewish 'purification rituals' of washing. One of the most significant examples is the 'Foot-Washing' that Jesus started in the Upper Room.[384]

The Blood of Christ:

This is the Biblical term for the *active spiritual agent* that accomplishes the following:

1. The original physical Blood of Jesus shed on the cross is the way God used to pay the entire price of sin, by that God made it available for all humanity for all time.

2. The contemporary *spiritual* distribution of Christ's Blood testifies to its enduring efficacy and value. The Holy Spirit transfers the forgiving power inherent in Christ's Blood. He applies the Blood to 'the doorposts and lintel' of every penitent human heart who confesses and forsakes (repents of) sin!

Believers must act biblically upon these precepts and to seek to obey the commands of Jesus Christ with all our heart for God to apply the benefits to us.[385]

The spiritual ministry of the Holy Spirit of Grace then *Cleanses the Believer, making them Holy* and provisionally places their lives in organic Union with Father God. See Bloodshed

The Body of Christ:

This manifold biblical term refers to all the following:

---

384   Ruth 3:3; 2 Kings 5:10–13; Isa. 1:6; Ezek. 23:40; Matt. 3:11,12; 6:17; Luke 7:38; John 9:7,11; 13:5–14; Acts 22:16
385   1 Pet, 1:2; 1 John 1:7,9

1. The sacrifice *Passover Lamb* of God who lived once as the personal 'flesh and blood' physical body of Jesus that walked this earth. God tells us that the collective sin of humankind is totally responsible for Jesus being crucified on the Cross, but God raised our Lord on the third day.

2. The intrinsic (spiritual) Real Presence of Jesus Christ that the Early Christians testified was present at the Love-Feasts mentioned by many period writers. The phrase 'Till He comes' reflects the understanding that at some point in time during the fellowship, the Holy Spirit would make the Manifest Presence of Christ personally real to them!

3. An *Active Spiritual Agent* that the Bread at *Communion* symbolizes. Similar to the Blood of Christ, which cleanses us from sin, the *Body of Christ IDENTIFIES the Believer for being spiritually UNITED with Christ.* This is the agent Paul refers to in Romans chapter six and seven and that reckons us dead unto sin when we obey Christ's New Covenant.

4. The Body of Christ is also the symbol of Christian Unity that Believers experience when they gather *in one accord.* Overall, Scripture defines the Universal Church as Christ's Body, which Scripture defines as the sum of all *true Christian* Believers throughout time and space.

5. We find another significant meaning of 'Real Presence' in Scripture in the eventual fulfilment of the Second Coming Event when Jesus Christ comes in Power and Glory.

However, we must beware of the following other facts as well concerning what the *true Body of Christ means:* One, Just because they call some group or organization a 'church' it does not always automatically follow that this group is necessarily a part of "The (true) Body of Christ." Two, We should know that membership in an organization does not qualify us for being part of Christ. Three, even an ardent sincere profession of faith by itself is insufficient!

Yes, We must go to New Testament Scripture to find what clearly defines the terms and conditions all Believers must satisfy to be "Part of Christ!" The essence is that we cannot trust any humanly generated or 'Organizational' definitions of spiritual things to be reliable, because of the wickedness and deception inherent in human nature. See *Church*, *EKKLESIA*, *Biblical Unity*

Casuistry/Casuist:

1. Webster's Dictionary defines a casuist as one who 'deals with moral cases' and 'matters of the conscience.' However, in Christianity a second application exists that is much more accurate, however far less flattering. Casuistry describes a primary activity of adept persons or organizations that employ sophisticated multi-level propaganda to ensure widespread belief in the 'party line' dogma espoused by an apostate Pseudo-Christianity. Their Casuistic leaders have used a plethora of complex syllogisms and clever argumentation to bolster untenable doctrines that totally lack any legitimate means to establish them according to New Testament Scripture. This activity may be good for lawyers in courtrooms where technicalities rule the day, but casuistry makes for a very dangerous game for the Christian Believer! Contrariwise, Simple comparison with the teachings of Jesus Christ and the early Apostolic writers will conclusively prove them wrong at every turn. Modern Bible Schools, Seminaries and Denominational organizations have become riddled with spiritual minefields sedulously laid by the religious mind benders that have come to dominate them. Over the years, Lucifer has used a host of religious spin-doctors who have worked overtime to produce a tangled web of confusion. In doing so, Religious authorities have literally paved and ornately decorated the Broad Way of destruction with pious platitudes, camouflaged moral conundrums and ornately festooned Machiavellian rationales justifying gross hypocrisy and false doctrine! *See the Judeo – Christian Tradition. Of course, we should know that casuists will go to any length to find an obscurantist reason to justify a blatant contradiction! They strain so hard at a thousand 'gnats,' but always end up swallowing the filthy camels of egregiously convoluted false doctrines. Tragically, most religious leaders continue to deceive gullible listless congregations with spiritual tripe. So many 'Beams in the eye' abound that it appears to have evolved to be a fashionable accessory that the masses all seem to envy! Most Christian leaders will apparently make themselves contort and bend over backward to the ground just to justify one false doctrine. Of course, the 'end justifies the means' as it brings crowds in the doors.

We know that Satan rewards the casuist well since all people pleasers covet praise and truckloads of cash.

You see them on TV patting themselves on the back giving themselves the glory hawking their 'personal fulfillment' books praising humanism that everybody seems to mindlessly lap up like Pavlovian dogs. Consequently, in the artificially maintained vacuum of spirit that prevails in mainstream apostate Christianity, rampant worldliness, false doctrines and hypocrisy prevail. Not only that, they zealously protect their cozy system with defense mechanisms with teeth. They vigorously slander and denounce as 'divisive' anyone who dares to preach *the really true Gospel* that upsets their 'Apple cart' and disrupts their immensely profitable 'gravy train.' Just challenge their status quo and at the very least you will get the 'Stonewall treatment.' Remember that the *real Jesus Christ is bad for business:* Just think for a moment about what the Jews of Jesus' time must have thought about someone who would dare upset the moneychangers' tables in the Temple! Religious people never change. Casuistry provides the ruling elite with a perfect cover. They are so busy with worldly pursuits that they fail to notice the price they must eventually pay for their willful iniquity. However, they are not the only ones to pay for contracting the incurable spiritual cancer that afflicts the life of all reprobates. Their pride is the lock and latch that binds them to the millstones they carry about their necks.

Christology:

Christology is that branch of *Theology* that deals specifically with the Nature of the Son, the Second Person of the Divine Trinity, Jesus Christ. The main points are as follows:

1. CHRIST IS ETERNALLY GOD. Christ is Coeternal with Father God and the Holy Spirit. He existed from *eternity past,* and Christ will continue to exist to *eternity future.* Christ is God and possesses all the attributes of God, starting with Omnipotence, Omniscience and Omnipresence.

2. TWO NATURES OF CHRIST EXIST. These are the following: One, the Divine and eternal Son and Two, the human person born to Mary in Bethlehem by sinless conception. This human-divine Jesus

Christ grew up and taught the precepts of God's Kingdom to the Disciples, who have recorded them in our New Testament.

3. Jesus Christ became the perfect human sacrifice we know as 'the Lamb of God' when He was crucified on Calvary. This awesome act of extending forgiveness of sin was promised in Scripture centuries before. Christ's Sacrifice paid for the entire sum God's justice demanded for sin for all mankind and for all time. After dying, Jesus then entered Sheol and ministered to the righteous Old Testament Saints.

4. Being the 'Firstborn from the dead' and the 'First-fruits' of them that sleep in Jesus, Christ arose bodily from the grave, Commissioned His followers and ascended to His rightful place at Father God's Right Hand on the Throne in Heaven. When He ascended into Heaven, Jesus also carried the Old Testament Saints away with him.

Communion:

The verb form of Communion originates from the Greek word Koinos, (Common) which means to share that which belongs to another. Communion and Fellowship are synonymous.

1. Communion points us to the spiritual reality that all Believers 'commonly' partake and share what belongs to Jesus Christ Who possesses the universal ownership and occupies that place of being the Lord (Head) of all Believers. New Testament Fellowship first grows out from Personal Communion with Father God by which we receive spiritual life. As Christians Brothers and Sisters share this bounty equilaterally, we become part of each other's lives. Body-Life grows from these relationships. What this spiritual dynamic teaches us is that God intends both personal Prayer and genuine New Testament Fellowship to be central activities integral to every Believer's life. The fact that genuine New Testament Fellowship (Body-Life) is so rare, shows how devastating the cumulative effects of the human factors of organization, selfishness and rebellion has been!

2. Christians commonly use the noun form of Communion to refer to the ceremony (Symbolic Observance or 'ordinance') of the Commemorative Celebration of the Lord's Supper.

3. Communion is also a term describing the *function of the human spirit we must learn to exercise to form a relationship with and receive spiritual life from God.* It is among the two components of the human spirit lost in the fall. Direct personal intervention is the only way God can replace it. Scripture calls this act Regeneration. Regeneration is only possible individually and is predicated upon the person confessing their sin and receiving the shed Blood Sacrifice of Jesus Christ. This places the Convert in a provisional state of initial Righteousness. However, Scripture also teaches us this: The New Covenant *requires subsequent on going acts of Repentance and Faith to prevent apostasy* for *us to retain that condition of Righteousness.* Continual use of this *regenerated* function is mandatory if a person is to maintain a consistent prayer life. See Worship

Conscience:

The Conscience is among the three organs of the human spirit: Intuition, Communion and *Conscience.* The human Conscience is the only vestige of the spirit left to unregenerate man. For very good reasons God has chosen to leave this function intact is so that man can receive Christ and be Saved. By the conscience we also discern right from wrong. Regenerated believers can gain so much more spiritual acumen by adding spiritual knowledge to expand the use of the Conscience. However, to maintain and build up that ability properly requires *discernment* in using knowledge rightly.

However, on the other hand, we can also diminish or 'sear the Conscience' by repeated acts of willful sin.

Conversion:

Three Greek words: *Strophe, Epistrophe and Epistrepho* describe Conversion as a *turning about or turning around.* Scripture teaches that the implication is that one must make a turn of one hundred and eighty –degrees or a reversal of course (in their way of life, attitude and lifestyle) by doing so.[386] Thus conversion describes and encompasses all the main goals of Christianity. To this end, Conversion always refers

---

386   Matt. 18:3; Luke 22:31,32; Acts 3:19; 1 Thess. 1:9; James 5:19, 20

us to the complex, difficult and usually painful process of Biblical Discipleship that God requires to produce it. Not only that, God fully intends for *every Christian* to attain the same goal, which is "The Image and stature of Jesus Christ." At this point, we must take note and beware of a false doctrine and a common semantical trap of thinking: This would be to blithely assume that the initial or *'Novice' Convert* could have immediately or automatically attained the status of being 'converted' or to the full stature of Christianity! We should see this as absurd since everything we receive that is worthwhile in the Kingdom of Heaven *requires time, constant cooperation and discipline on our part to develop.*

God's Spirit places a *(neophyte) Convert* in a probational and temporary condition (initial position based on Prevenient Grace) upon which God requires development contingent upon their subsequent active cooperation. Even one who has made a public declaration that they are a Christian does not make them one in God's eyes. Just claiming to be a 'Christian' does not prove we are one, even if we have done so for a long time. Scripture teaches that we must continue to fulfill the conditions specified in God's Word. In the world of physical nature, we know that a human baby must breathe for itself, learn to eat, walk and talk before they can survive and grow into adulthood.

Similarly, our full development into the Stature of Christ in turn also requires subsequent *continual cooperation* by the individual involved. Consequently, For a Believer to reach to the ultimate goal the process of *Conversion leads us to, God* demands our *total allegiance and total cooperation over an extended period, our whole lifetime!* [387]

Determinism (i.e., Predestination):

Introduction: Determinism is a common underlying tenet inherent in many forms of dogma and authoritarianism that the modern Church system has inherited. Scripture, however, proves it to be a false doctrine for Christians. Nonetheless, it is the root of other false doctrines religious leaders also carefully camouflage. Among these

---

387   *See main text. Chapter Three See also the 3-part series of papers entitled "Christian Conversion" and the Diagram/paper entitled "Figure One: Illustration/Comparison of Caterpillar/Butterfly to Conversion"*

are the following: 'Easy-Believeism,' 'Baptismal Regeneration,' 'Once Saved, always saved' and 'The Divine Right of kings,' where we find the modern Church's sycophantic approval of nationalistic doctrines, political leaders, sanctions on homicide and warfare, and hatred of enemies. This is also an unrecognized underlying cause of hypocrisy. Two major forms of Determinism exist, both using the synonym Predestination.

I. Double Predestination. (Double P.) is the hardline form of Determinism. This dogma underlies the main doctrines of both Catholicism and Protestantism. It falsely asserts that God has already decided who will be going to Heaven or Hell. This egregious doctrine also undercuts the main thrust of Christ's teachings about God's universal Love and of true Christianity, derailing it into a perverted form of fatalism that denies free will. See *Jesus Way* Appendix: Authority and Conscience. The reader should note that even simple logic can prove that it is necessary for God to retain the doctrine of human free will after the fall. This way God can uphold both His Love and Justice by simultaneously extending the olive branch of intended Salvation and holding all mankind accountable for their actions. Determinism is also known as 'Calvinism,' named after John Calvin, a major Swiss Reformer of the Sixteenth Century. His major work called Institutes also follows the flawed dualistic doctrines formulated by Augustine late in his life when he struggled to find resolution to the problem of evil in the world.

The resultant work, published in C. 426 A.D., is called *The City of God.* However, Augustine's book employed a pagan belief, Persian Dualism, in the vain attempt to justify what Jesus Christ would never be found doing or approving. Pope Leo the Great employed this pattern and his ways became the mantra of the imperialistic Church System we know as the Roman Catholic Church. They mercilessly persecuted all dissenters, including those who stood for the original truths of Jesus Christ, like Wycliffe and Huss. Not only that, all the major Protestant Reformers followed these same worldly themes justifying violence and murder 'to preserve order.'

Consequently most Christians have blindly followed this obviously humanistic philosophy for centuries, because their leaders kept teaching that Christ's hard sayings were 'impractical.' Yet, how could they justify teaching Christians to live like the world and still think they would 'make it' to Heaven? A true exegesis of Scripture refutes 'Once Saved always saved.' The following three major premises underlie Determinism/Predestination: Total Depravity, Irresistible Grace and Limited Atonement. The last two are totally false and the first is partially false because of gross misinterpretation regarding human free will.

II. Single-P. Single Predestination is a modified form of Double-P. It asserts that God only has decided who will go to Heaven, but has 'no particular mind' concerning all the rest. This 'Theology' is not much better than the former case.

III. Watch out: Those who falsely use the 'Doctrine of the Elect' and of various personal pronouns relating to this subject lead many astray. Advocates of determinism 'fall back' on an incorrect exegesis of Scriptures such as John six and ten, Romans' nine and Ephesians one. They teach a false impression of God to make people think that God arbitrarily 'chooses' who will be saved or damned or who will be a 'member' of the Church. Contrariwise, Scripture clearly teaches that "God is no respecter of persons."

IV. Summary. We must always be wise to properly discern the vast difference between Foreknowledge and Predestination. Remember that just because God knows the future and knows what a particular person will decide to do *does not mean that God makes that decision for them!* God holds all Human beings fully responsible and accountable for all actions they take *on the Basis of the rules contained within the New Covenant of Jesus Christ Our Lord!* See also entries on: *Agape Love*, *Antichrist*, *Apostasy/Apostate*, *Authority*, *Atonement*, *Basic Christian Doctrine*, *Casuist/Casuistry*, *Dualism*, *EKKLESIA/ Elec*, *Ethics*, *Hermeneutics*, *The Judeo-Christian Tradition*, *Probational*, *Reconciliation* and *Syncretism*.

Dualism: is the name for an array of philosophical tenets that originated from ancient paganism. It arose as man tried to explain the apparent contradictions in life and in those laws of the universe they could not explain. We can trace dualism to an ancient Babylonian cult called *Zoroaster*. This cult contained a strong theme of 'a cosmic struggle between good and evil' They saw this struggle personified in a mythical dramatic conflict. Conflicts between personages mirrored human affairs in the realm of 'the gods.' Later these ideas resurfaced as the "Emanation Theory" in the writings of Plato and Aristotle. The Platonism and Gnosticism of the Greco- Roman civilization provided fertile ground for such ideas. During the first century of the Common Era when Christianity first entered the scene, dualism was a commonly held belief. Worldly minds of that time thought dualism 'worked to explain' the disparities between the physical world of the senses and the ethereal world of 'the gods.' They saw the former to be 'evil,' while the latter they believed to be 'good,' however far removed from the affairs of man. In modern times, we can easily see this 'good vs. evil' motif. On the mass media they act it out in virtually every play, worldly movie and television series.

Their 'Situation dramas' always depict some perceived threat or 'evil,' and a 'hero' who saves others from 'the bad people' using violence or another method based on humanism, the universal idol-religion of the world. Dualism is the common philosophy behind these contrived situational 'what – if' questions we hear so frequently. They are also found in Sigmund Freud's 'Flight-Flight' depiction of alternatives. All beliefs relying on the idol of human power are false. Of course, they do not tell you that God has given Christians a *third path defined in the New Covenant!* The Bible teaches that matter is not evil, and that our Father God, creator of the universe, is very much involved with the daily affairs of human life. The truth of scripture teaches that the cloth of reality (physical and spiritual) contains no 'artificial split' within it! For our law, God has given Christians the New Covenant of Jesus Christ that is *universal in scope, consummated in the Teachings and Example of Jesus Christ.* We must take them seriously at face value as applying to all situations, whether private or public. What many Christians are frequently unaware of is that the poison of dualistic beliefs has deeply infiltrated *all religious organizations.* Because of the Determinism descending from Augustine's *City of God,* Dualism affects even those that many think are 'impregnable bastions of fundamentalism!'

Satan has deftly manipulated organized religion to the point that they routinely use dualism as a clever artifice to artificially divide the ethical rules applying to the physical from those that govern the Spiritual. In truth, the beliefs of many religious leaders have evolved such that *their real theology has become NOMINALISM.* Their 'spirituality' is mere perfunctory lip-service.

If you pin them down, you will find out that they only believe the realm of the senses is real. They truly do not believe spiritual things are real at all. This underlying *unbelief* is also the basis of all casuistry. Religious leaders use this often to 'justify' their counter-Christian doctrines justifying wars, glorifying and blessing soldiers going to battle and promoting idolatry by worshiping the symbols of the state. By doing so they have also declared their allegiance to the 'god of this World' whether they know it or not. Guess who that is and their destiny? I believe that many a Christian leader has adapted so much to the world such that they *believe the same as an atheist without even being aware of it!* It appears that the more knowledge 'religious people' have, as well as the higher their 'position,' the less they believe. Indeed, their hypocritical double standard sounds like the original sin, does not it? Even the world can easily detect their dissimulation. Hypocrisy is the same reason that Jesus spoke against the religious leaders so much. See Casuistry, Determinism (Predestination), Empiricism, Ethics, Nominalism. Platonism

EKKLESIA/Elect:

I. General background: EKKLESIA is the Greek word used in the New Testament for 'Church.' Originally it referred to a group of public officials who were 'Called out ones' separated out (chosen) and designated to serve at their own expense. As public servants, they were to accomplish a specified task for the Greek Assembly that met in Athens. New Testament writers picked up the word and used it in *the Christian sense. 'Church' designated a group of Believers who were 'Called out' by Jesus who met in a specific place to worship.* The word 'Church' developed from this context. The word "Elect" is also derived from the same Greek root. Scripture defines New Testament Churches, therefore, as separate and distinct organisms that are "Called out" from the world for the separate and distinct task of worshiping and serving the Lord Jesus Christ. The Church is part of Christ and the Kingdom of Heaven.[388]

Consequently, it can never be considered as *just as part of the surrounding community or culture. Nor, could the true Church be just some part of a religion attached to a Nation-state or Empire of this world.* Jesus told Pilate: "My Kingdom is not of this world…" The true Church is "Called out from the world" and is Holy unto the Lord. The true Church is a living organism composed of Believers called 'The Saints.' In various places Scripture verifies that God's Spirit is the *source* of all 'Callings' and roles in Christ's Body. God ordains their position as a 'Candlestick,' 'Nail' or 'Pillar' in God's House (His Temple). In Ephesians, Paul calls the collective whole (in all times and places) as 'the Family of God' on earth and Heaven. In Scripture God says they are the 'Children of God' or 'Sons of God,' and when taken as a whole, the Elect. Reader Note: We must understand that the term 'Elect' exists only as a product of two distinct choices: One is God's universal offer of Salvation and Two, man's free will decision to receive Christ. Always remember: God is no respecter of persons.[389]

II. The Church is in the world but not of the world: As such, the ongoing issue of *separation* is something with which every Believer must deal daily! Consequently, we must always be aware that this distinctiveness we have when we truly follow Jesus will inevitably draw down persecution in some way or other. Look at what happened to the early Christians.[390] Yes, God uses persecution to spread the Church and make it stronger. See how God used Philip the Evangelist. Consider Peter's experience that widened his outlook on 'outsiders.' Of course, we all know about Saul the persecutor's conversion that transformed him into Paul the Evangelist and Church planter![391]

---

388 Mat. 16:18; 18:20,21; John 18:36; Acts 2:38–47
389 Matt. 5:9; 18:3; 19:13,14; Mark 10:14,15; Luke 18:16,17; 20:36; John 1:10–14; 11:52; Rom. 8:14– 21 9:8,26; Gal. 3:26–29; Eph. 3:15; Phil. 2:15; 1 John 3:1– 10; 5:2 *See also Basic Christian Doctrine Areas Seven and Twelve*
390 Acts 4:1 ff; 5:17 ff.; 7:1–8:2
391 Acts 8:3–9:43; 10:1 ff.

III. The True Church is a living organism in the Spirit. All growth comes from one source: Jesus Christ, via the Holy Spirit. Jesus is also our Strong Deliverer. As members of Christ's Body, we are Partakers who share and actively participate in a very marvelous opportunity to manifest the love and power of our wonderful God in Christ![392]

However, you will quickly find out that any departure from the New Testament example of how Christians' Worship and serve God will destroy that precious gem of Body-Life in a hurry! Only one form of Governance works to his end: Everyone submits to Jesus first and then to each other. So learn to count the cost. No human device or structure can insulate the true Believer from the world's opposition, because God's Word tells us this is a given!

Moreover, No rule made by man, external 'Baptism ritual' or 'membership' in some human organization or corporation can suffice as the basis for identification in God's Kingdom. The one true Church is always Part of Christ (the Body of Christ). The *True Church always act as ONE in unison with Christ to fulfill Christ's Will.* Any entity that claims to be 'a Church' but fails that simple test is swearing falsely, such as any organization that calls for 'their members' to swear or 'pledge allegiance' to any worldly or National symbol which *leads us to give glory to man instead of God!* God's Word defines *swearing allegiance of any type* to be *a form of Worship* which demands an 'object of trust.' Verily, if that object we are trusting is *anything other than God, God's Word plainly tells us that IS Idolatry!* By definition, the New Testament tells Christians that *Our Lord Jesus Christ is God to us.* Consequently, if we persist in being guilty of willful and knowledgeable worship of any *false god,* which is idolatry, then we cannot be simultaneously part of God's Family, the Body of Christ. The ones who teach these false doctrines of worshiping the symbols of the State are *themselves* the lawbreakers and are in rebellion against God *They* have broken the First of the Ten Commandments and the Great Command.[393]

---

392   Matt. 16:18; Rom. 11:17; 15:27; 1 Cor. 9:9–13, 23; 10:17–21, 30; 2 Cor. 1:7; Eph. 3:6,7; Col. 1:12; 1 Tim. 6:2; 2 Tim. 1:8; Heb. 2:9–14; 3:1, 14; 6:4; 12:8–14; 1 Pet. 4:13–17; 5:1; 2 Pet. 1:4 *See also the paper entitled "The Doctrine of the Elect/Ekklesia"*

393   Ex. 20:3-6; Dan. 3:1-28, 6:4-27; Matt. 22:36,37; Acts 5:29-32

Jesus also told us that we cannot worship or serve more than one object of worship concurrently. We should know that since Christ is the second person of the Godhead, God the Son, Christ's authority is superior to any earthly power. Inspired by the Holy Spirit, Paul wrote that true Christian Believers have only "One Lord, One Faith and One Baptism." [394] Look also under the terms *The Body of Christ*, *Christian*, *Saints* and *The Doctrine of Sanctification*

Empiricism:

Empiricism is a combination of beliefs, methods and Philosophy including the disciplines of *Deductive and Inductive Reasoning (Logic)*. It works similarly to the Scientific Method, where conclusions are drawn based on information (Data) gathered under specific terms and conditions. We then compare this data with a previously determined *Hypothesis* or statement that is set up to explain a phenomenon or describe a mathematical, natural or physical relationship. Empiricism teaches that if the data *matches* the hypothesis, then the hypothesis was correct. However, if the data does not match precisely to the hypothesis, then we must alter the incorrect hypothesis to precisely match the pattern of data. We must repeat this process until the hypothesis reaches an exact match to the data. The Christian Believer, however, is presented with a serious problem with this *naturalism*. This is true since a major condition of obtaining data is that *the humanists insist that we must explain or measure it only using physical units* that we can detect by the senses. However, Naturalism cannot work to explain *Spiritual things. Neither can naturalism explain any quality of Faith nor anything that pertains to the Nature of God.* All humanistic methods are useful in the natural world *to a point. However,* whenever we encounter spiritual realities, all these methods fail us. Red lights should flash in our minds and trouble is always present whenever religious leaders attempt to decide doctrine or explain spiritual things using the limited ways of the natural! Scripture teaches that Spiritual Truths are *even more important than natural things! The most logical of methods fail us when we enter the realm of the Kingdom of Heaven,* simply because our ways of determining truth are woefully inadequate! *The flaw of*

---

394   Matt. 6:24; Eph. 4

Empiricism and of all humanistic ways is that its source is human and not Divine. Only God can adequately explain spiritual truths to man using the spirit of man via the Holy Spirit. Yes, for Christian Believers, human reason has its place, however, it must always take second place to true spiritual reality as defined by Scripture. *When we include all the data, true science always proves Scripture correct.* Jesus once said that "The words I speak to you are *spirit and life – the flesh profits nothing."* When we act in Faith to examine Scripture or doctrine, we can trust the Holy Spirit always to reveal to us the underlying truth.

Faith/Promise:

"Now, Faith is the substance of things for which we hope. (It is) the evidence of things not seen." Scripture plainly defines both Faith, *Trust* and belief synonymously. The Greek word *Pistis* defines Faith as a *firm persuasion or conviction of conscience based on hearing (the Word of God). Faith is a spiritual quantity!* "Faith comes by hearing, and hearing by the Word of God." 'Believing Faith' is first granted by God to every human so that they can believe God. Secondly, God transmits to Believers Subsequent Faith spiritually as a byproduct of our personal fellowship in the spirit. Constraints usually associated with 'ordinary human responses' do not hinder or limit Biblical Faith. Biblical Faith is as big as God! Consequently, as a Christian, it is no longer a valid excuse to follow the pressures of circumstance and the methods of all humanly attainable goals. No longer should we ever allow these things to control us or limit the ceiling of our belief and practice. This great fact also tells us that the way we base our belief system is crucial! God's Will is that we learn to *Trust* by receiving and assimilating God's Word into our spirit. Any form of 'Easy Believeism' that we base merely on Intellectual assent or any other human factor is worthless in the sight of God. The other New Covenant word related to Faith is Promise, for it is the *Promises of God that drive the engine of our Faith* to seek ever greater experiences in God's inexhaustible Treasure-house and Kingdom of Heaven! Yes the 'Promise of the Father' is for YOU![395]

---

395   Ex. 12:25; Psa. 105:42; Jer. 31:31–34; 32:32; 33:14; Luke 24:49; Acts 1:4; 2:33– 39; 7:17; 13:23,32; 32:21; 26:6,7; Rom. 4:13–20; 2 Cor. 1:20; Gal. 3:14–29; 4:28; Eph. 1:13; 2:12; 3:6; 6:2; 1 Tim. 4:8; 2 Tim. 1:1; Heb. 4:1; 6:12–17; 8:6; 9:11–15; 10:32–39; 11:1 ff.; 2 Pet. 1:4; 3:9–13; 1 John 2:25

Fellowship:

Fellowship is the English equivalent or synonym to relationship. The Greek word is the same for both terms. The idea for us to grasp is that scripture defines the New Covenant Church (the Body of Christ) for being a *cohesive community of Saints.* This community, in turn, is composed of two or more individual Believer-Priests that are *organically united to God.* All these Believers derive their central purpose in life and fellowship from a deeply personal relationship that flows from a spiritual bond of *Union with God that carries a profound identification with Jesus Christ.*

Truly *Christian* Fellowship is *also being a part of one another's lives!* Moreover, this central theme takes precedence in all the affairs of life of the Believer, despite whether they concern private or public things. See also The Body of Christ, Communion, EKKLESIA, *The Kingdom of Heaven*, (Biblical) Unity.

Foundation:

In Scripture, the foundation is the basis (The Rock or Cornerstone) upon which we place our Trust (Faith) and live our lives: As the hymm goes: 'The Church's One Foundation is Jesus Christ, her Lord.' Jesus' succinct Parable of the Two Houses in Luke six shows us the essence: The success or failure of our individual life and by extension, the collective life of the Church overall is directly decided by the *type of foundation* upon which that person or group builds.[396] All 'houses' are tested by 'fire and flood.' Another great illustration of Jesus is the 'Vine-Branch' analogy in John fifteen. This Scripture tells us that any person who comes to Christ must personally base their whole lifestyle on obedience to Jesus' Commands, i.e., Jesus' Way, or they will lose that (spiritual) life. That is the basis of the Root-Vine and Branch symbology of John fifteen.[397] See Stewardship

---

396   Luke 6:44–49; 1 Cor. 3:10–12
397   Matt. 16:21–26; John 15:1–6

The Archetype of the Garden:

The story of the "Garden of Eden" is not just some 'fairy tale.' It is a Biblical Archetype of how God works with man. It is where the two paths of Original sin and perseverance start. Think about is: If Adam 'walked with God' and could lose that relationship and contact with God (The human spirit's ability to relate to God), so can any Believer today and for the same reasons. The basic rules of Spirituality do not change! No ironclad guarantee of 'automatic Salvation' exists, even IF we have been Regenerated by God's Spirit at some point in time. The human spirit is composed of three organs: Intuition, Communion and Conscience. These correspond to their functions: Receiving from God, Worshiping God (and Prayer) and the innate knowledge of what is right and wrong. Paul told Timothy that some former Believers have had their consciences 'Seared with a hot iron.'[398]

The symbolism of the Garden teaches us that we are all the same. Adam had sweet fellowship with God, but he deliberately disobeyed God and lost that original ability and even went so far as to run and try to hide from God. 'Adam' is the Hebrew word for mankind that God uses to describe the human race. We are built the same: Triune in nature, spirit, soul and body. God originally designed us for the spirit to be in control and for us to worship and serve God. When man sinned, this contact was lost. The precious functions of Communion and Intuition formed a two-way street of communication and when this link was lost, man began depending on his own strength 'to survive,' but this predisposition led man further away from God. Adam's firstborn became a murderer and mankind spiraled downward into the darkness of sin. The only way to reverse this degradation is for one to find a way to restore (Regenerate) these lost functions so that God's life can again flow into their inner being. God has given every person *Free Will*.

Adam's fall has not diminished this ability to choose one iota. God wants man to choose his path. However, another element is in the mix: God still allows Satan to tempt, just like he did Eve, which led to Adam choosing the wrong path. Yet, that is still the way God allows it to remain. We must choose God over the temptation of Satan or any human desire, fear or ambition that would interpose. The "Garden" is

---

398   1 Tim. 4:2

not just a myth, or something we relegate to 'ancient history' – Verily it is the archetype or pattern that God uses in dealing with man. Yes a striking parallel exists between Adam's testing in the Garden and everyday life. Consider Jesus' Temptation sequence. Paul calls Jesus the 'Second Adam,' for it was Jesus that reversed the condition of hopelessness for man and gave us hope to bring us back to fellowship with God and to inherit the Eternal Life originally present in that 'Tree of Life.'

Yes, that Tree of Life is Jesus Christ![399] Receiving Jesus Christ enables God's Spirit to Restore the lost abilities and places us in God's Kingdom where we can then choose to follow Christ and reach the Stature of Christ in you, the Hope of Glory.

Grace:

In the New Testament, they translate the English word Grace form the Greek word *Charis,* which refers to the unmerited favor that God extends to man under the terms of the New Covenant. God personifies this Grace in the person and work of God's Son, Jesus Christ.[400] Grace also refers us to the *state or condition* that God places a Believer when they fulfill the specific conditions of Righteousness found in the New Covenant. Let us particularly note that *receiving* the Grace of God is *very conditional and dependent upon our attitude!* Scripture teaches that God observes free will continually. This means that *a Believer can resist (rebel against God) and forfeit our standing of righteousness at any given time!* For the Christian Believer, the New Covenant is the only context under which we can relate to God. God has fulfilled the Old Covenant dispensation (of the Law or Judaism) and replaced it with the New Covenant of Grace *in Christ,* which is the only way we can form a *personal Relationship to Father God.* By comparing Scripture with Scripture we can resolve and identify three types of Grace:

1. 'Prevenient Grace': This is the type of Grace is essentially the faith that God freely advances to all humans so that God can eventually save them. We must understand that this fact only guarantees that universal

399 Matt. 4. Luke 4; Rom. 5:14; 1 Cor. 15:22–58
400 John 1:16–18

opportunity to receive the sacrifice of Jesus Christ. It does not mean that God will automatically save everyone.[401]

'Salvation Grace': This is the 'start-up kit' included within the scope of prevenient Grace that God gives the individual *at the time of initial Salvation.* The general tone of the scripture will drive us to acknowledge that God's intent is for this initial limited gift to lead the person to an active faith relationship. Subsequently, God holds every individual Believer responsible for learning to employ *their own regenerated human spirit* to contact God and get renewed supplies of spiritual sustenance. This is what scripture teaches us is a *normal precondition of living the Christian life and maintaining spirituality!* Moreover, John tells us that when we initially receive the Sacrifice of Christ, God places the Believer in what we might call a provisional or "probationary" condition. We also know this period as *Discipleship.* During this crucial period God evaluates our attitudes and draws us by the Holy Spirit to exercise our reborn human spirit through the disciplines of Worship, Prayer and Scripture study. The Holy Spirit uses these tools and draws every regenerate person to *a Personal Relationship of Communion* and Spiritual Fellowship.

2. *Scripture teaches that the 'initial supply kit' is limited in scope and temporary in length.* This initial supply of Grace is only meant to "lead us to the inner Well of Salvation" where we will find the permanent supply source. This is the "Artesian Well" of spiritual life God tells us about in Scripture that 'springs up within' and eventually brings us to Eternal Life when we follow that path to its end! *Warning: If we fail to 'draw near to God' this way, Prevenient Grace will eventually expire!* What this means is that if *the person does not learn to exercise their own reborn spirit by choosing to enter a personal active faith relationship, they will lose that initial standing!* [402]

3. 'Infusion Grace': This is the only permanent 'ongoing form of Grace' that God makes freely accessible to Believers during the Discipleship/ Conversion process. However, it is only by the individual's choice can God's Spirit begin or continue the process of

401   John 1:12; Rom. 12:1–3
402   Isa. 12:3; Matt. 13; Luck 6:46–49; John 7:37–39; Heb. 6:1–8; 10:26–32 *See also the paper "Figure One: Illustration/Comparison of Caterpillar/Butterfly to Conversion"*

Infusion Grace. Yes, you must first learn to exercise the regenerated (reborn) human spirit *that you received when you first received Christ.* Thus enabled, it is God's intent that we continually abide in Christ and fully cooperate with the Holy Spirit. This discipleship/Conversion process is very costly and continually contingent upon our attitude toward God. Scripture teaches that the Believer must first count the cost and then endure all the way to the end for God to save us. The process is not complete until it fully permeates our entire being until this process transforms us to be like Christ. We must always remember that Grace always requires *continual active cooperation and obedience to assure its uninterrupted flow unto us.*[403]

Hermeneutics/(Hermeneutical):

Scholars coined these fancy terms that theologians employ to describe *how Believers are to understand and interpret the Scripture.* Yet, Scripture clearly defines the basis by which we understand it: "Thy Word is TRUTH." Jesus told the disciples in the Upper Room that the Comforter would come, and that this Comforter "(The Holy Spirit) would guide (instruct or teach) *them into ALL TRUTH.*" This means that God designed scripture so that anyone can understand it. In fact, Jesus spoke to the little children admonishing all hearers present that: "Unless you come as a little child, you will in no way enter the Kingdom of Heaven."[404]

High-minded scholasticism and detailed knowledge of Greek and Hebrew or even a Ph.D. in Theology will not gain you any special advantage in *the spiritual Kingdom in which true Christianity exists!* A little child can be just as wise in God's eyes as a philosopher or an epistemological expert! Consequently, we must beware of all *humanistic or (soulish) methods invented by man that coopt our allegiance to the Headship of Christ.* This warning applies to all devices that interfere with receiving and maintaining the *simplicity of the truth.* Savvy Believers know the God-ordained way that the Holy Spirit reveals the truth

403   Matt. 5:48; 11:25–30; 13:18:ff; 24:13; Luke 12:1 ff.; 14:26–3315:11–32; 17:20:ff.; 22:31,32; John 3:5–36; 4:14–24; 6:27–63; 7:15–18; 37–39; 8:31–36; 10:25–30; 12:32; 14–16
404   Matt. 18:1–11; John 14–17; 1 John 2:20–27; See also Isa. 28–30

of scripture to the inward SPIRIT that lies within every Regenerated human being (Born from Above).[405]

Modern Believers have inherited a colossal Problem: The growth and proliferation of 'Religious Organization' has caused a *major impediment to the Believer's understanding of both truth and Scripture.* Organization by religious hierarchies has led to an unbiblical monopoly within Christian circles. The obsessive desire by many religious leaders for controlling what is 'orthodox' doctrine has caused untold damage to the Body of Christ throughout many centuries worldwide. These overbearing monoliths have manipulated and bent the minds of millions, using authoritarian organizational methods of the world to effectively unsurp the role of the Holy Spirit. They have *wilfully substituted the flawed methods of humanism to maintain their power.*

These worldly methods and schemes all originate with the 'angelic order' system that Lucifer brought down to earth when God ejected him from Heaven. As Satan, he has deceived man from ancient times. The first mention we have chronicled in scripture is the original lie of Satan swallowed by Adam. Satan led him to believe that man could become his own god and could control everything by himself. Tribal units congealed this theme, expanding it with the master organizer Nimrod, who built the 'Tower of Babel' in Babylon. This was when God confused the languages of humankind to dissuade them from contacting demonic powers in their insatiable lust for forbidden knowledge and unwonted power. False prophets, Sorcerers, and 'witch doctors' abounded in the ancient world and have frequently led entire Nations astray throughout the centuries!

During the original founding period of Christianity described in the New Testament, writers like Paul frequently suffered from persecution by the powerful forces (strongholds) of religion and the occult. Even the religious orthodox Jews (Pharisees, Sadducees and Herodians) hated the Christians along with the pagans.

All those who love the lies of the world system will hate true Christians! That is what Jesus had warned the disciples about from the beginning. Religious organizations, including nearly all major

---

405   *See Jesus' Way, Appendix A, The Standard*

denominations calling themselves 'Christian', have evolved to be functionaries of the world system. Consequently, their doctrines always contain imbedded lies at some level within them. This is universally true because *religion exists to support human powers and to please people and not God!* That is why we can never define true Christianity as a 'religion.' *Religion* has always been part of the world system. Like the 'Trojan Horse,' Satan has deeply infiltrated and controlled the empty shell of what history originally describes as Christianity, turning it into a 'religion.' Consequently, it has mutated beyond recognition if you compare it with *the Standard of the New Testament.* Keeping these things in mind, let us now seek to properly define how Believers can independently interpret the meaning of scripture. When we approach Scripture, we must do so having specific and carefully understood underlying assumptions in mind:

1. Our Father always plays by the rules.

2. God has specified these rules in the New Covenant.

3. The New Covenant is primarily the New Testament.

4. We can learn to understand the entire Bible IF we view it *through the lens of Jesus Christ!*

5. Context is very important: Ask the 'Who, what, when, where and how' questions.

6. Consider the *type of scripture* you are reading: Many types exist: History (Chronicles of events), Prophecy, Law, Poetry, Epistle and Gospel.

7. The twofold general rule tells the following: *One, You must trust the Holy Spirit to 'interpret all scripture' to your spirit those things that God would have you see. Two you need to "Look at all Scripture through the lens of Jesus Christ."*

Summary: We must always remember that human traditions and religious dogma easily worm themselves in and corrupt the simplicity of the Gospel of Christ. That is why True Believers must always be on the lookout and to judge false doctrine for what it really is. See also *Discernment*, *Knowledge*, *Law*, *The lens of Jesus Christ*, *Logos*, *The Primary of Scripture*, *Revelation*, *Understanding*,

Wisdom, *The Word of God* and the paper entitled *Hermeneutics: Basic Principles of Scripture Interpretation.*

Humanism:

Humanism is the overall term used throughout the New Covenant series of books to refer to the worldwide Idol- Religion that contains the mantra of Antichrist. All over the world system, they teach this religion. Man worships himself, his works and other's personalities and works as 'god.' Yes, Humanism is the first cult. It is the personification of the original lie of Satan in the Garden. Humanism is what drove Nimrod to build the Tower of Babel. Via Paul, God also symbolically calls it 'the uncircumcision,' referring to the Gentiles (the world) who worship idols and rebel against God's authority. It is behind every belief that is counter-Christian, both outside and inside the organized religions, including 'pseudo' Christianity. Above all, humanism asserts selfishness and the control of man. Unbiblical control by organizations and their leaders result in oppression, opportunism (making merchandise of others), greed and lust for more power, usury and 'cultish' methods of dominating others. See *Antichrist*, *Empiricism*, *Nominalism*, *Platonism*, *The Reprobate mind*

Imputed, Impute:

This is an accounting term that involves 'counting' a credit or a debit to an 'account.' This 'account' contains the tally of *righteousness, the currency of God's Kingdom.* To save us, God requires a positive balance. Yes, God has created every human being with a personal account' and a free will to choose their thoughts and actions. In the Bible, God also gives man specific laws regarding these choices and holds every person responsible for knowing these. God's Word also tells us that when a person is first aware of moral choices at 'the Age of Accountability,' God 'counts' our choices from then on. However, because of our ancestor Adam's sin, every person born of a man comes into the world with a 'predisposition to sin.' That is what God's Word tells us about 'original sin.' Initially, God writes each soul in the Book called the Book of Life. However, God declares every person's account 'in arrears' and erases their name when they commit the first sin. God counts every act that the Bible defines as a transgression of the law (i.e., a sin), as a debit against that person's account.

Only a positive balance in that account represents 'righteousness' or right standing with God. Not only that, God's Word teaches us that even a single transgression creates a negative balance and is sufficient to condemn us to eternal punishment! The harsh truth is that unless something else atones for that sin in a biblical way that we must pay the consequences ourselves, which we can never do in our own power. God does not expiate any sin 'automatically.' We must choose to personally receive God's solution in the time allotted. However, this brings us to the beauty of the Original Gospel message! The centerpiece of that original Gospel message is that Jesus Christ has already offered up the Atoning Sacrifice that satisfies God that applies *for all sin, for all humankind for all time.* All we must do for God to forgive us of all our sin is to repent of our sin and individually choose to receive that one Sacrifice. Of course, we must realize that this only deals with *past sin.* Consequently, as we go on in life, to assure our account remains 'in the black,' we must be careful to observe what God commands us to pro-actively deal with all subsequent sin on a daily basis.[406] See the Age of Accountability, Sin, Righteousness, Unrighteousness

Infusion Grace:

Infusion Grace is that unique type of divine Grace that is potentially permanent. However, it requires continual human cooperation to fully enable it. See *Grace*, Paragraph 3.

Initial Salvation/Initial Faith:

This marks the beginning point or the 'baby stage' of the Christian life. During this crucial period, God advances many 'free samples' that show us how to open the package of spiritual life that is waiting for us. However, these inherent advantages advanced in 'Prevenient Grace' last for only for a temporary period. God's Word teaches us that we must learn for ourselves how to use the inner personal reborn (Regenerated) human spirit that God has given us. This is the way God opens the

---

406   Psa. 32; 51; Rom. 4:3; 6:16; 1 John 1:5–10; 2:1,2

spiritual life that we have available within when we receive the sacrifice of Christ. The Holy Spirit woos us to take maximum advantage of this new type of life, for this is how God works the New Covenant out in real lives. During this initial stage, the Holy Spirit often overlooks our mistakes. God's Word teaches us that seeking the presence of God is the way to attain mature spirituality through the gateway of Prayer that we enable by consistent scripture study and meditation. The upshot of all this is that we must choose to do these things in time. To reach the fullness of spiritual stature we must 'strive for mastery' and persevere diligently over a significant period. We face an ongoing inner battle with our fleshly nature that naturally resists the headship of Christ. However, these things will begin to sort out and get more familiar with time. The key is that we 'open up to God' inwardly and 'learn the ropes' of using our newly reborn spirit. You should never expect to get to the point where life is easy, but you *can reach a point when you sense the Spirit of God inside whom will assure you of 'spiritual confirmation'* [407] See *Christian*, *Conversion*, *Disciple*, *Faith*, *Grace*, *In Christ*, *Probational*.

Intuition:

Intuition is among the three functions of the fully functional human spirit: Intuition, communion and Conscience. The first two are functions that are necessary to form a personal relationship to God. Since Conscience is the only function remaining in unregenerate man, it follows that Intuition is a *spiritual function* that is only available and accessible with a reborn (regenerated) human spirit. The only way human beings can have these functions restored is for them to confess their sin and to receive the Sacrifice of Jesus Christ. The restore function of Intuition allows the Believer to *receive revelation directly from God's Spirit to their own spirit.* This is also how we understand scripture. We must acknowledge that human beings must learn to *differentiate spiritual things from soulish things.* Spiritual things are not available via the *intellect,* which is part of the SOUL. This is the reason that many Christians are confused about what true Doctrine consists. They depend on logic. They 'think intellectually' but have not the

---

407   John 1:12–14; 3:3–8; Rom. 8; 1 Cor. 12:12,13; Eph. 4:1–16; Heb. 5:11–14

wisdom that only *the spiritual understanding that God can give to us by His Spirit.*[408] Only God's Holy Spirit can give the spiritual meat that strengthens us to thrive in the Kingdom of Heaven. Yet God can only give this sustenance to those who have learned *the language of the spirit and have received the love of the Truth* in their own heart and mind! Jesus said that "The flesh profits nothing." See Worship/Praise, Inspiration; See also the papers "The Nature of Man" and "The Spiritual Laws of Revival," Chapter 2, Law Eight: the separation of the soul from the spirit.

The 'Judeo-Christian Tradition' (J.C.T.):

This doctrine is the confusing consequence of centuries of evolutionary casuistry that relies heavily on 'averaging' Judaism with Christianity. It is a loose term describing the Syncretic conglomeration of ethics, philosophy and dogma that apostate religion has handed down to modern Christians. A very egregious tenet in it is the recycling of the Old Testament practice of *Herem* or 'Holy War' they call "The Just War ethic," but it is a hoax from Hell! Carefully study the New Testament and Early Christian period writers: The heavenly spiritual wisdom the Holy Spirit imparts to open-hearted students easily exposes the underlying hypocrisy, contradictions, false doctrines and humanistic rationales that result from mixing both Biblical (ancient) and apocryphal (Talmudic**) Judaism with Christian doctrine. The J.C.T. exists primarily because the religious establishment is bent on retaining its power in the world.

To that end, they will use every form of propaganda and false doctrine to bolster their position. The J.C.T. clearly stands violating the spirit and essence of true Biblical Christianity. This traditionally held doctrine also strongly influences the underlying assumptions found in many counter-Christian doctrines and other 'pseudo-Christian' beliefs commonly found in both Catholic and Calvinistic (Reformed or Protestant) belief systems. The J.C.T. has also greatly influenced doctrine in both Evangelicals and Charismatic alike. **Talmudic

---

408   John 6:63,64; 1 Cor. 1:17–2:16 See the paper "The Spiritual Laws of Revival" Law Eight: "The Separation of the soul from spirit"

Judaism is the true religion of unbelieving Jews. It is based primarily on the writings of a medieval Rabbi, Moses Maimonides (1150–1204).

Judgment:

Scripture specifies several types of meaning for Judgment: Inevitably, some meanings overlap the area of condemnation, causing some confusion. See #s four and five below. However, we can offset this by distinguishing truth carefully by observing the proper contexts while comparing your reading of Scripture with the main focus points enumerated below:

1. The main idea of Biblical Judgment falls into the area of distinguishing between right or wrong. We derive the moral distinctions between right and wrong from different variations of the verb *Krino* (2919),* meaning to distinguish or make a value assessment. Also, it means to conclude, esteem, think or evaluate. Other words for this idea are *Krites* (2923) and *Diakrino* (1252). God intends all these words to center our minds on one thing: Discerning and contending for moral decisions, Lifestyle values and the distinguishing of meanings crucial to living the Christian life.[409]

2. *Horizo* (3724) means the setting of boundaries or the marking out of limits. *Kriterion* (2922)* means a rule of judging or the comparing to a standard. *Proorizo* (4309) prescribes a prior declaration or warning regarding the determination of standard, bounds or limits.[410]

3. The Greek noun *Krisis* (2920)*, meaning a decision, a violation (of the law), an accusation (and when life confronts us with a situation in which one must decide!)[411]

4. Sometimes they translate the Greek word *Krima* (2917)* as the English word 'judgment', although God's Spirit may not intend the context to refer to the specifics of condemnation. This does cause some difficulty in resolving the ultimate meaning, but the Holy Spirit always finds a way for the discerning student to find the truth. The word

---

409   Matt. 7:1,2; Luke 6:37 a; John 3:18; 7:24; Acts 13:27
410   1 Cor. 6:2–4
411   John 3:19; 5:24; 7:24

Krima usually (but not always) points us to the terms delineating how they prescribe (carry out) punishment for transgression of the law. We derive the English word crime from this root.[412]

5. Those used in the specification of punishment or vengeance are *Edikesis* (1738) and *Ekdikeo* (1556).[413]

6. God's Word also tell us about the case of a Reprobate mind as one who is subject to judgment. The Greek work *Adokimos* (96) would mean one who has failed the test.[414]

Paul uses this term in his letters to refer to the Symbol of ruined live: Castaway, Shipwreck, Perdition. These all have the common thread of a *mind-set that persistently rejects the Truth*. Another meaning of this would also fit the pattern of the attitude that God calls 'The Blasphemy of the Holy Spirit', i.e., one who persistently rejects Christ.

7. The Greek work *Katabrabeo* (2603)* means "to act as an unpire" against, or to deprive someone of the prize (i.e., to disqualify).[415] See also *Apostasy* and *Condemnation*

*Note: Numbers in parentheses are keyed to *Strong's Exhaustive Concordance of the Bible*

The Lens of Jesus Christ:

This is a *Hermeneutical* term that the Holy Spirit has revealed to the author. Like with a magnifying glass, when we 'look through Jesus at Scripture' God's Spirit will show us the most accurate meaning, including all the fine distinctions we need to observe. Remember Jesus promised that the Holy Spirit would take Jesus' Life and translate it to us!

When we follow this way, always looking at Scripture *as through Christ* the Holy Spirit will enhance and clarify the reader's understanding of all Scripture, so that we can properly discern how God desires how we apply any particular Scripture in the way of the New Covenant

---

412   Matt. 7:2; Luke 23:40; 24:20; 1 Tim. 3:6; James 3:1; Jude 4
413   Rom. 12:19; Heb. 10:20
414   1 Cor. 9:27; 2 Cor. 13:5–7; 2 Tim. 3:8; Titus 1:16
415   Col. 2:18

(Age of Grace). Always remember: Jesus Christ is the Word of God![416] See *Hermeneutics*, *Discernment*, *Exegesis*, *The Kingdom of Heaven*, *The New Covenant*, *Wisdom*

The Mark of the Beast:

This is the Biblical term used in Scripture as the *spiritual symbol* applying to those who are a part (citizens) of the World system. In Daniel and Revelation, Scripture defines the word 'beast' (a spiritual animal) for being a symbol of *a Political entity or an Empire.* Similarly, Scripture defines a Horn for being a Political leader, a demagogue, a dictator, President or Prime minister. Scripture also tells us that *every Nation of this World is also part of a larger whole or 'Zoo'* that we call the World System. Scripture inexorably links this World System we speak of with *Antichrist.* The Book of Revelation tells us that every person who serves the world system receives an 'identification symbol' that causes the world to support them.

They persecute every person who refuses this 'mark', making it very difficult for them to find or retain gainful employment, which is the world's way to control buying and selling. However, taking this 'Mark' also unequivocally associates that person with the world's final dark destiny of Hell. The 'Mark of the Beast is truly the opposite 'Counter-mark' to *The Mark of God* that the Holy Spirit gives the Believer. When a person truly receives Jesus Christ, God's Spirit Regenerates the person's inward human spirit and they are reborn with spiritual life *from above.* God also introduces all those who truly receive Christ as Citizens of the Kingdom of Heaven. Believers must also realize that 'The Mark of the Beast' is not just an outward thing, nor is it necessarily 'permanent.' Yes, people can repent of it! 'The Mark of the Beast is above all a symbol of an attitude. It is a humanist mind-set *(In the Forehead, symbol of what we think)* where that person having this attitude thinks like everybody else *in the World System.* Thus, they all conform to the crowd or 'herd mentality' of the masses, doing what the others do *(By the Right hand, where we do things).* The same Freudian phobias drive them all and they all conform to the same image and mold of the world.

---

416   Prov. 3:5,6; 8:1 ff.; John 14:6-27; 16:7–15; Rev. 19:10

Essentially, they all receive and believe all the doctrines of the world that Satan has encrypted into it. This is what the *prophetic symbolism of 666 conveys: Humanism* is the mantra of all activity. Six is the number applying to man' and *666 represents the tripling of the emphasis, which has led to the worldwide defacio worship of man* as his own savior. Prophetic Scripture tells us that in 'the end times' the World System will assiduously control all the business of *buying and selling by using the 'Mark of the Beast'.* One can easily deduce that they have already essentially accomplished this end. The regulation of employment and the licensing of sales by multinational conglomerates who dominate the global marketplace has ensured their monopoly. Global Capitalism controls nearly all avenues of making an income. They give jobs only to those who 'conform' (i.e., *Take the Mark of the Beast).* The world sedulously ostracizes all others who refuse to 'play ball' and by that keeps them on the outside. Religion fits handily into this mold as well, because the thematic definition of *all popular Religion* is man *trying to 'work his own way to God.'* Thus, you will find that they always give glory to human 'saviors' like professionals, politicians and soldiers. Contrariwise, Scripture teaches us that man can only find *Salvation when we submit to God and act in Faith trusting the One God has Sent, Jesus Christ. This is the only way God can justify or Save any person.* Religion and rituals are useless to save anyone. Complete Salvation in every context is available only in Jesus Christ. True Believers must learn the lifelong lesson: Accept the cost Jesus told us about and thus we learn to live by *Faith in God.*

Many deluded Believers nonetheless cling stubbornly to *Religious traditions and humanistic doctrines.* However, what many also fail to realize is that even *organized Religion labeled as 'Christianity' is nonetheless saturated with many world-serving counter-Christian doctrines, many of which they carefully camouflage. The most perfidious of these are those that teach unquestioning support and obedience to worldly political leaders. Thus they lead the masses to serve the State (The Antichrist or World System) by default!* These organizations include nearly all Mainline Denominations that claim to be 'Christian'. Yes, that means that *All Religions have essentially already 'Taken the Mark of the Beast!* The *truths* of Scripture concerning these facts are unavoidable: The New Testament teaches that *God only considers the true Body of Christ that is organically in Union with Jesus Christ, the Vine* for being not connected to the condemned world system.**

Everything else that connects itself to the World System in any way, however, shares its fate. Only those who are part of the true Body of Christ have refused *The Mark of the Beast* and consequently *do not follow the crowd mentality like the others!* God's Word clearly distinguishes two types of 'marks': Each one represents a diametrically opposite position to the other.*** No neutral grounds exist between them. Consequently, those who seek to avoid conflict by blindly following the teachings of organized religion (which is a part of the world system) will inevitably disqualify themselves for being part of Christ. This is because they consistently *refuse God's Mark* of true Faith that we can only prove by implicit Faith and obedience to Christ's Commands!

Consequently, all true Believers have learned by hard experience that it is worth the sacrifice to obey God rather than man. In the end, compromising or to conform to the mind-set of the world is never worthwhile for a Christian, for the price of our soul is simply too high.[417] **See *Jesus' Way* Chapter XVIII, 'Knowing the Difference' (Between the Church and the World) ***See also *Seal/Sign*

The Mosaic-Levitical-Sacrifice-System:

This is a term describing the methods that the Old Covenant of Judaism used in dealing with sin. It must be considered as a whole to properly understand the vast difference between this way and the *New Covenant Gospel*. This system includes all of the messy details regarding Blood Sacrifices, and Punishments meted out in an overall system that worked similarly to the financial arrangements in a *Mortgage*. God considered each sacrifice (whether it was an animal or human bloodshed) as an 'interest-only payment' that God held a marker or 'IOU' until Jesus Christ completed the full payment. Jesus accomplished this by the once for all sacrifice of *The Blood of Christ* Jesus shed on Calvary. On the cross, Jesus paid it ALL: *Both the original sums owed God along with all the accumulated interest* throughout the

417   John 18:36; Acts 4:11-22; 5:29-32; Rom. 12: 1–3; 2 Thess. 1,2; James 4:4–8; 1 John 2:15–17; 5:19; Rev. 13 *See also the book Jesus' Way Appendix B: "Authority and Conscience"*

Old Testament era. The New Covenant replaced this sacrifice system entirely when God removed (tore down) the veil in the Jewish temple at the precise moment that Jesus dismissed His Spirit, dying on the cross.[418] See also Atonement, Sacrifice and Bloodshed.

The New Covenant:

The New Covenant is the set of terms that describes the way Believers relate to God and man. It is also the New Testament Gospel of our Lord Jesus Christ, the Christian Covenant or the 'Constitution of the kingdom of Heaven'. The New Covenant contains the following components:

1. The Words (Teachings) and works of Jesus Christ.

2. The once-for-all-Atonement Sacrifice of Jesus Christ on Calvary.

3. The Bodily Resurrection of Jesus Christ.

4. The Ascension and High Priesthood of Jesus Christ.

5. The mediation of the Holy Spirit.

6. The Regeneration of the human spirit.

7. The teachings of the Early Apostles and New Testament writers.

8. The 'Carry-over doctrines' From the Old Testament that have New Testament corroboration.

See *Basic Christian Doctrine* and *Gospel*

For details, Refer to *Jesus' Way* Chapter X, 'The New Covenant' for the detailed exposition covering the main doctrinal areas defined by the basic elements of the Christian Covenant of Grace.

Orthodox/Orthodoxy:

This word does not occur in Scripture. However, many Christians believe it defines the 'Uniform Creedal Statements' of the 'Christian' religion [Sic.]. However, its most apparent rationale is decidedly

---

418   Matt. 27:50-52; Heb. 9:11–15

humanistic: Man has formulated 'orthodoxy' as a lever to control the masses by enforcing an artificial unity or conformance to a 'common doctrine' that they tell people describes "Christianity." Thus, they believe this maintains 'order'. However, the word 'orthodoxy' almost always relates to the State Religion, not to true Christianity. This term has also evolved considerably with time.

Especially after Constantine I, religious authorities assiduously sought to 'Reconcile' Christianity with the world vainly believing that they could 'popularize' it. What has happened is that religious leaders have "Redefined" and 'packaged' religion. Of course that is what the cults do. Consequently, many crucial Doctrines, terms and precepts of original Christianity have become grossly distorted and mutated so that people misunderstand them! See *Humanism*, *The Judeo-Christian Tradition*, *Nominalism* and *Syncretism*

Parable:

The Parable is a unique form of illustrative teaching that Jesus frequently used during his earthly ministry. Parables present a succinct and down-to-earth illustration of how crucial spiritual precepts work. Always, Jesus would present the Parable to the Disciples first. Then Jesus would make the general application in the hearing of the multitude. Parables employ the language of common everyday experience. Jesus' Parables always highlighted a specific issue germane to living the Christian life, illustrating the ever-present issues of faith, loyalty, obedience, diligence and stewardship. Jesus also told the Disciples that God's Spirit would reveal the underlying meaning only to those whose hearts are right before God!

To all the others, it would go 'Over their heads like water off a duck's back.' That is the way Jesus would teach about spiritual things. A few examples of the Parables Jesus taught are: 'The Sower and the Seed,' 'The Citizens and Talents', 'The Prodigal Son', 'The rich Man and Lazarus' and 'The Ten Virgins'.

See *stewardship* and the book *"Basic Christian Doctrine"*
See also the Paper entitled: *Jesus' Major Parables* Faith-based Pacifism=

The Patience of the Saints/Patience:

We can prove that this *Original* tenet *Doctrine of early Christianity* to be truly *equivalent to* New Covenant Faith-Based Christian Pacifism. * All the main elements are identical if we compare Jesus' Teachings with the essential components of nonviolence and Pacifism that include nonviolent resistance and fundamental *Trust in God,* describing the only way to solve humanity's deepest problems! The Early Christians taught and practiced Christian faith-based Pacifism from the beginning with Jesus Christ and the original Apostles including Paul. You can readily see this pattern in Luke's account in the Acts of the Apostles. After his conversion on the Damascus Road, we can see Paul's responses to repeated attacks always follows the pattern of nonviolent resistance consistent with Jesus' teaching: Faith-based Christian Pacifism. It is *easily provable* by both Scripture and historical period writers alike that the Early Christians practiced this doctrine. New Testament period writers also affirmed 'The Patience of the Saints' to be a Central Christian Doctrine.[419]

Patience in general is that Christian quality that 'abides under' (Gr.: *Hupomeno*) because of an all-encompassing faith that God is in control! A Synonym of this is 'longsuffering' (Gr.: *Makrothumai*), an adjunct to the fruit of the Spirit we call 'self-control' or inner strength. The overall references to patience are in this footnote.[420]

Prevenient Grace:

This is the 'startup package' that God makes available to every human being so that they can receive Christ if they so choose. It is also the type of Grace God gives to new Believers. It is unconditional, however temporary in nature and it will eventually lapse if the person who initially receives Christ fails to learn to use their reborn human spirit in worshipping God as the New Covenant teaches. See *Grace*, Paragraph 1, *Initial Salvation* and *Probational*

---

419 Matt. 5:39; Luke 21:8-19; John 18:36; Rom. 13:8 f.; Rev. 13:10; 14:10–12
420 Eccl. 7:8; Matt. 18:26,29; Luke 8:15; 21:19; Rom. 2:7; 5:1–5; 8:25;12:12–21; 15:4,5;2 Cor. 6:4–6; 1 Thess. 1:3,4; 5:14; 1 Tim. 6:11; 2 Tim. 2:24–26; Heb. 6:12–15; James 1:3,4; 5:7–11; 2 Pet. 1:6

Probational:

This term describes the contingencies that apply to the initial state of new converts and *initial Salvation*. During this crucial formative period we commonly call the *Discipleship Process or the Conversion period,* God is testing and evaluating the heart of the novice Believer. God's Will is that this process continues to its end: Until *an attitude of complete commitment has evidenced a True Conversion to the cause of Christ unto the death.* If this does not happen, the potential candidate risks the loss of whatever God had given them initially, up to and including the *lapse of *Prevenient Grace*.* During the formative period, God gives the novice *many opportunities to enter the most Holy Place of personal Relationship with God in their spirit.*

However, it behooves the initiate to quickly learn to use *their own Reborn* human spirit in the indeterminate time allotted by God. Whoever 'plays games with God' during this period places themselves in dangerous territory! Those who selfishly 'seek the bennies' of titillating gifts and 'temporal prosperity' are 'playing Russian Roulette' with their eternal souls. God is patient, but God is also Just and fair. Time runs out fast! We should know that Our God is an Awesome God who holds our destiny in His Hands! If we do not diligently seek the things that are above where Christ and the Kingdom of Heaven are, then you cannot guarantee that God will save you! "God is not mocked: Whatever a man sows, he also will reap." Not only that, Do not be so foolish as to think that a 'Double-minded' person will receive anything from God! You cannot 'play both sides against the middle' and succeed. You *must choose which master you will serve while you have the chance to decide.* No man owns Salvation. Salvation is only *IN CHRIST Alone. No Church can save you. No human being can save you.* See *Salvation* and the Position Papers *Christian Conversion, Part One: Introduction to Christian Conversion and Conditions for Salvation.*

Redeem, Redemption:

Redemption is a *financial term* that Scripture uses in a *theological context.* The verb form of the Greek word *Exagorazo means 'to buy out'.* The underlying premise of Redeeming or Redemption is that Christ has purchased each true Believer from the slave market where we were slaves of the world system with all its idolatrous mantras. In fact, The Blood of Christ is the 'purchasing agent' that recovers the title deed of the human soul of each Believer who receives the shed-Blood Sacrifice of Jesus Christ.[421]

A second Greek word is found in Scripture as the two forms of *Lutroo (v.i.)* and *Lutrosis (N.)*. They show to us that Christ's Blood has paid a Ransom to free the person from servitude.[422] Scripture says Redemption means that the Believer is set at liberty and delivered from all forms of bondage inherent in the world system and found in: Habits, sin, human traditions and in the various forms of others' will, choices or influence that they have unbiblically imposed upon them. A third form, *Apolutrosis,* is a strengthened form of the second. It applies specifically to our *physical deliverance from torture.* God also uses it as the basis of applying the *real-time forgiveness of sin and the expiation of guilt and punishment* for all penitents. Of course, we should know that Christ's Sacrifice removed the "curse of the Law." Viz., all Bloodshed penalties *that the Mosaic law required to pay for those sins.* Propitiation (full legal satisfaction of all the penalties) is a direct synonym.[423]

The Physical Deliverance of the Saints at the Rapture-Second Coming of Christ is another specific application.[424]

We must also remember that Jesus used spiritual applications of financial precepts frequently in the parabolic format of teaching. We can also see the precept of Redemption as a statement of assurance that Christ will always *take care of His Own!*

See *Atonement*, *The Blood of Christ*, *Bloodshed*, *Sacrifice*

---

421   Gal. 3:13; 4:5; Eph. 5:16; Col. 4:5
422   Luke 1:68; 2:38; 24:21; Titus 2:14; Heb. 9:12; 1 Pet. 1:18
423   Rom. 3:24; 6:4; Gal. 3:10–13; Eph. 1:7; Heb. 9:15; 11:35 *See also the entries *Bloodshed,* *The Blood of Christ* and *Remission* and the Papers entitled Fallacies of Determinism, Fulfilment Prophecy and How Does Christ's Blood Get to us Today*
424   Luke 21:28; Rom. 8:23; 2 Thess. 2:8

Regeneration:

Regeneration is the English translation of the Greek word *Palingenesis,* meaning New Birth. God uses this as the Biblical and spiritual language to denote being *Born from Above. Above* comes from the Greek word *Anothen,* which refers to *Heaven. This describes the process by which the Holy Spirit reinstates our human spirit with all its triune functions being intact: Intuition, Communion and Conscience.* This happens when the Believer confesses sin and first receives the Shed Blood Sacrifice of Jesus Christ. Regeneration marks the beginning point of the Discipleship/Conversion/ Sanctification process that we call the Christian life. However, we must beware of presumption: According to the New Covenant, Prevenient Salvation Grace advances the Regenerated functions of the human spirit in a probational condition. God's Spirit provides these for they are necessary to form a personal relationship to God in Christ by the spirit. God's will requires that Believers choose to *enter an ongoing personal relationship* that is lifelong. However, if we subsequently return to the ways of the flesh or persist in willful sin, God retains the right to end the relationship because of our abandonment or rebellion. Christians have no 'ironclad guarantee' that we can retain salvation if we relapse into unrepentant sin again. See Agape Love, Christian, Initial Salvation, Faith, Spiritual.

Remnant/Gather/Harvest:

God uses the Biblical term 'Remnant' in Scripture to apply to those who are *the remainder of faithful Believers that stay true to the terms of the Covenant God has cut to relate to them.* In the Old Testament, they were the ones in Israel who stuck to the terms of the *Mosaic Covenant (the Law)* while the vast majority compromised and fell into apostasy. We can find a good example in the time of Elijah the Prophet, C. 879 B.C.E., after he fled from 'Jezebel', a type of apostate (rebel) authority ruling God's people. In the cave where he hid, God said to Elijah that He had reserved *seven thousand* in Israel who had not bowed their knees to the Baal's. Baals are the generic term for territorial (National) Idols or deities worshiped by the masses. When you compare this figure with the closest census of the period in C. 808 B.C.E., you find the that 300,000 were in the two tribes of Judah and Benjamin.[425]

To find the average full number in all twelve tribes, based on that figure, we multiply by six, which brings the total of Israel to approximately 1,800,000. Now a simple calculation would place the Remnant of seven thousand as about 0.4% of the total. Elijah thought he was the only one. However when you think about the very small percentage that were serving God in comparison with the whole, then you can readily understand why he might have felt that way! He was not very far off, was he? Just read in detail about what has happened throughout Church history.

Then, think about how few contemporary Christians there are who Believe the terms of the Original New Covenant Gospel that God is holding all Believers responsible for obeying today! Yes, Me-thinks the same situation applies today as well. The Remnant is but part of God's great Promise to Gather His People. God has been 'sorting' people who are *zealous of Good Works!* [426]

God also prophesies that 'in the last days' He will gather all Nations against 'Israel.' This is all part of God's Master Plan or *Tapestry* the term the author uses to describe God's fore-intended pattern of Covenant History that unites his work with the Jews and Gentiles together in one Whole.[427]

Of particular significance to Believers, Scripture teaches that (after the Tribulation but before the Wrath sequence) God will send Jesus Christ back with an Angelic Host (Army) to "Gather His Elect from the four winds" unto himself. This is what Paul calls "The Blessed Hope."[428]

---

425   1 Kings 19:18; 1 Chron. 25:5

426   Isa. 43:1 ff.; 66:1 ff.; Jer.23:1 ff.; 29: 14; 31:8 ff.; 32:37; Ezek. 20:34–41; 33:30 37:28; Mic. 2:12; 4:1–6; Hab. 2:4,5; Zeph. 3:16–20; Zech. 10

427   Zech. 14:2; Matt. 3:23; 13:40–47; John 3:16; 14:6; Acts 10:1 ff.; 13:38-52; 15:1 ff.; 17:24-31; Rom. 8; 1 Cor. 15:20-28; Gal. 3; Eph. 2:11-3:21; Phil. 3

428   Matt. 24:21–31; Mark 13:24–27; Luke 21:25–36; John 11:52; Eph. 1:10; 1 Thess. 4:11–17

Repentance:

The Greek word *Metanoia* translates to mean the crucial act or choice when we *truly turn around and start going the opposite way.* It means *fully* changing one's mind (180 degrees). Repentance means a *total turnaround in attitude toward all things.* The point of Repentance is that point where we truly *make a radical change in the way we think and the way we look at things.* We reach the point of Repentance when God's Word *penetrates our heart, convicts us of our error, and we choose to respond to God by changing our ways!* Remember that just feeling sorry about the fact that you were 'caught' doing something does not mean that you have changed your position or your ways. Even if you confess that what you did was wrong is insufficient to qualify for being *Biblical Repentance! Confession is different. However, Confession is a Prerequisite we must have in place to lead us to the point of Repentance.* Tangible evidence accompanies Biblical Repentance proving that a fundamental lifestyle-level change has taken place![429]

See also *Conversion*, *Faith*, *Discipleship* and *Salvation*

The Reprobate mind:

Scripture defines the specific characteristics of this 'state of mind' that applies in two main ways: One is a person who has never believed in God and has been hardened to reject all other options. Two, is a person who had once known or had a relationship to God in Christ, and has subsequently apostatized and become wilfully set in that position. It is especially important that true Believers learn to recognize those in this latter case. These are the unfortunate souls who, having once tasted of the good things of *God's Kingdom,* have 'made shipwreck' of their lives and have become castaways, apostates and habitual 'Backsliders in heart', inured to their rebellious fallen ways, adamantly refusing correction continually. They are prideful, worshiping and serving humanistic ways and glorifying human abilities (Idolatry). In both cases, however, they have those traits that are common to all unbelievers. Because they are cut off from God,

---

429   Ezek. 18:30; Rom. 2:4; 2 Cor. 7:10

they fall into the common problem areas of unbelievers: Selfishness, rebellion, bitterness, disillusionment, amorality, resentment, deep-seated anger, failed expectations and disloyalty. They have frequently become opportunistic, self-serving power grabbers. Their poisonous spirit readily defiles others around them and that is why reprobates are so dangerous to Believers. They have frequently destroyed fellowships, because they foment division and hostility against God and Jesus Christ. They frequently try to blame-shift their problems on others. See *(Biblical) Unity* for explanation of differences between types of 'division'. Scripture is replete with warnings against falling into this deep ditch and snare of the soul![430]

In Scripture, the symbols of 'Jezebel' and 'Judas' exemplify the opportunistic extreme that reprobates use to get their way.[431]

Paul's succinct and detailed description in Romans is unmistakable. Let us pay particular attention to the phrase 'God gave them up...' Essentially, that means that it would literally take an 'act of God' to restore such a person to Salvation. His exhortation in his second letter to Timothy is also excellent.[432]

The only way to escape this pride-dominated trap is for the offender to freely confess their sin and truly repent of all unhealthy attitudes, recommitting their life to Faith in Christ and the truth. Intercessory prayer by righteous and faithful believers may also help.[433]

See *Idolatry*, *Humanism*, *Iniquity*, *Unbelief*

Righteousness:

The Greek word *Dikaosis* means Right-Relationship. Righteousness is 'the currency of the Kingdom of Heaven'. God must give this quality to a person. Each Believer receives it *by exercising Biblical Faith*. Not only that, Scripture tells us that Believers must continue to fulfill the

---

430   Psa. 66:18; 94:20; Isa. 44:20,21; 59:2; Jer. 6:30; Ezek. 3:18, 18:30; 33:8; 36:33; Matt. 7:21–23; 23:28; 24:12; Luke 13:27
431   1 King 18–21; 2 Kings 9; Acts 1:18; Rev. 2:20
432   Romans 1:17–2:18; 2 Cor. 13:5; 2 Tim. 2:19–3:8
433   Acts 3:19–26; 1 John 1:5–10; Neh.9; Dan. 9

requirements to maintain it for them to be a part of Christ or the Kingdom of Heaven. Just giving 'intellectual assent is *insufficient* by itself to qualify for Biblical Faith or to receive Righteousness. We should all know that the devils 'believe and tremble', but God definitely does not save them! To continue to be righteous before God, one must *actively trust Christ in all aspects of life, public and private.* Righteousness is a *spiritual quantity. We must continually receive for the Believer to remain in right-relation with God.* The Scripture teaches that we must actively pursue God by using all the disciplines of the spiritual life, beginning with learning to use our Reborn human spirit. When we Worship in spirit and in truth and remain 'United to the vine' by exercising 'prayer without ceasing' as a continual attitude we subsequently maintain that status.[434]

Salvation/Health:

I. Overall precepts: 'Salvation' is a general term found in Scripture that can refer concurrently to different contexts. First is the *physical Deliverance from evil or harm.* A second meaning refers to the Liberty or Freedom granted under the conditions of *Biblical Redemption,* described by the Greek words *Apolotrosis* and *Eleutheros.* See Redemption. Thirdly, Scripture defines a unique spiritual condition based on the New Birth of the human spirit. The complete Gospel of the New Testament teaches that this 'Salvation' is a result of an *ongoing personal relationship to God in the spirit.* This is the type that scripture calls *Soterion, or spiritual health,* which is only possible if the person maintains their relationship consistently according to the New Covenant. Only this type eventually leads to the inheritance of *Eternal Life* in Heaven. Scripture is clear that this Salvation is not like some 'Diploma' or certificate you can stuff in your back pocket and continue living the same way you always have. Christ's New Covenant teaches that Salvation is contingent upon many specific conditions we must satisfy. One of the most crucial of these is Conversion: The *Transformation of the mind and heart,* described by the Greek root *Metamrphoo.* To illustrate, the related word Metamophomai depicts the biological transformation of a caterpillar in a Butterfly. *The*

---

434   Hab. 2:4; Matt. 6:9–13; John 4:23,24; 14:21-26; 15:1-7; Rom. 4; 1 Thess. 5:17

goal of this transformation process, led by God's Spirit, is the spiritually advantageous condition that Scripture calls the *Saved Mind!* [435]

The Greek words' *Sophroneo* and *Sophronizo* describe the process through which the Holy Spirit purges our mind and attitude. Conversion is *conforming to God's way of thinking.* God promises that if the Believer fulfills those conditions, 'Enduring unto the end,' they will be saved. However, Jesus also says that we must 'Remain united to the Vine (Christ) or we will end up dying spiritually. If this happens, God cannot prevent us being cast off and burned as a dead branch.[436]

We do not 'own Salvation'. Only Jesus Christ owns Salvation. We can only be assured of Salvation if we Abide *In Christ,* which means we choose daily to remain united with Christ! [437]

II. Concerning Healing and Health, the general conditions for Health are synonymous to those of Salvation in both physical and spiritual contexts. What everyone must acknowledge is that Salvation/ Health is not something we can 'own'. Salvation belongs to Christ: Christ paid for it with His Precious Blood on Calvary and Jesus is the sole owner of it. Yes, Scripture teaches that human beings can *inherit* Salvation, but only IF they satisfy God's Terms, and 'Abide (endure) unto the end'! Another basic premise is that God is always Sovereign. We cannot 'demand things' from God! Yes, we can repeat back God's Word and say (pray): 'I claim that promise', however, it is still God's prerogative *how He grants that prayer.* God knows the end from the beginning and what is best for us. Our part is to obey His Word, expressed by Jesus Christ, the Son, and Trust God for the outcome![438] See *Initial Salvation*, Christian, Faith.

---

435   Rom. 12:1–3 *See the paper entitled "Figure One: Illustration/Comparison of Caterpillar/ Butterfly to Conversion"*

436   Matt. 24:13; John 15:1–7; 2 Tim. 2:11,12; Heb. 2:3-4:16; 6:3-12; 10:26-39

437   *See the book Basic Christian Doctrine and the papers entitled 'Conditions for Salvation' and 'God's Definition of Salvation'*

438   Deut. 32:39; Luke 17:11–19 *See also the book Jesus' Way, Chapter XIII: 'Ministry, Love and Healing'.*

(The Doctrine of) Sanctification: (Holiness)

This central New Covenant Doctrine is a *Carry-over Doctrine* that originated in Old Testament times. Sanctification (Holiness), defined by the Greek words *Hagiosune, Hagiotes* and *Hagiosmos,* involves and describes two main areas of the spiritual life: One, it presupposes that we are presently in a condition God would define as The State of (Being a receiver of God's) *Grace*. Two, Sanctification or Holiness is part of *an ongoing process* where we are progressively conforming to the image of Jesus Christ. In this second area, Sanctification merges with the concurrent spiritual process of *Discipleship and Conversion.* Within both these areas lay the underlying currents of *Cleansing and Purification. All these* require copious quantities of God's Grace, the essential ingredient we need most. God has initially given every person the Faith to believe God and to receive Jesus Christ. This is the beginning point when we first experience God's 'Prevenient Grace' and the *Initial Salvation* that 'Jump-Starts' our spiritual life by *Regeneration*, the New Birth of our human spirit. By that we receive the essential ingredients of *Justification* or *Righteousness* that bring us to the position of favor with God or *Grace*. *From that point on,* However, we are personally responsible for diligently following the disciplines God's Word teaches us are necessary to maintain spiritual life. Only by following these disciplines will God's Spirit release the power of *Infusion Grace* into our lives that gives ability to be like Jesus. As mentioned above, both elements are essential: Cleansing *(Katharizo, Katharismos, Katharos)* and Purification *(Hagnizmos, Hagnizo, Hagnos, Hagnotes),* are all central to the process of creating holiness. Cleansing is the initial stage of the process that God requires. The prerequisite for Cleansing of sin is that we *first confess that we have sinned*[439]   Purification takes this one step beyond mere confession, presupposing that we have learned that sin causes harm to us, and just confessing the same sin repeatedly again is insufficient to change our behavior. Not only that, we should never presume to keep on sinning and exploiting the Blood of Christ.[440]

---

439   1 John 1:7–9
440   Rom. 6:1

In seeking to be pure, we begin actively cooperating with God in making fundamental attitude changes. One of these is to eliminate inconsistencies in belief and conflicting priorities in us that James says cause us to be 'Double-Minded'. A Pure heart delights itself in obedience, making no selfish excuses. We should want to be pure in heart, pleasing God. Scripture declares that a very effective way for God's Spirit to make us pure is for us to continually saturate our minds with the Word of God. God makes us pure in a very effective way by *pruning our lives, removing things that cause us to go astray.*[441]

Moreover, God's Word tells us that we must be holy because God is holy. God requires us to seek to be holy as part of the deal we agreed to when we first received Christ. Without Holiness, we will never see the Lord! Finally, we must realize that holiness requires fertile ground that is *unfettered by worldly competition.* In this venue we find the issue of *separation.* The issue of separation is extremely important: Scripture tells us that while the Believer walks this earth, they are a stranger, a Pilgrim and a Sojourner. We are not of this world. The Greek words' *Paroika, Paroikos* and *Paraoikeo* depict a Heavenly minded attitude that recognizes that they are good Citizens of the Kingdom of Light above us where Christ is on the Throne.[442] True Believers are aliens that are only in this world because Jesus Christ has a Great Commission for us to discharge righteously. All other pursuits are incidental to this great purpose. Our New Testament defines a Christian as a foreign Ambassador that God sends to represent the Kingdom of Heaven, our true *Nationality of Origin!*[443]

Our *primary Allegiance is always to Jesus Christ our Lord, Savior and Commanding Officer!* As a Christian, If we are faithful in doing all these tasks, we will grow into the image and stature of Jesus Christ. This is what God intends for us all to reach and where God's Spirit will usher us into Christ's presence. This is the heart of the Doctrine of Sanctification. Other Biblical precepts and terms relating to the Doctrine of Sanctification are: Consecration, Dedication, Hallow, Stewardship, Sacred and Sanctuary. Related to Sanctification, we

---

441   Psalm 19; Psa. 51; Matt. 5:8; John 15:2; 2 Tim. 1:3; Heb. 9:11–15,22; James 4:1-10
442   Col. 3:1 f.
443   Matt. 6:9-15; Eph. 1:19–23; 2:18–22; 3:10, 11; Phil. 3:20, 21

also have the following Hebrew words and their Greek equivalents to amplify the meaning:

1. Qadesh (#6942, 44). This is a noun meaning a 'sacred' time, place, ground, person or object. This definition includes the human body, which God intends to be the venue of Worship, i.e., the Sanctuary, Temple or 'Holy of Holies.'[444]

The corresponding New Testament Greek word is *Naos, meaning the Holy of Holies.*[445]

2. Qadosh (#6918) A noun meaning a 'holy' person, group, church, people or nation (of God's people).[446]

The Geek word is *Hagios,* meaning *Saints*, a Holy Nation or a Kingdom of Priests.[447]

3. Mala. (#4390) (v.i.) They translate this word as meaning an act or process fulfilling, accomplishing, setting or confirming our Purpose in *being God's 'Special Cherished Possession.'* In this light, holiness includes our part in dedication, diligence, obedience and follow-through like in fulfilling a vow, a sacred pledge, an act of selfless sacrifice or to sanctify (Dedicate) oneself at the altar.[448]

4. The corresponding Greek word is *egkainizo,* saying the necessary cooperation of the Believer in the processes of Salvation and Renewal.[449]

Stewardship:

The Greek word *Oikonomia* depicts the delegation of a responsibility by a higher authority. Literally, it means the 'Rule of the House' or 'House Rules,'

For the Christian Believer, Our 'House' is the Kingdom of Heaven and The New Covenant contains our *House Rules,* which we also know as *the Complete Gospel* of our Lord Jesus Christ, the Messiah. Bible

---

444 Gen. 2:3; Ex. 3:15; 12:16; 28:3,41; 30:13,24; Lev. 27:3; Josh. 15:15; 1 Chr. 6:49; 16:10, 35; 29:16

445 1 Cor. 3:16

446 Lev. 19:2; 20:7, 26; Deut. 7 :6; 14:2, 21; 26:19; 28:9

447 Eph. 1:4; 2:21; 1 Pet. 2:9

448 Ex. 29:9, 22–35; 2 Chr. 29:31

449 John 10:22; Heb. 10:20

students commonly use the word *Dispensation* to describe stewardship. In Biblical history, God has employed many different 'dispensations,' however, they all focus on one *dispensation, the New Covenant, the covenant that contains the Promise of the Father, Jesus Christ!* This is the Covenant that God always intended to bring forward. God calls the ones who are the *keepers of the House Oikdomeo*=Stewards or as Jesus would have put it, *the Tenants.* Jesus' Parables are all pictures of the New Covenant. The parable of the Tenants teaches us that *God is the owner* and *not us.*

He has appointed Jesus Christ the Son as our Lord and Master who has written all the rules of the House in which for us to abide. Another word Jesus used to signify 'House' is *Vineyard.* Remember the Parable of the workers in the Vineyard?

According to the master set of rules God calls the New Covenant, only those who abide by the rules *will inherit the House/Vineyard.* Jesus also told the hearers that God would judge if they acted like the former tenants who drove the Son out of the vineyard and killed HIM! God has planned that all those who receive Christ as Savior and have followed Christ faithfully would share in our common *Calling (Kleroo, Kleros, Klesis)* or Heritage. Jesus inaugurated an entirely new way of dealing with things. Jesus Christ is the Legate of Father God, who has given all things to Christ. On earth, we are responsible for obeying *HIS Commands as our highest priority.* At the end of this age (Dispensation of Grace), Christ again will place those things back in the Father's hand. As for Believers, we enter the *Fellowship of the Gospel* by our obedience to what Christ tells us to do. That is how the Holy Spirit ushers us into the *Light where the Saints abide!* This is the fellowship *(Koinonia)* we can have *in the spirit* whenever we pray and worship in spirit and in truth.

Part of our Stewardship as a Christian Believer is the work or service in which God has especially crafted for each Kingdom Citizen to be engaged. Our *mission* or work is a part of that greater whole that God calls the Kingdom of Heaven. It is also part of our *Calling and Identity.* The early Christians used to call it the *Fellowship of the Gospel.* This fellowship has two main axes: The Vertical axis is our personal relationship to God in spirit, and is the fountainhead of all the spiritual

Gifts God grants under the dispensation of Grace. The Horizontal axis is our fellowship and service along with other Believers. When both axes are in harmony in our life., we become very effective at our task. Thus, it behooves all Christian Believers to take the work of God very seriously. On the day of the Judgment Seat of Christ, He will evaluate us all on how we did our jobs for Christ.

The writer would hope that the priorities of Heaven's Kingdom are uppermost in our daily thinking and planning. Jesus' Parable of the Sower and the Seed tells us about the results of our attitudes and Priorities.[450] See also Ekklesia and *Jesus' Way,* Appendix B.

Syncretism:

Webster's Dictionary* defines Syncretism as "The attempted union of contradictory parties or principles. In philosophy, Syncretism designates careless or illogical eclecticism. In Religion, the term is used BOTH for a serious attempt at reconciling, or in the more common disparaging sense, for *an egregious compromise.*" One Reformation period example was Lutheran George Calixtus' vain attempt to unify Protestant sects and Catholics all in a Lutheran framework. Richard Baxter (1615–1691) commented: "He is plotting a carnal *SYNCRETISM,* and attempting to reconcile Christ and Belial." Nonetheless, many such beliefs and doctrines, like spiritual Trojan Horses, have *already* done great damage to the Body of Christ! Consequently, in the general sense, when one begins to realize the widespread existence of Syncretic beliefs infiltrating the modern Church system, this should give us a stern warning: *If you are a True Christian, you must diligently avoid* all contradictory beliefs that are not consonant with the Spirit of Christ we find in the New Covenant! Also, a wise disciple will follow the admonitions of Christ's Teaching and those of Paul we find in Second Timothy.[451]

---

450   *Matt. 5-7,13,25; Luke 11-19; Rom. 8; 1 Cor. 15:20-28 See also the book Spiritual Guidelines for Restoration, "Historical Review" section and Chapter 14: "Stewardship" See also the paper "Jesus' Major Parables"*

451   *See the Paper entitled What is Syncretism*

ABOUT THE AUTHOR

Pastor David J. Bowers was raised in a Christian home by attentive parents who taught him to love God and to care about others. Early on, he was drawn to the Scriptures as an inexhaustible source of comfort and teaching. By delving into Scripture, God's spirit taught him that God's love for mankind was so great that He sent His only Son to give us a perfect example for living and to die for our sins. In his youth, he had the advantage of hearing the grand ideals of the Christian faith from conscientious pastors that fired his desire to serve God. Moreover, this idealism has not diminished with age, but rather intensified.

However, through the years he has also seen a "dark side" of Christians who are abusing others and hurting others because of the way churches are governed. Consequently, because of his knowledge of the Truth and strong determination to "make a difference," beginning in the seventies he became actively involved in home fellowships and in teaching basic Christianity in Bible studies. Not only that, he began writing position papers on biblical Christian doctrine and avidly taught the New Covenant way for church life and governance that encourages active participation and "body-life fellowship" by all believers.

Eventually, this led to the publishing of his first book, *Jesus' Way*, in 2009. Actually, *The Church in the Last Days* was originally written several years before this, but the writer thought that a basic treatise on the original doctrines of Christianity as taught in the New Testament should come first.

FOOTNOTES

Preface:

[1] Prov. 1:23

[2] Rev. 2:7, 11, 17, 29; 3:6, 13, 22

[3] Luke 8:18; 9:44. *Author Note: For more info on terms marked with *Asterisks* see Appendix E: Excerpts from Glossary of Terms*

[4] John 16:13–15.

[5] John 14:15–17,21–23; 1 John 2:20,27.

[6] John 7:15–17; 8:12–36

[7] Matt. 18:3.

[8] Ezek. 2:3–3:27

[9] Matt. 16:6–14; 2 Tim. 2–4

[10] Matt. 23; Luke 13,21

[11] Isa. 28–30; Jer. 4:1–4; Hosea 10:12; Matt. 15:1–20; John 8:12 ff.

[12] Prov. 28:13; Isa. 1,6; Jer. 2-11; Ezek. 3-18; Zech. 13:6; Matt. 13,16:21-26; Luke 11-14,16,19; John 12:37-50; Rom. 1,2; 2 Cor.11:12-15; 2 Thess. 2; 2 Tim. 3; 1 Pet. 1:18; 4:17,18 *See also the book "Spiritual Guidelines for Restoration,": "Historical Review" section and Chapter 20: "Spiritual Law Eight: The Separation of the soul from the spirit".*

[13] Heb. 12:1,2

[14] Matt. 6:33; 16:21–26

Chapter 1:

[15] Acts 17:24–31

[16] Read Isaiah 55:6–9 in *The Amplified Bible Version*

[17] Isaiah 53:6

[18] Psa. 32, 51; Isaiah 57:15

[19] Psa. 107; Matt. 9:13; 12:7

[20] 2 Cor. 2:14; James 2:13

[21] Romans 1–8; Galatians 2–5, and Hebrews 1, 7–10 *See the book Basic Christian Doctrine and the papers entitled "Fulfilment Prophecy" and "Principles of Fulfillment Theology"*

[22] Dan. 9:26; Luke 21:8–33; 1 Cor. 15:20–28; Phil. 1:6; 1 Thess. 4:13–17; Rev. 21

[23] James 2:10 ***See also the book Basic Christian Doctrine, Appendix F***

[24] Rom. 3:19–26; Gal. 2:16–21; Heb. 7:11–10:39

[25] Luke 9:23–26; John 1:1–14, 29–34; 3:3–8; 4:23,24; 5:19–30; 6:27 ff.; 8:12 ff.; Rom. 6:1–8:39;12:1 ff.; 1 Cor. 1:17–2:16; Col. 3:1; 2 Tim. 2: 11–13; Heb. 2:1– ; 3:14; 4:9–16; 6:4–12; 10:26–39; 2 Pet. 1:2–11 f. ***See the paper entitled "Figure One: Illustration–Comparison"***

[26] John 6:35–63

[27] James 4:13–17

[28] Matt. 7:13–29; Luke 6:46–49

[29] Matt. 24:13; Luke 19; Heb. 2:1–3; 3:1–6, 12–19; 6:3–12

[30] Ezek. 18:30; 33,34; Matt. 7:13–21; 25:1–13; Luke 21:34–36; John 15:1–7;2 Cor. 11; 1 Tim. 6; 2 Tim. 2; Heb. 3:1–6,12–14; 4:1–16; 6:1–7; 10:26–39; 12:1–18.

[31] Matt. 24:45,46; *Luke 18:8 *See also Appendix B.*

[32] Psa. 119:9–11; Matt. 6:9–13; 16:21–26

[33] Luke 10:38–42; 2 Cor. 4; Eph. 3; Col. 3,4

[34] Matt. 13:46 *See the paper entitled "Biblical Prosperity"*

[35] Luke 6:20 ff.; 1 Tim. 6:3–10; 2 Tim. 2:1 ff.

[36] 1 Tim. 6:12; Hebrews 11:23–29

[37] Matt. 5:43–48; Luke 2:34; 21:19; John 14:21–26; Acts 28:22; Rom. 12:9–21; 1 Tim. 6:3; 2 Tim. 2:10–15; 4:1–8 Heb. 12:1–3; 1 Pet. 2:12; Rev. 12:10,11; 14:12,13

[38] Matt. 7:13–21; 24:13

[39] Ibid. Footnote 21

[40] John 1:1–14; 3;27–30; 8:58; 10:30; 1 Cor. 1:17–2:16; Eph. 1:17–23; Phil. 1:19– 21; 2:5–11; Col. 1:12–2:10

[41] Matt. 24:1 ff.; 25:1 ff.; Luke 12–19; John 5:19-30; 9:39–41; Acts 10:36–43; 17:24–31; Rom. 2:11–16; 14:10; 2 Cor. 5:8–10; 1 Pet. 4:17,18.

[42] Isa. 30:15–21; Matt. 6:9–15; 1 John 1:5–10

[43] *See Appendix B and the papers "The Amazing Doctrine of God's Grace" and "Conditions of Salvation"*

[44] 1 Pet. 3:15

[45] Matt. 7:13–21; 24:1 ff.; 25:1 ff.; Heb. 6:1–7; 10:26–39; James 1:1–8, 17, 18, 21– 27; 2:14–26

Chapter 2:

[46] 2 Thess. 1:8–2:12; Rev. 13

[47] Matt. 24,25; Mark 13; Luke 13,21

[48] Isa. 14; Ezek. 28, 32; Matt. 25:41–46; Mark 9:42–48

[49] Jer. 9:3; 1 Tim. 4:1–5; 2 Tim. 3:1–9; 4:1 ff.

[50] Matt. 24:21–51; Luke 12:1–12; 21:7–19, 25–28, 34–36; Rom. 8:1 ff.; 1 Cor. 15:20–34; 2 Cor. 4:1– 6; 10:3–6; 11:10–15; Gal. 1:6–12; Eph. 1:7–10; Phil. 1:6; Col. 2:16–23; 2 Thess. 1:3–2:12; 1 Tim. 4:1–6; 2 Tim. 3:1–4:8 *See also Glossary of Terms entry *Determinism* and the papers entitled Christian Guidelines for Spiritual Warfare, Part Three: "Cracking the False Doctrine code" "The Doctrine of the Elect" and "Fallacies of Determinism."*

[51] Rom. 8; Eph. 1,2; Col. 1; Titus 2:11–15. *See the papers: "Conditions for Salvation" and "God's Definition of Salvation"*

[52] Matt. 6:24; Luke 10:22; John 1:12; Rom. 1:16,17; 6:1–8:39; 10:9,10; 2 Tim. 2:1 4:8 *See also Appendix A*

[53] Matt. 5:1–20; 24:13; John 7:15–18; 14:12–23; 15:10–12; Rom. 8:1–11; 1 Cor. 1:17–2:16; James 1:4–9; 2:14–26

[54] Luke 11:1–13; John 4:23,24 See also Psalms 1,5,8,9,15,17,24,27,34

[55] John 15:1 f.; 16:13–15; Phil. 1:6–21; Rom. 6–8; Gal. 5 2:12.13. *See also Appendix E Entry "Grace"*

[56] John 14:12–23; 15:10–12; 1 John 5:3.

[57] 1 John 1:5–10

[58] Matt. 5–7; Luke 6:20–49; Col. 3:1 f.; 1 Thess. 5:16–24; 1 Tim. 6.

[59] Luke 9:23–26; Rom. 6; 2 Tim. 2; 1 John 5:3. *See the papers entitled "an Analysis of Faith," "the Gravity of Sin," "How Does Christ's Blood get to us," "the Insidious Nature of Sin," "Living the Complete Gospel," "Obedience to Christ" and "the Way of the Cross"*

[60] Isa. 41–45; Eph. 2:8,9

61 **See Jesus's Major Parables, and the books entitled Basic Christian Doctrine (Area Twelve) and Spiritual Guidelines for Restoration (Chapter 20, Law #10)

62 Matt. 6:24; 10:32,33; 2 Tim. 2:11,12; Heb. 10:32–39

63 Josh. 24:13; Isa. 14; Ezek. 28, 32; Matt. 6:24; 20:25–28; James 4:1–8; 1 John 2:15–17.

64 Matt. 24:13; John 15:1 ff. (Matt.) 7:13–23… Rom. 6–8; Gal. 1:6–12; 2 Tim. 2:11 15; Heb. 2–4;6:3–12; 10:26–39

65 Heb. 12:16,17

66 Luke 12-16

67 Matt. 16:21–26

68 Matt. 13:44–51 *See also Appendix B" What Type of Christian are You?

69 Prov. 8:13; 16:18; Jer. 49:8; Mal. 1:3; Heb. 10:26–39; 12:1–17.

70 John 3:3–30; 1 Cor. 12–14; Gal. 5:22,23; James 1:17,18; 3:13–4:4.

71 Eph. 4:1 ff.; Phil. 2:1–11.

72 Gal. 1:6–12; Eph. 3:5–7; 1 Pet. 4:1–5:5.

73 John 17:11, 20–26

74 John 14:15; 15:10–12; Rom. 8:9; Acts 4:11-13.

75 John 3:27; Acts 2:1 ff.; Rom. 12:1 ff.; 1 Cor. 12,13; Eph. 4:1 ff. See also the paper entitled "Basics of Biblical Church Governance"

76 Rom. 8:9 **See also the paper entitled "(What is) The Body of Christ"

Chapter 3:

77 Luke 11:33–36; 22:31–53; John 13:1–8

78 Acts 1:1–11

79 Ezek. 18:30–32; Matt. 18:3–11; John 15:1–7; Acts 3:19–21; 1 Cor. 1:17–2:16; 9:27; Gal. 2:16–5:26; Heb. 12:1–14

80 See the book: Jesus Way, Chapter VII.: Basic Christian Ethics, Part One: 'Our View of God' and the booklet: A Seeker's Guide to Biblical Faith

81 Genesis 1–2 See also the papers "Destiny and Free Will" and "The Doctrine of the Elect"

82 Hebrews 1, 7–11 See also the papers entitled "Fulfilment Prophecy" an "Principles of Fulfillment Theology"

[83] 2 Chr. 16:9; Job 23:10; Jer. 29:11; Matt. 6:33; Rom. 8:28

[84] Neh. 9:20; Psa. 1, 19, 25, 27, 32, 86, 119; Rom. 8:28; Heb. 12:1 ff.

[85] John 14–17; 1 Cor. 13; 1 John 1–5

[86] John 3:16,17; 10:16,17; 13:34,35; 15:13; Rom. 5:5–8; 8:28–39; 2 Pet. 3:9; Rev. 21:7,8

[87] Rom. 1:18 ff.; 2 Thess. 2:10–12

[88] Eccl. 7:20; Psa. 51; Isa. 53:6; Hos. 14:9; Rom. 3:23; 6:23; Col. 1:21; Heb. 2:1- 4:16; 6:3-12; James 2;10 *See also the book: Basic Christian Doctrine, Appendix B: The Nature of Man*

[89] John 1:10–14, 29–34; Rom. 5:9–18; Phil. 2:1–11; Heb. 2:1-4:16; 6:3-12; 7:11– 10:23; 1 John 2:1,2 *See also the book: Basic Christian Doctrine, Appendix B: The Nature of Man*

[90] John 3:3–8; Rom. 12; 1 Cor. 12–14; Eph. 4

[91] Matt. 3:11,12; 6:27–68; 7:14–17; 16:18; 18:18–20; Rom. 6:1–11; Eph. 1–6; Col. 1–4; 1 Tim. 2:5; Heb. 7–11 *See the paper entitled "the Basics of Biblical Church Governance"*

[92] Matt. 10:32,33; Luke 12;8–10; John 9:22; 12:42; Rom. 10:9,10; Phil. 2:5–11; 2 Tim. 2:11–13; Heb. 10: 22–39; 1 John 4:1–6.

[93] Matt. 18:7–17; Acts 19:18; Rom. 3:23; James 5:13–16; 1 John 1:5–10.

[94] Matt. 3:2; 4:17; 21:28–32; Mark 1:15; 6:12; Luke 13:3; 15:4–7; 17:1–4; Acts 2:38,39; 3:19; 17:24–31.

[95] Luke 9:23–26; John 8:12–36; 12:35,36; Acts 9:31; Rom. 3:19–5:5; 6:1–11; 8:1 11; 2 Cor. 5:7–10; 10:1–6; Gal. 2:19–21; 5:16–25; Eph. 2:8–10; 4:1 ff.; 5:1 ff.; Phil. 2:12,13; 3:16–21; Col. 1:10; 2:6–10; 1 Thess. 1:1– 10; 2:12. *See the papers entitled "the Amazing Doctrine of God's Grace," "Conditions for Salvation" and "God's Definition of Salvation"*

[96] *See the book Jesus' Way and the three-part series entitled Christian Conversion "the Doctrine of Jesus Christ's Real Presence" and "Regarding Christ's Headship"*

[97] *See Jesus' Way, Appendix C: Kingdom of Heaven Diagram*

[98] Matt. 3:11,12; 16:18,19; 18:18–20; John 3:3–8; 6:27–68: 14–17; Rom. 6:1–11; 1 Cor. 12:12,13; 2 Cor. 3:17,18; Eph. 1–6; Phil. 1–4; Col. 1–4; 1 Tim. 2:5; Heb. 7–11.

[99] John 3:27; 16:13–15; Rom. 8:26-39; Heb. 2:1–3; 3:1–6,12–14; 6:3–12; James 1:17

[100] John 15

[101] Matt. 6:9–13; Luke 11:9–13; John 4:23,24; Eph. 6:18

[102] Matt. 5–7; 10:16–39; John 8:31–36; 14:15–26

[103] John 8:31–36; 14:15–24; 2 Tim. 2:15

[104] Matt. 22:37

[105] Jer. 29:11–13; John 15:11; 16:20–24; 17:13

[106] Matt. 5:14–16, 38–48; John 4:14; 7:37–39; Acts 4:11-13; Rom. 5:1–5; 12: 1ff. 1 Cor. 1:18–2:16; Gal. 5:22,23; Eph. 4:1–32; 6:18; Phil. 2:5–11; 3:7–15; Jude 20

Chapter 4:

[107] Mark 1:15; Acts 1:1 ff; Rom. 1:16 ff; 2 Cor. 11:1–4; Gal. 1:6–12 *See also the paper "Looking Through the Lens of Jesus Christ"*

[108] Deut. 4:2; Proverbs 8; Isa. 8:9–20; 28–30; Matt. 5:17–20; 2 Tim. 3:16; 2 Pet. 1:19–21; Rev. 22:18,19

[109] *See Glossary of Terms: Empiricism, Hermeneutics, Humanism, Nominalism, Platonism. **See also the paper "Hermeneutics: Basic Principles of Scripture Interpretation"*

[110] Matt. 23; Luke 13; 2 Cor. 11:12–15

[111] John 6:27–63; 7:15–18; 8:12–58; 14:21–26; 1 Cor. 10:1–13

[112] *See Glossary of Terms: Grace, Salvation*

[113] Universal Atonement: Matt. 26:26–29; Luke 22:14–23; John 1:1–18, 29–34 3:3– 8,16–18; 5:19– 30; 6:27–63; Acts 2:38,39; 3:19; Rom. 3:19–5:21; 1 Cor. 11:23 ff.; 2 Cor. 5:14–21; Eph. 1:3–3:9; Phil. 2:5–11; Col. 1:12–29; 1 Tim. 2:3–7; Heb. 1:1–9; 2:8–18; 5:6–10; 7:1–10:23; 2 Pet. 1:3; 1 John 2:1–6

[114] 1 Cor. 12:12,13

[115] Matt. 6:9–13; Luke 11:9–13; John 14–17

[116] Rom. 12; 1 Cor. 12–14; Eph. 4

[117] John 4:14–24; Eph. 4:23,24; Heb. 3:11–19; 4:11–16; 6:3–12; 10:26–39 *See also the paper entitled "the Lord's Supper, the New Covenant Passover"*

[118] *Repentance/Faith/Baptism:* Matt. 3:2; 5:17–20; 6:9–15; Luke 9:23–26; Joh 1:33; 4:14–24; 7:14– 18. 37–39; 14:21–16:15; Acts 1:8; 2:38,39; 3:19; *Rom. 3:19– 5:21; 6:1–11; 8:14–29; 10:1–15; 1 Cor. 10:16–18; 12:1–13; Gal. 2:15–3:28; 4:19–26; *Eph. 1:3–2:22; 3:10–21; 4:1–16,

21–24; 5:17–33; *Col. 1:22–29; 2:8–19; Heb. 4:9–5:14; 12:1–24; 1 John 1:5–10; 1 Pet. 1:1–2:10; Rev. 3:1 22

[119] *The Ministry of Reconciliation:* Matt 5–7; 28:18–20; John 12:23–17:26; Acts 1:1–4:37; 5:12–42; *Rom. 5:6–21; 8:1–39; 1 Cor. 13; *2 Cor. 5:14–21; Eph. 3:1–4:16; 6:10–18; *Phil. 2:5–18; 3:1–4:23; *Col. 1:12–29; 2 Tim. 1:6–14; 2:1–22; *Titus 2:11–15; 3:4–8; James 2:14–26; 1 Pet. 2:21–25; 3:18; 4:1 ff.; 1 John 3–5

[120] *See Jesus' Way: Chapter XIV The Circle of Love: Principle of the Kingdom*

[121] *See Jesus' Way: Chapter IX The Celebration of the Lord's Supper*

[122] *See the paper entitled "(What is) The Body of Christ"*

[123] John 1:1–14; 3:3–8; 13–17; Acts 4:8–13; Eph. 1–5; Rev. 21,22 *Se also the 3 part series of papers entitled "Christianity versus Religion"*

[124] Rom. 7:4

[125] *Matt. 18:20; John 15:1–11; Rom. 6:1–23; 7:7–8:39; *1 Cor. 11:23–32; 12:13; Eph. 2:1–22 *See also Glossary of Terms: *The Body of Christ*, the papers entitled "(What is) The Body of Christ," "the Christian Spirit," "Christian Worship and the True Temple," "The Doctrine of Jesus Christ's Real Presence," "the Evolution of Worship," "the Higher Laws of God," "Regarding Christ's Headship" and "Spirituality and Worship"*

[126] Rom. 6–8; Gal. 3:1–14; Eph. 2:4–10; 1 Pet. 1:2

[127] John 6:63; Rom. 3:19–26; 2 Cor. 13:5; 2 Pet. 1:2–11; 1 John 1:5–2:6

[128] Matt. 10:16–42; Luke 9:23–26; 14:26–33; John 1:12; 12:23–26; 15:1 ff.

[129] Matt. 27:52; Acts 9:32; Rom. 1:7; 8:27; 12:13; 15:25–31; 16:2,15; 1 Cor. 1:2;6:1,2; 14:33; 16:15; 2 Cor. 1:1; 8:4; 9:1,12; 13:13; Eph. 1:1,15,18; 2:13-22; Thess. 1:10; 1 Tim. 5:10; Philemon 5,7; Heb. 6:10; Rev. 5:8; 8:3,4; 11:18; 13:7–10; 14:10–12; 16:6; 17:6; 18:24; 19:8 *See also the position paper entitled: "What is the Body of Christ" and the book "Jesus' Way," Appendix C: the Kingdom of Heaven*

[130] Matt. 27:51–54; Luke 1:30–35; 2:8–14; 24:13–43; John 18:36–38; 21:15–35

[131] John 13:34,35; 14:1–15:26; Rom. 3:19–26; 12:1–3; 1 Cor. 12:12,13; Eph. 1–4; Phil. 2,3; 1 John 1–5

Chapter 5:

[1] Gen. 4:1-16; Psa. 32, 51; Matt. 23:29-39; John 3:16-30; Acts 17:24-31; Rom. 1:16 32; 3:9 ff.; 8:1 ff.; 1 John 2:1-6

[2] Jer. 17:9; 23:10 f.; Matt. 23; Rom. 1:18-32

[3] Prov. 16:7; Isa. 26:3,4,12; Matt. 5-7; Luke 6-14; Rom. 3, 5-8; 10:9,10; Eph. 2:83:21

[4] 2 Chr. 7:14; Isa. 48:18; 56:9-11; 59:1 ff; Matt. 23; Luke 21:19; John 3:36; Rom. 5:1-5;12:9-21; 1 Cor. 13; 2 Cor. 6:4-13; Col. 1:11; 2 Thess. 1:3-8; 1 Tim. 6:3-12; 2 Tim. 3:10-12;Heb. 6:12; 10:26-39; 12:1 -14; James 5:7,8; Rev. 2,3 *See also the author's book entitled Spiritual Guidelines for Restoration, "Historical Review" Section*

[5] Matt. 5-7; John 3:16; Rom. 5; 1 Cor. 13; Phil. 1-4; Col. 3:1 ff.; 1 John 2:1-6; 3:1 5:21

[6] Rom. 12:9-21; Eph. 6:10-12

[7] Psa. 2,110; Prov. 10:29; Isa. 1,2, 28:12-30:21; 52:13-53:12; 56:9-57:21; 59:1 ff.; Jer. 2-10; 11:9; 13:15-27; 17:1-10; 18:12; 23:9,10; 26:1-19; Ezek. 3,18,33,34; Hosea 14:9; Matt. 10:26-39; 23:1 ff.; Luke 2:33-35; 11:33-36; John 8:1-9:41; 1 Cor. 10

[8] John 8:31-36; 2 Cor. 3:17,18 *See also the paper entitled True Liberty is in Christ Alone, especially sect. II-B, the "List of Solas," those precepts in which Scripture points to the fundamental truth that Jesus Christ is the only Savior in all ways and venues.*

[9] 1Sam. 2:9; Psa. 1, 2, 32,49,51; 110:1 ff.; 115:1 ff.; 118:8,9; 146:1 ff.; Prov. 29:25; Isa. 2:1 ff.; 53:1 ff.; Jer. 10,17; Matt. 5-7; Luke 22:13-25; John 18:36-19:16; Rom. 12:9-21; Eph. 2:13 ff.; Col. 1:13 *See also the papers Emmanuel (1) and Emmanuel 2*

[10] Luke 4:18; John 8:31-36; Rom. 8:21; 2 Cor. 3:17,18; Gal. 5:1 *See the paper entitled True Liberty is in Christ Alone*

[11] CCLI #1126011

[12] Matt. 24:21,22; Mark 13:19,20; Luke 21:12 ff. *See also the papers entitled The Christian Epiphany and Facts of Scripture: The Church and the Tribulation*

[13] *See the papers entitled Are You Sure What you Believe is Truly Christian Doctrine, Authority and Conscience (a 2 Part series), The Beauty and Finesse of the New Covenant, Christianity Versus Religion (a 3 part series), Conditions for Salvation, Divergent Belief Systems, the Dynamics of Christian Discipleship,*

Every Believer can Independently Know the Truth of Scripture, God's Definition of Salvation, God Provides Everything we Need, How should we then Live (a 2 part series), Looking Through the Lens of Jesus Christ, the New Covenant, Only One Savior, Psychotic Hypocrisy, Retaining our Freedom requires Knowing and Applying the Truth and Serious Problems in Doctrine and practices still exist in many modern churches

[14] Exodus 20; Jer. 31; Ezek. 36; Matt. 5-7, 26; Luke 6-18, 21; Gal. 2-5; Hebrews 7-10,12; Rev. 13,17,18

[15] Jer. 4:4; 10:1 ff.; 17:1 ff.; 31:31-34; Luke 8:18; 11:33-36; John 14-17; James 1,2

[16] Matt. 16:21-26; Luke 9:23-26, 51-56; John 12:23-26

[17] *See the author's book Jesus' Way, c. 2009, Dorrance Publishing, Pittsburgh, PA.*

[18] *See the paper entitled The Higher Laws of God*

[19] *See the Book of Ecclesiastes*

[20] Matt. 5-7; 6:9-15; 10:26-39; John 8:9-11, 32-36; Rom. 5-8; 2 Cor. 5:14-21; Phil.1:21; 2:5-4:20

[21] Matt. 6:9-15, 22-24; Rom. 12:1 ff.

[22] 2 Cor. 4:3-6; 6:14-7:1; 10:3-6 *See also the 4 part series of papers entitled Christian Guidelines for Spiritual Warfare*

[23] Matt. 10:26-39; Luke 11:33-36; 12:8-10; John 5:24-30; 12:37-50; 14:1-17:26; 18:36-19:16; Acts 4:1-20; 5:29-32, 38-42; 17:24-31; Rom. 1:18-32; 6:1-8:39; Eph. 2:5-22; Phil. 2:5-13; Col. 1:12-29; 2:9,10; 3:1-17; 2 Tim. 2:10-12 *See also the paper Only One Savior*

[24] *See Glossary of Terms' entry *(the archetype of the) Garden**

[25] Gen. 15:6; Rom. 4:3

[26] *See Glossary of Terms' entry: The *Mosaic-Levitical-Sacrifice-System**

[27] Jer. 31; Ezek. 36; Matt. 26; Luke 22; John 2:19-21; Heb. 7-10 *See also the papers entitled Christian Worship and the True Temple: A New Covenant Perspective, Emmanuel (1) God is Dealing with His People, Emmanuel 2, the Higher Laws of God the Three Passovers of Scripture and Passover Sequence Chart*

[28] Matt. 10:26-39; Luke 12:8-10; 2 Tim. 2:10-12

[29] John 3:16; Rom. 5:1-11; 2 Cor. 5:14-21; Heb. 2:9-15; 1 John 2:1-6

[30] Matt. 13:12-15; Luke 8:18; 21:14-19; John 3:5-8, 27; 4:14,23,24; 6:27-63; 7:37-39;14:15-26; 15:26; 16:13-15; Acts 1:8; 2:38,39; 3:19; 4:7-

13; 5:29-32; Rom. 5:1-5; 8:1 ff; 1 Cor. 2:7-16; 12:1 ff.; 13:1 ff.; 14:1 ff.; 2 Cor. 3:3-5:21; Gal. 1:6-12; 5:14-25; Eph. 1:13; 2:13-3:21; 4:1-16,23,24; 5:17,18; 6:10-18; Heb. 2:3-14; 4:12-16; 8:10-13; 9:11-15; 1 Pet. 1:18-25; 1 John 4,5 *See also the papers entitled the Amazing Doctrine of God's Grace, Christian Worship and the True Temple, the Doctrine of Jesus Christ's Real Presence, Every Believer can Independently Know the Truth of Scripture, the Holy Spirit is God's Revelator, How does Christ's Blood get to us Today, the Progression of our Redemption requires Spiritual Development and Spirituality and Worship*

[31] Matt. 5:43-48

[32] Job 13:15; Psa. 18:2,30; 20:7; 25:1 f.; 27:1 ff.; 31:1 ff; 37:1 ff.; 40:4; 44:1-8; 91:1 ff.; 118:8,9; 146:3; Prov. 2:8; 3:5,6; 29:25; Matt. 21:18-22; Rom. 10:6-17

[33] Ruth 4:10; Acts 20:28; Eph. 1:14; Col. 1:12,13

[34] Matt. 16:21-26; John 8:31-36; Rom. 6:18; 2 Cor. 3:17,18; Gal. 5:1,13; Heb. 2:9-15; 1 Pet. 2:16 *See also the Hymn Faith of our Fathers, verse two.*

[35] *Ex. 6:6,7; *14:13,14; Isa. 42-45; Matt. 6:22-24; John 8:31-36; 2 Cor. 3:17,18; Phil. 2:5-11; Heb. 2:9-15 *See also the O.T. account of the Archetypal Passover in Exodus 3-15 and the paper True Liberty is in Christ Alone, especially Sect. II-B, the "Solas of Christ"*

[36] Rom. 14:23 *See also The Christian Epiphany and True Liberty is in Christ Alone*

[37] Matt. 10:16-42; Luke 8:18; 12:8-10; 14:26-33; 19:26; Rom. 1:16-32; 2 Cor. 12:9,10; Gal. 1:6-12; 2:19-21; 3:26-28; 6:14; Phil. 1:21-2:13; 3:7-15; Col. 1:23-29; 3:1-17; 1 Tim. 6:3- 12; 2 Tim. 1:7-12; 2:1 ff.; Heb. 2:9-15; 3:14; 4:12-16; 7:11-12:29; 1 John 5:3.

[38] Matt. 23; Luke 12:49,50; 1 Cor. 10:1-21; 11:23-31; 2 Thess. 1:8 f.; 2:3-12

[39] Matt. 5-7; Luke 5:12-14;6:20-42; 8:18; 9:23-26, 51-56; 11:9-13, 33-36; 12:8-10; John 3:18-21, 27; 5:22-30; 6:27-63; 8:12-58; 9:39-41; 12:23-50; 13:34-17:26; 18:36,37; Rom. 6:1- 8:39; 10:9,10 *See also the paper Principles of Fulfillment Theology*

[40] Matt. 10:26-39; Heb. 12:1 ff.; James 1:5-8; 2:8 ff.; 1 Pet. 1:3 ff.; 3:13-5:11

[41] Exodus 20,32; Psa. 115; Prov. 1:7; 9:10; Isa. 42-46; 57:15; Jer. 10,1-16,23;Acts 4:9-20

[42] Ex. 6-15; Psa. 23, 24, 27, 31, 37, 42, 46, 51, 59, 62, 71, 73, 84, 91,94,118; Isa. 40:31

⁴³ Exodus 6, 12-15; Judges 6,7; 2 Sam. 24:1 f.; 1 Kings 18:21; 1 Chr. 17:3-14; 21;1 f.;22:2-9; 2 Chr. 20; Zech. 4:6

⁴⁴ Psa. 20, 44, 83:18; 94, 118; Prov. 10:9,29; 14:12; 16:7; 21:30; Isa. 1-8, 28-34, 42-47; Jer. 2-19; Ezek. 18:30-32; 23:37-39; Dan. 3:1 ff.; 6:1 ff.; Hosea 10:12,13; 14:9; Matt. 5:43-48; John 18:36,37; Acts 4:11-15; 5:29-32; 16:16-34

⁴⁵ Exodus 20; Deut. 4:29-39; 6:4-6; 32:1-39; 1 Sam. 2:6-9; 15:22,23; Psa. 24, 95,96; 111:10; Prov. 1:7; 29:25; Isa. 30:1, 15-22 ; 42:1-9; 44:6-20; 45:5-12, 20-25; Jer. 10; Dan. 2:20- 22; Matt. 6:24; John 1:1-5; Acts 17:22-31; Rom. 1:18-32; 1 Cor. 2:4-16; 2 Cor. 4,5; Gal. 1:6-12; Phil. 2:5-11; Col. 1:12-27; Heb. 10-12; James 1:5-8; 2:10-26; 4:1-8; 1 John 5:19-21

⁴⁶ Exodus 14:13,14; 1 Sam. 2:6-10; Psa. 23-28, 31-37, 42, 44-46; 49-51, 55-57, 61-63, 71-73, 84, 91, 103, 145; Matt. 8:1-4; 28:20; Mark 1:40-42; 16:15-18; Luke 5:12-15; Rom. 8:26-39; 1 Cor. 10:12,13 *See also The Christian Epiphany, Sect. VI: "An Affidavit," Sect. A-5 for a list of God's "Protection Scriptures"*

⁴⁷ Matt. 6:24; 10:26-32; 16:21-26; Luke 12:8-10

⁴⁸ Josh. 5:13-15; Psa. 2,110; Matt. 28:18; John 1:1-18; Acts 4:1 f.; 5:29-32; Eph. 4:1-13;Corl. 1:12-29; 2:6 ff.; Rev. 4,5

⁴⁹ Ex. 20:1-7; Deut. 4:32-39; 1 Kings 18:21; Psa. 44, 94, 110, 115, 118; Isa. 43:10-12;44:6-10,20; 45:18-23; Jer. 10:1 ff.; 17:1-10; John 1:1-18; 18:36,37; Acts 5:29-32

⁵⁰ Matt. 10; Luke 9:23-26, 51-56; 14:25-33; John 15; Phil. 1:21; 3:7-15

⁵¹ Psa. 111:10; Prov. 1:7; 3:5,6; 9:10; 29:25; Matt. 10:16-39; John 18:36,37; Acts 4:12-20; 5:29-32

⁵² Gen. 18:14; Isa. 53:1; 59:1,2; Jer. 32:17,27; Matt. 19:26

⁵³ 1 Kings 18:21; 2 Chr. 7:14; Psa. 1,2; Prov. 1:7; 3:5,6; Isa. 53:1; 59:1,2; Ezek. 3,18,33,34; Matt. 6:24; Luke 16:13; 18:8; Rom. 1:16-25; 2 Cor. 3:17,18; Gal. 1:10; Phil. 2:5-11; James 4:4

⁵⁴ Matt. 5:3-48; 6:9-15; Luke 6:20 ff.; 17:1-4;

⁵⁵ Exodus 14:13,14; 15:26; Deut. 7:15; 1 Sam. 2:6-9; 1 Kings 18:21; Job. 28:28; Psa. 23-28, 31-37, 91; Prov. 1:7; 9:10; 29:25; Matt. 10:26-39; Luke 21:12-19

⁵⁶ 1 Sam. 2:1-10; 2 Sam.23:3; 2 Chr. 20:20,21; Neh. 5:9,15; Psa. 19:9; 111:10; Prov.1:7,33; 2:1-16; 8:13; 9:10; 10:27; 14:27; 19:22; 22:4;

23:17; Isa. 11:1 ff.; 33:6; Matt. 10:26-28;Luke 12:5; Rom. 11:16-23; Heb. 12:14-29; Rev. 15:4 *Then, contrast these to the following:* 1 Sam. 15:22,23; Psa. 36:1; Prov. 1:23-32; 29:25; Isa. 53:1-6; Jer. 10:1 ff.; 17:1-10; Rom. 1:18-32; 3:18

[57] Matt. 4:1-10; 6:22-24; Luke 4:1-8; 2 Cor. 4:1-6; 11:12-15 *See also the 3 part series of papers entitled Christianity Versus Religion and the 4 part series of papers entitled Christian Guidelines for Spiritual Warfare*

[58] Matt. 8:1-4; Mark 1:40-42; Luke 5:12-16

[59] Psa. 33:4; Phil. 1:6,21; 1 John 4:18

[60] Matt. 10:26-39; Luke 12:8-10; 2 Tim. 2:11-13

[61] Matt. 22:36,37

[62] Matt. 16:21-26; Luke 9:23-26; John 12:23-26

[63] Matt. 5:3 f.; Mark 12:40-44; Luke 6:20 f.; 14:13,21; Gal. 2:10

[64] Matt. 6:9-15; 18:21,22

[65] Matt. 5:43-48

[66] Matt.18:1-14; 19:13-15 *See also the author's book Jesus' Way Chapter XVI, "The Formula"*

[67] 2 Cor. 5:14-21

[68] 2 Thess. 1,2; 1 Tim. 4:1,2; 2 Tim. 3,4; Rev. 13,17,18

[69] Matt. 10:26-39; 24:21,22; Luke 12:8-10; John 16:33; 2 Tim. 2:11-13 \

Chapter 6:

[1] Daniel 2; Matt. 4:17; 9:35; 24:14; 26:13; 28:18-20; Mark 1:1,14,15 ; 8:34-38; 13:10-13; Rom. 1:16; 15:18-20; 1 Cor. 9:11-17; 2 Cor. 4:1-6; Gal. 1:6-12; 1 Tim. 6:3; Rev. 2,3 *See the book entitled Life-Songs in the Key of Jesus*

[2] Daniel 4,6; Amos 3:3; Matt. 7:13-21; 10:32-40; 16:24-26; 18:20; 24:9-13; Mark 4:11-14; Luke 2:33-35; 4:18,19; 6:20-49; 8:18; 9:23-26, 49-62; 10:16-27; 11:17-36; 12:8-12, 49-53;16:10-17; 18:16,17; 19:26; 21:8-18; John 1:1-18; 3:16-36; 4:14-24; 6:27-63; 8:12-58; 9:39-41;12:23-26,32,46; 13:34-17:26; 18:36,37; 21:15-17; Acts 4:12-20; 5:29-32; 2 Cor. 11:12-15; 1 Tim. 6:3; Rev. 2,3 See the books entitled *Basic Christian Doctrine, Life-Songs in the Key of Jesus* and *A Seeker's Guide to Biblical Faith* See also the papers entitled *Authority and Conscience* (A 2 part series), *Introduction to Christian Conversion* (A 3 Part series), *Christianity Versus Religion*(A 3 Part series), *Conditions for Salvation, the Doctrine*

of the Elect/ Ekklesia, Dynamics of Christian Discipleship, Every Believer can independently know the Truth of Scripture, Fallacies of Determinism, God's Definition of Salvation, Hermeneutics: Basic Principles of Scripture Interpretation (A 2 Part series), *the Higher Laws of God, Investigating the Symptoms of Latter day Problems, Jesus' Major Parables, Key Aspects of the Christian Gospel, the Key to Understanding Scripture is Spiritual Exegesis, the Kingdom of Heaven is the Highest Form of Civilization, Looking Through the 'Lens of Jesus Christ,' the New Covenant, Our Preparations for God's Service, Patriarchalism in the Church, Principles of Fulfilment Theology, Psychotic Hypocrisy, the Spiritual Laws of Revival* and *True Liberty is in Christ Alone*

3 Matt. 5:17-20; 6:9-13; 16:15-20; 18:20; Mark 2:21,22; 16:15-18; Luke 17:20-37; John 2:19-21; 4:23,24; 6:63: 14:6, 15-26; 16:13-15; 17:17; 18:36; Acts 7:48; 17:24-31; 1 Cor. 2:9-16;Rom. 8:1-11; Eph. 2:13-22; 2 Tim. 2:15-26; 2 Pet. 1:16-21 *See also Sect. III-G below and the papers entitled The Spiritual Laws of Revival and Spirituality and Worship*

4 Psa. 49:19; 97:11; 119:105; 130,; 139:12; Prov. 6:23; Isa. 5:20; Jer. 2-11,13,18; 23:9 ff.; 31:31-34; Ezek. 3,8,9,10,14,18, 20-22, 33,34,36; Matt. 4:16; 5:14-16; 6:22-24; Luke 11:33-36; John 1:4-18; 3:16-36; 7:15-18; 8:12-58; 9:5,9,10, 39-41; 12:35,36; 14:6-17:26; Rom. 8:1-18; 13:12; 2 Cor. 4:3-7; 11:12-15; Eph. 5:8,13; 2 Tim. 1:7-14; Heb. 1,2,7-12; 1 Pet. 2:22; 2 Pet. 1:2-11,19-21; 1 John 1:1 ff.; 4:1-6 *See also the 4 part series of papers entitled Christian Guidelines for Spiritual Warfare, Every Believer can Independently know the Truth of Scripture, From Whence do Lies come and God's "Universal Attitude Test"*

5 Ibid. Fn. #3 Acts 17:11 *See also the papers entitled Are You Sure What you Believe and Practice is Truly Christian Doctrine, (the 2 part series) Authority and Conscience, A Biblical Disclosure of Antichrist, (the 3 part series Christianity Versus Religion, The Dangers of Conformity and Do You Know Who You Are*

6 Gen. 12:1-9; 15:1-15; 21:1-7; 22:1-18; 32:22-30; 37:1-11; 40:1-41:57; Ex. 2-15; Numbers 11:1-30; Deut. 1-7; Dan. 2:19-45

7 Gen. 11

8 Acts 1:8; 2:1-39

9 Matt. 28:18-20; Mark 16:9-20; John 6:27-63: 14:15-26; 15:26; 16:13-15; Acts 1:8;2:1-39; Rom. 12:1-16; 1 Cor. 1:17-2:16; 12:1-14:40; 2 Cor. 1:20; Eph. 4:1-16

[10] Matt. 5:43-48; 26:51-56; Luke 6:20 ff.; 9:49-56; John 18:36,37; 1 John 3:15 f.; 4:7-21

[11] Exodus 20:13; Isa. 5:20-30; 8:20-22; 29:13,14; 30:8-22; Jer. 4:22; 11:17; 13:15-17; 17:5-10; Hos. 14:9; Matt. 6:22-24; 8:11,12; Mark 3:1-5; Luke 11:33-36; Rom. 12:9-21; Eph.5:5-11; 6:10-12; Col. 1:13; Heb. 11:13-16; 2 Pet. 2:1 ff.; 1 John 2:9-17; 3:11-15

[12] Matt. 4:1-10; 6:9-13; Luke 4:1-8; John 8:12, 31-36; 9:39-41; 18:36; 2 Cor. 3:17,18

[13] Ex. 6:6,7: 14:13,14; Deut. 1:26-33; 3:21,22; 32:39; Joshua 24:14-24; Ruth. 1:14-18; 1 Sam. 2:9; 1 Kings 18:21; Neh. 9; Psa. 20:6,7; 23:1 ff; 31-37; 46, 51, 61-63, 73, 84, 91, 118, 139; Isa. 42-46; Jer. 31:31-34; Ezek. 20-23, 36; Matt. 6:9-15, 24; 10:16-42; 23:1 ff.; Luke 6:20-49; 9:23-26, 51-56 (KJV); 11:33-36; 12:4-32; 14:15-33; 17:20-37; 19:8-27; John 3:3-8, 16-36; 4:13-26; 5:19-30; 6:27-63; 7:14-19; 8:12-48; 9:5, 9:24-41; 10:9-16, *27-30; 11:25,26; 12:23-32, 37-50; 13:34-17:26; 18:36,37; *Acts 16:25-35; Rom. 5:1-11; 6:1-8:39; 10:1-17; 1 Cor. 10:12-16; 13:1 ff.; 2 Cor. 4:1 ff.; 6:1-7:1; Gal. 1:6-12; 2:16-5:1; Eph. 1:3-2:22; Phil. 1-4; Col. 1:12-3:17; 1 Tim. 6:3-12; 2 Tim. 1:7-15; 2:15-26; Heb. 11:1-6, 12-16; James 1:5-8, 17-27; 4:1-8; 1 Pet. 1:3-25; 1 John 3,4 *See also the papers entitled The Amazing Doctrine of God's Grace and The Christian Epiphany*

[14] Matt. 5:39-48; John 18:36,37; Rom. 12:1 ff.; 2 Cor. 10:3-6; Eph. 6:10-18; Phil. 1:21; 3:7-20 *See also the 4 part series entitled Christian Guidelines for Spiritual Warfare*

[15] Job. 28:28; Psa. 111:10; Prov. 1:7; 8:13; 9:10; Isa. 11:2,3; 33:6; John 14:15-26;15:26; 16:14-15; 1 Cor. 1:17-2:16 *See also the paper entitled Every Believer can Independently know the Truth of Scripture*

[16] Luke 2:34,35; John 6:63; 14:15-26; 15:13-15; Heb. 4:12,13 *See also the paper entitled The Spiritual Laws of Revival Chapter 2, "Spiritual Law Eight is the Separation of soul from the spirit" and the book Jesus' Way*

[17] Isa. 1-6; 28:9-22; 29:13-30:21; 44:20,21; Jer. 3-33; Ezek. 3-34; Matt. 23:1 ff.; John 15:18-16:4; Rom. 8:1-11; 2 Thess. 2:3-12; Heb. 12:25-28; 2 Pet. 1:16-3:16; Rev. 13 *See also the Papers entitled Basics of Biblical Church Governance, Christian Guidelines for Spiritual Warfare, Part Three: "Cracking the False Doctrine Code," Facilitating Revival, The Fallacies of Determinism, Guidelines for Renewed Leadership and Psychotic Hypocrisy*

[18] Acts 17:26; Gal. 3:28 *See also the paper entitled Patriarchalism in the Church which identifies the original Greek words Paul used, exposing their lying doctrine that abuses women*

[19] Gen. 3:14-16; 1 Sam. 2:9; 1 Kings 18:21; Psa. 94:20-23; 118:8,9; 146:3; Matt. 5:38-48; 6:24; 7:13-15; 10:16 f.; 23:1 ff.; 24:4-13; Luke 2:34,35; John 18:36; Acts 4:12-20; 5:29-32;28:22; 1 Tim. 4:1,2; 2 Tim. 3:1-7; James 3,4; 2 Pet. 2:1 ff.; 1 John 4:1 ff.

[20] Cor. 4:1-5:17; 6:14-18; 10:1-7; 11:12-15 *See also the papers A Biblical Disclosure of Antichrist, (the 4 part series) Christian Guidelines for Spiritual Warfare and Christianity versus Religion, Part Two: The Dangers of Religious Catechism*

[21] 1 Thess. 5:23

[22] Psa. 3:8; 4:8; John 3:16,17; 8:31-36; 2 Cor. 1:20; 3:17,18; Heb. 4:16-19; 7:24,25; 10:22-39; *James 1:3-5 See also the papers The Christian Epiphany and True Liberty is in Christ Alone*

[23] *See the book Spiritual Guidelines for Restoration, "Historical Review" Section.*

[24] Psa. 18:26; 19:8; 24:4; Matt. 5:3-48; 6:9-13; 9:16,17; 10:16-42; Mark 2:21,22; 16:15-18; Lk. 2:34,35; 11:33-36; 17:20-37; John 4:23,24; 15:1-7; 18:36; Acts 7:48; 17:24-31;28:22; Rom. 12:1 ff.; 2 Cor. 6:14-7:1; 11:12-15; Gal. 1:6-12; Phil. 3:3,20,21; 4:6-8; 1 Tim. 3:9; 2 Tim. 2:10-26; Heb. 10:16-12:29; James 1:3-5, 27; 3:17; 1 John 3:1-4:21

[25] Matt. 7:13,14; John 10:27

[26] *Eph. 2:13-22 See also the papers entitled The Christian Epiphany, Conditions for Salvation and God's Definition of Salvation*

[27] *See the Papers entitled Basics of Biblical Church Governance and Guidelines for Renewed Leadership*

[28] Ex. 20:2-5; 34:14; Deut. 4:35,39; 8:19,20; 11:16; 30:17; 32:39; 33:26,27; 1 Sam. 2:2-10; 17:47; 1 Kings 18:21; 2 Kings 17:35-41; 18:5,6, 19-19:19; 1 Chr. 17:7-22; Psa. 2:1 ff.; 3:8; 4:8; 5:4-12; 11:1 ff.; 23:1 ff.; 27:1 ff.; 29:2; 31:23,24; 32:1 ff.; 33:1-34:22; 37:1 ff.; 40:1-41:2; 42:1-44:8; 45:1-46:11; 49:1 ff.; 50:2,14,15,23; 51:1 ff.; 59:16; 61-63; 66:5-12; 68:4,17-20; 73:16-26; 81:10; 83:18; 84:11; 86:2,11-13; 91:1 ff.; 94:12-23; 103:1 ff; 110:1 ff; 115:1-13; 118, 146; Isa. 6,12,26-30,42-46; Jer. 10; John 4:14-24; Phil. 2:5-11; Col. 2:8-13; 3:1-17; James 1:5 ff. *See the papers: (The 3 part series) Christianity Versus Religion and Spirituality and Worship See also the book Jesus' Way, Chapter X, Sect. III.: "The Glory of Worship"*

[29] Ex. 22:20; Lev. 20:7; Num. 23:9; Deut. 4:29-39; 5:6-11; 6:1-16; 10:17; 11:18-23;26:18,19; 2 Kings 17:36; Job. 28:28; Psa. 29:2; 45:11; 95:6,9; Prov. 1:7; 9:9,10, Isa. 42:8;43:10-15; 44:6-8; 45:5-12, 20-23; Dan. 3:10-18; Matt. 4:10; John 4:14-24; Rom. 5:1-5; 12:1-3;Phil. 2:10; 3:3

[30] *Matt. 7:7; 16:23-26; Luke 9:23-26; John 12:23-26 See also the papers entitled Destiny and Free Will and The Dynamics of Christian Discipleship*

[31] Matt. 13:1-23; 2 Tim. 2:11-26; Heb. 10:19-12:29; James 1:22-27

[32] Matt. 12:30; 27:15-29; Luke 23:1-18; John 15:18-16:4; 18:19-19:15; Acts 5:29-32; 1 Cor. 3:11 ff.; Col. 2:8, 18-20; 1 Tim. 4; 2 *Tim. 3:1-9 See the papers entitled The Christian Epiphany and True Liberty is in Christ Alone*

[33] 1 Sam. 8-10; Dan. 3,6; Matt. 6:9-13; Lk. 13:30-35; John 18:36,37; Acts 5:29-32

[34] Matt. 5:38-48; 6:9-13; Luke 9:51-56 (KJV); John 18:36,37; Rom. 8:1-11; 12:1 ff.; Eph. 6:10-12

[35] 1 Sam. 2; Joshua 2; Psa. 1, 2, 94, 110, 118, 146; Prov. 29:25; Jer. 5:1-5. 9, 20-22, 29-31; 6:10-19; 7:13,27; 8:4-11; 9:6-9; 10:1-11, 14-17; 11:10; 13:8-17; 17:5-10, 23; 18:11-16; Ezek. 3:3-11; 20:8-44; 21:24-27; 22:1 ff; 23:37-39; 36:16-32; Dan. 3,6; Luke 13:31,32; John 18:36-19:16*; Acts 5:29-32; Rom. 13:1-7* *Note in the asterisked refs that God's delegation of authority to humans is limited. Two examples are in Rom. 13:1: One, God is the greater power and two, the Greek word Tagma should have been translated Allowed, not 'ordained' The same principle applies to John 19:11 See the 2 part series of papers entitled Authority and Conscience*

[36] Isa. 1-6, 28-30, 42-46; 56:6-59:21; 63:7-65:25; Jer. 2-13; 17:5-10; *18:11-17; 23:9-40; Ezek. 3,7-14, 18, 20-22; 23:37-39*; 33,34,36; Hos. 1-14; Amos 3-9; Mic. 3,4; Mal. 2*; Matt. 5:38-48; 22:36,37; 23:1 ff.; Luke 6-14; John 14:15-26; Rom. 5:1-5; Phil. 4:13-19; 1 John 3-5 *See also the papers entitled Analysis of Church Governance and Questionnaire, the Christian Epiphany, Guidelines for Renewed Leadership and A Questionnaire for Church Leaders*

[37] John 8:31-36; 10:27; 2 Cor. 3:17,18

[38] Matt. 6:9-13; John 14-17; 18:36,37; Rom. 4:1-5:5; 6:1-8:39; 2 Cor. 1:20; Gal. 2:16-4:20; Eph. 1:7,19-23; 2:13-22; Phil. 3:2,20; Heb. 10:9-11:16

[39] Isa. 1-6; Jer. 2-18; Ezek. 3-36; Hos. 1-14; Mal. 2; Matt. 23; 1 Cor. 10

[40] Matt. 22:36 .37; Luke 22:31,32; John 21:15-17

[41] Matt. 18:20; John 13:34,35; 14:6-27; Acts 4:13; Rom. 5:1-5; 1 Cor. 2:9-16; 13;1 ff.;

[42] Matt. 5:38-48; Mark 3:4; Luke 9:51-56 (KJV); 11:33-36; Rom. 12:19-21

[43] *See the books entitled Basic Christian Doctrine, The Church in the Last Days, Jesus' Way and Spiritual Guidelines for Restoration*

[44] Ex. 6:6,7; 14:13,14; Deut. 1:26-33; 3:21,22; 32:39; 1 Sam. 2; 2 Chr. 20:11-24; Neh.9; Psa 20, 23, 24, 27, 31, 37, 42, 46, 51, 55, 56, 61, 63, 73, 84, 91, 94, 118, 146 Et., Al.; Jer. 31; Ezek. 36;Matt. 6:9-13; 10:16-42; 26:26-32, 51-54; Luke 22:15-32; John 1:1-18; 3:3-8, 16,17; 4:14-24;5:19-30; 6:27-63; 7:15-18, 37-39; 8:12-58; 9:39-41; 10:1-38; 11:25,26; 12:23-26,32-50; 13:34-17:26; 18:36-19:15; 20:19-23; 21:4-17; Acts 1:7-11; 2:1-7, 17-28, 32-41; 3:1-4:20; 5:29-32;7:37-60; 13:13-46; 17:24-31; 20:31-35; 26:9-18; Rom. 1:16-32; 3:4-5:11; 6:1-8:39; 12:1 ff.;1 Cor. 1:17-2:16; 2 Cor. 1-5; Gal. 1-6; Eph. 1,2; ... Heb. 7-12 *(and many more)*

[45] Jer. 31:31-34; Ezek. 36:16-32; Matt. 5:17-20; John 3:16,17; Heb.2:9-14; 7-12; 1 John 2:1-6 *See also the papers entitled The Christian Epiphany, Fulfilment Prophecy, Looking Through the Lens of Jesus Christ and True Liberty is in Christ Alone See also the Diagram entitled The Nine Ages*

[46] John 14:6; Gal. 1:6-12

[47] 2 Thess. 2:3-12 *See also the 2 part series of papers entitled Authority and Conscience*

[48] Joshua 2 (Rahab); Daniel 3,6; Matt. 4:1-10; 5:38-48; 6:9-13; 26:51-56; 28:18; Mark 3:4; Luke 4:1-8; 9:51-56 (KJV); John 18:36-38; Acts 4:11-20; 5:29-32; Phil. 1:27; 3:3,20; Heb. 11:13-16, 24-31

[49] Luke 2:34,35; John 15:18-16:4, 33; Acts 28:22; 2 Pet. 2:1-3

[50] Matt. 10:16-42; Phil. 4:6-19

[51] 2 Thess. 2:3-12; James 1:3-7; 4:1-8; 1 John 2:15-17

[52] Jer. 2-9, 18; Ezek. 3,18,33,34; Mic. 3, Mal. 2; Matt. 23; 1 Cor. 10

[53] John 15:18-16:4; 18:36-19:15 *See the paper Analysis of the causes and effects of apostasy, Divergent Belief Systems, (the 2 part series) How Should we Then Live and True Liberty is in Christ Alone*

[54] Psa. 37:3-5; Prov. 3:4,5; 13:15; 14:12; 16:25; 29:25; Isa. 30:10-21;; 45:5-23; Jer. 2:18-32; 23:10; Hos. 14:9; Mal. 2:1-9; Matt. 6:9-13; John 14:6-17:26; Rom. 6:1-8:39;1 John 5:4

[55] Rev. 2,3

[56] *See the book entitled Spiritual Guideline for Restoration, "Historical Review" Section*

Chapter 7:

[1] Matt. 5:43-48; 28:18-20; Luke 6:27-40; 9:51-56; Rom. 12:9-21

[2] Matt. 7:13-29; Rom. 12; 1 Cor. 12-15; Eph. 4:1-16

[3] Eph. 2:5-10; Phil. 3:7-15

[4] John 3:16; 1 John 2:1-6

[5] Psa. 32, 51; Matt. 23:31-39; John 18:36,37

[6] Eph. 6:12 *See also the paper entitled What is Collectivism*

[7] Matt. 6:24; Luke 16:13; John 4:23,24; Acts 4:13-20; 5:29-32

[8] Genesis 19; Joshua 1-12 *See also the way God obsoleted "judgment by murder" when He ordained Christ's *New Covenant* See Matt. 5-7; Luke 6:27-40; 9:51-56; John 18:36; Rom. 1:18-32; 1 Tim. 4:1,2; Heb. 7:11-10:23 See also the book Jesus' Way*

[9] Matt. 6:24; Luke 16:13 15; John 8:31-36; Romans 1:17-32; 2 Cor. 3:17,18

[10] Matt. 4:8-10; 5:43-48; Luke 4:5-8; 9:49-56; John 18:36,37; Acts 4:12-20; 5:29-32

[11] Psa. 3:3-8; 4:1-8; 9:9,10; 20:6,7; 27:1 ff.; 32:6-11; 46:1 ff.; 91:1 ff.; 1 Kings 18:21; Isa. 44:6-20; 45:20-23; Nah. 1:7; Matt. 6:24; Luke 16:13; 1 Cor. 10:14-22; 2 Cor. 6:14-18

[12] Joshua 24:15; Matt. 5-7; Rom. 8; 1 John 1-5

[13] John 3:16; 1 John 4:19

[14] 1 Sam. 15:22; John 14:15-27; Rom. 15:23

[15] Matt. 6:24; Luke 16:13; Rom. 8:1-11

[16] 1 Sam. 2:9; 15:23; Psa. 96:5; 106:36; 115:4; Isa. 2:8,18; 45:16; 48:5; 57:5; Jer. 2-10,17,18,23; Ezek. 2:1-3:11; 5:5-6:14; 8:10; 14:3,4,7; 16:36; 18:6-30; 21:24-27; 22:23-28;23:37-39; Hos. 4:17; 10:12,13; 14:9; Zech. 13:2; Mal. 2:1-13; Matt. 23; Luke 2:34,35; Acts 7:41-48; 17:16; 28:22; 1 Cor. 10:14; Gal. 5:1,13; Eph. 2:13-16; 1 Tim. 6:3-12; 2 Tim. 2:19

[17] Rom. 1:18-32

[18] Matt. 4:1-10; 6:9-13; Luke 4:1-8; 11:33-36; John 14:6; 18:36; Rom. 8:1-11; 2 Cor.4:3-7; Rev. 13

[19] Matt. 12:30; Luke 2:34; 11:33-36; John 14:15-27; Acts 28:22; Eph. 2:13,14; Phil.4:6-8

[20] Song 8:6,7; Matt. 5:38-48; Rom. 12:9-21; 2 Cor. 10:3-7; Eph. 6:10-12

[21] Matt. 5-7; Luke 6-12; John 8:31-36; Rom. 8:26-39

[22] Gen. 12-14, 22; 28:10-35:35; Exodus 3-15; Joshua 2:1 ff.; 24:14-27; Ruth 1:16-18;1 Sam. 2:1-10; 3:1-14; 1 Chr. 17; Psa. 18,19, 77:19; Isa. 43:16; Heb. 11

[23] Ex. 20; Deut. 4, 29-32; 1 Sam. 2; the Psalms, Proverbs, and the Prophets, including Jer. 31; Ezek. 36; Dan. 2:44,45; 4:3; 7:18-27; Matt. 5-7; 13:1 ff.; 16:18-26 et. Al.; Luke 1:33; 9:56-62; 11:33-36; John 1,3; 18:36; Acts 4,5, 14:22; 17:24-31; Rom. 4-8; 1 Cor. 4:20; 10:1 ff; Col. 1:13-16 *and so forth See also the books Jesus' Way, The Church in the Last Days, Basic Christian Doctrine and Spiritual Guidelines for Restoration and well as the Papers Emmanuel 1,2*

[24] Lev. 20:7; Psa. 9:10; 22:3; Isa. 6:13; Ezek. 22:26; 44:23; Hag. 2;11-14; Matt. 7:6; John17:11; Rom. 11:16; 1 Cor. 3:17; 2 Cor. 6:14-7:1; Col. 3:12; 2 Tim. 1:9; 1 Pet. 1:13-25

[25] Josh. 2; Psa. 94:20; 96:5; 118:8,9; Isa. 2:8,18,20; 28:5-23; 29:8-30:21; 42-46; Ezek. 6:4,5,13; 14:1-8; 18-23 (esp. 23:37-49); Dan. 2:44,45; 3:1 ff.; 6:1ff.; 7:13-28; Hos.4:17; 14:8,9; Matt. 6:9-13; Luke 13:24-35; Acts 4,5; 1 Cor. 3:16-32; 6:9-11; 10:1-13; 2 Cor. 6:14- 7:1; Phil. 3:20; Rev. 17:1-8; 21:8; 22:15

[26] Matt. 6:9-13; 10:16-42; 22:26,37; Luke 2:49; John 18:36; Acts 1-5. 7:48; 17:24-31; Rom. 8; Gal. 1,2; Phil. 1-4; Eph. 1-6; Col. 1-4

[27] John 14:6-17:26; Rom. 5-8; 1 Cor. 1:17-2:16

[28] Isa. 55:9; Acts 3:19; 1 John 1:5-10 *See also (the 3 part series) Christian Conversion, the Doctrine of Repentance, God's Definition of Salvation and the Role of Conscience*

[29] Gen. 12:1-3,8; 13:3; 14:22; 15:1-6, 12-18; 17:19-21; Rom. 4:9.13; Heb. 11

[30] Gen. 18:10-18; 22:1 ff.; 28:10-35:36; Jer. 7:23; John 3:16-36; 15:17

[31] Gen. 12:1 f. Cf. Heb. 11:12-16

[32] Ex. 20,34; Deut. 5

[33] Lev. 20:26; Num. 8:17; 23:9; Psa. 74:2; Isa. 43:1; John 10:14-18; Acts 20:26-32; Eph. 1:7-14 *See also the paper entitled The Three Passovers of Scripture*

[34] Joshua 24:13-20

[35] Psa. 18, 19,45; 1 Chr. 17:7-14, 20-22; Acts 13:22

[36] Matt. 17:20; 19:26 Cf. Luke 1:37; 18:27 and Jer. 32:17,27

[37] Matt. 6:9-13; 16:21-26; Luke 9:23-26; 11:33-36; John 8:12, 23-58; 12:23-26;18:36,37; Acts 5:29-32; Rom. 6:1-8:39; 12:1 ff.; 1 Cor. 1:17-2:16; 10:12-21; 2 Cor. 2:14-7:1;Gal. 1:6-12; 2:19-5:4; Eph. 2:8-22; Phil. 3:20; Col. 1:13-18; 2:8-3:17; Heb. 11:12-16; James 4:1-8; 1 John 2:15-17

[38] Luke 2:49; 9:23-26; John 14:6-16:26

[39] 1 Sam. 2:1-10; 1 Kings 18:21; Job. 19:25-27; Psa. 3:8; 4:8; 9:9,10; 16:1 ff.; 20:6,7; 23:1 ff.; 24:1. Ff.; 27:1 ff.; 31-37, 40-42, 45 (the Kings Daughter), 46, 50,51, 55, 61-63, 73, 84, 91, 94,95, 115,118, 146; Isa. 42-46; Jer. 31:31-34; Ezek. 33-36; Dan. 3,6,7; Zech. 4:6; Matt. 5-7; 10:16-42; John 11:25,26; 13:35-17:26; Acts 5:29-32; 17:24-31; 28:22; Rom. 1:16- 8:39; 1 Cor. 1:17-2:16; 15:20 ff.; Gal. 1:6-12; Eph. 1:7-14; 2:13,14; Phil. 2:5-11; 3:3,20; 1 Tim. 2:5; 6:3-12; 2 Tim. 1:7-14; 2:11-26; Heb. 1-4,10-12 *See also the papers entitled Are You Sure What You Believe is Truly Christian Doctrine, The Beauty and Finesse of the New Covenant, The Christian Epiphany, (the 3 part series) Christianity Versus Religion, Do You Truly Know and Believe the Complete Gospel of Jesus Christ, Fulfilment Prophecy, God's Kingdom is a Whole New World, (the 2 part series) How Should We Then Live, the Key to Understanding Scripture is Spiritual Exegesis, Looking Through the Lens of Jesus Christ, Major Missing Aspects of the Original Christian Gospel, Only One Savior, the Price of Living for Jesus, Principles of Fulfilment Theology, the Reality of God's Kingdom and Eternal Life, Regarding Christ's Headship, Retaining our Freedom requires Knowing and Applying the Truth and the Spiritual Laws of Revival*

[40] Matt. 6:9-13 *See also the paper The Spiritual Laws of Revival, Chapter 3, Law #11 and the writer's book Jesus' Way*

[41] *See the book Basic Christian Doctrine and* Gen. 1,2; Exodus 3,20; Deut. 4:32-42; 32:3,4,39; Josh. 24:14 ff.; 1 Sam. 2:1-10; Psa. 90, 121; Isa. 43-45; John 1:1-5; Acts 17:24-31

[42] Matt. 6:24; 10:32-40; 12:30; Mark 3:24-30; Luke 2:34; 11:17-23; 12:49-53; Acts 7:37 ff.; 13:21 ff.; 28:22; Rom. 8:1-11; Gal. 1:6-12; Eph. 6:12; Phil. 3:3,19-21; Heb. 12:1 ff. *See the papers Are You Sure What you believe is truly Christian Doctrine; the Beauty and Finesse of the New Covenant, Conditions for Salvation, Divergent Belief Systems, Examining the Original Imperatives of the Christian Gospel, Fallacies of Determinism and Living the Complete Gospel*

[43] Luke 10:22; Eph. 1:21,22; Phil. 2:5-11; 1 Tim. 2:5; Heb. 4:12-16; 9:9-15

[44] Matt. 4:8-10; Luke 4:5-8; Eph. 6:12

[45] Luke 10:18-23; 2 Cor. 10:3-6; Eph. 6:10-18

[46] Matt. 3:2; 4:17; 6:9-13; 12:30; 13: 10-17; 16:18-26; 19:13-26; Luke 12; John 3:36; 18:36,37; 1 Cor. 10:12-21; 2 Cor. 6:14-7:1; Phil. 3:20,21; Col. 1:13

[47] *Observing context, you should know that the word "Zealot" is another word for 'partisan' or 'patriot'*

[48] Matt. 5:43-48; 26:51,52; Luke 9:49-56; 21:8-19; John 18:36; James 3:13-4:8

[49] Matt. 6:24; John 3:36; 8:31-58; 10:27; 12:35-50; 14:27; 15:19; Rom. 12:1-3; 1 Cor. 2:1-16; 10:1 ff.; 2 Cor. 11:12-15; Gal. 6:14; Col. 2:6-3:10; 1 Tim. 2:5; 1 John 4:1-8; 5:4,5,19

[50] Ex. 20:1 f.; Josh. 2:1 ff; 24:14-21; 1 Sam. 2:5-9; 1 Knigs 18:21; Isa. 42-46; Jer. 5,7.10,17,18; Ezek. 18:30; 21:24-22:16; 28:1-19; Daniel 2,4,6,7,11; Matt. 24; Luke 16:13; 21;1 ff.; 2 Thess. 2; 2 Pet. 3; Jude 1

[51] Prov. 1:19; 15:27; 16:18; 22:7; 29:25; Isa. 8:9-20; 28:9-20; 29:9-16; 44:6-20; Jer. 10,17; Ezek. 21:25-27; 22:1 ff.; Matt. 16:26; 23:1 ff.; Mark 8:36; Luke 9:25; John 18:36; 2 Cor. 4:3-7; 10:3-7; 11:12-15; Eph. 6:1-12; Phil. 3:7-15; 1 Tim. 6:3-12; 2 Tim. 2:7-26; James 4:1-8; 1 John 2:15-17

[52] Compare 2 Chr. 7; Neh. 9; Jer. 2-18; Ezek. 3, 7-23,33-36 with Acts 20:25 ff.; Rev. 2,3 *See the papers entitled Emmanuel (1) and Emmanuel 2*

[53] Psa. 105; Luke 24:49; John 10:27; Acts 2:33-39; Rom. 4:13-20; 12:9-21; Gal. 3:14- 5:26* Cf. Matt. 5:17-20 *Notice that Gal. 3:19 says when the promised child, Jesus, came, the New Covenant became the rule of law for Christians*; See Eph. 1:13,14; 2:11-22; Heb. 6:13-20; 9:14,15; 10:19-39; 11:1 ff.; 12:26-29 *See also the book Jesus' Way, Chapter V, Sect. II*

[54] Matt. 5:38-48; 26:51,52; Mark 3:4; Rom. 8:1-11; 2 Cor. 4:3-7; 10:3-7; 11:12-15; Eph. 6:10-12

[55] Isa. 5:20; 8:20; Matt. 6:22-24; Luke 11:33-36; 16:13-15; John 1:4-9; 3:19-21; 8:12, 31-58; Gal. 1:6-12; 5:1-25; Eph. 2:13,14; 5:5-16; 1 Tim. 6:3-12; 2 Tim. 1-4; 1 John 1-5

[56] 1 Kings 18:21; Luke 11:33-36; John 1:1-18; Eph. 4; 1 Tim. 6:12 1 John 5:21

[57] Josh. 2; Dan. 3,6; Psa. 20:6,7; 46:1 ff.; 94:20; 95:6; 118:8,9; 146:1 ff.; Prov. 29:25; Song. 2:4; Isa. 42-46; Matt. 6:22-24; Luke 16:13; James 4:1-8;

1 John 2:15-17 *See also the papers entitled Authority and Conscience, the Basis of Liberty and True Liberty is in Christ Alone*

[58] Acts 5:29-32

[59] Song 2:4; Dan. 2:44,45; 4:24-27; 7:13-28; Matt. 4:1-10; 6:9-13, 22-24; Luke 4:1-8; 16:13; John 14:6-16:4; 18:36; 1 Cor. 13; Gal. 5:22,23; Eph. 6:10-12; Heb. 10:26-11:6; James 4

[60] Gen. 25:23-34; 27:1-40; Psa. 1,2,19,45,46, 110, 118, 146; Prov. 8; Jer. 31; Ezek. 36; Hosea 14:8,9; Zech. 4:6; Matt. 5-7; 26:41-52; Luke 2:34,35; 9:23-26, 49-56; 11:33-36; John 6:27-63; 8:12, 31-36; 18:36; Acts 2:38,39; 3:19; 4:12-20; 5:29-32; 7:48-60; 17:24-31; 20:28; 28:22; Rom. 1:16-32; 1 Cor. 1:17-2:16; 2 Cor. 4:3-7; 6:14-7:1; Gal. 1:6-12; Heb. 4,7-12

[61] See 1 Kings 18:21; Psa. 20,46,91, 94:20; 95:6; 118:8; Prov. 29:25; Dan. 2:44,45; 4:24-27; 7:13-28; Matt. 6:9-13; Luke 12:32; 19:12-15; 22:29; John 18:36; Phil. 3:20; Col. 1:13; Heb. 12:28; James 4:1-8; 1 John 2:15 17

[62] Mark 3:3,4

[63] Matt. 10:14; 16:21-26; 18:2-10; 19:13,14; Mark 10:13-16; Luke 9:23-26; 18:16,17

[64] Matt. 13:10-15, 37-46,52; Rom. 8:1-11

[65] John 1:12-18; 8:12, 31-36, 39-47; 14:6; 16:13-15; 18:36,37; Rom. 1:16-32; 2:7-11; 2 Cor. 4:1-7; Gal. 1:6-12; 2:1-6; 3:1-7; 4:1-19; Eph. 4:1-16; 6:10-14; 2 Thess. 2:3-13; 1 Tim. 2:4,5; 6:3-12; 2 Tim. 2:15-26; 3:7-9; 4:1-8; Heb. 10:26-39

[66] Luke 24:49; Acts 2:33-39; 3:19; Rom. 4:13-20; 2 Cor. 1:20; Gal. 3:14-29; 4:28; Eph. 1:13; 2:12-14; 3:6-13; Heb.6:12-17; 9:11-15; 10:36-39; 2 Pet. 1:4

[67] Matt. 6:9-13, 22-24; Luke 11:33-36; 16:13; John 18:36,37; Acts 5:29-32; Rom. 1:16- 32; 2 Cor. 4:3-7; 11:12-15; 2 Thess. 2:3-12

[68] Matt. 5-7; Luke 6-12; John 1-21; Rom. 8; James 1:5-8; 4:1-8; 1 John 2:15-17; Rev. 2:1-7; 3:14-22

[69] Gen. 15:6; Ex. 3-15; Deut. 4,7,8,11,12; Josh. 2,24; Ruth 1:16-18; 1 Sam. 2:1-10; 1 Chr. 17; 2 Chr. 7; Neh. 9; Various Psalms; Isa. 2,4,6,12, 28-30, 42-46; Jer. 2-18, 31; Ezek. 3,18,33-36; Dan. 2,3,6; Mark 3:4; Luke 6-12; John 5:24-30; 6:27-63; 7:15-18; 8:12,31-58; 10:1-16; 11:25,26; 1 Cor. 1:17-2:16; Gal. 1:6-12; 2:16-4:19; Eph. 1-4; Phil. 1-4; Col. 1-3; 1 Tim. 2:4,5; 6:3-12; 2 Tim. 1:7-2:26; Heb. 1-12

[70] Psa. 2,110; Isa. 42-46, 53; Matt. 5:38-48; 6:9-13; 17:5,6; John 8:12, 31-36; 18:36,37; Phil. 3:20; 1 Tim. 2:5; 2 Tim. 1:7-4:18

[71] Matt. 5:38-48; 6:9-13, 22-24; 26:47-54; Mark 3:4; Luke 2:34,35,49; 9:49-56; 11:33- 36; 16:13; John 1:1-18; 3:3-36; 4:14-24; 6:27-63; 7:15-18; 8:31-36; 9:39-41; 10:1-16; 14:6- 17:26; 18:36,37; Acts 4:12-20; 5:29-32; 7:48-59; 17:24-31; 20:26-38; 26:12-18; 28:22; Rom. 1:16-32; 12:9-21; Gal. 1:6-12; 2:16-4:19; Eph. 2:13,14; Phil. 3:3,20; Col. 1:13-16; 2 Thess. 2:3- 12; Heb. 11:12-16 *See also the papers entitled (the 2 part series) Authority and Conscience, The Christian Epiphany, (the 3 part series) Christianity Versus Religion, Divergent Belief Systems, Do You Truly Know and Believe the Complete Gospel of Jesus Christ, Every Believer can Independently know the Truth of Scripture, God's Kingdom is a Whole New World, the 'Higher Laws of God' that unify both Scripture and Doctrine, (the 2 part series) How should we then live, the Kingdom of Heaven is the Highest form of Civilization, Looking Through the Lens of Jesus Christ, Major Missing Aspects of the Original Christian Gospel, One Covenant for All, the Price of Living for Jesus, Principles of Fulfilment Theology, Psychotic Hypocrisy, Serious Problems in Doctrine and practice still exist in many modern churches and True Liberty is in Christ Alone*

[72] John 2:19-22; Acts 7:48; 17:24-31; 2 Cor. 6:14-7:1

[73] 1 Sam. 15:22,23; 1 Kings 18:21; Psa. 96:5; 106:7 ff.; 115:1 ff.; Isa. 2:1 ff.; 44:6-20; 45:15-23; 46:1,2; 56:9-57:13; Jer. 7:1 ff.; 10:1-10; 17:5-10; Ezek. 6:4,5,13; 14:3-7; 18:30-32; 21:24-27; 22:1 ff.; 23:37-39; 33:10-30; 36:16-32; 37:20-24; Hos. 4:17; 14:8,9; Mic. 3:1 ff.; Zech. 13:1-9; 1 Cor. 10:14-21; Gal. 5:20; 1 John 5:21

[74] Ex. 20:14; Deut. 5:18; Jer. 3:8,9; 7:1-11; 13:27; 23:9-14; Ezek. 16:15 ff.; Matt. 5:27; 15:19; 19:18; Gal. 5:19; 2 Pet. 2:14

[75] Matt. 5:38-48; Rom. 5:1-5

[76] Ezek. 20-23, 28-32; Dan. 2:44,45; Luke 24:44-49; Acts 17:24-31; 2 Thess. 2:3-12; 2 Pet. 3:7; Rev. 11:15-19

[77] Matt. 5-7; Luke 6-12, 15

[78] Psa. 84:4; Dan. 2:44,45; 7:15-27; Matt. 6:9-13; Heb. 12:28; Rev. 11:15 f.

[79] Eccl. 3:11; John 8:31-36; 11:25,26; Acts 4:12; Rom. 8:1,2; 1 Cor. 2:9-16; 2 Cor. 3:17,18

[80] Neh. 8:10

[81] See Matt. 24; Luke 21; 1 Cor. 10 *See also the book Spiritual Guidelines for Restoration, "Historical Review" Section and the papers entitled Emmanuel (1), Emmanuel 2*

[82] Rom. 15:4; 1 Cor. 10

[83] Ex. 32:9; 33:3; Deut. 9:13; 10:16; 2 Chr. 7:14; 30:8; Neh. 9; Matt. 23; John 9:39-41; Acts 7:48-60 Also, Ibid. Fn. #81 *and the paper entitled the Fallacies of Determinism*

[84] Matt. 5-7; Luke 6-12 *See also the papers entitled A Writer's Commentary, An Analysis of the Causes and Effects of Apostasy, Are You Sure what you Believe and Practice is Truly Christian Doctrine, Authority and Conscience (a 2 part series), Christianity Versus Religion (a 3 part series), Conditions for Salvation, the Dangers of Conformity, Divergent Belief Systems, Every believer can independently know the truth of Scripture, the Fallacies of Determinism, God's Definition of Salvation, God's Universal Attitude Test, Only One Savior, Regarding Christ's Headship, A Synopsis of Modern Idolatry among 'professing Christians' and What is Collectivism*

[85] Psa. 49; 119:105,130; Isa. 8:20; 9:1,2,6,7; Luke 1:76-79; 11:33-36; John 1:4,5,7-9; 3:19-21 (Isa. 5:20); 8:12, 31-36; 9:5, 39-41; 12:30-36,46; 18:36,37; Rom. 13:12; 2 Cor. 3:17,18; 4:4-6; Eph. 2:13,14; 5:8; Phil. 3:20; Col. 1:12-16; 2 Tim. 1:7-14; Heb. 11:12-16; 1 Pet. 2:9; 2 Pet. 1:19; 1 John 1:5-10; 2 :9-11,15-17; 3:11-17; 4:7-21

[86] Ex. 6:6,7; 14:13,14; Psa. 94:20; 118:8,9; 146:3; Prov. 3:5,6; Isa. 36,37; Jer. 7:4 f.; 10:1 ff.; 17:5-10; Matt. 5:1-12, 38-48; 6:9-15; Luke 1:75-79; John 8:31-36; 2 Cor. 3:17,18; Col. 1:13

[87] Eccl. 7:20; Prov. 28:13; Ezek. 18:30; Mark 1:15; Acts 2:38,39; 3:19; 17:24-31; 26:15- 18; Rom. 6:1-7:25

[88] *See the papers entitled The Christian Epiphany, Conditions for Salvation, The Conditions of God's Protection for Believers, God's Definition of Salvation and True Liberty is in Christ Alone*

[89] Matt. 5-7; 22:36,37; John 4:14-24 *See also the papers entitled The Dynamics of Christian Discipleship, The Higher Laws of God, The Spiritual Laws of Revival and Spirituality and Worship: A Study of Worship*

[90] Job 28:28; Psa. 2:1 ff.; 110:1 ff.; 111:10; Prov. 1:7: 9:9,10; Eccl. 12:13,14; Isa. 33:6; 42:1-46:13; Jer. 7:4 ff.; 10:1-0; 17:5-10; Mal. 2-4; Matt. 10:16-42; Luke 2:34,35; John 18:36,37; Acts 28:22; Rom. 1:18-32; 8:1 ff.; 1 Cor. 3:11-17; 11:23-32; 2 Cor. 11:12-15; Gal. 1:6-12; Phil. 3:3,20,21; Heb. 10-12

⁹¹ Matt. 4:1-10; Luke 4:1-8; Acts 5:29-32; Eph. 6:10-12; Col. 1:15,16; Rev. 13:1 ff. *See the 2 part series of papers entitled Authority and Conscience*

⁹² Josh. 2; Dan. 3,6; Acts 4:12-20; 5:29-32; Eph. 1:15-23; 6:10-18; Heb. 11:24-31

⁹³ Lev. 19:2; 20:7,26; Numbers 23:9,10; Deut. 7:6; 14:2,21; Josh. 24:14-19; 1 Sam. 2:5- 10; 1 Kings 18:21; Psa. 2:6; Isa. 6, 43-46; Matt. 4:1-10; 16:21-26; Mark 8:34-38; Luke 9:23-26, 49-56; John 8:12-58; 9:39- 10:18, 27,28; 12:23-36; 14:15-27; 15:1-16:4; 17:3 ff.; 18:36,37

⁹⁴ 1 Kings 18:21; Matt. 6:24; Luke 16:13; John 18:36,37; Rom. 12:1-3; Gal. 6:14-16

⁹⁵ Psa. 3:8; 4:8; 9:9,10; 37:1 ff.; 44:1 ff.; 46:1 ff.; 91:1 ff.; 94:20; 111:10; 115:1 ff.; 118:8,9; 146:1 ff.; Prov. 3:5,6; 14:12, 26; 16:25; 29:25; Matt. 19:16-42; 16:23-26

⁹⁶ Matt. 4:1-10; Mark 8:36; Luke 4:1-8; John 15:18-16:4; 17:5-16; 18:36,37; Rom. 12:1- 3; 1 Cor. 1:17-2:16; 3:18,19; 2 Cor. 4:3-6; Gal. 1:4,6-12; 4:3,4-16; 6:14; Eph. 6:11,12; Col. 2:6- 23; 2 Thess. 2:3-12; Heb. 10:26- 12:29; James 4:4; 2 Pet. 2,3; 1 John 2-5

⁹⁷ *See the two part series of papers entitled Authority and Conscience," the 3 part series Christianity Versus Religion and The Fallacies of Determinism*

⁹⁸ Psa. 3:8; 4:8; 9:9,10; 83:11; 94:20; 118:8,9; Prov. 29:25; Isa. 43-46; Matt. 4:1-10; 10:16-42; 12:30; Luke 4:1-8; 11:33-36; John 8:31-36; 18:36,37; 2 Cor. 3:17,18; Gal. 4:4-9,16; 1 John 5:18-21 *See also the papers entitled A Biblical Disclosure of Antichrist, the Basis of Liberty, the 4 part series Christian Guidelines for Spiritual Warfare, the Dangers of Conformity, Destiny and Free Will, Divergent Belief Systems, Do you Truly Believe that God is Real, Examining the Original Imperatives of the Christian Gospel, From Whence do Lies come, God's Universal Attitude Test, the 2 part series How Should We Then Live, Living the Complete Gospel, Looking Through the Lens of Jesus Christ, One Covenant for All, Principles of Fulfillment Theology, Retaining our Freedom requires Knowing and Applying the Truth, True Liberty is in Christ Alone and What is Collectivism*

⁹⁹ Num. 23:9; Josh. 2:1-7,14-18; Daniel 3,6; Matt. 4:1-10; 6:9-13; Luke 4:1- 8; John 18:36,37; Acts 4:12-20; 5:29-32; 2 Cor. 4:3-7; 10:3-7; Phil. 3:3,20,21; Col. 1:13-16; Heb. 11:13-16,24-31; James 1:5-8; 4:1-9; 1 John 2:15-17

¹⁰⁰ Jer. 2:1-13; 10:1-10; 17:5-10; Ezek. 7:1-12,19; 14:3-7; 18:30; 20:13 ff.; 21:24-27; 23:37-39; Hos.10:12,13; Mal. 2; Matt. 10:32,33; 11:28-30; 12:30; 23:1 ff.; Mark 3:3,4; Luke 11:33-36; 12:8-10; Rom. 8:1-11; 2

Thess. 2:3-12; Rev. 2:1-7, 12-3:6; 3:14-22 *See the papers Destiny and Free Will, Fallacies of Determinism and the 2 part series How Should We then Live?*

[101] Numbers 13,14; Prov. 10:29; 19:23; 28:18; 29:25; 30:5; Hosea 14:9; Matt. 6:22-24; 10:16-39; Luke 11:33-36; John 1:1-18; 8:12; 12:35,36, 46; Rom. 13:12; 1 Cor. 4:5; 2 Cor. 4:3-6; Col. 1:12,13; Heb. 10-12; 1 John 1

[102] Matt. 16:21-26; Luke 9:23-26; John 12:23-26; Acts 3:19

[103] Gen. 4; Psa. 32, 51; Matt. 5:38-48; 6:22-24; Luke 6:35-49; 9:51-56; 11:33-36; John 5:19-47; 7:24; 8:31-58; 9:39-41; 14:6-17:26; 18:36,37; Rom. 8:1 ff; Gal. 1:6-12; 2:16-21; 3:11- 4:20; 5:1, 14-26; 6:14-16; Phil. 3:3,7-21; 1 Tim. 6:3-16; 2 Tim. 1:7-14; Heb. 10:26-39; 1 John 3:7-15 *See also the paper entitled The Nature of Man and the book Basic Christian Doctrine*

[104] Ex. 6:6,7; 14:13,14; Deut. 3:22; 4:10; 5:29; 6:2-13,24; 10:12,20; 1 Sam. 2:1-10; 25:29; Psa. 1-5,9,17,20,23,31,34,37,44,46,51, 73,84, 111, 115, 118; Prov. 1:7; 2:5; 3:7; 9:10; 10:27; 14:26,27; 15:33; 16:6; 19:23; 29:25; Isa. 33:6; Matt. 5:38-48; 11:25-30; John 3:36; 8:31-58; 18:36,37; Acts 2:38,39; 3:19; Rom. 8:1-11; 12:1 ff.; 2 Cor. 3:17,18; 4:3-7; 10:14-18; 11:12-15; Gal. 5:1; Eph. 6:10-12

[105] John 15:1-17; 21:15-17; Rom. 5:1-5; Gal. 5:22,23; 1 John 4:7 ff.

[106] John 6:27-63; Rom. 12:9-21; 2 Cor. 10:3-7

[107] Luke 2:34,35; John 7:1-24; Rom. 8:1-11; Gal. 1:6-12; 2:19-5:13; Heb. 4:12,13 *See the paper entitled The Spiritual Laws of Revival, Ch. 2, Law #8: "The separation of the soul from the spirit"*

[108] Prov. 22:7 *See also the papers entitled True Liberty is in Christ Alone and What is Collectivism?*

[109] John 8:31-36; 14:6; Gal. 1:6-12; Eph. 4:4

[110] Matt. 4:1-10; Luke 4:1-8; 13:32; John 8:12-47; Acts 4:12-20; 5:29-32; Rom. *13:1 (*always know that God is the "Higher Power"); Eph. 6:10-12; 2 Cor. 3:1-4:7; 6:14-18; 10:3-7; 11:12-15; Gal. 1:6-12; Col. 1:15,16

[111] Psa. 3:8; 4:8; 9:9,10; 20:6,7; 27:1-3; 31:1 ff.; 32:7; 34:1 ff.; 37:1 ff.; 40:4; 41:1,2; 43:1-44: 46:1 ff.; 51:1 ff.; 56:4,11,13; 61:1-3; 84:1 ff; 91:1 ff.; 94:20; 115:9-11; 118:8,9; 146:1 ff. ; Prov. 3:5,6; Dan. 3,6; Jer. 5:1-9; 17:5-10; 18:6-12; Matt. 5:38-48; 6:9-15; 23:1 ff.; John 18:36,37; Acts 5:29-32; Rom. 12:9-21; 2 Cor. 6:14-18; 10:3-7; Eph. 6:10-12; 1 John 3:10-15

112 Ex. 6:6,7; 14:13,14; Deut. 4:32-40; 32:3,4,38,39; 1 Sam. 2:1-10; 25:29; 1 Kings 18:21; 2 Chron. 7:14; Job 28:28; Prov. 1:7; 9:10; 29:25; Isa. 33:6; 36-38

113 Psa. 44:1-8 *(notice also that, in the *New Covenant* God has translated the venue of war to spiritual warfare);* 94:20; 118:8,9; 146:1 ff.; Prov. 29:25; Isa. 42-46; Jer. 7:4-14; 10:1- 10; 17:5-10; Zech. 4:6

114 1 Kings 18:21; Zech. 4:6; Matt. 5:38-48; Luke 9:51-56; 11:33-36; 13:32; Acts 5:29- 32; 1 John 1:5-2:17

115 Matt. 21:22; Luke 1:34-37, 78,79; John 5:24; 8:47; Rom. 8:1 ff.; Phil. 2:5-11; 1 Tim. 2:5; Heb. 4:12,13

116 Matt. 5-7; Luke 6-12; Rom. 5:1-5; 8:1-18; Gal. 5:13-26; Eph. 2:1ff.

117 1 Sam. 2:1-10; 2 Sam. 22:33; Jer. 4:22; 5:1-5; 6:16,17; 18:12; Matt. 5:38-48; 10:16- 42; 26:51,52; Luke 6:20 ff.; 9:51-56; 11:33-36; John 18:36,37; Rom. 5:1-5; 8:1 ff.; 1 Cor. 1:17- 2:16; 2 Cor. 3:17,18; Phil. 1:21; 3:3,20,21; 1 Pet. 1:3-25; 2:21-25; 1 John 1-5

118 Eph. 6:7; James 1:5-8

119 Matt. 17:20; 19:26; Mark 10:27; Luke 18:27; *Heb. 6:4; 1 Pet. 3:15

120 Ex. 15:11; 1 Sam. 2:9; Psa. 5:14,15,23; 9:9,10; 23:1 ff.; 76:11; Isa. 35:4; Matt. 6:22-24; Luke 16:13-15; Eph. 2:13,14

121 Rom. 12:1-3

122 Matt. 5:8; 22:36,37; Rev. 22:1

123 Phil. 3:7-15; Heb. 7:11-10:23; Rev. 3:20 *See also the book Spiritual Guidelines for Restoration, "Historical Review" Section*

124 *See the paper The Higher Laws of God*

125 Matt. 24:13

Chapter 8:

132 *See the paper entitled Obedience to Christ*

133 Eph. 1:9–23; Col. 1:12–29

134 Mat. 5:3–7:29; 25:1 ff.; 28:18–20; Luke 6:46–49; 10:16–28; John 5:19–30; 13:34,35; 14:6–24; 15:10–17; Rom. 14:10; 1 Cor. 4:4,5; 2 Cor. 5:10 *See also the paper: "Jesus' Major Parables"*

135 Matt. 4:17–20; 8:19–22; 9:9; 16:21–26; Mark 1:14–17; 2:14 f.; 8:31–38; Luke 5:27 f.; 9:23–26, 51–62; 18:22

136 John 16:13–15; John 14:15-26

137 Matt. 11:25–30; Luke 11:1–13; John 3:3 ff.; 15:1–7; 17:7–15; Acts 4:10–20; 5:29–32; Rom. 8:1 ff.; Gal. 5:1–10; Phil. 2:5–11; 3:8–16; Col. 1:12–29; 2 Tim. 2–4

138 Matt. 5–7; Luke 6,12; 21:19; Rom. 12:9–21; 1 Tim. 4:7; 2 Tim. 2:1 ff.; Rev. 12;10,11; 14:12,13

139 Matt. 10:16–42; 16:21–28; Luke 9:23–26; 14:26–33; John 12:23–26; 2 Cor. 4:1– 18; Gal. 2:16–21; 6:12–14

140 Matt. 6:9-13; John 4:23,24; Rom. 6:1–8:15; 12:1 ff.; 1 Cor. 12–14; 2 Cor. 3:17– 4:18; Eph. 1–6

141 Matt. 10:16–39; 24:13; Mark 2:21,22; Luke 14:26–33; John 12:23–26; 13:3-38; 15:18–16:4; Phil. 2:5–3:21; Col. 1:10–29; 2 Tim. 2:1 ff. 1 Pet. 4:1 ff.

142 Matt. 16:18; 18:18–20; 20:20–28 *See also the paper: "What is the Body of Christ" See also the paper 'Basics of Biblical Church Governance'

143 Matt 5:38–48; Luke 9:51–56; John 15:1 ff.; Rom. 8:1 ff.; 12:19–21; 1 Cor. 13; 2 Cor. 4:4–6; 1 John 2–4; Rev 12: 19-21. See also Appendix E entry: *the patience of the saints*, viz., *faith-based pacifism*

Chapter 9:

144 Matt. 7:13–21; Rom. 1:18 ff.; 2 Cor. 11:1 ff.; 1 Tim. 1:18-20; 4:2; Jude 3–19. See Glossary of Terms' entry *casuistry*

145 John 7:24

146 Matt. 3:8; 7:13–21; 12:33–37; 25:14 ff.; Luke 3:8; John 7:7; 8:34–47; 10:25–30, 36–38; 9:4; 14:9–12; 15:24; Gal. 5:19–23; Eph. 5:1–21.

147 2 Cor. 4:1

148 Luke 12:15; 16:15; 1 Tim. 4:1,2; 2 Tim. 3:1–9.

149 Matt. 10:16–42; 16:21–26; Luke 9:23–26; 14:26–33; Rom. 1:18–2:16.

150 Ezek. 3,11, 18, 33, 34

151 Matt. 13; 15:6 14; 16:21–26; Rom. 8:1–11; 12:1–3; 1 Cor. 2:9–16; 1 John 1:1-10; 3:5–9.

152 John 5:6; Acts 9:34; Rom. 8:1 ff.; 12:1–3; Eph. 4:23,24; 1 Thess. 5:23. See also the papers entitled "the Higher Laws of God" and "The Spiritual Laws of Revival" and the book The Spiritual Man by Watchman Nee, Christian Fellowship Publishers, Inc., NY, 1977

153 John 4:23,24; Rom. 6:1 ff. 12:1–3

[154] Genesis 1:26,27; 2:7.

[155] Ibid footnotes 9–11 and Matt. 22:37; Luke 10:27; 1 Cor. 6:15–20; 1 Thess. 5:23; 2 Pet 1:3,4

[156] John 15:1–6; Rom. 1:16–2:15; 1 Cor. 9:24–27; Heb. 2:1–3; 3:6–4:16; 6:1–15; 9:11–15; 10:26–39; James 1:1 ff.; 2 Pet. 3:9. *See also the papers entitled "Conditions for Salvation, Destiny and Free Will," "The Fallacies of Determinism," "God's Definition of Salvation," and "The Spiritual Laws of Revival"*

[157] John 9:39–41; 1 Tim. 4:1,2; Titus 1:15,16 Cf. Ezek. 3,18, 33

[158] Acts 2:38,39; 3:19

Chapter 10:

[1] Matt. 13; 2 Cor. 5:14-21 *See also the author's book Jesus' Way, Chapter XI, "The New Covenant," Section Three: "Consider The Deeper Meaning of Atonement"*

[2] Matt. 11:25-30; 28:28; Mark 10:15; Luke 10:21-24; John 14:6; John 1:1-5, 10-18; 4:23,24; 5:22-27; 6:27-63; 8:31-36; 10:25-28; 11:25,26; 12:23-26; 14:6, 15-26; 15:26; 16:13-15; 17:14-24; 18:36; 2 Pet. 2:22; 1 John 5:3

[3] Psa. 23,46,91; Matt. 6:33 *(and many others!)*

[4] Isa. 1, 5,6; 28:9-20; 29:13-16; 30:9-22; 42:18-25; 44:6-20 48:17,18; 56:9-57:13; 59:1-18; 65:1-15; Jer. 5:5; 6:16; 8:8,9; 18:12; Ezek. 3,18,33,34; Hosea 1-14; Matt. 4:1-10; 13:1-30;16:23-26; 23:1 ff.; Luke 4:1-8; John 8:23; 14:27; 15:18-16:4,33; 18:36; Rom. 1:18 ff.; 1 Cor.1:17-2:16; 10:1-23; 2 Cor. 4:1-5:21; Gal. 4:1-5:4; 6:7-16; Phil. 2:5-16; Col. 2:6-12,18-23;Heb. 11; James 1:27; 3:13-4:8; 1 John 2:15-17 *See also Glossary of Terms' entry *(the Doctrine of) Sanctification* and the book Jesus' Way, Chapter XIX: "Knowing the Difference between the Church and the World"*

[5] Ex. 20:1-7; 1 Sam. 2:1-10; 1 Kings 18:21; Psa. 2:1 ff.; 3:8; 4:8; 20:6,7; 94:20; 115:1 ff.;118:8,9; Prov. 29:25; Isa. 2:8-20; 8:9-20; 28:9-20; 29:9-30:21; 44:6-46:13; Jer. 10:1-11; 17:1- 10; Ezek. 23:37-39; 33:1-36:38; Hos. 14:9; Matt. 27:15-26; John 18:36,37; 19:11-15; Acts 5:29-32; Rom. 1:16-32; 1 Cor. 10:1-22; 2 Cor. 10:3-7; Gal. 5:1; 6:14-16; Eph. 2:13,14; 6:10-12; Col. 1:12-3:15; 2 Thess. 2:3-12; 1 Tim. 6:3-12; 2 Tim. 1:7-15; 2:11 ff.; Heb. 10-12; James 4:1-8; 1 John 1-5

[6] Psa. 16:11; 23:1-6; 27:1-4, 11-14; 32:6,7; 33:4; 34:4 ff.; 36:9; 37:3-5, 18-31

[7] 2 Cor. 1:20

[8] John 6:45; 8:31-58; 9:17-41; 14:6-26; 18:36,37; Rom. 1:18-32; 2 Thess. 2:3-12

[9] Matt. 5:43-48; 10:26-39; 23:1 ff.; Luke 8:18; 11:33-36; 12:49-59; 14:25-33; 16:13-15; 19:26; John 8:21-47; Rom. 8:1-11; 2 Thess. 2:3-12; 1 Tim. 4:2; James 2:10; 1 John 3:15

[10] Rom. 8; Phil. 1:21

[11] Matt. 5:43-48; John 13:34,35; 1 John 3,4

[12] Matt. 17:20; 19:26; Mark 10:27; Luke 1:37; 18:27; 12:8-12: 21:8-19; John 14:12; Rom. 7:1-4; 8:1 ff.; 12:9-20; 2 Cor. 1:20; 5:6-21; 10:3-6; 12:9,10; Gal. 1:6-12; 2:19-21; 6:14; Eph. 2:13-16; 6:12-18; Phil. 1:21; 2:5-13; 3:7-14; Col. 1:12-29; 2:9,10; 2 Tim. 1:7-12; 2:3-13; Heb. 2:14,15; 4:6-16; 9:11-15, 27; 10:16-39; 12:1 ff.; James 1:5-8, 16-25; 3:13-18; 5:13-18; 1 Pet. 1:3-19; 4:12-19; 2 Pet. 1:1 ff.; 1 John 1:5-2:17; 4:4; 4:7-5:15 See also Footnote #1

[13] 2 Chr. 15:15; Psa. 119:10; Prov. 10:9,29; Hosea 14:9; John 4:23,24

[14] Gal. 1:6-12 *See also the paper entitled The Fallacies of Determinism*

[15] Mark 11:22,23; Rom. 8:26,27; 1 John 5:14,15

[16] Jer. 4:4; Hosea 10:12; Matt. 13; Mark 4; Luke 8

[17] 1 Chr. 16:29; Psa. 29:2; 30:4; 89:34,35; 96:9; 97:11,12; 110:3; Isa. 35:3-10; 63:9-19; Jer. 2,23,31; Mal. 2; Luke 1:67-79; Rom. 1:4; 6:19-22; 2 Cor. 7:1; Eph. 4:24; 1 Thess. 3:12,13; Heb. 2:10-14; 10:26-39; 12:1 ff.; 1 Pet. 13-19

[18] Psa. 1, 19, 23, 27, 34, 37, 40, 42, 45, 46, 50, 51, 56, 61-63, 73, 84, 91, 97, 103, 112, 115, 118, 119, 121, 139, 146; Isa. 32:17,18; 40:28-31; Matt. 11:25-30; John 13:34-17:26; Hebrews 4

[19] Isa. 8:9-20; 28:12-30:21; Matt. 7:13-23; 28:18; John 18:36,37; 1 Cor. 12:12,13; Phil. 3:20,21; 2 Tim. 2:3-12; 1 Pet. 3:15; 1 John 2:15-17

[20] Psa. 119:65-72; John 15:18-27; Acts 5:29-42; Rom. 8:17 ff.; 1 Cor. 10:12,13; 2 Cor. 1:1-11; 4:1-5:21; 7:9,10; Gal. 6:14; 2 Tim. 1:7-14; 2:3-12; 3:12; Heb. 10:26-39; 11:25; 12:1-29; 1 Pet. 4:1-19; 5:6-11; James 5:10,11 *See also Glossary of Terms' entry *Affliction* and the paper entitled The Indispensability of Affliction*

²¹ 1 Kings 18:21; 2 Chr. 20:19,20; Psa. 23, 24, 27, 31-42; Matt. 11:25-30; Heb. 4:9-16

²² Psa. 1,2; 37:3-5; 23,24; John 14-17; Phil. 1:6,21; Heb. 13:15; 1 John 2:15-17

²³ Isa. 26:3,4; 40:28-31; Phil. 3:7-14

²⁴ Psa. 2,110; Isa. 44-46; Jer. 10,17; John 2:19-21; 3:16,17; 11:25-52; 12:23 f; Rom. 1:18-32; 1 John 2:1-6 *See also the paper entitled True Liberty is in Christ Alone, especially Sect. II-B, which contains the list of "SOLA's," those benefits which come from Christ Alone*

²⁵ 1 Kings 18:21; Psa. 94:1 ff.; 110:1 ff.; 118:8,9; Isa. 43-46; Jer. 10,17; Ezek. 18:30-32; Matt. 28:18; John 14:6; 8:31-36; Acts 17:24-31; Rom. 1

²⁶ Matt. 6:9-15; John 3:3-8,16,17; 6:27-63; 2 Cor. 4:3-6; 10:2-6; Eph. 6:10-18

²⁷ Matt. 28:18; Luke 10:21-24; John 18:36,37; Phil. 3:20,21

²⁸ *See the papers entitled (the 2 part series) Authority and Conscience, (the 3 part series) Christianity Versus Religion and Regarding Christ's Headship*

²⁹ John 1:1-14; 14:1; Heb. 11:1-6

³⁰ John 14:6; Heb. 6:15-20; 1 Pet. 2:22

³¹ Luke 11:33-36; Acts 2:38,39; 3:19; Rom. 1:18-32; Gal. 1:6-12; Eph. 6:12; 2 Thess. 1,2; Heb. 7:11-10:23; 2 Pet. 1:2-21; Rev. 13,17 *See also the 4 part series of papers entitled Christian Guidelines for Spiritual Warfare and the book Spiritual Guidelines for Restoration, "Historical Review section"*

³² Matt. 5:43-48; 6:9-15, 22-24; 10:22-39; Luke 9:51-56; 12:8-10; John 8:12-58; 18:36,37; Rom. 12:9-21; 1 Cor. 13; 2:Cor. 10:3-6; 11:12-15; Eph. 6:10-18; 2 Thess. 2:3-12; 2 Tim. 2:11-13

³³ Luke 2:33-35; 21:8-24; Acts 2, 7; Heb. 4:12,13

³⁴ Rom. 12:1-3; Eph. 4:23,24

³⁵ Matt. 6:22; Luke 8:16-18; 11:33-36; John 1:1-18; 3:21; 6:27-63; Acts 26:12-18; Rom. 13:12; 2 Cor. 4:3-6; 5:14-21;10:3-6; Eph. 5:1-20; Col. 1:12,13; 2 Tim. 1:7-15; 2 Pet. 1:12-21

³⁶ Heb. 10:32; 11:24-28; 12:1-14

³⁷ Matt. 4:16; 5-7; 10:16-39; Luke 1:67-2:14; 9:23-26; John 8:31-47; 9:39-41; 12:23-26;14:15-16:33

³⁸ Luke 2:34,35; 6:22 ff.; John 3:19-21, 27-36; 15:18-25; 18:36,37; Acts 28:22; Rom. 1:18-2:16; 2 Cor. 4:2-6; 10:3-6; 11:10-15; 13:5-8; Gal.

1:6-12; 3:1; 4:16; Eph. 4:15-5:20; 6:14; 2 Thess. 2:3-12; 1 Tim. 2:5-7; 6:3-12; 2 Tim. 2:15-26; 3:1-8; 4:1-4; Heb. 10:26-39;; 2 Pet. 2:1-3

[39] Isa. 50:7; 54:17; 59:19; Acts 2:14-41; 7:1-60; 17:24-31; 2 Cor. 10:3-6

[40] Matt. 5:43-48; Rom. 12:9-21; Eph. 6:10-18

[41] John 10:25-30; 17:10-26; Acts 26:12-18; 2 Tim. 2:19-26; Heb. 2:9-15; 10:9-39; 12:1-17; 1 Pet. 1:3-2:10; 1 John 3:3 *See also the 4 part series of papers Christian Guidelines for Spiritual Warfare and Glossary of Terms' entry *(the Doctrine of) Sanctification* *

[42] 1 Sam. 2:6-9; Zech. 4:6; 1 Cor. 10:1-21

[43] 2 Tim. 1:7 f.; 1 Pet. 5:8

[44] John 5:24; Rom. 10:17; Heb. 11:6

[45] Rom. 12:19-21

[46] Matt. 6:14,15

[47] 1 Cor. 6:9-11, 16-20; Gal. 5:19-21

[48] Phil. 3:17-21

[49] James 4:1-8; 1 John 2:15-17

[50] Gal. 5:21 *(translated as 'witchcraft' in KJV)*

[51] Luke 2:34,35; Heb. 4:12,13 *See the paper The Spiritual Laws of Revival, Law #8: "the separation of soul from spirit"*

[52] Psa. 94:20; 115:11; 118:1-9; Prov. 29:25; Jer. 10,17; Matt. 6:22-24, 33; 10:26 39

[53] 2 Cor. 3:17,18

[54] Exodus 20:3; 1 Kings 18:21; Psa. 19, 119; Isa. 44:6-20; Jer. 10:1-15; 17:5-15; Matt. 4:10; 6:1-13, John 4:23,24; Acts 17:22-31; Rom. 1:16-2:16; James 1:5-8

[55] Psa. 94:20; 118:8,9; Dan. 3,6; Matt. 22:21; Acts 4:12-20; 5:29-32 *See also the 2 part series of papers entitled Authority and Conscience and Authority & Conscience Part Two: God has established a "Framework of Order"*

[56] John 7:16-39; 8:12-58;9:39-10:18; 13:35-17:26; Rom. 8:1-11; 1 Cor. 1:17-2:16; Heb. 8:6-12; Rev. 19:10-13

[57] Exodus 6:6,7; 14:13,14; *15:26; *Deut. 1:28,30; 3:22; 4:32-39; 7:15; 1 Sam. 2:6-10;*2 Chr. 7:14; 20:20; Psa. 5:11,12; 16:1 ff.; 18:2,6,16,17, 30,31, 46-49; 23:1 ff.; 25:1-12; 27:1 ff.; 31:1-15, 23,24; 32:6-8; 33:4, 18,19; 34:4 ff.; 37:3-5, 18,19, 23-25; 40:1-4; 41:1,2; 42:8; 44:1-8;

46:1 ff.; 50:14,15,23; 54:1 ff.; 59:16; 61:1 ff.; 62:1-8; 73:16,17, 24-28; 80:7; 84:11; *91:1 ff.;97:10,11; *103:1-5; *115:1 ff.; 116:6; *118:1-9; 121:1,2; 145:19,20; Prov. 2:8; 10:29; 12:28;19:23; 29:25; 30:5; Isa. 28:12-16; 29:9-30:21; 33:2-6; 42-46; 50:4-754:17; 59:19;*Matt. 8:1-4; 4:23,24; 9:20-30,35; 10:1; 14:35; *Mark 1:40-42; *16:15-18; *Luke 5:12-15; 6:17; 9:1; John 5:4; *Acts 28:1-6

58 Matt. 5:43-48; John 18:36; 1 John 3,4; Rev. 13,17

59 Matt. 24; Luke 21; 2 Thess. 2:3-12; 1 Tim. 3; 2 Tim. 2

60 Psa. 119:89; John 1:1; 14:21-26; 15:26; 16:11-15; 17:17

61 Jer. 30:7; Ezek. 5:9; Dan. 12:1; Matt. 24:21,22; Mark 13:19,20; Rom. 1:18-32;2 Thess. 2:3-12

62 *This reference is found in Gal. 5:20 with 'witchcraft' being the English translation of the Greek word Pharmakeia, which is also the root of the English word "Pharmaceutical"*

63 Psa. 15; Luke 21:8-19; 1 Cor. 10:1-21 Ibid. Footnote #6 above

64 Ezek. 18:30; Acts 3:19; 2 Cor. 7:9,10; 2 Thess. 2:3-12; 1 Tim. 4; 6:3-12; 2 Tim. 2,3

65 Matt. 6:9-13; 28:18; Luke 11:1-4; John 16:33

66 Matt. 27:50-53; 1 John 2:1-6

67 *Matt. 5:43-48; Luke 6:20 ff.; James 2:10 See also the papers entitled as follows: The 3 part series Christianity Versus Religion, Divergent Belief Systems, the 2 part series How Should we then Live and The New Covenant*

Chapter 11:

159 Matt. 5:6

160 John 14:6

161 Matt. 7:21; Rom. 2:11–16; 2 Thess. 2:10–12 *See also the books" Basic Christian Doctrine, The Doctrine of the Elect/ Ekklesia and Conditions for Salvation*

162 Rom. 1:18–2:16

163 John 12:42,43

164 Matt. 7:13–21; 10:32,33; 2 Tim. 2:11–13; Heb. 3:12–15; 6:4–6; 10:26–39

165 Rom. 8:9 ***See also Christian Conversion, Part One: Introduction to Christian Conversion and Figure One: Illustration-Comparison*

[166] Matt. 6:24; 24:13; Luke 10:22

[167] Matt. 16:21–25

[168] Matt. 6:24; James 1:5–8, 17–27; 2:14–26; 3:1–18

[169] Matt. 5:20–25; Mark 9:35–50; John 9:39–41. *See also the papers entitled 'Christian Conversion (a 3-part series), and 'Figure One: Illustration-Comparison of Caterpillar/ Butterfly to Conversion'*

[170] Matt. 5:20–25; 7:13–29; Mark 9:35–50; John 14:6; 15:1–7

[171] John 1:1–14; 3:3–8; Rom. 2:1–16; 8:1–16

[172] Matt. 7:13–21; Luke 13:23–30; 1 Cor. 1:18–2:16; 2 Cor. 2:11–16

[173] Compare Matt. 7:1 with John 7:24; **See also Glossary of Terms entry: Judgment*

[174] Luke 9:23–26; 1 John 1:5–10

[175] John 8:12; 9:39–41; 1 John 1:7

[176] John 14:15; 15:10–12

[177] Matt. 22:37–39

[178] Luke 9:51–56; Rom. 12:3–21; 1 Cor. 12,13; Eph. 4:1–16

[179] John 15:1–5; Gal. 5:22,23

[180] Matt. 8:11,12; 13:24–52; 22:1–14; 23:1 ff,; 14:36–51; 25:1 ff.; Luke 13:28; 2 Cor. 13:5; 2 Thess. 2:10–12; James 2:14–26; 2 Pet 1:3–10

[181] 1 Cor. 11:27–32; Heb. 2:1–3; 3:1–6,12–14; 6:1–9; 10:26–39

[182] Heb. 12:10–14

[183] Psa. 139:23,24

[184] Matt. 10:32,33; Heb. 10:26–39. *See the papers entitled "the Doctrine of Jesus Christ's Real Presence" and "Regarding Christ's Headship"*

[185] *Matt. 3:11,12; 6:9–13; John 1:29–34; 16:13–15; 1 Cor. 12:12,13; Eph. 1:19–23; 2:18–22*

[186] 1 Tim. 2:5; 1 John 2:1,2

[187] John 16:7–15

[188] Matt. 10:32,33; Eph. 4:30; Heb. 10:26–31, 38,39

[189] Matt. 24:13; 25:1–13; Luke 19:11–27; Acts 4:12; Rom. 10:10; Phil. 2:12,13; 1 Thess. 5:8; 2 Thess. 2:13; 1 Pet. 1:5–10

[190] Matt. 20; Luke 15

[191] Matt. 7:15; 10:32,33; 24:24; 2 Cor. 11:13–15,26; 13:5; Gal. 2:4; 2 Tim. 2:11–13; James 2:14–26. *See reference to Aesop in Bartlett's Familiar Quotations, Little, Brown and Co., Boston, NY, London, 17th Ed., 2002, Page 60#2*

Chapter 12:

[1] 2 Cor. 4:3-7 *See also the book entitled Spiritual Guidelines for Restoration, "Historical Review" Section.*

[2] Matt. 4:1-10; 7:15-29; 10:16-42; Mark 1:14-17; 3:1-6; Luke 1:78; 6:20 ff.; John 3:16-36; 6:27-63; 8:12, 31-58; 10:1-16; 12:32-50; 14:6-17:26

[3] Psa. 119:89; Rom. 1:16-32; 3:4

[4] Gen. 25:21-34; Mal. 2; Matt. 23; Luke 13:34,35; 2 Thess. 2:3-12

[5] *See the paper entitled The Spiritual Laws of Revival, Law #11*

[6] Ex. 19:5; Lev. 20:24-26; Num. 23:9; Deut. 14:2; 26:18; 1 Kings 18:21; Ezra 10:11; Neh. 9; Psa. 115:11; Matt. 4:1-10; Luke 4:1-8; Matt. 6:9-13; 12:30; John 18:36; Rom. 8:1-39; 2 Cor. 6:14-7:1; Eph. 5; Phil. 3:20; 1 Tim. 6:3-12; 2 Tim. 2; Titus 2:14; Heb. 11:12-16; James 4:1-8; 1 Pet. 1, 2* *(Note that 2:13,14 is conditioned by all the other Scriptures regulating our deportment in the world, however, it does not imply that we exalt worldly rulers and authority above God! God's Law is always above man's law whenever they conflict!)*

[7] Matt. 6:22-24; 7:13-29 *See the paper The Dynamics of Christian Discipleship*

[8] Neh. 9:6: Rom. 13:1-7; Col. 1:13-16; Titus 1:15,16; 1 Pet. 2:13,14 *See the 2 part series of papers entitled Authority and Conscience*

[9] Matt. 5:17-20 *See also the book Jesus' Way and the papers entitled Christian Conversion (a 3 part series), The Christian Epiphany, the Christian Spirit, Christianity versus Religion (a 3 part series), Destiny and Free Will, Do You Know Who You Are, Fallacies of Determinism, Fulfilment Prophecy, the Kingdom of Heaven is the Highest form of Civilization, Major Missing Aspects if the Original Christian Gospel, One Covenant for All and Seeing Through the Eyes of Jesus*

[10] Matt. 6:22-24; Luke 16:13-15

[11] Matt. 3:2; 4:17; 5:3-20; 6:9-13, 33; 7:21; 10:7; 11:11,12; 13:11-52; 16:18,19;18:3,4,20; 19:13,14,23-26; 20:1-16; 21:28-46; 22:1-22* (Notice the second half of vs. 21); 25:1-34; 26:17-29; Mark 1:14,15; 10:14-25; 12:28-34; 14:24-27; Luke 1:30-33; 6:20: ff.; 8:10; 12:8-12, 22-53; 13:18-30; 17:20,21; 18:16-27; 19:11-27; 22:15-32; John 3:3-8;

18:36; Acts 14:22;28:22,23; 1 Cor. 4:20; 15:20-28, 50; 2 Thess. 1:4 ff.; 2 Tim. 4:1 ff.; Heb. 1:8; 12:28; 2 Pet. 1:2-11; Rev. 1:9; 12;10

[12] Deut. 28: 15 ff.; 2 Kings 19:19; 2 Chr. 20:6; 36:23*; Ezra 1:2* *(note that in specific situations in the Old Testament, God did intervene, using temporal kingdoms for a temporary protector of His people, however, this must not be construed to be a 'general rule' extending to the present.); Psa. 2, 46,110; Isa. 10:5-25* (note also that at any time, because He is sovereign, God can also use 'heathen nations' to discipline His people when they go astray, reserving their judgment for a later time!)* Isa. 37:16-20; Jer. 10:1 ff.; 25:12 ff.; Ezek. 29:1 ff.; Dan. 2:44,45; 7:15 ff.; Zeph. 3:8; Matt. 4:1-10; Luke 4:1-8; Rom. 1:18-32; 2 Thess. 1:8; 2:3-12; 1 John 5:19; Rev. 13-18

[13] Rom. 1:20

[14] Matt. 23; Rom. 1:16-32; 2 Cor. 13:5-7; 2 Thess. 2:3-12; 2 Tim. 1:7-15; 3:8; Titus 1:15,16; 1 John 3,4; *(note that the reference to Cain and Abel in Ch. 3 that proves that all mankind are our brothers and sisters); Rev. 18 See the paper Fallacies of Determinism See also Glossary of Terms' entry *The Reprobate Mind**

[15] Psa. 51; Matt. 4:1-10; 6:24; 23:1 ff.; Luke 4:1-8; 9:23-26, 51-56 (KJV); 16:13-15;John 19:30; Heb. 2:9-15; 7:22-25; 8:6-13; 9:11-28; 10:12-39; 1 Pet. 2:21-25 *See also the paper entitled A Biblical Disclosure of Antichrist*

[16] Matt. 6:24; Rom. 6:1-23; 1 Cor. 7:21,22

[17] Exodus 6:6,7; 14:13,14 32:1 ff.; Numbers 13,14 and Deut. 1:30; 3:22

[18] *See the paper entitled What is Collectivism*

[19] Ex. 6:6,7; 14:13,14; Deut. 1:30; 3:22 *See also the Chart entitled "Behold the stark contrast between True Liberty and Slavery (Table One in the paper True Liberty is in Christ Alone) and Passover Sequence Chart which correlates the Precepts of the Passover and the paper The Three Passovers of Scripture*

[20] Contrast 1 Sam. 2 with 1 Sam. 8-10; 1 Kings 18; Psa. 94, 118; Prov. 29:25; Isa.1,2,6,8, 27-30; Jer. 10,17; Ezek, 36; Mic. 3,4; *See also the application to Christians found in John 6-8; 18:36; Rom. 8; 1 Cor. 10; Heb. 11:12-16; James 4 and 1 John 2*

[21] Prov. 29:25; Isa. 8:12-20; 26:3-12; 28:9-30:22; 32:1-18; 40-46, 48:17,18; Jer. 31:10-34; Lam. 3:22-24; Ezek. 23:37-39; 36:16:ff.; Hosea 14:9; Matt. 4:1-10; 23:1 ff.; Luke 4:1-8; 8:22-25; 2 Tim. 1:7-15; 2:1 ff.; 1

John 3,4 *See also the papers entitled Conditions for Salvation and God's Definition of Salvation*

[22] Matt. 5-7, 10; 11:28-30; 18:20; 22:36,37; Luke 6, 12; John 8:31-36; 13:34-17:26; Acts 2:42-47; Rom. 6:16-22; 12:1 ff.; 1 Cor. 7:20-24; 12-14; Gal. 5:1, 22,23; Eph. 4

[23] Matt. 6:22-24; Luke 16:13-15

[24] John 3:16; 12:32; Rom. 5:1-5; 12:9-21; 13:8-12; 2 Pet. 3:9; 1 John 2:1-6

[25] Lev.20:26; Num. 23:9; Isa. 42:1-4; 43:1-18; Jer. 31:31-34; Ezek. 36:16 ff.; Dan. 2:44,45; 7:9-14; Matt. 6:9-13; 28:18; Luke 9:51-62 (KJV); 12:31,32; 17:20,21; 18:9-31; 22:24-32; John 18:36; Acts 14:22; 28:22,23; Rom. 14:17; 2 Cor. 5:14-21; 2 Tim. 4; Heb. 1:8;10:1-12:29; 2 Pet. 1:2-11; Rev. 1:9; 12:10 *See also the paper Do You Know Who You Are*

[26] Matt. 28:18; John 18:36; Acts 4:10-20; 5:29-32 *See also the 2 parts series of papers entitled Authority and Conscience*

[27] Matt. 5-7; Luke 6,12; John 14:6-17:26

[28] Matt. 12:30; Luke 2:34,35; Acts 28:22; Rom.1:18-20; 6:3-23; 8:1-11; 2 Cor. 4; Gal. 1:6-12; Eph. 6:10-12; 2 Tim. 2:19-26; James 4:1-8; 1 John 2:15-17; 5:19-21 *See also the paper entitled A Biblical Disclosure of Antichrist*

[29] Matt. 28:18-20; Luke 22:31,32; Acts 3:19 *See the papers The Christian Epiphany, Facts of Scripture: The Church and the Tribulation and the book The Church and the Last Days*

[30] *Matt.* 5-7; Luke 6:20 ff.; 11:33-36; 12:1 ff.; John 1:1-18; 4:14-24; 5:19-30; 6:27-63; 7:15-18; 8:12, 31-58: 12:23-26; 13:34-17:26; Acts 2-7,17; Rom. 5:1-5; 6:1-8:39; 14:8; 1 Cor. 1,2,10,12-15; 2 Cor. 1-7; Gal. 1:6-12; 2:16-4:19; 5:1 f; Eph. 1-6; Phil. 1-4; Col. 1-3

[31] Matt. 5:38-49; 10:16-42; 16:21-26; Mark 3:1-5; Luke 9:23-26, 51-62; 11:33-36; Acts 4:9-20; 5:29-32; Rom. 6:1-22; 12:9-21; 2 Cor. 6:14-7:1; 10:3-7; Eph. 6:10-18; Col. 1:12-29; 2:9-24; 1 Tim. 2:5; 6:3-12; 2 Tim. 1:7-15; 2:1-4:8; Heb. 4:1-19; 6:3-12; 10:19-39; James 4:1-8;1 John 1-5

[32] Matt. 6:9-15; John 18:36; Phil. 3:20; Heb. 11:12-16; 12:1 ff.; James 4; John 2

[33] John 15:18-16:4,33; Acts 14:22; 26:13-18; 28:22; Rom. 5:3;; 12:12; 2 Cor. 1:4; 1 Thess. 1:4; Heb. 11:12-16; James 1:3-5, 21-27; 3:1-4:17; 5:11-20

34 Matt. 5:7; Luke 1:78,79; 2:14; John 14:26,27; 20:19-26; Rom. 8:6; 10:15; 14:17-19; Eph. 2:12-22; Phil. 4:7-9; Col. 1:20-24; 1 Thess. 5:23

35 Ex. 2:1-15; Psa. 4:8; 34:14; 119:165; Prov. 16:7; Isa. 9:6,7; 32:17,18; 48:16-19; Jer. 4:4; 12:14-17; Hosea 10:12; Matt. 5:38-48; 7:12-29; 2:51,52; Luke 2:14; 6:20 ff.; 12:1 ff.; John 4:14-38; 5:19-30; 6:27-64; 7:15-18; Acts 12-28; Rom. 12:1 ff.; 1 Cor. 15:30-33; 2 Cor. 4,6,11; Eph. 2:13,14; 2 Thess. 2:3-12; James 1,4; 1 Pet. 3:8-22; 1 John 1-5

36 Psa. 119:89; Prov. 27:6; Matt. 5:43-48; Mark 3:1-6; Luke 9:51-62: John 7:15-18; 8:31-36; 17:17

37 Isa. 1:18-2:22; 8:9-20; 30:9-22; Jer. 2:23 ff.; 3:16-4:4,22; 5:1-5,9,22-31; 6:13-7:29; 8:1-12; 10:1-11; 11:9-17; 13:8-17; 17:5-10; 23:9-14; Ezek. 18:23-32; 20:3-44; 21:24-22:31; 23:37-39; 33:30-33; John 3:16; 1 Cor. 10:1 ff.; 2 Cor. 5:14-21; Heb. 4;12,13; 8:6-12:29

38 *Read Jesus's main Discourses found in the Gospels*: Matt. 5-7,10,13,16,18,20; Mark 3,4; Luke 6-14, 19,21; John 3-17; Acts 1-17; Rom. 1-8; 1 Cor. 1-3,1-15; 2 Cor. 1-7,10,11; Gal. 1-5; Eph. 1-6; Phil. 1-4; Col. 1-3; 2 Tim. 1-4; Heb. 1-4, 6-12 *See also the book entitled Spiritual Guidelines for Restoration, "Historical Review" Section*

39 Matt. 6:9-13; John 14:6-17:26; 18:36; Acts 4:9-20; 5:29-32; Rom. 8,12; 2 Cor. 3:17,18; 11:12-15; Eph. 2:13,14; 6:10-12; Phil. 3:3, 20; Col. 1:12-29; 2 Tim. 2,3; Heb. 11:12-15; James 4:1-8; 1 John 2:15-17; 5:19-21

40 Matt. 16:21-26; John 8:31-36; 14:26,26; 2 Cor. 3:17,18; Eph. 2:13,14; Phil. 1:21

41 Ex. 3:11-14; Deut. 4:39; Psa. 2,110; Isa. 14, 42-46; Ezek. 28 *See also the book entitled Basic Christian Doctrine, Section I: "The Nature of God"*

42 *See the Chart entitled Passover Sequence Chart and the Papers entitled The New Covenant and The Three Passovers of Scripture*

43 *Start with the papers entitled Alive Forevermore, the Gift of God in Christ Jesus, the Amazing Doctrine of God's Grace, the Baptism of Jesus Christ, the Beauty and Finesse of the New Covenant, (the 3 parts series) Christian Conversion and Conditions for Salvation*

44 Matt. 5-7; 16:18,19; Matt. 18:19,20; John 8:31-58; Acts 17:24-31; Rom. 12:1 ff;1 Cor. 12,2,12-14; 2 Cor. 3-5; Gal. 1:6-12; Eph. 4:1-16; 1 Tim. 6:3-12; 2 Tim. 2:11-26; Heb. 1-4, 6-12

45 Luke 22:31,32; 1 Cor. 10; 2 Cor. 7:10; 2 Tim. 2:19-26

46 Matt. 6:9-13; 28:18; John 18:36

[47] Psa. 51; Ezek. 23:37-39; Matt. 23:29-39; John 3:16; 8:39-58; 1 John 3,4 (*Note in particular, the reference to Cain killing his brother extends to the present to include all humans on earth for being our "brothers and sisters!"*) *See the papers entitled A Writer's Commentary and The Main Missing Aspects of the Original Christian Gospel*

[48] Matt. 6:9-13; Luke 12:1-33; 13:18-35; John 18:36; 2 Cor. 3,4,6; 10:3-7; 11:12-15; Gal. 2:16-4:19; Eph. 6:10-18; Phil. 3:3:20; Heb. 11:12-16 *See also the paper entitled The Kingdom of Heaven is the Highest Form of Civilization*

[49] *See the paper entitled The Fallacies of *Determinism**

[50] Psa. 1-4, 8,9,15,16,18, 23-27, 31-37, 40-46, 55-57, 61-63, 73, 83,84, 89,91, 94-100, 103-107, 110, 121, 136, 146, Prov. 16:7; Matt. 5-7; 16:18,19; 18:19,20; John 3-17; 18:36,37;Acts 1-11; 17:24-31; Rom. 1:16,17; 5:1-8:39; 12:1 ff;; 1 Cor. 1-3, 10,12-15; 2 Cor. 1-7; Gal.1:6-12; 2:16-4:19; Eph. 1-4; Col. 1-3

[51] *See the papers entitled Facts of Scripture: The Church and the Tribulation and Fulfilment Prophecy*

[52] Matt. 25; Rom. 14:23; 2 Thess. 1:8; 2:3-12; Rev. 11:1-15

[53] *See the papers entitled Basics of Biblical Church Governance, Destiny and Free Will, Guidelines for Renewed Leadership, Questionnaire for Church Leaders and the Book entitled Spiritual Guidelines for Restoration, "Historical Review" Section*

[54] Jer. 4:4; Hosea 10:12; Matt. 24; Luke 21; John 15:18-16:4,33; Rom. 14:23; 2 Thess. 2:2-12; Rev. 2,3 *See also the papers entitled A Biblical Disclosure of Antichrist and Facts of Scripture: The Church and the Tribulation and the book entitled The Church in the Last Days*

[55] Matt. 23; 27:1-26; Mark 15:11-15; Luke 13:18-35; 23:13-25; John 18:36-19:15

[56] Matt. 5:43-48; 6:9-13, 22-14; Luke 16:13-15; Acts 5:29-32; Rom. 12:1-21; Gal. 1:6- 12; Eph. 6:10-12; Col. 1:13-16; Phil. 3:20; Heb. 10:18-39; 11:12-16 *See also the papers entitled The Christian Epiphany, Divergent Belief Systems, Do You Know Who You Are, Every Believer can independently know the Truth of Scripture, The Kingdom of Heaven is the Highest Form of Civilization, Looking Through the Lens of Jesus Christ and True Liberty is in Christ Alone*

[57] Joshua 2; 1 Kings 18; Daniel 3,6; Acts 5:29-32; Heb. 10:26-31; 1 John 5:19-21

[58] Matt. 27:1-6; Luke 22:15-20; John 8:31-36; 14:26,27; 2 Cor. 3:17,18; Eph. 2:13,14; Col. 1:20-24; Heb. 9:11-15; 10:26-31; 1 Pet. 1:19-21,

[59] John 6:27-63; Rom. 8:1-18

[60] Matt. 6:9-13; 22:21; John 18:36; Phil. 3:20; Heb. 11:12-16

[61] Gen. 12, 15, 22, 28, 32 35, 37-45; Ex. 3-15; Num. 6:22-27; Deut. 28-34; Josh. 1:5-9;24:1 ff.; 1 Sam. 2:1-10; 2 Sam. 22:1 ff.; 1 Chr. 16:1-17:27; 2 Chr 7:12-22; Neh. 1:4 ff.; 9:1 ff.; Psa. 1-9, 15-20, 23-37, 42-48, 51-57, 61-63, 68, 73, 84, 89-91, 94-98, 100-107, 110-119, 121, 130, 135-139, 145-147; Isa. 2,6,; 7:14; 9:6,7; 11:1-12:6; 25-32; 33:6; 35:1-38:22; 40-66; Jer. 31; Ezek. 36; Dan. 2:44,45; 7:9-28; Joel 2; Mic. 3-7; Matt. 5-7,10; 12:18-45; Luke 6,12; John 1:1-18; 4:14-24; 6:27-63; 7:15-18; 8:31-58; 10:1-16; 13:35-17:26; 18:36,37; Acts 17:24-31; Rom. 5-8; 1 Cor. 1,2,12-14; 2 Cor. 1-7; Gal. 2-5; Eph. 1-4; Phil. 1-4; Col. 1-3; 1 Tim. 2:5; 6:3- 12; 2 Tim. 1-4; Heb. 1-4, 9-12; 2 Pet. 1:2-11, 19 2:9, 20; 3:1 ff.; 1 John 1-5 See also Passover Sequence Chart and the papers entitled Fulfilment Prophecy and The Three Passovers of Scripture

[62] Matt. 26:26-29; Luke 22:20; John 8:31-36; 14:26,27; Rom. 5:1-5; Gal 5:1 f.; Eph. 2:13,14; Col. 1:20 f.; 3:1-7; Heb. 10:18-31 (espec. Vs. 19)

Chapter 13:

[192] Matt. 5:13–16; 13:1 ff.; John 7:37–39; 8:12. ff.; 13–17 *(Upper Room/ Gethsemane Dis.)*

[193] John 13:34,35; 15:1–12; Acts 4:11-13; 1 Cor. 13.

[194] Matt. 10:16–42; 16:21–28; Luke 10:1 ff.; 16:15.

[195] **Matt. 28:9–20; Mark 16:9–20; Luke 24:25–53; John 20:16–21:19; Acts 1:1-11

[196] John 13–17

[197] John 15:10–12

[198] Rom. 8:29

[199] Matt. 4:19; Mark 1:17; Luke 5:1–11.

[200] Matt. 14:1 f.; John 6:1 ff.; 21:15–17; Acts 20:28; 1 Pet. 5:1–5.

[201] Matt. 18:12; Luke 15:1 ff.; John 10:1 ff. *See also the paper: Jesus' Major Parables*

[202] Matt. 9:39–10:42; 20:1 f.; Luke 10:1 f.

²⁰³ Luke 6:46–49; Rom. 8:29; 1 Cor. 3:11–15; Eph. 2:13–3:21.

²⁰⁴ Matt. 16:18; Luke 6:46–49; 1 Cor. 3:11–15.

²⁰⁵ Acts 9:31; 1 Cor. 3:11–15; 8:1; 14:1–5; 2 Cor. 12:19; Eph. 4:1–16; Jude 20.

²⁰⁶ Zech. 4:6; Matt. 20:25–28; 25:34–40; John 15:5; Acts 1:8; 1 Cor. 15:10; 1 Pet.1.

²⁰⁷ *See the booklet: Guidelines for Renewed Leadership*

²⁰⁸ Matt. 25:1–13 See the paper "Jesus' Major Parables"

²⁰⁹ Matt. 10:16–42; Luke 14:26–33; 18:8; John 15:18–16:33; Acts 14:22; 2 Tim. 2:1 ff.

²¹⁰ Rom. 1:16,17

Chapter 14:

¹ Matt. 13:11; Mark 4:11; Luke 8:10; Eph. 1:9; 3:3-9; 6:19; Col. 1:26,27; 2:2,3; 4:3; Tim. 3:9,16

² Matt. 25:1-13; John 3:29,30; 10:13-16; Eph. 3:3-21; 5:22-30 See also the Paper entitled *Jesus' Major Parables*

³ John 1:1-14; 3:3-8, 16,17, 27; 10:1-18, 27-30; 1 Cor. 15:20-28; Eph. 1:9,10; 2:11-22;3:1-19 See also the Papers entitled *Fulfilment Prophecy* and *One Covenant for All*

⁴ Matt. 13:11; Mark 4:11; Luke 8:10

⁵ Matt. 18:3,4; 19:13,14; John 3:9-16,27; 1 Cor. 2:9-16; 4:1; Gal. 1:12; Eph. 1:3-14; 3:3-12; 6:19

⁶ Gen. 12,18,22; Acts 10:34-38 See also the Paper entitled *The Fulfillment of God's Promise* (to Abraham)

⁷ Luke 21:20-24; Acts 13:26-49; Romans 9-11; 16:25-27; Eph. 1:10; 2:11-22; 3:1-13;Col. 1:12-29; 2:2-4

⁸ Jer. 2:7; 6:15; 7:10; 8:12; Ezek. 6:11; 7:19; 8:6; 14:3-11; Dan. 9:27; 11:31; 12:11; Matt. 12:30,31; 24:15; Mark 3:28-30; 2 Thess. 2:7; Rev. 2:9; 17:5,7

⁹ Gen. 37,40; Dan. 2; Matt. 2; Gal. 1:12

¹⁰ *See the papers entitled Biblical Symbolism (Parts One and Two) and Jesus' Major Parables*

¹¹ *Dan. 9:26,27; 12:7; Matt. 24; Luke 21:24; Acts 13:17-49; Rom. 11:25; Rev. 10:7 *Observe that the "holy people's scattering" and the 70th Week*

both take place in two stages, following the "Law of Double fulfillments": One for the Jews and the second for Christians.

[12] Dan. 12:6,7 Cf. Dan. 9:24-27 *Again, note the last part of Dan. 9, Vss. 26 and 27 both point to " the scattering of the holy people's power" in two installments. Ibid. Fn. #11*

[13] Compare Dan. 12:8-13 with *Prophetic Chronology Two*, Sects. III and IV, *Contextually Comparing Elements ..., Sects. III, IV-B, C, F, VI-B, VII and Sequence of Events See also Fulfilment Prophecy, FIGURE ONE: "The Nine Ages" and Messiah Figures FIGURE ONE: "Seeing the Double Peaks of Teleos Vision"*

[14] Daniel 9,12; Matt. 24; Luke 21 *Together, these statements describe two stages: First, the events of the first century Jewish war of AD 67-70 (the 1st half of the 70th Week) with the 'Abomination of Desolation' (AOD) referring to the time when the Jewish Zealots desecrated the Temple by their indiscriminate bloodshed of innocent civilians. See Josephus' Wars of the Jews and the chart entitled Sequence of Events. The Second Fulfilment (2nd TOHY and 2nd Half of the 70th Week) takes place in the Great Tribulation Period, at the end of the "Age of Grace." See also Sect. III, Patterns in Prophetic Scripture II-A, IV-B-2, Cross Reference Guide IV-C, Fn#27,28 and Prophetic Chronology Two, Section IV "Correlating Prophetic Texts and Acrostics"*

[15] Acts 1:6-8 Cf. Isa. 52:13-53:12; Zech. 9:9,10; Matt. 16:15-23; 20:20-28; 23:1 ff.; Luke 24:25 ff.; John 10:24-38; 11:49-52 *See also the Papers entitled Conditions for Salvation Appendix C: "Sent Me Scripture List," Covenant Principles, Fulfilment Prophecy, Illustrating the Law of Multiple Fulfillments and Messiah Figures*

[16] Rev. 6:9-11

[17] Rev. 10:7 ***The text of paragraph B can also be found in the Paper entitled Patterns in Prophetic Scripture, Section IV-C, D. See also Appendix 1: Diagram One: "Correlating Last Days Events."*

[18] 2 Thess. 1,2; Rev. 5:5; 11:15 *See also the Papers entitled The Biblical Role of Israel, Facts Concerning the 70th Week of Daniel and The Messiah Figures*

[19] Genesis 12:1-3; 15:1-6; 17:1 ff.; 22:15-18; Psa. 2, 45, 110, 118:22; *Isa. 2,4, 8:9 20;9:6,7; 11-14, 24-35, 43-48, **61:1-3; Jer. 3-25, 31-36; Ezek. 7-25, 33,34, 36; Dan. 2:34,35,44,45; Joel 1-3; Amos 1-9; Mic. 2-5,7; Zeph. 1-3; Zech. 11-14; Mal. 3,4 *Note that many Old Testament Prophecies have multiple fulfillments that reiterate for as many subsequent generations and times, applying to both Jews and Gentiles, as are necessary to fulfill God's Grand Plan of Unification in Christ! **The reader should*

also note that, during his first appearing on earth as Messiah Lamb of God (MFLa), Christ stopped mid-sentence in the second verse. See Luke 4:18,19 Whereas, in Christ's Second Appearing as Messiah Lion of God (MFLi), the Judgment part is fulfilled. See 2 Thess. 1,2 See also the Papers entitled The Biblical Role of Israel, Fulfillment of God's Promise (to Abraham), Fulfilment Prophecy, Emmanuel 1 &2, Illustrating the "Law of Multiple Fulfillments" and The Messiah Figures

20 *Luke 21:20-24; Rom. 4:9-13, 20-5:5; 11:11-36; Gal. 3:6-29; Eph. 1:9,10; 2:11-22;3:1-11; 2 Thess. 1,2; 2 Pet. 1-3; Rev. 11:3-21 *See the Paper entitled Facts Concerning the 70th Week of Daniel (Especially Section I, Paragraphs B, C and Figure One which delineate the partitioning within Jesus' Prophetic Discourse that fits the "splitting" of the 70th Week into two separate fulfillment sequences. See also the Paper entitled Correlating Last Days Scriptures*

21 Psa. 110:1 ff. 118:22; *Isa. 28:16 (Chapters 26-30); Dan. 2:34,35,44,45; Matt. 21:42; Luke 20:40-44; 21:22-28

22 Dan. 9:26,27; 12:7 ff. * *See also the papers entitled The Biblical Role of Israel, Correlating Last Days Scriptures, The Doctrine of Last Things and Facts relating to the Fulfillment of God's Promise (to Abraham)*

23 *Zech. 12:9,10*

24 Matt. 23:29-39

25 Matt. 24:14,15

26 Matt. 24:29-31

27 Luke 21:24

28 John 10:16

29 Acts 1:6-8

30 Acts 17:31

31 Rom. 11:11-36 Cf. 9:6-10:13 *See also the Paper Destiny and Free Will*

32 1 Cor. 15:20-28; Rev. 11:15 Cf. Psa. 110:1 ff.; 118:22; Isa. 28:16

33 Gal. 3:1 ff.

34 Eph. 1:3-10; 2:11-22; 3:1-11

35 Phil. 3:3 f.; Cf. Gal. 6:14-16

36 Col. 1:15-29

37 Titus 2:11-15

38 Heb. 5:1-9; 7:1-10:23 Cf. Jer. 31:31-34; Ezek. 36:22-27 *See also the Papers entitled The Fulfillment of God's Promise (to Abraham), Fulfilment Prophecy, The New Covenant* and *One Covenant for All*

39 1 Pet. 2:5-10 Cf. Psa. 118:22; Isa. 28:16; Matt. 21:42; Acts 4:11

40 Rev. 10:7 Cf. Zech. 12:10; Matt. 5:17-20; Rom. 11:25; 16:25-27; Gal. 3:23-29 Ibid. *Footnote #17 See also the Paper entitled Prophetic Chronology Two Sect. IV: "Correlating Prophetic Texts and Acrostics"*

41 Rev. 11:15 Cf. John 10:16; 1 Cor. 15:20-28

42 Jer. 5-13,17,18, 20, 23; Matt. 24:4,5,11,24; Luke 21:8; Rom. 1:18-32; 2 Cor. 4:26; 11:12-15; 2 Tim. 3; Heb. 3:7-4:11

43 Compare Matt. 24 and Luke 21 with 2 Thess. 1,2 *See also Facts of Scripture*

44 Daniel 9:24-27; Matt. 23:33-24:15; 2 Thess. 2:3-12; Rev. 13,17 *See also the Papers entitled Emmanuel 2: God is Dealing with Israel/ the Jews* and *The Three Passovers of Scripture*

45 Isa. 8, 28-30, 40-66; Jer. 2-36; Ezek. 3-24, 33,34; Dan. 2,7,9,11,12; Matt. 23; Rom. 9-11; Gal. 2-5 See Footnotes #7, #21 **See also Sequence of Events, which includes references to Wars of the Jews, which is part of The Works of Flavius Josephus Translated By William Whiston, AP&A, Grand Rapids, 1971*

46 Ezek. 13,14; Zech. 11; Matt. 23:33 f.; Luke 21:20-24; Acts 13:26-52; Rom. 9:32,33; 11:25

47 Josh. 2; Dan. 3,6; Acts 4,5 *See the Paper entitled The Higher Laws of God This pattern can also be seen in Luke's account of the early Church's acts of bravery during the early persecutions of Christians by both Romans and apostate Jews.*

48 *Daniel 3,6 See also the Paper entitled Authority and Conscience*

49 Esther 1-10 *See also the book entitled The Works of Flavius Josephus,* which includes *Antiquities of the Jews* by Flavius Josephus, Bk. XI, Ch. VI, P. 12, AP&A, Grand Rapids, 1971

50 Daniel 12:1 ff.; 1 Cor. 15:20-28; Rev. 10-12 *See The Church in the Last Days' Chapter entitled: "End Time Analysis: The Tribulation Period, Part One " and The Biblical Role of Israel*

51 See the Papers entitled *The Biblical Role of Israel, Contextually Comparing the Elements of Prophetic Scripture, Emmanuel 1: God is Dealing with His People, Emmanuel 2: God is Dealing with Israel/ the Jews, The Fulfillment of*

God's Promise (to Abraham), Illustrating the "Law of Multiple Fulfillments" and Understanding Prophecy (a two part series)

[52] Dan. 7:19-28; 9:24-27; 12:7 ff. Matt. 24; Luke 21; Rom. 9:25,26; 2 Thess. 1,2

[53] Ibid Footnote #'s 12,21,45,49 See the papers entitled *Correlating Last Days Scriptures, The Biblical Role of Israel, Facts Concerning the 70th Week of Daniel* and *Prophetic Chronology Two: General Facts regarding the timing of "End Times Events"*

Chapter 15:

[211] Matt. 19:30

[212] Matt. 13:21; 24:21,29; John 16:33; Acts 14:22; Rom. 5:3; 8:35; 12:12; 2 Cor. 1:3. 213. *Compare John 16:33 with 1 Thess. 5:9 and use any Greek lexicon to look up the words for yourself*

[214] Matt. 24:9,10; 2 Thess. 2:1–7. *See the paper entitled "an Analysis of the Causes and Effects of Apostasy"*

[215] *2 Thess. 2:3*

[216] Matt. 24:14–28; Mark 2:21,22; Luke 21:34–36; 2 Thess. 2:1–12; 1 John 2:15– 23; Rev. 13:1–14:13. *See the book "The Pre-Wrath Rapture of the Church" by Marvin Rosenthal, Thomas Nelson, Nashville, 1990*

[217] Matt. 24;21–30; 25:1 ff.; Luke 21:8–27; 2 Cor. 5:8–10; Rev. 6:1–11:19.

[218] Matt. 24:4–13; 2 Thess. 2:3.

[219] Matt. 24:4–31; 1 Cor. 15:20–23; 1 Thess. 4:13–17; Rev. 1:7; 3:10; 6:1– 7:17.

[220] ***See Appendix C and Chapter 12, Section V*

[221] *Daniel 7:25; 9:24–27 (notice the prophetic 'week' is interrupted); 12:7;* Matt. 24:14–31; Rev. 11:2,3,9-11***Notice that John also uses the word 'days' in a similar prophetic context applying to the same period. See also the papers entitled "Contextually Comparing the Elements of Prophetic Scripture," "Correlating Last Days Scriptures, the Biblical Role of Israel," "the Doctrine of Last Things," "Facts Concerning the 70th Week of Daniel" and "Precepts Regarding the Interpretation of End Time Prophecies" Rev. 12:14;13:5*

[222] Ibid. Footnote #8; Daniel 12:10–12; Luke 21:24; Rom. 11:25,26; Rev. 10:7. *See also Appendix C*

[223] Matt. 24:21,22; Mark 13:19.

[224] See Chapter 12, Section V

[225] Rev. 6:1–3

[226] Rev. 6:4

[227] Rev. 6:5–7

[228] Rev. 6:8 Cf. Matt. 24:6–8; Mark 13:8; Luke 21:9–11; 1 Thess. 5:9.

[229] *See Sections VII and VIII See also Glossary of Terms' entry: the *Remnant**

[230] Matt. 24:9–12; Mark 13:9, 11–13; Luke 21:8, 12–18; 2 Thess. 2:1–8; Rev. 2:1-3:22.

[231] Matt. 24:29–31; 1 Cor. 15:20–23; 1 Thess. 4:13–17; Rev. 7:7–17

[232] Matt. 10:24–28; 17:23,24; Luke 12:1–12; Rev. 7:13–17; 13:10; 14:10–12.

[233] Rev. 14:1–15

[234] Psa. 2:6; 48:1,2; 87:1 f; Rev. 5:6–7:17; 12:10,11; 13:8.

[235] Mark 10:1–12; James 1:27; Heb. 13:4; 1 John 2:15–17.

[236] 1 Cor. 15:20–23; 1 John 3:1–3.

[237] Rom. 8:23–27; James 1:17,18.

[238] John 4:23–38; 6:27 ff.; 14:21–26; 15:1–6; 16:12–17:26

[239] *See also the entry *Ekklesia* in Appendix E: Excerpts from Glossary of Terms* 240 Matt. 24:29–31; 2 Cor. 5:8; 1 Thess. 4:13–17; 2 Tim. 4:8; 2 Pet. 3:9–18; Rev. 7:9–17

[241] Matt. 20:16; 22:14; 24:13; Mark 13:20; John 15:14–23; Rom. 8:23–39; 11:1–5; 1 Cor. 15:20–23; Heb. 2:1–4; 3:6; 6:3–12; James 5:7

[242] John 15:1–7; Rom. 11:16–32; Rev. 2:18–23 Cf. 1 Kings 17–19 See also *Glossary of Terms entry *Remnant/Gather/Harvest* See also Dan. 9:20–27 and the paper entitled "Facts Concerning the 70th Week of Daniel"*

Chapter 16:

[243] 1 John 2:15–24; 2 John 4–11 *Note that a "False Flag Operation" is a pre-planned event in which others are "set up" for the blame. See also What is Syncretism*

[244] Dan. 2:34,35,44,45; Luke 13:31–35; 21:8–19; Eph. 6:12; Rev. 12,13,17 *See also the author's book Spiritual Guidelines for Restoration, "Historical Review Section" and the references regarding John Wyclif and John Huss in the book The Reformation by Will Durant, Simon & Schuster, NY, 1957 Pages 30–37, 163–168*

[245] Rev. 13 *Viz., the "the Hegelian Dialectic." *See also Appendix A and the paper entitled "A Biblical Disclosure of Antichrist Ibid. Bartlett, Pages 554, #12 and 615, #2"*

[246] Matt. 5:38–48; 22:15–22; Luke 13:31–35; John 16:1–3,33; Gal. 1:6–12; 2 Thess. 1,2 *See also the book Spiritual Guidelines for Restoration Appendix A: "A Critique of Soul Power" See also the 3 part series of papers entitled "Christianity versus Religion"*

[247] Dan. 11:35,36; Matt. 7:13–21; John 18:36,37; 2 Cor. 4:4–6. *See the papers entitled "Basics of Biblical Church Governance" and "Guidelines for Renewed Leadership"*

[248] Matt. 7:13–29; 10:16–42; John 6:27–29; 7:15–27; 8:31–59; 10:1–30; 12:31–50; Acts 4:8–20; 5:17–32; 2 Cor. 4:4–6; 10:3–6; 11:2 ff.; Eph. 6:10–12; 1 John 2:1–20; 4:1–6; Rev. 12:1–13:7 *See also the book Jesus' Way, Appendix B*

[249] Psa. 101:7; Jer. 5:27; 8:5; 9:6; Dan. 8:12–14; 9:1 ff.; Mark 14:1; Luke 21:24; Col. 2:8

[250] Gen. 3:1; Dan. 8:23–26; Eph. 6:10–12; 1 John 3:8; Rev. 13:1 ff.

[251] Job 1:6; 2:1; Dan. 8:11; 11:36; Matt. 4:10; 16:23.

[252] *See Appendix D for more details*

[253] Compare Daniel 2:19–45 with Rev. 13:8 ff.

[254] Psa. 2,110, 118:22; Isa. 28:16; Dan. 2:19–45; Matt. 21:42; Luke 20:9–18; Rom. 9:33; Eph. 2:13–22; 2 Thess. 1,2; 1 Pet. 2;1–10; 4:12–19

Chapter 17:

[1] Luke 24:25-49; Rev. 19:10,13 See the Papers entitled *Covenant Principles, Fulfilment prophecy, Hermeneutics: Basic Principles of Scripture Interpretation, Hermeneutics, Part Two: Major Tools in Revealing Scripture, The Higher Laws of God, The Holy Spirit is God's Revelator, Illustrating the "Law of Multiple Fulfilments," Jesus' Major Parables, The Key ... is Spiritual Exegesis, Looking Through the 'Lens of Jesus Christ,' One Covenant for All, Principles of Fulfillment Theology, Prophetic Chronology* and *Prophetic Chronology Two*

[2] Mal. 3:16-18; John 10:1-16; Rom. 11:11-32; 1 Cor. 15:20-28 *See the Papers entitled The Biblical Precept of Mystery, The Biblical Role of Israel, Correlating Last Days Scriptures, The Doctrine of Last Things, Fulfilment Prophecy* and *The Three Passovers of Scripture*

3 Psa. 110; Daniel 2,7,9,12 *See also the Papers A Biblical Disclosure of Antichrist, Correlating Last Days Scriptures, "Correlating Major Events to Prophecy Chart," Emmanuel 2 and The Messiah Figures*

4 *Matt. 24*; Mark 13*; Luke 21*; Rev. 19:10,13 *With careful examination it is apparent that Jesus' Prophetic Discourse contains two levels of predictions, some applying to the Roman Jewish war of 67-70 AD, which was a direct judgment of Israel for rejecting Jesus as the "Lamb of God Messiah," (MFLa), forming the first half of the 70th Wk, and others which "look forward" to the Great Tribulation Period yet to come, associated with Jesus as the "Lion of God Messiah" (MFLi) in the second half of the 70th Wk. See Section III, Footnote #17 and the Papers entitled Correlating Last Days Scriptures, Sections II, IV and VIII, The Doctrine of Last Things, Section V and Facts of Scripture: The Church and the Tribulation*

5 *Isa. 53; Matt. 24:1,2, 32-35; John 1:29-34 (MFLa) and Dan. 2:34,35,44,45; Mal. 3:1-18; Matt. 24:14-31, 36-51; 2 Thess. 1,2; Rev. 5:5; 14:1-19:21 (MFLi) See also the Papers entitled The Biblical Precept of Mystery, Illustrating the "Law of Multiple Fulfillments" and The Messiah Figures*

6 *See sections II, III and IV below for details*

7 Dan. 7:25; 9:26; 12:7,11; Rev. 11:2,3; 12:14; 13:5

8 Dan. 9:26 *See the historical chronicles contained in The Works of Flavius Josephus, which includes the following section: Wars of the Jews, Bk. II, Ch. XVII-XXII*

9 Ibid. Fn. #5 **Note also that a footnote in Josephus' Antiquities of the Jews, Book XV, Chapter XI (Pg. 334) specifically states that the temple the Romans destroyed was the Third Temple! See the Set of Charts entitled Sequence of Events (leading to the destruction of Jerusalem in 70 AD). See also Section VI below*

10 Dan. 9:26; Matt. 24:1,2,34

11 Dan. 9:24; Matt. 23:37-39; Luke 21:24; Acts 13:38-52; Rom. 11:25

12 Ibid. Fn. #7

13 *See also the Papers entitled The Biblical Precept of Mystery, The Biblical Role of Israel, Contextually Comparing the Elements of Prophetic Scripture, Correlating the Prophecies concerning 'TOHY Periods,' The Fulfillment of God's Promise (to Abraham), Emmanuel 1, Emmanuel 2, Fulfilment Prophecy, Hermeneutics (1), Hermeneutics, Part Two, The Key to Understanding Scripture is Spiritual Exegesis, The Messiah Figures,*

Patterns in Prophetic Scripture, Prophetic Chronology One and *Prophetic Chronology Two*

[14] See the Papers entitled *Hermeneutics, Hermeneutics Part Two* and *The Key to Understanding Scripture is Spiritual Exegesis*

[15] Ibid. Footnote #14

[16] *For example, see The Biblical Precept of Mystery, Appendix 2: "Chronological Chart of 'Writing Periods' in Daniel*

[17] *See Appendix E: "Time Tag Scriptures"*

[18] *See the Papers entitled Contextually Comparing the Elements of Prophetic Scripture, Section VII, Correlating the Prophecies concerning 'TOHY Periods,' Patterns in Prophetic Scripture* and *Prophetic Chronology Two*

[19] *See the Paper entitled The Messiah Figures*

[20] *See the Papers entitled Facts of Scripture: The Church and the Tribulation* and *Prophetic Chronology One*

[21] John 10:7-16; 1 Cor. 15:20-28; Eph. 1-4 Ibid. Fn. #13 *See also refs on "God's Prophetic Time Line" in Correlating Last Days Scriptures and other related Papers*

[22] Dan. 9:26,27; Matt. 24:14; Luke 21:20-24; Acts 1:6-8; Rom. 11:7-33; Eph. 2:11-22; Rev. 11:1-3 *See also The Biblical Role of Israel and The Biblical Precept of Mystery and the Glossary of Terms' entry "The Judeo-Christian Tradition" found in the last Appendix*

[23] Matt. 24:1,2, 32-35; Luke 21:5,6, 20-24 *(1st half), with Luke 21:24 as pivotal verse and Vss. 8-19, 25-28, 33-36 pertaining to the 2nd half. See also the papers entitled Correlating the Prophecies concerning 'TOHY Periods,' Correlating Major Events to Prophecy Chart and Correlating the "Horns of the Fourth Beast" of Daniel seven ...*

[24] Dan. 7:25; 9:24-*27 In Matt. 24 and Luke 21 it appears that* Matt. 24:1,2, 32-35 (Luke 21:5,6,20-24) *apply to the first century tribulation/ war and that* Matt. 24:3-31, 36-51 (Luke 21:7-19, 25-28, 34-36) *apply to the last days' Great Tribulation Period along with Dan. 12:4-13; Rom. 11:25,26; Rev. 11:1-3,11; 12:6,14; 13:5* Ibid. Footnote #22

[25] Ibid. Footnote #4, #23 and #24 See also Fig. One: "Partition of 70th Week"

[26] John 2:19-21; 4:23,24 See also the Paper entitled *Christian Worship and the True Temple*

[27] Dan. 9:2, 24-27; Matt. 23:29-24:31; Luke 21:20-24 See also Isa. 52:13-53:12; John 1:29-34; Rev. 5:6-13

[28] Dan. 2:34,35,44,45; Zech. 12:9,10; Matt. 24; Rom. 11:7-33 *See also the Papers entitled Correlating Last Days' Scriptures, The Doctrine of Last Things and the book The Church in the Last Days*

[29] Compare Daniel 9:24-27; Matt. 24: Luke 21; John 10:7-16; 2 Thess. 2; Rev. 13,17

[30] Zech. 9:9,10; 11:12-14; 12:9,10; 13:6,7

[31] *See the book Jesus' Way: God's Guaranteed Blueprint*

[32] *See the papers entitled Looking Through the Lens of Jesus Christ, The New Covenant* and *Principles of Fulfilment Theology* as well as the book *Basic Christian Doctrine*

[33] Exodus 6-15; Deut. 1:30; 3:22; 4:39; 32:39; 1 Sam. 2:9: 1 Kings 18:21; Psa. 3:8; 4:8; 20, 23,27, Isa. 42-46; Hosea 10:12,13; Acts 16:*31 and may others See also the papers entitled The Christian Epiphany (espec. Sect. VI-A-5, Fn. #57), Conditions for Salvation, God's Definition of Salvation* and *True Liberty is in Christ Alone*

[34] Jer. 31:31-34; Ezek. 36:16-33; Matt. 26:26-29; Luke 22:15-32; Rom. 5:1-11; Eph. 1:7;2:13,14; Heb. 2:9-15; 6:17-20; 7:19-10:39; 11:12-31

[35] *See the paper entitled The Three Passovers of Scripture*

[36] Rom. 11:17-24

[37] 2 Pet. 3; Jude 8-16; Rev. 11:15 ff.; 16:17-18:24

[38] *See the Papers entitled Correlating Last Days' Scriptures, Correlating the Prophecies concerning 'TOHY Periods,' The Doctrine of Last Things, Patterns in Prophetic Scripture* and *Prophetic Chronology Two*

[39] *To understand this, let the reader observe the corrected syntax in the latter part of Daniel 9:26 and which is reiterated in verse 27, both which tell us that God is extending the Jew's Desolation unto the end (Consummation). Jesus' statement in Matt. 23:37-39 also confirms this. See also Section VI*

[40] Zech. 12:10; Dan. 12:7 f.; Matt. 23:37-39; Luke 21:20-24; Rom. 11:25,26 *See also the Papers entitled The Biblical Precept of Mystery, Sect. III, The Higher Laws of God, Sect. III, Illustrating the "Law of Multiple Fulfillments"and Prophetic Chronology Two, Sect. II*

[41] Compare Daniel 2 and 12 with Rev. 10, 11; Matt. 24, Luke 21; 1 Thess. 4 and 2 Thess. 2 See also the Papers entitled *Correlating Last Days Scriptures* and *The Doctrine of Last Things* (which includes the two "Last Days Time Line Charts")

[42] Compare Dan. 9:24-27 with Matt. 24:34; Luke 21:24; Rev. 10:2,3; 12:14; 13:5

[43] *See the Papers entitled Prophetic Chronology and The Three Passovers of Scripture*

[44] Dan. 9:25 Cf. Nehemiah 2-13 *See also the Papers entitled Correlating Last Days Scriptures, which includes "Correlating Major Events to Prophecy Chart" and Prophetic Chronology*

[45] Dan. 9:26a *See also The Works of Flavius Josephus: Antiquities of the Jews, Transl. By William Whiston, AP&A, Grand Rapids, 1971 Book XV, Ch. XI. P. 1 Note that the Editor's comment there confirms that the Temple the Romans destroyed in AD 70 was the Third Temple.*

[46] Dan. 9:26b, 27; 12:7; Matt. 23:37-24:2; 24:34; John 2:19-21; 4:14-24; 14:15-27; 16:13-15; Acts 1:8; 2:1 ff.; Rom. 8:11-17,26,27; 1 Cor. 12-14; Eph. 4:1-16 See also the Papers entitled *Illustrating the "Law of Multiple Fulfillments" and Messiah Figures*

[47] Zech. 12:9,10; Matt. 23:37-39; Rom. 11:11-32

[48] *See The Interlinear Bible by Jay Green, Vol. Three, AP&A, Evansville, IN., 1978*

[49] Compare Dan. 2:31-45 and Joel 2,3 with Matt. 21:28-46; Luke 21:20-24; *2 Thess. 1,2 and other references to the "Day of the Lord." See also Chapter 19: "The Event Sequence of the Second Coming of Jesus Christ" and the Papers Emmanuel 2: God is Dealing with Israel/ the Jews and Facts of Scripture: The Church and the Tribulation, Appendix 1*

[50] Dan. 9:26*; 1 Cor. 15:20-28; Rev. 11:15 Cf. Dan. 7:9-28 *The word used for 'end' here is Qets, meaning (to the) extremity, end, infinite or after. Note also that the New American Standard translation of the Bible has the correct syntax for this verse.*

[51] Dan. 9:27 Cf. Jer. 3-31; Ezek. 3-34; Zech. 12:9,10; Matt. 23:37-39; Rom. 11 *See Strongs Exhaustive Concordance of the Bible, Hebrew and Chaldee Dictionary section, #3671 and The Works of Flavius Josephus See also the set of Charts entitled Sequence of Events (leading to the destruction of Jerusalem)*

[52] 1 Sam. 2:1-9; 15:22,23; Matt. 5:43-48; 6:24; 23:1 ff.; 26:51,52; Mark 3:4; Luke 9:51-56 (KJV):16:13-15; Rom. 1:16-32; Gal. 1:6-12; 1 John 1-5 See the papers entitled *A Synopsis of Modern Idolatry among 'professing Christians', Are You Sure What You Believe is Truly Christian Doctrine,*

(the 3 pt. series) *Christianity Vs. Religion, Emmanuel (1)* and *Emmanuel 2*

[53] Dan. 11:31-35; Zech. 11:12-14; Matt. 24:14,15; Luke 20:17,18,; 21:24

[54] Dan. 2; Mal. 3,4; Msatt. 24: Luke 21; Acts 17:31; Rom. 2:16; 2 Thess. 1,2; 2 Pet.3 *A.K.A. Christ's Second Coming*

[55] Dan. 9; Matt. 23:36-39

[56] Matt. 24:3-31, 36-51 *(see also next Fn.)*

[57] Dan. 12; Zech. 12

[58] Isa. 53; Dan. 9; Zech. 9:9,10; 11:12-14

[59] Psa. 2, 110, 118:22; Dan.2:34,35,44,45; Matt. 21:42: Luke 20:17,18

[60] Dan. 9:2, 24-27

[61] Luke 21:24; Rom. 11:25,26

[62] Matt. 23:29-39; 24:34 *See also references in the following papers: The Biblical Precept of Mystery Pg. 9, Contextually Comparing the Elements of Prophetic Scripture Sect. IV, Pgs 11-18, Correlating Last Days Scriptures, Pg. 12, The Doctrine of Last Things Pgs 5,6,22, Fulfilment Prophecy Pg. 18, Illustrating the "Law of Multiple Fulfilments" Sect. III, Pg. 9, Prophetic Chronology One, Pg. 8, Fn. #26 and The Three Passovers of Scripture, Pgs 3,14*

[63] John 10:7-16; Rev.11:1-3

[64] Matt. 24:29-31 *Note that Jesus's statement "the tribulation of those days" refers to that portion of the Great Tribulation Period (GTP) prior to the "Day of te Lord" DTL, viz. Christ's Second Coming. Clue: An easy way to sort this out is to always remember that, during the GTP 'tribulation is man-caused, whereas 'wrath' is God-caused. This is also how we can accurately place the timing of the "Rapture of the Saints" (ROS). See also the book The Church and the Last Days and the papers entitled Correlating Last Days Scriptures and The Doctrine of Last Things*

[65] Dan. 7:25; 11:31-35; 12:6 ff.; Rev. 11:1-3; 12:6,14; 13:5

[66] Dan. 7:22; John 10:7-16; Eph. 2:11-22

Chapter 18:

[1] Exodus 3-15; Lev. 23

[2] Matt. 23:36; 24:29-34 *See also Passover Sequence Chart*

[3] *See the Papers Biblical Symbolism, Section III, Facts of Scripture' Section XII and Appendix 1, Fulfilment prophecy, Sections IV, V and VII, Emmanuel:*

God is Dealing with His People, Section III: "Exile and Gathering Part Two: The Passover and the End Times," Covenant principles, Section III-C-2, The Higher Laws of God and the book The Church and the Last Days, Chapter 12: "Event Sequence" (of the Second Coming of Jesus Christ), which includes the section entitled "Explanatory of the Term 'The Day of the Lord.'"

[4] Psa. 2, 5, 9, 10, 14, 37; 46, 53-59, 68, 73, 97, 109, 110, 137; Prov. 16:18; Eccl. 10:8; Isa. 24-26; Ezek. 22; Joel 2; Amos 6,8,9; Mic. 3; Nahum 1; Matt. 24; Luke 21;John 10:10; Gal. 6:8; 2 Thess. 1:3-10; 2 Pet. 3:7-18; Jude 3 ff. *See also Section IV-B below, and Footnote #18*

[5] Matt. 4; Luke 4; 2 Cor. 4:3-6; 10:3-6; 11:12-15; Eph. 3:10,11; 6:12; 1 John 3:8;5:19

[6] *Notice the sequence in points C to E are repeated several times in the book of Judges in the Old Testament. Remember also that Paul wrote the Corinthians that the things that were chronicled in the Old Testament were put there for our admonition so that we can learn from their (the Hebrew Nation that became ancient Israel) experiences. 1 Cor. 10; Cf. Ezek. 38:10*

[7] *Exodus 12; John 11:49-53 Cf. Matt. 23,24; Psa 118:22; Isa. 28:16; Jer. 2-10; Ezek. 24:21-27*

[8] *Matt. 4:1-1-; Luke 4:1-13; 10:18; Rev. 12-20 Cf. Isa. 14; Ezek. 28, 38 Note also that in Scripture, "Babylon," "Gog and Magog" and "Tyre" are spiritual symbols referring to occult sources or principalities that incite rebellion against God. See also Glossary of Terms' entry *(the archetype of the) Garden* See also the Paper A Biblical Disclosure of Antichrist*

[9] Isa. 14-30

[10] Jer. 10

[11] Ezek. 17, 21, 28, 29, 38* Cf. Rev. 13 *Magog is also the secret moniker for a well-known ex-President that belongs to the Satanic Cult of "Skull& Bones"*

[12] Hab. 2

[13] Esther 1-10

[14] Daniel 2

[15] Matt. 21:42-46; 24:1,2; 26:52; 27:19-25; Luke 19:41-48; 20:17,18; 21:5,6

[16] 2 Thess. 1,2

[17] Rev. 11:15-19; 19:1 f. Cf. Jer. 10:11; Joel 2

[18] Deut. 32:1 ff.; Psa. 1:1 ff.; 7:11-16; 94:13; Prov. 26:27; Isa. 61:1 f.; Mark 9:42-50; Luke 21:20-22; Rom. 12:19-21; Gal. 6:7,8; Rev. 12-21

[19] Ezek. 21:1 ff.; 32:17-32 Cf. Isa. 14; Ezek. 28; Rev. 19:11-21; 20:7-15; 21:8

[20] *See Glossary of Terms' entry *Kenosis**

[21] *Romans 1:18 ff.; 5:8 ff.; 9:17-23; 2 Thess. 1:4-2:12 See also the Papers entitled A Biblical Disclosure of Antichrist and Destiny and Free Will, the book Spiritual Guidelines for Restoration, Chapter 20, Spiritual Law #10 and the book The Church in the Last Days, Chapter 12, "The Event Sequence"*

[22] Matt. 24:29-31; 2 Thess. 1:7.f

[23] Prov. 21:1

[24] 1) Dan. 2:31-45; 7:7 ff.; 2) Matt. 21:42-26; 3) 2 Thess. 2:3-12; 4) 2 Pet. 3:9-13; 5) Rev. 13:11-18 Cf. Psa. 118:22; Isa. 28:14-22; Luke 20:17,18

[25] *See the book The Church in the Last Days*

[26] *In particular, compare Dan. 2:35, noticing the description of the destruction, with Matt. 21:44 See also Romans 9:17-23, keeping in mind that God's perfect foreknowledge is not the same as the "Calvinistic' misinterpretation of "predestination." See the Paper Destiny and Free Will*

[27] Dan. 2:34,35, 44,45; Matt. 21:42-46; Luke 20:17,18

[28] **2 Thess. 2:7-12 Cf. Rom. 1:18-32 *Note that God is not the source of evil or deception, but allows these things to happen to fulfill prophecies.*

[29] Rev. 8-11, 14-21

[30] Matt. 24:13; Rom. 12:19-21

[31] Psa. 78; Isa. 6, 30, 63; Jer. 31 *See the Paper Emmanuel: God is Dealing with His People*

[32] See Hebrews 11

[33] Matt. 20; 2 Pet. 3:9

[34] Heb. 12:14-17

[35] Luke 21:15-19; Rom.5:1-5; 8:23-28; Heb. 10:26-39; Rev. 12:10,11; 13:10

[36] Exodus 3-15; Ezek. 29:3 f. *See also Glossary of Terms' entry *Affliction**

[37] Isa. 52:13-53:12; Matt. 23:35; Luke 11:51 See also the Paper entitled *The Messiah Figures* and the set of Charts entitled *Catalogue of Events which includes the Passover Sequence Chart, which covers the details of Jesus' passion Week*

[38] Jer. 31:31-34; Matt. 26:26-29; Luke 22:15-20; John 19:30; Heb. 1,7-10

[39] Isa. 53; Jer. 31; Matt. 23,24

[40] *See the Paper entitled A Biblical Disclosure of Antichrist, the book Spiritual Guidelines for Restoration, "Historical Review" section and Appendix C: "Historical Timeline Chart*

[41] *See the book The Church in the Last Days and the Paper Facts of Scripture: The Church and the Tribulation*

[42] Matt. 24:13; John 10:27; Acts 20:17 ff.; Rom. 8; Col. 1:13,14; 2 Tim. 1-4; Heb. 10:26-39; 1 Pet. 1:1 ff.; 2 Pet. 1:2-11

[43] Matt. 26:52 Cf. Matt. 5:43-48; Luke 9:51-56

[44] 2 Thess. 1:3-12; Heb. 10:26-39; Rev. 21:6-8

[45] *See the Paper Christianity Versus Religion*

[46] *See the 1929 book Propaganda by Edward Bernays*

[47] Rev. 13:9-18

[48] *See the Papers A Biblical Disclosure of Antichrist, A Profile of Antichrist and What is Collectivism?*

[49] *The "Fractional Reserve" device is the practice of only requiring banks to keep a 'fraction' of the depositor's 'cash' on hand, while concurrently tallying 'on paper' or in computer files, the full amount of value they do not actually possess, but with which they nonetheless grant loans.*

[50] 2 Thess. 2:3-12; Rev. 13:9-18

[51] Prov. 22:7

[52] *For more reading on this subject see the book The Creature from Jekyll Island by G. Edward Griffin*

[53] *See the papers A Biblical Disclosure of Antichrist and What is Collectivism?*

[54] Matt. 5:43-48; 10:16; 26:52; Luke 22:53; John 1:1-5; 16:33; Rom. 12:19-21; 2 Cor. 10:3-6; Eph. 6:12

[55] Isa. 14:12-15; 24:17-23; 66:4,22-24; Jer. 10:11; Rom. 1:18-32; 3:10-18; Rev. 11:15-18

[56] Rev. 13:12-18

[57] Ezek. 8; 2 Cor. 11:12-15; Rev. 17:1 ff. *See also the Paper Authority and Conscience, also found in the writer's book Jesus' Way, Appendix B*

[58] Rom. 8; Heb. 12:14

[59] Rev. 19:10,13 *See also the Papers What is Liberty? and What is Collectivism?*

Chapter 19:

[255] Matt. 4:1–10; Luke 4:1–13.

[256] John 8:37–59; 10:10; Rom. 1:18–2:16

[257] Matt. 16:18; Rom. 1:18–2:16; 8:31–39; 12:1–3; 2 Cor. 10:1–9; Eph. 6:10–18; 2 Pet. 2.

[258] Rev. 12:10,11; 14:12,13

[259] Luke 4:18; John 3:16,17; 5:24,37–47; 6:27–29; 7:29; 8:16–18; 26–29; 13:16; Gal. 4:4. *See also the papers entitled "Are You Sure What You Believe is Truly Christian Doctrine," "Bonehead Christianity," "Divergent Belief Systems," the 2 part series "How Should We Then Live" and "Key Aspects of the Christian Gospel"*

[260] 2 Cor. 6:14–18; Gal. 4:30; Eph. 5:8; James 3:1–4:8; 1 John 2:15–17; Rev. 17.

[261] Matt. 10:16–42; 2 Tim. 2:1–12. ** *See the paper "Key Aspects of the Christian Gospel"*

[262] John 14:6:16:15; Eph. 1:19–23.

[263] Matt. 5:38–48; 16:21–26; Luke 9:23; John 12:23 ff.; Col. 3:1 f.; 1 John 1 ff.

[264] John 17:1 ff.; Rom. 12:9–21; 13:8 ff.; Col. 3:12,13; Titus 2:11–15; 1 John 2:1– 4:21.

[265] Matt. 18:18–20; 28:18–20; 2 Tim. 2:15–26; 1 Pet. 3:15.

[266] Rom. 8:28–39; Rev. 12:10,11

[267] *See the paper: "Christian Conversion, Part One: Introduction to Christian Conversion"*

[268] Matt. 5:27–48; 6:24; 12:39; 1 Cor. 6:9–20; Rev. 17:5 *See "What is the Body of Christ"*

[269] Matt. 6:22–24; 7:13–23; 13:24–30,36–43; 16:21–26; Luke 6:22; 9:51–62; 13:5–9; 22–35; 14:26– 33; 16:13; John 7:7,15–18; 12:23–26; 15:18–25; 17:1 ff.; Rom. 8:1 ff.; 1 Cor. 1:17–2:16; 2 Cor. 3:17–4:18 *See the papers "Basics of Biblical Church Governance," "Guidelines for Renewed Leadership" and "Two Divergent Belief Systems"*

[270] Matt. 13:24–30, 37–43; 2 Thess. 2:1–4; 1 John 4:1–6. *See the papers entitled "Analysis of the Causes and Effects of Apostasy,' 'an Analysis of Faith' and 'Investigating the Symptoms of latter-day Problems afflicting the Church'*

[271] Rev. 7:9–17

[272] 2 Tim. 4:1–8

[273] James 5:7,8; Rev. 12: 10,11

[274] Matt. 5:38–48; 1 John 2:1-11

[275] Song 2:4; John 13–17; Phil. 3:7–21; 1 John 2:12 f.;4:7-21; James 4:1 ff.

[276] Matt. 28:20; Acts 17:24–31; Rom. 8; 1 Cor. 10:12,13; 2 Cor. 5:8; 2 Tim. 1:7–12; 1 John 2:1–6; 4:1–6; 5:1–12.

[277] Matt. 10; 24:1 ff.; 28:18–20; Gal. 1:6–12; 2 Tim. 4:1–8.

[278] John 15:1 ff.

[279] Matt. 24:27–31; Luke 21:8 ff.; 1 Cor. 15:23; 1 Thess. 4:13–17; James 5:7–9; Rev. 1:7.

[280] John 16:33; Rom. 8:35–39; 1 John 4:1–6; Rev. 12:11; 13:10; 14:12.

[281] 1 Cor. 15:50–58; 1 Thess. 4:13–17; 5:1–11.

[282] Matt. 5:1–12; Rom. 14:10; 1 Cor. 3:9–16; 4:4,5; 2 Cor. 5:10.

[283] Luke 14:16–24; Rev. 19:6–13.

Chapter 20:

[284] Matt. 24:27 f.; Mark 13:24–37; Luke 21:27,28; Acts 1:11; 1 Cor. 1:7; 15:23–25; Phil. 1:6; Col. 3:3; 1 Thess. 1:3; 2:19; 3:13; 4:13–17; 5:2,3,23; 2 Thess. 1:6–10; 2:1; 3:5; 1 Tim. 6:12–14; 2 Tim. 1:10; James 5:7,8; 2 Pet. 3:4–13; Rev. 1:7.

[285] Matt. 24:29

[286] Matt. 24:27–31; Luke 21:27; Rev. 1:7; 6:12–17.

[287] Matt. 24:30; Rev. 6:15–17.

[288] Matt. 24:30; 1 Cor. 15:50–54; 1 Thess. 4:15; 2 Tim. 4:8.

[289] 1 Cor. 15:23; 1 Thess. 4:15,16.

[290] Matt. 24:27–31; Luke 21:27,28; 1 Thess. 4:17; Rev. 7:9–17. *See the papers entitled "Correlating Last Days Scriptures," "The Doctrine of Last Things" and "Facts of Scripture: the Church and the Tribulation"*

[291] Matt. 5:21,22; Rom. 14:10; 1 Cor. 4:1–5; 2 Cor. 5:8–10.

[292] 2 Thess. 1:6–10; 2 Pet. 3:3–12; Rev. 8:1–9:21; 14:14–18:24.

[293] Dan. 9:24–27; 12:10–12; Luke 21:24; Rom. 11:25,26; Rev. 10–12. *See also The Doctrine of the Elect/Ekklesia*

[294] *(Postulated timing)* Matt. 25:1–13; John 14:1–3; Rev. 19:1–10.

[295] Rev. 16:16

[296] Psa. 2,110; Eph. 1:17–23; 2 Thess. 1:6–10; Rev. 17:1–18:24; 19:11–21.

[297] Zech. 14:1–4; Matt. 12:1 ff.; 25:14 ff.; 28:20; Luke 19:11–27; Acts 1:11; Phil. 2:10,11; Rev. 11:15; 19:11–21; 20:1–6.

[298] Rev. 20:1–6

[299] Matt. 19:28; 25:14 ff.; Acts 17:31; Rom. 2:1–16; Rev. 2:26–29; 11:1–4; 12:5; 19:13

[300] Isa. 13:6–14:27; 34:8–17; Jer. 46:1 ff.; Ezek. 30:3 f.

[301] Isa. 1:1 ff.; Joel 1:1–2:32; Amos 5:6; Mal, 3,4; Isa. 2:12–22; Joel 3:1 f.; Obad. 1:15

[302] Zech 14:1–9 Cf. Zech. 9:9; 1 Cor. 15:20–28; Rev. 10:7–11:15

[303] Heb. 9:9,10

[304] Heb. 9:9–15

[305] Heb. 8:6–9

[306] Rev. 14:12,13

[307] 2 Thess. 1:1–12; Rev. 16:12,13 *See also Chapter 10, Sect. II and the paper entitled 'a Biblical Disclosure of Antichrist'*

[308] Rev. 17:1; 18:24

[309] Rev. 11:14–19;16:16,17 *Armageddon is the Hebrew: 'Ar Megiddo=Mt. Megiddo*

Chapter 21:

[310] John 15:1–12; Rom. 2:1–16.

[311] Matt. 13; 22:1–14; 25:1–13; 2 Cor. 11:2; 1 Pet. 4:17.

[312] Rom. 14:10; 2 Cor. 5:8–10.

[313] Matt. 19:28; 25:14 ff.; Acts 17:31; Rom. 2:11–16.

[314] Luke 10:22; John 5:22,23.

[315] Rom. 14:10; 2 Cor. 5:8–10.

[316] Matt. 5:10–12; 6:4,6,18; 10:42; 16:27; 25:1 ff.; Luke 6:23,35; 1 Cor. 3:1–4.

[317] Matt. 6:24; Heb. 12:1 ff.

[318] 1 John 5:3

319 Matt. 28:18–20; Luke 22:15–22; John 14:12–24; 15:10–17; Phil. 3:19–21; Col. 3:1–7; Heb. 11.

[320] Matt. 25:1 ff.; Acts 17:30,31; Rom. 2:1–16.

[321] Matt. 5:21,22; Luke 10:21,22; 21:36; John 5:22; 8:15,16; Acts 10:34–43; Eph. 6:9.

[322] 2 Cor. 5:1–21

[323] 1 Cor. 4:1–5

[324] 1 Cor. 11:23–32

[325] Gal. 5:13–25; 2 Tim. 2:1–14; 1 Pet. 4:17.

[326] Luke 6:46–49; 1 Cor. 3:9–17.

[327] See "Jesus's Major Parables"

[328] Luke 16

[329] Matt. 6:24

[330] **See Appendix B: What Type of Christian are you?

[331] Matt. 15:7–14 **See also the position paper: Authority and Conscience

[332] John 13–17; 1 Cor. 13; Gal. 5:22,23.

[333] Matt. 13:24–43; John 4:34–38

[334] Luke 14:7–24

[335] John 13:34,35; 1 Cor. 11:28–32

[336] Acts 20:17–38; 1 Cor. 1:17–2:16; 2 Cor. 3:1–4:7; Gal. 1:6–2:21; Col. 2:1 ff. See the papers entitled "Facilitating Revival," "Investigating the Symptoms of Latter-day Problems," and "Patriarchalism in the Church"

[337] 1 Cor. 3:1 ff.; 2 Tim. 2:19–26. See the papers entitled "Basics of Biblical Church Governance" and the 3 part series "Christianity Versus Religion"

[338] Matt. 24–38; 16:21–26; Luke 9:23–26; 14:26–33; Acts 20:19–38; Gal. 1:6–12; 2 Tim. 2:1–15. See the papers entitled "Failed Expectations" and "God's Universal Attitude Test"

[339] Matt. 5:10–12; 10:24–38; Luke 12:49–53 14:26–33; Eph. 6:10–18; 2 Tim. 2:1–15. See the papers entitled "the Baptism of Jesus Christ"

[340] Gen. 4:7; Matt. 5:22–25,38–48; 26:51,52; Luke 6:46–49; 9:51–56; Rom. 12:9– 21; Eph. 4:26–31; Col. 3:8; James 1:14,15; 1 John 3:1–15; 4:7–21 See Glossary of Terms entry *Faith-Based Pacifism* See also the author's book "Jesus' Way," Dorrance Publishing Co., Pittsburgh, 2009

Chapter 22:

[341] 2 Cor. 12:1–4

[342] 2 Pet. 3:9; Rev. 14:6,7

[343] Isa. 53:9; Matt. 5:1–7:29; 10:16; Luke 9:51–56; Phil. 2:12–16; Heb. 7:26; Rev. 12:10,11; 14:12,13.

[344] Matt. 24:27–31; 1 Cor. 15:23; 1 Thess. 4:13–17; James 5:7; Rev. 7:9-17

[345] 2 Thess. 1:6–10; 2:1–12; 2 Pet. 3:10 f.; Rev. 14:14 ff.

[346] Matt. 25:1–13; 1 Pet. 4:17.

[347] 2 Chr. 7:14; Dan. 9:4-19; Matt. 6:1–15,33; Luke 11:1–13; 1 Cor. 11:23–34

[348] 2 Chr. 7:14; Psalms 32, 51; Neh. 9; Dan. 9 *See the paper entitled "the Doctrine of Repentance"*

[349] Matt. 18:1 ff.; Luke 9:44–48; 2 Cor. 2:14–17.

[350] Mark 9:38–50; Luke 9:49,50. *See also the papers entitled Basics of Biblical Church Governance and Guidelines for Renewed Leadership*

[351] Matt. 15:1 f.; Mark 9:38–40; 1 Cor. 3:1 f.; Gal. 4:16. *See the paper entitled "Christian Guidelines for Spiritual Warfare, Part 4: Knowing Your Enemy" and the 3 part series entitled "Christianity Versus Religion"*

[352] Matt. 5:17–32; Mark 10:1–12. *See the 2 part series of papers entitled "Authority and Conscience"*

[353] Matt. 23; Luke 16:1–15.

Appendix A:

[354] Luke 11:29–14:35; 1 Cor. 4:8–21; Heb. 10:26–39; 12:1 ff. *See also the papers entitled "Two Divergent belief Systems" and "Facilitating Revival"*

[355] *Compare scriptures like:* Daniel 2:19–45; 11:30–12:4; Matt. 24; Luke 21; 2 Thess. 1,2; Revelation 6–20

[356] Rev. 13

[357] *See Chapter 10 and the paper "A Biblical Disclosure of Antichrist."*

[358] *Note that Scripture does not say that "Antichrist will make a covenant with Israel."*

[359] Rev. 13

[360] 1 Cor. 10:12,13

Appendix C:

[1] 1 John 4:1-6

[2] John 1:1 f.; 17:17; 1 John 1:1; 5:7; Rev. 19:10,13

[3] Jer. 31:31-34; Matt. 24:14; Acts 17:24-31; Heb. 1:1 f.

[4] Psa. 73; John 4:23,24; 8:31-36; 1 Cor. 1:17-2:16 See the Paper *Fulfilment Prophecy*

[5] For more details on these guidelines see the paper: *Hermeneutics: Basic Principles of Scripture Interpretation*

[6] Matt. 18:3.4; 19:13,14

[7] Matt. 15:1-14; 23:1 ff.; Luke 11-13 See also Footnotes 15,28,34

[8] *See A Seeker's Guide to Biblical Faith*

[9] **Note that the TOHY periods are a.k.a. "1260 Days," "42 Months," "a Time, Times and a Dividing (a half) of time," "in the midst of the week" and sometimes "3 ½ Days": Dan. 7:25; 9:27; 12:7; Rev. 11:2,11; 12:6,14; 13:5 See also the book The Church in the Last Days and the following: A Biblical Disclosure of Antichrist, Facts of Scripture: The Church and the Tribulation, The Doctrine of Last Things, The Three Passovers, Last Days Time Line Diagrams and Historical Time Line Chart See also Section IV and the Appendices*

[10] John 14:6-9, 15-26; 15:26; 16:7-15

[11] *See the diagram "Postulating Overlaps" in Appendices. See also The Church in the Last Days, Chapter 12: "Event Sequence" paragraph V: Explanatory on "The Day of the Lord."*

[12] Matt. 24; Mark 13; Luke 21,24

[13] Matt. 25:1-13

[14] *See the Paper Jesus; Major Parables*

[15] Matt. 18:10-14; 25:14 ff.; John 10:1-16

[16] John 16:33

[17] Rom. 11:25,26; 1 Cor. 15:20-28; 1 Thess. 4:13-18; 2 Thess. 1:7-2:12; 2 Tim. 3:1-7

[18] James 5:7,8

[19] 2 Pet. 2:2-3:10

[20] 1 John 2:15-27; Rev. 6:12-7:17; 11:1 f.; 12:1-11; 13:5

[21] Dan. 2:19-45; 7:25; 9:24-27; 12:7,11,12; Matt. 24; Luke 21

[22] *E. G., Ezek. 40-48 is a "pictorial vision – prophecy" written during the captivity that "looks forward" to the New Covenant. In that way it is similar to Ch. 37, Zechariah and Revelation. FYI.: See also the Paper Biblical Symbolism, Section D, #24-26 (Pgs 26-32)*

[23] *Ezek. 36:16-23; 37:1-1-3; Dan. 9:24-27 *See also the Paper entitled: The Three Passovers of Scripture, Paragraph VI: "Unique Aspects of Passover Chronology"*

[24] Psa. 68:18; Isa. 7:14; 9:6; Jer. 31:31-34; Ezek. 37: 4 ff.; Matt. 26:26-28; Luke 22:20-22

[25] Dan. 2:44.45; Matt. 10:24-42; Acts 17:24-31; Rom. 11:25,26; 1 Cor. 15:20-58; Phil. 2:5-11

[26] Daniel 7:25; 9:24-27; 12:7

[27] Daniel 12:11,12

[28] Zech. 3-6*; 9:9-17; 12:10 *Note: This Scripture* first applies physically to Nehemiah's/ Zerubbabel's rebuilding of the Jewish Temple (#2) and second, spiritually, to the cessation of "ritual Temple worship" and God's restoration of spiritual worship by the New Covenant way of Faith in Jesus Christ, The BRANCH. John 4:23,24 See also the Papers entitled Biblical Symbolism, Christian Worship and the True Temple and Spirituality and Worship*

[29] Matt. 24; Luke 21

[30] 1 Thess. 4:13-18; 2 Thess. 1:7-2:12

[31] Rev. 7:9-17; 11:1-4; 12:7; 13:5 Cf. Zech. 4

[32] *See the Papers entitled The Biblical Role of Israel, Sect. IV-D, The Doctrine of Last Things, Sect. VII, (Pg. 20, Footnote #33), Facts Concerning the 70th Week of Daniel, Sect. III and The Higher Laws of God, Pg. 7, Footnote #16*

[33] Matt. 13:10; Mark 4:11; Luke 8:10; 1 Cor. 1:17-2:16; 1 Tim. 3:16; Rev. 10:7 See the Papers entitled *The Biblical Precept of Mystery* and *The Key to Understanding Scripture,* Section II

[34] Job. 32:8; Prov. 1:7,23; 8:1 ff.; 9:10; Matt. 10:22; 24:13; Luke 21; Rom. 5:1-5; 8:1 ff.; 1 Cor. 4:1-5; 13:1 ff. ; Eph. 1:8,17; Col. 1:12-27; Heb. 1-4, 6, 9-12; James 1; 3:13-18; 2 Pet. 1:19-21; Rev. 12:10,11; 14:12

[35] John 10:1-16; Rom. 11:25,26; 1 Cor. 15:20-28, 51-58; Eph. 3:1-11; Col. 1:12-29; 2: 1-3; Heb. 1:1 f.; 10:12-39; 12:22-29; Rev. 10:7 *See the Paper entitled The Biblical Precept of Mystery, Sect. II-B and IV*

[36] Rev. 10:7 *See also the Papers entitled The Biblical Precept of Mystery, The Biblical Role of the Jews Sect. IV-D, The Doctrine of Last Things, Sect. VII, Facts Concerning the 70ᵗʰ Week of Daniel, Pg. 3, One Covenant for All, Sect. V-D, Patterns in Prophetic Scripture, Sect. IV-C & D, Prophetic Chronology Two, Sect. IV*

[37] Daniel 2:31-45; 9:24-27

[38] Daniel 7:7-28; 2 Thess. 2:3-12 *See also the Papers entitled: A Biblical Disclosure of Antichrist, The Higher Laws of God, A Historical Sketch of Antichrist Figures, and *Illustrating the 'Law of Multiple Fulfillments' Ibid. Footnotes #9 and #30*

[39] Zech. 3,4; 14:4-9; Rev. 10:7; 11:1-18 Cf. Jer. 31; Ezek. 36; John 10; 1 Cor. 15; Eph. 1-4; 1 Tim. 2:5 See also the Paper *Biblical Symbolism*, Sect. IV-C, P. 19-21, D, P. 24 and O, P. 3,4,10,11

[40] Rev. 12:1-14; 13:1 ff.; 17:1 ff.

[41] Dan. 9:24-27; Zech. 2; Matt. 24:15-22; Luke 21:20-28; *1 Thess. 5:9; Heb. 11; Rev. *7:9-17; 11:1-13 See the book *The Church in the Last Days* and the Paper entitled *Facts of Scripture: The Church and the Tribulation* See also *Fox's Book of Martyrs*

[42] Matt. 24:29-31; Luke 21:20-24; John 16:33; 1 Cor. 15:20-23; 1 Thess, 4:13-17;5:9; 2 Thess. 1:5-2:12; Rev. 7:14-17 *Notice also that all these Scriptures tell us that the Rapture comes after the Tribulation, taking place during Christ's Second Coming.*

[43] Matt. 24:21-31, 36,37,42-46; Mark 13:24-27; Luke 21:34-36; 2 Thess. 2:1-7; 2 Pet. 2:1-3; Rev. 2,3 *Notice that these warnings relate to a runaway apostasy in the church, rendering it impotent, neutralizing its influence against evil, thus unleashing antichrist. For more details concerning this see the papers entitled A Biblical Disclosure of Antichrist and Facts of Scripture: The Church and the Tribulation*

[44] Compare Daniel 9:24-26 to Matt. 24 and Luke 21

[45] John 17; Acts 17:24-31; Rom. 11; 1 Cor. 15:20-23; Phil. 1:6; 1 Thess. 4:13-5:12

[46] Isaiah 2; Joel 2; Micah 3,4; Matt. 24; Luke 21; 2 Thess. 1,2; Rev. 6,7

[47] Ezra 7:6-28; 8:32-36 *See The Chronological Bible by Edward Reese, c. 1977 Regal Publishers, Nashville, Pages 1161 and 1210 -1214*

[48] Jer. 3:12-19; Ezek. 20:33-24:27; Matt. 24:1 ff.; John 2:19-21; Acts 7:48;17:24-31

[49] Jer. 7:1-12; 31:31-34; Dan. 9:26,27; Matt. 27:50-54; John 2:19-21; 4:23,24 *For more info see the Paper entitled The Doctrine of Last Things *The Roman Prince, Titus*

[50] Dan. 2:44,45; 7:25; 9:24-27; 12:7,11,12; Zech. 12:10; Matt. 24; Luke 21; Rom. 11:25,26; Rev. 11:1-4,11; 12:14; 13:5 Ibid. *Footnote #9*

[51] Dan. 9:26,27; Matt. 24:2,3, 15 ff.; Luke 21:20-24 **See Figure One: "The Seventy Weeks" and "Correlating Major Events Chart" at the end of this Paper and the companion Paper: Sequence of Events (leading to the destruction of Jerusalem and the Great Temple in 70 AD).*

[52] John 2:19-21; Acts 7:48; Acts 17:24-31 See also the Paper *Christian Worship and the True Temple*

[53] Dan. 9:27; 2 Thess. 1:6-10; Rev. 11:15-18

[54] Dan. 2:31-45; 7:24,25; 9:24-27*; 12:7 *Verse 27 shows the "split point" occurring "in the midst of the week"*

[55] *Carefully read Matt. 24 and Luke 21 and you will see*

[56] *See the Papers entitled Correlating the Prophecies concerning TOHY Periods, The Doctrine of Last Things, Emmanuel 1* and *Emmanuel 2, Facts Concerning the 70th Week of Daniel* and *Fulfilment Prophecy*

[57] 1 Cor. 15:20,23 Cf. Matt. 24:29-31

[58] Matt. 24;29-31; Luke 21:5-28; Rom. 11:11-26; 1 Cor. 15:20-23; Phil. 1:6; 1 Thess. 4:13-17; 5:9; James 5:8

[59] Daniel 7:21,22; John 15:18-16:3; 16:33; Rom. 8:26-39; 1 Cor. 10:12,13; 2 Cor. 1:1-22; 2 Thess. 1:4-2:12; James 5:7,8; 2 Pet. 3:8-18

[60] Matt. 24:29-31; Luke 21:20-28; John 14:26; 15:26; 16:13-15; Gal. 1:6-12; 1 Tim. 6:3-5

[61] Psa. 110; 118:22; Isa. 28:16; Matt. 21:41-46; 1 Cor. 10:12,13

[62] Matt. 24:29-31; Luke 20:9-19; 21:24; Rom. 11:25,26; Rev. 10:7; 11:15-19; 15:1 16:21; 19:1 ff. *See also the Papers entitled Jesus' Major Parables, Correlating Prophecies concerning "TOHY" Periods* and *Facts Concerning the 70th Week of Daniel*

[63] **Dan. 9:24-27; Rev. 10:7; 11:1-4; 12:14; 13:5 See also the Papers entitled *Biblical Symbolism, The Doctrine of Last Things, The Higher Laws of God, Illustrating the "Law of Multiple Fulfillments"* and *The Key to Understanding Scripture is Spiritual Exegesis*

[64] Matt. 24:29-31; John 10:1-16; Gal. 2:16-5:25; *2 Thess. 1:3-2:12; 2 Tim. 3:1-7; 2 Pet. 2:3-3:13; 1 John 2:15-4:6; Rev. 2,3; 6:9-7:17; 11:1 ff.;

13:1-18:24 Ibid. *Footnotes 15,28,34 *Note also that the moniker 'man of sin' is a general characteristic germane to the negative consequences of humanism that afflict people worldwide: It does not necessarily indicate that 'antichrist' is an individual person, but rather a "global system of government" which fits perfectly with John's descriptions in Apocalypse. See also the Papers entitled Facts of Scripture: The Church and the Tribulation and Prophetic Chronology Two*

[65] Matt. 24:4-6*, 7-14, 24:15-28*; 29-51

Appendix C (2):

[1] Dan. 2:38

[2] Dan. 2:36-45

[3] Jer. 31:31-34; John 4:23,24

[4] Dan. 3; 4:1-3; Ezek. 33-48

[5] Daniel 4:4-37

[6] Cf. Daniel 2

[7] Dan. 5,6,9-12

[8] Jer. 32,33

[9] Ezra 7:6,7, 11-28 *The Chronological Bible by Edward Reese, Regal Publishers, Nashville, 1977, P. 1210,1211*

[10] Daniel 8

[11] *See The Story of Civilization, by Will Durant, Vol II, "The Life of Greece," chapters XXII to XXX*

[12] *See Flavius Josephus' Antiquities of the Jews Bk. XV, Ch. XI. P. 1*

[13] *See The Works of Flavius Josephus, Flavius Josephus, Translated by William Whiston, AP&A, Grand Rapids, 1971, Antiquities, Book XVII., Ch. VI., P. 4. See also Isa. 7:14; 9:6; Dan. 2:44,45; Mic. 5:2*

[14] John 2:20

[15] Dan. 9:25

[16] Isa. 53; Dan. 9:26

[17] Dan. 9:27 *a See also the Chart entitled Sequence of Events (Regarding the Jewish War of the First Century)*

[18] Dan. 2:41-43

[19] Dan. 9:27 b; Rev. 13:5; 17:1 ff.

[20] Dan. 2:44,45; Matt. 24:29-31; Acts 17:24-31; 2 Thess. 1,2; Rev. 11:15

Appendix D:

[1] *That is the following, in order of their appearance in Scripture: "A Time and Times and the Dividing of Time" (Dan. 7:25), "in the midst of the Week" (Dan. 9:27), "a Time, Times and a Half" (Dan. 12:7; Rev. 12:14), "a Thousand two hundred and threescore days" (Rev. 11:3; 12:6),* "Forty-Two Months" (Rev. 11:2; 13:5) and "Three Days and a half" (Rev.11:11) See also the Paper Prophetic Chronology Two, Sect. IV: "Chart One: Correlating Prophetic Texts and Acrostics" *Note: Jewish Ext. Period (JEP) adds 75 Days Cf. Dan. 12:11,12*

[2] *See the following Papers: The Biblical Role of Israel, Contextually Comparing the Elements of Prophetic Scripture, Correlating Last Days Scriptures, The Doctrine of Last Things, Emmanuel 1, Emmanuel 2; Facts Concerning the 70th Week of Daniel and Facts of Scripture: The Church and the Tribulation*

[3] *Rev. 10:7 This Scripture is part of a "parenthetical vision" including Revelation chapters ten to twelve. See line #4 in chart and the Paper entitled The Biblical Precept of Mystery*

[4] *Dan. 2:40-45; 7:7,8, 19-26 See the book entitled Wars of the Jews, by Flavius Josephus, translated by William Whiston, AP&A, Grand Rapids, 1971, Book III, Chapter I See also the writer's Historical Chart entitled Sequence of Events*

[5] Rev. 13 Ibid. Footnote #8

[6] Rev. 6-9

[7] Rev. 10-12 Cf. Dan. 9:26b,27; 12:11,12; Zech. 12:9,10: Matt. 23:37-39; Rom. 11:25 *See also line #6 in the chart (Section II below)*

[8] Rev. 13-18 Cf. Dan. 2:44,45; Matt. 21:33-44; 24:29-51; Luke 19-21; 2 Thess. 1,2; 2 Pet. 3:9-14 *See also line #3 in the chart and the Paper A Biblical Disclosure of Antichrist*

[9] Dan. 7:19-25

[10] Dan. 9:24-26

[11] *Dan. 12:1-10 Cf. Rev. 7:9-17; 12:6, 14; 13:5

[12] **Rev. 10:1-11:13 Cf. Matt. 23:37-39; Luke 21:24; Rom. 11:25 *See also next page line #5*

[13] Rev. 11:3 Cf. 12:14; 13:5 See also Zech. 4:1-5, 11-14

[14] Rev. 11:7-14 Cf. 7:9-17: 12:1 ff. *Apparently, all these Scriptures describe antichrists' persecution, "wearing down of the Saints" and the subsequent major event we call the "Rapture," in different terms and symbolism See also the book The Church in the Last Days, Chapters 9-12 and Facts of Scripture: The Church and the Tribulation

[15] Dan. 9:26,27; 12:11,12; Zech. 12:9,10; Matt. 23:39; Luke 21:24; Rom. 9:6-8; 11:11-33; Gal. 3:1 ff.; 4:19-26; 6:15,16; Rev. 14-18 *Ibid. Footnote #7 (Pg. 4)

[16] Rev. 11:15; 17:14 See also Appendix two

[17] Prov. 8; 1 Cor, 2:9-16

[18] Among these are the "Messianic Psalms," the prophecies of Isaiah, Jeremiah, Ezekiel, Daniel and Zechariah, Jesus' Prophetic Discourse in the Synoptics, Paul's letter to the Romans and second letter to the Thessalonians and John's Apocalypse (Revelation)

[19] Dan. 9:27; 12:1-13; Zech. 12:9,10; Matt. 23:37-24:51; Luke 21:20-24; Rom. 11:25

[20] Gen. 12:3; 22:18; Dan. 2:44,45; Acts 3:25; Gal. 3:8 See also the Papers The Fulfillment of God's Promise to Abraham, The Biblical Precept of Mystery, The Biblical Role of Israel, Fulfilment Prophecy (see the Diagram: "The Nine Ages") and The Messiah Figures

[21] Compare the contexts of the aforementioned "TOHY" references: Dan. 7:25; 9:27; 12:7; Rev. 11:2,3,11; 12:6,14; 13:5, associating them with the appropriate historical "Tribulation Type" period in which the reference or references applies, also considering the "multiple fulfillment" precept that underlies many prophecies.

[22] Dan. 2:44,45; Matt. 24,25; Luke 21; Rom. 9-11; 2 Thess. 1,2; Rev. 6-11, 12, 13 See Catalogue of Events, Correlating Last Days Scriptures Sect's II-IV, Destiny and Free Will, Emmanuel 1,2; Event Sequence, Fulfilment Prophecy and The Three Passovers of Scripture

[23] Matt. 24:29-31 See also the book The Church in the Last Days Chapters 8-12 and the Paper Facts of Scripture: The Church and the Tribulation

[24] Gal. 1:6-13; 1 Tim. 6:3

[25] See the books Jesus' Way: God's Guaranteed Blueprint, The Church and the Last Days and the reference entitled Basic Christian Doctrine. See also the Papers entitled A Biblical Disclosure of Antichrist, Are You Sure What You Believe and Practice is Truly Christian Doctrine, Authority and Conscience, Authority and Conscience 2, Basic Observations regarding God's Rules, The

Beauty and Finesse of the New Covenant, The Biblical Precept of Mystery, Biblical Prosperity: God's Definition Vs the World, Bonehead Christianity; The Three part Series on "Christian Conversion": Introduction to Christian Conversion, Christian Conversion Part Two: Factors in the Conversion Process and Christian Conversion Part Three: The Necessity of Conversion; Christian Conversion and the True Temple, Christianity Versus Religion (A Three Part Series), Cracking the False Doctrine Code, Destiny and Free Will, Divergent Belief Systems, The Doctrine of Repentance, Facts of Scripture: The Church and the Tribulation, Fallacies of Determinism, God's Definition of Salvation, God's Universal Attitude Test, The Higher Laws of God, The Holy Spirit is God's Revelator, How Should we then Live (A Two part Series), Jesus' Major Parables, Key Aspects of the Christian Gospel, The Key to Understanding (Scripture) is Spiritual Exegesis, Looking Through the Lens of Jesus Christ, The Major Elements of Biblical Salvation, The Messiah Figures, The New Covenant, One Covenant for All, The Primacy of the Christian Gospel, Principles of Fulfillment Theology, Regarding the Headship of Jesus Christ, The Role of Conscience, The Spiritual Laws of Revival, Spirituality and Worship and The Way of the Cross

[26] *See the Paper Facts Concerning the 70th Week of Daniel*

[27] *The Diagram entitled "Last Days Timeline Chart Part Two" is in the book The Church in the Last Days,* Appendix C. It can also be found in the Papers entitled *Facts of Scripture: The Church and the Tribulation,* Appendix 3 and *The Doctrine of Last Things,* CC. 2

[28] Rom. 11:25-33; Rev. 7:1-8 *(the 144k of Jewish Witnesses);* 14:1-7 *(the 144k of Gentile Witnesses);* 7:9-17 (the Rapture); 11:1-11 Cf. Zech. 4:1-7, 11-14

[29] 2 Thess. 2:3 f.; Gal. 6:15,16; Phil. 3:3; Rev. 10:7; 11: 1 ff.

[30] Dan. 9:26,27; 12:11,12; Matt. 23:37-39; Luke 21:24; John 10:7-16; Rom. 11:25; Gal. 3,4,6 *See The Church in the Last Days, Facts of Scripture and Facts concerning the 70th Week of Daniel*

Appendix E:

[361] *See the book entitled The Church in the Last days, Chapter 12, Paragraph V: "Explanation of the Term "The Day of the Lord."*

[362] Matt. 24:9–31; Luke 21:8–24; Rev. 11:3,9; 13:11–18

[363] Dan. 12:4–13; Rom. 11:25–27; Rev. 10:7

Appendix F:

[364] Matt. 24:4–8; Mark 13:5–8; Luke 21:8–19

[365] Matt. 24: 9–22; Mark 13:9–20; Luke 21:20–24

[366] Matt. 24:27–31; 25:1–13; Mark 13:24–27; Luke 21:25–33

[367] Zech. 14:4; Acts 1:7–11

[368] Matt. 25:14–30; Rom. 14:20; 2 Cor. 5:10

[369] Matt. 24:29–31; 1 Cor. 15:51–55; 1 Thess. 4:13–17; Rev. 7:9–17

[370] John 16:33; Rom. 1:18–32; 2:5–16; 1 Thess. 5:9

[371] 2 Thess. 1:6–10; Rev. 8:1–9, 21; 11:15–19; 14:14–18:24

[372] Daniel 12:4–13; Rev. 10:1–11:14

Appendix G:

[373] Jer. 31:31-34; Ezek. 36:26,27; Gal. 2-5; Heb. 7-11 *See also the book Jesus' Way: God's Guaranteed Blueprint*

[374] Matt. 28:18; John 1:12; Eph. 1:19-23; Col. 1:11-29; 2:9,10

[375] Daniel 4; Acts 4,5

[376] 1 Sam. 10; Psa. 94:20-23

[377] Matt. 5:43–48; 26:52: Luke 3:14, 15; 9:51–56; Acts 5:29-32; 1 John 3:11-15; 4:7-21; Rev. 13:9,10; 14:12,13 *See also the Papers entitled Authority and Conscience and Authority & Conscience, Part Two: God has established a Framework of Order*

[378] Gen. 6:18; 9:9–17; 17:7, 19,21; 1 Chron. 17; Daniel 2:44,45; Matt. 13,21; Mark 12; Luke 20

[379] Matt.21; Luke 19

[380] John 5:38; 6:29; 7:28,29; 8:26,29,42

[381] 1 Kings 22:19; 2 Chron. 18:18; Psa. 11:4; 45:6 (Heb. 1:8): 47:9; 89:14,29,36,44; 97:2; 103:19; Isa. 6:1; 22:23; 66:1 (Acts 7:49); Jer. 17:12; Ezek. 1:26; 10:1; Matt. 5:34; 19:28; 23:22; 25:31; Acts 2:30; Heb. 4:16: 8:1; 12:2: Rev. 4:1–10: 5:1–13; 7:17; 8:3; 14:3–5; 19:4,5

[382] Rev. 20:11

[383] 1 Cor. 12:12, 13; Eph. 4

[384] Ruth 3:3; 2 Kings 5:10–13; Isa. 1:6; Ezek. 23:40; Matt. 3:11,12; 6:17; Luke 7:38; John 9:7,11; 13:5–14; Acts 22:16

[385] 1 Pet, 1:2; 1 John 1:7,9

[386] Matt. 18:3; Luke 22:31,32; Acts 3:19; 1 Thess. 1:9; James 5:19, 20

[387] *See main text. Chapter Three See also the 3-part series of papers entitled "Christian Conversion" and the Diagram/paper entitled "Figure One: Illustration/Comparison of Caterpillar/Butterfly to Conversion"*

[388] Mat. 16:18; 18:20,21; John 18:36; Acts 2:38–47

[389] Matt. 5:9; 18:3; 19:13,14; Mark 10:14,15; Luke 18:16,17; 20:36; John 1:10–14; 11:52; Rom. 8:14– 21 9:8,26; Gal. 3:26–29; Eph. 3:15; Phil. 2:15; 1 John 3:1– 10; 5:2 *See also Basic Christian Doctrine Areas Seven and Twelve*

[390] Acts 4:1 ff; 5:17 ff.; 7:1–8:2

[391] Acts 8:3–9:43; 10:1 ff.

[392] Matt. 16:18; Rom. 11:17; 15:27; 1 Cor. 9:9–13, 23; 10:17–21, 30; 2 Cor. 1:7; Eph. 3:6,7; Col. 1:12; 1 Tim. 6:2; 2 Tim. 1:8; Heb. 2:9–14; 3:1, 14; 6:4; 12:8–14; 1 Pet. 4:13–17; 5:1; 2 Pet. 1:4 *See also the paper entitled "The Doctrine of the Elect/Ekklesia"*

[393] Ex. 20:3-6; Dan. 3:1-28, 6:4-27; Matt. 22:36,37; Acts 5:29-32

[394] Matt. 6:24; Eph. 4

[395] Ex. 12:25; Psa. 105:42; Jer. 31:31–34; 32:32; 33:14; Luke 24:49; Acts 1:4; 2:33– 39; 7:17; 13:23,32; 32:21; 26:6,7; Rom. 4:13–20; 2 Cor. 1:20; Gal. 3:14–29; 4:28; Eph. 1:13; 2:12; 3:6; 6:2; 1 Tim. 4:8; 2 Tim. 1:1; Heb. 4:1; 6:12–17; 8:6; 9:11–15; 10:32–39; 11:1 ff.; 2 Pet. 1:4; 3:9–13; 1 John 2:25

[396] Luke 6:44–49; 1 Cor. 3:10–12

[397] Matt. 16:21–26; John 15:1–6

[398] 1 Tim. 4:2

[399] Matt. 4. Luke 4; Rom. 5:14; 1 Cor. 15:22–58

[400] John 1:16–18

[401] John 1:12; Rom. 12:1–3

[402] Isa. 12:3; Matt. 13; Luck 6:46–49; John 7:37–39; Heb. 6:1–8; 10:26–32 *See also the paper "Figure One: Illustration/Comparison of Caterpillar/ Butterfly to Conversion"*

[403] Matt. 5:48; 11:25–30; 13:18:ff; 24:13; Luke 12:1 ff.; 14:26–3315:11–32; 17:20:ff.; 22:31,32; John 3:5–36; 4:14–24; 6:27–63; 7:15–18; 37–39; 8:31–36; 10:25–30; 12:32; 14–16

[404] Matt. 18:1–11; John 14–17; 1 John 2:20–27; See also Isa. 28–30

[405] *See Jesus' Way, Appendix A, The Standard*

[406] Psa. 32; 51; Rom. 4:3; 6:16; 1 John 1:5–10; 2:1,2

[407] John 1:12–14; 3:3–8; Rom. 8; 1 Cor. 12:12,13; Eph. 4:1–16; Heb. 5:11–14

[408] John 6:63,64; 1 Cor. 1:17–2:16 *See the paper "The Spiritual Laws of Revival" Law Eight: "The Separation of the soul from spirit"*

[409] Matt. 7:1,2; Luke 6:37 a; John 3:18; 7:24; Acts 13:27

[410] 1 Cor. 6:2–4

[411] John 3:19; 5:24; 7:24

[412] Matt. 7:2; Luke 23:40; 24:20; 1 Tim. 3:6; James 3:1; Jude 4

[413] Rom. 12:19; Heb. 10:20

[414] 1 Cor. 9:27; 2 Cor. 13:5–7; 2 Tim. 3:8; Titus 1:16

415 Col. 2:18

[416] Prov. 3:5,6; 8:1 ff.; John 14:6-27; 16:7–15; Rev. 19:10

[417] John 18:36; Acts 4:11-22; 5:29-32; Rom. 12: 1–3; 2 Thess. 1,2; James 4:4–8; 1 John 2:15–17; 5:19; Rev. 13 *See also the book Jesus' Way Appendix B: "Authority and Conscience"*

[418] Matt. 27:50-52; Heb. 9:11–15

[419] Matt. 5:39; Luke 21:8-19; John 18:36; Rom. 13:8 f.; Rev. 13:10; 14:10–12

[420] Eccl. 7:8; Matt. 18:26,29; Luke 8:15; 21:19; Rom. 2:7; 5:1–5; 8:25;12:12–21; 15:4,5;2 Cor. 6:4–6; 1 Thess. 1:3,4; 5:14; 1 Tim. 6:11; 2 Tim. 2:24–26; Heb. 6:12–15; James 1:3,4; 5:7–11; 2 Pet. 1:6

[421] Gal. 3:13; 4:5; Eph. 5:16; Col. 4:5

[422] Luke 1:68; 2:38; 24:21; Titus 2:14; Heb. 9:12; 1 Pet. 1:18

[423] Rom. 3:24; 6:4; Gal. 3:10–13; Eph. 1:7; Heb. 9:15; 11:35 *See also the entries *Bloodshed,* *The Blood of Christ* and *Remission* and the Papers entitled Fallacies of Determinism, Fulfilment Prophecy and How Does Christ's Blood Get to us Today*

[424] Luke 21:28; Rom. 8:23; 2 Thess. 2:8

[425] 1 Kings 19:18; 1 Chron. 25:5

[426] Isa. 43:1 ff.; 66:1 ff.; Jer.23:1 ff.; 29: 14; 31:8 ff.; 32:37; Ezek. 20:34–41; 33:30 37:28; Mic. 2:12; 4:1–6; Hab. 2:4,5; Zeph. 3:16–20; Zech. 10

[427] Zech. 14:2; Matt. 3:23; 13:40–47; John 3:16; 14:6; Acts 10:1 ff.; 13:38-52; 15:1 ff.; 17:24-31; Rom. 8; 1 Cor. 15:20-28; Gal. 3; Eph. 2:11-3:21; Phil. 3

[428] Matt. 24:21–31; Mark 13:24–27; Luke 21:25–36; John 11:52; Eph. 1:10; 1 Thess. 4:11–17

[429] Ezek. 18:30; Rom. 2:4; 2 Cor. 7:10

[430] Psa. 66:18; 94:20; Isa. 44:20,21; 59:2; Jer. 6:30; Ezek. 3:18, 18:30; 33:8; 36:33; Matt. 7:21–23; 23:28; 24:12; Luke 13:27

[431] 1 King 18–21; 2 Kings 9; Acts 1:18; Rev. 2:20

[432] Romans 1:17–2:18; 2 Cor. 13:5; 2 Tim. 2:19–3:8

[433] Acts 3:19–26; 1 John 1:5–10; Neh.9; Dan. 9

[434] Hab. 2:4; Matt. 6:9–13; John 4:23,24; 14:21-26; 15:1-7; Rom. 4; 1 Thess. 5:17

[435] Rom. 12:1–3 *See the paper entitled "Figure One: Illustration/Comparison of Caterpillar/Butterfly to Conversion"*

[436] Matt. 24:13; John 15:1–7; 2 Tim. 2:11,12; Heb. 2:3-4:16; 6:3-12; 10:26-39

[437] *See the book Basic Christian Doctrine and the papers entitled 'Conditions for Salvation' and 'God's Definition of Salvation'*

[438] Deut. 32:39; Luke 17:11–19 *See also the book Jesus' Way, Chapter XIII: 'Ministry, Love and Healing'.*

[439] 1 John 1:7–9

[440] Rom. 6:1

[441] Psalm 19; Psa. 51; Matt. 5:8; John 15:2; 2 Tim. 1:3; Heb. 9:11–15,22; James 4:1-10

[442] Col. 3:1 f.

[443] Matt. 6:9-15; Eph. 1:19–23; 2:18–22; 3:10, 11; Phil. 3:20, 21

[444] Gen. 2:3; Ex. 3:15; 12:16; 28:3,41; 30:13,24; Lev. 27:3; Josh. 15:15; 1 Chr. 6:49; 16:10, 35; 29:16

[445] 1 Cor. 3:16

[446] Lev. 19:2; 20:7, 26; Deut. 7 :6; 14:2, 21; 26:19; 28:9

[447] Eph. 1:4; 2:21; 1 Pet. 2:9

[448] Ex. 29:9, 22–35; 2 Chr. 29:31

[449] John 10:22; Heb. 10:20

[450] *Matt. 5-7,13,25; Luke 11-19; Rom. 8; 1 Cor. 15:20-28 See also the book Spiritual Guidelines for Restoration, "Historical Review" section and Chapter 14: "Stewardship" See also the paper "Jesus' Major Parables"*

[451] *See the Paper entitled What is Syncretism*

www.ingramcontent.com/pod-product-compliance
Lightning Source LLC
Chambersburg PA
CBHW051128120626

46547CB00012B/714

*9 7 9 8 8 9 3 5 6 4 0 8 2 *